NISSAN MAXIMA
1993-98 REPAIR MANUAL

Deleted

President	Dean F. Morgantini, S.A.E.
Vice President–Finance	Barry L. Beck
Vice President–Sales	Glenn D. Potere
Executive Editor	Kevin M. G. Maher, A.S.E.
Manager–Consumer Automotive	Richard Schwartz, A.S.E.
Manager–Marine/Recreation	James R. Marotta, A.S.E.
Production Specialists	Brian Hollingsworth, Melinda Possinger
Project Managers	Will Kessler, A.S.E., S.A.E., Thomas A. Mellon, A.S.E., S.A.E., Richard Rivele, Todd W. Stidham, A.S.E., Ron Webb
Editor	Christopher Bishop, A.S.E.

CHILTON™ Automotive Books

PUBLISHED BY **W. G. NICHOLS, INC.**

Manufactured in USA
© 1999 Chilton Nichols
1020 Andrew Drive
West Chester, PA 19380
ISBN 0-8019-8961-2
Library of Congress Catalog Card No. 99-072523
1234567890 8765432109

Contents

Contents

DRIVE TRAIN 7

SUSPENSION AND STEERING 8

BRAKES 9

BODY AND TRIM 10

GLOSSARY

MASTER INDEX

See last page for information on additional titles

SAFETY NOTICE

Proper service and repair procedures are vital to the safe, reliable operation of all motor vehicles, as well as the personal safety of those performing repairs. This manual outlines procedures for servicing and repairing vehicles using safe, effective methods. The procedures contain many NOTES, CAUTIONS and WARNINGS which should be followed, along with standard procedures to eliminate the possibility of personal injury or improper service which could damage the vehicle or compromise its safety.

It is important to note that repair procedures and techniques, tools and parts for servicing motor vehicles, as well as the skill and experience of the individual performing the work vary widely. It is not possible to anticipate all of the conceivable ways or conditions under which vehicles may be serviced, or to provide cautions as to all possible hazards that may result. Standard and accepted safety precautions and equipment should be used when handling toxic or flammable fluids, and safety goggles or other protection should be used during cutting, grinding, chiseling, prying, or any other process that can cause material removal or projectiles.

Some procedures require the use of tools specially designed for a specific purpose. Before substituting another tool or procedure, you must be completely satisfied that neither your personal safety, nor the performance of the vehicle will be endangered.

Although information in this manual is based on industry sources and is complete as possible at the time of publication, the possibility exists that some car manufacturers made later changes which could not be included here. While striving for total accuracy, NP/Chilton cannot assume responsibility for any errors, changes or omissions that may occur in the compilation of this data.

PART NUMBERS

Part numbers listed in this reference are not recommendations by Chilton for any product brand name. They are references that can be used with interchange manuals and aftermarket supplier catalogs to locate each brand supplier's discrete part number.

SPECIAL TOOLS

Special tools are recommended by the vehicle manufacturer to perform their specific job. Use has been kept to a minimum, but where absolutely necessary, they are referred to in the text by the part number of the tool manufacturer. These tools can be purchased, under the appropriate part number, from your local dealer or regional distributor, or an equivalent tool can be purchased locally from a tool supplier or parts outlet. Before substituting any tool for the one recommended, read the SAFETY NOTICE at the top of this page.

ACKNOWLEDGMENTS

Chilton expresses appreciation to Nissan Motor Co. for their generous assistance.

A special thanks to the fine companies who supported the production of this book. Hand tools, supplied by Craftsman, were used during all phases of vehicle teardown and photography. Many of the fine specialty tools used in procedures were provided courtesy of Lisle Corporation. Lincoln Automotive Products has provided their industrial shop equipment including jacks, engine stands and shop presses. A Rotary lift, the largest automobile lift manufacturer in the world offering the biggest variety of surface and inground lifts available, was also used.

1

GENERAL INFORMATION AND MAINTENANCE

HOW TO USE THIS BOOK

Chilton's Total Car Care manual for the 1993–98 Nissan Maxima is intended to help you learn more about the inner workings of your vehicle while saving you money on its upkeep and operation.

The beginning of the book will likely be referred to the most, since that is where you will find information for maintenance and tune-up. The other sections deal with the more complex systems of your vehicle. Operating systems from engine through brakes are covered to the extent that the average do-it-yourselfer becomes mechanically involved. This book will not explain such things as rebuilding a differential for the simple reason that the expertise required and the investment in special tools make this task uneconomical. It will, however, give you detailed instructions to help you change your own brake pads and shoes, replace spark plugs, and perform many more jobs that can save you money.

A secondary purpose of this book is a reference for owners who want to understand their vehicle and/or their mechanics better. In this case, no tools at all are required.

Where To Begin

Before removing any bolts, read through the entire procedure. This will give you the overall view of what tools and supplies will be required. There is nothing more frustrating than having to walk to the bus stop on Monday morning because you were short one bolt on Sunday afternoon. So read ahead and plan ahead. Each operation should be approached logically and all procedures thoroughly understood before attempting any work.

All sections contain adjustments, maintenance, removal and installation procedures, and in some cases, repair or overhaul procedures. When repair is not considered practical, we tell you how to remove the part and then how to install the new or rebuilt replacement. In this way, you at least save labor costs. "Backyard" repair of some components is just not practical.

Avoiding Trouble

Many procedures in this book require you to "label and disconnect . . ." a group of lines, hoses or wires. Don't be lulled into thinking you can remember where everything goes—you won't. If you hook up vacuum or fuel lines incorrectly, the vehicle may run poorly, if at all. If you hook up electrical wiring incorrectly, you may instantly learn a very expensive lesson.

You don't need to know the official or engineering name for each hose or line. A piece of masking tape on the hose and a piece on its fitting will allow you to assign your own label such as the letter A or a short name. As long as you remember your own code, the lines can be reconnected by matching similar letters or names. Do remember that tape will dissolve in gasoline or other fluids; if a component is to be washed or cleaned, use another method of identification. A permanent felt-tipped marker or a metal scribe can be very handy for marking metal parts. Remove any tape or paper labels after assembly.

Maintenance or Repair?

It's necessary to mention the difference between maintenance and repair. Maintenance includes routine inspections, adjustments, and replacement of parts which show signs of normal wear. Maintenance compensates for wear or deterioration. Repair implies that something has broken or is not working. A need for repair is often caused by lack of maintenance. Example: draining and refilling the automatic transmission fluid is maintenance recommended by the manufacturer at specific mileage intervals. Failure to do this can shorten the life of the transaxle, requiring very expensive repairs. While no maintenance program can prevent items from breaking or wearing out, a general rule can be stated: MAINTENANCE IS CHEAPER THAN REPAIR.

Two basic mechanic's rules should be mentioned here. First, whenever the left side of the vehicle or engine is referred to, it is meant to specify the driver's side. Conversely, the right side of the vehicle means the passenger's side. Second, screws and bolts are removed by turning counterclockwise, and tightened by turning clockwise unless specifically noted.

Safety is always the most important rule. Constantly be aware of the dangers involved in working on an automobile and take the proper precautions. See the information in this section regarding SERVICING YOUR VEHICLE SAFELY and the SAFETY NOTICE on the acknowledgment page.

Avoiding the Most Common Mistakes

Pay attention to the instructions provided. There are 3 common mistakes in mechanical work:

1. Incorrect order of assembly, disassembly or adjustment. When taking something apart or putting it together, performing steps in the wrong order usually just costs you extra time; however, it CAN break something. Read the entire procedure before beginning disassembly. Perform everything in the order in which the instructions say you should, even if you can't immediately see a reason for it. When you're taking apart something that is very intricate, you might want to draw a picture of how it looks when assembled at one point in order to make sure you get everything back in its proper position. We will supply exploded views whenever possible. When making adjustments, perform them in the proper order. One adjustment possibly will affect another.

2. Overtorquing (or undertorquing). While it is more common for overtorquing to cause damage, undertorquing may allow a fastener to vibrate loose causing serious damage. Especially when dealing with aluminum parts, pay attention to torque specifications and utilize a torque wrench in assembly. If a torque figure is not available, remember that if you are using the right tool to perform the job, you will probably not have to strain yourself to get a fastener tight enough. The pitch of most threads is so slight that the tension you put on the wrench will be multiplied many times in actual force on what you are tightening. A good example of how critical torque is can be seen in the case of spark plug installation, especially where you are putting the plug into an aluminum cylinder head. Too little torque can fail to crush the gasket, causing leakage of combustion gases and consequent overheating of the plug and engine parts. Too much torque can damage the threads or distort the plug, changing the spark gap.

There are many commercial products available for ensuring that fasteners won't come loose, even if they are not torqued just right (a very common brand is Loctite®). If you're worried about getting something together tight enough to hold, but loose enough to avoid mechanical damage during assembly, one of these products might offer substantial insurance. Before choosing a threadlocking compound, read the label on the package and make sure the product is compatible with the materials, fluids, etc. involved.

3. Crossthreading. This occurs when a part such as a bolt is screwed into a nut or casting at the wrong angle and forced. Crossthreading is more likely to occur if access is difficult. It helps to clean and lubricate fasteners, then to start threading the bolt, spark plug, etc. with your fingers. If you encounter resistance, unscrew the part and start over again at a different angle until it can be inserted and turned several times without much effort. Keep in mind that many parts, especially spark plugs, have tapered threads, so that gentle turning will automatically bring the part you're threading to the proper angle. Don't put a wrench on the part until it's been tightened a couple of turns by hand. If you suddenly encounter resistance, and the part has not seated fully, don't force it. Pull it back out to make sure it's clean and threading properly.

Be sure to take your time and be patient, and always plan ahead. Allow yourself ample time to perform repairs and maintenance. You may find maintaining your car a satisfying and enjoyable experience.

TOOLS AND EQUIPMENT

▶ **See Figures 1 thru 15**

Naturally, without the proper tools and equipment it is impossible to properly service your vehicle. It would also be virtually impossible to catalog every tool that you would need to perform all of the operations in this book. Of course, it would be unwise for the amateur to rush out and buy an expensive set of tools on the theory that he/she may need one or more of them at some time.

The best approach is to proceed slowly, gathering a good quality set of those tools that are used most frequently. Don't be misled by the low cost of bargain tools. It is far better to spend a little more for better quality. Forged wrenches, 6 or 12-point sockets and fine tooth ratchets are by far preferable to their less expensive counterparts. As any good mechanic can tell you, there are few worse experiences than trying to work on a vehicle with bad tools. Your monetary savings will be far outweighed by frustration and mangled knuckles.

Begin accumulating those tools that are used most frequently: those associated with routine maintenance and tune-up. In addition to the normal assortment of screwdrivers and pliers, you should have the following tools:

• Wrenches/sockets and combination open end/box end wrenches in sizes 3mm–19mm ¹³⁄₁₆ in. or ⅝ in. spark plug socket (depending on plug type).

➡If possible, buy various length socket drive extensions. Universal-joint and wobble extensions can be extremely useful, but be careful when using them, as they can change the amount of torque applied to the socket.

• Jackstands for support.
• Oil filter wrench.
• Spout or funnel for pouring fluids.
• Grease gun for chassis lubrication (unless your vehicle is not equipped with any grease fittings—for details, please refer to information on Fluids and Lubricants, later in this section).

• Hydrometer for checking the battery (unless equipped with a sealed, maintenance-free battery).
• A container for draining oil and other fluids.
• Rags for wiping up the inevitable mess.

In addition to the above items there are several others that are not absolutely necessary, but handy to have around. These include Oil Dry® (or an equivalent oil absorbent gravel—such as cat litter) and the usual supply of lubricants, antifreeze and fluids, although these can be purchased as needed. This is a basic list for routine maintenance, but only your personal needs and desire can accurately determine your list of tools.

After performing a few projects on the vehicle, you'll be amazed at the other tools and accessories on your workbench. Some useful household items are: a large turkey baster or siphon, empty coffee cans and ice trays (to store parts),a ball of twine, electrical tape for wiring, small rolls of colored tape for tagging lines or hoses, markers and pens, a note pad, golf tees (for plugging vacuum lines), metal coat hangers or a roll of mechanic's wire (to hold things out of the

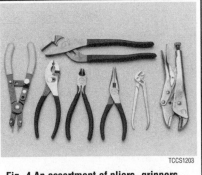
Fig. 1 All but the most basic procedures will require an assortment of ratchets and sockets
TCCS1200

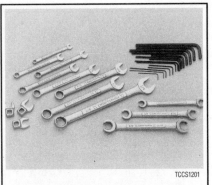
Fig. 2 In addition to ratchets, a good set of wrenches and hex keys will be necessary
TCCS1201

Fig. 3 A hydraulic floor jack and a set of jackstands are essential for lifting and supporting the vehicle
TCCS1202

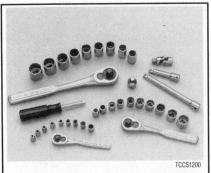
Fig. 4 An assortment of pliers, grippers and cutters will be handy for old rusted parts and stripped bolt heads
TCCS1203

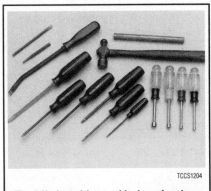
Fig. 5 Various drivers, chisels and prybars are great tools to have in your toolbox
TCCS1204

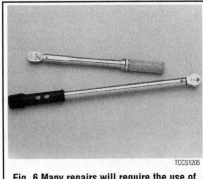
Fig. 6 Many repairs will require the use of a torque wrench to assure the components are properly fastened
TCCS1205

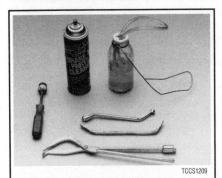
Fig. 7 Although not always necessary, using specialized brake tools will save time
TCCS1209

Fig. 8 A few inexpensive lubrication tools will make maintenance easier
TCCS1210

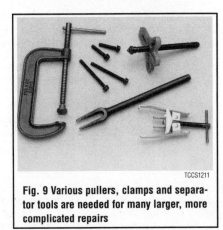
Fig. 9 Various pullers, clamps and separator tools are needed for many larger, more complicated repairs
TCCS1211

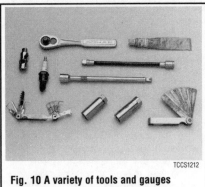

Fig. 10 A variety of tools and gauges should be used for spark plug gapping and installation

Fig. 11 Inductive type timing light

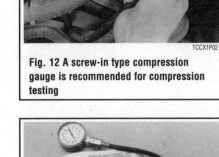

Fig. 12 A screw-in type compression gauge is recommended for compression testing

Fig. 13 A vacuum/pressure tester is necessary for many testing procedures

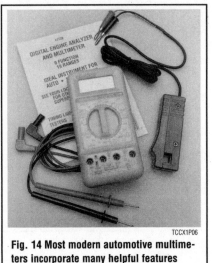

Fig. 14 Most modern automotive multimeters incorporate many helpful features

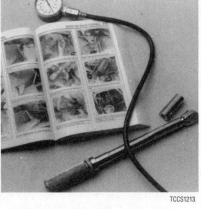

Fig. 15 Proper information is vital, so always have a Chilton Total Car Care manual handy

way), dental pick or similar long, pointed probe, a strong magnet, and a small mirror (to see into recesses and under manifolds).

A more advanced set of tools, suitable for tune-up work, can be drawn up easily. While the tools are slightly more sophisticated, they need not be outrageously expensive. There are several inexpensive tach/dwell meters on the market that are every bit as good for the average mechanic as a professional model. Just be sure that it goes to a least 1200–1500 rpm on the tach scale and that it works on 4, 6 and 8-cylinder engines. The key to these purchases is to make them with an eye towards adaptability and wide range. A basic list of tune-up tools could include:

- Tach/dwell meter.
- Spark plug wrench and gapping tool.
- Feeler gauges for valve adjustment.
- Timing light.

The choice of a timing light should be made carefully. A light which works on the DC current supplied by the vehicle's battery is the best choice; it should have a xenon tube for brightness. On any vehicle with an electronic ignition system, a timing light with an inductive pickup that clamps around the No. 1 spark plug cable is preferred.

In addition to these basic tools, there are several other tools and gauges you may find useful. These include:

- Compression gauge. The screw-in type is slower to use, but eliminates the possibility of a faulty reading due to escaping pressure.
- Manifold vacuum gauge.

- 12V test light.
- A combination volt/ohmmeter
- Induction Ammeter. This is used for determining whether or not there is current in a wire. These are handy for use if a wire is broken somewhere in a wiring harness.

As a final note, you will probably find a torque wrench necessary for all but the most basic work. The beam type models are perfectly adequate, although the newer click types (breakaway) are easier to use. The click type torque wrenches tend to be more expensive. Also keep in mind that all types of torque wrenches should be periodically checked and/or recalibrated. You will have to decide for yourself which better fits your bocketbook, and purpose.

Special Tools

Normally, the use of special factory tools is avoided for repair procedures, since these are not readily available for the do-it-yourself mechanic. When it is possible to perform the job with more commonly available tools, it will be pointed out, but occasionally, a special tool was designed to perform a specific function and should be used. Before substituting another tool, you should be convinced that neither your safety nor the performance of the vehicle will be compromised.

Special tools can usually be purchased from an automotive parts store or from your dealer. In some cases special tools may be available directly from the tool manufacturer.

SERVICING YOUR VEHICLE SAFELY

▶ **See Figures 16, 17, 18 and 19**

It is virtually impossible to anticipate all of the hazards involved with automotive maintenance and service, but care and common sense will prevent most accidents.

The rules of safety for mechanics range from "don't smoke around gasoline," to "use the proper tool(s) for the job." The trick to avoiding injuries is to develop safe work habits and to take every possible precaution.

Do's

- Do keep a fire extinguisher and first aid kit handy.
- Do wear safety glasses or goggles when cutting, drilling, grinding or prying, even if you have 20–20 vision. If you wear glasses for the sake of vision, wear safety goggles over your regular glasses.
- Do shield your eyes whenever you work around the battery. Batteries contain sulfuric acid. In case of contact with the eyes or skin, flush the area with water or a mixture of water and baking soda, then seek immediate medical attention.
- Do use safety stands (jackstands) for any undervehicle service. Jacks are for raising vehicles; jackstands are for making sure the vehicle stays raised until you want it to come down. Whenever the vehicle is raised, block the wheels remaining on the ground and set the parking brake.
- Do use adequate ventilation when working with any chemicals or hazardous materials. Like carbon monoxide, the asbestos dust resulting from some brake lining wear can be hazardous in sufficient quantities.
- Do disconnect the negative battery cable when working on the electrical system. The secondary ignition system contains EXTREMELY HIGH VOLTAGE. In some cases it can even exceed 50,000 volts.
- Do follow manufacturer's directions whenever working with potentially hazardous materials. Most chemicals and fluids are poisonous if taken internally.
- Do properly maintain your tools. Loose hammerheads, mushroomed punches and chisels, frayed or poorly grounded electrical cords, excessively worn screwdrivers, spread wrenches (open end), cracked sockets, slipping ratchets, or faulty droplight sockets can cause accidents.

- Likewise, keep your tools clean; a greasy wrench can slip off a bolt head, ruining the bolt and often harming your knuckles in the process.
- Do use the proper size and type of tool for the job at hand. Do select a wrench or socket that fits the nut or bolt. The wrench or socket should sit straight, not cocked.
- Do, when possible, pull on a wrench handle rather than push on it, and adjust your stance to prevent a fall.
- Do be sure that adjustable wrenches are tightly closed on the nut or bolt and pulled so that the force is on the side of the fixed jaw.
- Do strike squarely with a hammer; avoid glancing blows.
- Do set the parking brake and block the drive wheels if the work requires a running engine.

Don'ts

▶ **See Figure 20**

- Don't run the engine in a garage or anywhere else without proper ventilation—EVER! Carbon monoxide is poisonous; it takes a long time to leave the human body and you can build up a deadly supply of it in your system by simply breathing in a little every day. You may not realize you are slowly poisoning yourself. Always use power vents, windows, fans and/or open the garage door.
- Don't work around moving parts while wearing loose clothing. Short sleeves are much safer than long, loose sleeves. Hard-toed shoes with neoprene soles protect your toes and give a better grip on slippery surfaces. Jewelry such as watches, fancy belt buckles, beads or body adornment of any kind is not safe working around a vehicle. Long hair should be tied back under a hat or cap.
- Don't use pockets for toolboxes. A fall or bump can drive a screwdriver deep into your body. Even a rag hanging from your back pocket can wrap around a spinning shaft or fan.
- Don't smoke when working around gasoline, cleaning solvent or other flammable material.

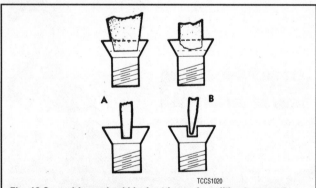

Fig. 16 Screwdrivers should be kept in good condition to prevent injury or damage which could result if the blade slips from the screw

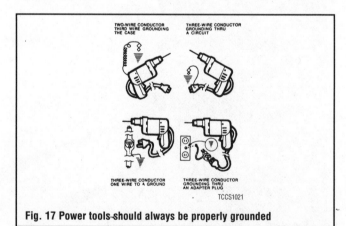

Fig. 17 Power tools should always be properly grounded

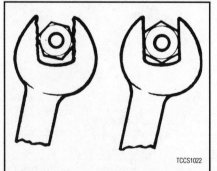

Fig. 18 Using the correct size wrench will help prevent the possibility of rounding off a nut

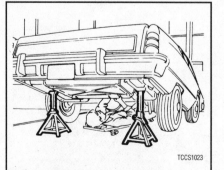

Fig. 19 NEVER work under a vehicle unless it is supported using safety stands (jackstands)

Fig. 20 Never work on a vehicle for so long that you lose your sense of reality

• Don't smoke when working around the battery. When the battery is being charged, it gives off explosive hydrogen gas.

• Don't use gasoline to wash your hands; there are excellent soaps available. Gasoline contains dangerous additives which can enter the body through a cut or through your pores. Gasoline also removes all the natural oils from the skin so that bone dry hands will suck up oil and grease.

• Don't service the air conditioning system unless you are equipped with the necessary tools and training. When liquid or compressed gas refrigerant is released to atmospheric pressure it will absorb heat from whatever it contacts. This will chill or freeze anything it touches, including your hands.

• Don't use screwdrivers for anything other than driving screws! A screwdriver used as a prying tool can snap when you least expect it, causing injuries. At the very least, you'll ruin a good screwdriver.

• Don't use an emergency jack (that little ratchet, scissors, or pantograph jack supplied with the vehicle) for anything other than changing a flat! These jacks are only intended for emergency use out on the road; they are NOT designed as a maintenance tool. If you are serious about maintaining your vehicle yourself, invest in a hydraulic floor jack of at least a 1½ ton capacity, and at least two sturdy jackstands.

FASTENERS, MEASUREMENTS AND CONVERSIONS

Bolts, Nuts and Other Threaded Retainers

▶ See Figures 21, 22, 23 and 24

Although there are a great variety of fasteners found in the modern car or truck, the most commonly used retainer is the threaded fastener (nuts, bolts, screws, studs, etc). Most threaded retainers may be reused, provided that they are not damaged in use or during the repair. Some retainers (such as stretch bolts or torque prevailing nuts) are designed to deform when tightened or in use and should not be reinstalled.

Whenever possible, we will note any special retainers which should be replaced during a procedure. But you should always inspect the condition of a retainer when it is removed and replace any that show signs of damage. Check all threads for rust or corrosion which can increase the torque necessary to achieve the desired clamp load for which that fastener was originally selected. Additionally, be sure that the driver surface of the fastener has not been compromised by rounding or other damage. In some cases a driver surface may

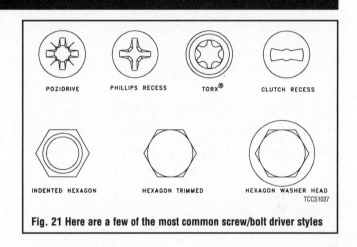

POZIDRIVE   PHILLIPS RECESS   TORX®   CLUTCH RECESS

INDENTED HEXAGON   HEXAGON TRIMMED   HEXAGON WASHER HEAD

TCCS1037

Fig. 21 Here are a few of the most common screw/bolt driver styles

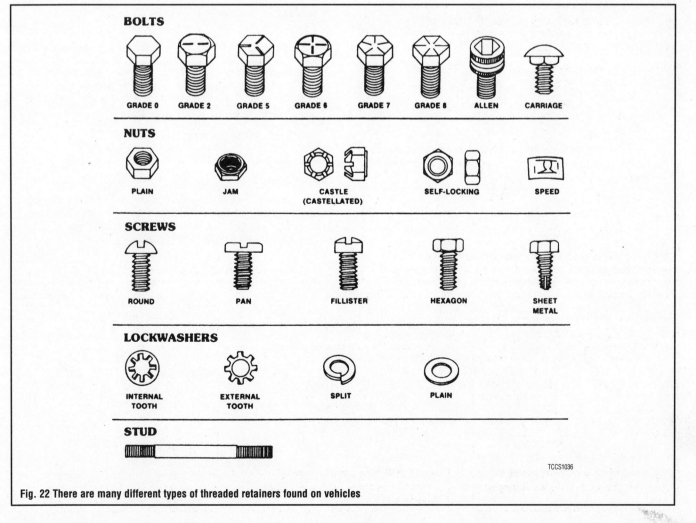

BOLTS

GRADE 0   GRADE 2   GRADE 5   GRADE 6   GRADE 7   GRADE 8   ALLEN   CARRIAGE

NUTS

PLAIN   JAM   CASTLE (CASTELLATED)   SELF-LOCKING   SPEED

SCREWS

ROUND   PAN   FILLISTER   HEXAGON   SHEET METAL

LOCKWASHERS

INTERNAL TOOTH   EXTERNAL TOOTH   SPLIT   PLAIN

STUD

TCCS1036

Fig. 22 There are many different types of threaded retainers found on vehicles

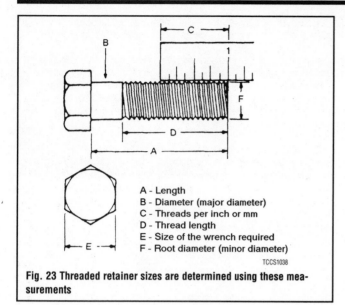

A - Length
B - Diameter (major diameter)
C - Threads per inch or mm
D - Thread length
E - Size of the wrench required
F - Root diameter (minor diameter)

TCCS1038

Fig. 23 Threaded retainer sizes are determined using these measurements

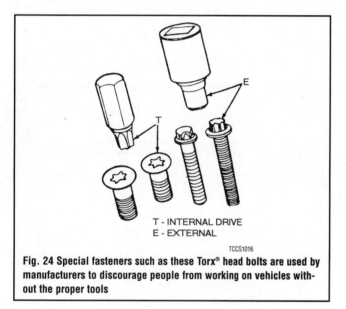

T - INTERNAL DRIVE
E - EXTERNAL

TCCS1016

Fig. 24 Special fasteners such as these Torx® head bolts are used by manufacturers to discourage people from working on vehicles without the proper tools

become only partially rounded, allowing the driver to catch in only one direction. In many of these occurrences, a fastener may be installed and tightened, but the driver would not be able to grip and loosen the fastener again. (This could lead to frustration down the line should that component ever need to be disassembled again).

If you must replace a fastener, whether due to design or damage, you must ALWAYS be sure to use the proper replacement. In all cases, a retainer of the same design, material and strength should be used. Markings on the heads of most bolts will help determine the proper strength of the fastener. The same material, thread and pitch must be selected to assure proper installation and safe operation of the vehicle afterwards.

Thread gauges are available to help measure a bolt or stud's thread. Most automotive and hardware stores keep gauges available to help you select the proper size. In a pinch, you can use another nut or bolt for a thread gauge. If the bolt you are replacing is not too badly damaged, you can select a match by finding another bolt which will thread in its place. If you find a nut which threads properly onto the damaged bolt, then use that nut to help select the replacement bolt. If however, the bolt you are replacing is so badly damaged (broken or drilled out) that its threads cannot be used as a gauge, you might start by looking for another bolt (from the same assembly or a similar location on your vehicle) which will thread into the damaged bolt's mounting. If so, the

other bolt can be used to select a nut; the nut can then be used to select the replacement bolt.

In all cases, be absolutely sure you have selected the proper replacement. Don't be shy, you can always ask the store clerk for help.

✳✳ WARNING

Be aware that when you find a bolt with damaged threads, you may also find the nut or recess it was threaded into has also been damaged. If this is the case, you may have to drill and tap the hole, replace the nut or otherwise repair the threads. NEVER try to force a replacement bolt to fit into the damaged threads.

Torque

Torque is defined as the measurement of resistance to turning or rotating. It tends to twist a body about an axis of rotation. A common example of this would be tightening a threaded retainer such as a nut, bolt or screw. Measuring torque is one of the most common ways to help assure that a threaded retainer has been properly fastened.

When tightening a threaded fastener, torque is applied in three distinct areas, the head, the bearing surface and the clamp load. About 50 percent of the measured torque is used in overcoming bearing friction. This is the friction between the bearing surface of the bolt head, screw head or nut face and the base material or washer (the surface on which the fastener is rotating). Approximately 40 percent of the applied torque is used in overcoming thread friction. This leaves only about 10 percent of the applied torque to develop a useful clamp load (the force which holds a joint together). This means that friction can account for as much as 90 percent of the applied torque on a fastener.

TORQUE WRENCHES

▶ **See Figures 25, 26 and 27**

In most applications, a torque wrench can be used to assure proper installation of a fastener. Torque wrenches come in various designs and most automotive supply stores will carry a variety to suit your needs. A torque wrench should be used any time we supply a specific torque value for a fastener. A torque wrench can also be used if you are following the general guidelines in the accompanying charts. Keep in mind that because there is no worldwide standardization of fasteners, the charts are a general guideline and should be used with caution. Again, the general rule of "if you are using the right tool for the job, you should not have to strain to tighten a fastener" applies here.

Beam Type

▶ **See Figure 28**

The beam type torque wrench is one of the most popular types. It consists of a pointer attached to the head that runs the length of the flexible beam (shaft) to a scale located near the handle. As the wrench is pulled, the beam bends and the pointer indicates the torque using the scale.

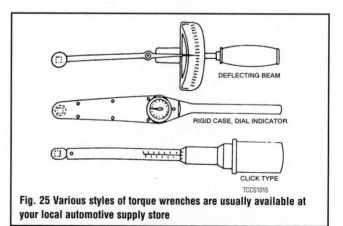

DEFLECTING BEAM

RIGID CASE, DIAL INDICATOR

CLICK TYPE

TCCS1015

Fig. 25 Various styles of torque wrenches are usually available at your local automotive supply store

Class	Diameter mm	Pitch mm	Hexagon head bolt			Hexagon flange bolt		
			N·m	kgf·cm	ft·lbf	N·m	kgf·cm	ft·lbf
4T	6	1	5	55	48 in.·lbf	6	60	52 in.·lbf
	8	1.25	12.5	130	9	14	145	10
	10	1.25	26	260	19	29	290	21
	12	1.25	47	480	35	53	540	39
	14	1.5	74	760	55	84	850	61
	16	1.5	115	1,150	83	—	—	—
5T	6	1	6.5	65	56 in.·lbf	7.5	75	65 in.·lbf
	8	1.25	15.5	160	12	17.5	175	13
	10	1.25	32	330	24	36	360	26
	12	1.25	59	600	43	65	670	48
	14	1.5	91	930	67	100	1,050	76
	16	1.5	140	1,400	101	—	—	—
6T	6	1	8	80	69 in.·lbf	9	90	78 in.·lbf
	8	1.25	19	195	14	21	210	15
	10	1.25	39	400	29	44	440	32
	12	1.25	71	730	53	80	810	59
	14	1.5	110	1,100	80	125	1,250	90
	16	1.5	170	1,750	127	—	—	—
7T	6	1	10.5	110	8	12	120	9
	8	1.25	25	260	19	28	290	21
	10	1.25	52	530	38	58	590	43
	12	1.25	95	970	70	105	1,050	76
	14	1.5	145	1,500	108	165	1,700	123
	16	1.5	230	2,300	166	—	—	—
8T	8	1.25	29	300	22	33	330	24
	10	1.25	61	620	45	68	690	50
	12	1.25	110	1,100	80	120	1,250	90
9T	8	1.25	34	340	25	37	380	27
	10	1.25	70	710	51	78	790	57
	12	1.25	125	1,300	94	140	1,450	105
10T	8	1.25	38	390	28	42	430	31
	10	1.25	78	800	58	88	890	64
	12	1.25	140	1,450	105	155	1,600	116
11T	8	1.25	42	430	31	47	480	35
	10	1.25	87	890	64	97	990	72
	12	1.25	155	1,600	116	175	1,800	130

TCCS1241

Fig. 27 Typical bolt torque for metric fasteners—WARNING: use only as a guide

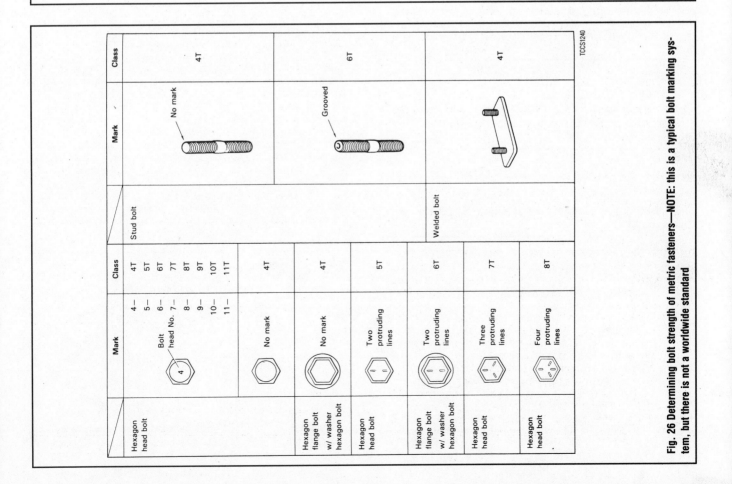

TCCS1240

Fig. 26 Determining bolt strength of metric fasteners—NOTE: this is a typical bolt marking system, but there is not a worldwide standard

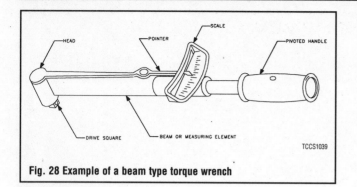

Fig. 28 Example of a beam type torque wrench

Click (Breakaway) Type

▶ See Figure 29

Another popular design of torque wrench is the click type. To use the click type wrench you pre-adjust it to a torque setting. Once the torque is reached, the wrench has a reflex signaling feature that causes a momentary breakaway of the torque wrench body, sending an impulse to the operator's hand.

Pivot Head Type

▶ See Figure 30

Some torque wrenches (usually of the click type) may be equipped with a pivot head which can allow it to be used in areas of limited access. BUT, it must be used properly. To hold a pivot head wrench, grasp the handle lightly, and as you pull on the handle, it should be floated on the pivot point. If the handle comes in contact with the yoke extension during the process of pulling, there is a very good chance the torque readings will be inaccurate because this could alter the wrench loading point. The design of the handle is usually such as to make it inconvenient to deliberately misuse the wrench.

➡ It should be mentioned that the use of any U-joint, wobble or extension will have an effect on the torque readings, no matter what type of wrench you are using. For the most accurate readings, install the socket directly

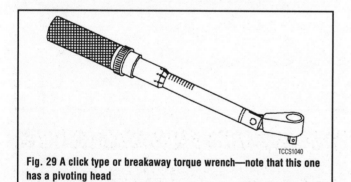

Fig. 29 A click type or breakaway torque wrench—note that this one has a pivoting head

on the wrench driver. If necessary, straight extensions (which hold a socket directly under the wrench driver) will have the least effect on the torque reading. Avoid any extension that alters the length of the wrench from the handle to the head/driving point (such as a crow's foot). U-joint or wobble extensions can greatly affect the readings; avoid their use at all times.

Rigid Case (Direct Reading)

▶ See Figure 31

A rigid case or direct reading torque wrench is equipped with a dial indicator to show torque values. One advantage of these wrenches is that they can be held at any position on the wrench without affecting accuracy. These wrenches are often preferred because they tend to be compact, easy to read and have a great degree of accuracy.

TORQUE ANGLE METERS

▶ See Figure 32

Because the frictional characteristics of each fastener or threaded hole will vary, clamp loads which are based strictly on torque will vary as well. In most applications, this variance is not significant enough to cause worry. But, in certain applications, a manufacturer's engineers may determine that more precise clamp loads are necessary (such is the case with many aluminum cylinder heads). In these cases, a torque angle method of installation would be specified. When installing fasteners which are torque angle tightened, a predetermined seating torque and standard torque wrench are usually used first to remove any compliance from the joint. The fastener is then tightened the specified additional portion of a turn measured in degrees. A torque angle gauge (mechanical protractor) is used for these applications.

Standard and Metric Measurements

▶ See Figure 33

Throughout this manual, specifications are given to help you determine the condition of various components on your vehicle, or to assist you in their installation. Some of the most common measurements include length (in. or cm/mm), torque (ft. lbs., inch lbs. or Nm) and pressure (psi, in. Hg, kPa or mm Hg). In most cases, we strive to provide the proper measurement as determined by the manufacturer's engineers.

Though, in some cases, that value may not be conveniently measured with what is available in your toolbox. Luckily, many of the measuring devices which are available today will have two scales so the Standard or Metric measurements may easily be taken. If any of the various measuring tools which are available to you do not contain the same scale as listed in the specifications, use the accompanying conversion factors to determine the proper value.

The conversion factor chart is used by taking the given specification and multiplying it by the necessary conversion factor. For instance, looking at the first line, if you have a measurement in inches such as "free-play should be 2 in." but your ruler reads only in millimeters, multiply 2 in. by the conversion factor of 25.4 to get the metric equivalent of 50.8mm. Likewise, if the specification was given only in a Metric measurement, for example in Newton Meters (Nm), then look at the center column first. If the measurement is 100 Nm, multiply it by the conversion factor of 0.738 to get 73.8 ft. lbs.

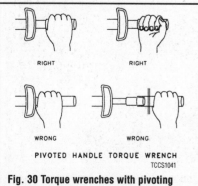

Fig. 30 Torque wrenches with pivoting heads must be grasped and used properly to prevent an incorrect reading

Fig. 31 The rigid case (direct reading) torque wrench uses a dial indicator to show torque

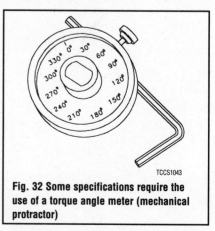

Fig. 32 Some specifications require the use of a torque angle meter (mechanical protractor)

CONVERSION FACTORS

LENGTH–DISTANCE

Inches (in.)	x 25.4	= Millimeters (mm)	x .0394	= Inches
Feet (ft.)	x .305	= Meters (m)	x 3.281	= Feet
Miles	x 1.609	= Kilometers (km)	x .0621	= Miles

VOLUME

Cubic Inches (in3)	x 16.387	= Cubic Centimeters	x .061	= in3
IMP Pints (IMP pt.)	x .568	= Liters (L)	x 1.76	= IMP pt.
IMP Quarts (IMP qt.)	x 1.137	= Liters (L)	x .88	= IMP qt.
IMP Gallons (IMP gal.)	x 4.546	= Liters (L)	x .22	= IMP gal.
IMP Quarts (IMP qt.)	x 1.201	= US Quarts (US qt.)	x .833	= IMP qt.
IMP Gallons (IMP gal.)	x 1.201	= US Gallons (US gal.)	x .833	= IMP gal.
Fl. Ounces	x 29.573	= Milliliters	x .034	= Ounces
US Pints (US pt.)	x .473	= Liters (L)	x 2.113	= Pints
US Quarts (US qt.)	x .946	= Liters (L)	x 1.057	= Quarts
US Gallons (US gal.)	x 3.785	= Liters (L)	x .264	= Gallons

MASS–WEIGHT

Ounces (oz.)	x 28.35	= Grams (g)	x .035	= Ounces
Pounds (lb.)	x .454	= Kilograms (kg)	x 2.205	= Pounds

PRESSURE

Pounds Per Sq. In. (psi)	x 6.895	= Kilopascals (kPa)	x .145	= psi
Inches of Mercury (Hg)	x .4912	= psi	x 2.036	= Hg
Inches of Mercury (Hg)	x 3.377	= Kilopascals (kPa)	x .2961	= Hg
Inches of Water (H_2O)	x .07355	= Inches of Mercury	x 13.783	= H_2O
Inches of Water (H_2O)	x .03613	= psi	x 27.684	= H_2O
Inches of Water (H_2O)	x .248	= Kilopascals (kPa)	x 4.026	= H_2O

TORQUE

Pounds–Force Inches (in–lb)	x .113	= Newton Meters (N·m)	x 8.85	= in–lb
Pounds–Force Feet (ft–lb)	x 1.356	= Newton Meters (N·m)	x .738	= ft–lb

VELOCITY

Miles Per Hour (MPH)	x 1.609	= Kilometers Per Hour (KPH)	x .621	= MPH

POWER

Horsepower (Hp)	x .745	= Kilowatts	x 1.34	= Horsepower

FUEL CONSUMPTION*

Miles Per Gallon IMP (MPG)	x .354	= Kilometers Per Liter (Km/L)	
Kilometers Per Liter (Km/L)	x 2.352	= IMP MPG	
Miles Per Gallon US (MPG)	x .425	= Kilometers Per Liter (Km/L)	
Kilometers Per Liter (Km/L)	x 2.352	= US MPG	

*It is common to covert from miles per gallon (mpg) to liters/100 kilometers (1/100 km), where mpg (IMP) x 1/100 km = 282 and mpg (US) x 1/100 km = 235.

TEMPERATURE

Degree Fahrenheit (°F)	= (°C x 1.8) + 32
Degree Celsius (°C)	= (°F – 32) x .56

TCCS1044

Fig. 33 Standard and metric conversion factors chart

SERIAL NUMBER IDENTIFICATION

Vehicle

♦ See Figures 34, 35, 36 and 37

The vehicle identification plate is located on the cowl at the rear of the engine compartment. The plate contains the model type, engine capacity, maximum horsepower, wheelbase and the engine and chassis serial numbers.

The vehicle or chassis serial number is broken down as shown in the illustration. The vehicle identification number is also reproduced on a plate on the upper left surface of the instrument panel and can be seen from the outside through the windshield. The V.I.N. is broken down as follows:

- First 3 digits/letters: Manufacturer
- Fourth letter: Engine type (H=VG30E, E=VE30DE, C=VQ30DE)
- Fifth letter: Vehicle line
- Sixth digit: Model change number
- Seventh digit: Body type (sedan)
- Eighth letter: Restraint system (S means standard; P means automatic)
- Ninth digit: Check digit
- Tenth letter: Model year in a letter code

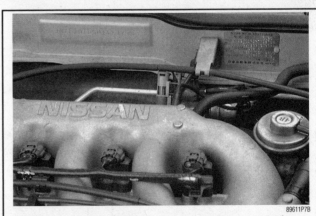

89611P7B

Fig. 34 The vehicle identification plate provides important information regarding features and specifications

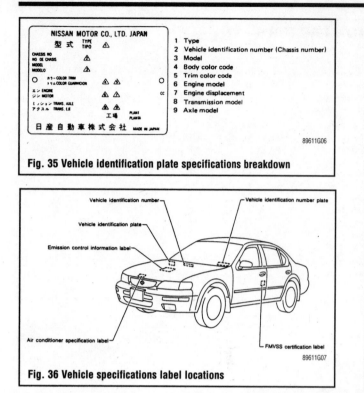

NISSAN MOTOR CO., LTD. JAPAN	1 Type
型式 TYPE TIPO △	2 Vehicle identification number (Chassis number)
CHASSIS NO	3 Model
NO. DE CHASIS △	4 Body color code
MODEL	5 Trim color code
MODELO △	6 Engine model
カラ - COLOR TRIM	7 Engine displacement
トリム COLOR GUARNICION	8 Transmission model
エン ENGINE	9 Axle model
ジン MOTOR	
ミッション TRANS. AXLE	
アクスル TRANS. LE	
日産自動車株式会社 MADE IN JAPAN	

Fig. 35 Vehicle identification plate specifications breakdown

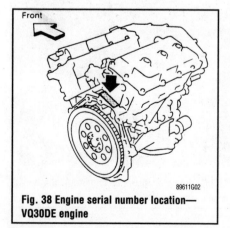

Fig. 36 Vehicle specifications label locations

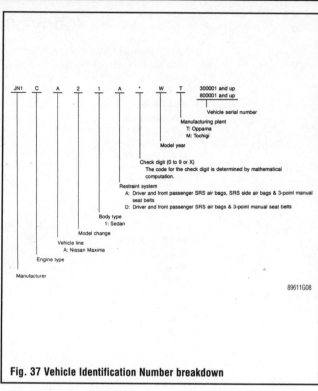

Fig. 37 Vehicle Identification Number breakdown

VEHICLE IDENTIFICATION CHART

	Engine Code						Model Year	
Code	Liters	Cu. In. (cc)	Cyl.	Fuel Sys.	Eng. Mfg.		Code	Year
H	3.0	180.5 (2960)	6	SMFI	Nissan		P	1993
E	3.0	180.5 (2960)	6	SMFI	Nissan		R	1994
LH	3.0	182.3 (2988)	6	SMFI	Nissan		S	1995
							T	1996
							V	1997
							W	1998

SMFI : Sequential Multi-port Fuel Injection

- Eleventh letter: Manufacturing plant code
- Last 6 digits: Vehicle serial (chassis) number

Engine

▶ See Figures 38, 39 and 40

The engine serial number can be found on the driver's side edge of the right rear cylinder bank.

Transaxle

▶ See Figures 41, 42 and 43

On the manual transaxle the serial number is stamped on the front upper face of the transaxle case. On the automatic transaxle the serial number is stamped on top of the transaxle housing, or on top of the valve body cover.

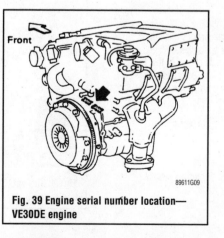

Fig. 38 Engine serial number location—VQ30DE engine

Fig. 39 Engine serial number location—VE30DE engine

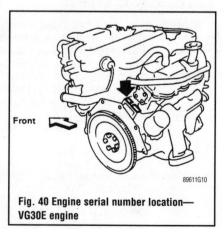

Fig. 40 Engine serial number location—VG30E engine

ENGINE IDENTIFICATION

Year	Model	Engine Displacement Liters (cc)	Engine Series (ID/VIN)	Fuel System	No. of Cylinders	Engine Type
1993	Maxima GXE	3.0L (2960)	VG30E / H	SMFI	6	OHC
	Maxima SE	3.0L (2960)	VE30DE / E	SMFI	6	OHC
1994	Maxima GXE	3.0L (2960)	VG30E / H	SMFI	6	OHC
	Maxima SE	3.0L (2960)	VE30DE / E	SMFI	6	OHC
1995	Maxima (all models)	3.0L (2988)	VQ30DE / LH	SMFI	6	OHC
1996	Maxima (all models)	3.0L (2988)	VQ30DE / LH	SMFI	6	OHC
1997	Maxima (all models)	3.0L (2988)	VQ30DE / LH	SMFI	6	OHC
1998	Maxima (all models)	3.0L (2988)	VQ30DE / LH	SMFI	6	OHC

SMFI : Sequential Multi-port Fuel Injection

89611C02

GENERAL ENGINE SPECIFICATIONS

Year	Engine ID/VIN	Engine Displacement Liters (cc)	Fuel System Type	Net Horsepower @ rpm	Net Torque @ rpm (ft. lbs.)	Bore x Stroke (in.)	Compression Ratio	Oil Pressure (lbs. @ rpm)
1993	VG30E / H	3.0L (2960)	SMFI	160 @ 5200	182 @ 2800	3.43 X 3.27	9.0:1	53-65 @ 3200
	VE30DE / E	3.0L (2960)	SMFI	190 @ 5600	190 @ 4000	3.43 X 3.27	10.0:1	60-74 @ 3000
1994	VG30E / H	3.0L (2960)	SMFI	160 @ 5200	182 @ 2800	3.43 X 3.27	9.0:1	53-65 @ 3200
	VE30DE / E	3.0L (2960)	SMFI	190 @ 5600	190 @ 4000	3.43 X 3.27	10.0:1	60-74 @ 3000
1995	VQ30DE / LH	3.0L (2988)	SMFI	190 @ 5600	205 @ 4000	3.66 X 2.89	10.0:1	63-80 @ 3000
1996	VQ30DE / LH	3.0L (2988)	SMFI	190 @ 5600	205 @ 4000	3.66 X 2.89	10.0:1	63-80 @ 3000
1997	VQ30DE / LH	3.0L (2988)	SMFI	190 @ 5600	205 @ 4000	3.66 X 2.89	10.0:1	63-80 @ 3000
1998	VQ30DE / LH	3.0L (2988)	SMFI	190 @ 5600	205 @ 4000	3.66 X 2.89	10.0:1	63-80 @ 3000

SMFI : Sequential Multi-port Fuel Injection

89611C03

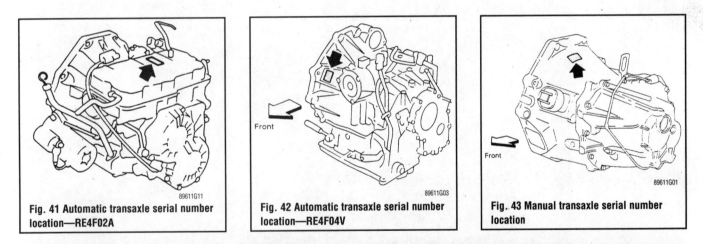

Fig. 41 Automatic transaxle serial number location—RE4F02A

Fig. 42 Automatic transaxle serial number location—RE4F04V

Fig. 43 Manual transaxle serial number location

ROUTINE MAINTENANCE AND TUNE-UP

Proper maintenance and tune-up is the key to long and trouble-free vehicle life, and the work can yield its own rewards. A maintenance schedule is provided by Nissan specifically for your Maxima. Strict adherence to this schedule will insure keeping the factory warranty in effect, as well as a long and reliable vehicle life. As a conscientious owner and driver, set aside a Saturday morning, say once a month, to check or replace items which could cause major problems later. Keep your own personal log to jot down which services you performed, the cost of the parts, the date, and the exact odometer reading at the time. Keep all receipts for such items as engine oil and filters, so that they may be referred to in case of related problems or to determine operating expenses. As a do-it-yourselfer, these receipts are the only proof you have that the required maintenance was performed. In the event of a warranty problem, these receipts will be invaluable. And, if you ever decide to sell your Nissan, thorough record keeping could sway a potential buyer, by showing that you have properly maintained your vehicle.

The literature provided with your Maxima when it was originally delivered includes the factory recommended maintenance schedule. If you no longer have this literature, replacement copies are usually available from a Nissan dealer. A maintenance schedule is provided later in this section, in case you do not have the factory literature.

MAINTENANCE COMPONENT LOCATIONS—1993–94 MODELS

1. Battery
2. Radiator expansion tank
3. Radiator cap
4. Power steering reservoir
5. Engine oil dipstick
6. Windshield washer fluid reservoir
7. Engine oil fill cap
8. Brake master cylinder
9. Fuel filter
10. Automatic transaxle fluid dipstick
11. Air cleaner housing (filter inside)

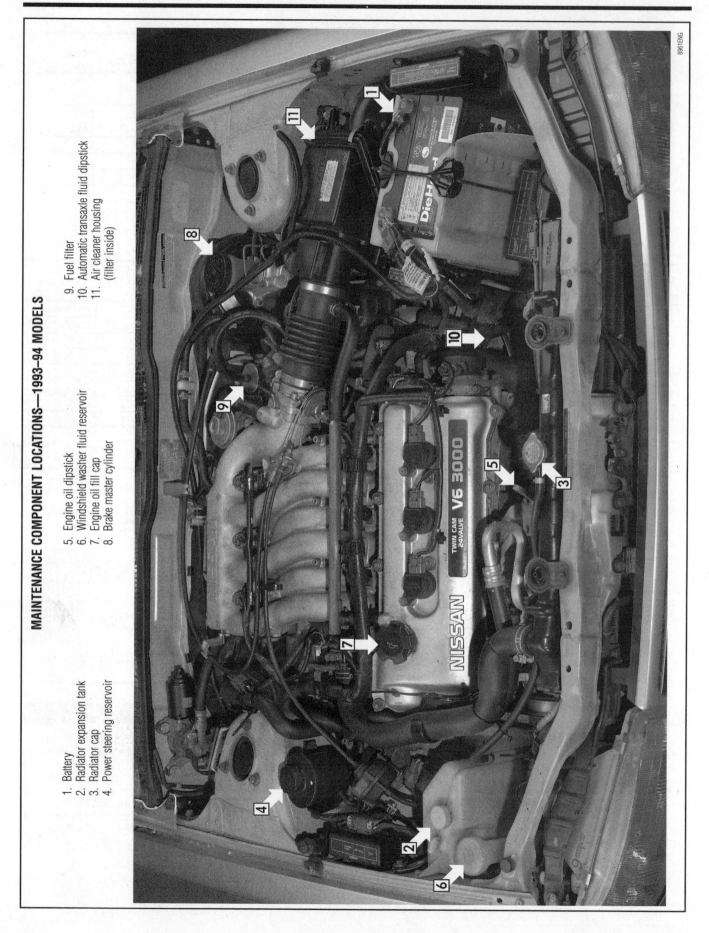

8961ENG

MAINTENANCE COMPONENT LOCATIONS—1995–98 ENGINES

1. Battery
2. Radiator expansion tank
3. Radiator cap
4. Power steering reservoir
5. Engine oil dipstick
6. Windshield washer fluid reservoir
7. Engine oil fill cap
8. Brake master cylinder reservoir
9. Automatic transaxle fluid dipstick
10. Air cleaner housing
   (filter inside)

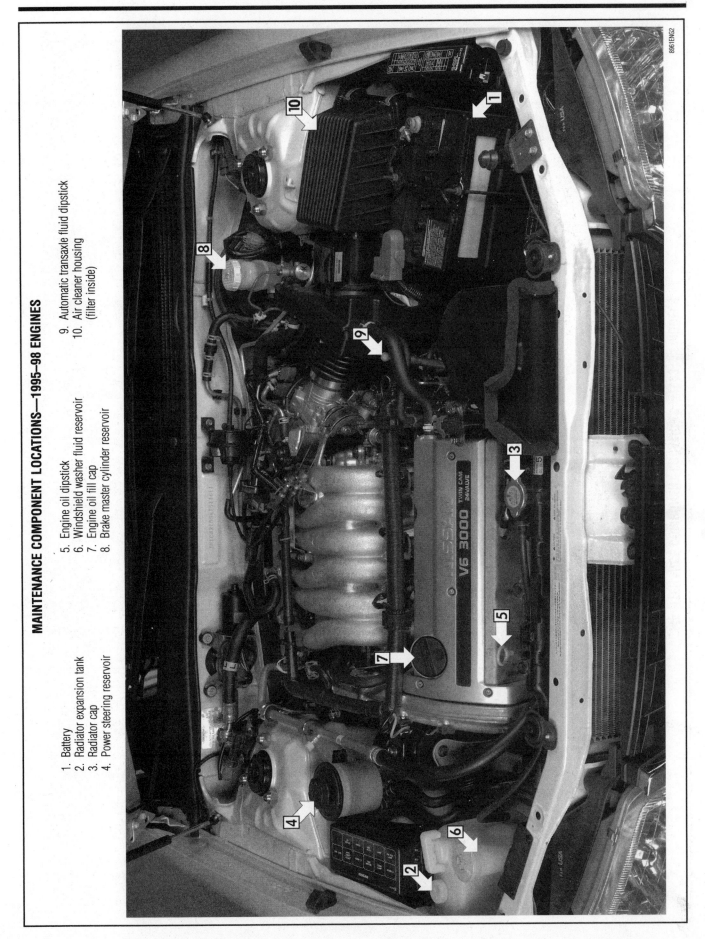

89611ENG2

Air Cleaner

An air cleaner is used to keep airborne dirt and dust out of the air flowing through the engine. Proper maintenance is vital, as a clogged element will restrict air flow and power, and allow excessive contamination of the oil with abrasives.

Maximas are equipped with a disposable, paper cartridge air filter element. The element should be checked at every tune-up or sooner if the vehicle is operated in a dusty area. Nissan does not recommend attempting to clean and reuse the element. The filter element should be replaced every 30,000 miles (48,000km).

REMOVAL & INSTALLATION

▶ **See Figures 44, 45 and 46**

1. Disengage the four clips on the sides of the air cleaner housing.
2. Lift up on the housing cover and remove the filter element.
3. Before installing the original or the replacement filter, wipe out the inside of the housing with a clean rag or paper towel.
   To install:
4. Install the paper air cleaner filter, seat the top cover on the bottom housing and tighten the wing nut(s), if equipped.

➡**Make sure the word UP is facing up when you install the filter element.**

Fuel Filter

The fuel filter is a disposable unit located in the engine compartment, next to the power brake booster. The filter should be replaced at least every 30,000 miles (48,000km). A dirty filter will starve the engine of fuel and cause driveability problems.

REMOVAL & INSTALLATION

▶ **See Figures 47, 48 and 49**

1. Remove the fuel pump fuse from the fuse panel.
2. Start the engine.
3. After the engine stalls, try to restart the engine. If the engine will not start, the fuel pressure has been released.
4. Turn the ignition switch **OFF**.
5. Using a shop rag to absorb the excess fuel, loosen the fuel filter's hose clamps, remove the hoses and the filter. Check the hoses for cracks and flexibility. Replace any hardened and/or cracked hoses.
6. Install a new fuel filter in the proper direction. Usually an arrow indicates the direction of fuel flow.

➡**Be sure to install a new high pressure fuel filter, not a carburetor type. Also, be sure to use new hose clamps.**

7. Install the fuel pump fuse.
8. Start the engine and check for leaks. It may be necessary to crank the engine for a time to build fuel pressure, so don't be alarmed if it doesn't start immediately.

Positive Crankcase Ventilation (PCV) Valve

▶ **See Figure 50**

This valve feeds crankcase blow-by gases into the intake manifold to be burned with the normal air/fuel mixture. The PCV valve has no strict interval for maintenance. However, it is wise to check the system occasionally in case of clogging, especially if you know that you have a vehicle that has been neglected. Make sure all PCV connections are tight. Check that the connecting hoses are clear and not clogged. Replace any brittle or broken hoses.

Fig. 44 The four spring clips on the edges of the air cleaner are disengaged by pulling back on the tabs

Fig. 45 Lift up on the upper filter housing, and slide out the filter element from the housing

Fig. 46 An example of a severely clogged filter element. A filter this dirty can hamper engine performance

Fig. 47 The fuel filter unclips from the bracket, allowing for easier replacement

Fig. 48 Be sure the filter is in the proper direction when attaching the hoses

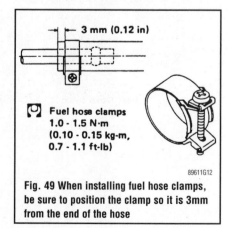

Fig. 49 When installing fuel hose clamps, be sure to position the clamp so it is 3mm from the end of the hose

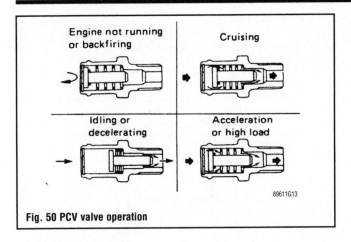

Fig. 50 PCV valve operation

REMOVAL & INSTALLATION

♦ **See Figure 51**

1. Squeeze the hose clamp with pliers and remove the hose.
2. If the valve has screw threads, use a wrench to unscrew it and remove the valve.
3. Disconnect the ventilation hoses; clean them if they are dirty.
4. Install the new PCV valve and replace the hoses and clamp.

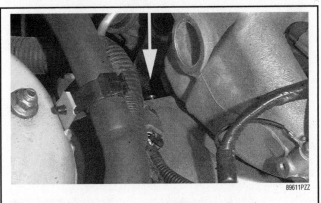

Fig. 51 PCV valve location on the VE30DE engine (arrow)

Evaporative Canister

SERVICING

♦ **See Figure 52**

The evaporation canister is maintenance free. Every 30,000 miles (48,000km), check the fuel and vapor lines for proper connections and correct routing as well as condition. Replace damaged or deteriorated parts as necessary.

Battery

PRECAUTIONS

Always use caution when working on or near the battery. Never allow a tool to bridge the gap between the negative and positive battery terminals. Also, be careful not to allow a tool to provide a ground between the positive cable/terminal and any metal component on the vehicle. Either of these conditions will cause a short circuit, leading to sparks and possible personal injury.

Do not smoke, have an open flame or create sparks near a battery; the gases contained in the battery are very explosive and, if ignited, could cause severe injury or death.

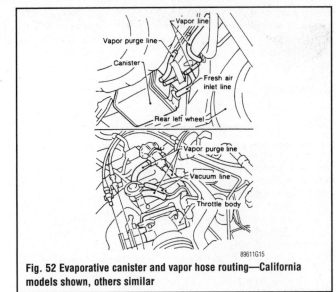

Fig. 52 Evaporative canister and vapor hose routing—California models shown, others similar

All batteries, regardless of type, should be carefully secured by a battery hold-down device. If this is not done, the battery terminals or casing may crack from stress applied to the battery during vehicle operation. A battery which is not secured may allow acid to leak out, making it discharge faster; such leaking corrosive acid can also eat away at components under the hood.

Always visually inspect the battery case for cracks, leakage and corrosion. A white corrosive substance on the battery case or on nearby components would indicate a leaking or cracked battery. If the battery is cracked, it should be replaced immediately.

GENERAL MAINTENANCE

♦ **See Figure 53**

A battery that is not sealed must be checked periodically for electrolyte level. You cannot add water to a sealed maintenance-free battery (though not all maintenance-free batteries are sealed); however, a sealed battery must also be checked for proper electrolyte level, as indicated by the color of the built-in hydrometer "eye."

Always keep the battery cables and terminals free of corrosion. Check these components about once a year..Refer to the removal, installation and cleaning procedures outlined in this section.

Keep the top of the battery clean, as a film of dirt can help completely discharge a battery that is not used for long periods. A solution of baking soda and water may be used for cleaning, but be careful to flush this off with clear water. DO NOT let any of the solution into the filler holes. Baking soda neutralizes battery acid and will de-activate a battery cell.

Batteries in vehicles which are not operated on a regular basis can fall victim to parasitic loads (small current drains which are constantly drawing current from the battery). Normal parasitic loads may drain a battery on a vehicle that is in storage

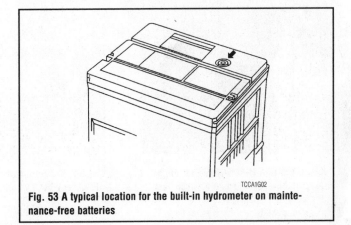

Fig. 53 A typical location for the built-in hydrometer on maintenance-free batteries

and not used for 6–8 weeks. Vehicles that have additional accessories such as a cellular phone, an alarm system or other devices that increase parasitic load may discharge a battery sooner. If the vehicle is to be stored for 6–8 weeks in a secure area and the alarm system, if present, is not necessary, the negative battery cable should be disconnected at the onset of storage to protect the battery charge.

Remember that constantly discharging and recharging will shorten battery life. Take care not to allow a battery to be needlessly discharged.

BATTERY FLUID

Check the battery electrolyte level at least once a month, or more often in hot weather or during periods of extended vehicle operation. On non-sealed batteries, the level can be checked either through the case on translucent batteries or by removing the cell caps on opaque-cased types. The electrolyte level in each cell should be kept filled to the split ring inside each cell, or the line marked on the outside of the case.

If the level is low, add only distilled water through the opening until the level is correct. Each cell is separate from the others, so each must be checked and filled individually. Distilled water should be used, because the chemicals and minerals found in most drinking water are harmful to the battery and could significantly shorten its life.

If water is added in freezing weather, the vehicle should be driven several miles to allow the water to mix with the electrolyte. Otherwise, the battery could freeze.

Although some maintenance-free batteries have removable cell caps for access to the electrolyte, the electrolyte condition and level on all sealed maintenance-free batteries must be checked using the built-in hydrometer "eye." The exact type of eye varies between battery manufacturers, but most apply a sticker to the battery itself explaining the possible readings. When in doubt, refer to the battery manufacturer's instructions to interpret battery condition using the built-in hydrometer.

➥**Although the readings from built-in hydrometers found in sealed batteries may vary, a green eye usually indicates a properly charged battery with sufficient fluid level. A dark eye is normally an indicator of a battery with sufficient fluid, but one which may be low in charge. And a light or yellow eye is usually an indication that electrolyte supply has dropped below the necessary level for battery (and hydrometer) operation. In this last case, sealed batteries with an insufficient electrolyte level must usually be discarded.**

Checking the Specific Gravity

▶ **See Figures 54, 55 and 56**

A hydrometer is required to check the specific gravity on all batteries that are not maintenance-free. On batteries that are maintenance-free, the specific gravity is checked by observing the built-in hydrometer "eye" on the top of the battery case. Check with your battery's manufacturer for proper interpretation of its built-in hydrometer readings.

☀ CAUTION

Battery electrolyte contains sulfuric acid. If you should splash any on your skin or in your eyes, flush the affected area with plenty of clear water. If it lands in your eyes, get medical help immediately.

The fluid (sulfuric acid solution) contained in the battery cells will tell you many things about the condition of the battery. Because the cell plates must be kept submerged below the fluid level in order to operate, maintaining the fluid level is extremely important. And, because the specific gravity of the acid is an indication of electrical charge, testing the fluid can be an aid in determining if the battery must be replaced. A battery in a vehicle with a properly operating charging system should require little maintenance, but careful, periodic inspection should reveal problems before they leave you stranded.

As stated earlier, the specific gravity of a battery's electrolyte level can be used as an indication of battery charge. At least once a year, check the specific gravity of the battery. It should be between 1.20 and 1.26 on the gravity scale. Most auto supply stores carry a variety of inexpensive battery testing hydrometers. These can be used on any non-sealed battery to test the specific gravity in each cell.

The battery testing hydrometer has a squeeze bulb at one end and a nozzle at the other. Battery electrolyte is sucked into the hydrometer until the float is lifted from its seat. The specific gravity is then read by noting the position of the float. If gravity is low in one or more cells, the battery should be slowly charged and checked again to see if the gravity has come up. Generally, if after charging, the specific gravity between any two cells varies more than 50 points (0.50), the battery should be replaced, as it can no longer produce sufficient voltage to guarantee proper operation.

CABLES

▶ **See Figures 57, 58, 59, 60 and 61**

Once a year (or as necessary), the battery terminals and the cable clamps should be cleaned. Loosen the clamps and remove the cables, negative cable first. On batteries with posts on top, the use of a puller specially made for this purpose is recommended. These are inexpensive and available in most auto parts stores. Side terminal battery cables are secured with a small bolt.

Clean the cable clamps and the battery terminal with a wire brush, until all corrosion, grease, etc., is removed and the metal is shiny. It is especially important to clean the inside of the clamp thoroughly (an old knife is useful here), since a small deposit of foreign material or oxidation there will prevent a sound electrical connection and inhibit either starting or charging. Special tools are available for cleaning these parts, one type for conventional top post batteries and another type for side terminal batteries. It is also a good idea to apply some dielectric grease to the terminal, as this will aid in the prevention of corrosion.

After the clamps and terminals are clean, reinstall the cables, negative cable last; DO NOT hammer the clamps onto battery posts. Tighten the clamps securely, but do not distort them. Give the clamps and terminals a thin external coating of grease after installation, to retard corrosion.

Check the cables at the same time that the terminals are cleaned. If the cable insulation is cracked or broken, or if the ends are frayed, the cable should be replaced with a new cable of the same length and gauge.

CHARGING

☀ CAUTION

The chemical reaction which takes place in all batteries generates explosive hydrogen gas. A spark can cause the battery to explode

TCCA1P07

Fig. 54 On non-maintenance-free batteries, the fluid level can be checked through the case on translucent models; the cell caps must be removed on other models

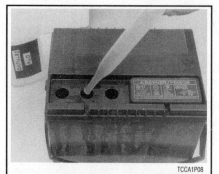

TCCA1P08

Fig. 55 If the fluid level is low, add only distilled water through the opening until the level is correct

TCCA1P09

Fig. 56 Check the specific gravity of the battery's electrolyte with a hydrometer

Fig. 57 Maintenance is performed with household items and with special tools like this post cleaner

Fig. 58 The underside of this special battery tool has a wire brush to clean post terminals

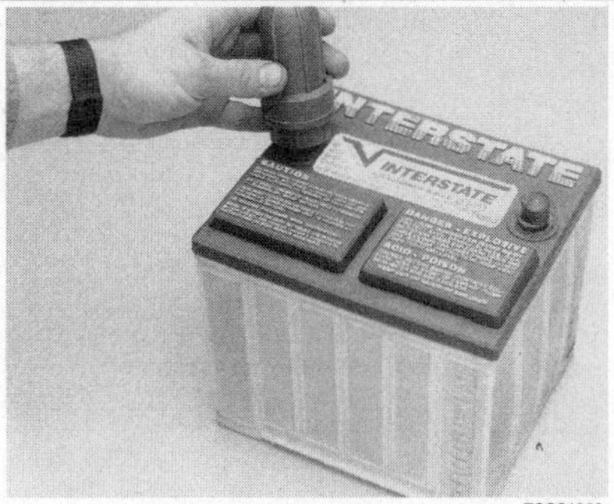

Fig. 59 Place the tool over the battery posts and twist to clean until the metal is shiny

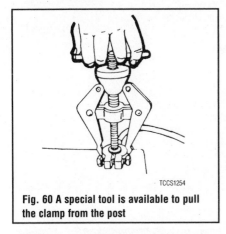

Fig. 60 A special tool is available to pull the clamp from the post

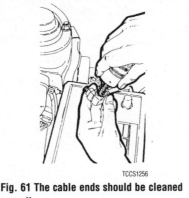

Fig. 61 The cable ends should be cleaned as well

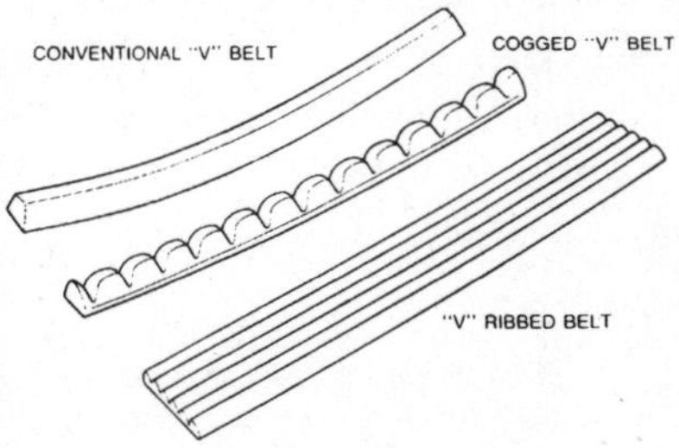

Fig. 62 There are typically 3 types of accessory drive belts found on vehicles today

and splash acid. **To avoid serious personal injury, be sure there is proper ventilation and take appropriate fire safety precautions when connecting, disconnecting, or charging a battery and when using jumper cables.**

A battery should be charged at a slow rate to keep the plates inside from getting too hot. However, if some maintenance-free batteries are allowed to discharge until they are almost "dead," they may have to be charged at a high rate to bring them back to "life." Always follow the charger manufacturer's instructions on charging the battery.

REPLACEMENT

When it becomes necessary to replace the battery, select one with an amperage rating equal to or greater than the battery originally installed. Deterioration and just plain aging of the battery cables, starter motor, and associated wires makes the battery's job harder in successive years. The slow increase in electrical resistance over time makes it prudent to install a new battery with a greater capacity than the old.

Belts

INSPECTION

▶ See Figures 62, 63, 64, 65 and 66

Inspect the belts for signs of glazing or cracking. A glazed belt will be perfectly smooth from slippage, while a good belt will have a slight texture of fabric visible. Cracks will usually start at the inner edge of the belt and run outward. All worn or damaged drive belts should be replaced immediately. It is best to replace all drive belts at one time, as a preventive maintenance measure, during this service operation.

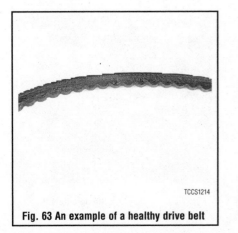

Fig. 63 An example of a healthy drive belt

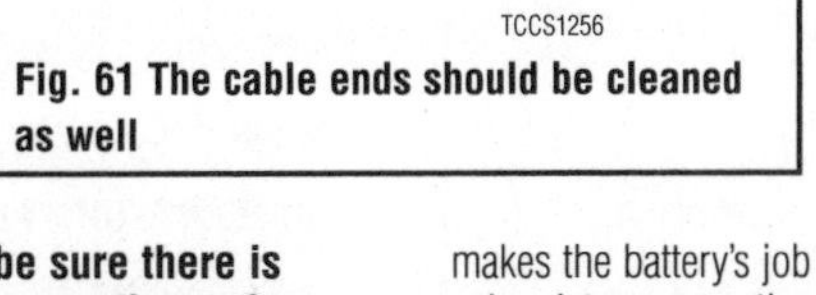

Fig. 64 Deep cracks in this belt that will eventually lead to belt failure

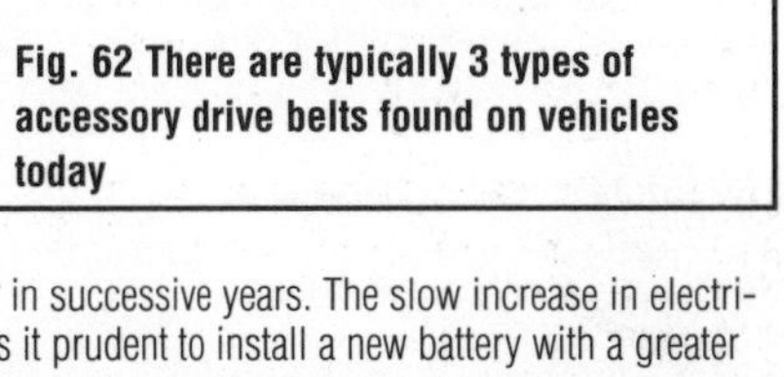

Fig. 65 Installing too wide a belt can result in serious belt wear and/or breakage

Fig. 66 The multi-ribbed belt on this VE30DE engine is in need of replacement; note the cracks on the belt

ADJUSTING

Belt deflection at the midpoint of the longest span between pulleys should not be more than ½ in. (13mm) with 22 lbs. (10kg) of pressure applied to the belt.

1993–94 Models

▶ See Figure 67

The belt tensions are adjusted using an adjustment bolt. The power steering pump and air compressor belt tensions are adjusted with the idler pulley.

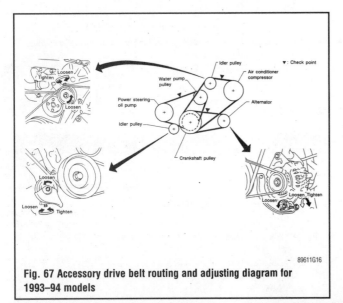

Fig. 67 Accessory drive belt routing and adjusting diagram for 1993–94 models

ALTERNATOR

▶ See Figures 68, 69 and 70

1. Disconnect the negative battery cable, for safety purposes.
2. Loosen the alternator's adjusting bolt locknut.
3. Loosen the alternator's pivot bolt.
4. Turn the adjusting bolt to adjust the belt tension.
5. Tighten the alternator's adjusting bolt locknut.
6. Tighten the alternator's mounting bolt.
7. Reconnect the negative battery cable.

AIR CONDITIONER COMPRESSOR

▶ See Figures 71 and 72

1. At the top of the idler pulley for the air conditioner, there is a bolt which is used to either raise or lower the pulley. To free the bolt for adjustment, it is necessary to loosen the locknut in the face of the idler pulley.
2. Loosen the idler pulley's mounting bolt.
3. Turn the adjusting bolt to adjust the belt tension.
4. After adjusting the belt tension, tighten the idler pulley's mounting bolt.

POWER STEERING PUMP

▶ See Figure 73

1. At the bottom of the idler pulley for the power steering pump, there is a bolt which is used to either raise or lower the pulley. To free the bolt for adjustment, it is necessary to loosen the locknut in the face of the idler pulley.
2. Loosen the idler pulley's mounting bolt.
3. Turn the adjusting bolt to adjust the belt tension.
4. After adjusting the belt tension, tighten the idler pulley's mounting bolt.
5. Reconnect the negative battery cable.

1995–98 Models

▶ See Figure 74

ALTERNATOR AND AIR CONDITIONING COMPRESSOR

▶ See Figure 75

1. Disconnect the negative battery cable.
2. Loosen the idler pulley bolt.
3. Turn the adjustment bolt at the top of the idler pulley bracket. Clockwise rotation will tighten the belt; counterclockwise will tighten it.

➡ **Keep the idler pulley bolt snug (but not tight) while adjusting belt tension. The adjustment bolt should turn with moderate force.**

4. After adjustment is satisfactory, tighten the idler pulley bolt, and then tighten the adjustment bolt.
5. Reconnect the negative battery cable.

POWER STEERING PUMP

1. Loosen the adjustment bolt locknut.
2. Loosen the pump pivot bolt.

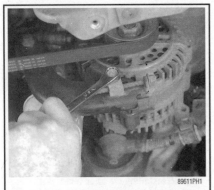

Fig. 68 Loosen the adjustment bolt locknut . . .

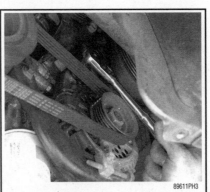

Fig. 69 . . . followed by the alternator pivot bolt . . .

Fig. 70 . . . then turn the adjustment bolt (arrow) to adjust the belt tension

Fig. 71 Loosen the mounting bolt just enough to allow the adjustment bolt to properly tension the belt

Fig. 72 After the tension is set with the adjustment bolt, tighten the mounting bolt and check the that the tension hasn't changed

Fig. 73 Loosen the pulley mounting bolt just enough to allow the adjustment bolt (arrow) to set the belt tension

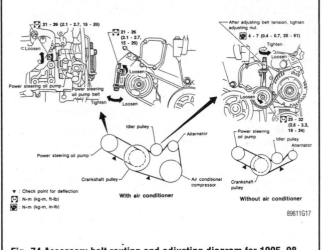

Fig. 74 Accessory belt routing and adjusting diagram for 1995–98 models

3. Turn the adjustment bolt to change the belt tension.
4. After adjustment is satisfactory, tighten the adjustment bolt locknut and the pump pivot bolt.
5. Check that the tension has not changed.

REMOVAL & INSTALLATION

♦ **See Figures 76 and 77**

The replacement of the inner belt on multi-belted engines may require the removal of the outer belts.

To replace a drive belt, loosen the adjusting and mounting bolts of the component which the belt is driving. Move the component inward to relieve the tension on the drive belt.

Slip the belt off the component pulley and match the new belt with the old belt for length and width. The old belt will be slightly longer. After a new belt is installed correctly, adjust the tension.

➡**When replacing more than 1 belt, it is a good idea to make note or mark what belt goes around what pulley; this will make installation easier if you mix up the belts.**

Timing Belts

SERVICING

Timing belts are typically only used on overhead camshaft engines. Timing belts are used to synchronize the crankshaft with the camshaft, similar to a timing chain on a overhead valve (pushrod) engine. Unlike a timing belt, a timing chain will normally last the life of the engine without needing service or replacement. Timing belts use raised teeth to mesh with sprockets to operate the valve train of an overhead camshaft engine.

Engines, chain or belt driven, can be classified as either free-running or interference. Depending on what would happen if the piston-to-valve timing is disrupted. A free-running engine has enough clearance between the piston and the valve to allow the crankshaft to turn (pistons still moving) while the camshaft stays in one position (several valves fully open). If this condition occurs normally, no internal engine damage will result. In an interference engine, there is not enough clearance between the pistons and valves to allow the crankshaft to turn without the camshaft being in time. Maximas from 1993–94 with the VG30E engine use a belt to drive the camshafts. The VG30E is also an interference type engine, which can suffer extensive internal damage if a timing belt fails. The piston design does not allow clearance for the valve to be fully open and the piston to be at the top of its stroke. If the belt fails, the piston will collide with the valve and will bend or break the valve, damage the

Fig. 75 Alternator and A/C compressor belt tensioner adjustment bolt

Fig. 76 After the tension on the belt is relieved, slip the belt from the pulley

Fig. 77 The replacement of some belts may require the removal of other belts

piston, and/or bend a connecting rod. When this type of failure occurs, the engine will need to be replaced or disassembled for further internal inspection; either choice costing approximately ten times the cost of replacing the timing belt.

The replacement interval for the VG30E engine timing belt is 60,000 miles (96,000km). But, if the timing belt is inspected earlier or more frequently than suggested, and shows signs of wear or defects, the belt should be replaced at that time.

Hoses

INSPECTION

▶ See Figures 78, 79, 80 and 81

The upper and lower radiator hoses and all heater hoses should be checked for deterioration, leaks and loose hose clamps every 15,000 miles (24,000Km). It is also wise to check the hoses periodically in early spring and at the beginning of the fall or winter when you are performing other maintenance. A quick visual inspection could discover a weakened hose which might have left you stranded if it had remained unrepaired.

Whenever you are checking the hoses, make sure the engine and cooling system are cold. Visually inspect for cracking, rotting or collapsed hoses, and replace as necessary. Run your hand along the length of the hose. If a weak or swollen spot is noted when squeezing the hose wall, the hose should be replaced.

REMOVAL & INSTALLATION

✷ CAUTION

When draining the coolant, keep in mind that cats and dogs are attracted by ethylene glycol antifreeze, and are quite likely to drink

TCCS1219
Fig. 78 The cracks developing along this hose are a result of age-related hardening

any that is left in an uncovered container or in puddles on the ground. This will prove fatal in sufficient quantity. Always drain the coolant into a sealable container. Coolant should be reused unless it is contaminated or several years old.

1. Remove the radiator pressure cap.

✷✷ CAUTION

Never remove the pressure cap while the engine is running, or personal injury from scalding hot coolant or steam may result. If possible, wait until the engine has cooled to remove the pressure cap. If this is not possible, wrap a thick cloth around the pressure cap and turn it slowly to the stop. Step back while the pressure is released from the cooling system. When you are sure all the pressure has been released, use the cloth to turn and remove the cap.

2. Position a clean container under the radiator and/or engine draincock or plug, then open the drain and allow the cooling system to drain to an appropriate level. For some upper hoses, only a little coolant must be drained. To remove hoses positioned lower on the engine, such as a lower radiator hose, the entire cooling system must be emptied.
3. Loosen the hose clamps at each end of the hose requiring replacement. Clamps are usually either of the spring tension type (which require pliers to squeeze the tabs and loosen) or of the screw tension type (which require screw or hex drivers to loosen). Pull the clamps back on the hose away from the connection.
4. Twist, pull and slide the hose off the fitting, taking care not to damage the neck of the component from which the hose is being removed.

➡If the hose is stuck at the connection, do not try to insert a screwdriver or other sharp tool under the hose end in an effort to free it, as the connection and/or hose may become damaged. Heater connections especially may be easily damaged by such a procedure. If the hose is to be replaced, use a single-edged razor blade to make a slice along the portion of the hose which is stuck on the connection, perpendicular to the end of the hose. Do not cut deep so as to prevent damaging the connection. The hose can then be peeled from the connection and discarded.

5. Clean both hose mounting connections. Inspect the condition of the hose clamps and replace them, if necessary.
   To install:
6. Dip the ends of the new hose into clean engine coolant to ease installation.
7. Slide the clamps over the replacement hose, then slide the hose ends over the connections into position.
8. Position and secure the clamps at least ¼ in. (6.35mm) from the ends of the hose. Make sure they are located beyond the raised bead of the connector.
9. Close the radiator or engine drains and properly refill the cooling system with the clean drained engine coolant or a suitable mixture of ethylene glycol coolant and water.
10. If available, install a pressure tester and check for leaks. If a pressure tester is not available, run the engine until normal operating temperature is reached (allowing the system to naturally pressurize), then check for leaks.

TCCS1220
Fig. 79 A hose clamp that is too tight can cause older hoses to separate and tear on either side of the clamp

TCCS1221
Fig. 80 A soft spongy hose (identifiable by the swollen section) will eventually burst and should be replaced

TCCS1222
Fig. 81 Hoses are likely to deteriorate from the inside if the cooling system is not periodically flushed

✳ CAUTION

If you are checking for leaks with the system at normal operating temperature, BE EXTREMELY CAREFUL not to touch any moving or hot engine parts. Once temperature has been reached, shut the engine OFF, and check for leaks around the hose fittings and connections which were removed earlier.

CV-Boots

INSPECTION

▶ See Figures 82 and 83

The CV (Constant Velocity) boots should be checked for damage each time the oil is changed and any other time the vehicle is raised for service. These boots keep water, grime, dirt and other damaging matter from entering the CV-joints. Any of these could cause early CV-joint failure which can be expensive to repair. Heavy grease thrown around the inside of the front wheel(s) and on the brake caliper/drum can be an indication of a torn boot. Thoroughly check the boots for missing clamps and tears. If the boot is damaged, it should be replaced immediately. Please refer to Section 7 for procedures.

Spark Plugs

▶ See Figure 84

A typical spark plug consists of a metal shell surrounding a ceramic insulator. A metal electrode extends downward through the center of the insulator and protrudes a small distance. Located at the end of the plug and attached to the side of the outer metal shell is the side electrode. The side electrode bends in at a 90° angle so that its tip is just past and parallel to the tip of the center electrode. The distance between these two electrodes (measured in thousandths of an inch or hundredths of a millimeter) is called the spark plug gap.

The spark plug does not produce a spark but instead provides a gap across which the current can arc. The coil produces anywhere from 20,000 to 50,000 volts (depending on the type and application) which travels through the wires to the spark plugs. The current passes along the center electrode and jumps the gap to the side electrode, and in doing so, ignites the air/fuel mixture in the combustion chamber.

SPARK PLUG HEAT RANGE

▶ See Figure 85

Spark plug heat range is the ability of the plug to dissipate heat. The longer the insulator (or the farther it extends into the engine), the hotter the plug will operate; the shorter the insulator (the closer the electrode is to the block's cooling passages) the cooler it will operate. A plug that absorbs little heat and remains too cool will quickly accumulate deposits of oil and carbon since it is not hot enough to burn them off. This leads to plug fouling and consequently to misfiring. A plug that absorbs too much heat will have no deposits but, due to the excessive heat, the electrodes will burn away quickly and might possibly lead to preignition or other ignition problems. Preignition takes place when plug tips get so hot that they glow sufficiently to ignite the air/fuel mixture before the actual spark occurs. This early ignition will usually cause a pinging during low speeds and heavy loads.

The general rule of thumb for choosing the correct heat range when picking a spark plug is: if most of your driving is long distance, high speed travel, use a colder plug; if most of your driving is stop and go, use a hotter plug. Original equipment plugs are generally a good compromise between the 2 styles and most people never have the need to change their plugs from the factory-recommended heat range.

REMOVAL & INSTALLATION

▶ See Figures 86 thru 92

A set of spark plugs usually requires replacement after about 20,000–30,000 miles (32,000–48,000 km), depending on your style of driving. In normal oper-

Fig. 82 CV-boots must be inspected periodically for damage

Fig. 83 A torn boot should be replaced immediately

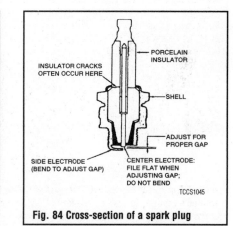

Fig. 84 Cross-section of a spark plug

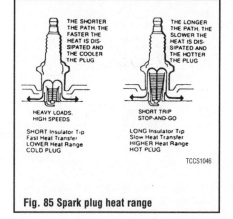

Fig. 85 Spark plug heat range

Fig. 86 The VQ30DE engines have a decorative facia that must be removed to access the coils and spark plugs

Fig. 87 Pinch the tab on the coil connector, then pull the head off it

Fig. 88 VQ30DE and VE30DE engines have individual coils for the spark plugs; you have to remove them to get to the spark plugs

Fig. 89 After the retainer screw is removed, carefully pull the coil out of the cylinder head

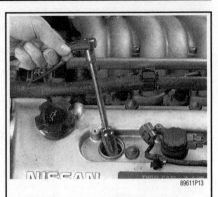

Fig. 90 Use a long extension with a locking end to remove the spark plugs

Fig. 91 When installing a spark plug, be careful not to bump the electrode out of adjustment

Fig. 92 Always use anti-seize compound on the spark plugs to prevent stripping out the aluminum threads

ation plug gap increases about 0.001 in. (0.025mm) for every 2500 miles (4000 km). As the gap increases, the plug's voltage requirement also increases. It requires a greater voltage to jump the wider gap and about two to three times as much voltage to fire the plug at high speeds than at idle. The improved air/fuel ratio control of modern fuel injection combined with the higher voltage output of modern ignition systems will often allow an engine to run significantly longer on a set of standard spark plugs, but keep in mind that efficiency will drop as the gap widens (along with fuel economy and power).

When you're removing spark plugs, work on one at a time. Don't start by removing the plug wires all at once, because, unless you number them, they may become mixed up. Take a minute before you begin and number the wires with tape.

1. Disconnect the negative battery cable, and if the vehicle has been run recently, allow the engine to thoroughly cool.

2. Carefully twist the spark plug wire boot to loosen it, then pull upward and remove the boot from the plug. Be sure to pull on the boot and not on the wire, otherwise the connector located inside the boot may become separated.

3. Using compressed air, blow any water or debris from the spark plug well to assure that no harmful contaminants are allowed to enter the combustion chamber when the spark plug is removed. If compressed air is not available, use a rag or a brush to clean the area.

➡Remove the spark plugs when the engine is cold, if possible, to prevent damage to the threads. If removal of the plugs is difficult, apply a few drops of penetrating oil or silicone spray to the area around the base of the plug, and allow it a few minutes to work.

4. Using a spark plug socket that is equipped with a rubber insert to properly hold the plug, turn the spark plug counterclockwise to loosen and remove the spark plug from the bore.

✳✳ WARNING

Do not to use a flexible extension on the socket. Use of a flexible extension may allow a shear force to be applied to the plug. A shear force could break the plug off in the cylinder head, leading to costly and frustrating repairs.

To install:

5. Inspect the spark plug boot for tears or damage. If a damaged boot is found, the spark plug wire must be replaced. If the engine has distributorless ignition, carefully look over the coils for any cracks or signs of arcing.

6. Using a wire feeler gauge, check and adjust the spark plug gap. When using a gauge, the proper size should pass between the electrodes with a slight drag. The next larger size should not be able to pass while the next smaller size should pass freely.

7. Carefully thread the plug into the bore by hand. If resistance is felt before the plug is almost completely threaded, back the plug out and begin threading again. In small, hard to reach areas, an old spark plug wire and boot could be used as a threading tool. The boot will hold the plug while you twist the end of the wire and the wire is supple enough to twist before it would allow the plug to crossthread.

8. Carefully tighten the spark plug. If the plug you are installing is equipped with a crush washer, seat the plug, then tighten about ¼ turn to crush the washer. If you are installing a tapered seat plug, tighten the plug to specifications provided by the vehicle or plug manufacturer.

9. Apply a small amount of silicone dielectric compound to the end of the spark plug lead or inside the spark plug boot to prevent sticking, then install the boot or coil onto the spark plug and push until it clicks into place. The click may be felt or heard, then gently pull back on the boot or coil to assure proper contact.

INSPECTION & GAPPING

▶ **See Figures 93, 94, 95, 96 and 97**

Check the plugs for deposits and wear. If they are not going to be replaced, clean the plugs thoroughly. Remember that any kind of deposit will decrease the efficiency of the plug. Plugs can be cleaned on a spark plug cleaning machine, which can sometimes be found in service stations, or you can do an acceptable job of cleaning with a stiff brush. If the plugs are cleaned, the electrodes must be filed flat. Use an ignition points file, not an emery board or the like, which will leave deposits. The electrodes must be filed perfectly flat with sharp edges; rounded edges reduce the spark plug voltage by as much as 50%.

A normally worn spark plug should have light tan or gray deposits on the firing tip.

A carbon fouled plug, identified by soft, sooty, black deposits, may indicate an improperly tuned vehicle. Check the air cleaner, ignition components and engine control system.

This spark plug has been **left in the engine too long,** as evidenced by the extreme gap- Plugs with such an extreme gap can cause misfiring and stumbling accompanied by a noticeable lack of power.

An oil fouled spark plug indicates an engine with worn poston rings and/or bad valve seals allowing excessive oil to enter the chamber.

A physically damaged spark plug may be evidence of severe detonation in that cylinder. Watch that cylinder carefully between services, as a continued detonation will not only damage the plug, but could also damage the engine.

A bridged or almost bridged spark plug, identified by a build-up between the electrodes caused by excessive carbon or oil build-up on the plug.

TCCA1P40

Fig. 93 Inspect the spark plug to determine engine running conditions

TCCS1212

Fig. 94 A variety of tools and gauges are needed for spark plug service

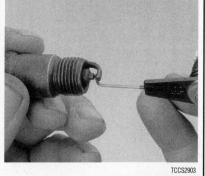

TCCS2903

Fig. 95 Checking the spark plug gap with a feeler gauge

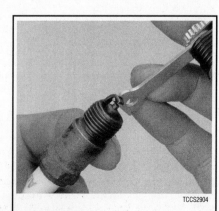

TCCS2904

Fig. 96 Adjusting the spark plug gap

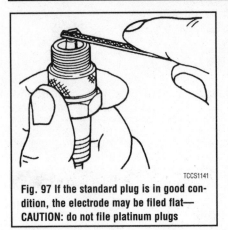

Fig. 97 If the standard plug is in good condition, the electrode may be filed flat— CAUTION: do not file platinum plugs

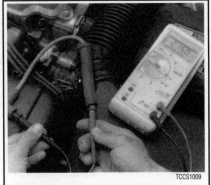

Fig. 98 Checking individual plug wire resistance with a digital ohmmeter

Fig. 99 VG30E distributor cap detail

Check spark plug gap before installation. The ground electrode (the L-shaped one connected to the body of the plug) must be parallel to the center electrode and the specified size wire gauge (please refer to the Tune-Up Specifications chart for details) must pass between the electrodes with a slight drag.

➡**NEVER adjust the gap or use a wire brush on a used platinum type spark plug.**

Always check the gap on new plugs as they are not always set correctly at the factory. Do not use a flat feeler gauge when measuring the gap on a used plug, because the reading may be inaccurate. A round-wire type gapping tool is the best way to check the gap. The correct gauge should pass through the electrode gap with a slight drag. If you're in doubt, try one size smaller and one larger. The smaller gauge should go through easily, while the larger one shouldn't go through at all. Wire gapping tools usually have a bending tool attached. Use that to adjust the side electrode until the proper distance is obtained. Absolutely never attempt to bend the center electrode. Also, be careful not to bend the side electrode too far or too often as it may weaken and break off within the engine, requiring removal of the cylinder head to retrieve it.

Spark Plug Wires

Every 15,000 miles (24,000 km) ,inspect the spark plug wires for burns, cuts or breaks in the insulation. Check the boots and the nipples on the distributor cap. Replace any damaged wiring.

Every 50,000 miles (80,000 km) or 60 months, the resistance of the wires should be checked with an ohmmeter. Wires with excessive resistance will cause misfiring, and may make the engine difficult to start in damp weather.

TESTING

▶ **See Figure 98**

1. Remove the distributor cap, leaving the wires in place.
2. Connect one lead of an ohmmeter to an electrode within the cap. Connect the other lead to the corresponding spark plug terminal (remove it from the spark plug for this test). Replace any wire which shows a resistance over 30,000 ohms. Resistance should not be over 25,000 ohms; 30,000 ohms must be considered the outer limit of acceptability.

➡**Resistance is also a function of length; the longer the wire, the greater the resistance. Thus, if the wires on your vehicle are longer than the factory originals, resistance will be higher, quite possibly outside the limits.**

REMOVAL & INSTALLATION

When installing new wires, replace them one at a time to avoid mix-ups. Start by replacing the longest one first. Install the boot firmly over the spark plug. Route the wire over the same path as the original. Insert the nipple firmly onto the tower on the distributor cap, then install the cap cover and latches to secure the wires.

Distributor Cap and Rotor

It is normally a good idea to inspect the distributor cap and rotor any time you perform a tune-up which includes checking the spark plug wires for wear, damage or excessive resistance. This procedure applies to VG30E engines only.

VE30DE and VQ30DE engines use a computer controlled distributorless ignition, with individual coils for each cylinder that attach directly to each spark plug.

REMOVAL & INSTALLATION

▶ **See Figure 99**

➡**Depending on the reason you have for removing the distributor cap, it may (in some cases) make more sense to leave the spark plug wires attached. This is handy if you are testing spark plug wires or if removal was necessary to access other components (and the length of the wires allows you to reposition the cap out of the way).**

1. Remove the distributor cover.
2. Tag the spark plug and ignition coil wires and the distributor cap for reassembly, then disconnect the wires from the cap. THIS STEP IS CRITICAL. Do not attempt to rewire the cap based only on a diagram, this too often leads to confusion and miswiring.
3. Remove the three screws that hold down the distributor cap.
4. Carefully lift the distributor cap STRAIGHT up and off the distributor in order to prevent damage to the rotor blade and spring.
5. Remove the rotor mounting screw, then grasp the rotor by hand and pull upward to remove it from the distributor shaft and armature.
6. Inspect both the distributor cap and rotor for damage and replace as necessary.

To install:
7. Place the rotor on the distributor shaft, then carefully align it with the threaded hole on the side of the shaft. Make sure the rotor is fully seated, but do not force it, as plastic components often break easily.
8. Install and tighten the rotor mounting screw snugly.
9. Position the distributor cap on the base and align the cap with the screw holes.
10. Secure the cap using the hold-down screws.
11. If removed, connect the spark plug wire leads as tagged during removal.
12. Connect the negative battery cable.

INSPECTION

After removing the distributor cap and rotor, clean the components (both inside and outside of the cap) using soap and water. If compressed air is available, carefully dry the components (wearing safety goggles) or allow the parts to air dry. You can dry them with a clean, soft cloth, just don't leave any lint or moisture behind.

Once the cap and rotor have been thoroughly cleaned, check for cracks, carbon tracks, burns or other physical damage. Make sure the carbon button inside the cap is free of damage. Check the cap terminals for dirt or corrosion. Always check the rotor blade and spring closely for damage. Replace any components where damage is found.

Ignition Timing

These vehicles use a complex electronic fuel injection system which is controlled by a series of temperature and air flow sensors which feed information into an Engine Control Module, or ECM. The ECM regulates ignition timing and fuel delivery based on the input of the engine sensors to achieve maximum performance and fuel economy.

The ignition timing on these vehicles is set at the factory, and does not normally require adjustment. The following procedures are included to check or reset the ignition timing if the distributor, crankshaft or camshaft position sensor have been replaced.

INSPECTION & ADJUSTMENT

VG30E Engine

▶ See Figure 100

1. Be sure all accessories (air conditioning, heater blower motor, radio, etc.) are off and the steering centered, with both manual and automatic transaxle models in the **N** position. Be sure to block the wheels and set the parking brake. The radiator cooling fan may cycle during this procedure. Be sure the radiator cooling fan is off. As the load on the electrical system is increased, engine speed is affected.

❊❊ CAUTION

The radiator cooling fan may cycle during this procedure. Be sure to keep your hands and tools away from the fan blades.

2. Locate the timing marks on the crankshaft pulley on the front of the engine.
3. Clean the timing marks, and the pointer which will indicate the timing when aligned with the correct notch on the crankshaft pulley.
4. Start the engine and allow it to reach normal operating temperature (water temperature gauge indicator pointing in the middle) while keeping the engine speed below 1000 rpm.
5. Raise the hood and run the engine at 2000 rpm for about two minutes.
6. If the engine runs smoothly, race the engine 2–3 times and then let it idle for one minute.
7. Turn the engine off and connect a timing light to the engine.
8. Start the engine and aim the timing light at the timing marks. If the marks on the pulley and the engine are aligned when the light flashes, the timing is correct.
9. If the timing is not within specifications, turn the engine off. Loosen the distributor hold-down bolt slightly, BUT DO NOT ALLOW THE DISTRIBUTOR TO MOVE. The distributor should be tight enough to remain in place when the engine is running.
10. Start the engine, and turn the distributor SLOWLY until the timing is correct. Tighten the distributor hold-down bolt when the timing is correct.

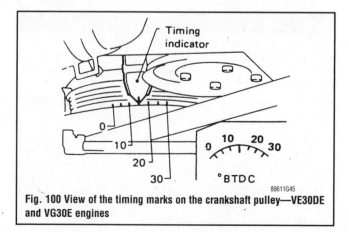

Fig. 100 View of the timing marks on the crankshaft pulley—VE30DE and VG30E engines

11. If the timing cannot be adjusted within specifications, perform the idle speed adjustment procedure, then readjust the timing as necessary.

VE30DE Engine

▶ See Figures 100 thru 106

1. Be sure all accessories (air conditioning, heater blower motor, radio, etc.) are off and the steering centered, with both manual and automatic transaxle models in the **Neutral** position. Be sure to block the wheels and set the parking brake. The radiator cooling fan may cycle during this procedure. Be sure the radiator cooling fan is off when checking the ignition timing. As the load on the electrical system is increased, engine speed is affected.

❊❊ CAUTION

The radiator cooling fan may cycle during this procedure. Be sure to keep your hands and tools away from the fan blades.

2. Locate the timing marks on the crankshaft pulley on the front of the engine.
3. Clean the timing marks, and the pointer which will indicate the timing when aligned with the correct notch on the crankshaft pulley.
4. Start the engine and allow it to reach normal operating temperature (water temperature gauge indicator pointing in the middle) while keeping the engine speed below 1000 rpm.
5. Raise the hood and run the engine at 2000 rpm for about two minutes.
6. Turn the engine off and unplug the Throttle Position Sensor (TPS) harness connector and the Auxiliary Air Control (AAC) valve harness connector.
7. Start the engine.
8. Race the engine 2–3 times and then let it idle for one minute.

Fig. 101 Clean the marks on the pulley and outline them with correction fluid to allow easier viewing

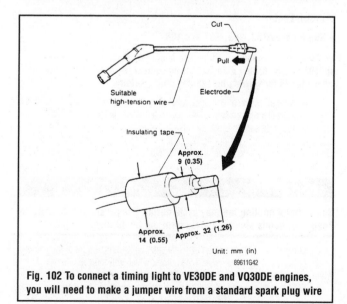

Fig. 102 To connect a timing light to VE30DE and VQ30DE engines, you will need to make a jumper wire from a standard spark plug wire

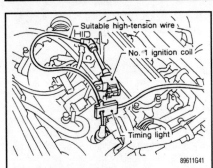

Fig. 103 The jumper wire will go between the individual plug coil and the plug itself, allowing attachment of an inductive pickup from a timing light

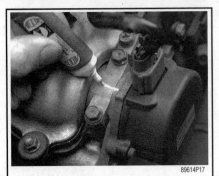

Fig. 104 It is advisable to mark the sensor for a reference point when adjusting the timing

Fig. 105 Loosen the bolts on the camshaft sensor just enough to move it by hand with moderate force

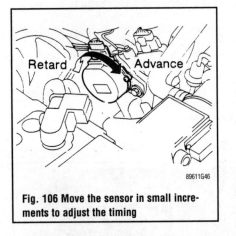

Fig. 106 Move the sensor in small increments to adjust the timing

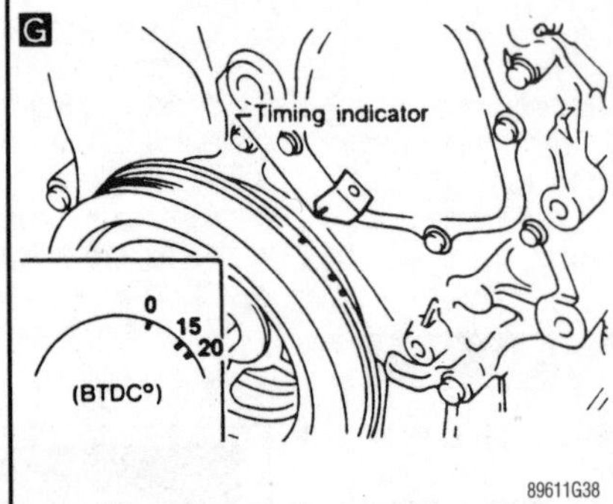

Fig. 107 View of the timing marks on the VQ30DE engine

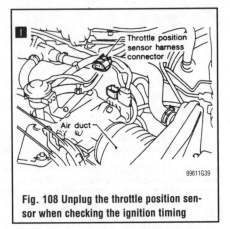

Fig. 108 Unplug the throttle position sensor when checking the ignition timing

9. Turn the engine off, and connect a timing light to the engine.

10. Start the engine and aim the timing light at the timing marks. If the marks on the pulley and the engine are aligned when the light flashes, the timing is correct.

11. If the timing is not within specifications, turn the engine off. Then loosen the camshaft position sensor hold-down bolt(s) slightly, BUT DO NOT ALLOW THE SENSOR TO MOVE.

12. Start the engine, and turn the camshaft position sensor SLOWLY until the timing is correct. Once the timing is correct, tighten the hold-down bolt(s).

13. If the timing cannot be adjusted within specifications, refer to section 4 for diagnostic procedures to check for faulty components.

VQ30DE Engine

♦ See Figures 102, 103, 107 and 108

➡The ignition timing on this engine is not adjustable. If not within specifications, further diagnostic inspection is required. The following procedure is for viewing the ignition timing setting.

1. Be sure all accessories (air conditioning, heater blower motor, radio, etc.) are off and the steering centered, with both manual and automatic transaxles in the **N** position. Be sure to block the wheels and set the parking brake. The radiator cooling fan may cycle during this procedure. Be sure the radiator cooling fan is off when checking the timing. As the load on the electrical system is increased, engine speed is affected.

✳✳ CAUTION

The radiator cooling fan may cycle during this procedure. Be sure to keep your hands and tools away form the fan blades.

2. Locate the timing marks on the crankshaft pulley on the front of the engine.

3. Clean the timing marks, and the pointer which will indicate the timing when aligned with the correct notch on the crankshaft pulley.

4. Start the engine and allow it to reach normal operating temperature (water

temperature gauge indicator pointing in the middle) while keeping the engine speed below 1000 rpm.

5. Raise the hood and run the engine at 2000 rpm for about two minutes.

6. Connect a timing light to the number one cylinder ignition wire on the engine.

7. Perform the following procedures:

   a. Race the engine at 2000 rpm for about two minutes under a no—load condition; make sure all of the accessories are turned off.

   b. Perform on board engine diagnostics and repair any fault code.

   c. Race the engine at 2000 rpm for about two minutes.

   d. Turn the engine off and disconnect the throttle position sensor.

   e. Start and race the engine 2–3 times under no–load then run the engine at idle speed.

8. Aim the timing light at the timing marks. If the mark on the pulley and the engine are aligned when the light flashes, the timing is correct.

9. If the timing cannot be adjusted within specifications, refer to section 4 for diagnostic procedures to check for faulty components.

Valve Lash

Maximas with VG30E and VE30DE engines use hydraulic type camshaft followers which are not adjustable. If the engine exhibits excessive valve noise, this may indicate valve train wear or clogged camshaft adjusters. These procedures apply only to the VQ30DE engines.

➡Check and adjust the valve clearances while the engine is cold and not running.

CHECKING

♦ See Figures 109, 110, 111, 112 and 113

1. Remove the intake manifold collector.
2. Remove the left and right rocker covers.
3. Remove the spark plugs.

4. Set the No. 1 cylinder at TDC on its compression stroke. Align the pointer with the TDC mark on the crankshaft pulley. Check that the valve lifters on the No. 1 cylinder are loose and valve lifters on the No. 4 cylinder are tight. If not, turn the crankshaft one revolution (360 degrees) and align the pointer with the TDC mark on the crankshaft pulley.

5. Check the following valves:
   a. Both No. 1 intake valves.
   b. Both No. 2 exhaust valves.
   c. Both No. 3 exhaust valves.
   d. Both No. 6 intake valves.

6. Using a feeler gauge, measure the clearance between the cam follower and the camshaft. Intake valve clearance (cold) is 0.010–0.013 in. (0.26–0.34mm) and exhaust valve clearance (cold) is 0.011–0.015 in. (0.29–0.37mm). The feeler gauge should fit between the cam lobe and the cam follower with slight resistance.

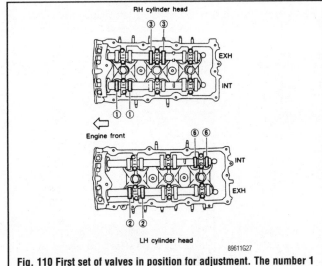

Fig. 109 Align the timing marks to put the number 1 cylinder at TDC on the compression stroke

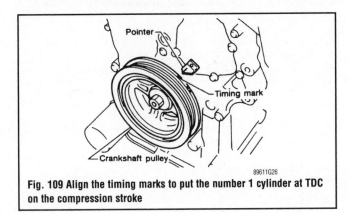

Fig. 110 First set of valves in position for adjustment. The number 1 cylinder should be at TDC on the compression stroke

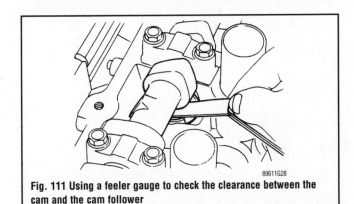

Fig. 111 Using a feeler gauge to check the clearance between the cam and the cam follower

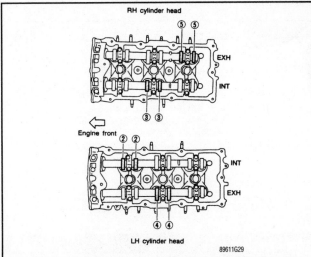

Fig. 112 Second set of valves in position for adjustment. The number 3 cylinder should be at TDC on the compression stroke

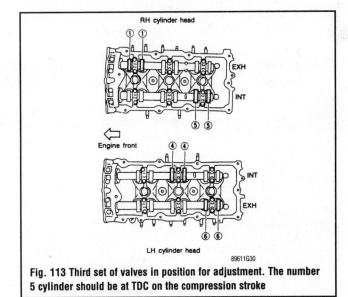

Fig. 113 Third set of valves in position for adjustment. The number 5 cylinder should be at TDC on the compression stroke

If the clearance is excessive, (or too little) select a thicker or thinner gauge until it fits appropriately, and then record the gauge thickness. It may be helpful to draw a diagram of each cylinder to keep track of your measurements.

7. Turn the crankshaft 240 degrees and set the No. 3 cylinder to TDC of its compression stroke.

8. Check the following valves:
   a. Both No. 2 intake valves.
   b. Both No. 3 intake valves.
   c. Both No. 4 exhaust valves.
   d. Both No. 5 exhaust valves.

9. Using a feeler gauge, measure the clearance between the cam follower and the camshaft.

10. Turn the crankshaft 240 degrees and set the No. 5 cylinder to TDC of its compression stroke.

11. Check the following valves:
   a. Both No. 1 exhaust valves.
   b. Both No. 4 intake valves.
   c. Both No. 5 intake valves.
   d. Both No. 6 exhaust valves.

12. Using a feeler gauge, measure the clearance between the cam follower and the camshaft.

13. If all the valve clearances are within specification, install the cylinder head covers, spark plugs, and the intake manifold collector.

ADJUSTING

♦ **See Figures 114, 115, 116 and 117**

If an adjustment is necessary, the valve clearance can be changed by replacing the shim(s). Valve adjustment will require special tool set, Nissan No. KV101151S0 The Camshaft Pliers will allow you to grip the camshaft and depress the cam follower. The Cam Follower Keeper allows the cam follower to remain depressed when the pliers are removed. These specialized tools are also made by aftermarket manufacturers and are usually available at most auto parts stores.

1. Turn the crankshaft CLOCKWISE so the camshaft lobe of the valve to be adjusted is pointed straight up.

2. Turn the cam follower so the notch is pointed towards the center of the cylinder head; this will facilitate the shim removal process.

3. Using the camshaft pliers, (tool No. KV10115110 or equivalent), push down on the cam follower and insert the cam follower keeper (tool No. KV10115120 or equivalent) on the edge of the cam follower to keep it in the depressed position.

※※ CAUTION

Be sure keeper tool is fully seated on the edge of the cam follower before removing the camshaft pliers. The keeper tool could slip off the cam follower from the valve spring pressure and become a projectile. Wear safety glasses during this procedure.

4. Remove the depressor tool and remove the shim with a magnet.

➡ **Compressed air can be blown into the hole of the cam follower to remove the adjusting shim.**

5. Determine the replacement adjusting shim size by using the following procedures and formula:

　　a. Using a micrometer, determine thickness of the removed shim.
　　b. Calculate the thickness of a new adjusting shim so valve clearance is within the specified values.

- Intake shim determination formula: N = R + (M—0.0118 in. or 0.30mm)
- Exhaust shim determination formula: N = R + (M—0.0130 in. or 0.33mm)
- R = thickness of the removed shim.
- N = thickness of the new shim.
- M = measured valve clearance.

　　c. Shims are available in 64 sizes from 0.0913–0.1161 in. (2.32–2.95mm) in steps of 0.004 in. (0.01mm). The thickness is stamped on the shim; this side is always installed facing down. Select new shims with thickness as close as possible to calculated value.

6. Install the new shim, then depress the cam follower with the camshaft pliers and remove the keeper tool. Check the valve clearance. Repeat this procedure for any other valves requiring adjustment.

Idle Speed and Mixture Adjustments

♦ **See Figure 118**

These vehicles use a complex electronic fuel injection system which is controlled by a series of temperature and air flow sensors which feed information into an Engine Control Module, or ECM. The ECM regulates ignition timing and fuel delivery based on the input of the engine sensors to achieve maximum performance and fuel economy.

The idle speed on these vehicles is set at the factory, and does not normally require adjustment. If the vehicle is not idling correctly, refer to Section 4 to diagnose faulty components. The following procedures are included to reset the idle speed if the throttle body has been replaced.

IDLE SPEED ADJUSTMENT

VG30E Engines

♦ **See Figures 119 and 120**

1. Be sure all accessories (air conditioning, heater blower motor, radio, etc.) are off and the steering centered, with both manual and automatic transaxle

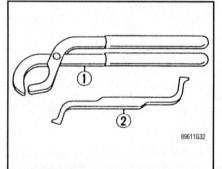

Fig. 114 These special tools, available from Nissan or the aftermarket, will be required to adjust the valves

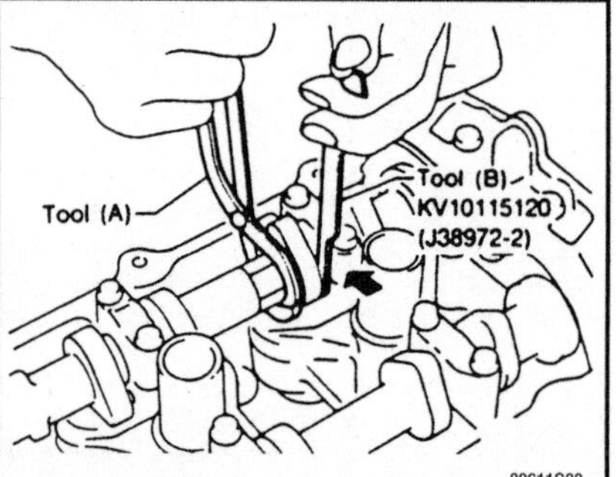

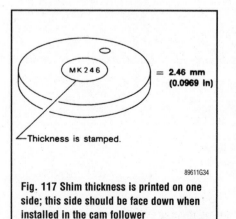

Thickness is stamped.

Fig. 117 Shim thickness is printed on one side; this side should be face down when installed in the cam follower

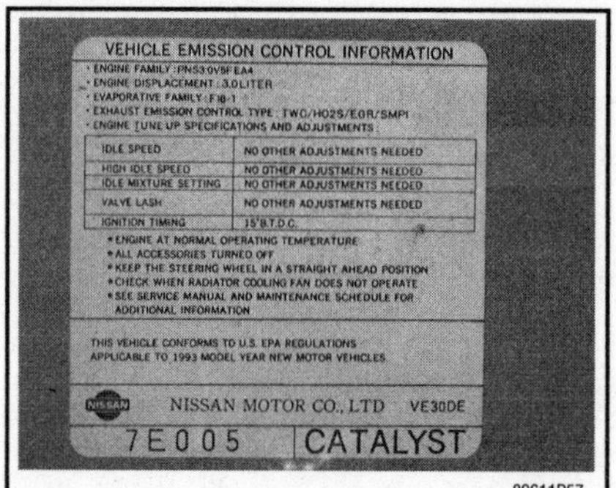

Fig. 115 Insert the keeper tool between the camshaft and the cam follower while pushing down with the pliers

Fig. 118 The vehicle emission control information sticker, usually on the inner hood panel, contains vital information for tune-ups

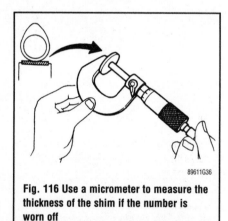

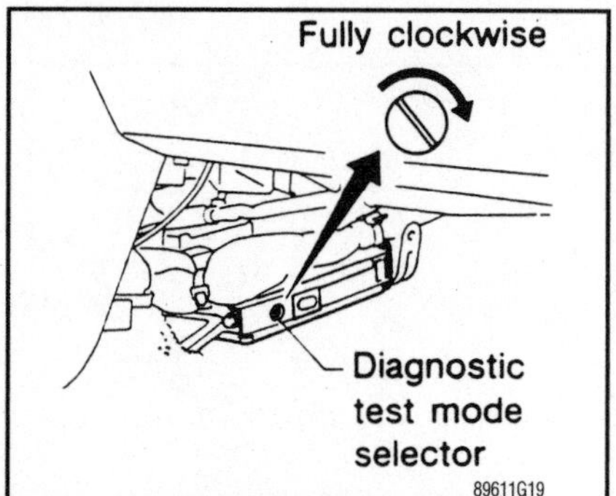

Fig. 116 Use a micrometer to measure the thickness of the shim if the number is worn off

Fig. 119 Turn the diagnostic test mode selector fully clockwise before adjusting the idle speed

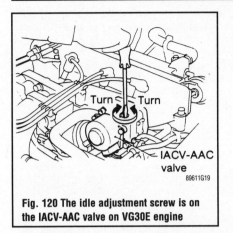

Fig. 120 The idle adjustment screw is on the IACV-AAC valve on VG30E engine

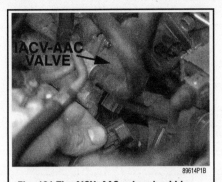

Fig. 121 The AICV–AAC valve should be unplugged when checking and adjusting the idle speed

Fig. 122 The throttle position sensor should also be disconnected when checking and adjusting the idle speed

models in the **N** position. Be sure to block the wheels and set the parking brake. Be sure the radiator cooling fan is off while checking and/or adjusting the timing and idle speed. As the load on the electrical system is increased, engine speed is affected.

2. Before adjusting the idle speed, visually check the following items first: air cleaner for being clogged, hoses and ducts for leaks, EGR valve for proper operation, all electrical connectors, gaskets and idle switch.

3. Start the engine and warm it to operating temperature, until water temperature indicator points to the middle of the gauge.

4. Then race the engine to 2000–3000 rpm a few times and then allow it to idle for one minute.

5. Check the ignition timing and adjust if necessary.

6. Close the Auxiliary Air Control (AAC) valve by turning the diagnostic mode selector on the ECM fully clockwise.

7. Correct the idle speed by turning the idle speed adjusting screw.

8. Operate the Auxiliary Air Control (AAC) valve by turning the diagnostic mode selector on the ECM fully counterclockwise and recheck the idle speed.

9. Run the engine at approximately 2000 rpm for about 2 minutes.

10. Verify that the idle speed is correct. If not, there may be faulty components within the engine management system. Refer to Section 4 for diagnostic procedures.

VE30DE Engines

▶ **See Figures 121, 122 and 123**

1. Be sure all accessories (air conditioning, heater blower motor, radio, etc.) are off and the steering centered, with both manual and automatic transaxle models in the **N** position. Be sure to block the wheels and set the parking brake. Be sure the radiator cooling fan is off while checking and/or adjusting the timing and idle speed. As the load on the electrical system is increased, engine speed is affected.

⁂ CAUTION

The radiator cooling fan may cycle during this procedure. Be sure to keep your hands and tools away from the fan blades.

2. Before adjusting the idle speed, visually check the following items first: air cleaner for being clogged, hoses and ducts for leaks, EGR valve for proper operation, all electrical connectors, gaskets and idle switch.

3. Unplug the Idle Air Control Valve/Auxiliary Air Control (IACV—AAC) valve harness connector and the Throttle Position Sensor (TPS) harness connector.

4. Start the engine and warm it to operating temperature (water temperature gauge indicator needle in the middle).

5. Race the engine 2–3 times (at 2000–3000 rpm) and them let it idle for one minute. The idle speed should be within the specifications of the Tune—up Specifications Chart. To correct the idle speed, turn the idle speed adjustment screw.

6. Turn the engine off and plug in the IACV—AAC valve and TPS harness connectors.

7. Start the engine and race it 2–3 times (at 2000–3000 rpm) and then let it idle for one minute.

8. Check that the idle speed is correct. If idling problems persist, refer to Section 4 to diagnose the electronic engine control system.

VQ30DE Engines

▶ **See Figure 124**

1. Be sure all accessories (air conditioning, heater blower motor, radio, etc.) are off and the steering centered, with both manual and automatic transaxle models in the **Neutral** position. Be sure to block the wheels and set the parking brake. Be sure the radiator cooling fan is off while checking and/or adjusting the timing and idle speed. As the load on the electrical system is increased, engine speed is affected.

⁂ CAUTION

The radiator cooling fan may cycle during this procedure. Be sure to keep your hands and tools away from the fan blades.

2. Before adjusting the idle speed, visually check the following items first: air cleaner for being clogged, hoses and ducts for leaks, EGR valve for proper operation, all electrical connectors, gaskets and idle switch.

3. Unplug the Throttle Position Sensor (TPS) connector.

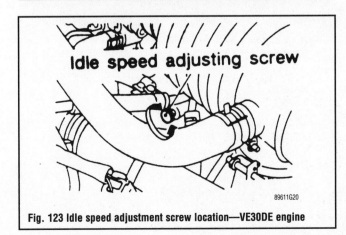

Fig. 123 Idle speed adjustment screw location—VE30DE engine

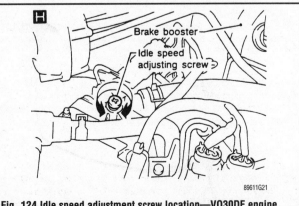

Fig. 124 Idle speed adjustment screw location—VQ30DE engine

TUNE-UP SPECIFICATIONS

Year	Engine ID/VIN	Engine Displacement Liters (cc)	Spark Plugs Gap (in.)	Ignition Timing (deg.) MT	Ignition Timing (deg.) AT	Fuel Pump (psi)	Idle Speed (rpm) MT	Idle Speed (rpm) AT	Valve Clearance In.	Valve Clearance Ex.
1993	H	3.0L (2960)	0.039–0.043	—	14–16 B	36.3 ①	— ②	750 ②	HYD	HYD
	E	3.0L (2960)	0.039–0.043	14–16 B	14–16 B	36 ①	750 ②	790 ②	HYD	HYD
1994	H	3.0L (2960)	0.039–0.043	—	14–16 B	36.3 ①	— ②	750 ②	HYD	HYD
	E	3.0L (2960)	0.039–0.043	14–16 B	14–16 B	36 ①	750 ②	790 ②	HYD	HYD
1995	LH	3.0L (2988)	0.039–0.043	14–16 B	14–16 B	34 ①	625 ②	700 ②	0.010–0.013 ③	0.011–0.015 ③
1996	LH	3.0L (2988)	0.039–0.043	14–16 B	14–16 B	34 ①	625 ②	700 ②	0.010–0.013 ③	0.011–0.015 ③
1997	LH	3.0L (2988)	0.039–0.043	14–16 B	14–16 B	34 ①	625 ②	700 ②	0.010–0.013 ③	0.011–0.015 ③
1998	LH	3.0L (2988)	0.039–0.043	14–16 B	14–16 B	34 ①	625 ②	700 ②	0.010–0.013 ③	0.011–0.015 ③

B : Before top dead center
① With regulator vacuum hose connected
② All accessories off, + or - 50 rpm
③ Engine COLD

89611C04

4. Start the engine and warm it to operating temperature (water temperature gauge indicator needle in the middle).

5. Race the engine 2–3 times (at 2000–3000 rpm) and them let it idle for one minute. The idle speed should be within the specifications of the Tune—up Specifications Chart. To correct the idle speed, turn the idle speed adjustment screw.

6. Turn the engine off and plug in the TPS connector.

7. Start the engine and race it 2–3 times (at 2000–3000 rpm) and then let it idle for one minute.

8. Check that the idle speed is correct. If necessary, refer to Section 4 to diagnose the electronic engine control system.

MIXTURE ADJUSTMENT

The air/fuel mixture is controlled by the ECM, and adjustment is not necessary or possible.

Air Conditioning System

SYSTEM SERVICE & REPAIR

➡It is recommended that the A/C system be serviced by an EPA Section 609 certified automotive technician utilizing a refrigerant recovery/recycling machine.

The do-it-yourselfer should not service his/her own vehicle's A/C system for many reasons, including legal concerns, personal injury, environmental damage and cost. The following are some of the reasons why you may decide not to service your own vehicle's A/C system.

According to the U.S. Clean Air Act, it is a federal crime to service or repair (involving the refrigerant) a Motor Vehicle Air Conditioning (MVAC) system for money without being EPA certified. It is also illegal to vent R-134a refrigerant into the atmosphere.

State and/or local laws may be more strict than the federal regulations, so be sure to check with your state and/or local authorities for further information. For further federal information on the legality of servicing your A/C system, call the EPA Stratospheric Ozone Hotline.

➡Federal law dictates that a fine of up to $25,000 may be levied on people convicted of venting refrigerant into the atmosphere. Additionally, the EPA may pay up to $10,000 for information or services leading to a criminal conviction of the violation of these laws.

When servicing an A/C system you run the risk of handling or coming in contact with refrigerant, which may result in skin or eye irritation or frostbite. Although low in toxicity (due to chemical stability), inhalation of concentrated refrigerant fumes is dangerous and can result in death; cases of fatal cardiac arrhythmia have been reported in people accidentally subjected to high levels of refrigerant. Some early symptoms include loss of concentration and drowsiness.

Also, refrigerants can decompose at high temperatures (near gas heaters or open flame), which may result in hydrofluoric acid, hydrochloric acid and phosgene (a fatal nerve gas).

R-134a refrigerant is a greenhouse gas which, if allowed to vent into the atmosphere, will contribute to global warming (the Greenhouse Effect).

It is usually more economically feasible to have a certified MVAC automotive technician perform A/C system service to your vehicle. While it is illegal to service an A/C system without the proper equipment, the home mechanic would have to purchase an expensive refrigerant recovery/recycling machine to service his/her own vehicle.

PREVENTIVE MAINTENANCE

Although the A/C system should not be serviced by the do-it-yourselfer, preventive maintenance can be practiced and A/C system inspections can be performed to help maintain the efficiency of the vehicle's A/C system. For preventive maintenance, perform the following:

• The easiest and most important preventive maintenance for your A/C system is to be sure that it is used on a regular basis. Running the system for five minutes each month (no matter what the season) will help ensure that the seals and all internal components remain lubricated.

➡Some newer vehicles automatically operate the A/C system compressor whenever the windshield defroster is activated. When running, the compressor lubricates the A/C system components; therefore, the A/C system would not need to be operated each month.

• In order to prevent heater core freeze-up during A/C operation, it is necessary to maintain a proper antifreeze protection. Use a hand-held coolant tester (hydrometer) to periodically check the condition of the antifreeze in your engine's cooling system.

➡Antifreeze should not be used longer than the manufacturer specifies.

• For efficient operation of an air conditioned vehicle's cooling system, the radiator cap should have a holding pressure which meets manufacturer's specifications. A cap which fails to hold these pressures should be replaced.

• Any obstruction of or damage to the condenser configuration will restrict air flow which is essential to its efficient operation. It is, therefore, a good rule to keep this unit clean and in proper physical shape.

➡Bug screens which are mounted in front of the condenser (unless they are original equipment) are regarded as obstructions.

• The condensation drain tube expels any water, which accumulates on the bottom of the evaporator housing, into the engine compartment. If this tube is obstructed, the air conditioning performance can be restricted and condensation buildup can spill over onto the vehicle's floor.

SYSTEM INSPECTION

Although the A/C system should not be serviced by the do-it-yourselfer, preventive maintenance can be practiced and A/C system inspections can be performed to help maintain the efficiency of the vehicle's A/C system. For A/C system inspection, perform the following:

The easiest and often most important check for the air conditioning system consists of a visual inspection of the system components. Visually inspect the air conditioning system for refrigerant leaks, damaged compressor clutch, abnormal compressor drive belt tension and/or condition, plugged evaporator drain tube, blocked condenser fins, disconnected or broken wires, blown fuses, corroded connections and poor insulation.

A refrigerant leak will usually appear as an oily residue at the leakage point in the system. The oily residue soon picks up dust or dirt particles from the surrounding air and appears greasy. Through time, this will build up and appear to be a heavy dirt impregnated grease.

For a thorough visual and operational inspection, check the following:
* Check the surface of the radiator and condenser for dirt, leaves or other material which might block air flow.
* Check for kinks in hoses and lines. Check the system for leaks.
* Make sure the drive belt is properly tensioned. When the air conditioning is operating, make sure the drive belt is free of noise or slippage.
* Make sure the blower motor operates at all appropriate positions, then check for distribution of the air from all outlets with the blower on **HIGH** or **MAX**.

➡️**Keep in mind that under conditions of high humidity, air discharged from the A/C vents may not feel as cold as expected, even if the system is working properly. This is because vaporized moisture in humid air retains heat more effectively than dry air, thereby making humid air more difficult to cool.**

* Make sure the air passage selection lever is operating correctly. Start the engine and warm it to normal operating temperature, then make sure the temperature selection lever is operating correctly.

Windshield Wipers

ELEMENT (REFILL) CARE & REPLACEMENT

▶ See Figures 125 thru 134

For maximum effectiveness and longest element life, the windshield and wiper blades should be kept clean. Dirt, tree sap, road tar and so on will cause streaking, smearing and blade deterioration if left on the glass. It is advisable to wash the windshield carefully with a commercial glass cleaner at least once a month. Wipe off the rubber blades with the wet rag afterwards. Do not attempt to move wipers across the windshield by hand; damage to the motor and drive mechanism will result.

To inspect and/or replace the wiper blade elements, place the wiper switch in the **LOW** speed position and the ignition switch in the **ACC** position. When the wiper blades are approximately vertical on the windshield, turn the ignition switch to **OFF**.

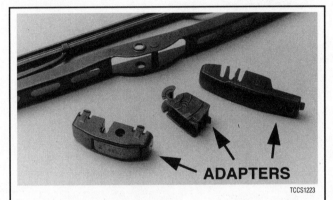

Fig. 125 Bosch® wiper blade and fit kit

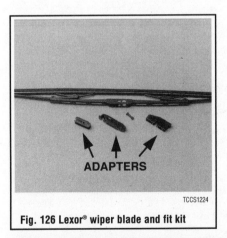

Fig. 126 Lexor® wiper blade and fit kit

Fig. 127 Pylon® wiper blade and adapter

Fig. 128 Trico® wiper blade and fit kit

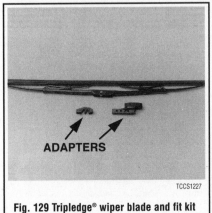

Fig. 129 Tripledge® wiper blade and fit kit

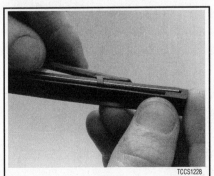

Fig. 130 To remove and install a Lexor® wiper blade refill, slip out the old insert and slide in a new one

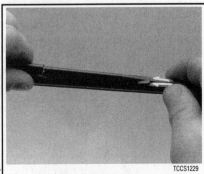

Fig. 131 On Pylon® inserts, the clip at the end has to be removed prior to sliding the insert off

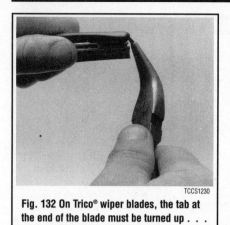

Fig. 132 On Trico® wiper blades, the tab at the end of the blade must be turned up . . .

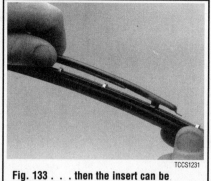

Fig. 133 . . . then the insert can be removed. After installing the replacement insert, bend the tab back

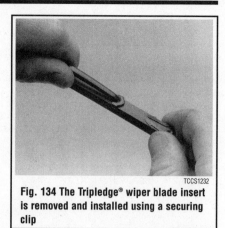

Fig. 134 The Tripledge® wiper blade insert is removed and installed using a securing clip

Examine the wiper blade elements. If they are found to be cracked, broken or torn, they should be replaced immediately. Replacement intervals will vary with usage, although ozone deterioration usually limits element life to about one year. If the wiper pattern is smeared or streaked, or if the blade chatters across the glass, the elements should be replaced. It is easiest and most sensible to replace the elements in pairs.

If your vehicle is equipped with aftermarket blades, there are several different types of refills and your vehicle might have any kind. Aftermarket blades and arms rarely use the exact same type blade or refill as the original equipment. Here are some typical aftermarket blades; not all may be available for your vehicle:

The Anco® type uses a release button that is pushed down to allow the refill to slide out of the yoke jaws. The new refill slides back into the frame and locks in place.

Some Trico® refills are removed by locating where the metal backing strip or the refill is wider. Insert a small screwdriver blade between the frame and metal backing strip. Press down to release the refill from the retaining tab.

Other types of Trico® refills have two metal tabs which are unlocked by squeezing them together. The rubber filler can then be withdrawn from the frame jaws. A new refill is installed by inserting the refill into the front frame jaws and sliding it rearward to engage the remaining frame jaws. There are usually four jaws; be certain when installing that the refill is engaged in all of them. At the end of its travel, the tabs will lock into place on the front jaws of the wiper blade frame.

Another type of refill is made from polycarbonate. The refill has a simple locking device at one end which flexes downward out of the groove into which the jaws of the holder fit, allowing easy release. By sliding the new refill through all the jaws and pushing through the slight resistance when it reaches the end of its travel, the refill will lock into position.

To replace the Tridon® refill, it is necessary to remove the wiper blade. This refill has a plastic backing strip with a notch about 1 in. (25mm) from the end. Hold the blade (frame) on a hard surface so that the frame is tightly bowed. Grip the tip of the backing strip and pull up while twisting counterclockwise. The backing strip will snap out of the retaining tab. Do this for the remaining tabs until the refill is free of the blade. The length of these refills is molded into the end and they should be replaced with identical types.

Regardless of the type of refill used, be sure to follow the part manufacturer's instructions closely. Make sure that all of the frame jaws are engaged as the refill is pushed into place and locked. If the metal blade holder and frame are allowed to touch the glass during wiper operation, the glass will be scratched.

Tire and Wheels

Common sense and good driving habits will afford maximum tire life. Fast starts, sudden stops and hard cornering are hard on tires and will shorten their useful life span. Make sure that you don't overload the vehicle or drive with incorrect pressure in the tires. Both of these practices will increase tread wear.

➡**For optimum tire life, keep the tires properly inflated, rotate them often and have the wheel alignment checked periodically.**

Inspect your tires frequently. Be especially careful to watch for bubbles in the tread or sidewall, deep cuts or underinflation. Replace any tires with bubbles in the sidewall. If cuts are so deep that they penetrate to the cords, discard the tire. Any cut in the sidewall of a radial tire renders it unsafe. Also look for uneven tread wear patterns that may indicate the front end is out of alignment or that the tires are out of balance.

TIRE ROTATION

◆ **See Figures 135, 136 and 137**

Tires must be rotated periodically to equalize wear patterns that vary with a tire's position on the vehicle. Tires will also wear in an uneven way as the front steering/suspension system wears to the point where the alignment should be reset.

Rotating the tires will ensure maximum life for the tires as a set, so you will not have to discard a tire early due to wear on only part of the tread. Typically, the right front tire will wear the quickest. This is a result of the convex shape of most road surfaces.

Nissan recommends rotating tires every 7,500 miles (12,000km). When rotating "unidirectional tires," make sure that they always roll in the same direction. This means that a tire used on the left side of the vehicle must not be switched to the right side and vice-versa. Such tires should only be rotated

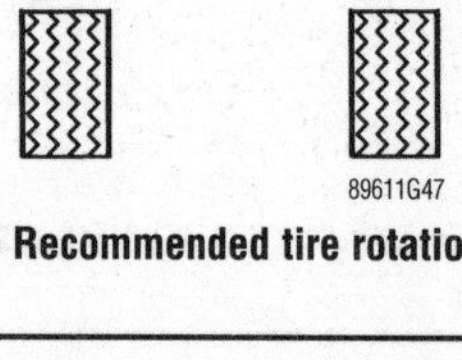

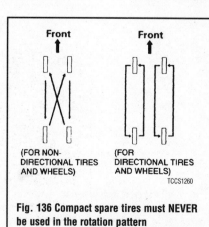

Fig. 135 Recommended tire rotation pattern

Fig. 136 Compact spare tires must NEVER be used in the rotation pattern

Fig. 137 Unidirectional tires are identifiable by sidewall arrows and/or the word "rotation"

front-to-rear or rear-to-front, while always remaining on the same side of the vehicle. These tires are marked on the sidewall as to the direction of rotation; observe the marks when reinstalling the tire(s).

Some styled or "mag" wheels may have different offsets front to rear. In these cases, the rear wheels must not be used up front and vice-versa. Furthermore, if these wheels are equipped with unidirectional tires, they cannot be rotated unless the tire is remounted for the proper direction of rotation.

➥The compact or space-saver spare is strictly for emergency use. It must never be included in the tire rotation or placed on the vehicle for everyday use.

TIRE DESIGN

◆ **See Figure 138**

For maximum satisfaction, tires should be used in sets of four. Mixing of different types (radial, bias-belted, fiberglass belted) must be avoided. In most cases, the vehicle manufacturer has designated a type of tire on which the vehicle will perform best. Your first choice when replacing tires should be to use the same type of tire that the manufacturer recommends.

When radial tires are used, tire sizes and wheel diameters should be selected to maintain ground clearance and tire load capacity equivalent to the original specified tire. Radial tires should always be used in sets of four.

❄❄ CAUTION

Radial tires should never be used on only the front axle.

When selecting tires, pay attention to the original size as marked on the tire. Most tires are described using an industry size code sometimes referred to as P-Metric. This allows the exact identification of the tire specifications, regardless of the manufacturer. If selecting a different tire size or brand, remember to check the installed tire for any sign of interference with the body or suspension while the vehicle is stopping, turning sharply or heavily loaded.

Snow Tires

Good radial tires can be an advantage in slippery weather, but in snow, a street radial tire does not have sufficient tread to provide traction and control. The small grooves of a street tire quickly pack with snow and the tire behaves like a billiard ball on a marble floor. The more aggressive, chunky tread of a snow tire will self-clean as the tire turns, providing much better grip on snowy surfaces.

To satisfy municipalities requiring snow tires during weather emergencies, most snow tires carry either an M + S designation after the tire size stamped on the sidewall, or the designation "all-season." In general, no change in tire size is necessary when buying snow tires.

Most manufacturers strongly recommend the use of 4 snow tires on their vehicles for reasons of stability. If snow tires are fitted only to the drive wheels, the opposite end of the vehicle may become very unstable when braking or turning on slippery surfaces. This instability can lead to unpleasant endings if the driver can't counteract a slide in time.

Note that snow tires will affect vehicle handling in all non-snow situations. The stiffer, heavier snow tires will noticeably change the turning and braking

characteristics of the vehicle on dry pavement. Once the snow tires are installed, you must re-learn the behavior of the vehicle and drive accordingly.

➥Consider buying extra wheels on which to mount the snow tires. Once done, the "snow wheels" can be installed and removed as needed. This eliminates the potential damage to tires or wheels from seasonal removal and installation. Even if your vehicle has styled wheels, check if inexpensive steel wheels are available. Although the look of the vehicle will change, the expensive wheels will be protected from salt, curb hits and pothole damage during the winter months.

TIRE STORAGE

If they are mounted on wheels, store the tires at proper inflation pressure. All tires should be kept in a cool, dry place. If they are stored in the garage or basement, do not let them stand on a concrete floor; set them on strips of wood, a mat or a large stack of newspaper. Keeping them away from direct moisture is of paramount importance. Tires should not be stored upright, but in a flat position.

INFLATION & INSPECTION

◆ **See Figures 139 thru 146**

The importance of proper tire inflation cannot be overemphasized. A tire employs air as part of its structure. It is designed around the supporting strength of the air at a specified pressure. For this reason, improper inflation drastically reduces the tire's ability to perform as intended. A tire will lose some air in day-to-day use; having to add a few pounds of air periodically is not necessarily a sign of a leaking tire.

Two items should be a permanent fixture in every glove compartment: an accurate tire pressure gauge and a tread depth gauge. Check the tire pressure (including the spare) regularly with a pocket type gauge. Too often, the gauge on the end of the air hose at your corner garage is not accurate because it suffers too much abuse. Always check tire pressure when the tires are cold, as pressure increases with temperature. Never counteract excessive pressure build-up by bleeding off air pressure (letting some air out). This will cause the tire to run hotter and wear quicker. If you must move the vehicle to check the tire inflation, do not drive more than a mile before checking. A cold tire is generally one that has not been driven for more than three hours.

A plate or sticker is normally provided somewhere in the vehicle (door post, hood, tailgate or trunk lid) which shows the proper pressure for the tires.

❄❄ CAUTION

Never exceed the maximum tire pressure embossed on the tire! This is the pressure to be used when the tire is at maximum loading, but it is rarely the correct pressure for everyday driving. Consult the owner's manual or the tire pressure sticker for the correct tire pressure.

Once you've maintained the correct tire pressures for several weeks, you'll be familiar with the vehicle's braking and handling personality. Slight adjustments in tire pressures can fine-tune these characteristics, but never change the cold pressure specification by more than 2 psi. A slightly softer tire pressure will give a softer ride but also yield lower fuel mileage. A slightly harder tire will give crisper dry road handling but can cause skidding on wet surfaces. Unless you're fully attuned to the vehicle, stick to the recommended inflation pressures.

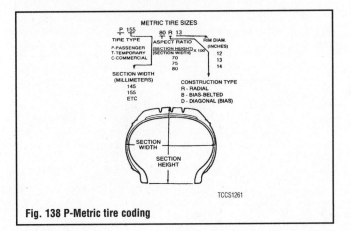

Fig. 138 P-Metric tire coding

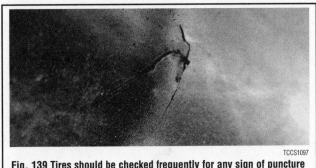

Fig. 139 Tires should be checked frequently for any sign of puncture or damage

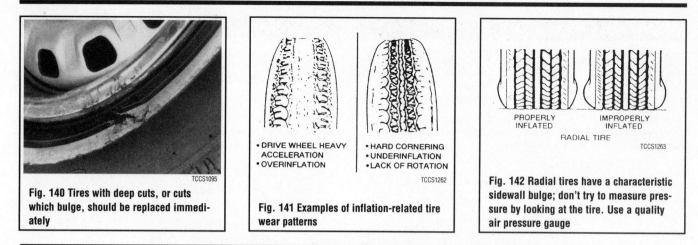

Fig. 140 Tires with deep cuts, or cuts which bulge, should be replaced immediately

Fig. 141 Examples of inflation-related tire wear patterns

Fig. 142 Radial tires have a characteristic sidewall bulge; don't try to measure pressure by looking at the tire. Use a quality air pressure gauge

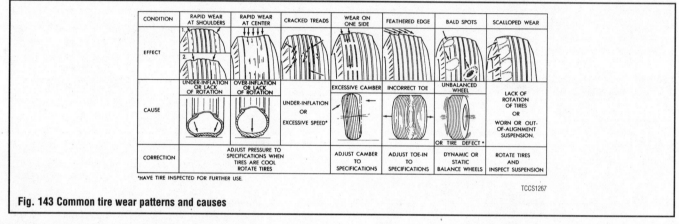

Fig. 143 Common tire wear patterns and causes

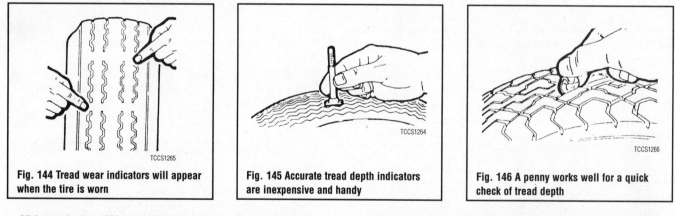

Fig. 144 Tread wear indicators will appear when the tire is worn

Fig. 145 Accurate tread depth indicators are inexpensive and handy

Fig. 146 A penny works well for a quick check of tread depth

All tires made since 1968 have built-in tread wear indicator bars that show up as ½ in. (13mm) wide smooth bands across the tire when 1/16 in. (1.5mm) of tread remains. The appearance of tread wear indicators means that the tires should be replaced. In fact, many states have laws prohibiting the use of tires with less than this amount of tread.

You can check your own tread depth with an inexpensive gauge or by using a Lincoln head penny. Slip the Lincoln penny (with Lincoln's head upside-down) into several tread grooves. If you can see the top of Lincoln's head in 2 adjacent grooves, the tire has less than 1/16 in. (1.5mm) tread left and should be replaced. You can measure snow tires in the same manner by using the "tails" side of the Lincoln penny. If you can see the top of the Lincoln memorial, it's time to replace the snow tire(s).

CARE OF SPECIAL WHEELS

If you have invested money in magnesium, aluminum alloy or sport wheels, special precautions should be taken to make sure your investment is not wasted and that your special wheels look good for the life of the vehicle.

Special wheels are easily damaged and/or scratched. Occasionally check the rims for cracking, impact damage or air leaks. If any of these are found, replace the wheel. But in order to prevent this type of damage and the costly replacement of a special wheel, observe the following precautions:

- Use extra care not to damage the wheels during removal, installation, balancing, etc. After removal of the wheels from the vehicle, place them on a mat or other protective surface. If they are to be stored for any length of time, support them on strips of wood. Never store tires and wheels upright; the tread may develop flat spots.
- When driving, watch for hazards; it doesn't take much to crack a wheel.
- When washing, use a mild soap or non-abrasive dish detergent (keeping in mind that detergent tends to remove wax). Avoid cleansers with abrasives or the use of hard brushes. There are many cleaners and polishes for special wheels.
- If possible, remove the wheels during the winter. Salt and sand used for snow removal can severely damage the finish of a wheel.
- Make certain the recommended lug nut torque is never exceeded or the wheel may crack. Never use snow chains on special wheels; severe scratching may occur.

FLUIDS AND LUBRICANTS

Fluid Disposal

Used fluids such as engine oil, transmission fluid, antifreeze and brake fluid are hazardous wastes and must be disposed of properly. Before draining any fluids, consult with your local authorities; in many areas, waste oil, antifreeze, etc. are being accepted as a part of recycling programs. A number of service stations and auto parts stores are also accepting waste fluids for recycling.

Be sure of the recycling center's policies before draining any fluids, as many will not accept different fluids that have been mixed together.

Fuel and Engine Oil Recommendations

OIL

♦ See Figures 147 and 148

The SAE (Society of Automotive Engineers) grade number indicates the viscosity of the engine oil and thus its ability to lubricate at a given temperature. The lower the SAE grade number, the lighter the oil. The lower the viscosity, and the easier it is to crank the engine in cold weather.

Oil viscosities should be chosen from those oils recommended for the lowest anticipated temperatures during the oil change interval.

Fig. 147 Look for the API oil identification label when choosing your engine oil

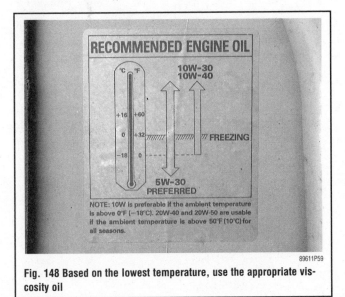

Fig. 148 Based on the lowest temperature, use the appropriate viscosity oil

Multi-viscosity oils (5W30, 10W40, etc.) offer the important advantage of being adaptable to temperature extremes. They allow easy starting at low temperatures, yet they give good protection at high speeds and engine temperatures. This is a decided advantage in changeable climates or in long distance touring.

Choose the viscosity range carefully, based upon the lowest expected temperature for the time of year. If the lowest expected temperature is below 0°F (-18°C), you should use 5W30. In the summer months, 10W30 can be used for the extra guarantee of sufficient viscosity at high temperatures.

The API (American Petroleum Institute) designation indicates the classification of engine oil used under certain given operating conditions. Only oils designated for use Service SG should be used. Oils of the SG type perform a variety of functions inside the engine in addition to the basic function as a lubricant. Through a balanced system of metallic detergents and polymeric dispersants, the oil prevents the formation of high and low temperature deposits and also keeps sludge and particles of dirt in suspension. Acids, particularly sulfuric acid, as well as other by-products of combustion, are neutralized. Both the SAE grade number and the API designation can be found on top of the oil can.

➡The API has come out with a new designation of motor oil, SJ. Oils designated for use Service SJ are equally acceptable in your Nissan. Non-detergent or straight mineral oils should not be used in your vehicle.

SYNTHETIC OIL

There are excellent synthetic and fuel efficient oils available that, under the right circumstances, can help provide better fuel mileage and better engine protection. However, these advantages come at a price, which can be 3 to 4 times the price per quart of conventional motor oils.

Before pouring any synthetic oils into your vehicle's engine, you should consider the condition of the engine and the type of driving you do. Also, check the vehicle's warranty conditions regarding the use of synthetics.

Generally, it is best to avoid the use of synthetic oil in both brand new and older, high mileage engines. New engines require a proper break-in, and the synthetics are so slippery that they can prevent this. Most manufacturers recommend that you wait at least 5000 miles before switching to a synthetic oil. Conversely, older engines are looser and tend to use more oil. Synthetics will slip past worn parts more readily than regular oil, and will be used up faster. If your vehicle already leaks and/or uses oil (due to worn parts and bad seals or gaskets), it will leak and use more with a slippery synthetic oil inside.

Consider your type of driving. If most of your accumulated mileage is on the highway at higher, steadier speeds, a synthetic oil will reduce friction and probably help deliver better fuel mileage. Under such ideal highway conditions, the oil change interval can be extended, as long as the oil filter will operate effectively for the extended life of the oil. If the filter can't do its job for this extended period, dirt and sludge will build up in your engine's crankcase, sump, oil pump and lines, no matter what type of oil is used. If using synthetic oil in this manner, you should continue to change the oil filter at the recommended intervals.

Vehicles used under harder, stop-and-go, short hop circumstances should always be serviced more frequently, and for these vehicles synthetic oil may not be a wise investment. Because of the necessary shorter change interval needed for this type of driving, you cannot take advantage of the long recommended change interval of most synthetic oils.

FUEL

The minimum octane requirement for all engines using unleaded fuel is 91 RON (87 CLC). All unleaded fuels sold in the U.S. are required to meet this minimum octane rating.

The use of a fuel too low in octane (a measurement of anti-knock quality) will result in spark knock. Since many factors such as altitude, terrain, air temperature and humidity affect operating efficiency, knocking may result even though the recommended fuel is being used. If persistent knocking occurs, it may be necessary to switch to a higher grade of fuel. Continuous or heavy knocking may result in engine damage.

➡Your engine's fuel requirement can change with time, mainly due to carbon buildup, which will in turn increase the temperatures in the combustion chamber and change the compression ratio. If your engine pings, knocks or runs on, switch to a higher grade of fuel. Sometimes just changing brands will cure the problem. Using a higher grade of fuel is always recommended.

Engine

OIL LEVEL CHECK

▶ **See Figures 149, 150, 151 and 152**

The best time to check the engine oil is before operating the engine or after it has been sitting for at least 10 minutes in order to obtain an accurate reading. This will allow the oil to drain back in the crankcase. To check the engine oil level, make sure the vehicle is resting on a level surface, remove the oil dipstick, wipe it clean and reinsert the stick firmly for an accurate reading. The oil dipstick has two marks to indicate high and low oil level. If the oil is at or below the "low level" mark on the dipstick, oil should be added as necessary. The oil level should be maintained in the safety margin, neither going above the "high level" mark or below the "low level" mark.

OIL & FILTER CHANGE

▶ **See Figures 153 thru 160**

The Nissan factory maintenance intervals (every 7500 miles or 6 months) specify changing the oil filter at every second oil change after the initial service. We recommend replacing the oil filter with every oil change. For the small price of an oil filter, it's cheap insurance to replace the filter at every oil change. One of the larger filter manufacturers points out in its advertisements that not chang-

Fig. 149 Be sure to push the dipstick all the way down to obtain an accurate reading

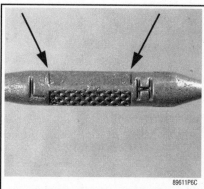

Fig. 150 The engine oil level should ALWAYS be maintained between the marks

Fig. 151 Unscrew the cap on the front valve cover to add oil to the engine

Fig. 152 Add oil in small increments; overfilling the engine with oil can damage internal components

Fig. 153 Always use the proper size wrench when loosening or tightening the drain plug

Fig. 154 After the drain plug is loosened, unscrew it by hand while pushing in . . .

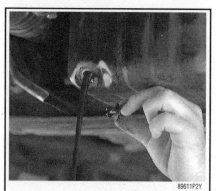

Fig. 155 . . . then quickly pull it away, and let the oil drain

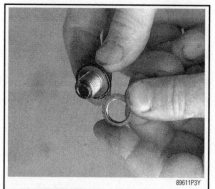

Fig. 156 The copper washer should be replaced to ensure a leak-free seal

Fig. 157 Carefully clean any dirt around the drain hole that would interfere with the copper washer

Fig. 158 Use an oil filter wrench to loosen the filter

Fig. 159 This is another example of an oil filter wrench. Select the type which best suits your application

Fig. 160 After the oil filter is loosened with a wrench, spin it off the housing. Keeping the filter upright will minimize spillage

ing the filter leaves 1 quart (0.9L) of dirty oil in the engine. This claim is true and should be kept in mind when changing your oil.

1. Run the engine until it reaches normal operating temperature.
2. Raise and safely support the vehicle and support it on safety stands if necessary to gain access to the filter.
3. Slide a drain pan of at least 6 quarts (6L) capacity under the oil pan.

❄❄ CAUTION

The EPA warns that prolonged contact with used engine oil may cause a number of skin disorders, including cancer! You should make every effort to minimize your exposure to used engine oil. Protective gloves should be worn when changing the oil. Wash your hands and any other exposed skin areas as soon as possible after exposure to used engine oil. Soap and water, or waterless hand cleaner should be used.

4. Loosen the drain plug. Turn the plug out by hand. By keeping an inward pressure on the plug as you unscrew it, oil won't escape past the threads and you can remove it without being burned by hot oil.
5. Allow the oil to drain completely and then install the drain plug. Don't overtighten the plug or you'll be buying a new pan or a trick replacement plug for damaged threads.
6. Using an oil filter wrench, remove the oil filter. Keep in mind that it's holding about 1 quart (0.9L) of dirty, hot oil.
7. Empty the old filter into the drain pan and dispose of the filter and old oil.

➡**One ecologically desirable solution to the used oil disposal problem is to find a cooperative gas station owner who will allow you to dump your used oil into his tank or take the oil to a reclamation center (often at garages and gas stations).**

8. Using a clean rag, wipe off the filter adapter on the engine block. Be sure the rag doesn't leave any lint which could clog an oil passage.
9. Coat the rubber gasket on the filter with fresh oil. Spin it onto the engine by hand; when the gasket touches the adapter surface give it another ½–¾ turn. No more or you'll squash the gasket and it will leak.
10. Refill the engine with the correct amount of fresh oil.
11. Crank the engine over several times and then start it. If the oil pressure indicator light doesn't go out or the pressure gauge shows zero, shut the engine down and find out what's wrong.
12. If the oil pressure is OK and there are no leaks, shut the engine off and lower the vehicle.

Manual Transaxle

FLUID RECOMMENDATION

▶ **See Figure 161**

For manual transaxles be sure to use fluid with an API GL4 rating.

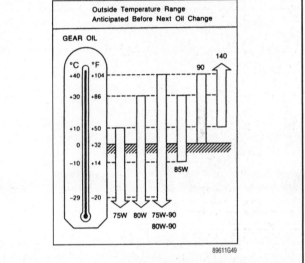

Fig. 161 Select the appropriate gear oil for the ambient temperature

LEVEL CHECK

▶ **See Figure 162**

You should inspect the manual transaxle gear oil at 12 months or 15,000 miles, at this point you should correct the level or replace the oil as necessary. The lubricant level should be even with the bottom of the filler hole. Push in on the filler plug when unscrewing it. When you are sure all of the threads of the plug are free of the transaxle case, move the plug away from the case slightly. If lubricant begins to flow out of the transaxle, then you know it is full. If not, add the correct gear oil as necessary

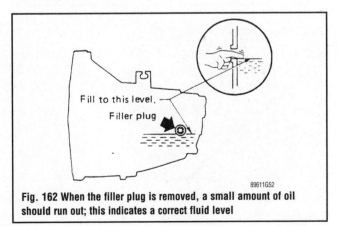

Fig. 162 When the filler plug is removed, a small amount of oil should run out; this indicates a correct fluid level

DRAIN & REFILL

▶ **See Figure 163**

➡ **It is recommended that the manual transmission fluid be changed every 30,000 miles if the vehicle is used in severe service. You may also want to change it if you have bought your vehicle used or if it has been driven in water deep enough to reach the transaxle case.**

1. Run the engine until it reaches normal operating temperature then turn key to the off position.
2. Raise and safely support the vehicle.
3. Remove the filler plug from the left side of the transaxle to provide a vent.
4. The drain plug is located on the bottom of the transaxle case. Place a pan under the drain plug and remove it.

✲✲ CAUTION

The oil will be HOT. Push up against the threads as you unscrew the plug to prevent leakage.

5. Allow the oil to drain completely. Clean off the plug and replace it; do not overtighten the plug.
6. Fill the transaxle with gear oil through the filler plug hole. Use API service GL4 gear oil of the proper viscosity. This oil usually comes in a squeeze bottle with a long nozzle. If yours isn't, use a plastic squeeze bottle (the type used in the kitchen). Refer to the "Capacities" chart for the amount of oil needed.
7. The oil level should come up to the edge of the filler hole. You can stick your finger in to verify this. Watch out for sharp threads.
8. Replace the filler plug. Lower the vehicle, dispose of the old oil in the same manner as old engine oil.
9. Test drive the vehicle, stop and check for leaks.

Automatic Transaxle

FLUID RECOMMENDATIONS

All automatic transaxles, use Dexron III®ATF (automatic transmission fluid).

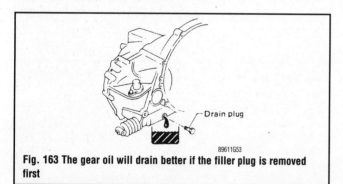

Fig. 163 The gear oil will drain better if the filler plug is removed first

LEVEL CHECK

▶ **See Figures 164, 165 and 166**

The fluid level in the automatic transaxle should be checked every 12 months or 15,000 miles, whichever comes first. The transaxle has a dipstick for fluid level checks.

1. Drive the vehicle until it is at normal operating temperature. The level should not be checked immediately after the vehicle has been driven for a long time at high speed or in city traffic in hot weather. In those cases, the transaxle should be given a ½ hour to cool down.
2. Stop the vehicle, apply the parking brake, then shift slowly through all gear positions, ending in **P**. Let the engine idle for about 5 minutes with the transaxle in **P**. The vehicle should be on a level surface.
3. With the engine still running, remove the dipstick, wipe it clean, then reinsert it, pushing it fully into the tube.
4. Pull the dipstick again and, holding it horizontally, read the fluid level.
5. Cautiously feel the end of the dipstick to determine the temperature. Note that on Nissans there is a scale on each side, HOT on one, COLD on the other. If the fluid level is not in the correct area, more will have to be added.
6. Fluid is added through the dipstick tube. You will probably need the aid of a spout or a long necked funnel. Be sure whatever you pour through is perfectly clean and dry. Use an automatic transmission fluid marked Dexron III®. Add fluid slowly, and in small amounts, checking the level frequently between additions. Do not overfill, which will cause foaming, slippage or possible transaxle damage. It takes only 1 pint (473mL) to raise the level from **L** to **H** when the transaxle is hot.

DRAIN & REFILL

▶ **See Figures 167, 168 and 169**

➡ **It is recommended that the automatic transmission fluid be changed every 30,000 miles if the vehicle is used in severe service. You may also want to change it if you have bought your vehicle used and are unsure of the last time it was changed.**

1. Raise the car and support it securely on jackstands.
2. Place a large drain pan under the transaxle.
3. Loosen the drain plug on the transaxle. Unscrew the drain plug from the pan by hand while pushing inward. When the threads are free, quickly pull the drain plug away and drain the fluid from the transaxle.
4. After the fluid is fully drained, install drain plug. On RE4F04 models, the copper gasket should be replaced. Tighten the drain plug to 22–29 ft.lbs. (29–39 Nm.). Do not overtighten the plug, or the threads may be stripped, requiring costly repair.
5. Lower the vehicle from the jackstands.
6. Fill the transaxle with Dexron III®or Genuine Nissan ATF specified for your vehicle until the dipstick registers at the MAX mark.
7. Start the engine and move the gear selector through all gears in the shift pattern. Allow the engine to idle for five minutes.
8. Check the fluid level. Add ATF, as necessary, to obtain the correct level.

Fig. 164 The dipstick for the automatic transaxle is located near the air filter element housing

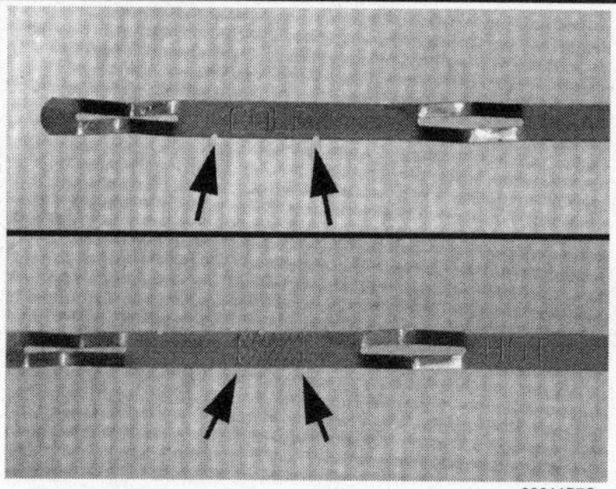

Fig. 165 For proper transaxle operation, always maintain the fluid level between the levels on the dipstick

Fig. 166 ATF is added through the dipstick tube. Add fluid in small amounts to avoid overfilling

Fig. 167 Drain plug location on RE4F02 model transaxles

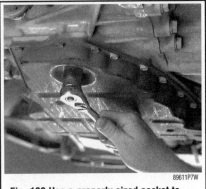

Fig. 168 Use a properly sized socket to loosen the drain plug . . .

Fig. 169 . . . then unscrew it by hand and allow the fluid to drain. Be sure to replace the copper washer to ensure a leak-free seal

PAN & FILTER SERVICE

RE4F02 Models

➡ RE4F02 model transaxles use filters which are placed within the valve body inside the transaxle. Changing these filters would require valve body disassembly, which should be performed by a qualified transmission repair shop.

RE4F04 Models

♦ See Figures 170 thru 178

1. Raise the car and support it securely on jackstands.
2. Place a large drain pan under the transaxle.
3. Loosen the drain plug on the transaxle fluid pan. Unscrew the drain plug from the pan by hand while pushing inward. When the threads are free, quickly

pull the drain plug away and drain the fluid from the transaxle. Discard the drain plug gasket.

4. Using a new gasket, install the drain plug and tighten it to 22–29 ft.lbs. (29–39 Nm.).
5. Loosen all of the pan attaching bolts to within a few turns of complete removal, then carefully break the gasket seal, allowing any excess fluid to drain over the edge of the pan.

> **✳✳ WARNING**
>
> DO NOT force the pan while breaking the gasket seal. DO NOT allow the pan flange to become bent or otherwise damaged.

6. Remove the pan bolts and carefully lower the pan. Keep in mind there may still be traces of fluid in the pan even though it has been drained.
7. Clean the transaxle oil pan thoroughly using a safe solvent, then allow it

Fig. 170 To access the filter, remove the bolts around the perimeter of the pan . . .

Fig. 171 . . . then carefully lower it from the transaxle. Keep in mind there will be a small amount of fluid in the pan after it is drained

Fig. 172 There are 11 bolts and 1 nut that mount the transaxle filter

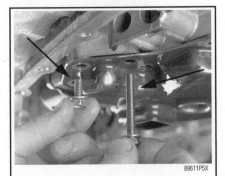

Fig. 173 Note the different lengths of the filter bolts; there are three different lengths

Fig. 174 After the fasteners are removed, carefully lower the filter and drain out any excess fluid inside

Fig. 175 Inspect the electrical wires inside the transaxle while the pan is removed

Fig. 176 Be sure to clean the magnet in the transaxle pan. Note the indentation in the pan to keep the magnet in position

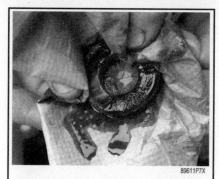

Fig. 177 The fine particles gathered on the magnet are normal for high mileage vehicles; any large chunks indicate damage

Fig. 178 Use a gasket scraper to clean the old gasket from the pan; always use a new gasket

to air dry. DO NOT use a cloth to dry the pan, since it might leave behind bits of lint. Discard the old pan gasket.

8. Remove the filter mounting bolts, then remove the filter by pulling it down and off of the valve body. Make sure any gaskets or seals are removed with the old filter.

9. Install the new filter, making sure all gaskets are in place, then secure it with the retaining bolts. Make sure the bolts are installed in their correct locations, as they are different lengths. Torque the bolts to 6.9 –6.5 ft. lbs. (7–9 Nm.).

10. Place a new gasket on the pan, then install the pan to the transaxle. Use new bolts, as they are special self-sealing bolts. Tighten the pan bolts to 6.9 –6.5 ft. lbs. (7–9 Nm.).

11. Remove the jackstands and carefully lower the vehicle.

12. Fill the transaxle, through the dipstick hole, with Dexron III®Automatic Transmission Fluid (ATF) or Genuine Nissan ATF specified for your vehicle.

13. Start the engine and move the gear selector through all gears in the shift pattern. Allow the engine to idle for five minutes.

14. Check the fluid level. Add ATF, as necessary, to obtain the correct level.

Cooling System

FLUID RECOMMENDATION

The cooling fluid, or antifreeze, should be changed every 30,000 miles or 24 months. When replacing the fluid, use a mixture of 50 percent distilled water and 50 percent ethylene glycol antifreeze. On 1993–1995 models, Nissan recommends a modified mixture of 70 percent water and 30 percent cooling fluid.

Check the freezing protection rating at least once a year, preferably just before the winter sets in. This can be done with an antifreeze tester (most service stations will have one on hand and will probably check it for you, if not, they are available at an auto parts store). Maintain a protection rating of at least

-20°F (-29°C) to prevent serious engine damage as a result of freezing and to assure the proper engine operating temperature.

It is also a good idea to check the cooling system for leaks. A pressure test gauge is available to perform such a task. This is an excellent tool for locating small pinhole leaks and loose hose connections, which could lead to an overheated engine.

LEVEL CHECK

▶ **See Figures 179, 180, 181 and 182**

Check the coolant level every 3000 miles or once a month. In hot weather operation, it may be a good idea to check the level once a week. Check for loose connections and signs of deterioration of the coolant hoses. Maintain the coolant level between the **MAX** and **MIN** marks on the coolant expansion (recovery) tank. If the coolant expansion tank is empty, check the coolant level in the radiator. if the level is below the filler neck, refill the radiator, then refill the expansion tank to the proper level with the appropriate mixture of coolant and water.

❋❋ CAUTION

Never remove the radiator cap when the vehicle is hot or overheated. Wait until it has cooled. Place a thick cloth over the radiator cap to shield yourself from the heat and turn the radiator cap, slightly, until the sound of escaping pressure can be heard. Do not turn any more; allow the pressure to release gradually. When no more pressure can be heard escaping, remove the cap with the heavy cloth, cautiously.

➡**Never add cold water to an overheated engine while the engine is not running.**

After filling the radiator, run the engine until it reaches normal operating temperature, to make sure the thermostat has opened and all the air is free from the system.

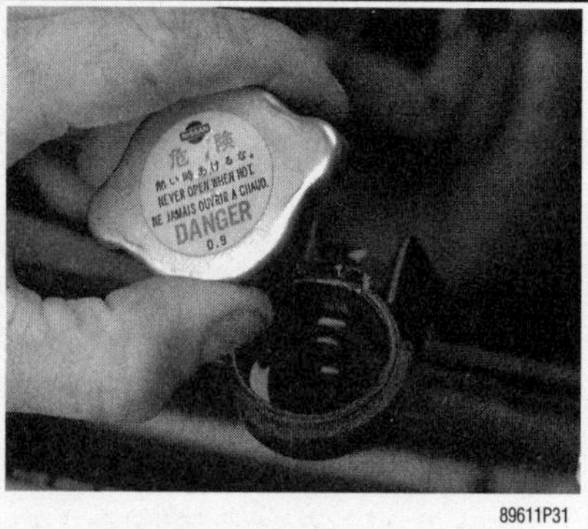

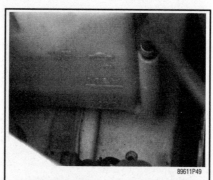

Fig. 179 NEVER open the radiator cap when the engine is hot

Fig. 180 The engine coolant level should always be maintained between the MIN and MAX markings on the expansion tank

Fig. 181 When adding coolant, use of a funnel is advised to prevent any spillage onto the accessory drive belts, which will cause slippage

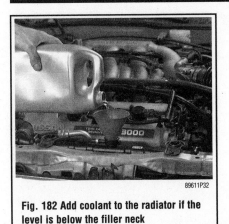

Fig. 182 Add coolant to the radiator if the level is below the filler neck

Fig. 183 Unscrew the petcock on the bottom of the radiator to drain the coolant

Fig. 184 When draining the radiator, make sure the air bleed port plug and the radiator cap are removed to allow quick draining

DRAIN & REFILL

♦ **See Figures 183, 184, 185, 186 and 187**

To drain the cooling system, allow the engine to cool down before attempting to remove the radiator cap. Then turn the cap until it hisses. Wait until all pressure is off the cap before removing it completely.

✳✳ CAUTION

To avoid burns and scalding, always handle a warm radiator cap with a heavy rag.

1. If equipped with a manual air conditioning, set the heater TEMP control lever to the fully HOT position. If equipped with automatic air conditioning turn ignition switch **ON** and set temperature at MAXIMUM. Then turn the ignition switch **OFF**.
2. With the radiator cap removed, drain the radiator by loosening the petcock at the bottom of the radiator.
3. Remove the drain plugs from both sides of the engine block.

✳✳ CAUTION

When draining the coolant, keep in mind that cats and dogs are attracted by the ethylene glycol antifreeze, and are quite likely to drink any that is left in an uncovered container or in puddles on the ground. This will prove fatal in sufficient quantity. Always drain the coolant into a sealable container.

4. Close the petcock. Be careful not to damage the petcock when closing.
5. Install the drain plugs to both sides of the engine block.
6. Remove the air bleed port plug.
7. Refill the system with a 50/50 mix of ethylene glycol antifreeze; fill the system to ¾–1¼ in. 1938mm) from the bottom of the filler neck on the radiator. Reinstall the radiator cap and the air bleed port drain plug.
8. Fill the coolant expansion tank to the **MAX** level.

9. Operate the engine at 2000 rpm for a few minutes and check the system for signs of leaks and for the correct level.

FLUSHING & CLEANING THE SYSTEM

To flush the system you must first, drain the cooling system but do not close the petcock valve on the bottom of the radiator. You can insert a garden hose, in the filler neck, turn the water pressure on moderately then start the engine. After about 10 minutes or less the water coming out of the bottom of the radiator should be clear. Shut off the engine and water supply, allow the radiator to drain then refill and bleed the system as necessary.

➡**Do not allow the engine to overheat. The supply of water going in the top must be equal in amount to the water draining from the bottom, this way the radiator will always be full when the engine us running.**

Usually flushing the radiator using water is all that is necessary to maintain the proper condition in the cooling system.

Radiator flush is the only cleaning agent that can be used to clean the internal portion of the radiator. Radiator flush can be purchased at any auto supply store. Follow the directions on the label.

Also, there are a number of radiator flush "kits" available, that include a fitting to connect a garden hose into the engine cooling system. Once this fitting is installed, future radiator flushing is simplified by unscrewing a cap and fastening a garden hose. Use your own judgment with these kits, as they are not recommended by Nissan, and could possibly void the factory warranty.

Brake and Clutch Master Cylinder

FLUID RECOMMENDATION

When adding or changing the fluid in the systems, use a quality brake fluid of the DOT 3 specifications.

➡**Never reuse old brake fluid.**

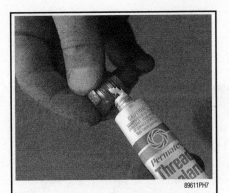

Fig. 185 Removing the engine block drain plugs will allow for a more thorough coolant change

Fig. 186 Always use thread sealer on the block drain plugs to prevent leaks

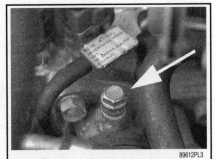

Fig. 187 The air bleed port plug should always be removed when adding coolant to a fully drained engine to prevent air pockets

LEVEL CHECK

▶ **See Figures 188, 189 and 190**

The brake and clutch master cylinders are located under the hood, in the left rear section of the engine compartment. They are made of translucent plastic so the levels may be checked without removing the tops. The fluid level in both reservoirs should be checked at least every 15,000 miles. The fluid level should be maintained at the upper most mark on the side of the reservoir. Any sudden decrease in the level indicates a possible leak in the system and should be checked out immediately.

When making additions of brake fluid, use only fresh, uncontaminated brake fluid meeting or exceeding DOT 3 standards. Be careful not to spill any brake fluid on painted surfaces, as it eats the paint. Do not allow the brake fluid container or the master cylinder reservoir to remain open any longer than necessary. Brake fluid absorbs moisture from the air, reducing its effectiveness and causing corrosion in the lines.

Power Steering System

FLUID RECOMMENDATION

When adding or changing the power steering fluid, use Dexron III ®Automatic Transmission Fluid (ATF).

LEVEL CHECK

▶ **See Figures 191, 192, 193, 194 and 195**

The power steering hydraulic fluid level is checked with a dipstick inserted into the pump reservoir cap. The level can be checked with the fluid either warm or cold. The vehicle should be parked on a level surface. Check the fluid level every 12 months or 15,000 miles, whichever comes first.

1. With the engine **OFF**, unscrew the dipstick and check the level. If the

Fig. 188 Never allow the fluid in the reservoir to fall below the MIN mark

Fig. 189 Always add fresh brake fluid to the reservoir. If the fluid in the reservoir is dirty, it should be promptly flushed

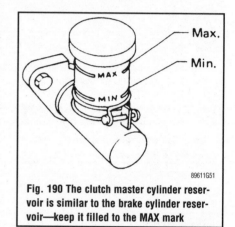

Fig. 190 The clutch master cylinder reservoir is similar to the brake cylinder reservoir—keep it filled to the MAX mark

Fig. 191 The dipstick for the power steering fluid reservoir is on the inside of the cap

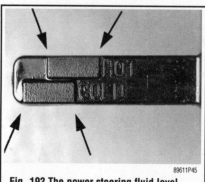

Fig. 192 The power steering fluid level should always be between the marks on the dipstick

Fig. 193 Later model Maximas have a translucent reservoir to view the fluid level

Fig. 194 Check the filter for debris before adding fluid to the reservoir

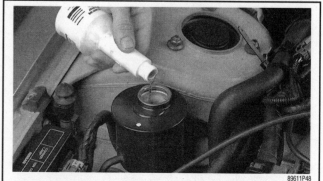

Fig. 195 Add power steering fluid as required to correct the reservoir level

engine is warm, the level should be within the proper range on the **HOT** scale. If the engine is cold, the level should be within the proper range on the **COLD** scale.

2. If the level is low, add Dexron III®Automatic Transmission Fluid (ATF), or a superceding compatible ATF its until correct. Be careful not to overfill, which will cause fluid loss and seal damage.

Chassis Greasing

The manufacturer doesn't install lubrication fittings in lube points on the steering linkage or suspension. You can buy metric threaded fittings to grease these points or use a pointed, rubber tip end on your grease gun. Lubricate all joints equipped with a plug, every 15,000 miles or once a year with NLGI No. 2 (Lithium base) grease. Replace the plugs after lubrication.

Body Lubrication

Lubricate all locks and hinges with multipurpose grease every 7500 miles.

Wheel Bearings

The 1993–98 Maximas use sealed wheel bearings that do not require maintenance. If there is noise or excessive play from a bearing, it must be replaced. For information on wheel bearing removal and installation, refer to Section 7 of this manual.

TRAILER TOWING

General Recommendations

Your vehicle was primarily designed to carry passengers and cargo. It is important to remember that towing a trailer will place additional loads on your vehicle's engine, drive train, steering, braking and other systems. However, if you find it necessary to tow a trailer, using the proper equipment is a must.

Local laws may require specific equipment such as trailer brakes or fender mounted mirrors. Check your local laws.

➡**A brochure with information on trailer towing, special equipment required and optional equipment available can be obtained from your Nissan dealer.**

Trailer Weight

Never allow the total trailer load to exceed 1000 lbs. (454kg) The total trailer load equals trailer weight plus its cargo weight.

Hitch Weight

Figure the hitch weight to select a proper hitch. Hitch weight is usually 9 to 11 percent of the trailer gross weight and should be measured with the trailer loaded. Hitches fall into 3 types: those that mount on the frame and rear bumper or the bolt-on or weld-on distribution type used for larger trailers. Axle mounted or clamp-on bumper hitches should never be used.

Check the gross weight rating of your trailer. Tongue weight is usually figured as 10 percent of gross trailer weight. Therefore, a trailer with a maximum gross weight of 1000 lbs. (454kg) will have a maximum tongue weight of 110 lbs. (45.4kg) Class I trailers fall into this category.

When you've determined the hitch that you'll need, follow the manufacturer's installation instructions, exactly, especially when it comes to fastener torque. The hitch will subjected to a lot of stress and good hitches come with hardened bolts. Never substitute an inferior bolt for a hardened bolt.

Cooling

ENGINE

One of the most common, if not THE most common, problems associated with trailer towing is engine overheating.

Aftermarket engine oil coolers are helpful for prolonging engine oil life and reducing overall engine temperatures. Both of these factors increase engine life.

While not absolutely necessary in towing Class I and some Class II trailers, they are recommended for heavier Class II and all Class III towing.

Engine oil cooler systems consist of an adapter, screwed on in place of the oil filter, a remote filter mounting and a multi-tube, finned heat exchanger, which is mounted in front of the radiator or air conditioning condenser.

TRANSAXLE

An automatic transaxle is usually recommended for trailer towing. Modern automatics have proven reliable and, of course, easy to operate, in trailer towing.

The increased load of a trailer, however, causes an increase in the temperature of the automatic transmission fluid. Heat is the worst enemy of an automatic transaxle. As the temperature of the fluid increases, the life of the fluid decreases.

It is essential, therefore, that you install an automatic transaxle cooler.

The cooler, which consists of a multi-tube, finned heat exchanger, is usually installed in front of the radiator or air conditioning compressor and hooked in line with the transaxle cooler tank inlet line. Follow the cooler manufacturer's installation instructions.

Select a cooler of at least adequate capacity, based upon the combined gross weights of the vehicle and trailer.

Cooler manufacturers recommend that you use an aftermarket cooler in addition to, and not instead of, the present cooling tank within your radiator. If you do want to use it in place of the radiator cooling tank, get a cooler at least 2 sizes larger than normally necessary.

➡**A transaxle cooler can, sometimes, cause slow or harsh shifting in the transaxle during cold weather, until the fluid has a chance to come up to normal operating temperature. Some coolers can be purchased with or retrofitted with a temperature bypass valve which will allow fluid flow through the cooler only when the fluid has reached operating temperature or above.**

Handling A Trailer

Towing a trailer with ease and safety requires a certain amount of experience. It's a good idea to learn the feel of a trailer by practicing turning, stopping and backing in an open area such as an empty parking lot to gain experience in handling the extra weight and length of the trailer. Take enough time to get the feel of the vehicle/trailer combination under a variety of situations.

Skillful backing requires practice. Back up slowly with an assistant acting as a guide and watching for obstructions. Make small corrections, instead of exaggerated ones, as a slight movement of the steering wheel will result in a much larger movement of the rear of the trailer.

Allow considerable more room for stopping when a trailer is attached to the vehicle. Keep in mind, the car/trailer combination is a considerable increase in the weight that your car's brakes have to bring to a stop. If you have a manual brake controller, lead with the trailer brakes when approaching a stop. Trailer brakes are also handy for correcting side sway. Apply the trailer brakes for a moment without using your vehicle brakes; the trailer should track straight again.

Check everything before starting out on the road, then stop after you've traveled about 50 miles and double-check the trailer hitch and electrical connections to make sure everything is still secured. Listen for sounds like chains dragging on the ground (indicating that a safety chain has come loose) and check your rear view mirrors frequently to make sure the trailer is tracking properly.

Remember that a car/trailer combination is more sensitive to cross winds; slow down when crossing bridges or wide open expanses in gusty wind conditions. Exceeding the speed limit while towing a trailer is not only illegal, it is foolhardy and invites disaster. A strong gust of wind can send a speeding car/trailer combination out of control.

Because the trailer wheels are closer than the towing vehicle wheels to the inside of a turn, drive slightly beyond the normal turning point when negotiating a sharp turn at a corner. Allow extra distance for passing other vehicles and downshift if necessary for better acceleration. Allow at least the equivalent of one vehicle and trailer length combined for each 10 mph of road speed.

Finally, remember to check the height of the loaded car/trailer, allowing for luggage racks, antenna, etc. mounted on the roof and take note of low bridges or parking garage clearances.

TOWING THE VEHICLE

Towing

On front wheel drive vehicles never tow with rear wheels raised (with front drive wheels on the ground) as this may cause serious and expensive damage to the transaxle. On front wheel drive models Nissan recommends that the vehicle be towed with the driving (front) wheels off the ground.

On all models there are towing hooks under the vehicle to aid in towing. If any question concerning towing are in doubt, check with the Towing Procedure Manual, available from Nissan.

JUMP STARTING A DEAD BATTERY

♦ See Figure 196

Whenever a vehicle is jump started, precautions must be followed in order to prevent the possibility of personal injury. Remember that batteries contain a small amount of explosive hydrogen gas which is a by-product of battery charging. Sparks should always be avoided when working around batteries, especially when attaching jumper cables. To minimize the possibility of accidental sparks, follow the procedure carefully.

✳ CAUTION

NEVER hook the batteries up in a series circuit or the entire electrical system will be destroyed!

Vehicles equipped with a diesel engine may utilize two 12 volt batteries. If so, the batteries are connected in a parallel circuit (positive terminal to positive terminal, negative terminal to negative terminal). Hooking the batteries up in parallel circuit increases battery cranking power without increasing total battery voltage output. Output remains at 12 volts. On the other hand, hooking two 12 volt batteries up in a series circuit (positive terminal to negative terminal, positive terminal to negative terminal) increases total battery output to 24 volts (12 volts plus 12 volts).

Jump Starting Precautions

• Be sure that both batteries are of the same voltage. Vehicles covered by this manual and most vehicles on the road today utilize a 12 volt charging system.
• Be sure that both batteries are of the same polarity (have the same terminal, in most cases NEGATIVE grounded).
• Be sure that the vehicles are not touching or a short could occur.
• On serviceable batteries, be sure the vent cap holes are not obstructed.
• Do not smoke or allow sparks anywhere near the batteries.
• In cold weather, make sure the battery electrolyte is not frozen. This can occur more readily in a battery that has been in a state of discharge.
• Do not allow electrolyte (battery acid) to contact your skin or clothing.

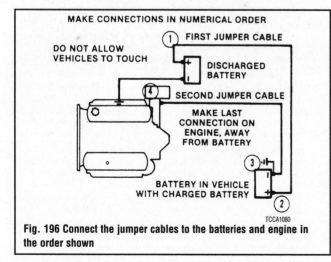

MAKE CONNECTIONS IN NUMERICAL ORDER

DO NOT ALLOW VEHICLES TO TOUCH

① FIRST JUMPER CABLE

DISCHARGED BATTERY

④ SECOND JUMPER CABLE

MAKE LAST CONNECTION ON ENGINE, AWAY FROM BATTERY

③ ② BATTERY IN VEHICLE WITH CHARGED BATTERY

TCCA1080

Fig. 196 Connect the jumper cables to the batteries and engine in the order shown

Jump Starting Procedure

1. Make sure that the voltages of the 2 batteries are the same. Most batteries and charging systems are of the 12 volt variety.
2. Pull the jumping vehicle (with the good battery) into a position so the jumper cables can reach the dead battery and that vehicle's engine. Make sure that the vehicles do NOT touch.
3. Place the transaxles of both vehicles in **Neutral** (MT) or **P** (AT), as applicable, then firmly set their parking brakes.

➡**If necessary for safety reasons, the hazard lights on both vehicles may be operated throughout the entire procedure without significantly increasing the difficulty of jumping the dead battery.**

4. Turn all lights and accessories OFF on both vehicles. Make sure the ignition switches on both vehicles are turned to the **OFF** position.
5. Cover the battery cell caps with a rag, but do not cover the terminals.
6. Make sure the terminals on both batteries are clean and free of corrosion or proper electrical connection will be impeded. If necessary, clean the battery terminals before proceeding.
7. Identify the positive (+) and negative (-) terminals on both batteries.
8. Connect the first jumper cable to the positive (+) terminal of the dead battery, then connect the other end of that cable to the positive (+) terminal of the booster (good) battery.
9. Connect one end of the other jumper cable to the negative (-) terminal on the booster battery and the final cable clamp to an engine bolt head, alternator bracket or other solid, metallic point on the engine with the dead battery. Try to pick a ground on the engine that is positioned away from the battery in order to minimize the possibility of the 2 clamps touching should one loosen during the procedure. DO NOT connect this clamp to the negative (-) terminal of the bad battery.

✳ CAUTION

Be very careful to keep the jumper cables away from moving parts (cooling fan, belts, etc.) on both engines.

10. Check to make sure that the cables are routed away from any moving parts, then start the donor vehicle's engine. Run the engine at moderate speed for several minutes to allow the dead battery a chance to receive some initial charge.
11. With the donor vehicle's engine still running slightly above idle, try to start the vehicle with the dead battery. Crank the engine for no more than 10 seconds at a time and let the starter cool for at least 20 seconds between tries. If the vehicle does not start in 3 tries, it is likely that something else is also wrong or that the battery needs additional time to charge.
12. Once the vehicle is started, allow it to run at idle for a few seconds to make sure that it is operating properly.
13. Turn ON the headlights, heater blower and, if equipped, the rear defroster of both vehicles in order to reduce the severity of voltage spikes and subsequent risk of damage to the vehicles' electrical systems when the cables are disconnected. This step is especially important to avoid damage to the vehicles' computer control modules.
14. Carefully disconnect the cables in the reverse order of connection. Start with the negative cable that is attached to the engine ground, then the negative cable on the donor battery. Disconnect the positive cable from the donor battery and finally, disconnect the positive cable from the formerly dead battery. Be careful when disconnecting the cables from the positive terminals not to allow the alligator clips to touch any metal on either vehicle or a short and sparks will occur.

JACKING

▶ **See Figures 197 thru 202**

Never use the tire changing jack (the little jack supplied with the vehicle) for anything other than changing a flat out on the road. These jacks are simply not safe enough for any type of vehicle service except tire changing!

The service operations in this book often require that one end or the other, or both, of the vehicle be raised and safely supported. For this reason a hydraulic floor jack of at least 1½ ton capacity is as necessary as a spark plug socket to you, the do-it-yourself owner/mechanic. The cost of these jacks (invest in a good quality unit) is actually quite reasonable considering how they pay for themselves again and again over the years.

Along with a hydraulic floor jack should be at least two sturdy jackstands.

These are a necessity if you intend to work underneath the vehicle. Never work under the vehicle when it is only supported by a jack!

Drive-on ramps are an alternative method of raising the front end of the vehicle. They are commercially available or can be fabricated from heavy lumber or steel. Be sure to always block the wheels when using ramps.

✳✳ CAUTION

NEVER use concrete cinder blocks to support the vehicle. They are likely to break if the load is not evenly distributed. They should never be trusted when you are under the vehicle!

Fig. 197 Raise the front of the vehicle with a floor jack beneath the front crossmember . . .

Fig. 198 . . . and support the vehicle with jackstands beneath the body rails

Fig. 199 Raise the rear of the vehicle with the jack under the rear suspension cross-support. Note the protrusion for jacking

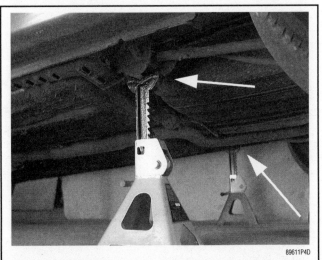

Fig. 200 Support the rear of the vehicle with jackstands beneath the rear suspension link pivots

Fig. 201 The pantograph jack should only be used for changing a tire in an emergency; NEVER use this jack for servicing

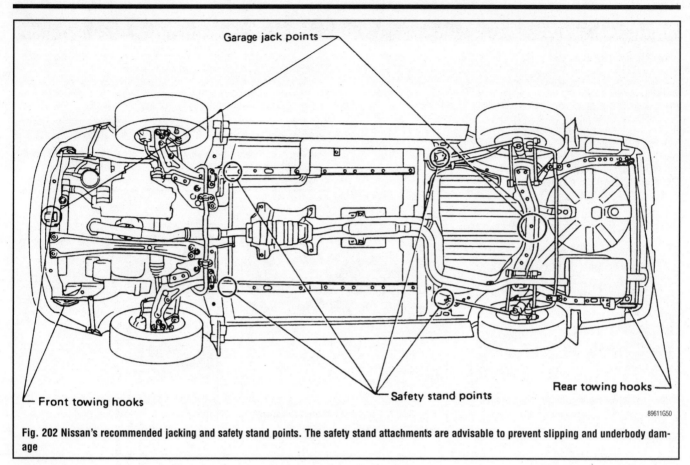

Garage jack points

Front towing hooks

Safety stand points

Rear towing hooks

89611G50

Fig. 202 Nissan's recommended jacking and safety stand points. The safety stand attachments are advisable to prevent slipping and underbody damage

CAPACITIES

Year	Model	Engine ID/VIN	Engine Displacement Liters (cc)	Engine Oil with Filter (qts.)	Transaxle Man ①	Transaxle Auto. ②	Transfer Case (pts.)	Drive Axle Front (pts.)	Drive Axle Rear (pts.)	Fuel Tank (gal.)	Cooling System wo/AC (qts.) ④	Cooling System w/AC (qts.) ④
1993	GXE	VG30E / H	3.0L (2960)	4.12	—	7.875	—	—	—	18.5	8.75	8.75
	SE	VE30DE / E	3.0L (2960)	4	③	10.12	—	—	—	18.5	11.25	11.25
1994	GXE	VG30E / H	3.0L (2960)	4.12	—	7.875	—	—	—	18.5	8.75	8.75
	SE	VE30DE / E	3.0L (2960)	4	③	10.12	—	—	—	18.5	11.25	11.25
1995	All models	VQ30DE / LH	3.0L (2988)	4.25	③	10	—	—	—	18.5	9	9
1996	All models	VQ30DE / LH	3.0L (2988)	4.25	③	10	—	—	—	18.5	9	9
1997	All models	VQ30DE / LH	3.0L (2988)	4.25	③	10	—	—	—	18.5	9	9
1998	All models	VQ30DE / LH	3.0L (2988)	4.25	③	10	—	—	—	18.5	9	9

① Capacity given is for pints
② Capacity give is for quarts
③ RS5F50V transaxle = 9.125-9.500 pts.
   RS5F50A transaxle = 9.250-10.125 pts.
④ Capacity given includes the reservoir

89611C05

MAINTENENACE INTERVALS

If a vehicle is operated under any of the following conditions it is considered severe service:

- Towing a trailer or using a camper or car-top carrier.
- Repeated short trips of less than 5 miles in temperatures below freezing, or trips of less than 10 miles in any temperature.
- Extensive idling or low-speed driving for long distances as in heavy commercial use, such as delivery, taxi or police cars.
- Operating on rough, muddy or salt-covered roads.
- Operating on unpaved or dusty roads.
- Driving in extremely hot (over 90°) conditions.

NORMAL MAINTENANCE INTERVALS—1993–94 MODELS

Abbreviations: R = Replace. I = Inspect. Correct or replace if necessary.   [ ]: At the mileage intervals only

MAINTENANCE OPERATION	Miles x 1,000	7.5	15	22.5	30	37.5	45	52.5	60
Perform at number of miles, kilometers or months, whichever comes first.	(km x 1,000)	(12)	(24)	(36)	(48)	(60)	(72)	(84)	(96)
	Months	6	12	18	24	30	36	42	48
Emission control system maintenance									
Drive belts	See NOTE (1)								I*
Air cleaner filter					[R]				[R]
Vapor lines					I*				I*
Fuel lines					I*				I*
Fuel filter	See NOTE (2)*								
Engine coolant	See NOTE (3)				R*				R*
Engine oil		R	R	R	R	R	R	R	R
Engine oil filter	See NOTE (4)	R	R	R	R	R	R	R	R
Spark plugs — VE30DE engine (Use PLATINUM-TIPPED type)									[R]
Spark plugs — VG30E engine					[R]				[R]
Timing belt (VG30E engine only)									[R]
Chassis and body maintenance									
Brake lines & cables		I	I	I	I	I	I	I	I
Brake pads, discs, drums & linings		I	I	I	I	I	I	I	I
Manual & automatic transaxle oil		I	I	I	I	I	I	I	I
Steering gear linkage, axle & suspension parts		I	I	I	I	I	I	I	I
Exhaust system		I	I	I	I	I	I	I	I
Drive shaft boots		I	I	I	I	I	I	I	I
Air bag system	See NOTE (5)								

NOTE: (1) After 60,000 miles (96,000 km) or 48 months, inspect every 15,000 miles (24,000 km) or 12 months.
(2) If vehicle is operated under extremely adverse weather conditions or in areas where ambient temperatures are either extremely low or extremely high, the filters might become clogged. In such an event, replace them immediately.
(3) After 60,000 miles (96,000 km) or 48 months, replace every 30,000 miles (48,000 km) or 24 months.
(4) Use Part No. 15208-60U00 or equivalent on VE30DE engine, and Nissan PREMIUM type or equivalent on VG30E engine.
(5) Inspect the air bag system 10 years after the date of manufacture as noted on the F.M.V.S.S. certification label.
(6) Maintenance items and intervals with "*" are recommended by NISSAN for reliable vehicle operation. The owner need not perform such maintenance in order to maintain the emission warranty or manufacturer recall liability. Other maintenance items and intervals are required.

89611M01

SEVERE MAINTENANCE INTERVALS—1993–94 MODELS

Abbreviations: R = Replace. I = Inspect. Correct or replace if necessary.

[ ]: At the mileage intervals only

MAINTENANCE OPERATION		MAINTENANCE INTERVAL															
Perform at number of miles, kilometers or months, whichever comes first.	Miles x 1,000	3.75	7.5	11.25	15	18.75	22.5	26.25	30	33.75	37.5	41.25	45	48.75	52.5	56.25	60
	(km x 1,000)	(6)	(12)	(18)	(24)	(30)	(36)	(42)	(48)	(54)	(60)	(66)	(72)	(78)	(84)	(90)	(96)
	Months	3	6	9	12	15	18	21	24	27	30	33	36	39	42	45	48
Emission control system maintenance																	
Drive belts	See NOTE (1)																I*
Air cleaner filter	See NOTE (2)								[R]								[R]
Vapor lines									I*								I*
Fuel lines									I*								I*
Fuel filter	See NOTE (3)*																
Engine coolant	See NOTE (4)																R*
Engine oil	See NOTE (5)	R	R	R	R	R	R	R	R	R	R	R	R	R	R	R	R
Engine oil filter		R	R	R	R	R	R	R	R	R	R	R	R	R	R	R	R
Spark plugs VE30DE engine (Use PLATINUM-TIPPED type)																	[R]
Spark plugs VG30E engine									[R]								[R]
Timing belt (VG30E engine only)																	[R]
Chassis and body maintenance																	
Brake lines & cables					I				I				I				I
Brake pads, discs, drums & linings			I		I		I		I		I		I		I		I
Manual & automatic transaxle oil	See NOTE (6)				I				I				I				I
Steering gear & linkage, axle & suspension parts					I				I				I				I
Steering linkage ball joints & front suspension ball joints									I								I
Exhaust system					I				I				I				I
Drive shaft boots					I				I				I				I
Air bag system	See NOTE (7)																I*

NOTE: (1) After 60,000 miles (96,000 km) or 48 months, inspect every 15,000 miles (24,000 km) or 12 months.
(2) If operating mainly in dusty conditions, more frequent maintenance may be required.
(3) If vehicle is operated under extremely adverse weather conditions or in areas where ambient temperatures are either extremely low or extremely high, the filters might become clogged. In such an event, replace them immediately.
(4) After 60,000 miles (96,000 km) or 48 months, replace every 30,000 miles (48,000 km) or 24 months.
(5) Use Part No. 15208-60U00 or equivalent on VE30DE engine, and Nissan PREMIUM type or equivalent on VG30E engine.
(6) If towing a trailer, using a camper or a car-top carrier, or driving on rough or muddy roads, change (not just inspect) oil at every 30,000 miles (48,000 km) or 24 months.
(7) Inspect the air bag system 10 years after the date of manufacture as noted on the F.M.V.S.S. certification label.
(8) Maintenance items and intervals with "*" are recommended by NISSAN for reliable vehicle operation. The owner need not perform such maintenance in order to maintain the emission warranty or manufacturer recall liability. Other maintenance items and intervals are required.

89611M02

ENGLISH TO METRIC CONVERSION: MASS (WEIGHT)

Current mass measurement is expressed in pounds and ounces (lbs. & ozs.). The metric unit of mass (or weight) is the kilogram (kg). Even although this table does not show conversion of masses (weights) larger than 15 lbs, it is easy to calculate larger units by following the data immediately below.

To convert ounces (oz.) to grams (g): multiply th number of ozs. by 28
To convert grams (g) to ounces (oz.): multiply the number of grams by .035

To convert pounds (lbs.) to kilograms (kg): multiply the number of lbs. by .45
To convert kilograms (kg) to pounds (lbs.): multiply the number of kilograms by 2.2

lbs	kg	lbs	kg	oz	kg	oz	kg
0.1	0.04	0.9	0.41	0.1	0.003	0.9	0.024
0.2	0.09	1	0.4	0.2	0.005	1	0.03
0.3	0.14	2	0.9	0.3	0.008	2	0.06
0.4	0.18	3	1.4	0.4	0.011	3	0.08
0.5	0.23	4	1.8	0.5	0.014	4	0.11
0.6	0.27	5	2.3	0.6	0.017	5	0.14
0.7	0.32	10	4.5	0.7	0.020	10	0.28
0.8	0.36	15	6.8	0.8	0.023	15	0.42

ENGLISH TO METRIC CONVERSION: TEMPERATURE

To convert Fahrenheit (°F) to Celsius (°C): take number of °F and subtract 32; multiply result by 5; divide result by 9

To convert Celsius (°C) to Fahrenheit (°F): take number of °C and multiply by 9; divide result by 5; add 32 to total

Fahrenheit (F)		Celsius (C)		Fahrenheit (F)		Celsius (C)		Fahrenheit (F)		Celsius (C)	
°F	°C	°C	°F	°F	°C	°C	°F	°F	°C	°C	°F
−40	−40	−38	−36.4	80	26.7	18	64.4	215	101.7	80	176
−35	−37.2	−36	−32.8	85	29.4	20	68	220	104.4	85	185
−30	−34.4	−34	−29.2	90	32.2	22	71.6	225	107.2	90	194
−25	−31.7	−32	−25.6	95	35.0	24	75.2	230	110.0	95	202
−20	−28.9	−30	−22	100	37.8	26	78.8	235	112.8	100	212
−15	−26.1	−28	−18.4	105	40.6	28	82.4	240	115.6	105	221
−10	−23.3	−26	−14.8	110	43.3	30	86	245	118.3	110	230
−5	−20.6	−24	−11.2	115	46.1	32	89.6	250	121.1	115	239
0	−17.8	−22	−7.6	120	48.9	34	93.2	255	123.9	120	248
1	−17.2	−20	−4	125	51.7	36	96.8	260	126.6	125	257
2	−16.7	−18	−0.4	130	54.4	38	100.4	265	129.4	130	266
3	−16.1	−16	3.2	135	57.2	40	104	270	132.2	135	275
4	−15.6	−14	6.8	140	60.0	42	107.6	275	135.0	140	284
5	−15.0	−12	10.4	145	62.8	44	112.2	280	137.8	145	293
10	−12.2	−10	14	150	65.6	46	114.8	285	140.6	150	302
15	−9.4	−8	17.6	155	68.3	48	118.4	290	143.3	155	311
20	−6.7	−6	21.2	160	71.1	50	122	295	146.1	160	320
25	−3.9	−4	24.8	165	73.9	52	125.6	300	148.9	165	329
30	−1.1	−2	28.4	170	76.7	54	129.2	305	151.7	170	338
35	1.7	0	32	175	79.4	56	132.8	310	154.4	175	347
40	4.4	2	35.6	180	82.2	58	136.4	315	157.2	180	356
45	7.2	4	39.2	185	85.0	60	140	320	160.0	185	365
50	10.0	6	42.8	190	87.8	62	143.6	325	162.8	190	374
55	12.8	8	46.4	195	90.6	64	147.2	330	165.6	195	383
60	15.6	10	50	200	93.3	66	150.8	335	168.3	200	392
65	18.3	12	53.6	205	96.1	68	154.4	340	171.1	205	401
70	21.1	14	57.2	210	98.9	70	158	345	173.9	210	410
75	23.9	16	60.8	212	100.0	75	167	350	176.7	215	414

TCCS1C01

ENGLISH TO METRIC CONVERSION: LENGTH

To convert inches (ins.) to millimeters (mm): multiply number of inches by 25.4
To convert millimeters (mm) to inches (ins.): multiply number of millimeters by .04

Inches	Decimals	Milli-meters	Inches to millimeters: inches	mm	Inches	Decimals	Milli-meters	Inches to millimeters: inches	mm
1/64	0.015625	0.3969	0.0001	0.00254	33/64	0.515625	13.0969	0.6	15.24
1/32	0.03125	0.7937	0.0002	0.00508	17/32	0.53125	13.4937	0.7	17.78
3/64	0.046875	1.1906	0.0003	0.00762	35/64	0.546875	13.8906	0.8	20.32
1/16	0.0625	1.5875	0.0004	0.01016	9/16	0.5625	14.2875	0.9	22.86
5/64	0.078125	1.9844	0.0005	0.01270	37/64	0.578125	14.6844	1	25.4
3/32	0.09375	2.3812	0.0006	0.01524	19/32	0.59375	15.0812	2	50.8
7/64	0.109375	2.7781	0.0007	0.01778	39/64	0.609375	15.4781	3	76.2
1/8	0.125	3.1750	0.0008	0.02032	5/8	0.625	15.8750	4	101.6
9/64	0.140625	3.5719	0.0009	0.02286	41/64	0.640625	16.2719	5	127.0
5/32	0.15625	3.9687	0.001	0.0254	21/32	0.65625	16.6687	6	152.4
11/64	0.171875	4.3656	0.002	0.0508	43/64	0.671875	17.0656	7	177.8
3/16	0.1875	4.7625	0.003	0.0762	11/16	0.6875	17.4625	8	203.2
13/64	0.203125	5.1594	0.004	0.1016	45/64	0.703125	17.8594	9	228.6
7/32	0.21875	5.5562	0.005	0.1270	23/32	0.71875	18.2562	10	254.0
15/64	0.234375	5.9531	0.006	0.1524	47/64	0.734375	18.6531	11	279.4
1/4	0.25	6.3500	0.007	0.1778	3/4	0.75	19.0500	12	304.8
17/64	0.265625	6.7469	0.008	0.2032	49/64	0.765625	19.4469	13	330.2
9/32	0.28125	7.1437	0.009	0.2286	25/32	0.78125	19.8437	14	355.6
19/64	0.296875	7.5406	0.01	0.254	51/64	0.796875	20.2406	15	381.0
5/16	0.3125	7.9375	0.02	0.508	13/16	0.8125	20.6375	16	406.4
21/64	0.328125	8.3344	0.03	0.762	53/64	0.828125	21.0344	17	431.8
11/32	0.34375	8.7312	0.04	1.016	27/32	0.84375	21.4312	18	457.2
23/64	0.359375	9.1281	0.05	1.270	55/64	0.859375	21.8281	19	482.6
3/8	0.375	9.5250	0.06	1.524	7/8	0.875	22.2250	20	508.0
25/64	0.390625	9.9219	0.07	1.778	57/64	0.890625	22.6219	21	533.4
13/32	0.40625	10.3187	0.08	2.032	29/32	0.90625	23.0187	22	558.8
27/64	0.421875	10.7156	0.09	2.286	59/64	0.921875	23.4156	23	584.2
7/16	0.4375	11.1125	0.1	2.54	15/16	0.9375	23.8125	24	609.6
29/64	0.453125	11.5094	0.2	5.08	61/64	0.953125	24.2094	25	635.0
15/32	0.46875	11.9062	0.3	7.62	31/32	0.96875	24.6062	26	660.4
31/64	0.484375	12.3031	0.4	10.16	63/64	0.984375	25.0031	27	690.6
1/2	0.5	12.7000	0.5	12.70					

ENGLISH TO METRIC CONVERSION: TORQUE

To convert foot-pounds (ft. lbs.) to Newton-meters: multiply the number of ft. lbs. by 1.3
To convert inch-pounds (in. lbs.) to Newton-meters: multiply the number of in. lbs. by .11

in lbs	N-m	in lbs	N-m	in lbs	N-m	in lbs	N-m	in lbs	N-m
0.1	0.01	1	0.11	10	1.13	19	2.15	28	3.16
0.2	0.02	2	0.23	11	1.24	20	2.26	29	3.28
0.3	0.03	3	0.34	12	1.36	21	2.37	30	3.39
0.4	0.04	4	0.45	13	1.47	22	2.49	31	3.50
0.5	0.06	5	0.56	14	1.58	23	2.60	32	3.62
0.6	0.07	6	0.68	15	1.70	24	2.71	33	3.73
0.7	0.08	7	0.78	16	1.81	25	2.82	34	3.84
0.8	0.09	8	0.90	17	1.92	26	2.94	35	3.95
0.9	0.10	9	1.02	18	2.03	27	3.05	36	4.0

TCCS1C02

ENGLISH TO METRIC CONVERSION: TORQUE

Torque is now expressed as either foot-pounds (ft./lbs.) or inch-pounds (in./lbs.). The metric measurement unit for torque is the Newton-meter (Nm). This unit—the Nm—will be used for all SI metric torque references, both the present ft./lbs. and in./lbs.

ft lbs	N-m	ft lbs	N-m	ft lbs	N-m	ft lbs	N-m
0.1	0.1	33	44.7	74	100.3	115	155.9
0.2	0.3	34	46.1	75	101.7	116	157.3
0.3	0.4	35	47.4	76	103.0	117	158.6
0.4	0.5	36	48.8	77	104.4	118	160.0
0.5	0.7	37	50.7	78	105.8	119	161.3
0.6	0.8	38	51.5	79	107.1	120	162.7
0.7	1.0	39	52.9	80	108.5	121	164.0
0.8	1.1	40	54.2	81	109.8	122	165.4
0.9	1.2	41	55.6	82	111.2	123	166.8
1	1.3	42	56.9	83	112.5	124	168.1
2	2.7	43	58.3	84	113.9	125	169.5
3	4.1	44	59.7	85	115.2	126	170.8
4	5.4	45	61.0	86	116.6	127	172.2
5	6.8	46	62.4	87	118.0	128	173.5
6	8.1	47	63.7	88	119.3	129	174.9
7	9.5	48	65.1	89	120.7	130	176.2
8	10.8	49	66.4	90	122.0	131	177.6
9	12.2	50	67.8	91	123.4	132	179.0
10	13.6	51	69.2	92	124.7	133	180.3
11	14.9	52	70.5	93	126.1	134	181.7
12	16.3	53	71.9	94	127.4	135	183.0
13	17.6	54	73.2	95	128.8	136	184.4
14	18.9	55	74.6	96	130.2	137	185.7
15	20.3	56	75.9	97	131.5	138	187.1
16	21.7	57	77.3	98	132.9	139	188.5
17	23.0	58	78.6	99	134.2	140	189.8
18	24.4	59	80.0	100	135.6	141	191.2
19	25.8	60	81.4	101	136.9	142	192.5
20	27.1	61	82.7	102	138.3	143	193.9
21	28.5	62	84.1	103	139.6	144	195.2
22	29.8	63	85.4	104	141.0	145	196.6
23	31.2	64	86.8	105	142.4	146	198.0
24	32.5	65	88.1	106	143.7	147	199.3
25	33.9	66	89.5	107	145.1	148	200.7
26	35.2	67	90.8	108	146.4	149	202.0
27	36.6	68	92.2	109	147.8	150	203.4
28	38.0	69	93.6	110	149.1	151	204.7
29	39.3	70	94.9	111	150.5	152	206.1
30	40.7	71	96.3	112	151.8	153	207.4
31	42.0	72	97.6	113	153.2	154	208.8
32	43.4	73	99.0	114	154.6	155	210.2

TCCS1C03

ENGLISH TO METRIC CONVERSION: FORCE

Force is presently measured in pounds (lbs.). This type of measurement is used to measure spring pressure, specifically how many pounds it takes to compress a spring. Our present force unit (the pound) will be replaced in SI metric measurements by the Newton (N). This term will eventually see use in specifications for electric motor brush spring pressures, valve spring pressures, etc.

To convert pounds (lbs.) to Newton (N): multiply the number of lbs. by 4.45

lbs	N	lbs	N	lbs	N	oz	N
0.01	0.04	21	93.4	59	262.4	1	0.3
0.02	0.09	22	97.9	60	266.9	2	0.6
0.03	0.13	23	102.3	61	271.3	3	0.8
0.04	0.18	24	106.8	62	275.8	4	1.1
0.05	0.22	25	111.2	63	280.2	5	1.4
0.06	0.27	26	115.6	64	284.6	6	1.7
0.07	0.31	27	120.1	65	289.1	7	2.0
0.08	0.36	28	124.6	66	293.6	8	2.2
0.09	0.40	29	129.0	67	298.0	9	2.5
0.1	0.4	30	133.4	68	302.5	10	2.8
0.2	0.9	31	137.9	69	306.9	11	3.1
0.3	1.3	32	142.3	70	311.4	12	3.3
0.4	1.8	33	146.8	71	315.8	13	3.6
0.5	2.2	34	151.2	72	320.3	14	3.9
0.6	2.7	35	155.7	73	324.7	15	4.2
0.7	3.1	36	160.1	74	329.2	16	4.4
0.8	3.6	37	164.6	75	333.6	17	4.7
0.9	4.0	38	169.0	76	338.1	18	5.0
1	4.4	39	173.5	77	342.5	19	5.3
2	8.9	40	177.9	78	347.0	20	5.6
3	13.4	41	182.4	79	351.4	21	5.8
4	17.8	42	186.8	80	355.9	22	6.1
5	22.2	43	191.3	81	360.3	23	6.4
6	26.7	44	195.7	82	364.8	24	6.7
7	31.1	45	200.2	83	369.2	25	7.0
8	35.6	46	204.6	84	373.6	26	7.2
9	40.0	47	209.1	85	378.1	27	7.5
10	44.5	48	213.5	86	382.6	28	7.8
11	48.9	49	218.0	87	387.0	29	8.1
12	53.4	50	222.4	88	391.4	30	8.3
13	57.8	51	226.9	89	395.9	31	8.6
14	62.3	52	231.3	90	400.3	32	8.9
15	66.7	53	235.8	91	404.8	33	9.2
16	71.2	54	240.2	92	409.2	34	9.4
17	75.6	55	244.6	93	413.7	35	9.7
18	80.1	56	249.1	94	418.1	36	10.0
19	84.5	57	253.6	95	422.6	37	10.3
20	89.0	58	258.0	96	427.0	38	10.6

TCCS1C04

ENGLISH TO METRIC CONVERSION: LIQUID CAPACITY

Liquid or fluid capacity is presently expressed as pints, quarts or gallons, or a combination of all of these. In the metric system the liter (l) will become the basic unit. Fractions of a liter would be expressed as deciliters, centiliters, or most frequently (and commonly) as milliliters.

To convert pints (pts.) to liters (l): multiply the number of pints by .47
To convert liters (l) to pints (pts.): multiply the number of liters by 2.1
To convert quarts (qts.) to liters (l): multiply the number of quarts by .95
To convert liters (l) to quarts (qts.): multiply the number of liters by 1.06
To convert gallons (gals.) to liters (l): multiply the number of gallons by 3.8
To convert liters (l) to gallons (gals.): multiply the number of liters by .26

gals	liters	qts	liters	pts	liters
0.1	0.38	0.1	0.10	0.1	0.05
0.2	0.76	0.2	0.19	0.2	0.10
0.3	1.1	0.3	0.28	0.3	0.14
0.4	1.5	0.4	0.38	0.4	0.19
0.5	1.9	0.5	0.47	0.5	0.24
0.6	2.3	0.6	0.57	0.6	0.28
0.7	2.6	0.7	0.66	0.7	0.33
0.8	3.0	0.8	0.76	0.8	0.38
0.9	3.4	0.9	0.85	0.9	0.43
1	3.8	1	1.0	1	0.5
2	7.6	2	1.9	2	1.0
3	11.4	3	2.8	3	1.4
4	15.1	4	3.8	4	1.9
5	18.9	5	4.7	5	2.4
6	22.7	6	5.7	6	2.8
7	26.5	7	6.6	7	3.3
8	30.3	8	7.6	8	3.8
9	34.1	9	8.5	9	4.3
10	37.8	10	9.5	10	4.7
11	41.6	11	10.4	11	5.2
12	45.4	12	11.4	12	5.7
13	49.2	13	12.3	13	6.2
14	53.0	14	13.2	14	6.6
15	56.8	15	14.2	15	7.1
16	60.6	16	15.1	16	7.6
17	64.3	17	16.1	17	8.0
18	68.1	18	17.0	18	8.5
19	71.9	19	18.0	19	9.0
20	75.7	20	18.9	20	9.5
21	79.5	21	19.9	21	9.9
22	83.2	22	20.8	22	10.4
23	87.0	23	21.8	23	10.9
24	90.8	24	22.7	24	11.4
25	94.6	25	23.6	25	11.8
26	98.4	26	24.6	26	12.3
27	102.2	27	25.5	27	12.8
28	106.0	28	26.5	28	13.2
29	110.0	29	27.4	29	13.7
30	113.5	30	28.4	30	14.2

TCCS1C05

ENGLISH TO METRIC CONVERSION: PRESSURE

The basic unit of pressure measurement used today is expressed as pounds per square inch (psi). The metric unit for psi will be the kilopascal (kPa). This will apply to either fluid pressure or air pressure, and will be frequently seen in tire pressure readings, oil pressure specifications, fuel pump pressure, etc.

To convert pounds per square inch (psi) to kilopascals (kPa): multiply the number of psi by 6.89

Psi	kPa	Psi	kPa	Psi	kPa	Psi	kPa
0.1	0.7	37	255.1	82	565.4	127	875.6
0.2	1.4	38	262.0	83	572.3	128	882.5
0.3	2.1	39	268.9	84	579.2	129	889.4
0.4	2.8	40	275.8	85	586.0	130	896.3
0.5	3.4	41	282.7	86	592.9	131	903.2
0.6	4.1	42	289.6	87	599.8	132	910.1
0.7	4.8	43	296.5	88	606.7	133	917.0
0.8	5.5	44	303.4	89	613.6	134	923.9
0.9	6.2	45	310.3	90	620.5	135	930.8
1	6.9	46	317.2	91	627.4	136	937.7
2	13.8	47	324.0	92	634.3	137	944.6
3	20.7	48	331.0	93	641.2	138	951.5
4	27.6	49	337.8	94	648.1	139	958.4
5	34.5	50	344.7	95	655.0	140	965.2
6	41.4	51	351.6	96	661.9	141	972.2
7	48.3	52	358.5	97	668.8	142	979.0
8	55.2	53	365.4	98	675.7	143	985.9
9	62.1	54	372.3	99	682.6	144	992.8
10	69.0	55	379.2	100	689.5	145	999.7
11	75.8	56	386.1	101	696.4	146	1006.6
12	82.7	57	393.0	102	703.3	147	1013.5
13	89.6	58	399.9	103	710.2	148	1020.4
14	96.5	59	406.8	104	717.0	149	1027.3
15	103.4	60	413.7	105	723.9	150	1034.2
16	110.3	61	420.6	106	730.8	151	1041.1
17	117.2	62	427.5	107	737.7	152	1048.0
18	124.1	63	434.4	108	744.6	153	1054.9
19	131.0	64	441.3	109	751.5	154	1061.8
20	137.9	65	448.2	110	758.4	155	1068.7
21	144.8	66	455.0	111	765.3	156	1075.6
22	151.7	67	461.9	112	772.2	157	1082.5
23	158.6	68	468.8	113	779.1	158	1089.4
24	165.5	69	475.7	114	786.0	159	1096.3
25	172.4	70	482.6	115	792.9	160	1103.2
26	179.3	71	489.5	116	799.8	161	1110.0
27	186.2	72	496.4	117	806.7	162	1116.9
28	193.0	73	503.3	118	813.6	163	1123.8
29	200.0	74	510.2	119	820.5	164	1130.7
30	206.8	75	517.1	120	827.4	165	1137.6
31	213.7	76	524.0	121	834.3	166	1144.5
32	220.6	77	530.9	122	841.2	167	1151.4
33	227.5	78	537.8	123	848.0	168	1158.3
34	234.4	79	544.7	124	854.9	169	1165.2
35	241.3	80	551.6	125	861.8	170	1172.1
36	248.2	81	558.5	126	868.7	171	1179.0

TCCS1006

ENGLISH TO METRIC CONVERSION: PRESSURE

The basic unit of pressure measurement used today is expressed as pounds per square inch (psi). The metric unit for psi will be the kilopascal (kPa). This will apply to either fluid pressure or air pressure, and will be frequently seen in tire pressure readings, oil pressure specifications, fuel pump pressure, etc.

To convert pounds per square inch (psi) to kilopascals (kPa): multiply the number of psi by 6.89

Psi	kPa	Psi	kPa	Psi	kPa	Psi	kPa
172	1185.9	216	1489.3	260	1792.6	304	2096.0
173	1192.8	217	1496.2	261	1799.5	305	2102.9
174	1199.7	218	1503.1	262	1806.4	306	2109.8
175	1206.6	219	1510.0	263	1813.3	307	2116.7
176	1213.5	220	1516.8	264	1820.2	308	2123.6
177	1220.4	221	1523.7	265	1827.1	309	2130.5
178	1227.3	222	1530.6	266	1834.0	310	2137.4
179	1234.2	223	1537.5	267	1840.9	311	2144.3
180	1241.0	224	1544.4	268	1847.8	312	2151.2
181	1247.9	225	1551.3	269	1854.7	313	2158.1
182	1254.8	226	1558.2	270	1861.6	314	2164.9
183	1261.7	227	1565.1	271	1868.5	315	2171.8
184	1268.6	228	1572.0	272	1875.4	316	2178.7
185	1275.5	229	1578.9	273	1882.3	317	2185.6
186	1282.4	230	1585.8	274	1889.2	318	2192.5
187	1289.3	231	1592.7	275	1896.1	319	2199.4
188	1296.2	232	1599.6	276	1903.0	320	2206.3
189	1303.1	233	1606.5	277	1909.8	321	2213.2
190	1310.0	234	1613.4	278	1916.7	322	2220.1
191	1316.9	235	1620.3	279	1923.6	323	2227.0
192	1323.8	236	1627.2	280	1930.5	324	2233.9
193	1330.7	237	1634.1	281	1937.4	325	2240.8
194	1337.6	238	1641.0	282	1944.3	326	2247.7
195	1344.5	239	1647.8	283	1951.2	327	2254.6
196	1351.4	240	1654.7	284	1958.1	328	2261.5
197	1358.3	241	1661.6	285	1965.0	329	2268.4
198	1365.2	242	1668.5	286	1971.9	330	2275.3
199	1372.0	243	1675.4	287	1978.8	331	2282.2
200	1378.9	244	1682.3	288	1985.7	332	2289.1
201	1385.8	245	1689.2	289	1992.6	333	2295.9
202	1392.7	246	1696.1	290	1999.5	334	2302.8
203	1399.6	247	1703.0	291	2006.4	335	2309.7
204	1406.5	248	1709.9	292	2013.3	336	2316.6
205	1413.4	249	1716.8	293	2020.2	337	2323.5
206	1420.3	250	1723.7	294	2027.1	338	2330.4
207	1427.2	251	1730.6	295	2034.0	339	2337.3
208	1434.1	252	1737.5	296	2040.8	240	2344.2
209	1441.0	253	1744.4	297	2047.7	341	2351.1
210	1447.9	254	1751.3	298	2054.6	342	2358.0
211	1454.8	255	1758.2	299	2061.5	343	2364.9
212	1461.7	256	1765.1	300	2068.4	344	2371.8
213	1468.7	257	1772.0	301	2075.3	345	2378.7
214	1475.5	258	1778.8	302	2082.2	346	2385.6
215	1482.4	259	1785.7	303	2089.1	347	2392.5

TCCS1007

2

ENGINE
ELECTRICAL

DISTRIBUTOR IGNITION SYSTEM

→**For information on understanding electricity and troubleshooting electrical circuits, please refer to Section 6 of this manual.**

Maximas from 1993–94 with the VG30E engine are the only models that use a distributor type ignition system. For all other engine models, refer to the Distributorless Ignition System heading within this section.

General Information

The VG30E engines use a distributor ignition system that works in conjunction with the Engine Control Module (ECM). The various sensors attached to the engine send information to the ECM, which manipulates the ignition timing to achieve maximum power and efficiency.

When the ignition switch is turned **ON**, voltage from the battery is applied to the ignition coil. As the shaft of the distributor rotates, the crankshaft sensor sends a signal to the ECM. This signal activates the power transistor to cause ignition coil primary winding current flow from the negative terminal through the power transistor to ground repeatedly. This interruption induces high voltage in the ignition coil secondary windings, which is sent through the distributor, spark plug cable, and finally, the spark plug.

Diagnosis and Testing

SERVICE PRECAUTIONS

▶ **See Figure 1**

- Always turn the key **OFF** and isolate both ends of a circuit whenever testing for a short or continuity.
- Always disconnect solenoids and switches from the harness before measuring for continuity, resistance or energizing with a 12 volt source.
- Be careful with connectors; Before attaching them, inspect the terminals for corrosion and bending. Check that the terminals are not pushed out from the back of the connector.

SECONDARY SPARK TEST

▶ **See Figure 2**

This procedure is performed best with a spark tester. Two types of spark testers are commonly available; both available from most auto parts stores. The neon bulb type is connected to the spark plug wire and flashes with each ignition pulse. The air gap type must be adjusted to match the spark plug gap required for the engine. This type will allow you to see the condition of the spark as well as checking for spark itself. If the spark is orange/yellow, this indicates a weak spark; blue would be a strong spark.

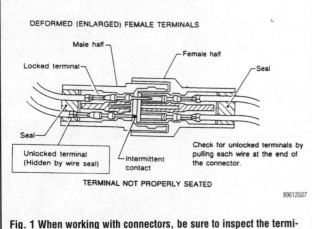

Fig. 1 When working with connectors, be sure to inspect the terminals. Check for proper seating within the connector

1. Disconnect a spark plug wire, and install the spark tester.
2. Ground the tester at a good location on the engine.
3. Crank the engine and check for spark at the tester.
4. If spark occurs at the tester, the ignition system is functioning properly.
5. If there is no spark at the tester, remove the distributor cap and verify the rotor is turning when the engine is cranked.
6. If the rotor is turning, check for spark at the ignition coil by installing the tester in the coil wire.
7. If no spark exists, test the ignition coil, power transistor and related wiring.

Ignition Coil

The ignition coil is located on the front of the engine, in front of the distributor.

TESTING

▶ **See Figure 3**

1. Disconnect the negative battery cable.
2. Disconnect the electrical harness connector from the ignition coil.
3. Using an ohmmeter, adjust it to the low range.
4. Attach the probes to terminals **1** and **2**; there should be resistance of approximately 1.0 ohms. If not, replace the ignition coil.
5. Connect the electrical harness connector to the ignition coil.
6. Connect the negative battery cable.

REMOVAL & INSTALLATION

1. Disconnect the negative battery cable.
2. Unplug the electrical harness connector from the ignition coil.
3. Disconnect the ignition coil wire.
4. Remove the ignition coil bolts and the coil.
To install:
5. Mount the ignition coil to the engine and tighten the bolts.
6. Plug in the harness connector, and the coil ignition wire.
7. Connect the negative battery cable.
8. Start the engine and check for proper operation.

Power Transistor (Ignition Module)

The power transistor is located on the front of the engine, in front of the distributor.

TESTING

▶ **See Figure 4**

1. Disconnect the negative battery cable.
2. Disconnect the electrical harness connector from the power transistor.
3. Using an ohmmeter, adjust the setting to the low range, approximately 1.0 ohms.
4. To test the power transistor, perform the following procedures:
   a. Place the positive probe on terminal **a** and the negative probe on terminal **b**; there should be continuity.
   b. Place the positive probe on terminal **a** and the negative probe on terminal **c**; there should be continuity.
   c. Place the negative probe on terminal **a** and the positive (+) probe on terminal **b**; there should not be continuity.
   d. Place the negative probe on terminal **a** and the positive (+) probe on terminal **c**; there should not be continuity.
5. If the power transistor does not perform according to the test, replace it.
6. Reconnect the electrical harness connector to the power transistor.
7. Connect the negative battery cable.

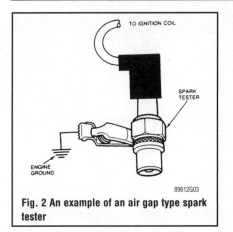

Fig. 2 An example of an air gap type spark tester

Fig. 3 Checking the VG30E ignition coil with an ohmmeter

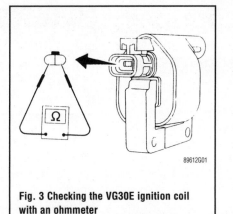

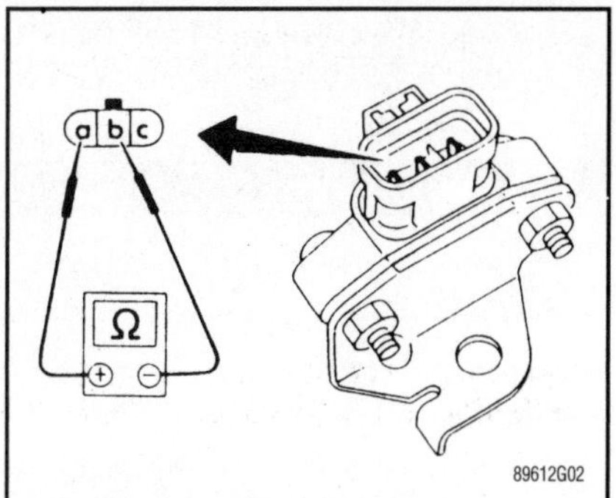

Fig. 4 Checking the power transistor with an ohmmeter—VG30E engine

REMOVAL & INSTALLATION

1. Disconnect the negative battery cable.
2. Disconnect the electrical harness connectors from the power transistor.
3. Remove the power transistor bolts and the transistor.
To install:
4. Install the power transistor and tighten the bolts.
5. Connect the electrical harness connectors to the power transistor.
6. Connect the negative battery cable.
7. Start the engine and check the operation.

Distributor

REMOVAL

If a distributor is not keyed for installation with only one orientation, it could have been removed previously and rewired. The resultant wiring would hold the correct firing order, but could change the relative placement of the plug towers in relation to the engine. For this reason it is imperative that you label all wires before disconnecting any of them. Also, before removal, compare the current wiring with the accompanying illustrations. If the current wiring does not match, make notes in your book to reflect how your engine is wired.

1. Disconnect the negative battery cable.
2. Set the engine to Top Dead Center (TDC) with the number 1 piston on compression stroke.
3. Remove and label the distributor spark plug wires from the distributor cap.
4. Remove the distributor cap and scribe a mark on the engine block to show both rotor and distributor position prior to removal.
5. Disconnect and label the wiring connections to the distributor.
6. Remove the bolt(s) holding distributor to engine.
7. Pull the distributor upward to remove from cylinder block.

➥**Do not disturb the camshaft or crankshaft position after the distributor is removed from the engine. If any of the components are moved, TDC on cylinder 1 will have to be found again before reinstalling the distributor.**

DISTRIBUTORLESS IGNITION SYSTEM

General Information

Maximas with the VE30DE and VQ30DE engines use a distributorless ignition system that is controlled by the Engine Control Module (ECM). The ECM receives a signal from the crankshaft sensor, and processes the signal based on inputs from other various engine sensors. Then the ECM sends signals to each of the individual coils in the proper firing order.

This system is more efficient than a distributor, and has less moving parts. The high voltage coils are directly attached to each spark plug, allowing a higher energy spark within the cylinder. A high energy spark means a faster, more thorough burning of the air/fuel mixture, which produces more power and less emissions.

INSTALLATION

Engine Not Disturbed

1. Install a new distributor housing O-ring.
2. Install the distributor in the engine so the rotor is aligned with the match-mark on the housing and the housing is aligned with the matchmark on the engine. Make sure the distributor is fully seated and the distributor gear is fully engaged.
3. Install and snug the hold-down bolt.
4. Connect the distributor pickup lead wires.
5. Install the distributor cap and tighten the screws.
6. Install the spark plug wires and the splash shield.
7. Connect the negative battery cable.
8. After the ignition timing has been adjusted, tighten the hold-down bolt(s) to 80–104 inch lbs. (9–11 Nm).

Engine Disturbed

1. Install a new distributor housing O-ring.
2. Position the engine so the No. 1 piston is at TDC of its compression stroke and the mark on the vibration damper is aligned with **0** on the timing indicator.
3. Install the distributor in the engine so the rotor is aligned with the position of the No. 1 ignition wire on the distributor cap. Make sure the distributor is fully seated and that the distributor shaft is fully engaged.
4. Install and snug the hold-down bolt.
5. Connect the distributor pickup lead wires.
6. Install the distributor cap and tighten the screws.
7. Install the spark plug wires, and the splash shield, if equipped.
8. Connect the negative battery cable.
9. After the ignition timing has been adjusted, tighten the hold-down bolt(s) to 80–104 inch lbs.

Crankshaft Position Sensor

The crankshaft position sensor on VG30E engines is located inside the distributor. For information on removal and installation and testing, refer to Section 4.

Diagnosis and Testing

For diagnostic procedures on distributorless ignition, refer to Section 4.

SECONDARY SPARK TEST

1. Remove the ignition coil.
2. Remove the spark plug.
3. Install the spark plug to the ignition coil, then attach the coil wiring.
4. Ground the plug at a good ground location on the engine.
5. Crank the engine and check for spark.

6. If spark occurs, the ignition system is functioning properly.

7. If no spark exists, test the ignition coil, power transistor and related wiring.

Ignition Coil(s)

TESTING

▶ **See Figures 5 and 6**

1. Disconnect the negative battery cable.
2. Unplug the electrical connector(s) from the ignition coil(s).
3. Remove the coil securing bolt and lift the coil from the spark plug.
4. Using an ohmmeter, adjust it to the low range, and attach the probes to terminal **1** and terminal **2**.
5. Measure the resistance; it should read around 0.8 ohms.

REMOVAL & INSTALLATION

▶ **See Figures 7, 8, 9 and 10**

1. Remove the decorative facia on the valve cover, if equipped.
2. Unplug the coil harness connector.
3. Unbolt the coil retaining fastener(s). Some models have only one bolt, while others have two fasteners.
4. Carefully pull the coil assembly out of the engine.

To install:

5. Place the coil into the spark plug recess. Make certain the tip of the coil is seated on the spark plug, and not beside it.
6. Fasten the coil with the retaining bolt(s).
7. Plug the harness connector onto the coil.
8. Replace the decorative facia, if equipped.

➡**If you are removing more than one coil at a time, be sure to label each coil, harness connector and cylinder.**

Power Transistor

On VQ30DE engines, the power transistor is integrated with the individual-ized coils for each spark plug.

The power transistor on VE30DE is located next to the crankshaft position sensor, at the rear of the right cylinder bank.

TESTING

VE30DE Engines

▶ **See Figures 11 and 12**

1. Disconnect the negative battery cable.
2. Disconnect the electrical harness connector(s) from the power transistor.

➡**If necessary, remove the power transistor from the engine.**

3. Using an ohmmeter, adjust it to the low range and perform the following procedures:

a. Attach the positive probe to terminal **d** and with the negative probe, touch terminals **a**, **b**, **c**, **e**, **f** and **g**; the resistance of each terminal should not be 0 or infinity.

b. Attach the negative probe to terminal **d** and with the positive probe, touch terminals **a**, **b**, **c**, **e**, **f** and **g**; the resistance of each terminal should not be 0 or infinity.

c. Attach the positive probe to terminal **d** and with the negative probe, touch terminals **1**, **2**, **3**, **4**, **5** and **6**; the resistance of each terminal should not be 0 or infinity.

d. Attach the negative probe to terminal **d** and with the positive probe, touch terminals **1**, **2**, **3**, **4**, **5** and **6**; the resistance of each terminal should be infinity.

e. Attach the positive probe to terminal **a** and the negative probe to ter-minal **1**; the resistance should not be 0 or infinity.

f. Attach the negative probe to terminal **a** and the positive probe to ter-minal **1**; the resistance should be infinity.

Fig. 5 Checking an ignition coil resis-tance—note the locations of the test probes

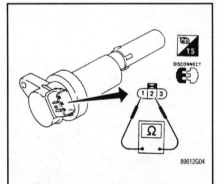

Fig. 6 Be sure to use terminals 1 and 2 when checking the ignition coils

Fig. 7 Some engines have a decorative panel on the front valve cover that needs to be removed to access the front coils

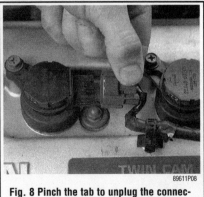

Fig. 8 Pinch the tab to unplug the connec-tor . . .

Fig. 9 . . . then remove the retainer bolts . . .

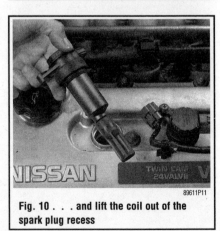

Fig. 10 . . . and lift the coil out of the spark plug recess

g. Attach the positive probe to terminal **b** and the negative probe to terminal **2**; the resistance should not be 0 or infinity.

h. Attach the negative probe to terminal **b** and the positive probe to terminal **2**; the resistance should be infinity.

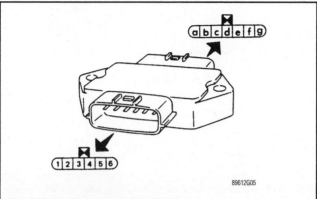

Fig. 11 Power transistor pin identification

Fig. 12 Certain models have slightly different markings; 1-2-3-G-4-5-6 would be equivalent to A-B-C-D-E-F-G

i. Attach the positive probe to terminal **c** and the negative probe to terminal **3**; the resistance should not be 0 or infinity.

j. Attach the negative probe to terminal **c** and the positive probe to terminal **3**; the resistance should be infinity.

k. Attach the positive probe to terminal **e** and the negative probe to terminal **4**; the resistance should not be 0 or infinity.

l. Attach the negative probe to terminal **e** and the positive probe to terminal **4**; the resistance should be infintiy.

m. Attach the positive probe to terminal **f** and the negative probe to terminal **5**; the resistance should not be 0 or infinity.

n. Attach the negative probe to terminal **f** and the positive probe to terminal **5**; the resistance should be infinity.

o. Attach the positive probe to terminal **g** and the negative probe to terminal **6**; the resistance should not be 0 or infinity.

p. Attach the negative probe to terminal **g** and the positive probe to terminal **6**; the resistance should be infinity.

4. If the any of the test results do not agree, replace the power transistor.
5. Connect the electrical harness connectors to the power transistor.
6. Connect the negative battery cable.

REMOVAL & INSTALLATION

VE30DE Engine

♦ See Figures 13, 14 and 15

1. Disconnect the negative battery cable.
2. Disconnect the electrical harness connectors from the power transistor.
3. Remove the power transistor-to-engine bolts and the transistor.

To install:

4. Install the power transistor and tighten the bolts.
5. Connect the electrical harness connectors to the power transistor.
6. Connect the negative battery cable.
7. Start the engine and check the operation.

Camshaft and Crankshaft Position Sensors

For information on diagnostics and removal and installation of these sensors, refer to Section 4.

Fig. 13 Unplug the power transistor upper plug . . .

Fig. 14 . . . followed by the lower plug. Push down on the tab and pull the connector to unplug it from the power transistor

Fig. 15 Removing the power transistor from the bracket will make testing easier

FIRING ORDER

♦ See Figures 16 and 17

➡ **To avoid confusion, remove and tag the spark plug wires one at a time, for replacement.**

If a distributor is not keyed for installation with only one orientation, it could have been removed previously and rewired. The resultant wiring would hold the correct firing order, but could change the relative placement of the plug towers in relation to the engine. For this reason it is imperative that you label all wires before disconnecting any of them. Also, before removal, compare the current wiring with the accompanying illustrations. If the current wiring does not match, make notes in your book to reflect how your engine is wired.

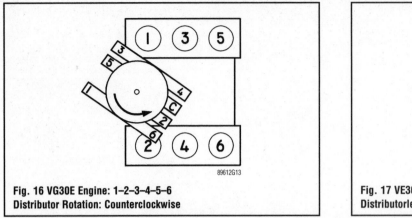

Fig. 16 VG30E Engine: 1–2–3–4–5–6
Distributor Rotation: Counterclockwise

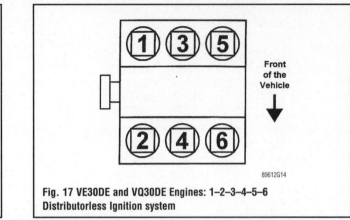

Front of the Vehicle

Fig. 17 VE30DE and VQ30DE Engines: 1–2–3–4–5–6
Distributorless Ignition system

CHARGING SYSTEM

General Information

The charging system is a negative (-) ground system that consists of an alternator, a voltage regulator, a charge indicator, a storage battery, wiring connecting the components, and fuse link wire.

The alternator is driven by a belt from the engine. Energy is supplied from the alternator/regulator system to the rotating field through two brushes to two slip-rings. The slip-rings are mounted on the rotor shaft and are connected to the field coil. This energy supplied to the rotating field from the battery is called excitation current and is used to initially energize the field to begin the generation of electricity. Once the alternator starts to generate electricity, the excitation current comes from its own output rather than the battery.

The alternator produces power in the form of alternating current (AC). The alternating current is rectified by diodes into direct current (DC). The direct current is used to charge the battery and power the rest of the electrical system.

When the ignition key is turned **ON**, current flows from the battery, through the charging system indicator light on the instrument panel, to the voltage regulator, and to the alternator. Since the alternator is not producing any current, the alternator warning light will flash. When the engine is started, the alternator begins to produce current, turning off the alternator light. As the alternator turns and produces current, the current is divided in two ways: one part to charge the battery and power the electrical components of the vehicle, and the rest is returned to the alternator to enable it to increase its output. In this situation, the alternator is receiving current from the battery and from itself. A voltage regulator is wired into the current supply to the alternator to prevent it from receiving too much current, which, in turn, would cause it to produce too much current. Conversely, if the voltage regulator does not allow the alternator to receive enough current, the battery will not be fully charged and will eventually drain.

The battery is connected to the alternator at all times, whether the ignition key is turned **ON** or not. If the battery were shorted to ground, the alternator would also be shorted. This would damage the alternator. To prevent this, a fusible link is installed in the wiring between the battery and the alternator. If the battery is shorted, the fusible link melts, thereby protecting the alternator.

Alternator Precautions

To prevent damage to the alternator and regulator, the following precautions should be taken when working with the electrical system:
- Never reverse the battery connections.
- Booster batteries for starting must be connected properly: positive-to-positive and negative-to-ground.
- Disconnect the battery cables before using a fast charger; the charger has a tendency to force current through the diodes in the opposite direction for which they were designed. This burns out the diodes.
- Never use a fast charger as a booster for starting the vehicle.
- Never disconnect the voltage regulator while the engine is running.
- Avoid long soldering times when replacing diodes or transistors. Prolonged heat is damaging to AC generators.
- Do not use test lamps of more than 12 volts for checking diode continuity.
- Do not short across or ground any of the terminals on the AC generator.

- The polarity of the battery, generator, and regulator must be matched and considered before making any electrical connections within the system.
- Never operate the alternator on an open circuit. Make sure that all connections within the circuit are clean and tight.
- Never disconnect the battery while the engine is running.
- Disconnect the battery terminals when performing any service on the electrical system. This will eliminate the possibility of accidental reversal of polarity.
- Disconnect the battery if arc welding is to be done on any part of the vehicle.

Alternator

TESTING

The easiest way to test the performance of the alternator is to perform a regulated voltage test.
1. Start the engine and allow it to reach operating temperature.
2. Connect a voltmeter between the positive and negative terminals of the battery.
3. Voltage should be 14.1–14.7 volts.
4. If voltage is higher or lower than specification, connect a voltmeter between the battery positive (B+) voltage output terminal of the alternator and a good engine ground.
5. Voltage should be 14.1–14.7 volts.
6. If voltage is still out of specification, a problem exists in the alternator or voltage regulator.
7. If voltage is now within specification, a problem exists in the wiring to the battery or in the battery itself.

➡**Many automotive parts stores have alternator bench testers available for use by customers. An alternator bench test is the most definite way to determine the condition of your alternator.**

REMOVAL & INSTALLATION

1993–94 Models

◆ See Figures 18, 19, 20, 21 and 22

1. Disconnect the negative battery cable, for safety purposes.
2. Remove the right side splash guard from under the vehicle.
3. Disconnect the alternator lead wires and connections. Label them if you are unsure of their locations.
4. Loosen the drive belt adjusting bolt and slip the belt off the pulley.
5. Remove the lower adjustment bolt, followed by the upper pivot bolt.
6. Lower the alternator from the vehicle.
To install:
7. Using a C-clamp and a socket, push the upper pivot bushing back in it's bore until it bottoms out.
8. Raise the alternator into the engine bracket, and push the upper pivot bolt all the way through the bracket to support it.

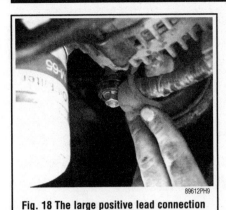

Fig. 18 The large positive lead connection is protected by a rubber boot

Fig. 19 Make sure the alternator ground wire is also removed

Fig. 20 Remove the lower adjustment bolt . . .

Fig. 21 . . . followed by the upper pivot bolt. Make sure you support the alternator

Fig. 22 Using a C-clamp to push in the pivot bushing will make installation easier

9. Install the lower adjustment bolt, followed by the upper pivot nut.
10. Place the belt on the alternator pulley, and tighten the belt.
11. Tighten the upper and lower mounting bolts.
12. Engage the alternator lead wires and connections.
13. Connect the negative battery cable.
14. Start the vehicle, and check for proper operation.
15. Readjust the belt tension, if necessary. Install the lower splash guard.

1995–98 Models

1. Disconnect the negative battery terminal.
2. Remove the splash guard on the right side of the vehicle.
3. Loosen the alternator belt idler pulley.
4. Slip the drive belt off the alternator pulley.
5. Remove the four air conditioning compressor mounting bolts.
6. Remove the radiator fan and fan shroud.
7. Move the air conditioning compressor forward.
8. Disconnect the alternator harness connector.
9. Remove the alternator mounting bolts, and lower the alternator from the vehicle.

To install:
10. Hold the alternator in place and install the mounting bolts.
11. Plug in the alternator harness connector.
12. Move the air conditioning compressor back into location.
13. Install the radiator cooling fan and shroud.
14. Install the air conditioning compressor mounting bolts.
15. Place the drive belt on the alternator pulley.
16. Tighten the drive belt to the proper tension with the idler pulley.
17. Install the splash guard.
18. Connect the negative battery terminal.

➡**Proper belt tension is important. A belt that is too tight may cause alternator bearing failure; one that is too loose will cause a gradual battery discharge and/or belt slippage, resulting in belt breakage from overheating.**

Voltage Regulator

The voltage regulator is located inside the alternator, and alternator disassembly is required for replacement. Replacement of the entire unit is recommended.

STARTING SYSTEM

General Information

The starting system includes the battery, starter motor, solenoid, ignition switch, circuit protection and wiring connecting the components. An inhibitor switch is included in the starting system to prevent the vehicle from being started with the vehicle in gear.

When the ignition key is turned to the **START** position, current flows and energizes the starter's solenoid coil. The solenoid plunger and clutch shift lever are activated, and the clutch pinion engages the ring gear on the flywheel. The switch contacts close and the starter cranks the engine until it starts. To prevent damage caused by excessive starter armature rotation when the engine starts, the starter incorporates an over-running clutch in the pinion gear.

Vehicles with a manual transaxle are equipped with a clutch pedal switch in the starter circuit, which is designed to prevent the starter motor from operating unless the clutch pedal is depressed. Vehicles equipped with automatic transaxles use a Park/Neutral position switch in the starter circuit. These switches prevent the starter motor from functioning unless the transmission range selector lever is in Neutral (**N**) or Park (**P**).

Heavy cables, connectors and switches are utilized by the starting system because of the large amount of amperage this system is required to handle while cranking the engine. For premium starter motor function, the resistance in the starting system must be kept to an absolute minimum.

A discharged or faulty battery, loose or corroded connections, or partially broken cables will result in slower-than-normal cranking speeds. The amount of damage evident may even prevent the starter motor from rotating the engine at all.

Starter

Maximas use a gear reduction starter has a set of ratio reduction gears; the brushes on the gear reduction starter are located on a plate behind the starter drive housing. The extra gears make the starter pinion gear turn at about ½ the speed of the starter, giving the starter twice the turning power of a conventional starter.

The starting system is comprised of the following components:
- Permanent magnet gear-reduction starter motor with a solenoid-actuated drive
- Battery
- Remote control starter switch (part of the ignition switch)
- Park/Neutral Position switch (Automatic models)
- Clutch Pedal Position switch (on manual transmission models)
- Starter relay
- Heavy circuit wiring

TESTING

The easiest way to test the performance of the starter is to perform a voltage drop test.

➡**The battery must be in good condition and fully charged prior to performing this test.**

1. Connect a voltmeter between the positive and negative terminals of the battery.
2. Turn the ignition key to the **START** position and note the voltage drop on the meter.
3. If voltage drops below 11.5 volts, there is high resistance in the starting system.
4. Check for proper connections at the battery and starter.
5. Check the resistance of the battery cables and replace as necessary.
6. If all other components in the system are functional, the starter may be faulty.

➡**Many automotive parts stores have starter bench testers available for use by customers. A starter bench test is the most definitive way to determine the condition of your starter.**

REMOVAL & INSTALLATION

▶ **See Figures 23 and 24**

1. Disconnect the negative battery cable from the battery.
2. On the VE30DE and VQ30DE engines, remove the air duct.

SENDING UNITS AND SENSORS

➡**This section describes the operating principles of sending units, warning lights and gauges. Sensors that provide information to the Electronic Control Module (ECM) are covered in Section 4 of this manual.**

Several types of sending units exist, however most can be characterized as being either a pressure type or a resistance type. Pressure type sending units convert liquid pressure into an electrical signal that is sent to the gauge. Resistance type sending units are most often used to measure temperature and use variable resistance to control the current flow back to the indicating device. Both types of sending units are connected in series by a wire to the battery (through the ignition switch). When the ignition is turned **ON**, current flows from the battery through the indicating device and on to the sending unit.

Oil Pressure Switch

The oil pressure switch is located underneath the front of the engine, next to oil filter. This switch sends a signal to the oil light on the instrument cluster, warning of low oil pressure.

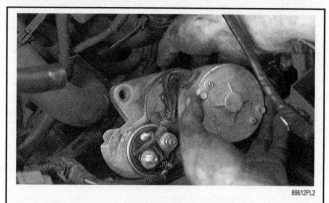

Fig. 23 Removing the starter (automatic transaxle)

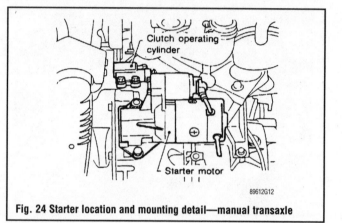

Fig. 24 Starter location and mounting detail—manual transaxle

3. Disconnect the starter wiring at the starter, taking note of the positions for correct installation.
4. On the VE30DE engine, remove the connector brackets.
5. Remove the starter-to-engine bolts ,and remove the starter from the vehicle.

To install:

6. Holding the starter in position, insert and tighten the attaching bolts. Be careful not overtorque the mounting bolts as this will crack the nose of the starter case.
7. Install the starter wiring in the correct location.
8. On the VE30DE engine, install the air duct and the connector brackets.
9. Connect the negative battery cable.
10. Start the engine a few times to make sure of proper operation.

TESTING

▶ **See Figures 25 and 26**

✳✳ CAUTION

During this procedure, the engine will running; use extreme caution. Keep clear of moving parts.

➡**The engine should be at normal operating temperature before performing this procedure.**

1. Turn off the engine.
2. Unplug the oil pressure switch connector.
3. Using an ohmmeter, check the continuity between the terminal and ground; there should be continuity.
4. Start the engine and let it idle. Check the continuity between the terminal

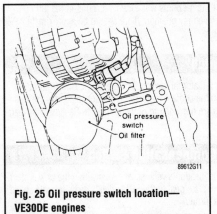

Fig. 25 Oil pressure switch location—VE30DE engines

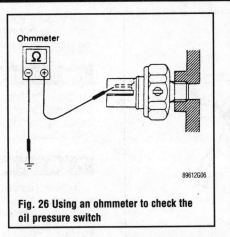

Fig. 26 Using an ohmmeter to check the oil pressure switch

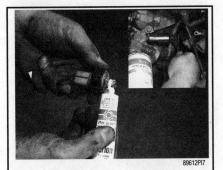

Fig. 27 Location of the oil pressure switch; the alternator is removed for clarity

and ground; there should not be continuity. If not within specifications, replace the switch.

REMOVAL & INSTALLATION

▶ See Figures 27 and 28

➡ If the engine is hot, allow it to cool before performing this procedure.

1. Disconnect the negative battery cable.
2. Raise and safely support the vehicle.
3. Disconnect the electrical connector from the oil pressure switch.
4. Remove the oil pressure switch from the engine.

To install:

5. Using proper sealant, lubricate the oil pressure switch threads.
6. Install the oil pressure switch and torque it to 9–12 ft. lbs. (13–17 Nm).
7. Connect the electrical connector to the oil pressure switch.
8. Connect the negative battery cable.

Thermal Transmitter (Coolant Temperature Sender Unit)

▶ See Figure 29

The Thermal Transmitter is used to send a signal to the temperature gauge on the instrument cluster, indicating engine coolant temperature.

TESTING

▶ See Figure 30

✴✴ CAUTION

During this procedure, the engine will running; use extreme caution. Keep clear of moving parts.

➡ The engine should be at normal operating temperature before performing this procedure.

1. Turn off the engine.
2. Disconnect the transmitter sender wire.
3. Using an ohmmeter, check the resistance between the transmitter wire terminal and ground.
4. The resistance between the terminal and ground should be between 70–90 ohms when the coolant temperature is approximately 140°F (60°C).
5. When the coolant temperature is approximately 212°F (100°C), there should be between 21 to 24 ohms of resistance between the transmitter wire terminal and ground.
6. If the resistance is not within specifications, it should be replaced.
7. Connect the transmitter sender wire.

REMOVAL & INSTALLATION

1. Disconnect the transmitter sender wire.
2. Unscrew the thermal transmitter from the engine.

To install:

3. Dress the threads of the thermal transmitter with sealant.
4. Screw the transmitter into the housing, and attach the wire.

Fuel Level Sender

The Fuel Level Sender is integrated with the fuel pump, which is mounted inside the fuel tank. Refer to Section 5 for removal and installation procedures.

TESTING

▶ See Figures 31 and 32

✴✴ CAUTION

Observe all applicable safety precautions when working around fuel. Whenever servicing the fuel system, always work in a

Fig. 28 Use thread sealer on the switch to prevent leaks. Be careful not to over-tighten the switch

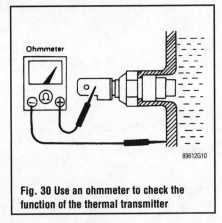

Fig. 29 Location of the thermal sending unit (A) next to the coolant temperature sensor (B)

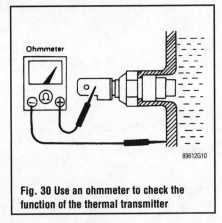

Fig. 30 Use an ohmmeter to check the function of the thermal transmitter

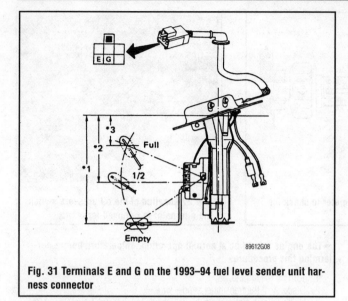

Fig. 31 Terminals E and G on the 1993–94 fuel level sender unit harness connector

well ventilated area. **Do not allow fuel spray or vapors to come in contact with a spark or open flame. Keep a dry chemical fire extinguisher near the work area. Always keep fuel in a container specifically designed for fuel storage; also, always properly seal fuel containers to avoid the possibility of fire or explosion.**

Using an ohmmeter, check the resistance between terminals **G** and **E**. When the float rod in the full (up) position, the resistance should be between 4 and 8 ohms. When the float rod is in the empty (down) position, there should be between 78 to 85 ohms of resistance.

For vehicles with digital instrumentation, the resistance between terminals **G**

and **E** should be between 15 to 18 ohms when the float rod is in the full position. With the float rod in the empty position, there should be approximately 929 and 1,009 ohms of resistance.

Radiator Fan Switch

Maximas do not have a radiator fan switch. The Electronic Control Module (ECM) uses the signal from the coolant temperature sensor to control the radiator fans. If the radiator fans are not working properly, refer to Section 4 for diagnostic procedures.

Power Steering Compensation Switch

The power steering compensation switch senses load within the power steering system. This switch sends a signal to the ECM, which keeps the idle speed steady when the steering is turned.

TESTING

▶ **See Figure 33**

1. Unplug the connector on the switch.
2. Using an ohmmeter, attach probes to each terminal.
3. Start the engine. With the steering centered, there should not be continuity.
4. When the steering wheel is turned, continuity should exist.
5. If the switch does not function properly, it should be replaced.

REMOVAL & INSTALLATION

▶ **See Figure 34**

1. Unplug the connector on the switch.
2. Using the appropriately sized socket, unscrew it from the pipe. Be sure to use a wrench to hold the pipe while loosening, or damage could occur to the pipe.
3. When installing a new switch, be sure to apply thread sealer.

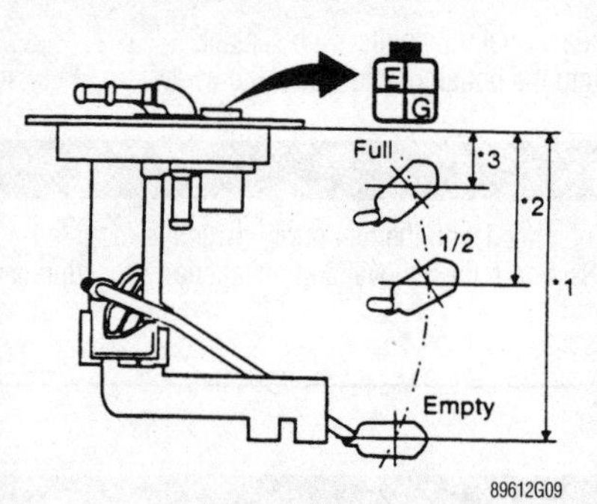

Fig. 32 Terminals E and G on the 1995–98 fuel level sender unit harness connector

Fig. 33 With the engine idling, have an assistant turn the steering wheel; there should be continuity in the switch

Fig. 34 Unplugging the wiper motor connector will allow for better access to the switch

Troubleshooting Basic Starting System Problems

Problem	Cause	Solution
Starter motor rotates engine slowly	• Battery charge low or battery defective	• Charge or replace battery
	• Defective circuit between battery and starter motor	• Clean and tighten, or replace cables
	• Low load current	• Bench-test starter motor. Inspect for worn brushes and weak brush springs.
	• High load current	• Bench-test starter motor. Check engine for friction, drag or coolant in cylinders. Check ring gear-to-pinion gear clearance.
Starter motor will not rotate engine	• Battery charge low or battery defective	• Charge or replace battery
	• Faulty solenoid	• Check solenoid ground. Repair or replace as necessary.
	• Damaged drive pinion gear or ring gear	• Replace damaged gear(s)
	• Starter motor engagement weak	• Bench-test starter motor
	• Starter motor rotates slowly with high load current	• Inspect drive yoke pull-down and point gap, check for worn end bushings, check ring gear clearance
	• Engine seized	• Repair engine
Starter motor drive will not engage (solenoid known to be good)	• Defective contact point assembly	• Repair or replace contact point assembly
	• Inadequate contact point assembly ground	• Repair connection at ground screw
	• Defective hold-in coil	• Replace field winding assembly
Starter motor drive will not disengage	• Starter motor loose on flywheel housing	• Tighten mounting bolts
	• Worn drive end busing	• Replace bushing
	• Damaged ring gear teeth	• Replace ring gear or driveplate
	• Drive yoke return spring broken or missing	• Replace spring
Starter motor drive disengages prematurely	• Weak drive assembly thrust spring	• Replace drive mechanism
	• Hold-in coil defective	• Replace field winding assembly
Low load current	• Worn brushes	• Replace brushes
	• Weak brush springs	• Replace springs

TCCS2C01

Troubleshooting Basic Charging System Problems

Problem	Cause	Solution
Noisy alternator	• Loose mountings • Loose drive pulley • Worn bearings • Brush noise • Internal circuits shorted (High pitched whine)	• Tighten mounting bolts • Tighten pulley • Replace alternator • Replace alternator • Replace alternator
Squeal when starting engine or accelerating	• Glazed or loose belt	• Replace or adjust belt
Indicator light remains on or ammeter indicates discharge (engine running)	• Broken belt • Broken or disconnected wires • Internal alternator problems • Defective voltage regulator	• Install belt • Repair or connect wiring • Replace alternator • Replace voltage regulator/alternator
Car light bulbs continually burn out—battery needs water continually	• Alternator/regulator overcharging	• Replace voltage regulator/alternator
Car lights flare on acceleration	• Battery low • Internal alternator/regulator problems	• Charge or replace battery • Replace alternator/regulator
Low voltage output (alternator light flickers continually or ammeter needle wanders)	• Loose or worn belt • Dirty or corroded connections • Internal alternator/regulator problems	• Replace or adjust belt • Clean or replace connections • Replace alternator/regulator

TCCS2C02

3

ENGINE AND ENGINE OVERHAUL

ENGINE MECHANICAL

VG30E ENGINE MECHANICAL SPECIFICATIONS

Description	English Specifications	Metric Specifications
General Information		
Displacement	180.62 cu in.	2,960 cu.cm
Bore and stroke	3.43 x 3.27 in.	87 x 83mm
Valve arrangement	Single Overhead Camshaft (OHC)	
Firing order	1-2-3-4-5-6	
Number of piston rings		
Compression	2	
Oil	1	
Number of main bearings	4	
Compression ratio	9.0 to 1	
Compression pressure		
Standard	173 psi/300 rpm	1,196 kPa/300 rpm
Minimum	128 psi/300 rpm	883 kPa/300 rpm
Differential limit between cylinders	14 psi/300 rpm	98 kPa/300 rpm
Inspection and Adjustment		
Cylinder Head		
Head surface distortion		
Standard	Less than 0.0012 in.	Less than 0.03mm
Limit	0.004 in.	0.1mm
Nominal cylinder head height	4.205-4.220 in.	106.8-107.2mm
Limit (total amount of cylinder head resurfacing plus cylinder block resurfacing)	0.008 in.	0.2mm
Valve		
Valve head diameter		
Intake	1.654-1.661 in.	42.0-42.2mm
Exhaust	1.378-1.386 in.	35.0-35.2mm
Valve length		
Intake	4.933-4.957 in.	125.3-125.9mm
Exhaust	4.890-4.913 in.	124.2-124.8mm
Valve stem diameter		
Intake	0.2742-0.2748 in.	6.965-6.980mm
Exhaust	0.3136-0.3138 in.	7.965-7.970mm
Valve seat angle (Intake & Exhaust)	45°15'-45°45'	
Valve margin		
Intake	0.0453-0.0571 in.	1.15-1.45mm
Exhaust	0.0531-0.0650 in.	1.35-1.65mm
Valve margin limit	More than 0.020 in.	More than 0.5mm
Valve stem end surface grinding limit	Less than 0.008 in.	Less than 0.2mm
Valve Spring		
Free height		
Outer	2.016 in.	51.2mm
Inner	1.736 in.	44.1mm
Pressure		
Outer	117.7 lbs. at 1.181 in.	523.7 N at 30.0mm
Inner	57.3 lbs. at 0.984 in.	255.0 N at 25.0mm
Out-of-square		
Outer	0.087 in.	2.2mm
Inner	0.075 in.	1.9mm

89613C01

VG30E ENGINE MECHANICAL SPECIFICATIONS

Description		English Specifications	Metric Specifications
Hydraulic Lash Adjuster			
Outer diameter		0.6278-0.6282 in.	15.947-15.957mm
Inner diameter		0.6299-0.6304 in.	16.000-16.013mm
Clearance between adjuster and guide		0.0017-0.0026 in.	0.043-0.066mm
Valve Guide			
Valve guide			
Outer diameter			
Intake	Standard	0.4340-0.4344 in.	11.023-11.034mm
	Service	0.4418-0.4423 in.	11.223-11.234mm
Exhaust	Standard	0.4733-0.4738 in.	12.023-12.034mm
	Service	0.4812-0.4817 in.	12.233-12.234mm
Valve guide			
Inner diameter (Finished size)			
Intake		0.2756-0.2763 in.	7.000-7.018mm
Exhaust		0.3150-0.3157 in.	8.000-8.018mm
Cylinder head valve guide hole diameter			
Intake	Standard	0.4321-0.4329 in.	10.975-10.996mm
	Service	0.4400-0.4408 in.	11.175-11.196mm
Exhaust	Standard	0.4321-0.4329 in.	11.975-11.996mm
	Service	0.4793-0.4802 in.	12.175-12.196mm
Interference fit of valve guide			
Intake		0.0011-0.0023 in.	0.027-0.059mm
Exhaust		0.0011-0.0023 in.	0.027-0.059mm
Stem-to-guide clearance			
Intake	Standard	0.0008-0.0021 in.	0.020-0.053mm
	Limit	0.0039 in.	0.10mm
Exhaust	Standard	0.0016-0.0029 in.	0.040-0.073mm
	Limit	0.0039 in.	0.10mm
Valve deflection limit		0.0079 in.	0.20mm
Valve Clearance Adjustment			
Valve clearance			
Intake		hydraulic	
Exhaust		hydraulic	
Valve Seat			
Cylinder head seat recess diameter			
Intake	Standard	n/a	n/a
	Service	1.7520-1.7526 in.	44.500-44.516mm
Exhaust	Standard	n/a	n/a
	Service	1.4764-1.4770 in.	37.500-37.516mm

89613C02

VG30E ENGINE MECHANICAL SPECIFICATIONS

Description		English Specifications	Metric Specifications
Cylinder Block			
Distortion			
Standard		Less than 0.0012 in.	Less than 0.03mm
Limit		0.004 in.	0.1mm
Cylinder bore			
Inner diameter			
Grade 1	Standard	3.4252-3.4256 in.	87.000-87.010mm
	Limit	0.008 in.	0.2mm
Grade 2	Standard	3.4256-3.4260 in.	87.010-87.020mm
	Limit	0.008 in.	0.2mm
Grade 3	Standard	3.4260-3.4264 in.	87.020-87.030mm
	Limit	0.008 in.	0.2mm
Out-of-round		Less than 0.0006 in.	Less than 0.015mm
Taper		Less than 0.0006 in.	Less than 0.015mm
Difference in inner diameter between cylinders			
Standard		Less than 0.0020 in.	Less than 0.05mm
Nominal cylinder bore height			
Standard		9.7224-9.7264 in.	100.00mm
Limit (total amount of cylinder head resur-facing plus cylinder block resurfacing)		0.008 in.	0.2mm
Camshaft and Camshaft Bearing			
Cam Height			
Intake		1.5566-1.5641 in.	39.537-39.727mm
Exhaust		1.5566-1.5641 in.	39.537-39.727mm
Wear limit of cam height		0.0059 in.	0.15mm
Camshaft journal-to-bearing clearance		0.0018-0.0035 in.	0.045-0.090mm
Inner diameter of camshaft bearing			
#1 journal		1.8898-1.8907 in.	48.000-48.025mm
#2 to #4 journal		1.8504-1.8514 in.	47.000-47.025mm
#5 journal		1.6732-1.6742 in.	42.500-42.525mm
Outer diameter of camshaft journal			
#1 journal		1.8866-1.8874 in.	47.920-47.940mm
#2 to #4 journal		1.8472-1.8480 in.	46.920-46.940mm
#5 journal		1.6701-1.6709 in.	42.420-42.440mm
Camshaft run-out (Total indicator reading)			
Standard		Less than 0.0016 in.	Less than 0.04mm
Limit		0.004 in.	0.1mm
Camshaft end-play		0.0012-0.0024 in.	0.03-0.06mm
Piston, Piston Ring and Piston Pin			
Piston			
Piston skirt diameter			
Standard	Grade No. 1	3.4238-3.4242 in.	86.965-86.975mm
	Grade No. 2	3.4242-3.4246 in.	86.975-86.985mm
	Grade No. 3	3.4246-3.4250 in.	86.985-86.995mm
Service (Oversize)			

89613C03

VG30E ENGINE MECHANICAL SPECIFICATIONS

Description	English Specifications	Metric Specifications
Bearing Clearance		
Main bearing clearance		
Standard	0.0011-0.0022 in.	0.028-0.055mm
Limit	0.0035 in.	0.90mm
Connecting rod bearing clearance		
Standard	0.0006-0.0021 in.	0.014-0.054mm
Limit	0.0035 in.	0.09mm
Miscellaneous Components		
Camshaft sprocket run-out (Total indicator reading)	Less than 0.004 in.	Less than 0.10mm
Flywheel run-out (Total indicator reading)	Less than 0.0059 in.	Less than 0.15mm
Drive plate run-out (Total indicator reading)	Less than 0.0059 in.	Less than 0.15mm

89613C05

VG30E ENGINE MECHANICAL SPECIFICATIONS

Description	English Specifications	Metric Specifications
Piston skirt diameter (cont.)		
0.0098 in./0.25mm	3.4337-3.4356 in.	87.215-87.265mm
0.0197 in./0.50mm	3.4435-3.4455 in.	87.465-87.515mm
Piston pin hole diameter	0.8255-0.8260 in.	20.969-20.981mm
Piston clearance to cylinder block	0.0006-0.0014 in.	0.015-0.035mm
Piston pin		
Piston pin outer diameter	0.8256-0.8261 in.	20.971-20.983mm
Interference fit of piston pin-to-piston	0-0.0002 in.	0-0.004mm
Piston pin-to-connecting rod bearing clearance	0.0002-0.0007 in.	0.005-0.017mm
Piston ring		
Side clearance		
Top		
Standard	0.0016-0.0029 in.	0.040-0.073mm
Limit	0.004 in.	0.1mm
2nd		
Standard	0.0012-0.0025 in.	0.030-0.063mm
Limit	0.004 in.	0.1mm
Oil (rail ring)	0.0006-0.0075 in.	0.015-0.19mm
Ring gap		
Top		
Standard	0.0083-0.0173 in.	0.21-0.44mm
Limit	0.039 in.	1.0mm
2nd		
Standard	0.0171-0.0173 in.	0.18-0.44mm
Limit	0.039 in.	1.0mm
Oil (rail ring)		
Standard	0.0079-0.0299 in.	0.20-0.76mm
Limit	0.039 in.	1.0mm
Connecting Rod		
Center distance (Standard)	6.067-6.071 in.	154.1-154.2mm
Bend per 3.94 in./100mm (Limit)	0.0039 in.	0.10mm
Torsion 3.94 in./100mm (Limit)	0.0039 in.	0.10mm
Piston pin bushing inner diameter (Installed)	0.8261-0.8265 in.	20.982-20.994mm
Side Clearance		
Standard	0.0079-0.0138 in.	0.20-0.35mm
Limit	0.0157 in.	0.40mm
Crankshaft		
Main journal diameter		
Grade No. 0	2.4790-2.4793 in.	62.967-62.975mm
Grade No. 1	2.4787-2.4790 in.	62.959-62.967mm
Grade No. 2	2.4784-2.4787 in.	62.951-62.959mm
Pin journal diameter	1.9667-1.9675 in.	49.955-49.974mm
Center distance	1.634 in.	41.5mm
Taper of journal and pin (Standard)	Less than 0.0002 in.	Less than 0.005mm
Out-of-round of journal and pin (Standard)	Less than 0.0002 in.	Less than 0.005mm
Run-out - Total indicator reading (Standard)	Less than 0.0039 in.	Less than 0.10mm
Free end-play		
Standard	0.0020-0.0067 in.	0.050-0.170mm
Limit	0.0118 in.	0.30mm

89613D04

VE30DE ENGINE MECHANICAL SPECIFICATIONS

Description	English Specifications	Metric Specifications
Valve Guide		
Valve guide		
Outer diameter		
Standard	0.3946-0.3950 in.	10.023-10.034mm
Service	0.4025-0.4029 in.	10.223-10.234mm
Valve guide		
Inner diameter (Finished size)	0.2362-0.2369 in.	6.000-6.018mm
Cylinder head valve guide hole diameter		
Standard	0.3927-0.3935 in.	9.975-9.996mm
Service	0.4006-0.4014 in.	10.175-10.196mm
Interference fit of valve guide	0.0011-0.0023 in.	0.027-0.059mm
Stem-to-guide clearance		
Intake		
Standard	0.0008-0.0017 in.	0.020-0.043mm
Limit	0.0031 in.	0.08mm
Exhaust		
Standard	0.0016-0.0025 in.	0.040-0.063mm
Limit	0.004 in.	0.10mm
Valve deflection limit	0.0079 in.	0.20mm
Valve guide projection (top)	0.535-0.543 in.	13.6-13.8mm
Valve Clearance Adjustment		
Valve clearance		
Intake	hydraulic	
Exhaust	hydraulic	
Valve Seat		
Cylinder head seat recess diameter		
Intake		
Standard	1.4173-1.4179 in.	36.000-36.016mm
Service	1.4370-1.4376 in.	36.500-36.516mm
Exhaust		
Standard	1.2402-1.2408 in.	31.500-31.516mm
Service	1.2598-1.2605 in.	32.000-32.016mm
Valve seat interference fit		
Intake	0.0032-0.0044 in.	0.081-0.113mm
Exhaust	0.0025-0.0038 in.	0.064-0.096mm
Valve seat outer diameter		
Intake		
Standard	1.4211-1.4218 in.	36.097-36.113mm
Service	1.4408-1.4415 in.	36.597-36.613mm
Exhaust		
Standard	1.2433-1.2439 in.	31.580-31.596mm
Service	1.2630-1.2636 in.	32.080-32.096mm
Depth		
Intake and exhaust	0.232-0.240 in.	5.9-6.1mm
Height		
Intake and Exhaust	0.232-0.236 in.	5.9-6.0mm

89613C07

VE30DE ENGINE MECHANICAL SPECIFICATIONS

Description	English Specifications	Metric Specifications
Valve Guide		
Valve guide		
Outer diameter		
Standard	0.3946-0.3950 in.	10.023-10.034mm
Service	0.4025-0.4029 in.	10.223-10.234mm
Valve guide		
Inner diameter (Finished size)	0.2362-0.2369 in.	6.000-6.018mm
Cylinder head valve guide hole diameter		
Standard	0.3927-0.3935 in.	9.975-9.996mm
Service	0.4006-0.4014 in.	10.175-10.196mm
Interference fit of valve guide	0.0011-0.0023 in.	0.027-0.059mm
Stem-to-guide clearance		
Intake		
Standard	0.0008-0.0017 in.	0.020-0.043mm
Limit	0.0031 in.	0.08mm
Exhaust		
Standard	0.0016-0.0025 in.	0.040-0.063mm
Limit	0.004 in.	0.10mm
Valve deflection limit	0.0079 in.	0.20mm
Valve guide projection (top)	0.535-0.543 in.	13.6-13.8mm
Valve Clearance Adjustment		
Valve clearance		
Intake	hydraulic	
Exhaust	hydraulic	
Valve Seat		
Cylinder head seat recess diameter		
Intake		
Standard	1.4173-1.4179 in.	36.000-36.016mm
Service	1.4370-1.4376 in.	36.500-36.516mm
Exhaust		
Standard	1.2402-1.2408 in.	31.500-31.516mm
Service	1.2598-1.2605 in.	32.000-32.016mm
Valve seat interference fit		
Intake	0.0032-0.0044 in.	0.081-0.113mm
Exhaust	0.0025-0.0038 in.	0.064-0.096mm
Valve seat outer diameter		
Intake		
Standard	1.4211-1.4218 in.	36.097-36.113mm
Service	1.4408-1.4415 in.	36.597-36.613mm
Exhaust		
Standard	1.2433-1.2439 in.	31.580-31.596mm
Service	1.2630-1.2636 in.	32.080-32.096mm
Depth		
Intake and exhaust	0.232-0.240 in.	5.9-6.1mm
Height		
Intake and Exhaust	0.232-0.236 in.	5.9-6.0mm

89613C06

VE30DE ENGINE MECHANICAL SPECIFICATIONS

Description					English Specifications	Metric Specifications
Cylinder Block						
Distortion						
	Standard				Less than 0.0012 in.	Less than 0.03mm
	Limit				0.0039 in.	0.1mm
Cylinder bore						
	Inner diameter					
		Grade 1				
			Standard		3.4252-3.4256 in.	87.000-87.010mm
			Limit		0.0079 in.	0.2mm
		Grade 2				
			Standard		3.4256-3.4260 in.	87.010-87.020mm
			Limit		0.0079 in.	0.2mm
		Grade 3				
			Standard		3.4260-3.4264 in.	87.020-87.030mm
			Limit		0.0079 in.	0.2mm
	Out-of-round				Less than 0.0006 in.	Less than 0.015mm
	Taper				Less than 0.0004 in.	Less than 0.010mm
Difference in inner diameter between cylinders					Less than 0.0020 in.	Less than 0.05mm
Nominal cylinder bore height					9.7224-9.7264 in.	100.00mm
Limit (total amount of cylinder head resurfacing plus cylinder block resurfacing)					0.008 in.	0.2mm
Camshaft and Camshaft Bearings						
Cam Height						
	Intake				1.4834-1.4909 in.	37.678-37.868mm
	Exhaust				1.4834-1.4909 in.	37.678-37.868mm
Wear limit of cam height					0.0020 in.	0.05mm
Camshaft journal-to-bearing clearance						
	Standard				0.0018-0.0034 in.	0.045-0.086mm
	Limit				0.0059 in.	0.15mm
Inner diameter of camshaft bearing					1.0236-1.0244 in.	26.000-26.021mm
Outer diameter of camshaft journal					1.0211-1.0218 in.	25.935-25.955mm
Camshaft run-out (Total indicator reading)						
	Standard				Less than 0.0008 in.	Less than 0.02mm
	Limit				0.0020 in.	0.15mm
Camshaft end-play						
	Standard				0.0028-0.0058 in.	0.070-0.148mm
	Limit				0.0079 in.	0.20mm
Camshaft sprocket runout					Less than 0.0059 in.	Less than 0.15mm
Piston, Piston Ring and Piston Pin						
Piston						
	Piston skirt diameter					
		Standard				
			Grade No. 1		3.4242-3.4246 in.	86.975-86.985mm
			Grade No. 2		3.4246-3.4250 in.	86.985-86.995mm
			Grade No. 3		3.4250-3.4254 in.	86.995-87.005mm
		Service (Oversize)				
			0.0098 in./0.25mm		3.4340-3.4360 in.	87.225-87.275mm
			0.0197 in./0.50mm		3.4439-3.4459 in.	87.475-87.525mm
Piston pin hole diameter					0.8656-0.8661 in.	21.987-21.999mm
Piston clearance to cylinder block					0.0006-0.0014 in.	0.015-0.035mm

89613C08

VE30DE ENGINE MECHANICAL SPECIFICATIONS

Description			English Specifications	Metric Specifications
Piston pin				
Piston pin outer diameter			0.8657-0.8662 in.	21.989-22.001mm
Interference fit of piston pin-to-piston			0-0.0002 in.	0-0.004mm
Piston pin-to-connecting rod bearing clearance			0.0002-0.0007 in.	0.005-0.017mm
Piston ring				
Side clearance				
	Top			
		Standard	0.0016-0.0031 in.	0.040-0.080mm
		Limit	0.004 in.	0.1mm
	2nd			
		Standard	0.0012-0.0025 in.	0.030-0.063mm
		Limit	0.004 in.	0.1mm
Ring gap				
	Top			
		Standard	0.0083-0.0157 in.	0.21-0.40mm
		Limit	0.039 in.	1.0mm
	2nd			
		Standard	0.0197-0.0272 in.	0.50-0.69mm
		Limit	0.039 in.	1.0mm
	Oil (rail ring)			
		Standard	0.0079-0.0272 in.	0.20-0.69mm
		Limit	0.039 in.	1.0mm
Connecting Rod				
Center distance (Standard)			6.067-6.071 in.	154.1-154.2mm
Bend per 3.94 in./100mm (Limit)			0.0059 in.	0.15mm
Torsion 3.94 in./100mm (Limit)			0.0118 in.	0.30mm
Piston pin bushing inner diameter (Installed)			0.8661-0.8666 in.	22.000-22.012mm
Connecting rod big end inner diameter			2.0866-2.0871 in.	53.000-53.013mm
Side Clearance				
	Standard		0.0079-0.0138 in.	0.20-0.35mm
	Limit		0.0157 in.	0.40mm
Crankshaft				
Main journal diameter				
	Grade No. 0		2.4790-2.4793 in.	62.967-62.975mm
	Grade No. 1		2.4787-2.4790 in.	62.959-62.967mm
	Grade No. 2		2.4784-2.4787 in.	62.951-62.959mm
Pin journal diameter			1.9667-1.9675 in.	49.955-49.974mm
Center distance			1.634 in.	41.5mm
Taper of journal and pin (Standard)			Less than 0.0002 in.	Less than 0.005mm
Out-of-round of journal and pin (Standard)			Less than 0.0002 in.	Less than 0.005mm
Run-out - Total indicator reading (Standard)			Less than 0.0039 in.	Less than 0.10mm
Free end-play				
	Standard		0.0020-0.0067 in.	0.050-0.170mm
	Limit		0.0118 in.	0.30mm

89613C09

VE30DE ENGINE MECHANICAL SPECIFICATIONS

Description	English Specifications	Metric Specifications
Bearing Clearance		
Main bearing clearance		
Standard	0.0011-0.0022 in.	0.028-0.055mm
Limit	0.0035 in.	0.90mm
Connecting rod bearing clearance		
Standard	0.0011-0.0019 in.	0.028-0.048mm
Limit	0.0035 in.	0.08mm
Miscellaneous Components		
Flywheel run-out (Total indicator reading)	Less than 0.0059 in.	Less than 0.15mm
Drive plate run-out (Total indicator reading)	Less than 0.0059 in.	Less than 0.15mm

89613C10

VQ30DE ENGINE MECHANICAL SPECIFICATIONS

Description	English Specifications	Metric Specifications
General Information		
Displacement	182.33 cu. in.	2,988 cu.cm
Bore and stroke	3.66 x 2.886 in.	93 x 73.3mm
Valve arrangement	Dual Overhead Camshaft (DOHC)	
Firing order	1-2-3-4-5-6	
Number of piston rings		
Compression	2	
Oil	1	
Number of main bearings	4	
Compression ratio	10.0 to 1	
Compression pressure		
Standard	185 psi/300 rpm	1,275 kPa/300 rpm
Minimum	142 psi/300 rpm	981 kPa/300 rpm
Differential limit between cylinders	14 psi/300 rpm	98 kPa/300 rpm
Inspection and Adjustment		
Cylinder Head		
Head surface distortion		
Standard	Less than 0.0012 in.	Less than 0.03mm
Limit	0.004 in.	0.1mm
Nominal cylinder head height	4.972-4.980 in.	126.3-126.5mm
Limit (total amount of cylinder head resurfacing plus cylinder block resurfacing)	0.008 in.	0.2mm
Valve		
Valve head diameter		
Intake	1.417-1.429 in.	36.0-36.3mm
Exhaust	1.228-1.240 in.	31.2-31.5mm
Valve length		
Intake	3.8315-3.8512 in.	97.32-97.82mm
Exhaust	3.7342-3.7539 in.	94.85-95.35mm
Valve stem diameter		
Intake	0.2348-0.2354 in.	5.965-5.980mm
Exhaust	0.2341-0.2346 in.	5.945-5.960mm
Valve seat angle (Intake & Exhaust)	45°15'-45°45'	
Valve margin		
Intake	0.0374-0.0492 in.	0.95-1.25mm
Exhaust	0.0453-0.0571 in.	1.15-1.45mm
Valve margin limit	More than 0.020 in.	More than 0.5mm
Valve stem end surface grinding limit	Less than 0.008 in.	Less than 0.2mm
Valve Spring		
Free height	1.8476 in.	46.93mm
Pressure	102.1 lbs. at 1.0846 in.	454.0 N at 27.55mm
Out-of-square	Less than 0.079 in.	Less than 2.0mm
Cam follower		
Outer diameter	1.3764-1.3770 in.	34.960-34.975mm
Guide diameter	1.3780-1.3788 in.	35.000-35.021mm
Clearance	0.0010-0.0024 in.	0.025-0.061mm

89613C11

VQ30DE ENGINE MECHANICAL SPECIFICATIONS

Description					English Specifications	Metric Specifications
Valve Guide						
Valve guide						
	Outer diameter					
		Standard			0.3946-0.3950 in.	10.023-10.034mm
		Service			0.4025-0.4029 in.	10.223-10.234mm
Valve guide						
	Inner diameter (Finished size)				0.2362-0.2369 in.	6.000-6.018mm
Cylinder head valve guide hole diameter						
		Standard			0.3927-0.3935 in.	9.975-9.996mm
		Service			0.4006-0.4014 in.	10.175-10.196mm
Interference fit of valve guide					0.0011-0.0023 in.	0.027-0.059mm
Stem-to-guide clearance						
	Intake					
		Standard			0.0008-0.0021 in.	0.020-0.053mm
		Limit			0.0031 in.	0.08mm
	Exhaust					
		Standard			0.0016-0.0029 in.	0.040-0.073mm
		Limit			0.004 in.	0.10mm
Valve deflection limit						
	Intake				0.0094 in.	0.24mm
	Exhaust				0.0110 in.	0.28mm
Valve guide projection (top)					0.496-0.504 in.	12.6-12.8mm
Valve Clearance Adjustment						
Valve clearance (cold)						
	Intake				0.010-0.013 in.	0.26-0.34mm
	Exhaust				0.011-0.015 in.	0.29-0.37mm
Valve Seat						
Cylinder head seat recess diameter						
	Intake					
		Standard			1.4567-1.4573 in.	37.000-37.016mm
		Service			1.4764-1.4770 in.	37.500-36.516mm
	Exhaust					
		Standard			1.2677-1.2683 in.	32.200-32.216mm
		Service			1.2874-1.2880 in.	32.700-32.716mm
Valve seat interference fit						
	Intake				0.0032-0.0044 in.	0.061-0.113mm
	Exhaust				0.0025-0.0038 in.	0.064-0.096mm
Valve seat outer diameter						
	Intake					
		Standard			1.4605-1.4611 in.	37.097-37.113mm
		Service			1.4802-1.4808 in.	37.597-37.613mm
	Exhaust					
		Standard			1.2709-1.2715 in.	32.280-32.296mm
		Service			1.2905-1.2912 in.	32.780-32.796mm

89613C12

VQ30DE ENGINE MECHANICAL SPECIFICATIONS

Description					English Specifications	Metric Specifications
Valve seat height						
	Intake					
		Standard			0.232-0.236 in.	5.9-6.0mm
		Service			0.1988-0.2028 in.	5.05-5.15mm
	Exhaust					
		Standard			0.232-0.236 in.	5.9-6.0mm
		Service			0.1949-0.1988 in.	4.95-5.05mm
Valve seat recess depth						
	Intake and Exhaust				0.232-0.240 in.	5.9-6.1mm
Cylinder Block						
Distortion						
		Standard			Less than 0.0012 in.	Less than 0.03mm
		Limit			0.0039 in.	0.1mm
Cylinder bore						
	Inner diameter					
		Grade 1				
			Standard		3.6614-3.6618 in.	93.000-93.010mm
			Limit		0.0079 in.	0.2mm
		Grade 2				
			Standard		3.6618-3.6622 in.	93.010-93.020mm
			Limit		0.0079 in.	0.2mm
		Grade 3				
			Standard		3.6622-3.6626 in.	93.020-93.030mm
			Limit		0.0079 in.	0.2mm
	Out-of-round				Less than 0.0006 in.	Less than 0.015mm
	Taper				Less than 0.0004 in.	Less than 0.010mm
Difference in inner diameter between cylinders					Less than 0.0012 in.	Less than 0.03mm
Nominal cylinder bore height						
	Standard				3.94 in.	100.00mm
	Limit (total amount of cylinder head resurfacing plus cylinder block resurfacing)				0.008 in.	0.2mm
Camshaft and Camshaft Bearings						
Cam Height-1995 engines only						
	Intake				1.7305-1.7380 in.	43.955-44.145mm
	Exhaust				1.7305-1.7380 in.	43.955-44.145mm
Cam Height-1996 through 1998 engines						
	Intake				1.7299-1.7374 in.	43.940-44.130mm
	Exhaust				1.7299-1.7374 in.	43.940-44.130mm
Wear limit of cam height					0.008 in.	0.2mm
Camshaft journal-to-bearing clearance						
		Standard			0.0018-0.0034 in.	0.045-0.086mm
		Limit			0.0069 in.	0.15mm
Inner diameter of camshaft bearing						
	#1 journal				1.0236-1.0244 in.	26.000-26.021mm
	#2,3,4 journal				0.9252-0.9260 in.	23.500-23.521mm
Outer diameter of camshaft journal						
	#1 journal				1.0211-1.0218 in.	25.935-25.955mm
	#2,3,4 journal				0.9226-0.9234 in.	23.435-23.455mm

89613C13

VQ30DE ENGINE MECHANICAL SPECIFICATIONS

Description	English Specifications	Metric Specifications
Camshaft run-out (Total indicator reading)		
Standard	Less than 0.0008 in.	Less than 0.02mm
Limit	0.0020 in.	0.05mm
Camshaft end-play		
Standard	0.0045-0.0074 in.	0.115-0.188mm
Limit	0.0094 in.	0.24mm
Camshaft sprocket runout	Less than 0.0059 in.	Less than 0.15mm
Piston, Piston Ring and Piston Pin		
Piston		
Piston skirt diameter		
Standard		
Grade No. 1	3.6606-3.6610 in.	92.979-92.990mm
Grade No. 2	3.6610-3.6614 in.	92.990-93.000mm
Grade No. 3	3.6614-3.6618 in.	93.000-93.009mm
Service (Oversize)	0.0079 in./0.20mm	
Piston pin hole diameter	3.6685-3.6697 in.	93.180-93.210mm
Piston pin outer diameter	0.8656-0.8661 in.	21.987-21.999mm
Piston clearance to cylinder block	0.0004-0.0012 in.	0.010-0.030mm
Piston pin		
Piston pin outer diameter	0.8657-0.8662 in.	21.989-22.001mm
Interference fit of piston-to-piston	0.0002-0.0006 in.	0.001-0.002mm
Piston pin-to-connecting rod bearing clearance	0.0002-0.0007 in.	0.005-0.017mm
Piston ring		
Side clearance		
Top Standard	0.0016-0.0031 in.	0.040-0.060mm
Limit	0.0043 in.	0.11mm
2nd Standard	0.0012-0.0028 in.	0.030-0.070mm
Limit	0.004 in.	0.1mm
Ring gap		
Top Standard	0.0087-0.0126 in.	0.22-0.32mm
Limit	0.0217 in.	0.055mm
2nd Standard	0.0126-0.0185 in.	0.32-0.47mm
Limit	0.0335 in.	0.85mm
Oil (rail ring) Standard	0.0079-0.0236 in.	0.20-0.60mm
Limit	0.0374 in.	0.95mm
Connecting Rod		
Center distance (Standard)	5.8110-5.8149 in.	147.60-147.70mm
Bend per 3.94 in./100mm (Limit)	0.0059 in.	0.15mm
Torsion 3.94 in./100mm (Limit)	0.0118 in.	0.30mm
Piston pin bushing inner diameter (Installed)	0.8661-0.8666 in.	22.000-22.012mm
Connecting rod small end inner diameter	0.9441-0.9449 in.	23.980-24.000mm
Connecting rod big end inner diameter	1.8898-1.8903 in.	48.000-48.013mm
Side Clearance		

89613C14

VQ30DE ENGINE MECHANICAL SPECIFICATIONS

Description	English Specifications	Metric Specifications
Side clearance (cont.)		
Standard	0.0079-0.0138 in.	0.20-0.35mm
Limit	0.0157 in.	0.40mm
Crankshaft		
Main journal diameter		
Grade No. 0	2.3610-2.3612 in.	59.969-59.975mm
Grade No. 1	2.3607-2.3610 in.	59.963-59.969mm
Grade No. 2	2.3605-2.3607 in.	59.957-59.963mm
Grade No. 3	2.3603-2.3605 in.	59.951-59.957mm
Pin journal diameter		
Grade No. 0	1.7704-1.7706 in.	44.968-44.974mm
Grade No. 1	1.7702-2.7704 in.	44.962-44.968mm
Grade No. 2	1.7699-1.7702 in.	44.956-44.962mm
Center distance	1.4413-1.4445 in.	36.61-36.69mm
Taper of journal and pin (Standard)	Less than 0.0001 in.	Less than 0.002mm
Out-of-round of journal and pin (Standard)	Less than 0.0001 in.	Less than 0.002mm
Run-out - Total indicator reading (Standard)	Less than 0.0039 in.	Less than 0.10mm
Free end-play		
Standard	0.0020-0.0067 in.	0.050-0.170mm
Limit	0.0118 in.	0.30mm
Bearing Clearance		
Main bearing clearance-1995 and 1996 engines		
Standard	0.0014-0.0021 in.	0.035-0.053mm
Limit	0.0026 in.	0.065mm
Main bearing clearance-1997 and 1998 engines		
Standard	0.0005-0.0012 in.	0.012-0.030mm
Limit	0.0026 in.	0.065mm
Connecting rod bearing clearance-1995 and 1996 engines		
Standard	0.0013-0.0023 in.	0.034-0.059mm
Limit	0.0028 in.	0.070mm
Connecting rod bearing clearance-1997 and 1998 engines		
Standard	0.0008-0.0018 in.	0.020-0.045mm
Limit	0.0028 in.	0.070mm
Miscellaneous Components		
Flywheel run-out (Total indicator reading)	Less than 0.0059 in.	Less than 0.15mm
Drive plate run-out (Total indicator reading)	Less than 0.0059 in.	Less than 0.15mm

89613C15

Engine

In the process of removing the engine, you will come across a number of steps which call for the removal of a separate component or system, such as "disconnect the exhaust system" or "remove the radiator." In most instances, a detailed removal procedure can be found elsewhere in this manual.

It is virtually impossible to list each individual wire and hose which must be disconnected, simply because so many different model and engine combinations have been manufactured. Careful observation and common sense are the best possible approaches to any repair procedure.

Removal and installation of the engine can be made easier if you follow these basic points:

• If you have to drain any of the fluids, use a suitable container.

• Always tag any wires or hoses and, if possible, the components they came from before disconnecting them.

• Because there are so many bolts and fasteners involved, store and label the retainers from components separately in muffin pans, jars or coffee cans. This will prevent confusion during installation.

• If it is necessary to disconnect the air conditioning system, have this service performed by a qualified technician using a recovery/recycling station. If the system does not have to be disconnected, unbolt the compressor and set it aside.

• When unbolting the engine mounts, always make sure the engine is properly supported. When removing the engine, make sure that any lifting devices are properly attached to the engine. If your engine does not have lifting hooks, your local Nissan dealer can order them for you. DO NOT attempt to remove the engine/transaxle assembly without the proper lifting hooks; you could damage the cylinder heads. Use extreme caution when removing and installing the engine/transaxle assembly.

• compartment slowly, checking that no hoses, wires or other components are still connected.

• After the engine is clear of the compartment, place it on an engine stand or workbench.

• After the engine has been removed, you can perform a partial or full teardown of the engine using the procedures outlined in this manual.

REMOVAL & INSTALLATION

▶ **See Figures 1, 2, 3 and 4**

It is recommended the engine and transaxle be removed as a single unit. The engine and transaxle can be separated after removal.

➡**On vehicles with air conditioning, it is vital to refer to Section 1 prior to performing this procedure.**

1. Matchmark the hood hinge relationship and remove the hood.
2. Release the fuel system pressure.
3. Disconnect the negative battery cable.
4. Raise and safely support the vehicle.

➡**The vehicle will have to be raised high enough to remove the engine/transaxle assembly from underneath the vehicle. Make certain the vehicle will not slip off the jackstands. Keep in mind the center of gravity will change drastically when the engine/transaxle assembly is removed; use extreme caution.**

5. Tag and detach all engine harness connectors.
6. Drain the coolant from the cylinder block and the radiator.
7. Drain the crankcase and the transaxle.

✳✳ CAUTION

The EPA warns that prolonged contact with used engine oil may cause a number of skin disorders, including cancer! You should make every effort to minimize your exposure to used engine oil. Protective gloves should be worn when changing the oil. Wash your hands and any other exposed skin areas as soon as possible after exposure to used engine oil. Soap and water, or waterless hand cleaner should be used.

8. Remove the radiator and fan assembly.
9. Tag and disconnect all vacuum hoses, wires, and harness connectors attached to the engine /transaxle assembly.

✳✳ CAUTION

Observe all applicable safety precautions when working around fuel. Whenever servicing the fuel system, always work in a well ventilated area. Do not allow fuel spray or vapors to come in contact with a spark or open flame. Keep a dry chemical fire extinguisher near the work area. Always keep fuel in a container specifically designed for fuel storage; also, always properly seal fuel containers to avoid the possibility of fire or explosion.

10. Disconnect the exhaust system from the engine.
11. Remove the driveshafts.
12. Remove the alternator, power steering pump and air conditioning compressor from the engine.

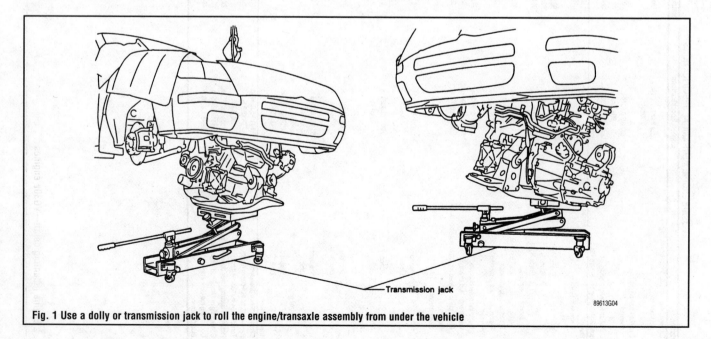

Transmission jack

89613G04

Fig. 1 Use a dolly or transmission jack to roll the engine/transaxle assembly from under the vehicle

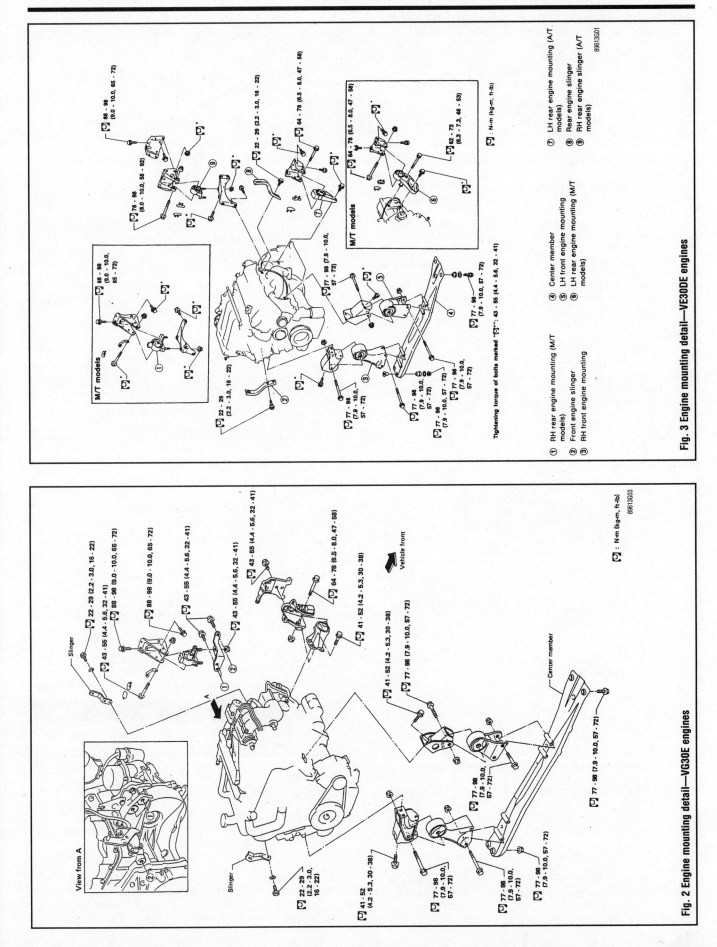

Fig. 3 Engine mounting detail—VE30DE engines

Fig. 2 Engine mounting detail—VG30E engines

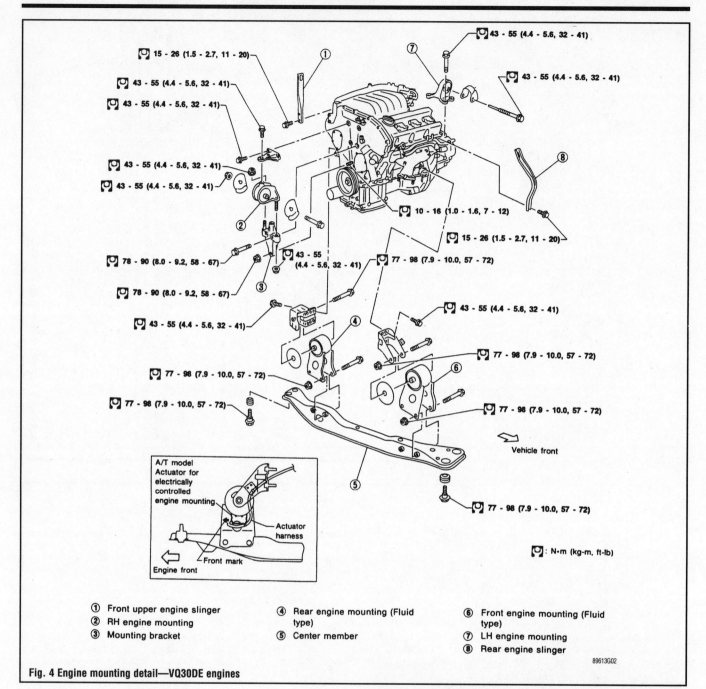

① Front upper engine slinger
② RH engine mounting
③ Mounting bracket
④ Rear engine mounting (Fluid type)
⑤ Center member
⑥ Front engine mounting (Fluid type)
⑦ LH engine mounting
⑧ Rear engine slinger

A/T model
Actuator for electrically controlled engine mounting.
Actuator harness
Front mark
Engine front

Vehicle front

⚙ : N•m (kg-m, ft-lb)

89613G02

Fig. 4 Engine mounting detail—VQ30DE engines

13. Disconnect the shift linkage (or control cable—automatic models) from the transaxle.

14. Attach a hoist to the engine.

15. Remove the bolts from the motor mount brackets, and lower the engine/transaxle assembly onto a dolly.

16. Roll the engine/transaxle assembly from underneath the vehicle.

To install:

17. Installation is the reverse of the removal procedure; but note the following steps:

• Do NOT start the engine without filling it with the proper type of and amount of new engine oil, and a new oil filter. Otherwise, severe engine damage will result.

• Be sure to have the battery fully charged. The engine will have to be cranked for longer then usual to achieve oil pressure before starting the engine.

• Crank the engine with the fuel pump fuse removed to achieve oil pressure before the engine is started. Do not crank the starter for more than 15 seconds at a time; wait at least 10 seconds between each use. After the oil pressure light goes out, install the fuel pump fuse and start the engine.

Rocker Arm (Valve) Cover

REMOVAL & INSTALLATION

VG30E Engine

FRONT BANK

1. Disconnect the air intake duct from the dual duct housing.

2. Disconnect the electrical connectors from the throttle body, the step motor AAC valve and the exhaust gas temperature sensor.

3. Disconnect and label the hoses from the valve cover, the throttle body, the step motor AAC valve, the EGR control valve and the air cut valve.

4. If the spark plug wires are in the way, disconnect them and move them aside. Disconnect the accelerator cable from the throttle body.

5. Remove the upper intake manifold collector-to-intake manifold bolts, in sequence, and lift the assembly from the intake manifold. Discard the gasket.

6. Remove the valve cover-to-cylinder head bolts and the valve cover; discard the gasket.

To install:

7. Clean the gasket mounting surfaces.

8. Install a new valve cover gasket. Install the valve cover and torque the bolts to 0.7–2.2 ft. lbs. (1–3 Nm).

9. Use a new gasket and install the upper intake manifold collector-to-intake manifold; torque the bolts, in sequence, to 5.1–5.8 ft. lbs. (7–8 Nm).

10. Connect the spark plug wires, if disconnected. Connect the accelerator cable to the throttle body.

11. Connect the hoses to the valve cover, the throttle body, the step motor AAC valve, the EGR control valve and the air cut valve.

12. Connect the electrical connectors to the throttle body, the step motor AAC valve and the exhaust gas temperature sensor.

13. Connect the negative battery cable.

14. Start the engine and check for oil leaks.

REAR BANK

1. Remove the breather hose from the valve cover.

2. If the spark plug wires are in the way, disconnect them and move them aside.

3. Tag and disconnect any hoses or lines in the way of removing the valve cover.

4. Remove the valve cover-to-cylinder head bolts and the valve cover; discard the gasket(s).

To install:

5. Clean the gasket mounting surfaces.

6. Install a new valve cover gasket. Install the valve cover and torque the bolts to 0.7–2.2 ft. lbs. (1–3 Nm).

7. Install the spark plug wires, if disconnected.

8. Install the breather hose to the valve cover.

9. Connect any hoses or lines that were removed.

10. Connect the negative battery cable.

11. Start the engine and check for oil leaks.

VE30DE Engine

FRONT BANK

▶ See Figures 5, 6, 7 and 8

1. Disconnect the negative battery cable.

2. Disconnect the electrical connectors from the ignition coils.

3. Remove the ignition coil-to-valve cover bolts and the ignition coils.

4. If necessary, disconnect the electrical connectors from the camshaft sensor and the power transistor.

5. Remove the valve cover-to-cylinder head nuts and the valve cover. Discard the gasket.

To install:

6. Clean the gasket mounting surfaces.

7. Using liquid gasket sealant, apply a continuous bead to the cylinder head and the valve cover.

8. Using a new gasket, install it onto the cylinder head. Install the valve cover and torque the nuts in the following order:

a. Torque the nuts, in the following sequence: 1, 2, 12, 11, 9 and 14 to 2.9 ft. lbs. (4 Nm).

b. Torque the nuts, in the sequence of 1 through 14 to 5.8–7.2 ft. lbs. (8–10 Nm).

9. Connect the electrical connectors to the camshaft position sensor and the power transistor, if disconnected.

10. Install the ignition coils and torque the ignition coil-to-valve cover bolts to 2.7–3.7 ft. lbs. (3.7–5.0 Nm).

11. Connect the electrical connectors to the ignition coils.

12. Connect the negative battery cable.

13. Start the engine and check for oil leaks.

REAR BANK

▶ See Figure 9

1. Disconnect the negative battery cable.

2. Label and disconnect the hoses from the throttle body, the EGR valve, the EGR control solenoid valve, the intake manifold collector, the power valve control solenoid valve (if equipped with a manual transaxle) and the power valve actuator (if equipped with a manual transaxle).

3. Label and disconnect the electrical connectors from the throttle position sensor, the exhaust gas temperature sensor, power valve actuator, etc.

4. Disconnect the accelerator cable from the throttle body.

5. Remove the intake manifold collector support-to-intake manifold collector and the intake manifold collector support-to-cylinder head bolts and the supports.

6. Remove the intake manifold collector-to-intake manifold bolts and the intake manifold collector.

7. Disconnect the electrical connectors from the ignition coils.

8. Remove the ignition coil-to-valve cover bolts and the ignition coils.

9. Remove the valve cover-to-cylinder head nuts and the valve cover. Discard the gasket.

To install:

10. Thoroughly clean the gasket mounting surfaces.

11. Using liquid gasket sealant, apply a continuous bead to the cylinder head and the valve cover.

12. Using a new valve cover gasket, install it onto the cylinder head. Install the valve cover and torque the nuts in the following order:

a. Torque the nuts, in the following sequence: 1, 2, 12, 11, 9 and 14 to 2.9 ft. lbs. (4 Nm).

b. Torque the nuts, in the sequence of 1 through 14 to 5.8–7.2 ft. lbs. (8–10 Nm).

13. Install the ignition coils and torque the ignition coil-to-valve cover bolts to 2.7–3.7 ft. lbs. (3.7–5.0 Nm).

14. Using a new gasket, install the intake manifold collector and torque the intake manifold collector-to-intake manifold bolts, in sequence, to 13–16 ft. lbs. (18–22 Nm).

15. Install the intake manifold collector support and torque the bolts to 12–15 ft. lbs. (16–21 Nm).

16. Connect the accelerator cable to the throttle body.

17. Connect the hoses to the throttle body, the EGR valve, the EGR control solenoid valve, the intake manifold collector, the power valve control solenoid valve (if equipped with a manual transaxle) and the power valve actuator (if equipped with a manual transaxle).

Fig. 5 Remove the nuts and the special washers, and lift the valve cover from the cylinder head

Fig. 6 The valve cover gasket lifts out of the recessed perimeter of the valve cover

Fig. 7 Use a small amount of RTV type sealant in the corners of the camshaft bearing caps to prevent leaks

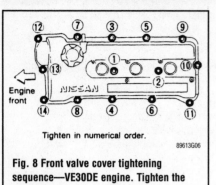

Tighten in numerical order.

89613G06

Fig. 8 Front valve cover tightening sequence—VE30DE engine. Tighten the valve cover in the proper sequence to prevent leaks

Tighten in numerical order.

89613G05

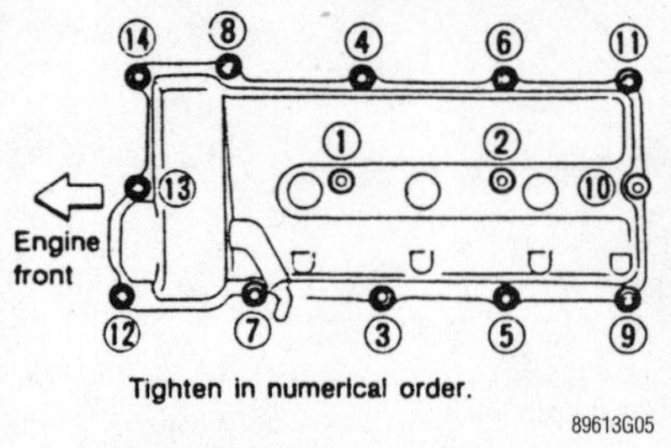

Fig. 9 Rear valve cover tightening sequence—VE30DE Engine. Tighten the valve cover in the proper sequence to prevent leaks

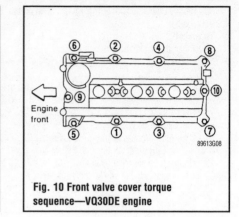

89613G08

Fig. 10 Front valve cover torque sequence—VQ30DE engine

18. Connect the electrical connectors from the throttle position sensor, the exhaust gas temperature sensor, etc.
19. Connect the negative battery cable.
20. Start the engine and check for leaks.

VQ30DE Engine

FRONT BANK

▶ **See Figure 10**

1. Disconnect the negative battery cable.
2. Remove the decorative facia on the valve cover.
3. Disconnect the electrical connectors from the ignition coils.
4. Remove the ignition coil-to-valve cover bolts and the ignition coils.
5. If necessary, disconnect the electrical connectors from the camshaft sensor and the power transistor.
6. Remove the valve cover-to-cylinder head nuts and the valve cover. Discard the gasket.
   To install:
7. Clean the gasket mounting surfaces.
8. Using liquid gasket sealant, apply a continuous bead to the cylinder head and the valve cover.
9. Using a new gasket, install it onto the cylinder head. Install the valve cover and torque the nuts in the following order:
   a. Torque the nuts, 1 through 10, in sequence, to 9–36 in.lbs. (1–3 Nm.).
   b. Torque the nuts, 1 through 10, in sequence, to 47.7–65.1 in.lbs. (5.4–7.4 Nm.).
10. Connect the electrical connectors to the camshaft sensor and the power transistor, if disconnected.
11. Install the ignition coils and tighten the ignition coil-to-valve cover bolts.
12. Connect the electrical connectors to the ignition coils.
13. Install the decorative facia cover.
14. Connect the negative battery cable.
15. Start the engine and check for oil leaks.

REAR BANK

▶ **See Figure 11**

1. Disconnect the negative battery cable.
2. Label and disconnect the hoses from the throttle body, the EGR valve, the EGR control solenoid valve, the intake manifold collector, the power valve control solenoid valve (if equipped with a manual transaxle) and the power valve actuator (if equipped with a manual transaxle).
3. Label and disconnect the electrical connectors from the throttle position sensor, the exhaust gas temperature sensor, power valve actuator, etc.
4. Disconnect the accelerator cable from the throttle body.
5. Remove the intake manifold collector support-to-intake manifold collector and the intake manifold collector support-to-cylinder head bolts and the supports.
6. Remove the intake manifold collector-to-intake manifold bolts and the intake manifold collector.
7. Disconnect the electrical connectors from the ignition coils.
8. Remove the ignition coil-to-valve cover bolts and the ignition coils.
9. Remove the valve cover-to-cylinder head nuts and the valve cover. Discard the gasket.

To install:
10. Thoroughly clean the gasket mounting surfaces.
11. Using liquid gasket sealant, apply a continuous bead to the cylinder head and the valve cover.
12. Using a new valve cover gasket, install the valve cover onto the cylinder head. Torque the nuts in the following order:
   a. Torque the nuts, 1 through 10, in sequence, to 9–36 in.lbs. (1–3 Nm.).
   b. Torque the nuts, 1 through 10, in sequence, to 47.7–65.1 in.lbs. (5.4–7.4 Nm.).
13. Using a new gasket, install the intake manifold collector.
14. Install the ignition coils and tighten the ignition coil-to-valve cover bolts.
15. Connect the accelerator cable to the throttle body.
16. Connect the hoses to the throttle body, the EGR valve, the EGR control solenoid valve, the intake manifold collector, the power valve control solenoid valve (if equipped with a manual transaxle) and the power valve actuator (if equipped with a manual transaxle).
17. Connect the electrical connectors from the throttle position sensor, the exhaust gas temperature sensor, etc.
18. Connect the negative battery cable.
19. Start the engine and check for leaks.

Rocker Arms/Shafts

REMOVAL & INSTALLATION

VG30E Engine

▶ **See Figure 12**

1. Turn the crankshaft to position the No. 1 piston on the TDC of it's compression stroke.
2. Remove the intake manifold collector.
3. Remove the valve cover.
4. Remove the rocker arm/shaft assembly-to-cylinder head bolts by loosening the bolts in 2–3 steps.
5. Remove the rocker arm/shaft assembly from the cylinder head.
   To install:

✳✳ WARNING

Be sure to lubricate all of the moving surfaces with fresh oil before installation.

6. With the No. 1 piston set on the TDC of it's compression stroke, install the left side rocker arm/shaft assembly and torque the rocker arm/shaft assembly-to-cylinder head bolts, in 2–3 steps, to 13–16 ft. lbs. (18–22 Nm).

➡**When installing the rocker arm/shaft assembly to cylinder head bolts, dip the threaded portion of each bolt in fresh engine oil before installation. This will ensure a correct torque reading.**

7. Rotate the crankshaft 360° and position the No. 4 piston on the TDC of it's compression stroke. Install the right side rocker arm/shaft assembly and torque the rocker arm/shaft assembly-to-cylinder head bolts, in 2–3 steps, to 13–16 ft. lbs. (18–22 Nm).

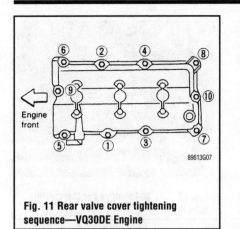

Fig. 11 Rear valve cover tightening sequence—VQ30DE Engine

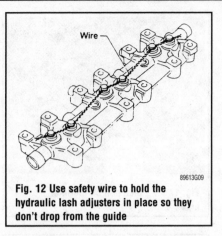

Fig. 12 Use safety wire to hold the hydraulic lash adjusters in place so they don't drop from the guide

Fig. 13 The VE30DE engine uses a floating rocker arm with a hydraulic lash adjuster to operate the valves

➡The right side of the engine incorporates cylinders No. 1, 3 and 5. The left side of the engine incorporates cylinders No. 2, 4 and 6.

8. Install the valve cover.
9. Connect the negative battery cable. Start the engine and check the engine operation.

VE30DE Engine

♦ See Figure 13

The VE30DE engine is equipped with floating rocker arms which can only be removed when the camshaft(s) are removed.

VQ30DE Engine

The VQ30DE engine does not use a rocker arm assembly. The camshafts are placed directly over the valves, with a bucket type camshaft follower that actuates each valve.

Thermostat

REMOVAL & INSTALLATION

VG30E Engine

♦ See Figure 14

➡It may be necessary to remove radiator shroud, coolant fan assembly and water suction pipe retaining bolts to gain access to the thermostat housing.

The thermostat is located at the front of the engine, directly above the water pump.

1. Disconnect the negative battery cable.
2. Drain the cooling system to a level below the thermostat housing.
3. Disconnect the water hose from the water outlet housing.
4. Remove the water outlet housing-to-thermostat housing bolts. Separate the water outlet housing from the thermostat housing. Remove the thermostat from the thermostat housing.

To install:

5. Clean the gasket mounting surfaces.
6. Using liquid sealant, apply a bead to the water outlet housing.
7. Install the thermostat into the thermostat housing with the thermostat spring facing the hose and the thermostat pintle in the upward direction.
8. Install the water outlet housing and torque the water outlet housing-to-thermostat housing bolts to 12–15 ft. lbs. (16–21 Nm).
9. Reconnect the hose to the front housing.
10. Refill the cooling system.
11. Connect the negative battery cable.
12. Start the engine and allow it to reach normal operating temperatures; then check for leaks. After cooling, recheck the coolant level.

VE30DE Engine

♦ See Figures 15 thru 21

The thermostat is located at the rear of the engine, directly above the transaxle bell housing.

1. Disconnect the negative battery cable.
2. Drain the cooling system to a level below the thermostat housing.
3. Disconnect the radiator hose from the water inlet housing.
4. Remove the water inlet housing-to-thermostat housing bolts. Separate the water inlet housing from the thermostat housing. Remove the thermostat from the thermostat housing.

To install:

5. Clean the gasket mounting surfaces.

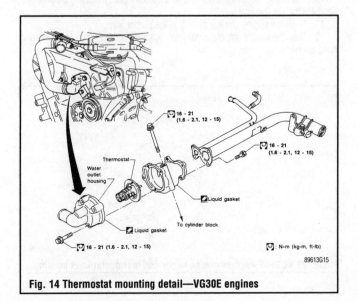

Fig. 14 Thermostat mounting detail—VG30E engines

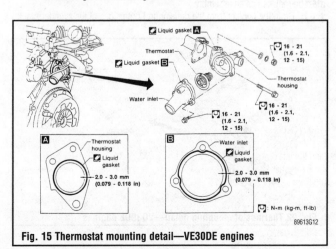

Fig. 15 Thermostat mounting detail—VE30DE engines

Fig. 16 Remove the inlet hose and the three inlet pipe bolts . . .

Fig. 17 . . . then pull off the inlet pipe . . .

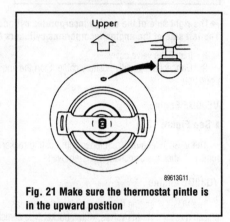

Fig. 18 . . . and remove the thermostat from the housing

Fig. 19 Use liquid gasket to form a seal on the inlet pipe

Fig. 20 Aftermarket gaskets are also available

Fig. 21 Make sure the thermostat pintle is in the upward position

6. Using liquid sealant, apply a bead to the water inlet housing.

7. Install the thermostat into the thermostat housing with the thermostat spring facing the thermostat housing and the thermostat pintle in the upward direction.

8. Install the water inlet housing and torque the water inlet housing-to-thermostat housing bolts.

9. Reconnect the radiator hose to the water inlet housing.

10. Refill the cooling system.

11. Connect the negative battery cable.

12. Start the engine and allow it to reach normal operating temperatures; then check for leaks. After cooling, recheck the coolant level.

VQ30DE Engine

▶ See Figures 22 and 23

The thermostat on the VQ30DE engine is located on the front of the right cylinder head. The water inlet pipe and the thermostat are an integrated unit, and must be replaced as an assembly.

1. Drain the coolant from the radiator and both sides of the cylinder block.

2. Remove the accessory drive belts and the idler pulley bracket.

3. Remove the water pump drain plug on the pump side of the engine.

4. Remove the lower radiator hose from the water inlet pipe/thermostat assembly.

5. Remove the 3 retaining nuts, and carefully pull the assembly away from the housing. Do not reuse the gasket.

To install:

6. Place a new gasket on the pump housing.

7. Place the thermostat assembly on the engine and tighten the nuts to 74.6–99 in. lb.(.086–1.14 Nm).

8. Install the lower radiator hose to the water inlet pipe/thermostat assembly.

9. Install the water pump drain plug on the pump side of the engine.

10. Install the accessory drive belts and the idler pulley bracket. Be sure to set them the tension properly.

11. Refill the engine cooling system to the proper level.

12. Start the engine and check for leaks around the thermostat assembly and hose connections.

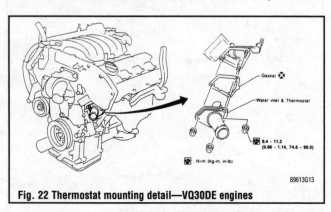

Fig. 22 Thermostat mounting detail—VQ30DE engines

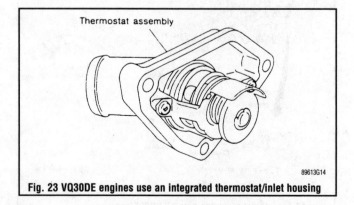

Fig. 23 VQ30DE engines use an integrated thermostat/inlet housing

Intake Manifold

REMOVAL & INSTALLATION

VG30E Engine

▶ **See Figure 24**

1. Relieve the fuel system pressure.
2. Disconnect the negative battery cable.
3. Disconnect the air intake duct from the dual duct housing.
4. Unplug the electrical connectors from the throttle body, the step motor AAC valve and the exhaust gas temperature sensor.
5. Disconnect and label the hoses from the valve cover, the throttle body, the step motor AAC valve, the EGR control valve and the air cut valve.
6. If the spark plug wires are in the way, disconnect them and move them aside. Disconnect the accelerator cable from the throttle body.
7. Remove the upper intake manifold collector-to-intake manifold bolts, in sequence, and lift the assembly from the intake manifold. Discard the gasket.
8. Remove the lower intake manifold collector-to-intake manifold bolts, in sequence, and lift the assembly from the intake manifold. Discard the gasket.
9. If the fuel injector assembly is in the way, perform the following procedures:
   a. Disconnect the electrical connectors from the fuel injectors.
   b. Disconnect the fuel injector assembly from the fuel lines.

❋❋ CAUTION

Observe all applicable safety precautions when working around fuel. Whenever servicing the fuel system, always work in a well ventilated area. Do not allow fuel spray or vapors to come in contact with a spark or open flame. Keep a dry chemical fire extinguisher near the work area. Always keep fuel in a container specifically designed for fuel storage; also, always properly seal fuel containers to avoid the possibility of fire or explosion.

   c. Remove the fuel rail-to-cylinder head bolts.
   d. Remove the fuel rail assembly from the engine.
10. Remove the intake manifold-to-engine bolts, in sequence, lift the intake manifold from the engine and discard the gasket.
   To install:
11. Clean the gasket mounting surfaces.
12. Use a new gasket and install the intake manifold by performing the following procedures:
   a. Torque the intake manifold-to-engine nuts/bolts, in sequence, to 2.2–3.6 ft. lbs. (3–5 Nm).
   b. Torque the intake manifold-to-engine nuts/bolts, in sequence, to 12–14 ft. lbs. (16–20 Nm).
   c. Finally, torque the intake manifold-to-engine nuts/bolts, in sequence, to 17–20 ft. lbs. (24–27 Nm).
13. If the fuel injector assembly was removed, perform the following procedures:
   a. Install the fuel rail assembly to the engine.
   b. Install the fuel rail-to-cylinder head bolts and torque the bolts to 1.8–2.4 ft. lbs. (2.5–3.2 Nm).
   c. Connect the fuel injector assembly to the fuel lines.
   d. Connect the electrical connectors to the fuel injectors.
14. Use a new gasket and install the lower intake manifold collector; torque the lower intake manifold collector-to-intake manifold bolts, in 2–3 steps, in sequence, to 13–16 ft. lbs. (18–22 Nm).
15. Use a new gasket and install the upper intake manifold collector-to-intake manifold; torque the bolts to 5.1–5.8 ft. lbs. (7–8 Nm).
16. Connect the spark plug wires, if disconnected. Connect the accelerator cable to the throttle body.
17. Connect the hoses to the valve cover, the throttle body, the step motor AAC valve, the EGR control valve and the air cut valve.
18. Plug in the electrical connectors to the throttle body, the step motor AAC valve and the exhaust gas temperature sensor.

19. Connect the negative battery cable.
20. Start the engine and check for oil leaks.

VE30DE Engine

▶ **See Figures 25 thru 41**

❋❋ CAUTION

Observe all applicable safety precautions when working around fuel. Whenever servicing the fuel system, always work in a well ventilated area. Do not allow fuel spray or vapors to come in contact with a spark or open flame. Keep a dry chemical fire extinguisher near the work area. Always keep fuel in a container specifically designed for fuel storage; also, always properly seal fuel containers to avoid the possibility of fire or explosion.

1. Relieve the fuel system of pressure.
2. Disconnect the negative battery cable.
3. Unplug the electrical connectors from the throttle position sensor, the exhaust gas temperature sensor, etc.
4. Label and disconnect the hoses from the throttle body, the EGR valve, the EGR control solenoid valve, the intake manifold collector, the power valve control solenoid valve (if equipped with a manual transaxle) and the power valve actuator (if equipped with a manual transaxle).
5. Remove the three ignition coils from the rear cylinder bank.
6. Disconnect the accelerator cable and cruise control cable, if equipped, from the throttle body.
7. Unbolt the rear manifold collector support brackets.
8. Remove the intake manifold collector-to-intake manifold bolts and the intake manifold collector.
9. If necessary, unplug the electrical connector from the camshaft position sensor and the power transistor.
10. Disconnect the electrical connectors from the fuel injectors.
11. Disconnect the fuel injector assembly from the fuel lines.
12. Remove the fuel rail-to-cylinder head bolts.
13. Remove the fuel rail assembly from the engine.
14. Unbolt the water pipe from the lower manifold.
15. Remove the intake manifold-to-engine bolts, in sequence, by reversing the torquing sequence. Lift the intake manifold from the engine and discard the gasket.
   To install:
16. Clean the gasket mounting surfaces.
17. Install the intake manifold and torque the intake manifold-to-engine, in sequence, bolts to 12–14 ft. lbs. (16–20 Nm) and the nuts to 17–20 ft. lbs. (24–27 Nm).
18. Install the fuel rail assembly to the engine.
19. Install the fuel rail-to-cylinder head bolts and torque the bolts to 12–14 ft. lbs. (16–20 Nm).
20. Connect the fuel injector assembly to the fuel lines.
21. Connect the electrical connectors to the fuel injectors.
22. Using a new gasket, install the intake manifold collector and torque the intake manifold collector-to-intake manifold bolts, in sequence, to 13–16 ft. lbs. (18–22 Nm).
23. Install the intake manifold collector support and torque the bolts to 12–15 ft. lbs. (16–21 Nm).
24. Connect the accelerator cable and cruise control cable, if equipped, to the throttle body.
25. Connect the hoses to the throttle body, the EGR valve, the EGR control solenoid valve, the intake manifold collector, the power valve control solenoid valve (if equipped with a manual transaxle) and the power valve actuator (if equipped with a manual transaxle).
26. If disconnected, plug in the electrical connectors to the camshaft position sensor and the power transistor.
27. Install the ignition coils to the rear cylinder bank.
28. Plug in the electrical connectors from the throttle position sensor, the exhaust gas temperature sensor, etc.
29. Connect the negative battery cable.
30. Start the engine and check for leaks.

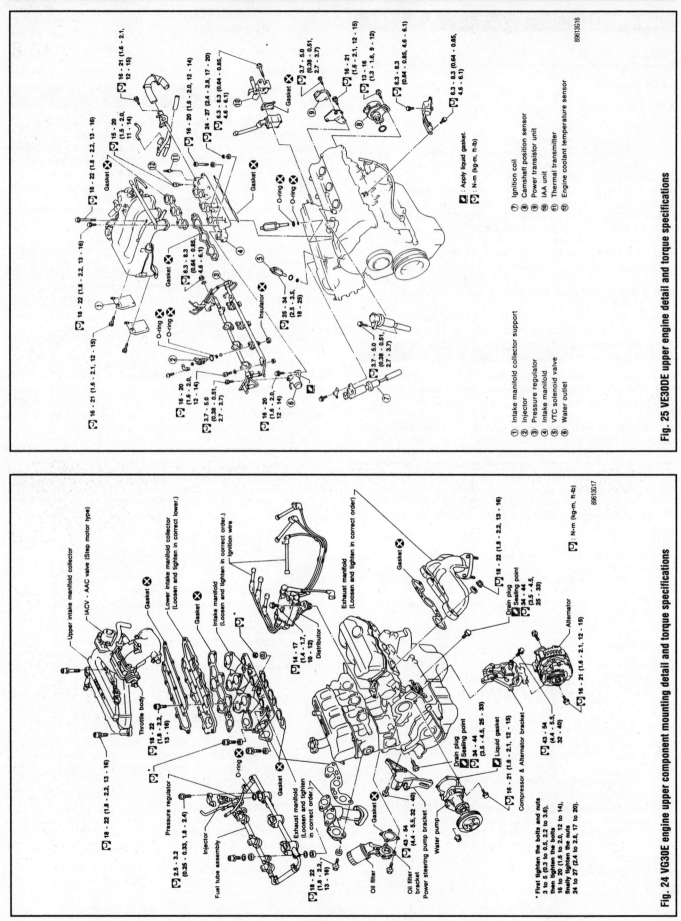

Fig. 25 VE30DE upper engine detail and torque specifications

① Intake manifold collector support
② Injector
③ Pressure regulator
④ Intake manifold
⑤ VTC solenoid valve
⑥ Water outlet
⑦ Ignition coil
⑧ Camshaft position sensor
⑨ Power transistor unit
⑩ IAA unit
⑪ Thermal transmitter
⑫ Engine coolant temperature sensor

Fig. 24 VG30E engine upper component mounting detail and torque specifications

Fig. 26 Detach the components secured to the manifold collector for removal

Fig. 27 Use pliers to remove the spring-type clips that secure the hoses onto the manifold collector

Fig. 28 Unbolt the EGR control valve bracket and set it aside

Fig. 29 Remove the bolts from the manifold collector brackets and any bracket on the rear of the manifold

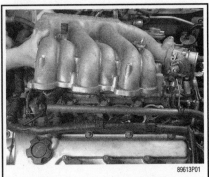

Fig. 30 After the bolts are removed, lift the manifold collector from the engine

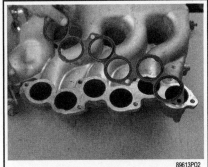

Fig. 31 Replace the manifold gasket whenever the manifold collector is removed

Fig. 32 Use towels or rags in the intake ports to keep debris from entering the engine

Fig. 33 Use plugs on the fuel lines to contain any excess fuel in the fuel lines

Fig. 34 The fuel rail assemblies have washers under the mounting points to provide a cushion for the injectors

Fig. 35 The fuel rail must be removed to remove the lower manifold from the engine

Fig. 36 The water pipe attached to the manifold can be unbolted and moved away for manifold removal

Fig. 37 The lower manifold uses special washers for mounting; be sure they are installed in the direction they are removed

Fig. 38 Carefully lift the manifold from the engine

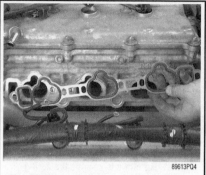

Fig. 39 Always replace the gaskets after removing the manifold

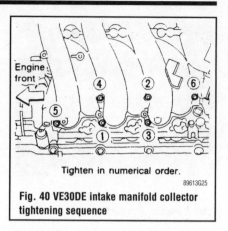

Tighten in numerical order.

Fig. 40 VE30DE intake manifold collector tightening sequence

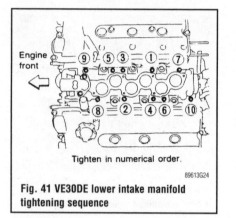

Tighten in numerical order.

Fig. 41 VE30DE lower intake manifold tightening sequence

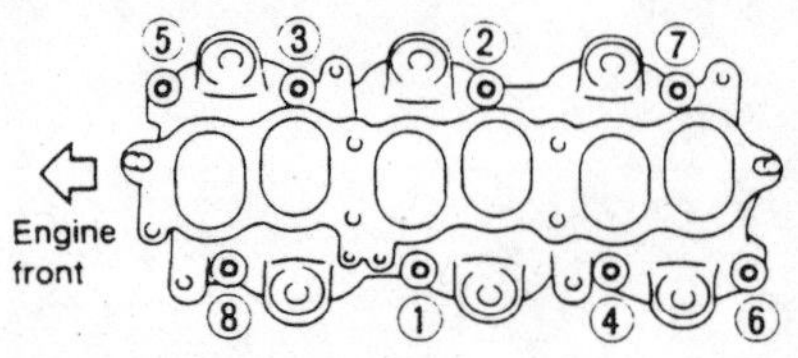

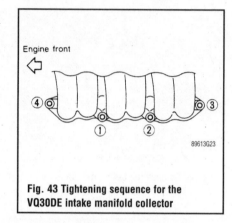

Fig. 42 VQ30DE Lower intake manifold tightening sequence

Fig. 43 Tightening sequence for the VQ30DE intake manifold collector

VQ30DE Engine

♦ **See Figures 42, 43, 44, 45 and 46**

✳✳ CAUTION

Observe all applicable safety precautions when working around fuel. Whenever servicing the fuel system, always work in a well ventilated area. Do not allow fuel spray or vapors to come in contact with a spark or open flame. Keep a dry chemical fire extinguisher near the work area. Always keep fuel in a container specifically designed for fuel storage; also, always properly seal fuel containers to avoid the possibility of fire or explosion.

1. Relieve the fuel system of pressure.
2. Disconnect the negative battery cable.
3. Drain the coolant from the engine.
4. Remove the air intake duct from the throttle body.
5. Unplug the throttle position sensor connectors and the ignition coils.
6. Tag and disconnect any hoses that would interfere with manifold removal.
7. Unbolt the EGR tube from the manifold collector.
8. Unbolt the manifold collector supports that connect to the rear cylinder head.
9. Remove the intake manifold collector bolts and lift it from the engine.
10. Unplug the fuel injector harness connectors. If necessary, mark them for identification to avoid mixing them up.
11. Remove the fuel rail assembly.
12. Remove the intake manifold in the reverse order of installation. Refer to the illustration. Discard the gaskets.
   To install:
13. Using new gaskets, place the lower intake manifold onto the engine.
14. Torque the lower intake manifold, in two steps, as shown in the illustration. First, tighten the bolts and nuts in order to 3.6–7.2 ft.lbs. (5–10 Nm.). Tighten the bolts and nuts again to 20–23 ft.lbs. (26–31 Nm.). Go over the sequence at least five times to ensure equal torque on all fasteners.
15. Using new O-rings on the injectors, install the fuel rail to the manifold.

Follow the illustration and torque the fuel rail bolts to 6.9–8.0 ft.lbs. (9.3–10.8 Nm.). Tighten the bolts again to 15–20 ft.lbs. (21–26 Nm.).
16. Plug in the fuel injector harness connectors.
17. Using a new gasket, install the intake manifold collector. Following the sequence shown in the illustration, torque the bolts to 13–16 ft.lbs. (18–22 Nm.).
18. Install the EGR guide tube to the manifold collector.
19. Connect any hoses that were previously removed.
20. Plug in the throttle position sensor connectors and the ignition coils.
21. Install the air intake duct to the throttle body.
22. Refill the engine with coolant.
23. Connect the negative battery cable.
24. Start the engine and check for proper engine operation.

Exhaust Manifold(s)

REMOVAL & INSTALLATION

VG30E Engine

♦ **See Figures 47 and 48**

1. Disconnect the negative battery cable.
2. Raise and safely support the vehicle.

➡ **To make removing the exhaust manifolds easier, soaking the exhaust pipe retaining bolts with penetrating oil is recommended.**

3. Disconnect the exhaust pipes from the exhaust manifolds.
4. Remove both exhaust manifolds-to-engine bolts, in sequence. Discard the gaskets.
   To install:
5. Clean all gasket mounting surfaces. Install new gaskets.
6. Install the exhaust manifolds to the engine and torque the exhaust manifold-to-engine bolts, alternately in 2 stages, in the exact reverse order of removal to 13–16 ft. lbs. (16–22 Nm).

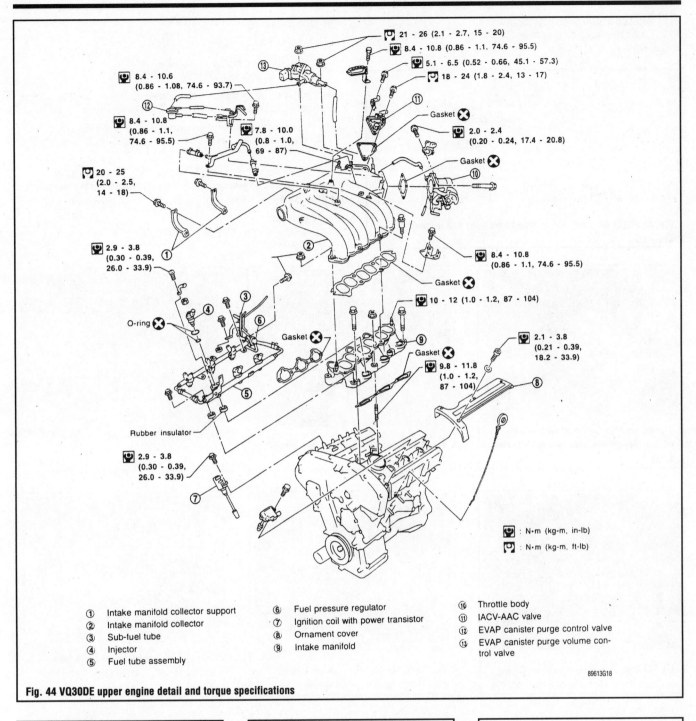

21 - 26 (2.1 - 2.7, 15 - 20)
8.4 - 10.8 (0.86 - 1.1, 74.6 - 95.5)
5.1 - 6.5 (0.52 - 0.66, 45.1 - 57.3)
18 - 24 (1.8 - 2.4, 13 - 17)
8.4 - 10.6 (0.86 - 1.08, 74.6 - 93.7)
8.4 - 10.8 (0.86 - 1.1, 74.6 - 95.5)
7.8 - 10.0 (0.8 - 1.0, 69 - 87)
Gasket
2.0 - 2.4 (0.20 - 0.24, 17.4 - 20.8)
Gasket
20 - 25 (2.0 - 2.5, 14 - 18)
2.9 - 3.8 (0.30 - 0.39, 26.0 - 33.9)
8.4 - 10.8 (0.86 - 1.1, 74.6 - 95.5)
Gasket
O-ring
Gasket
10 - 12 (1.0 - 1.2, 87 - 104)
Gasket
2.1 - 3.8 (0.21 - 0.39, 18.2 - 33.9)
9.8 - 11.8 (1.0 - 1.2, 87 - 104)
Rubber insulator
2.9 - 3.8 (0.30 - 0.39, 26.0 - 33.9)

: N•m (kg-m, in-lb)
: N•m (kg-m, ft-lb)

① Intake manifold collector support
② Intake manifold collector
③ Sub-fuel tube
④ Injector
⑤ Fuel tube assembly
⑥ Fuel pressure regulator
⑦ Ignition coil with power transistor
⑧ Ornament cover
⑨ Intake manifold
⑩ Throttle body
⑪ IACV-AAC valve
⑫ EVAP canister purge control valve
⑬ EVAP canister purge volume control valve

89613G18

Fig. 44 VQ30DE upper engine detail and torque specifications

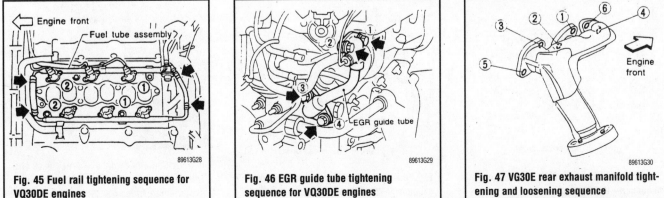

Engine front
Fuel tube assembly

89613G28

Fig. 45 Fuel rail tightening sequence for VQ30DE engines

EGR guide tube

89613G29

Fig. 46 EGR guide tube tightening sequence for VQ30DE engines

Engine front

89613G30

Fig. 47 VG30E rear exhaust manifold tightening and loosening sequence

7. Install the exhaust pipes to the manifolds.
8. Connect the negative battery cable. Start the engine and check for exhaust leaks.

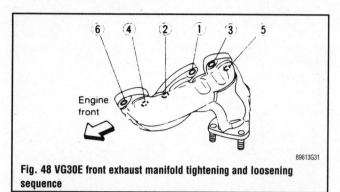

Fig. 48 VG30E front exhaust manifold tightening and loosening sequence

VE30DE Engine

▶ **See Figures 49 thru 57**

1. Disconnect the negative battery cable.
2. Raise and safely support the vehicle.

➡ **To make removing the exhaust manifolds easier, soaking the exhaust pipe retaining bolts with penetrating oil is recommended.**

3. Disconnect the exhaust pipes from the exhaust manifolds.
4. Remove the exhaust manifold-to-engine bolts, in the opposite order of the tightening sequence. Discard the gaskets.

➡ **It may be necessary to unbolt the air conditioning compressor to remove the front exhaust manifold if the stud nearest to the compressor comes out with the nut.**

To install:

5. Clean all gasket mounting surfaces. Install new gaskets.

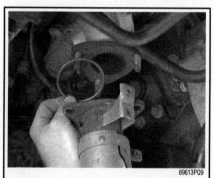

Fig. 49 Soaking the manifold nuts with penetrating oil will help to avoid breaking studs

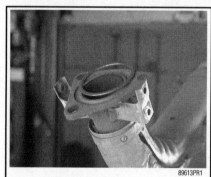

Fig. 50 Loosen the bolts and remove the front heat shield . . .

Fig. 51 . . . followed by the rear shield

Fig. 52 Always replace the copper O-ring between the header pipe and the manifold

Fig. 53 Notice the recess in the header pipe flange for the copper O-ring

Fig. 54 A universal swivel and a long extension will make removal and installation of the nuts easier

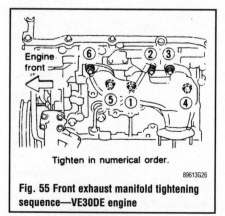

Fig. 55 Front exhaust manifold tightening sequence—VE30DE engine

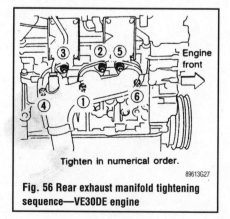

Fig. 56 Rear exhaust manifold tightening sequence—VE30DE engine

Fig. 57 Sometimes the studs may back out with the nuts; use locking compound when installing them to keep them in place

6. Install the exhaust manifold to the engine. Torque the exhaust manifold-to-engine bolts, in sequence, to 13–16 ft. lbs. (16–22 Nm).
7. Install the exhaust pipes to the manifolds.
8. Connect the negative battery cable. Start the engine and check for exhaust leaks.

VQ30DE Engine

1. Disconnect the negative battery cable.
2. Raise and safely support the vehicle.

➡To make removing the exhaust manifolds easier, soaking the exhaust pipe retaining bolts with penetrating oil is recommended.

3. Remove the exhaust manifold heat shields.
4. Disconnect the exhaust pipes from the exhaust manifolds.
5. Remove the exhaust manifold-to-engine bolts, in the opposite order of the tightening sequence. Discard the gaskets.

To install:

6. Clean all gasket mounting surfaces. Install new gaskets.
7. Install the exhaust manifold to the engine. Torque the exhaust manifold-to-engine bolts to 13–16 ft. lbs. (16–22 Nm).
8. Install the exhaust pipes to the manifolds.
9. Install the exhaust manifold heat shields.
10. Connect the negative battery cable. Start the engine and check for exhaust leaks.

Radiator

REMOVAL & INSTALLATION

➧ See Figures 58 thru 64

1. Remove the splash shield underneath the vehicle. This makes access to the lower hose easier.
2. Disconnect the upper and lower radiator hoses.
3. Disconnect the radiator overflow hose.

⁂ CAUTION

Never open, service or drain the radiator or cooling system when hot; serious burns can occur from the steam and hot coolant. Also, when draining engine coolant, keep in mind that cats and dogs are attracted to ethylene glycol antifreeze and could drink any that is left in an uncovered container or in puddles on the ground. This will prove fatal in sufficient quantities. Always drain coolant into a sealable container. Coolant should be reused unless it is contaminated or is several years old.

4. Disconnect the automatic transaxle cooler lines from the radiator (automatic models).

89613PE6

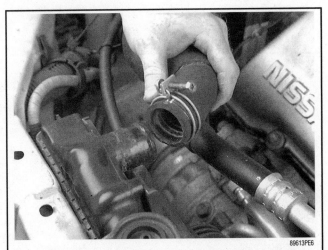

Fig. 58 Twist the hose while pulling away to disconnect it from the radiator

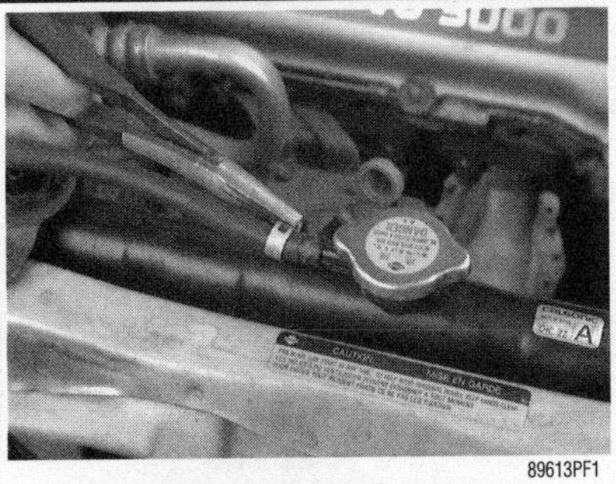

89613PF1

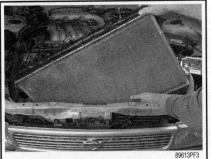

Fig. 59 Pinch the clamp with pliers to loosen it; then pull it back to remove the hose

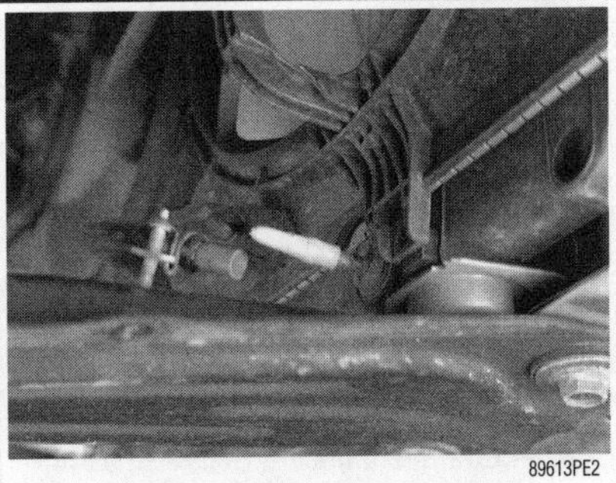

89613PE2

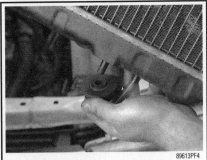

Fig. 60 After the automatic transaxle cooler lines are removed, use plugs to keep any ATF from spilling

89613PF2

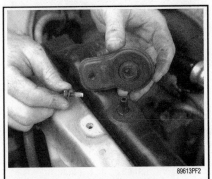

Fig. 61 Remove the bolt and pull the upper bracket from the pin on the radiator

89613PF3

Fig. 62 When lifting the radiator out of the engine compartment, be careful not to damage the cooling fins

89613PF4

Fig. 63 Make sure the rubber spacers are installed properly on the bottom radiator pins . . .

89613PF5

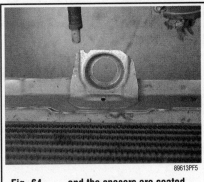

Fig. 64 . . . and the spacers are seated properly in the radiator mounts

5. Remove the radiator mounting brackets.

6. Remove the fan/shroud assembly. Don't forget to unplug the cooling fans.

7. Carefully lift the radiator from the engine compartment.

To install:

8. Lower the radiator into the engine compartment. Be sure the rubber spacers on the bottom of the radiator are properly seated in the holes in the body.

9. Install the radiator mounting brackets.

10. Connect the automatic transaxle cooler lines from the radiator (automatic models).

11. Install the fan/shroud assembly. Be sure to plug in the cooling fans.

12. Install the upper and lower radiator hoses.

13. Install the splash shield underneath the vehicle.

14. Refill the cooling system with the appropriate antifreeze/water mix and bleed the system.

15. Run the engine and check the cooling system for leaks.

Engine Fan

REMOVAL & INSTALLATION

♦ **See Figures 65 thru 71**

1. Disconnect the negative battery cable.

2. Remove the cap and drain the radiator via the drain plug in the bottom tank to a level below the upper radiator hose.

❊❊❊ CAUTION

Never open, service or drain the radiator or cooling system when hot; serious burns can occur from the steam and hot coolant. Also, when draining engine coolant, keep in mind that cats and dogs are attracted to ethylene glycol antifreeze and could drink any that is

Fig. 65 The upper radiator hose must be disconnected from the radiator to remove the fan assembly

Fig. 66 Press on the tab and pull the connector to disengage it from the radiator fan shroud

Fig. 67 There are four bolts that secure the radiator; two on the top of the radiator . . .

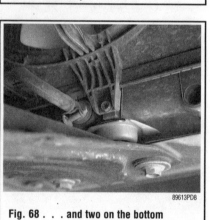

Fig. 68 . . . and two on the bottom

Fig. 69 After the bolts are removed, unclip the fan shroud from the radiator . . .

Fig. 70 . . . and lift the radiator fan shroud from the vehicle

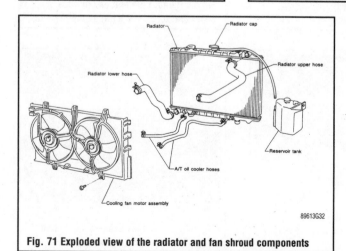

Fig. 71 Exploded view of the radiator and fan shroud components

left in an uncovered container or in puddles on the ground. This will prove fatal in sufficient quantities. Always drain coolant into a sealable container. Coolant should be reused unless it is contaminated or is several years old.

3. Remove the upper radiator hose.

4. Disconnect the electrical connectors from the electrical cooling fans.

5. Remove the fan/shroud assembly from the radiator.

To install:

6. Position the fan/shroud assembly in the vehicle and attach it to the radiator.

7. Connect the upper radiator hose.

8. Connect the electrical connectors to the electrical cooling fans.

9. Refill the cooling system with 50/50 antifreeze/water mix and bleed the system.

10. Connect the negative battery cable.

11. Run engine and check the cooling system for leaks.

Water Pump

REMOVAL & INSTALLATION

VG30E Engine

♦ **See Figure 72**

The water pump is located in the front center of the engine.

➡**Be careful not to spill coolant on the timing belt when performing this procedure.**

1. Drain the cooling system through the drain plug at the bottom of the radiator, and the drain plugs on both sides of the block.

✳✳ CAUTION

Never open, service or drain the radiator or cooling system when hot; serious burns can occur from the steam and hot coolant. Also, when draining engine coolant, keep in mind that cats and dogs are attracted to ethylene glycol antifreeze and could drink any that is left in an uncovered container or in puddles on the ground. This will prove fatal in sufficient quantities. Always drain coolant into a sealable container. Coolant should be reused unless it is contaminated or is several years old.

2. Remove the upper radiator hose.
3. Loosen and remove the drive belt(s) from the water pump pulley.
4. To make the operation easier, remove the timing belt cover. If necessary, remove the thermostat housing and gasket for access.
5. Remove the water pump-to-engine bolts (noting different lengths) and remove the pump. If the water pump has excessive end play or rough operation, replace it.

To install:
6. Clean the gasket mounting surfaces.
7. Use a new gasket and coat the gasket with sealant. Reinstall the pump and torque the water pump-to-engine bolts evenly to 12–15 ft. lbs. (16–21 Nm).
8. If the thermostat housing was removed, install it with a new gasket. Install the cruise control unit if removed.
9. Install the tensioner, tensioner bracket, air conditioning belt and adjust the belt correctly.
10. Install the upper radiator hose.
11. Refill the cooling system. Connect the negative battery cable.
12. Start the engine, run to normal operating temperature and check for the correct coolant level and for leaks.

VE30DE Engine

♦ **See Figures 73 thru 78**

The water pump is located in the front center of the engine.
1. Remove the splash shield on the passenger side of the vehicle.
2. Drain the cooling system.

✳✳ CAUTION

Never open, service or drain the radiator or cooling system when hot; serious burns can occur from the steam and hot coolant. Also, when draining engine coolant, keep in mind that cats and dogs are attracted to ethylene glycol antifreeze and could drink any that is left in an uncovered container or in puddles on the ground. This will prove fatal in sufficient quantities. Always drain coolant into a sealable container. Coolant should be reused unless it is contaminated or is several years old.

3. Remove the upper radiator hose to access the upper water pump bolts.
4. Remove the small hose attached the upper part of the water pump.

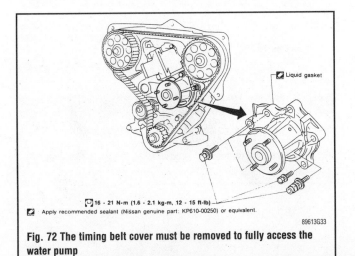

Fig. 72 The timing belt cover must be removed to fully access the water pump

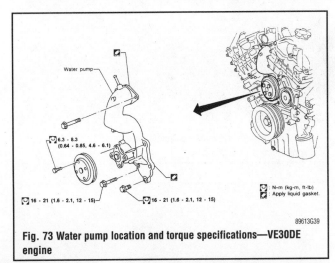

Fig. 73 Water pump location and torque specifications—VE30DE engine

Fig. 74 Removing the upper radiator hose will allow better access to the upper bolts and the small hose attached to the pump

Fig. 75 Removing the A/C belt tensioner will allow more room to remove the pump once it's unbolted from the engine

Fig. 76 Use a prybar with a square edge to hold the pulley in place while loosening the bolts; then unscrew them by hand

Fig. 77 The water pump has to be carefully positioned for removal

Fig. 78 Use locking pliers and carefully twist out the timing pointer if pump removal is difficult

5. Remove the drive belts from the front of the engine.
6. Remove the tensioner pulley for the air conditioning compressor belt.

➡It is recommended that the crankshaft damper be removed to make water pump removal and installation easier.

7. Remove the water pump pulley-to-water pump bolts, followed by the pulley.
8. Remove the water pump-to-engine bolts. Label each bolt, noting location, and bolt length.

✳✳ WARNING

Failure to install the bolts of different lengths in their proper locations could result in a cracked timing chain cover, requiring time consuming and costly repair. Be sure to label each bolt and its location.

9. Remove the water pump from the engine. If the water pump has excessive end play or rough operation, replace it.

To install:
10. Clean the gasket mounting surfaces and grooves.
11. Using liquid sealant, apply a continuous bead to the gasket mounting surfaces of the water pump.
12. Install the water pump and torque water pump-to-engine bolts to 12–15 ft. lbs. (16–21 Nm).
13. Install the water pump pulley and torque the water pump pulley-to-water pump bolts to 4.6–6.1 ft. lbs. (6.3–8.3 Nm).
14. Install the tensioner pulley for the air conditioning compressor belt.
15. Install the crankshaft damper, if removed.
16. Install the timing pointer, if removed.
17. Install the drive belts from the engine and set the proper tension.
18. Install the splash shield on the passenger side of the vehicle.
19. Attach the hoses to the upper water pump and the main inlet pipe.
20. Refill the cooling system to the appropriate capacity.
21. Start the engine, run to normal operating temperature and check for the correct coolant level and for leaks.

VQ30DE Engine

▶ **See Figures 79, 80, 81, 82 and 83**

1. Remove the splash shields from under the vehicle.
2. Drain the coolant system.

✳✳ CAUTION

Never open, service or drain the radiator or cooling system when hot; serious burns can occur from the steam and hot coolant. Also, when draining engine coolant, keep in mind that cats and dogs are

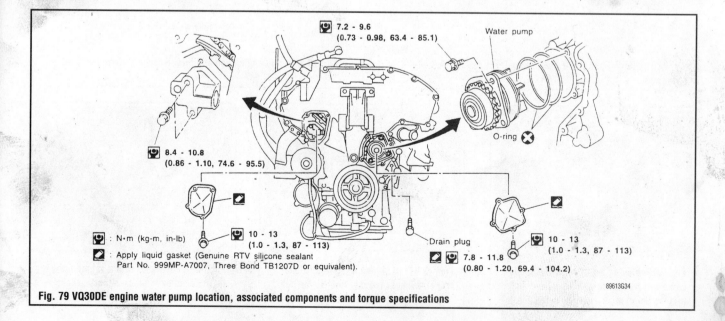

Fig. 79 VQ30DE engine water pump location, associated components and torque specifications

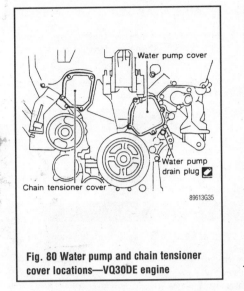

Fig. 80 Water pump and chain tensioner cover locations—VQ30DE engine

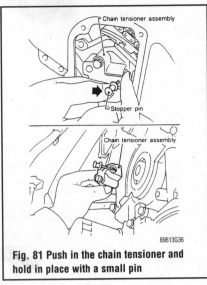

Fig. 81 Push in the chain tensioner and hold in place with a small pin

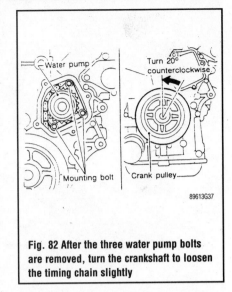

Fig. 82 After the three water pump bolts are removed, turn the crankshaft to loosen the timing chain slightly

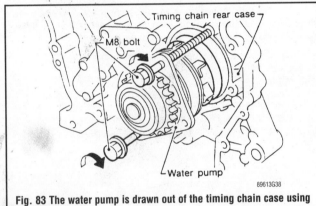

Fig. 83 The water pump is drawn out of the timing chain case using two long bolts

attracted to ethylene glycol antifreeze and could drink any that is left in an uncovered container or in puddles on the ground. This will prove fatal in sufficient quantities. Always drain coolant into a sealable container. Coolant should be reused unless it is contaminated or is several years old.

3. Remove the right side motor mount and bracket assembly. Use a jack or an engine support to hold the engine in place while the mount is removed.
4. Remove the drive belts and the idler pulley bracket.
5. Remove the water pump drain plug.
6. Remove the chain tensioner cover and the water pump cover.
7. Using a suitable tool, push in the timing chain tensioner sleeve. Use a small pin to stop the tensioner from returning.
8. Remove the three water pump bolts. To relax the tension on the timing chain, turn the crankshaft damper approximately 20° counterclockwise.
9. Using two longer bolts, carefully draw the pump out of the housing. Turn each bolt no more than one half turn each time, or the pump and housing may be damaged.
10. Remove the water pump assembly from the engine. Discard the O-rings.
11. Inspect the assembly for excessive corrosion, rough operation or end play. Replace as necessary.
   To install:
12. Place a small amount of coolant on the O-rings to lubricate them.
13. Carefully push the water pump assembly into the housing.

✳✳ WARNING

Be sure not to cut the O-rings on the pump housing when installing the pump assembly. Be sure to lubricate the O-rings before assembly.

14. Tighten the water pump assembly bolts to 5.1–7.2 ft. lb. (7–10 Nm.).
15. Return the crankshaft to its original position by turning it 20° forward.
16. Install the timing chain tensioner. Tighten the two bolts to 6.2–8.0 ft. lb. (8.4–10.8 Nm.). Remove the retainer pin from the tensioner.
17. Clean the mating surfaces of the chain tensioner cover and water pump cover. Apply a fresh bead of appropriate liquid gasket to each cover.
18. Install the covers, and torque the bolts to 7–9 ft. lb. (10–13 Nm.).
19. Install the water pump drain plug.
20. Install the drive belts and the idler pulley bracket Be sure to set belt tension properly.
21. Install the right side motor mount and bracket assembly.
22. Refill the coolant system.

Cylinder Head

REMOVAL & INSTALLATION

➡ To prevent distortion or warping of the cylinder head, allow the engine to cool completely before removing the head bolts.

VG30E Engine

♦ See Figures 84 thru 91

➡ To remove or install the cylinder head, you'll need a cylinder head bolt tool, No. ST10120000 (J2423901). This tool may be available through aftermarket manufacturers, available at most auto supply stores.

➡ The collector assembly and intake manifold have special bolt sequence for removal and installation.

1. Disconnect the negative battery cable for safety purposes.
2. The distributor assembly is located in the left cylinder head. Mark and remove it, if necessary.
3. Release the fuel system pressure.

✳✳ CAUTION

Observe all applicable safety precautions when working around fuel. Whenever servicing the fuel system, always work in a well ventilated area. Do not allow fuel spray or vapors to come in contact with a spark or open flame. Keep a dry chemical fire extinguisher near the work area. Always keep fuel in a container specifically designed for fuel storage; also, always properly seal fuel containers to avoid the possibility of fire or explosion.

4. Rotate the crankshaft to position the No. 1 piston on TDC of it's compression stroke.

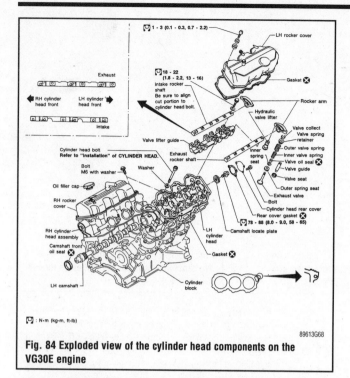

Fig. 84 Exploded view of the cylinder head components on the VG30E engine

5. Drain the cooling system. Disconnect all the electrical connectors, vacuum hoses and water hoses connected to the intake manifold collector.

✳✳ CAUTION

Never open, service or drain the radiator or cooling system when hot; serious burns can occur from the steam and hot coolant. Also, when draining engine coolant, keep in mind that cats and dogs are attracted to ethylene glycol antifreeze and could drink any that is left in an uncovered container or in puddles on the ground. This will prove fatal in sufficient quantities. Always drain coolant into a sealable container.

6. Remove the timing belt. Refer to the Timing Belt, Removal and Installation procedure.

➥ Do not rotate either the crankshaft or camshaft from this point onward or the valves could be bent by hitting the pistons.

7. Remove the intake manifold collector cover.
8. Remove the intake manifold and fuel rail assembly.
9. Remove the exhaust manifold collector bracket. Remove the exhaust manifold covers. Disconnect the exhaust manifold when it connects to the exhaust connecting tube.
10. Remove the camshaft pulleys and the rear timing cover securing bolts.
11. Loosen the cylinder head bolts, in sequence, using 2–3 steps.

✳✳ WARNING

A warped or cracked cylinder head could result from removing the bolts in incorrect order.

12. Remove the cylinder head with the exhaust manifold attached. If you need to remove the exhaust manifold, refer to the procedure in this section.

➥ Don't set the cylinder head face down on any surface. The protruding valves could bend. Use small blocks of wood on each side of the head to keep the valves from hitting the work surface.

13. Check the positions of the timing marks and camshaft sprockets to make sure they have not shifted.

To install:
14. Use rubbing alcohol or brake cleaner to clean the gasket mounting surfaces. Inspect the cylinder head(s) for warpage, wear, cracks and/or damage.
15. Make the following checks by performing the following procedures:
   a. If the engine was disturbed, rotate the crankshaft to position the No. 1 piston on the TDC of it's compression stroke.
   b. Align the mark on the crankshaft sprocket with the mark on the oil pump body.
   c. Make sure the knock pin on the camshaft is set at the top.

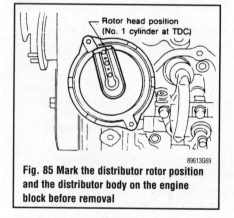

Fig. 85 Mark the distributor rotor position and the distributor body on the engine block before removal

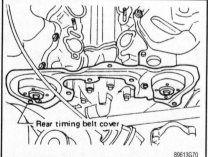

Fig. 86 Be sure to unbolt the rear timing belt cover before removing the cylinder heads

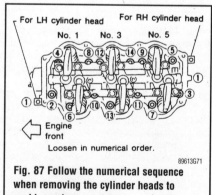

Fig. 87 Follow the numerical sequence when removing the cylinder heads to avoid warping

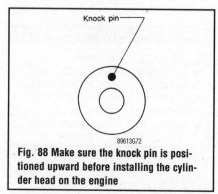

Fig. 88 Make sure the knock pin is positioned upward before installing the cylinder head on the engine

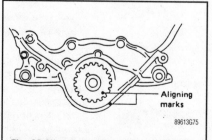

Fig. 89 Align the marks on the crankshaft damper and the oil pump body to set the number one piston at TDC

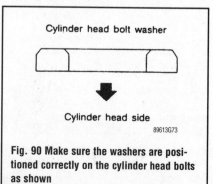

Fig. 90 Make sure the washers are positioned correctly on the cylinder head bolts as shown

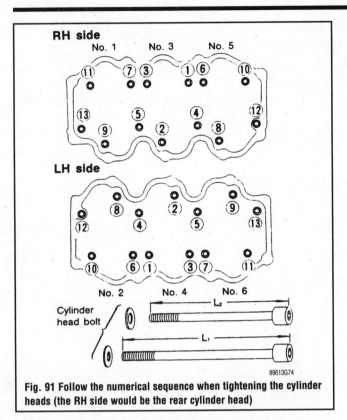

Fig. 91 Follow the numerical sequence when tightening the cylinder heads (the RH side would be the rear cylinder head)

➡️It is suggested, but not required, that the cylinder head bolts be replaced when installing a cylinder head. This will ensure proper torque, preventing any head gasket leakage.

16. Using a new gasket, install the cylinder head to the block.. Apply clean engine oil to the threads and seats of the bolts and install the bolts with washers in the correct position. Note that bolts 4, 5, 12, and 13 are 5.00 in. (127mm) long. The other bolts are 4.17 in. (106mm) long.

17. Torque the bolts according to the pattern for the cylinder head on each side in the following stages:

    a. Torque all bolts, in order, to 22 ft. lbs. (29 Nm).

    b. Torque all bolts, in order, to 43 ft. lbs. (59 Nm).

    c. Loosen all bolts completely.

    d. Torque all bolts, in order, to 22 ft. lbs. (29 Nm).

    e. Torque all bolts, in order, to 40–47 ft. lbs. (54–64 Nm). If you have a special wrench available that torques bolts to a certain angle, turn them 60–65°.

18. Install the rear timing cover bolts. Install the camshaft pulleys and torque the camshaft pulley-to-camshaft bolts to 58–65 ft. lbs. (78–88 Nm). Make sure the pulley marked R3 goes on the right and that marked L3 goes on the left.

19. Align the timing marks, if necessary, and then install the timing belt and adjust the belt tension.

20. Install the front upper and lower belt covers.

21. Make sure the valve cover bolts, trays and washers are free of oil. Then, install the valve covers.

22. Torque the intake manifold-to-engine bolts as follows:

    a. Torque, in sequence, to 2.2–3.6 ft. lbs. (3–5 Nm).

    b. Torque, in sequence, to 12–14 ft. lbs. (16–20 Nm).

    c. Torque, in sequence, to 17–20 ft. lbs. (24–27 Nm).

23. Install the exhaust manifold, if removed from the cylinder head.

24. Connect the exhaust manifold to the exhaust pipe connection. Install the exhaust collector bracket.

25. Install the intake manifold collector and intake manifold collector cover.

26. Connect all the vacuum hoses and water hoses to the intake collector.

27. Refill the cooling system.

28. Connect the negative battery cable.

29. Start the engine check the engine timing. After the engine reaches the normal operating temperature check for the correct coolant level.

30. Road test the vehicle for proper operation.

VE30DE Engine

◆ See Figures 92 thru 109

➡️To remove or install the cylinder head, you'll need a cylinder head bolt tool, No. ST10120000 (J2423901). This tool may be available through aftermarket manufacturers, available at most auto supply stores.

1. Disconnect the negative battery cable for safety purposes.

2. Release the fuel system pressure.

✳✳ CAUTION

Observe all applicable safety precautions when working around fuel. Whenever servicing the fuel system, always work in a well ventilated area. Do not allow fuel spray or vapors to come in contact with a spark or open flame. Keep a dry chemical fire extinguisher near the work area. Always keep fuel in a container specifically designed for fuel storage; also, always properly seal fuel containers to avoid the possibility of fire or explosion.

3. Rotate the crankshaft to position the No. 1 piston on TDC of it's compression stroke.

4. Drain the cooling system. Unplug and label all the electrical connectors, vacuum hoses and water hoses connected to the intake manifold collector.

✳✳ CAUTION

Never open, service or drain the radiator or cooling system when hot; serious burns can occur from the steam and hot coolant. Also, when draining engine coolant, keep in mind that cats and dogs are attracted to ethylene glycol antifreeze and could drink any that is left in an uncovered container or in puddles on the ground. This will prove fatal in sufficient quantities. Always drain coolant into a sealable container.

5. The camshaft position sensor is located in the rear of the left (front) cylinder head. Mark it's position, unplug the electrical connector from it and remove it.

6. Remove the intake manifold collector.

7. Remove the upper timing chain.

➡️Do not rotate either the crankshaft or camshaft from this point onward or the valves could be bent by hitting the pistons.

8. Remove the intake manifold and fuel rail assembly.

9. Remove the exhaust manifold(s)-to-cylinder head(s) bolts and the exhaust manifolds.

10. Remove the camshaft sprockets-to-camshafts bolts and the camshaft sprockets.

11. Remove the exhaust camshafts, the camshaft brackets and the rocker arms.

12. Loosen the cylinder head-to-engine bolts, in sequence, using 2–3 steps. Failure to do this could result in cylinder head warpage.

13. Lift the cylinder head(s) from the engine.

➡️Don't set the cylinder head face down on any surface; the protruding valves could bend. Use small blocks of wood on each side of the head to keep the valves from hitting the work surface.

To install:

14. Scrape the old gasket material away from the cylinder head and the block.

15. Use rubbing alcohol or brake cleaner to clean the gasket mounting surfaces. Inspect the cylinder head(s) for warpage, wear, cracks and/or damage.

16. Apply sealant to the front part of the head gasket, where it seals the timing chain cover. DO NOT apply sealant to any other area of the gasket.

➡️It is suggested, but not required, that the cylinder head bolts be replaced when installing a cylinder head. This will ensure proper torque, preventing any head gasket leakage.

17. Install the cylinder head(s) and torque the head bolts by performing the following procedures:

    a. Torque all bolts, in sequence, to 29 ft. lbs. (39 Nm).

    b. Torque all bolts, in sequence, to 90 ft. lbs. (123 Nm).

    c. Loosen all bolts.

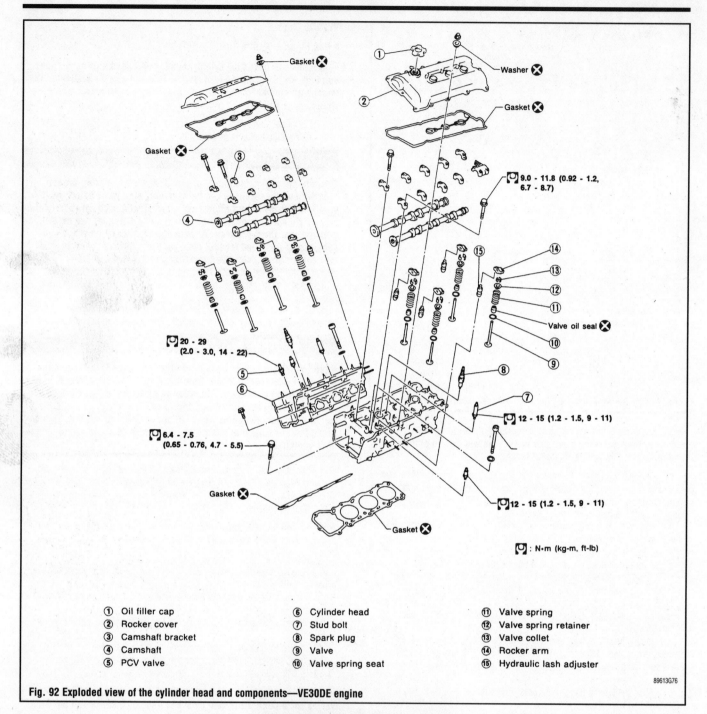

Fig. 92 Exploded view of the cylinder head and components—VE30DE engine

① Oil filler cap
② Rocker cover
③ Camshaft bracket
④ Camshaft
⑤ PCV valve
⑥ Cylinder head
⑦ Stud bolt
⑧ Spark plug
⑨ Valve
⑩ Valve spring seat
⑪ Valve spring
⑫ Valve spring retainer
⑬ Valve collet
⑭ Rocker arm
⑮ Hydraulic lash adjuster

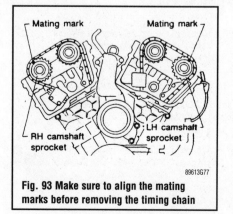

Fig. 93 Make sure to align the mating marks before removing the timing chain

Fig. 94 The exhaust camshafts must be removed to allow access to the cylinder head bolts

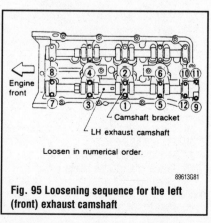

Fig. 95 Loosening sequence for the left (front) exhaust camshaft

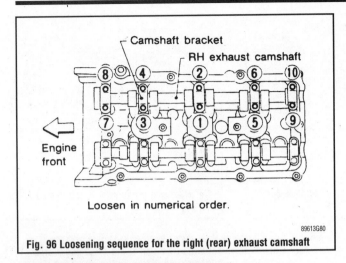

Fig. 96 Loosening sequence for the right (rear) exhaust camshaft

Fig. 97 A large breaker bar will provide the leverage necessary to loosen the cylinder head bolts

Fig. 98 The three small bolts at the front of the cylinder head are easily forgotten; be sure to remove them

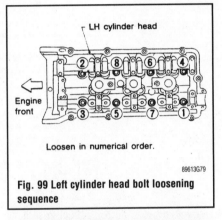

Fig. 99 Left cylinder head bolt loosening sequence

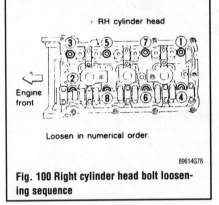

Fig. 100 Right cylinder head bolt loosening sequence

Fig. 101 Be sure to lubricate the head bolt threads when installing the cylinder head to obtain a correct torque reading

Fig. 102 Have an assistant available to aid in removing the cylinder head from the engine block

Fig. 103 Place the cylinder head on blocks as shown to prevent any damage to the valves

Fig. 104 Pull the head gasket from the cylinder block and discard it

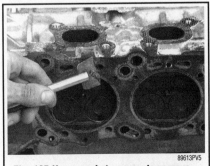

Fig. 105 Use a gasket scraper to remove any residual gasket material from the cylinder head . . .

Fig. 106 . . . and the cylinder block mating surface

Fig. 107 Hold the torque wrench by the handle only; placing a hand on the wrench tube could affect the torque value

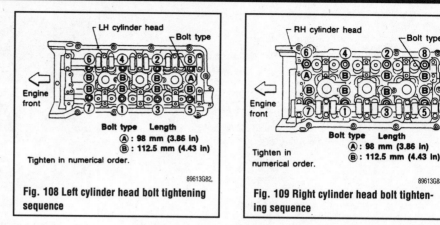

Fig. 108 Left cylinder head bolt tightening sequence

Fig. 109 Right cylinder head bolt tightening sequence

d. Torque all bolts, in sequence, to 25–33 ft. lbs. (34–44 Nm).

e. Torque all bolts, in sequence, to 87–94 ft. lbs. (118–127 Nm).

18. Install the outside cylinder head-to-engine bolts.

19. Install the exhaust camshafts, camshaft brackets and rocker arms; the right exhaust camshaft is identified with **96E RE** and the left exhaust camshaft is identified with **96E LE**.

20. Using a gasket sealant, apply a continuous bead to the mating surface of the left exhaust camshaft end bracket. Torque the exhaust camshaft bracket-to-cylinder head bolts to 6.7–8.7 ft. lbs. (9.0–11.0 Nm).

21. Position the right exhaust camshaft key at about 10 o'clock position and the left camshaft key at about 12 o'clock position.

22. Install the timing chains and sprockets; torque the timing chain sprocket-to-camshaft bolts to 80–87 ft. lbs. (108–118 Nm).

23. Install the exhaust manifold(s) and the exhaust manifold(s)-to-cylinder head(s) bolts.

24. Install the intake manifold and fuel rail assembly.

25. Install the intake manifold collector.

26. Align and install the camshaft position sensor to the rear of the left cylinder head, and connect the electrical connector.

27. Plug in all the electrical connectors, vacuum hoses and water hoses to the intake manifold collector.

28. Refill the cooling system.

29. Connect the negative battery cable.

30. Start the engine check the engine timing. After the engine reaches the normal operating temperature check for the correct coolant level.

31. Road test the vehicle for proper operation.

VQ30DE Engines

▶ **See Figures 110 thru 120**

➡ **To remove or install the cylinder head, you'll need a cylinder head bolt tool, No. ST10120000 (J2423901). This tool may be available through aftermarket manufacturers, available at most auto supply stores.**

1. Relieve the fuel system pressure.

⁑⁑ **CAUTION**

Observe all applicable safety precautions when working around fuel. Whenever servicing the fuel system, always work in a well ventilated area. Do not allow fuel spray or vapors to come in contact with a spark or open flame. Keep a dry chemical fire extinguisher near the work area. Always keep fuel in a container specifically designed for fuel storage; also, always properly seal fuel containers to avoid the possibility of fire or explosion.

2. Disconnect the negative battery cable for safety purposes.

3. Drain the engine oil and the cooling system. Be sure to drain the engine block and the radiator.

⁑⁑ **CAUTION**

Never open, service or drain the radiator or cooling system when hot; serious burns can occur from the steam and hot coolant. Also,

when draining engine coolant, keep in mind that cats and dogs are attracted to ethylene glycol antifreeze and could drink any that is left in an uncovered container or in puddles on the ground. This will prove fatal in sufficient quantities. Always drain coolant into a sealable container.

➡ **Before disconnecting any hoses or connectors, use tape or other means to identify components for reassembly.**

4. Remove the intake manifold collector.

5. Remove the fuel rail assembly.

6. Remove the intake manifold.

7. Remove the cylinder head covers.

8. Remove the drive belts and idler pulley.

9. Remove the steel (lower) and aluminum (upper) oil pans.

10. Remove the water pump cover.

11. Remove the timing chain case cover.

12. Remove the timing chains, camshaft sprockets and related components.

13. Remove the crankshaft sprocket.

14. Loosen the bolts that secure the rear timing chain case. The bolts must be loosened in the reverse order of installation sequence.

15. Using seal cutter tool, remove the rear timing case cover.

➡ **Remove the O-rings from the front of the engine block.**

16. Remove the camshafts. Loosen the camshaft brackets in numerical order in several steps.

17. Remove the cylinder head bolts in the reverse order of the tightening sequence. The bolts should be loosened in 2–3 steps.

⁑⁑ **WARNING**

A warped or cracked cylinder head could result from removing the bolts in incorrect order.

18. Remove the cylinder head(s) from the vehicle.

➡ **Don't set the cylinder head face down on any surface. The protruding valves could bend. Use small blocks of wood on each side of the head to keep the valves from hitting the work surface.**

19. Remove and discard the head gaskets.

20. Remove all traces of liquid gasket from the timing chain case and from the water pump covers.

21. Remove all traces of liquid gasket from the engine block.

22. Inspect the timing chain for excessive wear or damage and replace as necessary.

To install:

23. Turn the crankshaft until the No. 1 piston is set 240 degrees before TDC on compression stroke.

24. Use rubbing alcohol or brake cleaner to clean the gasket mounting surfaces. Inspect the cylinder head(s) for warpage, wear, cracks and/or damage.

25. Using new head gaskets, install the cylinder heads.

➡ **It is suggested, but not required, that the cylinder head bolts be replaced when installing a cylinder head. This will ensure proper torque, preventing any head gasket leakage.**

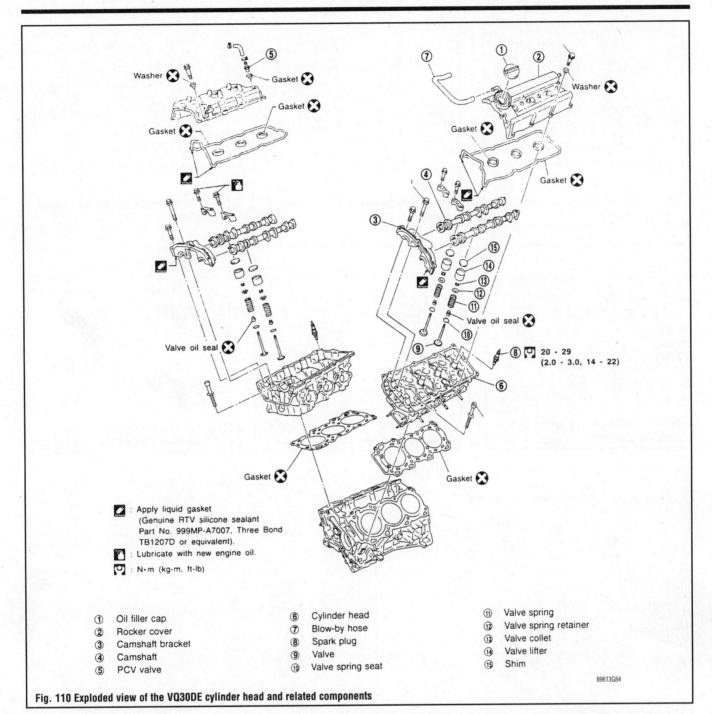

Washer ⊗   ⑤   Gasket ⊗

Gasket ⊗

Gasket ⊗

⑦   ①   ②   Washer ⊗

Gasket ⊗

Gasket ⊗

④

③

⑮
⑭
⑬
⑫
⑪

Valve oil seal ⊗

Valve oil seal ⊗

⑩

⑨

⑧   20 - 29
(2.0 - 3.0, 14 - 22)

⑥

Gasket ⊗   Gasket ⊗

✎ : Apply liquid gasket
(Genuine RTV silicone sealant
Part No. 999MP-A7007, Three Bond
TB1207D or equivalent).

🛢 : Lubricate with new engine oil.

⊙ : N·m (kg-m, ft-lb)

① Oil filler cap
② Rocker cover
③ Camshaft bracket
④ Camshaft
⑤ PCV valve

⑥ Cylinder head
⑦ Blow-by hose
⑧ Spark plug
⑨ Valve
⑩ Valve spring seat

⑪ Valve spring
⑫ Valve spring retainer
⑬ Valve collet
⑭ Valve lifter
⑮ Shim

89613G84

Fig. 110 Exploded view of the VQ30DE cylinder head and related components

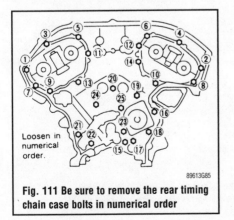

Loosen in
numerical
order.

89613G85

**Fig. 111 Be sure to remove the rear timing
chain case bolts in numerical order**

KV10111100
(J37228)

89613G86

**Fig. 112 Use an oil pan seal cutter to sep-
arate the rear timing chain case from the
engine block**

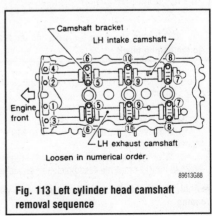

Camshaft bracket

LH intake camshaft

Engine
front

LH exhaust camshaft

Loosen in numerical order.

89613G88

**Fig. 113 Left cylinder head camshaft
removal sequence**

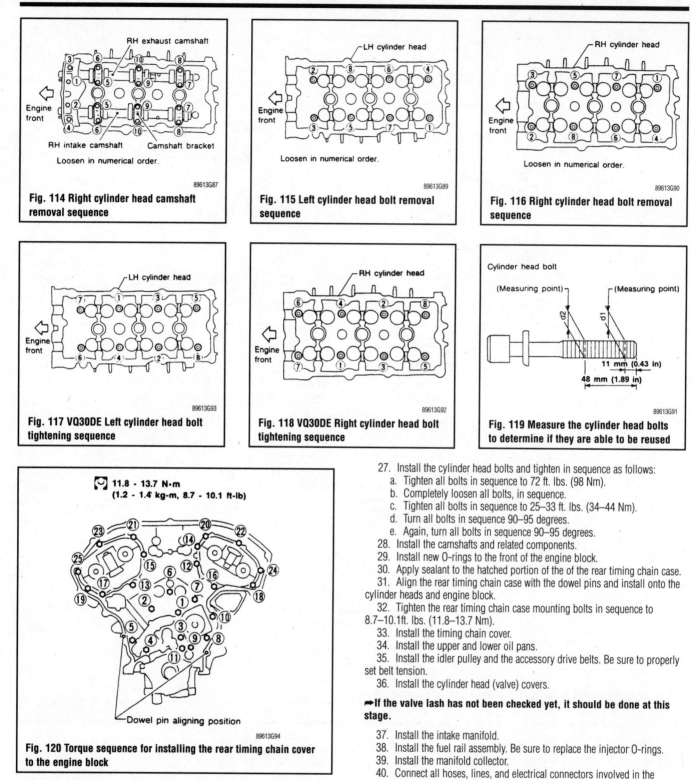

Fig. 114 Right cylinder head camshaft removal sequence

Fig. 115 Left cylinder head bolt removal sequence

Fig. 116 Right cylinder head bolt removal sequence

Fig. 117 VQ30DE Left cylinder head bolt tightening sequence

Fig. 118 VQ30DE Right cylinder head bolt tightening sequence

Fig. 119 Measure the cylinder head bolts to determine if they are able to be reused

Fig. 120 Torque sequence for installing the rear timing chain cover to the engine block

26. If replacement of the head bolts is not possible, perform the following bolt measurement:

   a. Measure the diameter of the head bolt 0.43 in. (11mm) from the bottom of the bolt.

   b. Measure the diameter of the head bolt 1.89 in. (48mm) from the bottom of the bolt.

   c. Whenever the size difference between the two measurements exceeds 0.0043 in. (0.11mm) the head bolts must be replaced.

➡️**Apply fresh oil to the cylinder head bolts to obtain an accurate torque reading.**

27. Install the cylinder head bolts and tighten in sequence as follows:

   a. Tighten all bolts in sequence to 72 ft. lbs. (98 Nm).

   b. Completely loosen all bolts, in sequence.

   c. Tighten all bolts in sequence to 25–33 ft. lbs. (34–44 Nm).

   d. Turn all bolts in sequence 90–95 degrees.

   e. Again, turn all bolts in sequence 90–95 degrees.

28. Install the camshafts and related components.

29. Install new O-rings to the front of the engine block.

30. Apply sealant to the hatched portion of the of the rear timing chain case.

31. Align the rear timing chain case with the dowel pins and install onto the cylinder heads and engine block.

32. Tighten the rear timing chain case mounting bolts in sequence to 8.7–10.1ft. lbs. (11.8–13.7 Nm).

33. Install the timing chain cover.

34. Install the upper and lower oil pans.

35. Install the idler pulley and the accessory drive belts. Be sure to properly set belt tension.

36. Install the cylinder head (valve) covers.

➡️**If the valve lash has not been checked yet, it should be done at this stage.**

37. Install the intake manifold.

38. Install the fuel rail assembly. Be sure to replace the injector O-rings.

39. Install the manifold collector.

40. Connect all hoses, lines, and electrical connectors involved in the removal process.

41. Replace the oil filter, and fill the engine with fresh oil.

42. Fill the coolant system with the proper mix of distilled water and coolant. Bleed the air from the system.

43. Connect the negative battery cable.

44. Start the engine and run at 3000 RPM under no load to purge the air from the high pressure chamber in the timing chain tensioners. The engine may produce a rattling noise. This indicates that air still remains in the chamber and is not a matter of concern.

45. Verify that there are no leaks.

46. Road test the vehicle for proper operation.

Oil Pan

REMOVAL & INSTALLATION

VG30E and VE30DE Engine

▶ See Figures 121 thru 129

1. Raise and safely support the vehicle.
2. Connect a lifting device to the engine and apply upward pressure to take the engine weight off the engine mounts or support the engine by using the crankshaft damper.
3. Remove the oil pan plug and drain the oil into a container.

✳✳ CAUTION

The EPA warns that prolonged contact with used engine oil may cause a number of skin disorders, including cancer! You should make every effort to minimize your exposure to used engine oil. Protective gloves should be worn when changing the oil. Wash your hands and any other exposed skin areas as soon as possible after exposure to used engine oil. Soap and water or waterless hand cleaner should be used.

4. Remove the splash shields from under the engine.
5. Remove the exhaust pipe-to-exhaust manifold bolts and lower the exhaust pipe.
6. Remove the engine mount insulator-to-crossmember nuts and bolts.
7. Remove the center crossmember-to-chassis bolts and the crossmember.
8. Remove the oil pan-to-engine bolts, in sequence.

9. Using the oil pan removal tool KV10111100 or equivalent, separate the oil pan from the engine.

✳✳ WARNING

Do not drive the seal cutter into the oil pump or rear oil seal retainer portion, for the aluminum mating surfaces will be damaged. Do not use a prybar, for the oil pan flange will be deformed. Use caution when pulling the oil pan free from the engine.

To install:
10. Clean the mating surfaces of the engine and oil pan.
11. Apply sealant to the 4 joints on the lower surface of the block. Apply sealant to the corresponding areas of the oil pan gasket on both upper and lower surfaces.
12. Apply a continuous bead of liquid gasket (Nissan part #999MP-A7007 or equivalent RTV silicone sealant) 3.5 to 4.5 mm wide to the mating surface of the oil pan.
13. Install the oil pan and torque the oil pan-to-engine bolts, by reversing the removal sequence, to 5.1–5.8 ft. lbs. (7–8 Nm).
14. Install the exhaust pipe connections.
15. Install the center crossmember. Torque the center crossmember-to-body nuts/bolts and engine mount-to-crossmember nuts/bolts to 57–72 ft. lbs. (77–98 Nm).
16. After 30 minutes of gasket curing time, refill the oil pan with the specified quantity of clean oil. Operate the engine and check for leaks.

✳✳ WARNING

Operating the engine without the proper amount and type of engine oil will result in severe engine damage.

17. Install the splash shields under the vehicle.

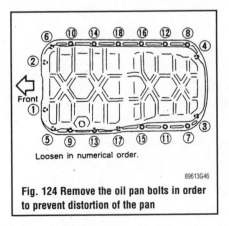

Fig. 121 Disconnect the exhaust pipes at the manifolds and lower the pipe to allow clearance to remove the oil pan

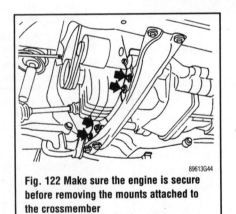

Fig. 122 Make sure the engine is secure before removing the mounts attached to the crossmember

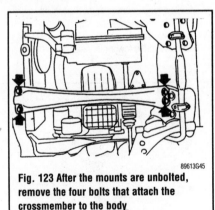

Fig. 123 After the mounts are unbolted, remove the four bolts that attach the crossmember to the body

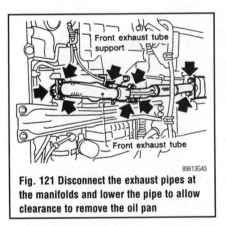

Fig. 124 Remove the oil pan bolts in order to prevent distortion of the pan

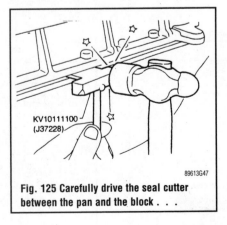

Fig. 125 Carefully drive the seal cutter between the pan and the block . . .

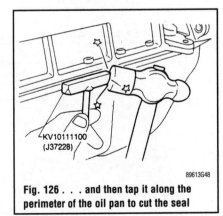

Fig. 126 . . . and then tap it along the perimeter of the oil pan to cut the seal

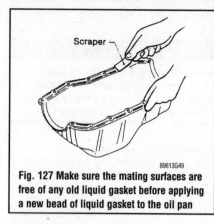

Fig. 127 Make sure the mating surfaces are free of any old liquid gasket before applying a new bead of liquid gasket to the oil pan

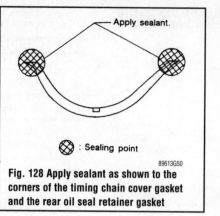

Fig. 128 Apply sealant as shown to the corners of the timing chain cover gasket and the rear oil seal retainer gasket

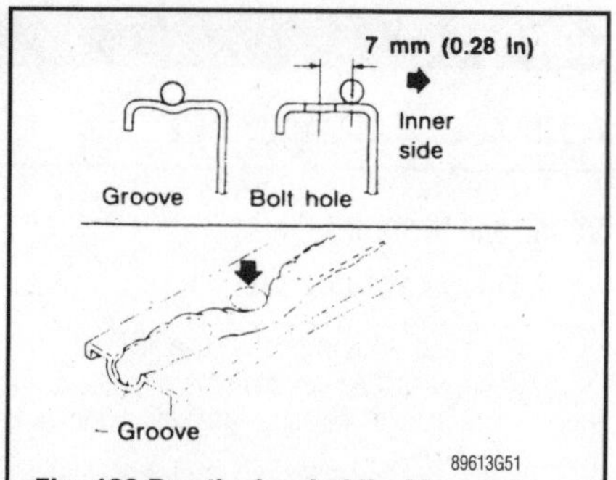

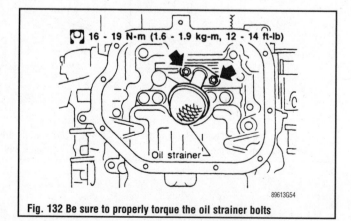

Fig. 129 Run the bead of liquid gasket around the inside of the corners of the bolt holes on the oil pan

VQ30DE Engine

LOWER OIL PAN

♦ See Figures 130 and 131

※※ CAUTION

The EPA warns that prolonged contact with used engine oil may cause a number of skin disorders, including cancer! You should make every effort to minimize your exposure to used engine oil. Protective gloves should be worn when changing the oil. Wash your hands and any other exposed skin areas as soon as possible after exposure to used engine oil. Soap and water, or waterless hand cleaner should be used.

1. Raise and safely support the vehicle.
2. Drain the oil from the engine.
3. Remove the lower splash shields from the vehicle.
4. Remove the lower oil pan bolts, in the reverse order of the tightening sequence.

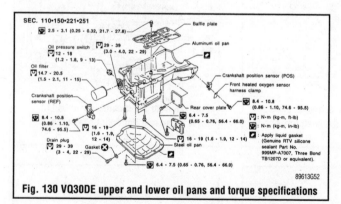

Fig. 130 VQ30DE upper and lower oil pans and torque specifications

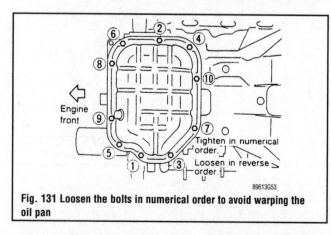

Fig. 131 Loosen the bolts in numerical order to avoid warping the oil pan

5. Using the oil pan gasket separator tool, (Nissan #KV10111100 or equivalent) break the seal between the upper and lower oil pans. Do NOT use a screwdriver to pry on the edge of the pan; the mating surfaces may be deformed.

6. Lower the oil pan from the engine. Keep in mind there may still be some oil in the pan even though the oil has been drained. Have a receptacle handy to drain any excess oil from the pan.

To install:

7. Clean the mating surfaces of the upper and lower oil pans.
8. Apply a continuous bead of liquid gasket (Nissan part #999MP-A7007 or equivalent RTV silicone sealant) 3.5 to 4.5 mm wide to the mating surface of the oil pan.
9. Install the oil pan and torque the oil pan-to-engine bolts, by reversing the removal sequence, to 4.7–5.5 ft.lbs. (6.4–7.5 Nm.).
10. After 30 minutes of gasket curing time, refill the oil pan with the specified quantity of clean oil.
11. Operate the engine and check for leaks.

※※ WARNING

Operating the engine without the proper amount and type of engine oil will result in severe engine damage.

12. Install the splash shields under the vehicle.

UPPER OIL PAN

♦ See Figures 132 thru 141

1. Remove the lower oil pan.
2. Remove the oil strainer from the oil pump housing.
3. Remove the two crankshaft sensors (POS and REF) from the upper oil pan. Use caution when removing the sensors; the edges of the sensors and signal plate teeth can be easily damaged.
4. Disconnect the oil pressure switch.
5. Remove the oil filter.
6. Disconnect the exhaust system header pipe and remove it from the vehicle.

Fig. 132 Be sure to properly torque the oil strainer bolts

7. Using an engine hoist or a jack carefully placed under the crankshaft damper, support the engine so the center member can be removed.

8. Unbolt the front and rear engine mounts, and the bolts that attach the center member to the body. Remove the center member from the vehicle.

9. Remove the accessory drive belts.

10. Unbolt the A/C compressor and mounting bracket. Use wire to hang the A/C compressor in position.

11. Remove the rear cover plate.

12. Remove the upper oil pan-to-engine block bolts, in the sequence shown in the illustration. Take note that the removal sequence differs from the tightening sequence.

13. Remove the transaxle-to-upper oil pan bolts.

14. Using a suitable tool, use the notch on the side of the oil pan to break it free from the engine.

15. Remove and discard the O-rings from the engine block and oil pump body.

To install:

16. Thoroughly clean all traces of liquid gasket from the engine block, oil pan mating surface, and the bolt holes.

17. Apply liquid gasket sealant (Nissan part #999MP-A7007 or equivalent RTV silicone sealant) to the timing chain cover gasket and rear oil seal retainer gasket.

18. Apply A bead of liquid gasket to the mating surface of the upper oil pan.

19. Install new O-Rings on the engine block and oil pump body.

20. Install the upper oil pan to the engine. Torque the bolts to 12–14 ft.lbs (116–19 Nm.) in order as shown in the illustration.

21. Install the bolts that attach the upper oil pan to the transaxle. Torque the bolts to 26–35 ft.lbs (35.1–47.1 Nm.).

22. Install the rear cover plate.

23. Attach the A/C compressor bracket and compressor to the engine. torque the bolts to 34–44 ft. lbs. (45–60 Nm.).

24. Install the accessory drive belts and set them to the proper tension.

25. Install the center member to the engine mounts and to the body. Tighten the bolts and nuts to 57–72 ft. lbs. (77–98 Nm.).

26. Install the two crankshaft position sensors (POS and REF) and the front oxygen sensor harness clamp.

27. Connect the oil pressure switch connector.

28. Install the exhaust header pipe and support. Be sure to use new gaskets to prevent exhaust leaks.

29. Install the oil strainer to the oil pump inlet.

30. Install the lower oil pan.

31. After waiting at least 30 minutes for the liquid gasket to cure, install a new oil filter and fill the engine with fresh oil.

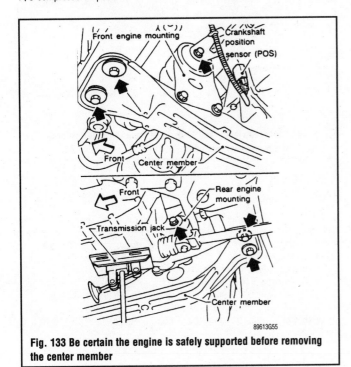

Fig. 133 Be certain the engine is safely supported before removing the center member

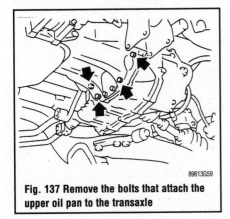

Fig. 134 Remove the bolts (arrows) and hang the A/C compressor aside

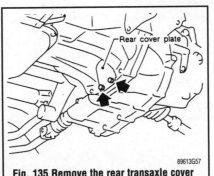

Fig. 135 Remove the rear transaxle cover plate—the bolts attach the upper oil pan to the transaxle

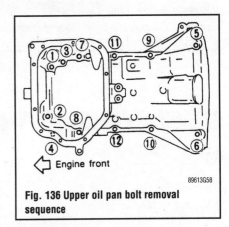

Fig. 136 Upper oil pan bolt removal sequence

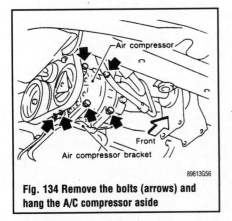

Fig. 137 Remove the bolts that attach the upper oil pan to the transaxle

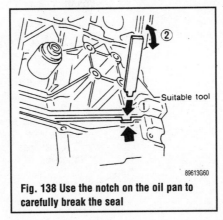

Fig. 138 Use the notch on the oil pan to carefully break the seal

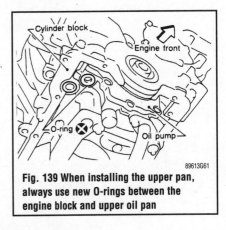

Fig. 139 When installing the upper pan, always use new O-rings between the engine block and upper oil pan

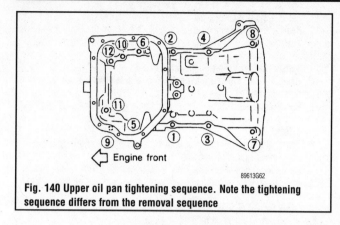

Fig. 140 Upper oil pan tightening sequence. Note the tightening sequence differs from the removal sequence

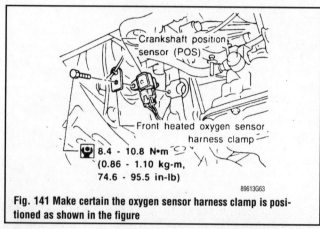

Fig. 141 Make certain the oxygen sensor harness clamp is positioned as shown in the figure

❊❊ WARNING

Operating the engine without the proper amount and type of engine oil will result in severe engine damage.

32. Start the engine and check that there are no leaks from the oil pan mating surfaces.
33. Install the lower splash shields to the vehicle.

Oil Pump

REMOVAL & INSTALLATION

VG30E Engine

▶ See Figure 142

1. Remove all accessory drive belts and the alternator.
2. Remove the timing belt covers and remove the timing belt.
3. Drain the engine oil and remove the oil pan.
4. Remove the oil pump assembly-to-engine bolts, along with the oil strainer, and remove the assembly from the engine.

To install:
5. Pack the oil pump full of petroleum jelly to prevent the pump from cavitating when the engine is started.
6. Install the oil pump and torque the oil pump-to-engine long bolts to 9–12 ft. lbs. (12–16 Nm) and short bolts to 4.3–5.1 ft. lbs. (6–7 Nm).
7. Using a new O-ring, install the strainer and torque the strainer-to-oil pump bolts to 12–15 ft. lbs. (16–21 Nm) and the strainer-to-engine bolt to 4.6–6.1 ft. lbs. (6.3–8.3 Nm).
8. Install the oil pan.
9. Install the timing belt and covers.
10. Install the alternator and all drive belts.
11. Start engine and check for oil leaks.

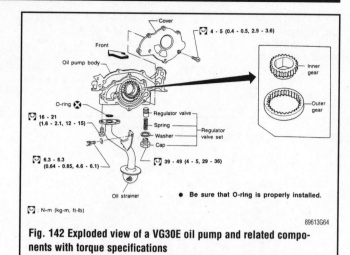

Fig. 142 Exploded view of a VG30E oil pump and related components with torque specifications

VE30DE Engine

▶ See Figure 143

The oil pump is an integral part of the timing chain cover. The cylinder heads and the oil pan must be removed to remove the timing chain cover. Refer to the Timing Chain heading within this section for information on removal of the timing chain cover.

1. Remove all accessory drive belts and the alternator.
2. Remove the cylinder heads.
3. Remove the crankshaft damper-to-crankshaft bolt and the damper.
4. Drain the engine oil and remove the oil pan.
5. Remove the oil strainer-to-engine bolt, oil strainer-to-oil pump bolts and the strainer.
6. Remove the timing chain cover-to-engine bolts and the timing chain cover.
7. Remove the oil pump assembly-to-engine bolts, along with the oil strainer, and remove the assembly from the timing chain cover.
8. Clean the gasket mating surfaces.

To install:
9. Pack the oil pump full of petroleum jelly to prevent the pump from cavitating when the engine is started.
10. Apply a bead of liquid sealant to the timing chain cover mating surfaces.
11. Install the oil pump to the timing chain cover.
12. Install the timing chain cover and torque the timing chain cover-to-engine bolts to 4.6–6.1 ft. lbs. (6.3–8.3 Nm) except for bolt above oil filter housing and 12–15 ft. lbs. (16–21 Nm) for bolt above oil filter housing.
13. Using a new gasket, install the strainer and torque the strainer-to-timing chain cover bolts to 12–15 ft. lbs. (16–21 Nm) and the strainer-to-engine bolt to 4.6–6.1 ft. lbs. (6.3–8.3 Nm).
14. Install the oil pan.
15. Install the cylinder heads.
16. Install the alternator and all drive belts.
17. Start engine and check for oil leaks.

VQ30DE Engine

▶ See Figure 144

The oil pump on the VQ30DE engine is located on the crankshaft behind the timing chain cover. The oil pans and the timing chain cover and timing chain must be removed to access the oil pump.

1. Remove the upper and lower oil pans.
2. Remove the water pump cover.
3. Remove the timing chain cover.
4. Remove the timing chain.
5. Unbolt the oil pump strainer.
6. Unbolt the oil pump assembly from the engine block.

To install:
7. Pack the oil pump full of petroleum jelly to prevent the pump from cavitating when the engine is started.
8. Bolt the oil pump assembly to the engine block. Torque the bolts to 74.6–95.5 in.lbs. (8.43–10.8 Nm.).

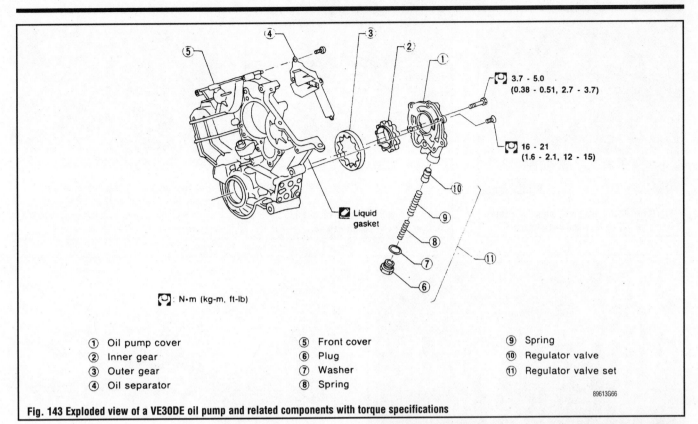

Fig. 143 Exploded view of a VE30DE oil pump and related components with torque specifications

Torque specifications shown:
- 3.7 - 5.0 (0.38 - 0.51, 2.7 - 3.7)
- 16 - 21 (1.6 - 2.1, 12 - 15)

: N·m (kg-m, ft-lb)

Liquid gasket

1. Oil pump cover
2. Inner gear
3. Outer gear
4. Oil separator
5. Front cover
6. Plug
7. Washer
8. Spring
9. Spring
10. Regulator valve
11. Regulator valve set

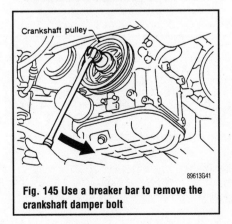

Fig. 144 Exploded view of a VQ30DE oil pump and related components with torque specifications

Labels:
- Oil pump body
- Outer gear
- Inner gear
- Oil pump cover
- 8.43 - 10.8 (0.86 - 1.10, 74.6 - 95.5)
- Gasket
- Oil strainer
- O-ring
- Regulator valve
- Regulator valve set
- Spring
- Regulator plug
- 16 - 19 (1.6 - 1.9, 12 - 14)
- 5.9 - 7.9 (0.60 - 0.81, 52.1 - 70.3)
- 39 - 69 (4.0 - 7.0, 29 - 51)
- : N·m (kg-m, in-lb)
- : N·m (kg-m, ft-lb)

9. Install the oil strainer. Be sure to use a new gasket.
10. Install the timing chain.
11. Install the timing chain cover.
12. Install the water pump cover.
13. Install the upper and lower oil pans.

Crankshaft Damper/Pulley

REMOVAL & INSTALLATION

◆ See Figures 145 thru 151

1. Remove the drive belts from the crankshaft damper.
2. Remove the crankshaft damper-to-crankshaft bolt. Hold the crankshaft stationary by placing a suitable tool in the ring gear teeth on the flywheel.
3. Remove the crankshaft damper from the crankshaft by pulling it straight off the shaft. A puller may be required to remove the damper from the shaft. Be careful not to lose the woodruff key when removing the crankshaft damper.

➡ If working on a VE30DE or VQ30DE engine, it would be a good idea to replace the crankshaft oil seal when the crankshaft damper is removed.

To install:

4. Install the crankshaft damper onto the shaft, making sure the woodruff key is in place. Dip the damper bolt in fresh oil and torque the crankshaft damper-to-crankshaft bolt to the following specifications:
- VG30E engine—90–98 ft.lbs. (123–132 Nm.)
- VE30DE engine—123–130 ft.lbs. (167–177 Nm.)

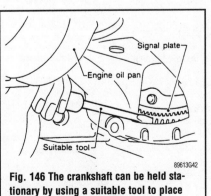

Fig. 145 Use a breaker bar to remove the crankshaft damper bolt

Fig. 146 The crankshaft can be held stationary by using a suitable tool to place between the flywheel teeth

Fig. 147 Be sure to lubricate the threads of the crankshaft damper bolt to obtain a proper torque reading

Fig. 148 The crankshaft damper can sometimes be pulled from the shaft by hand

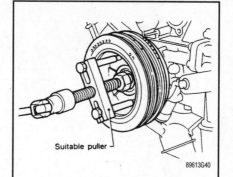

Fig. 149 A puller may be required to remove the crankshaft damper

Fig. 150 The timing chain cover oil seal should be replaced whenever the crankshaft damper is removed; this seal is leaking severely

Fig. 151 This crankshaft damper may have a problem sealing properly due to the groove that was worn into it from the seal

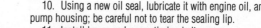

Fig. 152 Exploded view of VG30E timing belt and related components

• VQ30DE engine—29–36 ft.lbs. (39–49 Nm.) followed by 60–66° clockwise angle torque

5. Install the drive belts to the crankshaft damper; be sure to properly set belt tension.

Timing Belt Cover and Seal

REMOVAL & INSTALLATION

VG30E Engine

▶ See Figures 152 and 153

1. Raise and safely support the vehicle.
2. Remove the engine under covers and drain engine coolant from the radiator; be careful not to allow coolant to contact drive belts.
3. Remove the front right side wheel and tire assembly. Remove the engine side cover.
4. Remove the engine coolant reservoir tank and radiator hoses.
5. Remove the A.S.C.D. (speed control device) actuator.
6. Remove all the drive belts from the engine. When removing the power steering drive belt, loosen the idler pulley from the right side wheel housing.
7. Remove the idler bracket of the A/C compressor drive belt.
8. Remove the crankshaft damper and the woodruff key. Remove the timing belt covers.
9. Using a prybar, pry the oil seal from the oil pump; be careful not to scratch the crankshaft or oil pump housing sealing surface.

To install:

10. Using a new oil seal, lubricate it with engine oil, and press it into the oil pump housing; be careful not to tear the sealing lip.
11. Install lower and upper timing belt covers.
12. Install crankshaft damper and idler bracket of the compressor drive belt. Tighten the crankshaft damper bolt to 90–98 ft. lbs. (123–132 Nm).
13. Install the drive belts.
14. Install the coolant reservoir tank, radiator hoses, A.S.C.D. actuator.
15. Install the right front wheel. Install engine under cover and side covers.
16. Refill the cooling system.
17. Check ignition timing and road test for proper operation.

Timing Chain Cover and Seal

REMOVAL & INSTALLATION

VE30DE Engine

The timing chain (front) cover is an integral part of the oil pump housing. The cylinder heads and the oil pan must be removed in order for the timing chain cover to be removed. Refer to the Timing Chain procedure in this section for removal of the timing chain cover.

➡The front crankshaft seal can be replaced without removing the timing chain cover.

1. Using a small prybar, pry the oil seal from the timing chain cover; be careful not to scratch the timing chain cover sealing surface.
2. Using a new oil seal, lubricate it with engine oil and press it into the timing chain cover.

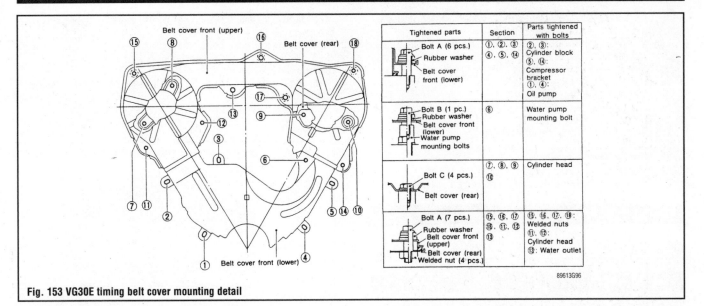

Tightened parts	Section	Parts tightened with bolts
Bolt A (6 pcs.) Rubber washer Belt cover front (lower)	①, ②, ③ ④, ⑤, ⑭	②, ③: Cylinder block ⑤, ⑭: Compressor bracket ①, ④: Oil pump
Bolt B (1 pc.) Rubber washer Belt cover front (lower) Water pump mounting bolts	⑥	Water pump mounting bolt
Bolt C (4 pcs.) Belt cover (rear)	⑦, ⑧, ⑨ ⑩	Cylinder head
Bolt A (7 pcs.) Rubber washer Belt cover front (upper) Belt cover (rear) Welded nut (4 pcs.)	⑮, ⑯, ⑰ ⑱, ⑪, ⑫ ⑬	⑮, ⑯, ⑰, ⑱: Welded nuts ⑪, ⑫: Cylinder head ⑬: Water outlet

89613G96

Fig. 153 VG30E timing belt cover mounting detail

3. When installing the timing chain cover; be careful not to tear the oil seal's sealing lip on the crankshaft.

VQ30DE Engine

♦ See Figures 154, 155, 156 and 157

The engine mount on the front (passenger side) of the engine and the lower and upper oil pans must be removed to remove the timing chain cover.

Refer to the Oil Pan Procedure and the Timing Chain procedure for more information.

1. Raise and safely support the front of the vehicle securely on jackstands.
2. Drain the engine oil and coolant from the engine.
3. Remove the splash shields from under the vehicle.
4. Remove the drive belts and the idler pulley bracket.
5. Remove the power steering pump.
6. Remove the camshaft and crankshaft position sensors.

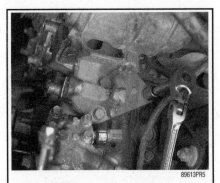

Fig. 154 Unbolt the A/C compressor bracket from the engine . . .

Fig. 155 . . . and use wire to support it while unbolted

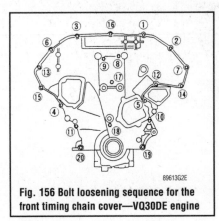

Fig. 156 Bolt loosening sequence for the front timing chain cover—VQ30DE engine

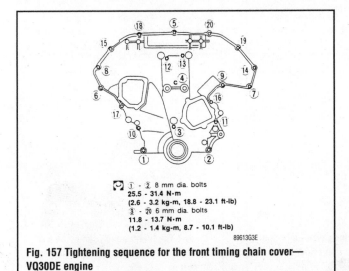

① - ② 8 mm dia. bolts
25.5 - 31.4 N·m
(2.6 - 3.2 kg-m, 18.8 - 23.1 ft-lb)
③ - ⑳ 6 mm dia. bolts
11.8 - 13.7 N·m
(1.2 - 1.4 kg-m, 8.7 - 10.1 ft-lb)

89613G3E

Fig. 157 Tightening sequence for the front timing chain cover—VQ30DE engine

7. Remove the intake manifold collector.
8. Remove the crankshaft damper.
9. Remove the air conditioning compressor and bracket. Use safety wire to support it while it is unbolted from the engine.
10. Remove the lower and upper oil pans.
11. Remove the water pump cover.
12. Remove the timing chain cover bolts, in the sequence shown in the illustration.
13. Using the notch on the top of the timing chain case, insert a suitable tool and carefully separate the front timing chain cover from the rear cover.
14. Using a small prybar, pry the oil seal from the timing chain cover; be careful not to scratch the timing chain cover sealing surface.
15. Using a new oil seal, lubricate it with engine oil and press it into the timing chain cover so the seal is flush with the cover surface. Be sure to apply a small amount of grease to the inner lip of the seal upon installation of the cover.

To install:

16. Clean the gasket material from the front and rear timing chain cases, including the bolt holes.
17. Apply liquid gasket to the timing chain cover.

18. Following the tightening sequence shown in the illustration, tighten the timing chain cover bolts to the specified torque.

19. Apply liquid gasket to the water pump cover and install it to the front timing chain cover.

20. Install the upper and lower oil pans.

21. Install the exhaust header pipe.

22. Install the engine mount and bracket.

23. Install the center member assembly. Remove the engine from the hoist.

24. Install the crankshaft damper.

25. Install the crankshaft and camshaft position sensors.

26. Install the A/C compressor and bracket to the engine block.

27. Install the power steering pump.

28. Install the accessory drive belts and the idler pulley.

29. Fill the engine with the appropriate quantity of engine oil and coolant.

Timing Belt

REMOVAL & INSTALLATION

✳✳ WARNING

Timing belt maintenance is extremely important! VG30E engines utilize an interference-type, non-free-wheeling engine. If the timing belt breaks, the valves in the cylinder head may strike the pistons, causing potentially serious (also time-consuming and expensive) engine damage. The recommended replacement interval for the timing belt is 60,000 miles (96,000 km), or sooner.

VG30E Engine

▶ See Figures 158 thru 164

1. Raise and safely support the vehicle.

2. Remove the engine under covers and drain engine coolant from the radiator; be careful not to allow coolant to contact drive belts.

3. Remove the front right side wheel and tire assembly. Remove the engine side cover.

4. Remove the drive belts from the engine.

5. Rotate the crankshaft to position the No. 1 cylinder at the TDC of it's compression stroke.

6. Remove the upper radiator hose and the water inlet hose. Remove the water pump pulley.

7. Remove the idler bracket of the compressor drive belt.

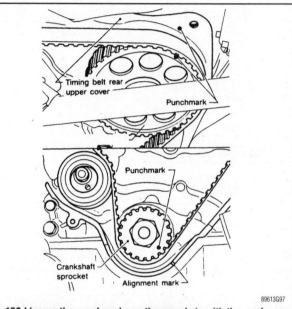

Fig. 158 Line up the punchmarks on the sprockets with the marks on the rear timing belt cover before removal of the belt

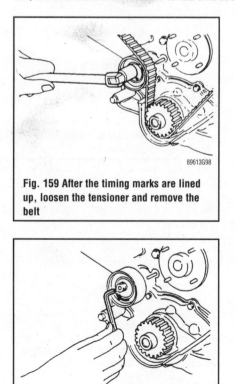

Fig. 159 After the timing marks are lined up, loosen the tensioner and remove the belt

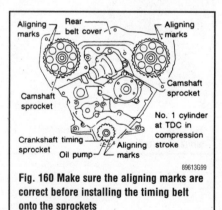

Fig. 160 Make sure the aligning marks are correct before installing the timing belt onto the sprockets

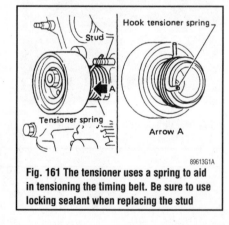

Fig. 161 The tensioner uses a spring to aid in tensioning the timing belt. Be sure to use locking sealant when replacing the stud

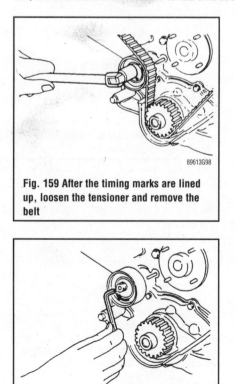

Fig. 162 Lock the tensioner in position after turning it clockwise to allow for belt installation

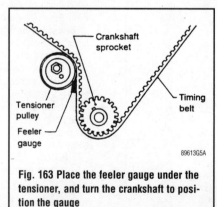

Fig. 163 Place the feeler gauge under the tensioner, and turn the crankshaft to position the gauge

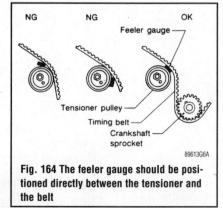

Fig. 164 The feeler gauge should be positioned directly between the tensioner and the belt

8. Remove the crankshaft damper. It may be necessary to use a puller to remove the crankshaft damper from the crankshaft.

9. Remove the upper and lower timing belt covers.

10. Make sure the punch marks on the camshaft sprockets align with the punch marks on the rear timing belt cover and the punch mark on the crankshaft sprocket aligns with the punch mark on the oil pump.

11. Loosen the timing belt idler pulley bolt. Using a hexagon wrench, rotate the idler pulley to release it's tension and remove the timing belt.

➡ **Be careful not to bend the new belt installing it. Timing belts are designed to flex only the way they turn around the pulleys.**

To install:

➡ **After removing timing belt, do not rotate crankshaft and camshaft separately, because valves will hit piston heads.**

12. Confirm that No. 1 cylinder is at TDC on its compression stroke. Install tensioner and tensioner spring. If stud is removed apply locking sealant to threads before installing.

13. Swing tensioner fully clockwise with hexagon wrench and temporarily tighten locknut.

14. Set timing belt, align the arrow on the timing belt forward. Align the white lines on the timing belt with the punch marks on all 3 pulleys.

➡ **There are 133 total timing belt teeth. If timing belt is installed correctly there will be 40 teeth between left and right camshaft sprocket timing marks. There will be 43 teeth between left camshaft sprocket and crankshaft sprocket timing marks.**

15. Loosen tensioner locknut, keeping tensioner steady with a hexagon wrench.

16. Swing tensioner 70–80° clockwise with hexagon wrench and temporarily tighten locknut.

17. Remove the spark plugs. Turn crankshaft clockwise 2–3 times, then slowly set No. 1 cylinder at TDC on its compression stroke.

18. Push middle of timing belt between right camshaft sprocket and tensioner pulley with a force of 22 lbs. (98 N).

19. Loosen tensioner locknut, keeping tensioner steady with a hexagon wrench.

20. Using a feeler gauge or equivalent, which is 0.0138 in. (0.35mm) thick and 0.500 in. (13mm) wide, set the gauge at the bottom of tensioner pulley and timing belt. Turn crankshaft clockwise and position the gauge completely between tensioner pulley and timing belt. The timing belt will move about 2.5 teeth.

21. Tighten tensioner locknut, keeping tensioner steady with a hexagon wrench.

22. Turn crankshaft clockwise or counterclockwise and remove the gauge.

23. Rotate the engine 3 times, then set No. 1 at TDC on its compression stroke. Verify that the marks line up in the proper positions on the sprockets.

24. Measure the deflection of the timing belt between the two camshaft sprockets. The belt should deflect 0.51–0.59 in. (13–15 mm) with 22 lbs. of force. If the tension is incorrect, reset the tension as required.

25. Install the upper and lower belt covers.

26. Install the crankshaft damper.

27. Install the idler bracket of the A/C compressor drive belt.

28. Install the upper radiator hose and the water inlet hose. Install the water pump pulley.

29. Install the drive belts from the engine. Be sure to properly set the belt tension.

30. Install the front right side wheel and tire assembly.

31. Install the engine splash shield.

32. Refill the engine with the proper quantity of coolant.

33. Start the engine and check for proper operation.

Timing Chain and Sprockets

REMOVAL & INSTALLATION

VE30DE Engine

▶ **See Figures 165 thru 190**

➡ **The cylinder heads and the oil pan must be removed in order for the lower timing chain to be removed.**

1. Remove the upper intake manifold collector.

2. Remove the fuel rail.

3. Remove the valve covers.

4. Remove the upper chain guides between the camshafts.

5. Remove the upper chain covers on the cylinder heads.

6. Set the number one piston at TDC on the compression stroke by aligning the timing marks on the crankshaft damper.

7. Check that the mating marks on the sprockets are aligned as shown in the illustration. If not, the crankshaft should be rotated another 360°.

8. Remove the camshaft position sensor. Mark the position of the sensor before removal to help keep the ignition timing correct.

9. Remove the upper chain tensioners.

10. Using a back up wrench, remove the bolts which retain the camshaft sprockets.

11. Remove the exhaust camshafts. Follow the numerical sequence.

12. Remove the both cylinder heads.

13. Remove the oil pan.

14. Remove the crankshaft damper.

15. Remove the water pipe.

16. Remove the water pump pulley and the water pump.

17. Remove the oil pan, the crankshaft damper, the oil strainer and the oil filter bracket.

18. Remove the timing chain cover, the alternator adjusting bar and the upper timing chains.

19. Remove the lower timing chain guides, the idler sprockets and the lower timing chain.

To install:

20. Install the crankshaft sprocket on the crankshaft.

21. Make sure the No. 1 cylinder is at the TDC of it's compression stroke.

22. Install the right idler sprocket and timing chain guides.

23. Position the lower timing chain on the right idler sprocket by aligning the mating mark on the right idler sprocket with the silver mating mark on the lower timing chain.

24. Install the left idler sprocket with the lower timing chain; align the mating marks on the lower timing chain with the mating marks on the left idler sprocket and crankshaft sprocket. Install the chain guide and the chain tensioner.

25. Position the upper timing chains on the idler sprockets by aligning the mating marks on the idler sprockets with the gold mating marks on the upper timing chains.

26. Install the oil pump drive spacer, the timing chain cover and the alternator adjusting bar by performing the following procedures:

a. Remove all traces of sealant from the mating surfaces of the timing chain cover and the engine block.

b. Using liquid sealant, apply a continuous bead to the mating surface of the timing chain cover.

c. Wipe excessive sealant from the cylinder head mounting surfaces.

27. Install the oil filter bracket, the oil strainer, the crankshaft damper and the oil pan.

28. Install the water pump by performing the following procedures:

a. Remove all traces of sealant from the mating surface of the water pump.

b. Remove all traces of sealant from the mating surface of the engine.

c. Using liquid sealant, apply a continuous bead to the mating surface of the water pump.

29. Install the water pump pulley.

30. Install the water pipe by performing the following procedures:

a. Torque bolt **a** and **b** finger-tight.

b. Torque bolt **c** to 12–15 ft. lbs. (16–21 Nm).

c. Torque bolt **a** to 2.2–6.5 ft. lbs. (3–9 Nm).

d. Torque bolt **b** to 12–15 ft. lbs. (16–21 Nm).

e. Torque bolt **a** to 12–15 ft. lbs. (16–21 Nm).

31. Rotate the crankshaft counterclockwise, until the No. 1 piston is set at approx. 120° before TDC on the compression stroke, to prevent interference of the valves and pistons.

32. Install the cylinder heads.

33. Install the camshafts, the camshaft brackets and the rocker arms.

34. Position the right side exhaust camshaft at about 10 o'clock position and the left side exhaust camshaft at about 12 o'clock position.

35. Install the right side VTC assembly and the right camshaft sprocket. Align the mating marks on the right upper timing chain with the mating marks on the right VTC assembly and the right camshaft sprocket.

36. Install the right timing chain tensioner. Before installing the chain ten-

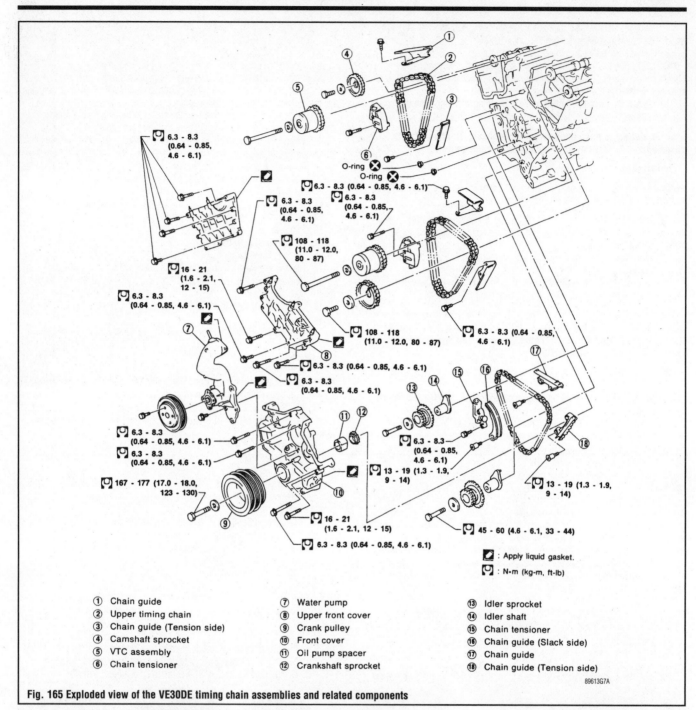

6.3 - 8.3
(0.64 - 0.85,
4.6 - 6.1)

6.3 - 8.3 (0.64 - 0.85, 4.6 - 6.1)

6.3 - 8.3
(0.64 - 0.85,
4.6 - 6.1)

6.3 - 8.3
(0.64 - 0.85,
4.6 - 6.1)

O-ring

O-ring

108 - 118
(11.0 - 12.0,
80 - 87)

16 - 21
(1.6 - 2.1,
12 - 15)

6.3 - 8.3
(0.64 - 0.85, 4.6 - 6.1)

108 - 118
(11.0 - 12.0, 80 - 87)

6.3 - 8.3 (0.64 - 0.85,
4.6 - 6.1)

6.3 - 8.3 (0.64 - 0.85, 4.6 - 6.1)

6.3 - 8.3
(0.64 - 0.85, 4.6 - 6.1)

6.3 - 8.3
(0.64 - 0.85, 4.6 - 6.1)

6.3 - 8.3
(0.64 - 0.85,
4.6 - 6.1)

6.3 - 8.3
(0.64 - 0.85, 4.6 - 6.1)

13 - 19 (1.3 - 1.9,
9 - 14)

13 - 19 (1.3 - 1.9,
9 - 14)

167 - 177 (17.0 - 18.0,
123 - 130)

16 - 21
(1.6 - 2.1, 12 - 15)

45 - 60 (4.6 - 6.1, 33 - 44)

6.3 - 8.3 (0.64 - 0.85, 4.6 - 6.1)

: Apply liquid gasket.

: N·m (kg-m, ft-lb)

① Chain guide
② Upper timing chain
③ Chain guide (Tension side)
④ Camshaft sprocket
⑤ VTC assembly
⑥ Chain tensioner
⑦ Water pump
⑧ Upper front cover
⑨ Crank pulley
⑩ Front cover
⑪ Oil pump spacer
⑫ Crankshaft sprocket
⑬ Idler sprocket
⑭ Idler shaft
⑮ Chain tensioner
⑯ Chain guide (Slack side)
⑰ Chain guide
⑱ Chain guide (Tension side)

89613G7A

Fig. 165 Exploded view of the VE30DE timing chain assemblies and related components

89613PS5

Fig. 166 Remove the three bolts retaining the upper chain guides . . .

89613PS6

Fig. 167 . . . and lift it from the cylinder head

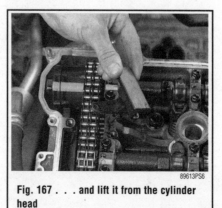

89613PT1

Fig. 168 To allow access to the camshaft sprocket bolts, unbolt the upper timing chain cover . . .

Fig. 169 . . . and carefully pry the cover away from the cylinder head

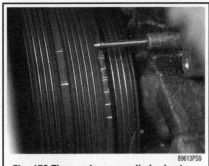

Fig. 170 The number one cylinder is at TDC when the timing marks are aligned as shown

Fig. 171 It may be helpful to paint marks on the chain and sprockets if the marks are not easily visible

Fig. 172 Remove the two bolts attaching the upper timing chain tensioners

Fig. 173 When installing the chain tensioners, carefully press the tensioner in and lock it in position with the clip

Fig. 174 Always use a back up wrench on the camshaft when removing the sprocket bolts; NEVER use the chain to provide tension

Fig. 175 Remove the intake and exhaust camshaft sprockets and set the timing chain under the camshafts

Fig. 176 Always lubricate the threads of the camshaft sprocket bolts to obtain a correct torque reading

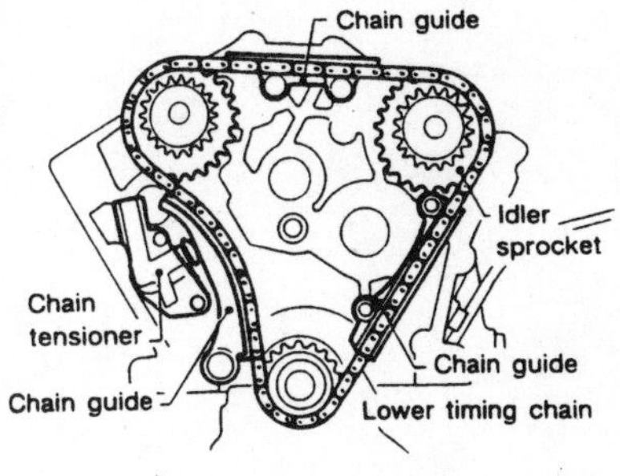

Fig. 177 Lower timing chain and related components

sioner, press-in sleeve until the hook can be engaged on the pin; make sure the hook used to retain the chain tensioner is released.

➡ There are 2 types of chain tensioners; be careful not to install the left chain tensioner onto the right cylinder head.

37. Rotate the crankshaft clockwise to set the No. 1 piston at the TDC of it's compression stroke.

38. Install the left side VTC assembly and the left camshaft sprocket. Align the mating marks on the left upper timing chain with the mating marks on the left VTC assembly and the left camshaft sprocket.

39. Install the left chain tensioner; make sure the upper timing chains are in the correct positions.

40. Install the camshaft position sensor; make sure the position of the camshaft and rotor position of the camshaft position sensor are aligned.

41. Install the upper timing chain covers.

42. Install the upper chain guides on both cylinder heads.

43. Install the valve covers.

44. Install any parts removed in the reverse order of removal. When installing the VTC solenoid valve, always use new O-rings and lubricate the O-rings with engine oil.

VQ30DE Engine

◆ See Figures 191 thru 204

1. Drain the engine oil and coolant from the engine.
2. Remove the splash shields from under the vehicle.
3. Remove the drive belts and the idler pulley bracket.
4. Remove the power steering pump.
5. Remove the camshaft and crankshaft position sensors.
6. Remove the intake manifold collector.
7. Remove the fuel rail assembly.
8. Remove the valve covers from the cylinder heads.
9. Set the number 1 piston at Top Dead Center (TDC) on the compression stroke by rotating the crankshaft until the marks are in line. The cam lobes for the number 1 cylinder should be pointing outward. Do not rotate the engine from this step onward.

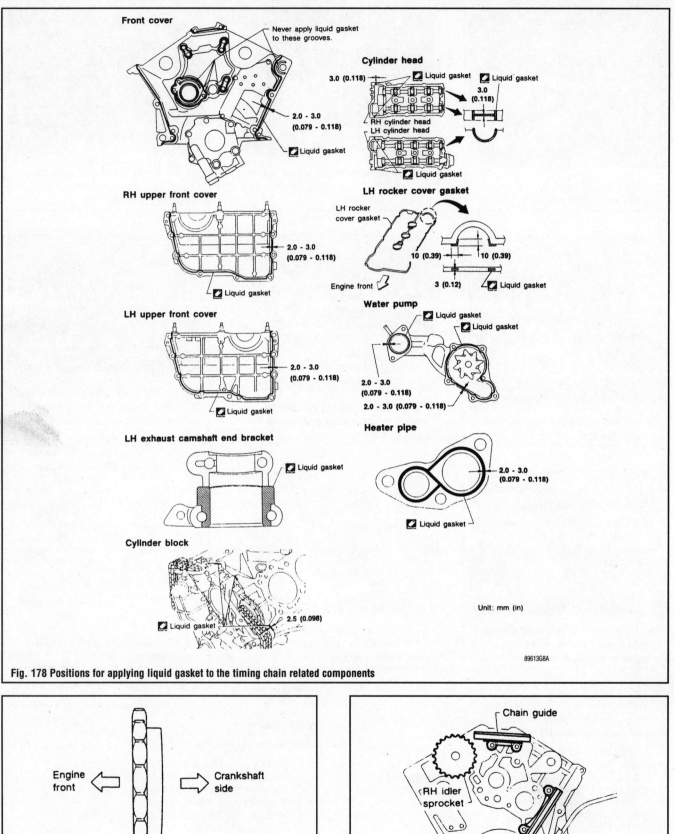

Front cover

Never apply liquid gasket to these grooves.

2.0 - 3.0
(0.079 - 0.118)

Liquid gasket

Cylinder head

3.0 (0.118) Liquid gasket Liquid gasket

3.0
(0.118)

RH cylinder head
LH cylinder head

Liquid gasket

RH upper front cover

2.0 - 3.0
(0.079 - 0.118)

Liquid gasket

LH rocker cover gasket

LH rocker
cover gasket

10 (0.39) 10 (0.39)

Engine front

3 (0.12) Liquid gasket

LH upper front cover

2.0 - 3.0
(0.079 - 0.118)

Liquid gasket

Water pump

Liquid gasket
Liquid gasket

2.0 - 3.0
(0.079 - 0.118)

2.0 - 3.0 (0.079 - 0.118)

LH exhaust camshaft end bracket

Liquid gasket

Heater pipe

2.0 - 3.0
(0.079 - 0.118)

Liquid gasket

Cylinder block

Unit: mm (in)

Liquid gasket 2.5 (0.098)

89613G8A

Fig. 178 Positions for applying liquid gasket to the timing chain related components

Engine
front Crankshaft
side

Crankshaft sprocket

89613G2B

Fig. 179 Make sure the crankshaft sprocket is installed in the proper direction

Chain guide

RH idler
sprocket

Chain guide

89613G1B

Fig. 180 Install the lower timing chain guides and the right side idler sprocket to the engine block

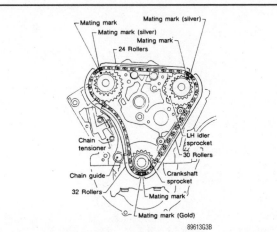

Fig. 181 Line up the mating marks on the lower timing chain with the marks on the sprockets

10. Remove the crankshaft damper.

11. Remove the air conditioning compressor and bracket. Use safety wire to support it while it is unbolted from the engine.

12. Remove the water pump cover.

13. Remove the timing chain cover bolts, in the sequence shown in the illustration.

14. Using the notch on the top of the timing chain case, insert a suitable tool and carefully separate the timing chain front cover from the rear cover.

15. Remove the internal chain guide and the upper chain guide.

16. Remove the timing chain tensioner and slack side chain guide. Use a pin to retain the timing chain tensioner.

17. Remove the right and left hand sprocket 1ST bolts.

18. Mark the sprockets and the chain with paint for proper alignment during installation.

19. Remove the sprockets and the timing chain.

20. Remove the lower chain guide near the crankshaft.

21. Using small pins, push the camshaft tensioners inward and lock them in place.

22. Apply paint to the camshaft sprockets and chains to mark their positions for proper alignment during installation.

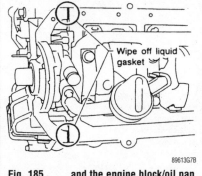

Fig. 182 Have an assistant hold the upper timing chains in position while installing the lower timing chain cover

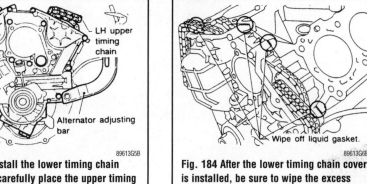

Fig. 183 Install the lower timing chain cover and carefully place the upper timing chains over the sprockets

Fig. 184 After the lower timing chain cover is installed, be sure to wipe the excess liquid gasket from the cylinder heads . . .

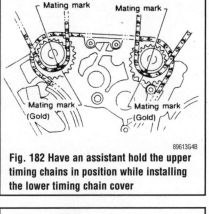

Fig. 185 . . . and the engine block/oil pan mating surface

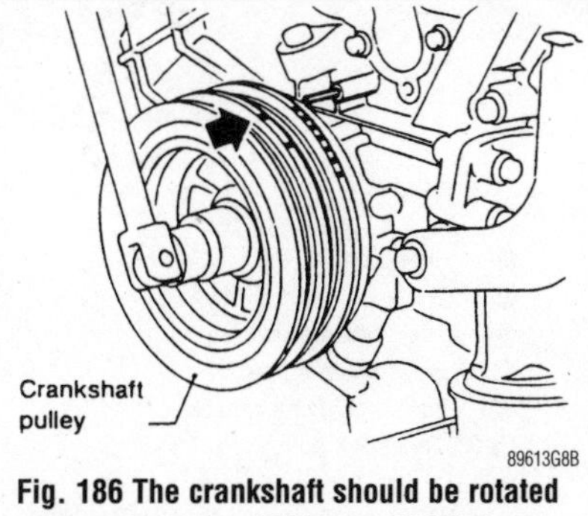

Fig. 186 The crankshaft should be rotated counterclockwise 120° from TDC before cylinder head installation

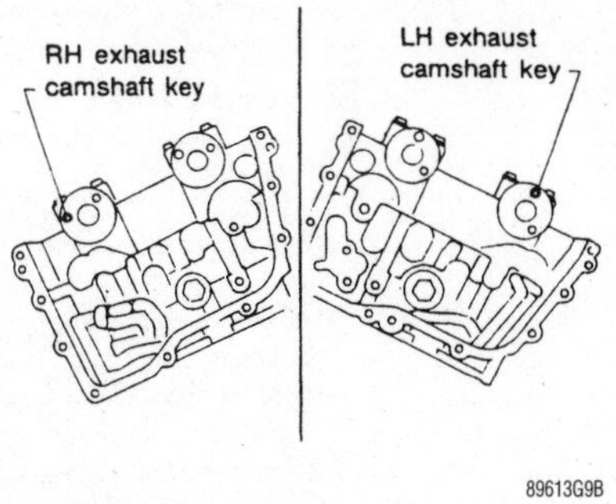

Fig. 187 Position the camshafts as shown before tightening the brackets

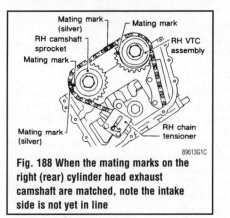

Fig. 188 When the mating marks on the right (rear) cylinder head exhaust camshaft are matched, note the intake side is not yet in line

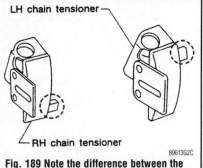

Fig. 189 Note the difference between the two upper chain tensioners; be careful not to install them incorrectly

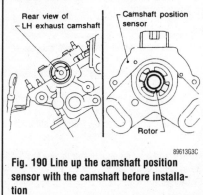

Fig. 190 Line up the camshaft position sensor with the camshaft before installation

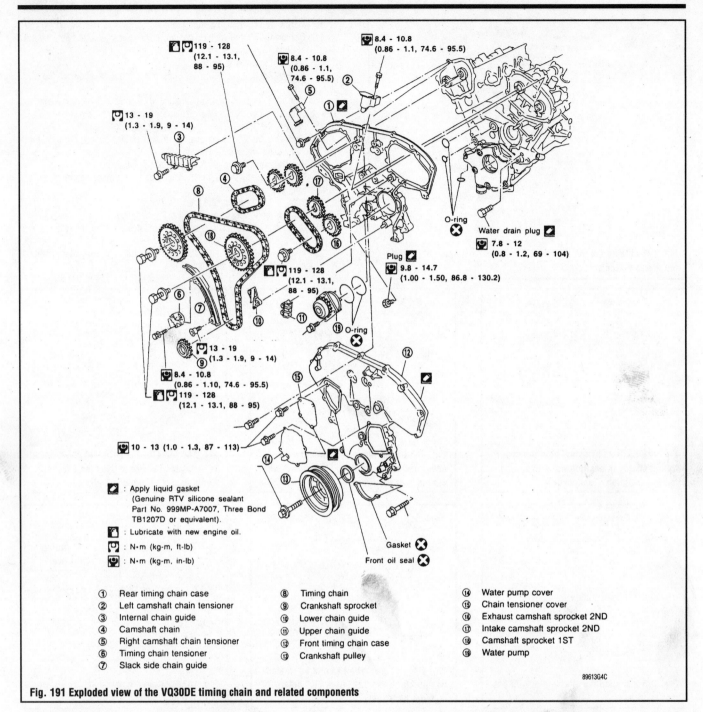

Fig. 191 Exploded view of the VQ30DE timing chain and related components

① Rear timing chain case
② Left camshaft chain tensioner
③ Internal chain guide
④ Camshaft chain
⑤ Right camshaft chain tensioner
⑥ Timing chain tensioner
⑦ Slack side chain guide

⑧ Timing chain
⑨ Crankshaft sprocket
⑩ Lower chain guide
⑪ Upper chain guide
⑫ Front timing chain case
⑬ Crankshaft pulley

⑭ Water pump cover
⑮ Chain tensioner cover
⑯ Exhaust camshaft sprocket 2ND
⑰ Intake camshaft sprocket 2ND
⑱ Camshaft sprocket 1ST
⑲ Water pump

89613G4C

23. Using a wrench on the camshafts, hold the camshaft stationary while loosening the sprocket bolts.

24. Remove the sprockets and chains from the camshafts.

To install:

25. Clean the gasket material from the front and rear timing chain cases, including the bolt holes.

26. Install the crankshaft sprocket. Make sure the mating marks on the sprocket are facing to the front of the engine.

27. Install the lower chain guide on the dowel pin. Make sure the "front" mark on the guide is facing up.

28. Align the marks on the camshaft sprockets as shown in the illustration and install them to the camshafts.

➡**Be careful not to confuse the intake and exhaust camshaft sprockets. The exhaust camshaft sprockets are thicker than the intake camshaft sprockets.**

29. Remove the pins from the camshaft chain tensioners.

30. Install the main timing chain on the crankshaft sprocket and water pump sprocket. Then install the camshaft drive sprockets as shown in the illustration. Dip the camshaft sprocket bolts in fresh engine oil and torque them to 88–95 ft.lbs. (119–128 Nm).

31. Install the chain guides. Install the main timing chain tensioner.

➡**After checking that all of the mating marks on the chains and sprockets are correct, temporarily install the crankshaft damper and SLOWLY rotate the engine by hand at least one full revolution to verify the camshaft/crankshaft timing is correct. If the crankshaft stops suddenly, a piston is hitting a valve. Do NOT force the engine to rotate; bent valves will result. Check the mating marks on the sprockets and the chains, and perform any procedures as necessary to correct misalignment.**

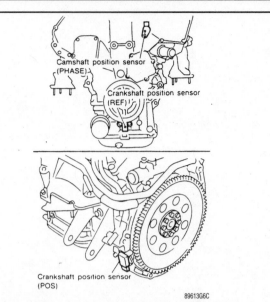

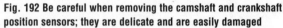

Fig. 192 Be careful when removing the camshaft and crankshaft position sensors; they are delicate and are easily damaged

32. Apply liquid gasket to the timing chain cover as shown in the illustration.

33. Following the tightening sequence shown in the illustration, tighten the timing chain cover bolts to the specified torque.

34. Apply liquid gasket to the water pump cover and install it to the front timing chain cover.

35. Install the rocker (valve) covers.

36. Install the intake manifold collector.

37. Install the upper and lower oil pans.

38. Install the exhaust header pipe.

39. Install the engine mount and bracket.

40. Install the center member assembly. Remove the engine from the hoist.

41. Install the crankshaft damper.

42. Install the crankshaft and camshaft position sensors.

43. Install the A/C compressor and bracket to the engine block.

44. Install the power steering pump.

45. Install the accessory drive belts and the idler pulley.

46. Fill the engine with the appropriate quantity of engine oil and coolant.

➡**The engine may produce a rattling noise when it is started. Run the engine at around 3,000 RPM in neutral to purge the air from the hydraulic chain tensioner.**

47. Start the engine and check for leaks from the sealing surfaces.

48. Install the timing chain cover.

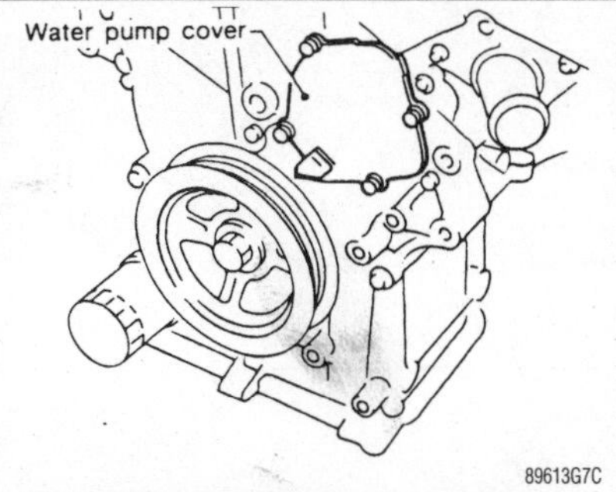

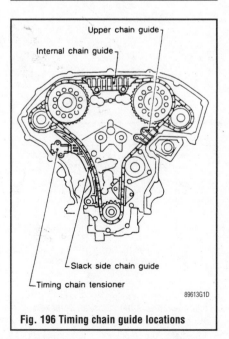

Fig. 193 The water pump cover should be removed to remove the front timing chain cover

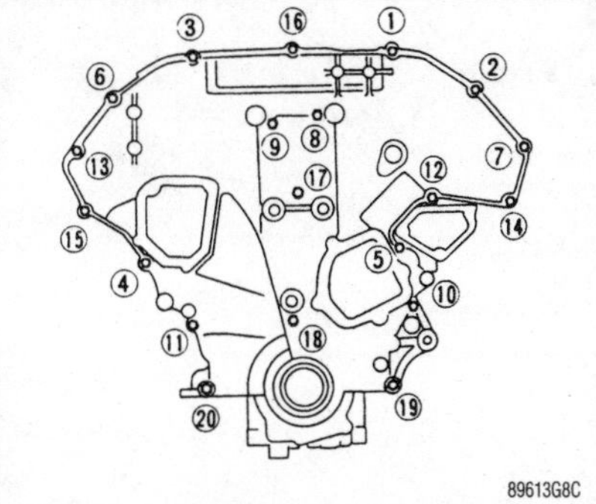

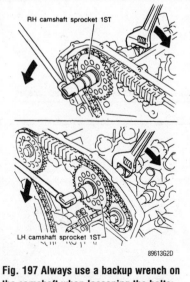

Fig. 194 Front timing chain cover bolt removal sequence

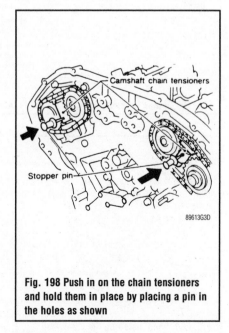

Fig. 195 Use the notch in the front timing chain cover to pry it from the rear cover

Fig. 196 Timing chain guide locations

Fig. 197 Always use a backup wrench on the camshaft when loosening the bolts; NEVER use the chain to provide tension

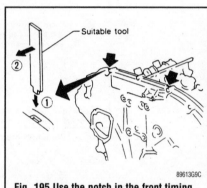

Fig. 198 Push in on the chain tensioners and hold them in place by placing a pin in the holes as shown

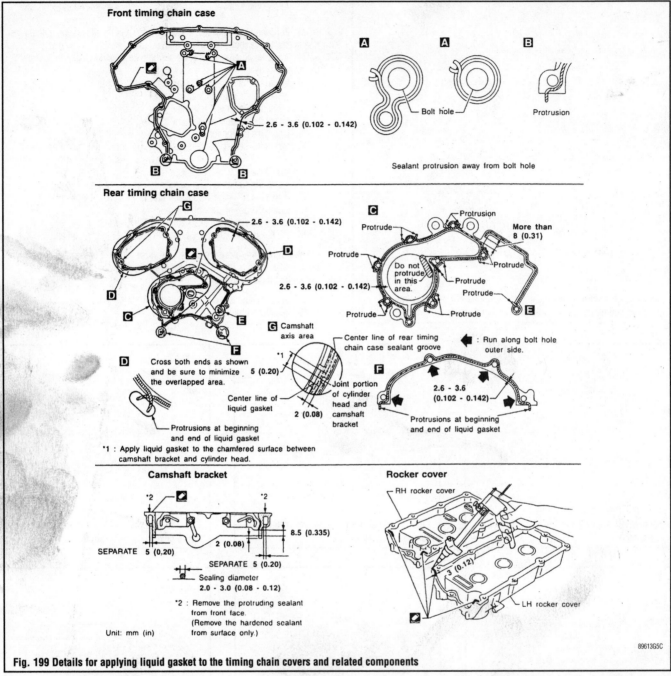

Front timing chain case

2.6 - 3.6 (0.102 - 0.142)

Ⓐ Ⓐ Ⓑ

Bolt hole

Protrusion

Sealant protrusion away from bolt hole

Rear timing chain case

Ⓖ

2.6 - 3.6 (0.102 - 0.142)

Ⓓ

Ⓓ

Ⓒ

Ⓔ

Ⓕ

Ⓒ

Protrusion

Protrude

More than 8 (0.31)

2.6 - 3.6 (0.102 - 0.142)

Do not protrude in this area.

Protrude

Protrude

Protrude

Protrude

Ⓔ

Protrude

Protrude

Ⓓ

Cross both ends as shown and be sure to minimize the overlapped area.

Protrusions at beginning and end of liquid gasket

Ⓖ Camshaft axis area

*1

5 (0.20)

Center line of liquid gasket

2 (0.08)

Center line of rear timing chain case sealant groove

Joint portion of cylinder head and camshaft bracket

← : Run along bolt hole outer side.

Ⓕ

2.6 - 3.6 (0.102 - 0.142)

Protrusions at beginning and end of liquid gasket

*1 : Apply liquid gasket to the chamfered surface between camshaft bracket and cylinder head.

Camshaft bracket

*2   *2

8.5 (0.335)

SEPARATE 5 (0.20)

2 (0.08)

SEPARATE 5 (0.20)

Sealing diameter 2.0 - 3.0 (0.08 - 0.12)

*2 : Remove the protruding sealant from front face. (Remove the hardened sealant from surface only.)

Unit: mm (in)

Rocker cover

RH rocker cover

3 (0.12)

LH rocker cover

89613G5C

Fig. 199 Details for applying liquid gasket to the timing chain covers and related components

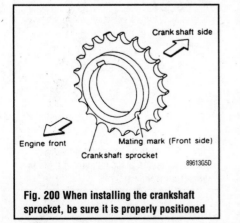

Crank shaft side

Engine front

Mating mark (Front side)

Crankshaft sprocket

89613G5D

Fig. 200 When installing the crankshaft sprocket, be sure it is properly positioned

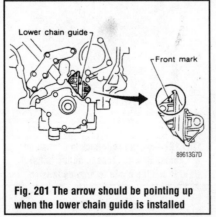

Lower chain guide

Front mark

89613G7D

Fig. 201 The arrow should be pointing up when the lower chain guide is installed

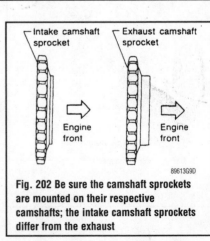

Intake camshaft sprocket

Exhaust camshaft sprocket

Engine front

Engine front

89613G9D

Fig. 202 Be sure the camshaft sprockets are mounted on their respective camshafts; the intake camshaft sprockets differ from the exhaust

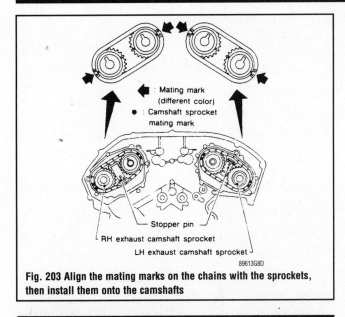

Fig. 203 Align the mating marks on the chains with the sprockets, then install them onto the camshafts

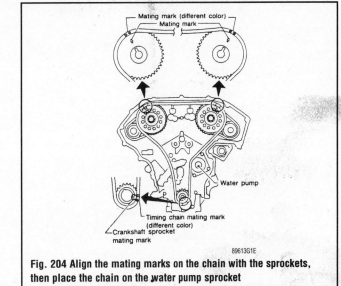

Fig. 204 Align the mating marks on the chain with the sprockets, then place the chain on the water pump sprocket

Camshaft, Bearings and Rocker Arms

REMOVAL & INSTALLATION

VG30E Engine

♦ See Figure 205

The cylinder heads must be removed from the engine to remove the camshafts.

1. Remove the timing belt.
2. Drain the coolant by removing drain plug on the cylinder block.
3. Remove the intake manifold assembly.
4. Remove the cylinder head from the engine.
5. With cylinder head mounted on a suitable workbench, remove the rocker shafts with rocker arms. Bolts should be loosened in 2–3 steps.
6. Remove the hydraulic lash adjusters and guide.

➡**Hold hydraulic lash adjusters with wire so they will not drop from the guide.**

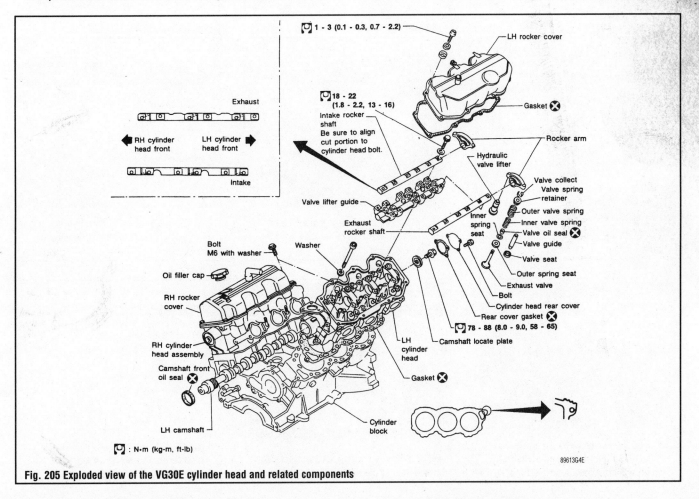

Fig. 205 Exploded view of the VG30E cylinder head and related components

7. Remove the camshaft front oil seal and slide camshaft out of the cylinder head.

To install:

8. Install camshaft, locate plate, cylinder head rear cover and front oil seal. Set camshaft knock pin at 12 o'clock position.

9. Install the cylinder head(s).

10. Install valve adjuster guide assembly. Assemble the hydraulic adjusters in their original position. After installing them in the correct location remove the wire holding them in the guide.

11. Install the rocker shafts in correct position with the rocker arms. Tighten bolts in 2–3 stages to 13–16 ft. lbs. Before tightening, be sure to set camshaft lobe at the position where lobe is not lifted or the valve closed. You can set each cylinder one at a time or follow the procedure below (timing belt must be installed in the correct position):

    a. Set No. 1 piston at TDC on its compression stroke and tighten rocker shaft bolts for No. 2, No. 4 and No. 6 cylinders.

    b. Set No. 4 piston at TDC on its compression stroke and tighten rocker shaft bolts for No. 1, No. 3 and No. 5 cylinders.

    c. Torque specification for the rocker shaft retaining bolts is 13–16 ft. lbs.

12. Install the intake manifold and collector assembly.

13. Install rear timing belt cover and camshaft sprocket. The left and right camshaft sprockets are different parts. Install the correct sprocket in the correct position.

14. Install the timing belt.

VE30DE Engine

♦ See Figures 206 thru 219

The upper timing chains must be removed to allow for camshaft removal. Refer to the Timing Chain procedure in this section.

1. Remove the valve cover. If removing the rear camshaft, the intake manifold collector must be removed.

2. Remove the upper timing chain cover(s) on the front of the cylinder head(s).

3. Set the engine to TDC on the number one cylinder on the compression stroke.

4. Mark the timing chain and sprockets for proper alignment during installations.

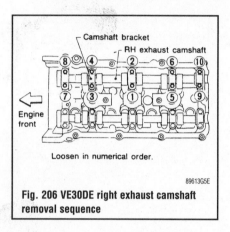

Fig. 206 VE30DE right exhaust camshaft removal sequence

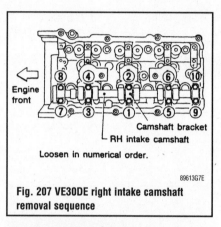

Fig. 207 VE30DE right intake camshaft removal sequence

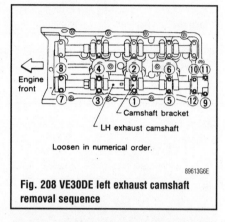

Fig. 208 VE30DE left exhaust camshaft removal sequence

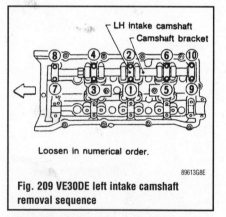

Fig. 209 VE30DE left intake camshaft removal sequence

Fig. 210 Keep the camshaft brackets in order when removing them; they are NOT interchangeable

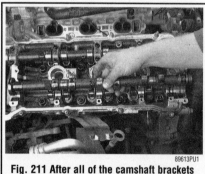

Fig. 211 After all of the camshaft brackets removed, lift the camshaft straight out of the cylinder head

Fig. 212 The rocker arms can easily be removed by popping them off of the hydraulic lash adjusters

Fig. 213 The hydraulic lash adjusters lift directly out of their bores

Fig. 214 It is recommended that the hydraulic lash adjusters be stored in oil to prevent air from entering them

5. Remove the timing chain tensioners and upper chain guides.

6. Using a back-up wrench on the camshafts, remove the camshaft sprocket bolts and the sprockets.

7. Loosen the camshaft brackets in numerical order as shown in the illustration. Be sure not to mix up the camshaft brackets.

8. Lift the camshaft(s) from the cylinder heads.

9. The rocker arms and hydraulic lash adjusters can be removed after the camshafts are removed.

➡**Do not lay the lifters on their sides; there is a chance of air entering them. Keep them upright, or store them in clean engine oil. Be sure to keep them in the order they were removed from the cylinder heads.**

To install:

10. Using engine assembly lubricant, lightly coat the bearing surfaces of each of the camshafts.

11. Install the camshaft brackets. Tighten the brackets in numerical order as shown in the illustrations.

12. Using a back-up wrench on the camshafts, install the camshaft sprocket

bolts and the sprockets. Dip the sprocket bolts in fresh engine oil and torque the bolts to 80–87 ft.lbs. (108–118 Nm.).

13. Install the timing chain tensioners and upper chain guides.

14. Install the upper timing chain cover(s) on the front of the cylinder head(s).

15. Install the valve cover(s). If the camshafts on the rear cylinder head were removed, install the intake manifold collector.

VQ30DE Engine

♦ **See Figures 220, 221, 222, 223 and 224**

The front and rear timing chain cover and timing chains must be removed to allow for camshaft removal. Refer to the Timing Chain procedure in this section.

1. Remove the rear timing chain case bolts.

2. Remove the rear timing chain case from the engine block.

3. Loosen the intake and exhaust camshaft brackets, in several steps as shown in the illustrations. Be sure to mark the positions of the camshaft brackets prior to removal.

4. Remove the camshafts from the cylinder heads.

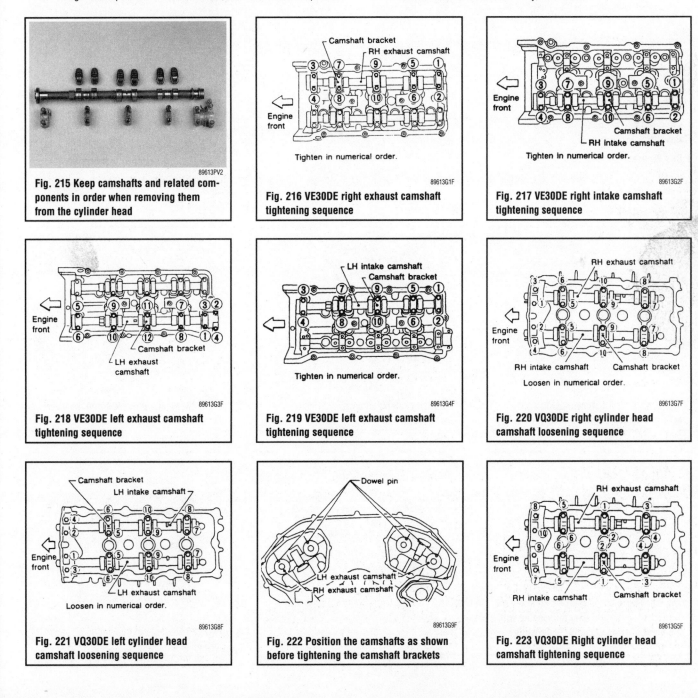

Fig. 215 Keep camshafts and related components in order when removing them from the cylinder head

Fig. 216 VE30DE right exhaust camshaft tightening sequence

Fig. 217 VE30DE right intake camshaft tightening sequence

Fig. 218 VE30DE left exhaust camshaft tightening sequence

Fig. 219 VE30DE left exhaust camshaft tightening sequence

Fig. 220 VQ30DE right cylinder head camshaft loosening sequence

Fig. 221 VQ30DE left cylinder head camshaft loosening sequence

Fig. 222 Position the camshafts as shown before tightening the camshaft brackets

Fig. 223 VQ30DE Right cylinder head camshaft tightening sequence

5. Remove the bucket-type cam followers from the cylinder heads. Be sure not to mix up the shims. Use egg cartons or other means to keep the followers and shims in the proper order. All camshaft components should always be installed in their original locations.

To install:

6. Using engine assembly lubricant, lightly coat the followers with engine oil and install them into the cylinder heads.

7. Using engine assembly lubricant, lightly coat the bearing surfaces and the cam lobes.

8. Install the camshafts to the cylinder heads. Position the dowel pins as shown in the illustration.

9. Tighten the camshaft brackets in three stages:

• Step 1: Tighten numbers 7–10 to 17 in.lbs (1.96 Nm), followed by numbers 1–6 to17 in.lbs (1.96 Nm)

• Step 2: Tighten all bolts in numerical order, to 52 in.lbs. (6 Nm.).

• Step 3: Tighten all bolts in numerical order, to 79.9–104.2 in.lbs. (9.02–11.8 Nm.).

10. Clean the mating surfaces of the rear timing chain cover and the cylinder block.

11. Install new O-rings to the cylinder block.

12. Apply a bead of liquid gasket to the mating surface of the timing chain case.

13. Mount the rear timing chain case to the engine block. Torque the bolts to 8.7–10.1 ft.lbs. (11.8–13.7 Nm.) in numerical order as shown in the illustration.

14. Install the timing chain.

INSPECTION

Camshafts

▶ **See Figures 225 thru 230**

1. Visually check the camshaft for scratches, seizures and/or wear; if necessary, replace the camshaft.

➡**Refer to the Engine Specifications Chart for measurements and specifications.**

2. To check the camshaft runout, position camshaft in a set of "V" blocks.

3. Mount a dial indicator so it contacts the camshaft at a 90° angle to the bearing surfaces.

4. Rotate the camshaft to measure the cam bearing journal runout.

5. To check the camshaft lobe height, use a micrometer to check cam (lobe) height, making sure the anvil and the spindle of the micrometer are positioned directly on the heel and tip of the cam lobe.

6. To check the camshaft journals, measure them with a micrometer.

7. Install the camshaft brackets and torque them to the specified torque.

8. Using an internal micrometer, measure the cylinder head camshaft bearing journals.

9. If the measurements are less than the limits listed, the camshaft will have to be replaced, since the camshafts in all of the engines covered in this guide run directly on the cylinder head surface; no actual bearings or bushings are used, so no oversize bearings or bushings are available.

10. To check the camshaft end play, perform the following procedures:

a. Install the camshaft into the cylinder head.

b. Using a dial micrometer, mount it at a 90° angle to the end of the camshaft. Move the camshaft in and out, then, measure the end play. Refer to the Engine Specifications Chart.

c. If the end play is out of range, install another locate plate to bring the tolerance within specifications.

Camshaft Followers

▶ **See Figures 231 and 232**

1. Visually inspect the contact and sliding areas of the follower. Replace as necessary.

2. Using a micrometer, measure the diameter of the follower.

3. Using an internal micrometer, measure the follower bore in the cylinder head. Refer to the Engine Specifications Chart for specifications.

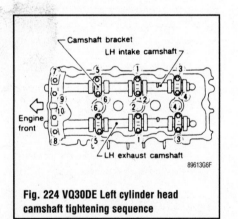

Fig. 224 VQ30DE Left cylinder head camshaft tightening sequence

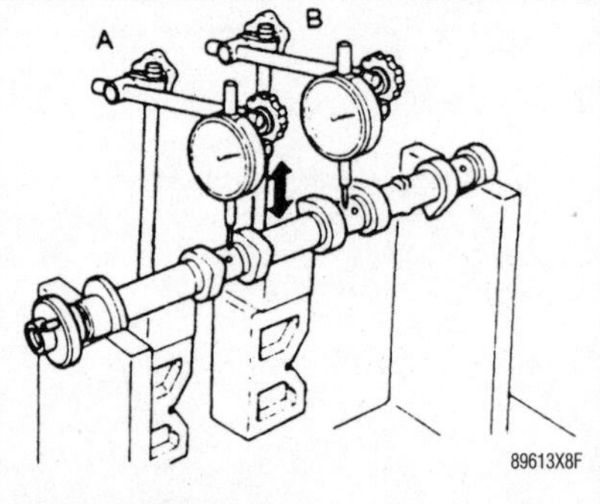

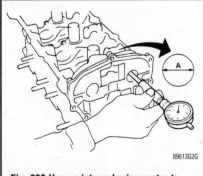

Fig. 225 Example of a camshaft set up to measure runout

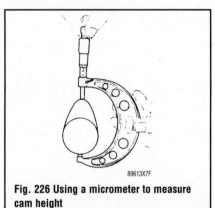

Fig. 226 Using a micrometer to measure cam height

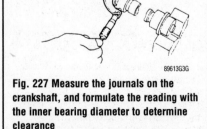

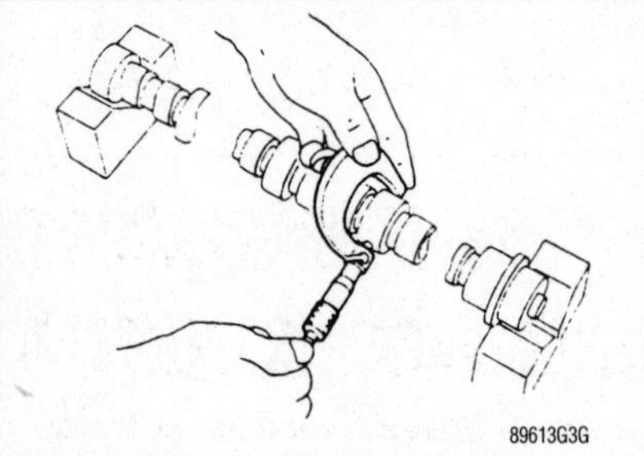

Fig. 227 Measure the journals on the crankshaft, and formulate the reading with the inner bearing diameter to determine clearance

Fig. 228 Use an internal micrometer to measure the camshaft bearing surface

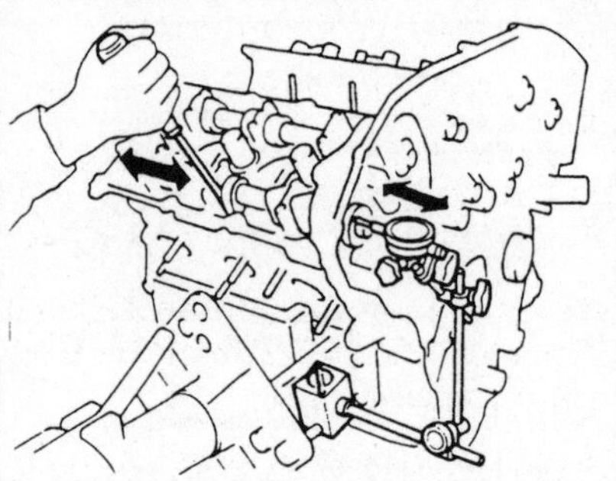

Fig. 229 Example of measuring a camshaft for end play

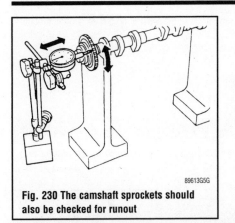

Fig. 230 The camshaft sprockets should also be checked for runout

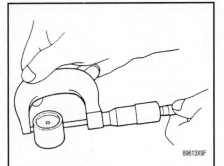

Fig. 231 Measure the diameter of the camshaft follower . . .

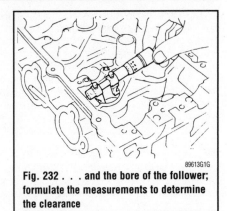

Fig. 232 . . . and the bore of the follower; formulate the measurements to determine the clearance

Rear Main Oil Seal

REMOVAL & INSTALLATION

◆ See Figures 233, 234 and 235

1. Remove the transaxle.
2. Remove the flywheel/flexplate.
3. Remove the bolts holding the rear oil seal retainer to the engine block and remove the oil seal retainer.

➡The rear main oil seal can be removed by using a pry tool to remove it from the retainer, if desired. When removing the seal, be careful not to score the crankshaft.

4. Clean the mating surfaces of the engine block and the retainer.

To install:

5. Using a large chisel, carefully drive the oil seal from the retainer.
6. Lightly apply oil to the outer surface of the seal, and drive the seal into the retainer plate with a seal driver. The seal should be flush with the surface of the retainer plate.
7. Apply grease to the inner lip of the seal, and install the retainer plate with the new seal to the engine using a new gasket. Torque the bolts to 74.6–95.5 in. lbs. (8.4–10.8 Nm.).

8. Install the flywheel/flexplate.
9. Install the transaxle.

Flywheel/Flexplate

REMOVAL & INSTALLATION

The transaxle must be removed for flywheel/flexplate removal.

1. Remove the clutch assembly from the flywheel.
2. Remove the flywheel bolts. loosen them in a criss-cross pattern in several stages.
3. Remove the flywheel from the crankshaft.

❊❊ CAUTION

Keep any magnetized objects away from the signal plate.

To install:

4. Clean the mating surface of the flywheel/flexplate.
5. Mount the flywheel/flexplate onto the crankshaft and torque the bolts to 61–69 ft. lbs. (83–93 Nm.). Be sure to lubricate the bolts when installing them.

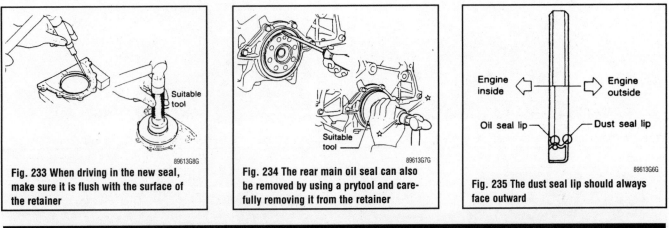

Fig. 233 When driving in the new seal, make sure it is flush with the surface of the retainer

Fig. 234 The rear main oil seal can also be removed by using a prytool and carefully removing it from the retainer

Fig. 235 The dust seal lip should always face outward

EXHAUST SYSTEM

Inspection

◆ See Figures 236 thru 242

➡Safety glasses should be worn at all times when working on or near the exhaust system. Older exhaust systems will almost always be covered with loose rust particles which will shower you when disturbed. These particles are more than a nuisance and could injure your eye.

❊❊ CAUTION

DO NOT perform exhaust repairs or inspection with the engine or exhaust hot. Allow the system to cool completely before attempting any work. Exhaust systems are noted for sharp edges, flaking metal and rusted bolts. Gloves and eye protection are required. A healthy supply of penetrating oil and rags is highly recommended.

Your vehicle must be raised and supported safely to inspect the exhaust system properly. By placing 4 safety stands under the vehicle for support should provide enough room for you to slide under the vehicle and inspect the system completely. Start the inspection at the exhaust manifold or turbocharger pipe where the header pipe is attached and work your way to the back of the vehicle. On dual exhaust systems, remember to inspect both sides of the vehicle. Check the complete exhaust system for open seams, holes loose connections, or other deterioration which could permit exhaust fumes to seep into the passenger compartment. Inspect all mounting brackets and hangers for deterioration, some models may have rubber O-rings that can be overstretched and non-supportive. These components will need to be replaced if found. It has always been a practice to use a pointed tool to poke up into the exhaust system where the deterioration spots are to see whether or not they crumble. Some models may have heat shield covering certain parts of the exhaust system , it will be necessary to remove these shields to have the exhaust visible for inspection also.

REPLACEMENT

▶ **See Figures 243 and 244**

There are basically two types of exhaust systems. One is the flange type where the component ends are attached with bolts and a gasket in-between. The other exhaust system is the slip joint type. These components slip into one another using clamps to retain them together.

✳✳ CAUTION

Allow the exhaust system to cool sufficiently before spraying a solvent exhaust fasteners. Some solvents are highly flammable and could ignite when sprayed on hot exhaust components.

Before removing any component of the exhaust system, ALWAYS squirt a liquid rust dissolving agent onto the fasteners for ease of removal. A lot of knuckle skin will be saved by following this rule. It may even be wise to spray the fasteners and allow them to sit overnight.

Flange Type

▶ **See Figure 245**

✳✳ CAUTION

Do NOT perform exhaust repairs or inspection with the engine or exhaust hot. Allow the system to cool completely before attempting

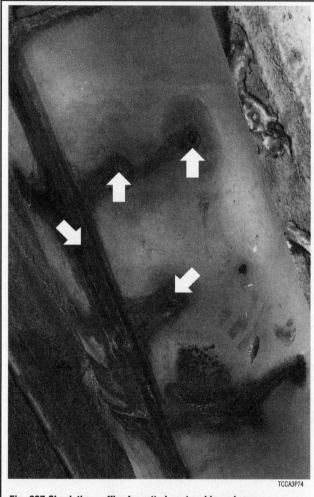
Fig. 237 Check the muffler for rotted spot welds and seams

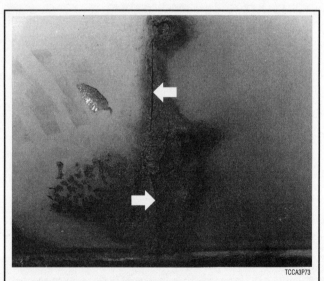
Fig. 236 Cracks in the muffler are a guaranteed leak

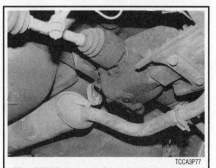
Fig. 238 Make sure the exhaust components are not contacting the body or suspension

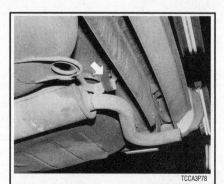
Fig. 239 Check for overstretched or torn exhaust hangers

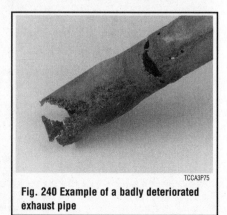
Fig. 240 Example of a badly deteriorated exhaust pipe

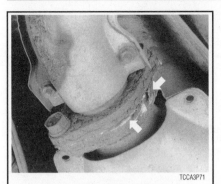

Fig. 241 Inspect flanges for gaskets that have deteriorated and need replacement

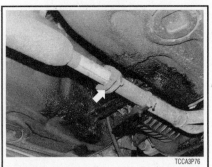

Fig. 242 Some systems, like this one, use large O-rings (donuts) in between the flanges

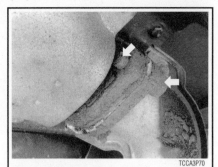

Fig. 243 Nuts and bolts will be extremely difficult to remove when deteriorated with rust

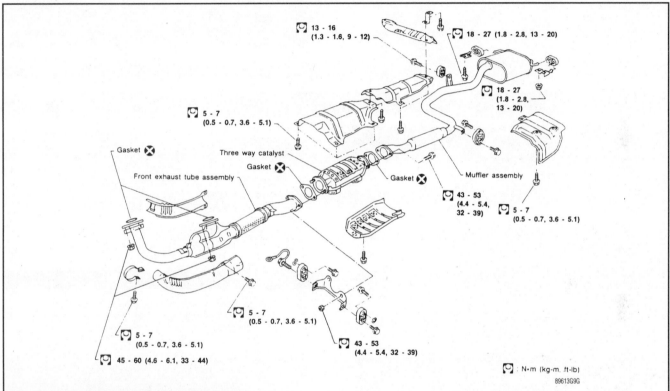

Fig. 244 Exploded view of the Maxima exhaust system

Fig. 245 Example of a flange type exhaust system joint

any work. Exhaust systems are noted for sharp edges, flaking metal and rusted bolts. Gloves and eye protection are required. A healthy supply of penetrating oil and rags is highly recommended. Never spray liquid rust dissolving agent onto a hot exhaust component.

Before removing any component on a flange type system, ALWAYS squirt a liquid rust dissolving agent onto the fasteners for ease of removal. Start by unbolting the exhaust piece at both ends (if required). When unbolting the headpipe from the manifold, make sure that the bolts are free before trying to remove them. if you snap a stud in the exhaust manifold, the stud will have to be removed with a bolt extractor, which often means removal of the manifold itself. Next, disconnect the component from the mounting; slight twisting and turning may be required to remove the component completely from the vehicle. You may need to tap on the component with a rubber mallet to loosen the component. If all else fails, use a hacksaw to separate the parts. An oxy-acetylene cutting torch may be faster but the sparks are DANGEROUS near the fuel tank, and at the very least, accidents could happen, resulting in damage to the under-car parts, not to mention yourself.

Slip Joint Type

▶ **See Figure 246**

Before removing any component on the slip joint type exhaust system, ALWAYS squirt a liquid rust dissolving agent onto the fasteners for ease of removal. Start by unbolting the exhaust piece at both ends (if required). When unbolting the headpipe from the manifold, make sure that the bolts are free before trying to remove them. if you snap a stud in the exhaust manifold, the stud will have to be removed with a bolt extractor, which often means removal of the manifold itself. Next, remove the mounting U-bolts from around the exhaust pipe you are extracting from the vehicle. Don't be surprised if the U-bolts break while removing the nuts. Loosen the exhaust pipe from any mounting brackets retaining it to the floor pan and separate the components.

Safety Precautions

For a number of reasons, exhaust system work can be dangerous. Always observe the following precautions:
1. Raise and safely support the vehicle.
2. Wear safety goggles to protect your eyes from metal chips that may fly free while working on the exhaust system.
3. If you are using a torch be careful not to come close to any fuel lines.
4. Always use the proper tool for the job.

Fig. 246 Example of a common slip joint type system

ENGINE RECONDITIONING

Determining Engine Condition

Anything that generates heat and/or friction will eventually burn or wear out (i.e. a light bulb generates heat, therefore its life span is limited). With this in mind, a running engine generates tremendous amounts of both; friction is encountered by the moving and rotating parts inside the engine and heat is created by friction and combustion of the fuel. However, the engine has systems designed to help reduce the effects of heat and friction and provide added longevity. The oiling system reduces the amount of friction encountered by the moving parts inside the engine, while the cooling system reduces heat created by friction and combustion. If either system is not maintained, a break-down will be inevitable. Therefore, you can see how regular maintenance can affect the service life of your vehicle. If you do not drain, flush and refill your cooling system at the proper intervals, deposits will begin to accumulate in the radiator, thereby reducing the amount of heat it can extract from the coolant. The same applies to your oil and filter; if it is not changed often enough it becomes laden with contaminates and is unable to properly lubricate the engine. This increases friction and wear.

There are a number of methods for evaluating the condition of your engine. A compression test can reveal the condition of your pistons, piston rings, cylinder bores, head gasket(s), valves and valve seats. An oil pressure test can warn you of possible engine bearing, or oil pump failures. Excessive oil consumption, evidence of oil in the engine air intake area and/or bluish smoke from the tail pipe may indicate worn piston rings, worn valve guides and/or valve seals. As a general rule, an engine that uses no more than one quart of oil every 1000 miles is in good condition. Engines that use one quart of oil or more in less than 1000 miles should first be checked for oil leaks. If any oil leaks are present, have them fixed before determining how much oil is consumed by the engine, especially if blue smoke is not visible at the tail pipe.

COMPRESSION TEST

▶ **See Figure 247**

A noticeable lack of engine power, excessive oil consumption and/or poor fuel mileage measured over an extended period are all indicators of internal engine wear. Worn piston rings, scored or worn cylinder bores, blown head gaskets, sticking or burnt valves, and worn valve seats are all possible culprits. A check of each cylinder's compression will help locate the problem.

➡ **A screw-in type compression gauge is more accurate than the type you simply hold against the spark plug hole. Although it takes slightly longer to use, it's worth the effort to obtain a more accurate reading.**

1. Make sure that the proper amount and viscosity of engine oil is in the crankcase, then ensure the battery is fully charged.

2. Warm-up the engine to normal operating temperature, then shut the engine **OFF**.
3. Disable the ignition system so the engine does not start.
4. Label and disconnect all of the spark plug wires from the plugs/coils.
5. Thoroughly clean the cylinder head area around the spark plug ports, then remove the spark plugs.
6. Set the throttle plate to the fully open (wide-open throttle) position. You can block the accelerator linkage open for this, or you can have an assistant fully depress the accelerator pedal.
7. Install a screw-in type compression gauge into the No. 1 spark plug hole until the fitting is snug.

✳✳ WARNING

Be careful not to crossthread the spark plug hole.

8. According to the tool manufacturer's instructions, connect a remote starting switch to the starting circuit.
9. With the ignition switch in the **OFF** position, use the remote starting switch to crank the engine through at least five compression strokes (approximately 5 seconds of cranking) and record the highest reading on the gauge.

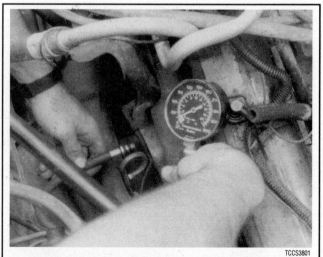

Fig. 247 A screw-in type compression gauge is more accurate and easier to use without an assistant

10. Repeat the test on each cylinder, cranking the engine approximately the same number of compression strokes and/or time as the first.

11. Compare the highest readings from each cylinder to that of the others. The indicated compression pressures are considered within specifications if the lowest reading cylinder is within 75 percent of the pressure recorded for the highest reading cylinder. For example, if your highest reading cylinder pressure was 150 psi (1034 kPa), then 75 percent of that would be 113 psi (779 kPa). So the lowest reading cylinder should be no less than 113 psi (779 kPa).

12. If a cylinder exhibits an unusually low compression reading, pour a tablespoon of clean engine oil into the cylinder through the spark plug hole and repeat the compression test. If the compression rises after adding oil, it means that the cylinder's piston rings and/or cylinder bore are damaged or worn. If the pressure remains low, the valves may not be seating properly (a valve job is needed), or the head gasket may be blown near that cylinder. If compression in any two adjacent cylinders is low, and if the addition of oil doesn't help raise compression, there is leakage past the head gasket. Oil and coolant in the combustion chamber, combined with blue or constant white smoke from the tail pipe, are symptoms of this problem. However, don't be alarmed by the normal white smoke emitted from the tail pipe during engine warm-up or from cold weather driving. There may be evidence of water droplets on the engine dipstick and/or oil droplets in the cooling system if a head gasket is blown.

OIL PRESSURE TEST

Check for proper oil pressure at the sending unit passage with an externally mounted mechanical oil pressure gauge (as opposed to relying on a factory installed dash-mounted gauge). A tachometer may also be needed, as some specifications may require running the engine at a specific rpm.

1. With the engine cold, locate and remove the oil pressure sending unit.
2. Following the manufacturer's instructions, connect a mechanical oil pressure gauge and, if necessary, a tachometer to the engine.
3. Start the engine and allow it to idle.
4. Check the oil pressure reading when cold and record the number. You may need to run the engine at a specified rpm, so check the specifications chart located earlier in this section.
5. Run the engine until normal operating temperature is reached (upper radiator hose will feel warm).
6. Check the oil pressure reading again with the engine hot and record the number. Turn the engine **OFF**.
7. Compare your hot oil pressure reading to that given in the chart. If the reading is low, check the cold pressure reading against the chart. If the cold pressure is well above the specification, and the hot reading was lower than the specification, you may have the wrong viscosity oil in the engine. Change the oil, making sure to use the proper grade and quantity, then repeat the test.

Low oil pressure readings could be attributed to internal component wear, pump related problems, a low oil level, or oil viscosity that is too low. High oil pressure readings could be caused by an overfilled crankcase, too high of an oil viscosity or a faulty pressure relief valve.

Buy or Rebuild?

If you have determined that your engine is worn out, you must make some decisions. The question of whether or not an engine is worth rebuilding is largely a subjective matter and one of personal worth. Is the engine a popular one, or is it an obsolete model? Are parts available? Will it get acceptable gas mileage once it is rebuilt? Is the car it's being put into worth keeping? Would it be less expensive to buy a new engine, have your engine rebuilt by a pro, rebuild it yourself or buy a used engine from a salvage yard? Or would it be simpler and less expensive to buy another car? If you have considered all these matters and more, and have still decided to rebuild the engine, then it is time to decide how you will rebuild it.

➡ **The editors at Chilton feel that most engine machining should be performed by a professional machine shop. Don't think of it as wasting money, rather, as an assurance that the job has been done right the first time. There are many expensive and specialized tools required to perform such tasks as boring and honing an engine block or having a valve job done on a cylinder head. Even inspecting the parts requires expensive micrometers and gauges to properly measure wear and clearances. Also, a machine shop can deliver to you clean, and ready to assemble parts, saving you time and aggravation. Your maximum savings will**

come from performing the removal, disassembly, assembly and installation of the engine and purchasing or renting only the tools required to perform the above tasks. Depending on the particular circumstances, you may save 40 to 60 percent of the cost doing these yourself.

A complete rebuild or overhaul of an engine involves replacing all of the moving parts (pistons, rods, crankshaft, camshaft, etc.) with new ones and machining the non-moving wearing surfaces of the block and heads. Unfortunately, this may not be cost effective. For instance, your crankshaft may have been damaged or worn, but it can be machined undersize for a minimal fee.

So, as you can see, you can replace everything inside the engine, but, it is wiser to replace only those parts which are really needed, and, if possible, repair the more expensive ones. Later in this section, we will break the engine down into its two main components: the cylinder head and the engine block. We will discuss each component, and the recommended parts to replace during a rebuild on each.

Engine Overhaul Tips

Most engine overhaul procedures are fairly standard. In addition to specific parts replacement procedures and specifications for your individual engine, this section is also a guide to acceptable rebuilding procedures. Examples of standard rebuilding practice are given and should be used along with specific details concerning your particular engine.

Competent and accurate machine shop services will ensure maximum performance, reliability and engine life. In most instances it is more profitable for the do-it-yourself mechanic to remove, clean and inspect the component, buy the necessary parts and deliver these to a shop for actual machine work.

Much of the assembly work (crankshaft, bearings, piston rods, and other components) is well within the scope of the do-it-yourself mechanic's tools and abilities. You will have to decide for yourself the depth of involvement you desire in an engine repair or rebuild.

TOOLS

The tools required for an engine overhaul or parts replacement will depend on the depth of your involvement. With a few exceptions, they will be the tools found in a mechanic's tool kit (see Section 1 of this manual). More in-depth work will require some or all of the following:

- A dial indicator (reading in thousandths) mounted on a universal base
- Micrometers and telescope gauges
- Jaw and screw-type pullers
- Scraper
- Valve spring compressor
- Ring groove cleaner
- Piston ring expander and compressor
- Ridge reamer
- Cylinder hone or glaze breaker
- Plastigage®
- Engine stand

The use of most of these tools is illustrated in this section. Many can be rented for a one-time use from a local parts jobber or tool supply house specializing in automotive work.

Occasionally, the use of special tools is called for. See the information on Special Tools and the Safety Notice in the front of this book before substituting another tool.

OVERHAUL TIPS

Aluminum has become extremely popular for use in engines, due to its low weight. Observe the following precautions when handling aluminum parts:

- Never hot tank aluminum parts. The caustic hot tank solution will eat the aluminum.
- Remove all aluminum parts (identification tag, etc.) from engine parts prior to the tanking.
- Always coat threads lightly with engine oil or anti-seize compounds before installation, to prevent seizure.
- Never overtighten bolts or spark plugs especially in aluminum threads.

When assembling the engine, any parts that will be exposed to frictional contact must be prelubed to provide lubrication at initial start-up. Any product specifically formulated for this purpose can be used, but engine oil is not recommended as a prelube in most cases.

When semi-permanent (locked, but removable) installation of bolts or nuts is desired, threads should be cleaned and coated with Loctite® or another similar, commercial non-hardening sealant.

CLEANING

▶ **See Figures 248, 249, 250 and 251**

Before the engine and its components are inspected, they must be thoroughly cleaned. You will need to remove any engine varnish, oil sludge and/or carbon deposits from all of the components to insure an accurate inspection. A crack in the engine block or cylinder head can easily become overlooked if hidden by a layer of sludge or carbon.

Most of the cleaning process can be carried out with common hand tools and readily available solvents or solutions. Carbon deposits can be chipped away using a hammer and a hard wooden chisel. Old gasket material and varnish or sludge can usually be removed using a scraper and/or cleaning solvent. Extremely stubborn deposits may require the use of a power drill with a wire brush. If using a wire brush, use extreme care around any critical machined surfaces (such as the gasket surfaces, bearing saddles, cylinder bores, etc.). USE OF A WIRE BRUSH IS NOT RECOMMENDED ON ANY ALUMINUM COMPONENTS. Always follow any safety recommendations given by the manufacturer of the tool and/or solvent. You should always wear eye protection during any cleaning process involving scraping, chipping or spraying of solvents.

An alternative to the mess and hassle of cleaning the parts yourself is to drop them off at a local garage or machine shop. They will, more than likely, have the necessary equipment to properly clean all of the parts for a nominal fee.

※ CAUTION

Always wear eye protection during any cleaning process involving scraping, chipping or spraying of solvents.

Remove any oil galley plugs, freeze plugs and/or pressed-in bearings and carefully wash and degrease all of the engine components including the fasteners and bolts. Small parts such as the valves, springs, etc., should be placed in a metal basket and allowed to soak. Use pipe cleaner type brushes, and clean all passageways in the components. Use a ring expander and remove the rings from the pistons. Clean the piston ring grooves with a special tool or a piece of broken ring. Scrape the carbon off of the top of the piston. You should never use a wire brush on the pistons. After preparing all of the piston assemblies in this manner, wash and degrease them again.

※ WARNING

Use extreme care when cleaning around the cylinder head valve seats. A mistake or slip may cost you a new seat.

When cleaning the cylinder head, remove carbon from the combustion chamber with the valves installed. This will avoid damaging the valve seats.

REPAIRING DAMAGED THREADS

▶ **See Figures 252, 253, 254, 255 and 256**

Several methods of repairing damaged threads are available. Heli-Coil® (shown here), Keenserts® and Microdot® are among the most widely used. All involve basically the same principle—drilling out stripped threads, tapping the hole and installing a prewound insert—making welding, plugging and oversize fasteners unnecessary.

Two types of thread repair inserts are usually supplied: a standard type for most inch coarse, inch fine, metric course and metric fine thread sizes and a spark lug type to fit most spark plug port sizes. Consult the individual tool manufacturer's catalog to determine exact applications. Typical thread repair kits will contain a selection of prewound threaded inserts, a tap (corresponding to the outside diameter threads of the insert) and an installation tool. Spark plug inserts usually differ because they require a tap equipped with pilot threads and a combined reamer/tap section. Most manufacturers also supply blister-packed thread repair inserts separately in addition to a master kit containing a variety of taps and inserts plus installation tools.

Before attempting to repair a threaded hole, remove any snapped, broken or damaged bolts or studs. Penetrating oil can be used to free frozen threads. The offending item can usually be removed with locking pliers or using a screw/stud

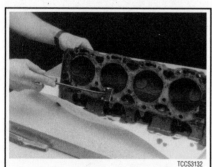

Fig. 248 Use a gasket scraper to remove the old gasket material from the mating surfaces

Fig. 249 Use a ring expander tool to remove the piston rings

Fig. 250 Clean the piston ring grooves using a ring groove cleaner tool, or . . .

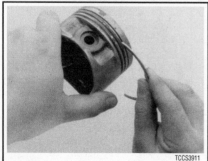

Fig. 251 . . . use a piece of an old ring to clean the grooves. Be careful, the ring can be quite sharp

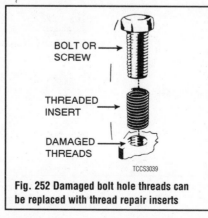

Fig. 252 Damaged bolt hole threads can be replaced with thread repair inserts

Fig. 253 Standard thread repair insert (left), and spark plug thread insert

Fig. 254 Drill out the damaged threads with the specified size bit. Be sure to drill completely through the hole or to the bottom of a blind hole

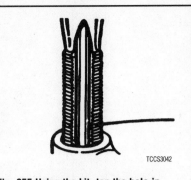

Fig. 255 Using the kit, tap the hole in order to receive the thread insert. Keep the tap well oiled and back it out frequently to avoid clogging the threads

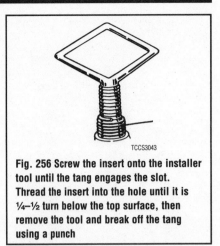

Fig. 256 Screw the insert onto the installer tool until the tang engages the slot. Thread the insert into the hole until it is ¼–½ turn below the top surface, then remove the tool and break off the tang using a punch

extractor. After the hole is clear, the thread can be repaired, as shown in the series of accompanying illustrations and in the kit manufacturer's instructions.

Engine Preparation

To properly rebuild an engine, you must first remove it from the vehicle, then disassemble and diagnose it. Ideally you should place your engine on an engine stand. This affords you the best access to the engine components. Follow the manufacturer's directions for using the stand with your particular engine. Remove the flywheel or flexplate before installing the engine to the stand.

Now that you have the engine on a stand, and assuming that you have drained the oil and coolant from the engine, it's time to strip it of all but the necessary components. Before you start disassembling the engine, you may want to take a moment to draw some pictures, or fabricate some labels or containers to mark the locations of various components and the bolts and/or studs which fasten them. Modern day engines use a lot of little brackets and clips which hold wiring harnesses and such, and these holders are often mounted on studs and/or bolts that can be easily mixed up. The manufacturer spent a lot of time and money designing your vehicle, and they wouldn't have wasted any of it by haphazardly placing brackets, clips or fasteners on the vehicle. If it's present when you disassemble it, put it back when you assemble, you will regret not remembering that little bracket which holds a wire harness out of the path of a rotating part.

You should begin by unbolting any accessories still attached to the engine, such as the water pump, power steering pump, alternator, etc. Then, unfasten any manifolds (intake or exhaust) which were not removed during the engine removal procedure. Finally, remove any covers remaining on the engine such as the rocker arm, front or timing cover and oil pan. Some front covers may require the vibration damper and/or crank pulley to be removed beforehand. The idea is to reduce the engine to the bare necessities (cylinder head(s), valve train, engine block, crankshaft, pistons and connecting rods), plus any other `in block' components such as oil pumps, balance shafts and auxiliary shafts.

Finally, remove the cylinder head(s) from the engine block and carefully place on a bench. Disassembly instructions for each component follow later in this section.

Cylinder Head

There are two basic types of cylinder heads used on today's automobiles: the Overhead Valve (OHV) and the Overhead Camshaft (OHC). The latter can also be broken down into two subgroups: the Single Overhead Camshaft (SOHC) and the Dual Overhead Camshaft (DOHC). Generally, if there is only a single camshaft on a head, it is just referred to as an OHC head. Also, an engine with an OHV cylinder head is also known as a pushrod engine.

Most cylinder heads these days are made of an aluminum alloy due to its light weight, durability and heat transfer qualities. However, cast iron was the material of choice in the past, and is still used on many vehicles today. Whether made from aluminum or iron, all cylinder heads have valves and seats. Some use two valves per cylinder, while the more hi-tech engines will utilize a multi-valve configuration using 3, 4 and even 5 valves per cylinder. When the valve contacts the seat, it does so on precision machined surfaces, which seals the

combustion chamber. All cylinder heads have a valve guide for each valve. The guide centers the valve to the seat and allows it to move up and down within it. The clearance between the valve and guide can be critical. Too much clearance and the engine may consume oil, lose vacuum and/or damage the seat. Too little, and the valve can stick in the guide causing the engine to run poorly if at all, and possibly causing severe damage. The last component all cylinder heads have are valve springs. The spring holds the valve against its seat. It also returns the valve to this position when the valve has been opened by the valve train or camshaft. The spring is fastened to the valve by a retainer and valve locks (sometimes called keepers). Aluminum heads will also have a valve spring shim to keep the spring from wearing away the aluminum.

An ideal method of rebuilding the cylinder head would involve replacing all of the valves, guides, seats, springs, etc. with new ones. However, depending on how the engine was maintained, often this is not necessary. A major cause of valve, guide and seat wear is an improperly tuned engine. An engine that is running too rich, will often wash the lubricating oil out of the guide with gasoline, causing it to wear rapidly. Conversely, an engine which is running too lean will place higher combustion temperatures on the valves and seats allowing them to wear or even burn. Springs fall victim to the driving habits of the individual. A driver who often runs the engine rpm to the redline will wear out or break the springs faster then one that stays well below it. Unfortunately, mileage takes it toll on all of the parts. Generally, the valves, guides, springs and seats in a cylinder head can be machined and re-used, saving you money. However, if a valve is burnt, it may be wise to replace all of the valves, since they were all operating in the same environment. The same goes for any other component on the cylinder head. Think of it as an insurance policy against future problems related to that component.

Unfortunately, the only way to find out which components need replacing, is to disassemble and carefully check each piece. After the cylinder head(s) are disassembled, thoroughly clean all of the components.

DISASSEMBLY

▶ See Figures 257 and 258

Whether it is a single or dual overhead camshaft cylinder head, the disassembly procedure is relatively unchanged. One aspect to pay attention to is careful labeling of the parts on the dual camshaft cylinder head. There will be an intake camshaft and followers as well as an exhaust camshaft and followers and they must be labeled as such. In some cases, the components are identical and could easily be installed incorrectly. DO NOT MIX THEM UP! Determining which is which is very simple; the intake camshaft and components are on the same side of the head as was the intake manifold. Conversely, the exhaust camshaft and components are on the same side of the head as was the exhaust manifold.

CUP TYPE CAMSHAFT FOLLOWERS

▶ See Figures 259, 260 and 261

Most cylinder heads with cup type camshaft followers will have the valve spring, retainer and locks recessed within the follower's bore. You will need a C-clamp style valve spring compressor tool, an OHC spring removal tool (or equivalent) and a small magnet to disassemble the head.

Fig. 257 Exploded view of a valve, seal, spring, retainer and locks from an OHC cylinder head

Fig. 258 Example of a multi-valve cylinder head. Note how it has 2 intake and 2 exhaust valve ports

1. If not already removed, remove the camshaft(s) and/or followers. Mark their positions for assembly.

2. Position the cylinder head to allow use of a C-clamp style valve spring compressor tool.

Fig. 259 C-clamp type spring compressor and an OHC spring removal tool (center) for cup type followers

Fig. 260 Most cup type follower cylinder heads retain the camshaft using bolt-on bearing caps

Fig. 261 Position the OHC spring tool in the follower bore, then compress the spring with a C-clamp type tool

➡It is preferred to position the cylinder head gasket surface facing you with the valve springs facing the opposite direction and the head laying horizontal.

3. With the OHC spring removal adapter tool positioned inside of the follower bore, compress the valve spring using the C-clamp style valve spring compressor.

4. Remove the valve locks. A small magnetic tool or screwdriver will aid in removal.

5. Release the compressor tool and remove the spring assembly.

6. Withdraw the valve from the cylinder head.

7. If equipped, remove the valve seal.

➡Special valve seal removal tools are available. Regular or needlenose type pliers, if used with care, will work just as well. If using ordinary pliers, be sure not to damage the follower bore. The follower and its bore are machined to close tolerances and any damage to the bore will effect this relationship.

8. If equipped, remove the valve spring shim. A small magnetic tool or screwdriver will aid in removal.

9. Repeat Steps 3 through 8 until all of the valves have been removed.

ROCKER ARM TYPE CAMSHAFT FOLLOWERS

♦ See Figures 262 thru 270

Most cylinder heads with rocker arm-type camshaft followers are easily disassembled using a standard valve spring compressor. However, certain models may not have enough open space around the spring for the standard tool and may require you to use a C-clamp style compressor tool instead.

1. If not already removed, remove the rocker arms and/or shafts and the camshaft. If applicable, also remove the hydraulic lash adjusters. Mark their positions for assembly.

2. Position the cylinder head to allow access to the valve spring.

3. Use a valve spring compressor tool to relieve the spring tension from the retainer.

Fig. 262 Example of the shaft mounted rocker arms on some OHC heads

Fig. 263 Another example of the rocker arm type OHC head. This model uses a follower under the camshaft

Fig. 264 Before the camshaft can be removed, all of the followers must first be removed . . .

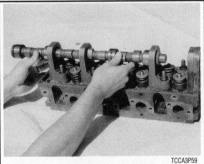

Fig. 265 . . . then the camshaft can be removed by sliding it out (shown), or unbolting a bearing cap (not shown)

Fig. 266 Compress the valve spring . . .

Fig. 267 . . . then remove the valve locks from the valve stem and spring retainer

Fig. 268 Remove the valve spring and retainer from the cylinder head

Fig. 269 Remove the valve seal from the guide. Some gentle prying or pliers may help to remove stubborn ones

Fig. 270 All aluminum and some cast iron heads will have these valve spring shims. Remove all of them as well

➡ **Due to engine varnish, the retainer may stick to the valve locks. A gentle tap with a hammer may help to break it loose.**

4. Remove the valve locks from the valve tip and/or retainer. A small magnet may help in removing the small locks.

5. Lift the valve spring, tool and all, off of the valve stem.

6. If equipped, remove the valve seal. If the seal is difficult to remove with the valve in place, try removing the valve first, then the seal. Follow the steps below for valve removal.

7. Position the head to allow access for withdrawing the valve.

➡ **Cylinder heads that have seen a lot of miles and/or abuse may have mushroomed the valve lock grove and/or tip, causing difficulty in removal of the valve. If this has happened, use a metal file to carefully remove the high spots around the lock grooves and/or tip. Only file it enough to allow removal.**

8. Remove the valve from the cylinder head.

9. If equipped, remove the valve spring shim. A small magnetic tool or screwdriver will aid in removal.

10. Repeat Steps 3 though 9 until all of the valves have been removed.

INSPECTION

Now that all of the cylinder head components are clean, it's time to inspect them for wear and/or damage. To accurately inspect them, you will need some specialized tools:

- A 0–1 in. micrometer for the valves
- A dial indicator or inside diameter gauge for the valve guides
- A spring pressure test gauge

If you do not have access to the proper tools, you may want to bring the components to a shop that does.

Springs, Retainers and Valve Locks

▶ **See Figures 273 and 274**

The first thing to check is the most obvious, broken springs. Next check the free length and squareness of each spring. If applicable, insure to distinguish between intake and exhaust springs. Use a ruler and/or carpenters square to measure the length. A carpenters square should be used to check the springs for squareness. If a spring pressure test gauge is available, check each springs rating and compare to the specifications chart. Check the readings against the specifications given. Any springs that fail these inspections should be replaced.

The spring retainers rarely need replacing, however they should still be checked as a precaution. Inspect the spring mating surface and the valve lock retention area for any signs of excessive wear. Also check for any signs of cracking. Replace any retainers that are questionable.

Valve locks should be inspected for excessive wear on the outside contact area as well as on the inner notched surface. Any locks which appear worn or broken and its respective valve should be replaced.

Cylinder Head

There are several things to check on the cylinder head: valve guides, seats, cylinder head surface flatness, cracks and physical damage.

VALVE GUIDES

▶ **See Figure 275**

Now that you know the valves are good, you can use them to check the guides, although a new valve, if available, is preferred. Before you measure anything, look at the guides carefully and inspect them for any cracks, chips or breakage. Also if the guide is a removable style (as in most aluminum

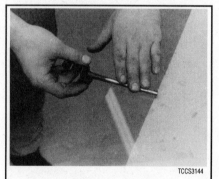

Fig. 271 Valve stems may be rolled on a flat surface to check for bends

TCCS3144

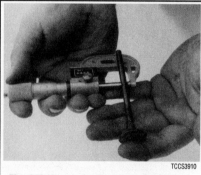

Fig. 272 Use a micrometer to check the valve stem diameter

TCCS3910

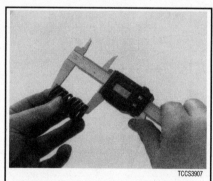

Fig. 273 Use a caliper to check the valve spring free-length

TCCS3907

Valves

▶ **See Figures 271 and 272**

The first thing to inspect are the valve heads. Look closely at the head, margin and face for any cracks, excessive wear or burning. The margin is the best place to look for burning. It should have a squared edge with an even width all around the diameter. When a valve burns, the margin will look melted and the edges rounded. Also inspect the valve head for any signs of tulipping. This will show as a lifting of the edges or dishing in the center of the head and will usually not occur to all of the valves. All of the heads should look the same, any that seem dished more than others are probably bad. Next, inspect the valve lock grooves and valve tips. Check for any burrs around the lock grooves, especially if you had to file them to remove the valve. Valve tips should appear flat, although slight rounding with high mileage engines is normal. Slightly worn valve tips will need to be machined flat. Last, measure the valve stem diameter with the micrometer. Measure the area that rides within the guide, especially towards the tip where most of the wear occurs. Take several measurements along its length and compare them to each other. Wear should be even along the length with little to no taper. If no minimum diameter is given in the specifications, then the stem should not read more than 0.001 in. (0.025mm) below the specification. Any valves that fail these inspections should be replaced.

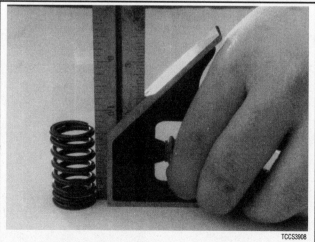

Fig. 274 Check the valve spring for squareness on a flat surface; a carpenter's square can be used

TCCS3908

heads), check them for any looseness or evidence of movement. All of the guides should appear to be at the same height from the spring seat. If any seem lower (or higher) from another, the guide has moved. Mount a dial indicator onto the spring side of the cylinder head. Lightly oil the valve stem and insert it into the cylinder head. Position the dial indicator against the valve stem near the tip and zero the gauge. Grasp the valve stem and wiggle towards and away from the dial indicator and observe the readings. Mount the dial indicator 90 degrees from the initial point and zero the gauge and again take a reading. Compare the two readings for a out of round condition. Check the readings against the specifications given. An Inside Diameter (I.D.) gauge designed for valve guides will give you an accurate valve guide bore measurement. If the I.D. gauge is used, compare the readings with the specifications given. Any guides that fail these inspections should be replaced or machined.

VALVE SEATS

A visual inspection of the valve seats should show a slightly worn and pitted surface where the valve face contacts the seat. Inspect the seat carefully for severe pitting or cracks. Also, a seat that is badly worn will be recessed into the cylinder head. A severely worn or recessed seat may need to be replaced. All cracked seats must be replaced. A seat concentricity gauge, if available, should be used to check the seat run-out. If run-out exceeds specifications the seat must be machined (if no specification is given use 0.002 in. or 0.051mm).

CYLINDER HEAD SURFACE FLATNESS

▶ **See Figures 276 and 277**

After you have cleaned the gasket surface of the cylinder head of any old gasket material, check the head for flatness.

Place a straightedge across the gasket surface. Using feeler gauges, determine the clearance at the center of the straightedge and across the cylinder head at several points. Check along the centerline and diagonally on the head surface. If the warpage exceeds 0.003 in. (0.076mm) within a 6.0 in. (15.2cm) span, or 0.006 in. (0.152mm) over the total length of the head, the cylinder head must be resurfaced. After resurfacing the heads of a V-type engine, the intake manifold flange surface should be checked, and if necessary, milled proportionally to allow for the change in its mounting position.

CRACKS AND PHYSICAL DAMAGE

Generally, cracks are limited to the combustion chamber, however, it is not uncommon for the head to crack in a spark plug hole, port, outside of the head or in the valve spring/rocker arm area. The first area to inspect is always the hottest; the exhaust seat/port area.

A visual inspection should be performed, but just because you don't see a crack does not mean it is not there. Some more reliable methods for inspecting for cracks include Magnaflux®, a magnetic process or Zyglo®, a dye penetrant. Magnaflux® is used only on ferrous metal (cast iron) heads. Zyglo® uses a spray on fluorescent mixture along with a black light to reveal the cracks. It is strongly recommended to have your cylinder head checked professionally for cracks, especially if the engine was known to have overheated and/or leaked or consumed coolant. Contact a local shop for availability and pricing of these services.

Physical damage is usually very evident. For example, a broken mounting ear from dropping the head or a bent or broken stud and/or bolt. All of these defects should be fixed or, if unrepairable, the head should be replaced.

Camshaft and Followers

Inspect the camshaft(s) and followers as described earlier in this section.

REFINISHING & REPAIRING

Many of the procedures given for refinishing and repairing the cylinder head components must be performed by a machine shop. Certain steps, if the inspected part is not worn, can be performed yourself inexpensively. However, you spent a lot of time and effort so far, why risk trying to save a couple bucks if you might have to do it all over again?

Valves

Any valves that were not replaced should be refaced and the tips ground flat. Unless you have access to a valve grinding machine, this should be done by a machine shop. If the valves are in extremely good condition, as well as the valve seats and guides, they may be lapped in without performing machine work.

It is a recommended practice to lap the valves even after machine work has been performed and/or new valves have been purchased. This insures a positive seal between the valve and seat.

LAPPING THE VALVES

➡**Before lapping the valves to the seats, read the rest of the cylinder head section to insure that any related parts are in acceptable enough condition to continue.**

➡**Before any valve seat machining and/or lapping can be performed, the guides must be within factory recommended specifications.**

1. Invert the cylinder head.
2. Lightly lubricate the valve stems and insert them into the cylinder head in their numbered order.
3. Raise the valve from the seat and apply a small amount of fine lapping compound to the seat.
4. Moisten the suction head of a hand-lapping tool and attach it to the head of the valve.
5. Rotate the tool between the palms of both hands, changing the position of the valve on the valve seat and lifting the tool often to prevent grooving.
6. Lap the valve until a smooth, polished circle is evident on the valve and seat.
7. Remove the tool and the valve. Wipe away all traces of the grinding compound and store the valve to maintain its lapped location.

✳✳ WARNING

Do not get the valves out of order after they have been lapped. They must be put back with the same valve seat with which they were lapped.

Fig. 275 A dial gauge may be used to check valve stem-to-guide clearance; read the gauge while moving the valve stem

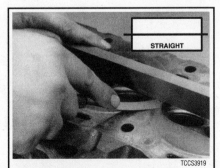

Fig. 276 Check the head for flatness across the center of the head surface using a straightedge and feeler gauge

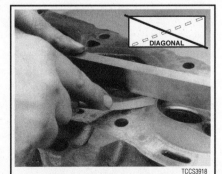

Fig. 277 Checks should also be made along both diagonals of the head surface

Springs, Retainers and Valve Locks

There is no repair or refinishing possible with the springs, retainers and valve locks. If they are found to be worn or defective, they must be replaced with new (or known good) parts.

Cylinder Head

Most refinishing procedures dealing with the cylinder head must be performed by a machine shop. Read the sections below and review your inspection data to determine whether or not machining is necessary.

VALVE GUIDE

➡**If any machining or replacements are made to the valve guides, the seats must be machined.**

Unless the valve guides need machining or replacing, the only service to perform is to thoroughly clean them of any dirt or oil residue.

There are only two types of valve guides used on automobile engines: the replaceable-type (all aluminum heads) and the cast-in integral-type (most cast iron heads). There are four recommended methods for repairing worn guides.

* Knurling
* Inserts
* Reaming oversize
* Replacing

Knurling is a process in which metal is displaced and raised, thereby reducing clearance, giving a true center, and providing oil control. It is the least expensive way of repairing the valve guides. However, it is not necessarily the best, and in some cases, a knurled valve guide will not stand up for more than a short time. It requires a special knurlizer and precision reaming tools to obtain proper clearances. It would not be cost effective to purchase these tools, unless you plan on rebuilding several of the same cylinder head.

Installing a guide insert involves machining the guide to accept a bronze insert. One style is the coil-type which is installed into a threaded guide. Another is the thin-walled insert where the guide is reamed oversize to accept a split-sleeve insert. After the insert is installed, a special tool is then run through the guide to expand the insert, locking it to the guide. The insert is then reamed to the standard size for proper valve clearance.

Reaming for oversize valves restores normal clearances and provides a true valve seat. Most cast-in type guides can be reamed to accept an valve with an oversize stem. The cost factor for this can become quite high as you will need to purchase the reamer and new, oversize stem valves for all guides which were reamed. Oversize guides are generally 0.003 to 0.030 in. (0.076 to 0.762mm), with 0.015 in. (0.381mm) being the most common.

To replace cast-in type valve guides, they must be drilled out, then reamed to accept replacement guides. This must be done on a fixture which will allow centering and leveling off of the original valve seat or guide, otherwise a serious guide-to-seat misalignment may occur making it impossible to properly machine the seat.

Replaceable-type guides are pressed into the cylinder head. A hammer and a stepped drift or punch may be used to install and remove the guides. Before removing the guides, measure the protrusion on the spring side of the head and record it for installation. Use the stepped drift to hammer out the old guide from the combustion chamber side of the head. When installing, determine whether or not the guide also seals a water jacket in the head, and if it does, use the recommended sealing agent. If there is no water jacket, grease the valve guide and its bore. Use the stepped drift, and hammer the new guide into the cylinder head from the spring side of the cylinder head. A stack of washers the same thickness as the measured protrusion may help the installation process.

VALVE SEATS

➡**Before any valve seat machining can be performed, the guides must be within factory recommended specifications.**

➡**If any machining or replacements were made to the valve guides, the seats must be machined.**

If the seats are in good condition, the valves can be lapped to the seats, and the cylinder head assembled. See the valves section for instructions on lapping.

If the valve seats are worn, cracked or damaged, they must be serviced by a machine shop. The valve seat must be perfectly centered to the valve guide, which requires very accurate machining.

CYLINDER HEAD SURFACE

If the cylinder head is warped, it must be machined flat. If the warpage is extremely severe, the head may need to be replaced. In some instances, it may be possible to straighten a warped head enough to allow machining. In either case, contact a professional machine shop for service.

➡**Any OHC cylinder head that shows excessive warpage should have the camshaft bearing journals align bored after the cylinder head has been resurfaced.**

⁕⁕ WARNING

Failure to align bore the camshaft bearing journals could result in severe engine damage including but not limited to: valve and piston damage, connecting rod damage, camshaft and/or crankshaft breakage.

CRACKS AND PHYSICAL DAMAGE

Certain cracks can be repaired in both cast iron and aluminum heads. For cast iron, a tapered threaded insert is installed along the length of the crack. Aluminum can also use the tapered inserts, however welding is the preferred method. Some physical damage can be repaired through brazing or welding. Contact a machine shop to get expert advice for your particular dilemma.

ASSEMBLY

The first step for any assembly job is to have a clean area in which to work. Next, thoroughly clean all of the parts and components that are to be assembled. Finally, place all of the components onto a suitable work space and, if necessary, arrange the parts to their respective positions.

OHC Engines

▶ **See Figure 278**

CUP TYPE CAMSHAFT FOLLOWERS

To install the springs, retainers and valve locks on heads which have these components recessed into the camshaft follower's bore, you will need a small screwdriver-type tool, some clean white grease and a lot of patience. You will also need the C-clamp style spring compressor and the OHC tool used to disassemble the head.

1. Lightly lubricate the valve stems and insert all of the valves into the cylinder head. If possible, maintain their original locations.
2. If equipped, install any valve spring shims which were removed.
3. If equipped, install the new valve seals, keeping the following in mind:
* If the valve seal presses over the guide, lightly lubricate the outer guide surfaces.

TCCA3P64

Fig. 278 Once assembled, check the valve clearance and correct as needed

- If the seal is an O-ring type, it is installed just after compressing the spring but before the valve locks.

4. Place the valve spring and retainer over the stem.

5. Position the spring compressor and the OHC tool, then compress the spring.

6. Using a small screwdriver as a spatula, fill the valve stem side of the lock with white grease. Use the excess grease on the screwdriver to fasten the lock to the driver.

7. Carefully install the valve lock, which is stuck to the end of the screwdriver, to the valve stem then press on it with the screwdriver until the grease squeezes out. The valve lock should now be stuck to the stem.

8. Repeat Steps 6 and 7 for the remaining valve lock.

9. Relieve the spring pressure slowly and insure that neither valve lock becomes dislodged by the retainer.

10. Remove the spring compressor tool.

11. Repeat Steps 2 through 10 until all of the springs have been installed.

12. Install the followers, camshaft(s) and any other components that were removed for disassembly.

ROCKER ARM TYPE CAMSHAFT FOLLOWERS

1. Lightly lubricate the valve stems and insert all of the valves into the cylinder head. If possible, maintain their original locations.

2. If equipped, install any valve spring shims which were removed.

3. If equipped, install the new valve seals, keeping the following in mind:

- If the valve seal presses over the guide, lightly lubricate the outer guide surfaces.
- If the seal is an O-ring type, it is installed just after compressing the spring but before the valve locks.

4. Place the valve spring and retainer over the stem.

5. Position the spring compressor tool and compress the spring.

6. Assemble the valve locks to the stem.

7. Relieve the spring pressure slowly and insure that neither valve lock becomes dislodged by the retainer.

8. Remove the spring compressor tool.

9. Repeat Steps 2 through 8 until all of the springs have been installed.

10. Install the camshaft(s), rockers, shafts and any other components that were removed for disassembly.

Engine Block

GENERAL INFORMATION

A thorough overhaul or rebuild of an engine block would include replacing the pistons, rings, bearings, timing belt/chain assembly and oil pump. The block would then have the cylinders bored and honed oversize (or if using removable cylinder sleeves, new sleeves installed) and the crankshaft would be cut undersize to provide new wearing surfaces and perfect clearances. However, your particular engine may not have everything worn out. What if only the piston rings have worn out and the clearances on everything else are still within factory specifications? Well, you could just replace the rings and put it back together, but this would be a very rare example. Chances are, if one component in your engine is worn, other components are sure to follow, and soon. At the very least, you should always replace the rings, bearings and oil pump. This is what is commonly called a "freshen up".

Cylinder Ridge Removal

Because the top piston ring does not travel to the very top of the cylinder, a ridge is built up between the end of the travel and the top of the cylinder bore.

Pushing the piston and connecting rod assembly past the ridge can be difficult, and damage to the piston ring lands could occur. If the ridge is not removed before installing a new piston or not removed at all, piston ring breakage and piston damage may occur.

➡It is always recommended that you remove any cylinder ridges before removing the piston and connecting rod assemblies. If you know that new pistons are going to be installed and the engine block will be bored oversize, you may be able to forego this step. However, some ridges may actually prevent the assemblies from being removed, necessitating its removal.

There are several different types of ridge reamers on the market, none of which are inexpensive. Unless a great deal of engine rebuilding is anticipated, borrow or rent a reamer.

1. Turn the crankshaft until the piston is at the bottom of its travel.

2. Cover the head of the piston with a rag.

3. Follow the tool manufacturers instructions and cut away the ridge, exercising extreme care to avoid cutting too deeply.

4. Remove the ridge reamer, the rag and as many of the cuttings as possible. Continue until all of the cylinder ridges have been removed.

DISASSEMBLY

▶ **See Figures 279 and 280**

The engine disassembly instructions following assume that you have the engine mounted on an engine stand. If not, it is easiest to disassemble the engine on a bench or the floor with it resting on the bellhousing or transmission mounting surface. You must be able to access the connecting rod fasteners and turn the crankshaft during disassembly. Also, all engine covers (timing, front, side, oil pan, whatever) should have already been removed. Engines which are seized or locked up may not be able to be completely disassembled, and a core (salvage yard) engine should be purchased.

If not done during the cylinder head removal, remove the timing chain/belt and/or gear/sprocket assembly. Remove the oil pick-up and pump assembly and, if necessary, the pump drive. If equipped, remove any balance or auxiliary shafts. If necessary, remove the cylinder ridge from the top of the bore. See the cylinder ridge removal procedure earlier in this section.

Rotate the engine over so that the crankshaft is exposed. Use a number punch or scribe and mark each connecting rod with its respective cylinder number. The cylinder closest to the front of the engine is always number 1. However, depending on the engine placement, the front of the engine could either be the flywheel or damper/pulley end. Generally the front of the engine faces the front of the vehicle. Use a number punch or scribe and also mark the main bearing caps from front to rear with the front most cap being number 1 (if there are five caps, mark them 1 through 5, front to rear).

✳✳ WARNING

Take special care when pushing the connecting rod up from the crankshaft because the sharp threads of the rod bolts/studs will score the crankshaft journal. Insure that special plastic caps are installed over them, or cut two pieces of rubber hose to do the same.

Again, rotate the engine, this time to position the number one cylinder bore (head surface) up. Turn the crankshaft until the number one piston is at the bottom of its travel, this should allow the maximum access to its connecting rod. Remove the number one connecting rods fasteners and cap and place two

TCCS3803
Fig. 279 Place rubber hose over the connecting rod studs to protect the crankshaft and cylinder bores from damage

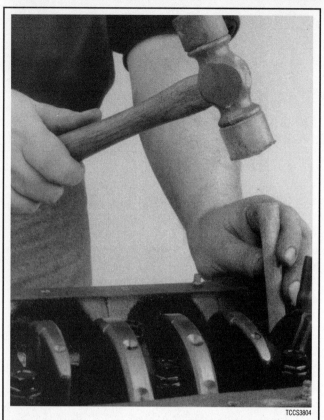

Fig. 280 Carefully tap the piston out of the bore using a wooden dowel

lengths of rubber hose over the rod bolts/studs to protect the crankshaft from damage. Using a sturdy wooden dowel and a hammer, push the connecting rod up about 1 in. (25mm) from the crankshaft and remove the upper bearing insert. Continue pushing or tapping the connecting rod up until the piston rings are out of the cylinder bore. Remove the piston and rod by hand, put the upper half of the bearing insert back into the rod, install the cap with its bearing insert installed, and hand-tighten the cap fasteners. If the parts are kept in order in this manner, they will not get lost and you will be able to tell which bearings came form what cylinder if any problems are discovered and diagnosis is necessary. Remove all the other piston assemblies in the same manner. On V-style engines, remove all of the pistons from one bank, then reposition the engine with the other cylinder bank head surface up, and remove that banks piston assemblies.

The only remaining component in the engine block should now be the crankshaft. Loosen the main bearing caps evenly until the fasteners can be turned by hand, then remove them and the caps. Remove the crankshaft from the engine block. Thoroughly clean all of the components.

INSPECTION

Now that the engine block and all of its components are clean, it's time to inspect them for wear and/or damage. To accurately inspect them, you will need some specialized tools:

• Two or three separate micrometers to measure the pistons and crankshaft journals
• A dial indicator
• Telescoping gauges for the cylinder bores
• A rod alignment fixture to check for bent connecting rods

If you do not have access to the proper tools, you may want to bring the components to a shop that does.

Generally, you shouldn't expect cracks in the engine block or its components unless it was known to leak, consume or mix engine fluids, it was severely overheated, or there was evidence of bad bearings and/or crankshaft damage. A visual inspection should be performed on all of the components, but just because you don't see a crack does not mean it is not there. Some more reliable methods for inspecting for cracks include Magnaflux®, a magnetic process or

Zyglo®, a dye penetrant. Magnaflux® is used only on ferrous metal (cast iron). Zyglo® uses a spray on fluorescent mixture along with a black light to reveal the cracks. It is strongly recommended to have your engine block checked professionally for cracks, especially if the engine was known to have overheated and/or leaked or consumed coolant. Contact a local shop for availability and pricing of these services.

Engine Block

ENGINE BLOCK BEARING ALIGNMENT

Remove the main bearing caps and, if still installed, the main bearing inserts. Inspect all of the main bearing saddles and caps for damage, burrs or high spots. If damage is found, and it is caused from a spun main bearing, the block will need to be align-bored or, if severe enough, replacement. Any burrs or high spots should be carefully removed with a metal file.

Place a straightedge on the bearing saddles, in the engine block, along the centerline of the crankshaft. If any clearance exists between the straightedge and the saddles, the block must be align-bored.

Align-boring consists of machining the main bearing saddles and caps by means of a flycutter that runs through the bearing saddles.

DECK FLATNESS

The top of the engine block where the cylinder head mounts is called the deck. Insure that the deck surface is clean of dirt, carbon deposits and old gasket material. Place a straightedge across the surface of the deck along its centerline and, using feeler gauges, check the clearance along several points. Repeat the checking procedure with the straightedge placed along both diagonals of the deck surface. If the reading exceeds 0.003 in. (0.076mm) within a 6.0 in. (15.2cm) span, or 0.006 in. (0.152mm) over the total length of the deck, it must be machined.

CYLINDER BORES

▶ See Figure 281

The cylinder bores house the pistons and are slightly larger than the pistons themselves. A common piston-to-bore clearance is 0.0015–0.0025 in. (0.0381mm–0.0635mm). Inspect and measure the cylinder bores. The bore should be checked for out-of-roundness, taper and size. The results of this inspection will determine whether the cylinder can be used in its existing size and condition, or a rebore to the next oversize is required (or in the case of removable sleeves, have replacements installed).

The amount of cylinder wall wear is always greater at the top of the cylinder than at the bottom. This wear is known as taper. Any cylinder that has a taper of 0.0012 in. (0.305mm) or more, must be rebored. Measurements are taken at a number of positions in each cylinder: at the top, middle and bottom and at two points at each position; that is, at a point 90 degrees from the crankshaft centerline, as well as a point parallel to the crankshaft centerline. The measurements are made with either a special dial indicator or a telescopic gauge and micrometer. If the necessary precision tools to check the bore are not available, take the block to a machine shop and have them measure it. Also if you don't have the tools to check the cylinder bores, chances are you will not have the necessary devices to check the pistons, connecting rods and crankshaft. Take these components with you and save yourself an extra trip.

For our procedures, we will use a telescopic gauge and a micrometer. You will need one of each, with a measuring range which covers your cylinder bore size.

1. Position the telescopic gauge in the cylinder bore, loosen the gauges lock and allow it to expand.

➡️**Your first two readings will be at the top of the cylinder bore, then proceed to the middle and finally the bottom, making a total of six measurements.**

2. Hold the gauge square in the bore, 90 degrees from the crankshaft centerline, and gently tighten the lock. Tilt the gauge back to remove it from the bore.

3. Measure the gauge with the micrometer and record the reading.

4. Again, hold the gauge square in the bore, this time parallel to the crankshaft centerline, and gently tighten the lock. Again, you will tilt the gauge back to remove it from the bore.

5. Measure the gauge with the micrometer and record this reading. The difference between these two readings is the out-of-round measurement of the cylinder.

6. Repeat steps 1 through 5, each time going to the next lower position, until you reach the bottom of the cylinder. Then go to the next cylinder, and continue until all of the cylinders have been measured.

The difference between these measurements will tell you all about the wear in your cylinders. The measurements which were taken 90 degrees from the crankshaft centerline will always reflect the most wear. That is because at this position is where the engine power presses the piston against the cylinder bore the hardest. This is known as thrust wear. Take your top, 90 degree measurement and compare it to your bottom, 90 degree measurement. The difference between them is the taper. When you measure your pistons, you will compare these readings to your piston sizes and determine piston-to-wall clearance.

Crankshaft

Inspect the crankshaft for visible signs of wear or damage. All of the journals should be perfectly round and smooth. Slight scores are normal for a used crankshaft, but you should hardly feel them with your fingernail. When measuring the crankshaft with a micrometer, you will take readings at the front and rear of each journal, then turn the micrometer 90 degrees and take two more readings, front and rear. The difference between the front-to-rear readings is the journal taper and the first-to-90 degree reading is the out-of-round measurement. Generally, there should be no taper or out-of-roundness found, however, up to 0.0005 in. (0.0127mm) for either can be overlooked. Also, the readings should fall within the factory specifications for journal diameters.

If the crankshaft journals fall within specifications, it is recommended that it be polished before being returned to service. Polishing the crankshaft insures that any minor burrs or high spots are smoothed, thereby reducing the chance of scoring the new bearings.

Pistons and Connecting Rods

PISTONS

♦ **See Figure 282**

The piston should be visually inspected for any signs of cracking or burning (caused by hot spots or detonation), and scuffing or excessive wear on the skirts. The wristpin attaches the piston to the connecting rod. The piston should move freely on the wrist pin, both sliding and pivoting. Grasp the connecting rod securely, or mount it in a vise, and try to rock the piston back and forth along the centerline of the wristpin. There should not be any excessive play evident between the piston and the pin. If there are C-clips retaining the pin in the piston then you have wrist pin bushings in the rods. There should not be any excessive play between the wrist pin and the rod bushing. Normal clearance for the wrist pin is approx. 0.001–0.002 in. (0.025mm–0.051mm).

Use a micrometer and measure the diameter of the piston, perpendicular to the wrist pin, on the skirt. Compare the reading to its original cylinder measurement obtained earlier. The difference between the two readings is the piston-to-wall clearance. If the clearance is within specifications, the piston may be used as is. If the piston is out of specification, but the bore is not, you will need a new piston. If both are out of specification, you will need the cylinder rebored and oversize pistons installed. Generally if two or more pistons/bores are out of specification, it is best to rebore the entire block and purchase a complete set of oversize pistons.

CONNECTING ROD

You should have the connecting rod checked for straightness at a machine shop. If the connecting rod is bent, it will unevenly wear the bearing and piston, as well as place greater stress on these components. Any bent or twisted connecting rods must be replaced. If the rods are straight and the wrist pin clearance is within specifications, then only the bearing end of the rod need be checked. Place the connecting rod into a vice, with the bearing inserts in place, install the cap to the rod and torque the fasteners to specifications. Use a telescoping gauge and carefully measure the inside diameter of the bearings. Compare this reading to the rods original crankshaft journal diameter measurement. The difference is the oil clearance. If the oil clearance is not within specifications, install new bearings in the rod and take another measurement. If the clearance is still out of specifications, and the crankshaft is not, the rod will need to be reconditioned by a machine shop.

➡**You can also use Plastigage® to check the bearing clearances. The assembling section has complete instructions on its use.**

Camshaft

Inspect the camshaft and hydraulic lash adjusters/followers as described earlier in this section.

Bearings

All of the engine bearings should be visually inspected for wear and/or damage. The bearing should look evenly worn all around with no deep scores or pits. If the bearing is severely worn, scored, pitted or heat blued, then the bearing, and the components that use it, should be brought to a machine shop for inspection. Full-circle bearings (used on most camshafts, auxiliary shafts, balance shafts, etc.) require specialized tools for removal and installation, and should be brought to a machine shop for service.

Oil Pump

➡**The oil pump is responsible for providing constant lubrication to the whole engine and so it is recommended that a new oil pump be installed when rebuilding the engine.**

Completely disassemble the oil pump and thoroughly clean all of the components. Inspect the oil pump gears and housing for wear and/or damage. Insure that the pressure relief valve operates properly and there is no binding or sticking due to varnish or debris. If all of the parts are in proper working condition, lubricate the gears and relief valve, and assemble the pump.

REFINISHING

♦ **See Figure 283**

Almost all engine block refinishing must be performed by a machine shop. If the cylinders are not to be rebored, then the cylinder glaze can be removed with a ball hone. When removing cylinder glaze with a ball hone, use a light or penetrating type oil to lubricate the hone. Do not allow the hone to run dry as this may cause excessive scoring of the cylinder bores and wear on the hone. If new pistons are required, they will need to be installed to the connecting rods. This should be performed by a machine shop as the pistons must be installed in the correct relationship to the rod or engine damage can occur.

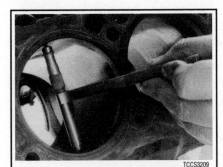

TCCS3209

Fig. 281 Use a telescoping gauge to measure the cylinder bore diameter—take several readings within the same bore

TCCS3210

Fig. 282 Measure the piston's outer diameter, perpendicular to the wrist pin, with a micrometer

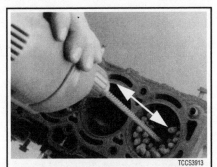

TCCS3913

Fig. 283 Use a ball type cylinder hone to remove any glaze and provide a new surface for seating the piston rings

Pistons and Connecting Rods

▶ **See Figure 284**

Only pistons with the wrist pin retained by C-clips are serviceable by the home-mechanic. Press fit pistons require special presses and/or heaters to remove/install the connecting rod and should only be performed by a machine shop.

All pistons will have a mark indicating the direction to the front of the engine and the must be installed into the engine in that manner. Usually it is a notch or arrow on the top of the piston, or it may be the letter F cast or stamped into the piston.

1. Note the location of the forward mark on the piston and mark the connecting rod in relation.
2. Remove the C-clips from the piston and withdraw the wrist pin.

➡ **Varnish build-up or C-clip groove burrs may increase the difficulty of removing the wrist pin. If necessary, use a punch or drift to carefully tap the wrist pin out.**

3. Insure that the wrist pin bushing in the connecting rod is usable, and lubricate it with assembly lube.
4. Remove the wrist pin from the new piston and lubricate the pin bores on the piston.
5. Align the forward marks on the piston and the connecting rod and install the wrist pin.
6. The new C-clips will have a flat and a rounded side to them. Install both C-clips with the flat side facing out.
7. Repeat all of the steps for each piston being replaced.

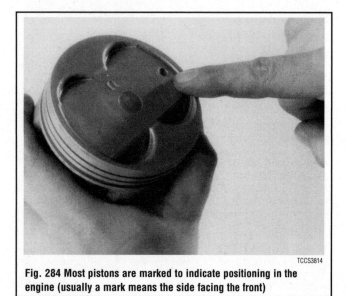

Fig. 284 Most pistons are marked to indicate positioning in the engine (usually a mark means the side facing the front)

ASSEMBLY

Before you begin assembling the engine, first give yourself a clean, dirt free work area. Next, clean every engine component again. The key to a good assembly is cleanliness.

Mount the engine block into the engine stand and wash it one last time using water and detergent (dishwashing detergent works well). While washing it, scrub the cylinder bores with a soft bristle brush and thoroughly clean all of the oil passages. Completely dry the engine and spray the entire assembly down with an anti-rust solution such as WD-40® or similar product. Take a clean lint-free rag and wipe up any excess anti-rust solution from the bores, bearing saddles, etc. Repeat the final cleaning process on the crankshaft. Replace any freeze or oil galley plugs which were removed during disassembly.

Crankshaft

▶ **See Figures 285, 286, 287 and 288**

1. Remove the main bearing inserts from the block and bearing caps.
2. If the crankshaft main bearing journals have been refinished to a definite

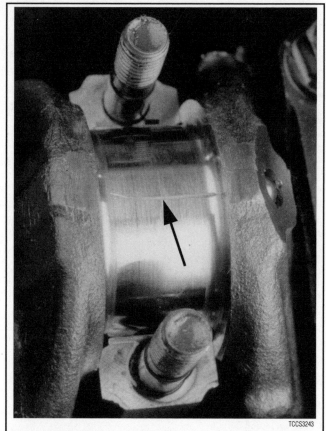

Fig. 285 Apply a strip of gauging material to the bearing journal, then install and torque the cap

undersize, install the correct undersize bearing. Be sure that the bearing inserts and bearing bores are clean. Foreign material under inserts will distort bearing and cause failure.

3. Place the upper main bearing inserts in bores with tang in slot.

➡ **The oil holes in the bearing inserts must be aligned with the oil holes in the cylinder block.**

4. Install the lower main bearing inserts in bearing caps.
5. Clean the mating surfaces of block and rear main bearing cap.
6. Carefully lower the crankshaft into place. Be careful not to damage bearing surfaces.
7. Check the clearance of each main bearing by using the following procedure:

    a. Place a piece of Plastigage® or its equivalent, on bearing surface across full width of bearing cap and about ¼ in. off center.

    b. Install cap and tighten bolts to specifications. Do not turn crankshaft while Plastigage® is in place.

    c. Remove the cap. Using the supplied Plastigage® scale, check width of Plastigage® at widest point to get maximum clearance. Difference between readings is taper of journal.

    d. If clearance exceeds specified limits, try a 0.001 in. or 0.002 in. undersize bearing in combination with the standard bearing. Bearing clearance must be within specified limits. If standard and 0.002 in. undersize bearing does not bring clearance within desired limits, refinish crankshaft journal, then install undersize bearings.

8. After the bearings have been fitted, apply a light coat of engine oil to the journals and bearings. Install the rear main bearing cap. Install all bearing caps except the thrust bearing cap. Be sure that main bearing caps are installed in original locations. Tighten the bearing cap bolts to specifications.
9. Install the thrust bearing cap with bolts finger-tight.
10. Pry the crankshaft forward against the thrust surface of upper half of bearing.
11. Hold the crankshaft forward and pry the thrust bearing cap to the rear. This aligns the thrust surfaces of both halves of the bearing.

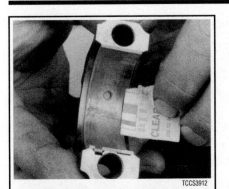

Fig. 286 After the cap is removed again, use the scale supplied with the gauging material to check the clearance

Fig. 287 A dial gauge may be used to check crankshaft end-play

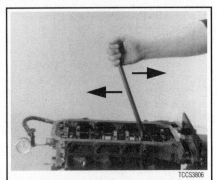

Fig. 288 Carefully pry the crankshaft back and forth while reading the dial gauge for end-play

12. Retain the forward pressure on the crankshaft. Tighten the cap bolts to specifications.

13. Measure the crankshaft end-play as follows:

a. Mount a dial gauge to the engine block and position the tip of the gauge to read from the crankshaft end.

b. Carefully pry the crankshaft toward the rear of the engine and hold it there while you zero the gauge.

c. Carefully pry the crankshaft toward the front of the engine and read the gauge.

d. Confirm that the reading is within specifications. If not, install a new thrust bearing and repeat the procedure. If the reading is still out of specifications with a new bearing, have a machine shop inspect the thrust surfaces of the crankshaft, and if possible, repair it.

14. Rotate the crankshaft so as to position the first rod journal to the bottom of its stroke.

Pistons and Connecting Rods

▶ See Figures 289, 290, 291 and 292

1. Before installing the piston/connecting rod assembly, oil the pistons, piston rings and the cylinder walls with light engine oil. Install connecting rod bolt protectors or rubber hose onto the connecting rod bolts/studs. Also perform the following:

a. Select the proper ring set for the size cylinder bore.

b. Position the ring in the bore in which it is going to be used.

c. Push the ring down into the bore area where normal ring wear is not encountered.

d. Use the head of the piston to position the ring in the bore so that the ring is square with the cylinder wall. Use caution to avoid damage to the ring or cylinder bore.

e. Measure the gap between the ends of the ring with a feeler gauge. Ring gap in a worn cylinder is normally greater than specification. If the ring gap is greater than the specified limits, try an oversize ring set.

f. Check the ring side clearance of the compression rings with a feeler gauge inserted between the ring and its lower land according to specifica-

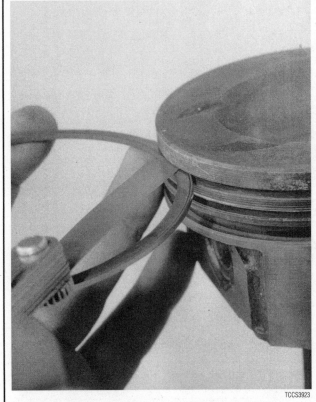

Fig. 289 Checking the piston ring-to-ring groove side clearance using the ring and a feeler gauge

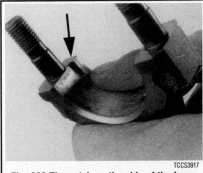

Fig. 290 The notch on the side of the bearing cap matches the tang on the bearing insert

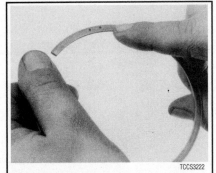

Fig. 291 Most rings are marked to show which side of the ring should face up when installed to the piston

Fig. 292 Install the piston and rod assembly into the block using a ring compressor and the handle of a hammer

tion. The gauge should slide freely around the entire ring circumference without binding. Any wear that occurs will form a step at the inner portion of the lower land. If the lower lands have high steps, the piston should be replaced.

2. Unless new pistons are installed, be sure to install the pistons in the cylinders from which they were removed. The numbers on the connecting rod and bearing cap must be on the same side when installed in the cylinder bore. If a connecting rod is ever transposed from one engine or cylinder to another, new bearings should be fitted and the connecting rod should be numbered to correspond with the new cylinder number. The notch on the piston head goes toward the front of the engine.

3. Install all of the rod bearing inserts into the rods and caps.

4. Install the rings to the pistons. Install the oil control ring first, then the second compression ring and finally the top compression ring. Use a piston ring expander tool to aid in installation and to help reduce the chance of breakage.

5. Make sure the ring gaps are properly spaced around the circumference of the piston. Fit a piston ring compressor around the piston and slide the piston and connecting rod assembly down into the cylinder bore, pushing it in with the wooden hammer handle. Push the piston down until it is only slightly below the top of the cylinder bore. Guide the connecting rod onto the crankshaft bearing journal carefully, to avoid damaging the crankshaft.

6. Check the bearing clearance of all the rod bearings, fitting them to the crankshaft bearing journals. Follow the procedure in the crankshaft installation above.

7. After the bearings have been fitted, apply a light coating of assembly oil to the journals and bearings.

8. Turn the crankshaft until the appropriate bearing journal is at the bottom of its stroke, then push the piston assembly all the way down until the connecting rod bearing seats on the crankshaft journal. Be careful not to allow the bearing cap screws to strike the crankshaft bearing journals and damage them.

9. After the piston and connecting rod assemblies have been installed, check the connecting rod side clearance on each crankshaft journal.

10. Prime and install the oil pump and the oil pump intake tube.

11. Install the auxiliary/balance shaft(s)/assembly(ies).

CYLINDER HEAD(S)

1. Install the cylinder head(s) using new gaskets.
2. Install the timing sprockets/gears and the belt/chain assemblies.

Engine Covers and Components

Install the timing cover(s) and oil pan. Refer to your notes and drawings made prior to disassembly and install all of the components that were removed. Install the engine into the vehicle.

Engine Start-up and Break-in

STARTING THE ENGINE

Now that the engine is installed and every wire and hose is properly connected, go back and double check that all coolant and vacuum hoses are connected. Check that you oil drain plug is installed and properly tightened. If not already done, install a new oil filter onto the engine. Fill the crankcase with the proper amount and grade of engine oil. Fill the cooling system with a 50/50 mixture of coolant/water.

1. Connect the vehicle battery.
2. Start the engine. Keep your eye on your oil pressure indicator; if it does not indicate oil pressure within 10 seconds of starting, turn the vehicle off.

❋❋ WARNING

Damage to the engine can result if it is allowed to run with no oil pressure. Check the engine oil level to make sure that it is full. Check for any leaks and if found, repair the leaks before continuing. If there is still no indication of oil pressure, you may need to prime the system.

3. Confirm that there are no fluid leaks (oil or other).
4. Allow the engine to reach normal operating temperature (the upper radiator hose will be hot to the touch).
5. If necessary, set the ignition timing.
6. Install any remaining components such as the air cleaner (if removed for ignition timing) or body panels which were removed.

BREAKING IT IN

Make the first miles on the new engine, easy ones. Vary the speed but do not accelerate hard. Most importantly, do not lug the engine, and avoid sustained high speeds until at least 100 miles. Check the engine oil and coolant levels frequently. Expect the engine to use a little oil until the rings seat. Change the oil and filter at 500 miles, 1500 miles, then every 3000 miles past that.

ENGINE TORQUE SPECIFICATIONS

Component	English Specification	Metric Specification
Rocker arm cover		
VG30E	.07–2.2 ft. lbs.	1–3 Nm
VE30DE ①		
1. Bolts 1,2,12,11,9,14	2.9 ft. lbs.	4 Nm
2. Bolts 1 through 14	5.8–7.2 ft. lbs.	8–10 Nm
VQ30DE ①		
1. Bolts 1 through 10	.07–2.2 ft. lbs.	1–3 Nm
2. Bolts 1 through 10	4.0–5.5 ft. lbs.	5.4–7.4 Nm
Rocker arm shaft		
VG30E	13–16 ft. lbs.	18–22 Nm
Thermostat		
VG30E	12–15 ft. lbs.	16–21 Nm
VE30DE	12–15 ft. lbs.	16–21Nm
VQ30DE	6.2–8.3 ft. lbs.	8.4–11.2 Nm

ENGINE TORQUE SPECIFICATIONS

Component	English Specification	Metric Specification
Intake manifold		
VG30E ②		
Lower	17–20 ft. lbs.	24–27 Nm
Upper	13–16 ft. lbs.	18–22 Nm
VE30DE ②		
Lower		
Bolts	12–14 ft. lbs.	16–20 Nm
Nuts	17–20 ft. lbs.	24–27 Nm
Upper	13–16 ft. lbs.	18–22 Nm
VQ30DE ②		
Lower	20–23 ft. lbs.	26–31 Nm
Upper	13–16 ft. lbs.	18–22 Nm
Exhaust manifold		
VG30E	13–16 ft. lbs.	16–22 Nm
VE30DE	13–16 ft. lbs.	16–22 Nm
VQ30DE	13–16 ft. lbs.	16–22 Nm
Water pump		
VG30E	12–15 ft. lbs.	16–21 Nm
VE30DE	12–15 ft. lbs.	16–21 Nm
VQ30DE	5.1–7.2 ft. lbs.	7–10 Nm
Cylinder head		
VG30E ②		
Step 1	22 ft. lbs.	29 Nm
Step 2	43 ft. lbs.	59 Nm
Step 3	Loosen all bolts completely	
Step 4	22 ft. lbs.	29 Nm
Step 5	40–47 ft. lbs.	54–64 Nm
VE30DE ②		
Step 1	29 ft. lbs.	39 Nm
Step 2	90 ft. lbs.	123 Nm
Step 3	Loosen all bolts completely	
Step 4	25–33 ft. lbs.	34–44 Nm
Step 5	87–94 ft. lbs.	118–127 Nm
VQ30DE ②		
1	72 ft. lbs.	98 Nm
2	Loosen all bolts completely	
3	25–35 ft. lbs.	34–44 Nm
4	90-95 deg. clockwise	
5	90-95 deg. clockwise	
Oil pan		
VG30E ①	5.1–5.8 ft. lbs.	7–8 Nm
VE30DE A	5.1–5.8 ft. lbs.	7–8 Nm
VQ30DE ①		
Lower	4.7–5.5 ft. lbs.	6.4–7.5 Nm
Upper	12–14 ft. lbs.	16–19 Nm

89613CA7

ENGINE TORQUE SPECIFICATIONS

Component	English Specification	Metric Specification
Oil pump		
VG30E		
Long bolts	12–14 ft. lbs.	12–16 Nm
Short bolts	4.3–5.1 ft. lbs.	6–7 Nm
VE30DE	12–15 ft. lbs.	16–21 Nm
VQ30DE	6.2–8.0 ft. lbs.	8.43–10.8 Nm
Oil strainer		
VG30E	12–15 ft. lbs.	16–21 Nm
VE30DE	12–15 ft. lbs.	16–21 Nm
VQ30DE	12–14 ft. lbs.	16–19 Nm
Crankshaft damper		
VG30E	90–98 ft. lbs.	123–132 Nm
VE30DE	123–132 ft. lbs.	167–177 Nm
VQ30DE		
1	29–36 ft. lbs.	39–49 Nm
2	60-66 deg. clockwise angle torque	
Timing chain cover		
VE30DE ①		
Lower cover	4.6–6.1 ft. lbs.	6.3–8.3 Nm
Upper covers	4.6–6.1 ft. lbs.	6.3–8.3 Nm
VQ30DE ①		
Rear cover	8.7–10.1 ft. lbs.	11.8–13.7 Nm
Front cover		
Bolts 1 and 2 (8mm)	18.8–23.1 ft. lbs.	25.5–31.4 Nm
Bolts 3 through 20 (6mm)	8.7–10.1 ft. lbs.	11.8–13.7 Nm
Camshaft bearing caps		
VE30DE ②	6.7–8.7 ft. lbs.	9.0–11.8 Nm
VQ30DE ②		
Step 1	4.4 ft. lbs.	6 Nm
Step 2	6.7–8.7 ft. lbs.	9.02–11.8 Nm
Camshaft sprocket bolts		
VG30E	58–65 ft. lbs.	78–88 Nm
VE30DE	80–87 ft. lbs.	108–118 Nm
VQ30DE	88–95 ft. lbs.	119–128 Nm
Flywheel/Flexplate	61–69 ft. lbs.	83–93 Nm
Engine mounts		
Center member-to-body	57-72 ft. lbs.	77-98 Nm
Engine mount-to-center member	57-72 ft. lbs.	77-98 Nm
Engine mount bracket-to-engine block	32-41 ft. lbs	43-55 Nm
Engine mount-to-bracket through bolts	57-72 ft. lbs	77-98 Nm
Right side engine mount (VQ30DE) ③	58-67 ft. lbs	78-90 Nm

① Refer to text for numerical sequence.

② Tighten in stages. Refer to the text for further information.

③ Refer to the illustrations for further information.

89613CA8

USING A VACUUM GAUGE

White needle = steady needle   *Dark needle = drifting needle*

The vacuum gauge is one of the most useful and easy-to-use diagnostic tools. It is inexpensive, easy to hook up, and provides valuable information about the condition of your engine.

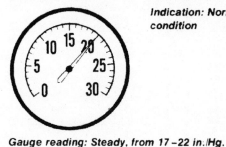

Indication: Normal engine in good condition

Gauge reading: Steady, from 17–22 in./Hg.

Indication: Sticking valve or ignition miss

Gauge reading: Needle fluctuates from 15–20 in./Hg. at idle

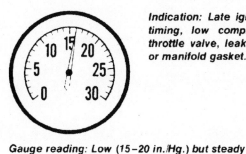

Indication: Late ignition or valve timing, low compression, stuck throttle valve, leaking carburetor or manifold gasket.

Gauge reading: Low (15–20 in./Hg.) but steady

Indication: Improper carburetor adjustment, or minor intake leak at carburetor or manifold

NOTE: Bad fuel injector O-rings may also cause this reading.

Gauge reading: Drifting needle

Indication: Weak valve springs, worn valve stem guides, or leaky cylinder head gasket (vibrating excessively at all speeds).

NOTE: A plugged catalytic converter may also cause this reading.

Gauge reading: Needle fluctuates as engine speed increases

Indication: Burnt valve or improper valve clearance. The needle will drop when the defective valve operates.

Gauge reading: Steady needle, but drops regularly

Indication: Choked muffler or obstruction in system. Speed up the engine. Choked muffler will exhibit a slow drop of vacuum to zero.

Gauge reading: Gradual drop in reading at idle

Indication: Worn valve guides

Gauge reading: Needle vibrates excessively at idle, but steadies as engine speed increases

TCCS3C01

Troubleshooting Engine Mechanical Problems

Problem	Cause	Solution
External oil leaks	Cylinder head cover RTV sealant broken or improperly seated	Replace sealant; inspect cylinder head cover sealant flange and cylinder head sealant surface for distortion and cracks
	Oil filler cap leaking or missing	Replace cap
	Oil filter gasket broken or improperly seated	Replace oil filter
	Oil pan side gasket broken, improperly seated or opening in RTV sealant	Replace gasket or repair opening in sealant; inspect oil pan gasket flange for distortion
	Oil pan front oil seal broken or improperly seated	Replace seal; inspect timing case cover and oil pan seal flange for distortion
	Oil pan rear oil seal broken or improperly seated	Replace seal; inspect oil pan rear oil seal flange; inspect rear main bearing cap for cracks, plugged oil return channels, or distortion in seal groove
	Timing case cover oil seal broken or improperly seated	Replace seal
	Excess oil pressure because of restricted PCV valve	Replace PCV valve
	Oil pan drain plug loose or has stripped threads	Repair as necessary and tighten
	Rear oil gallery plug loose	Use appropriate sealant on gallery plug and tighten
	Rear camshaft plug loose or improperly seated	Seat camshaft plug or replace and seal, as necessary
Excessive oil consumption	Oil level too high	Drain oil to specified level
	Oil with wrong viscosity being used	Replace with specified oil
	PCV valve stuck closed	Replace PCV valve
	Valve stem oil deflectors (or seals) are damaged, missing, or incorrect type	Replace valve stem oil deflectors
	Valve stems or valve guides worn	Measure stem-to-guide clearance and repair as necessary
	Poorly fitted or missing valve cover baffles	Replace valve cover
	Piston rings broken or missing	Replace broken or missing rings
	Scuffed piston	Replace piston
	Incorrect piston ring gap	Measure ring gap, repair as necessary
	Piston rings sticking or excessively loose in grooves	Measure ring side clearance, repair as necessary
	Compression rings installed upside down	Repair as necessary
	Cylinder walls worn, scored, or glazed	Repair as necessary

TCCS3C02

Troubleshooting Engine Mechanical Problems

Problem	Cause	Solution
Excessive oil consumption (cont.)	Piston ring gaps not properly staggered	Repair as necessary
	Excessive main or connecting rod bearing clearance	Measure bearing clearance, repair as necessary
No oil pressure	Low oil level	Add oil to correct level
	Oil pressure gauge, warning lamp or sending unit inaccurate	Replace oil pressure gauge or warning lamp
	Oil pump malfunction	Replace oil pump
	Oil pressure relief valve sticking	Remove and inspect oil pressure relief valve assembly
	Oil passages on pressure side of pump obstructed	Inspect oil passages for obstruction
	Oil pickup screen or tube obstructed	Inspect oil pickup for obstruction
	Loose oil inlet tube	Tighten or seal inlet tube
Low oil pressure	Low oil level	Add oil to correct level
	Inaccurate gauge, warning lamp or sending unit	Replace oil pressure gauge or warning lamp
	Oil excessively thin because of dilution, poor quality, or improper grade	Drain and refill crankcase with recommended oil
	Excessive oil temperature	Correct cause of overheating engine
	Oil pressure relief spring weak or sticking	Remove and inspect oil pressure relief valve assembly
	Oil inlet tube and screen assembly has restriction or air leak	Remove and inspect oil inlet tube and screen assembly. (Fill inlet tube with lacquer thinner to locate leaks.)
	Excessive oil pump clearance	Measure clearances
	Excessive main, rod, or camshaft bearing clearance	Measure bearing clearances, repair as necessary
High oil pressure	Improper oil viscosity	Drain and refill crankcase with correct viscosity oil
	Oil pressure gauge or sending unit inaccurate	Replace oil pressure gauge
	Oil pressure relief valve sticking closed	Remove and inspect oil pressure relief valve assembly
Main bearing noise	Insufficient oil supply	Inspect for low oil level and low oil pressure
	Main bearing clearance excessive	Measure main bearing clearance, repair as necessary
	Bearing insert missing	Replace missing insert
	Crankshaft end-play excessive	Measure end-play, repair as necessary
	Improperly tightened main bearing cap bolts	Tighten bolts with specified torque
	Loose flywheel or drive plate	Tighten flywheel or drive plate attaching bolts
	Loose or damaged vibration damper	Repair as necessary

TCCS3C03

Troubleshooting Engine Performance

Problem	Cause	Solution
Hard starting (engine cranks normally)	Faulty engine control system component	Repair or replace as necessary
	Faulty fuel pump	Replace fuel pump
	Faulty fuel system component	Repair or replace as necessary
	Faulty ignition coil	Test and replace as necessary
	Improper spark plug gap	Adjust gap
	Incorrect ignition timing	Adjust timing
	Incorrect valve timing	Check valve timing; repair as necessary
Rough idle or stalling	Incorrect curb or fast idle speed	Adjust curb or fast idle speed (if possible)
	Incorrect ignition timing	Adjust timing to specification
	Improper feedback system operation	Refer to Chapter 4
	Faulty EGR valve operation	Test EGR system and replace as necessary
	Faulty PCV valve air flow	Test PCV valve and replace as necessary
	Faulty TAC vacuum motor or valve	Repair as necessary
	Air leak into manifold vacuum	Inspect manifold vacuum connections and repair as necessary
	Faulty distributor rotor or cap	Replace rotor or cap (Distributor systems only)
	Improperly seated valves	Test cylinder compression, repair as necessary
	Incorrect ignition wiring	Inspect wiring and correct as necessary
	Faulty ignition coil	Test coil and replace as necessary
	Restricted air vent or idle passages	Clean passages
	Restricted air cleaner	Clean or replace air cleaner filter element
Faulty low-speed operation	Restricted idle air vents and passages	Clean air vents and passages
	Restricted air cleaner	Clean or replace air cleaner filter element
	Faulty spark plugs	Clean or replace spark plugs
	Dirty, corroded, or loose ignition secondary circuit wire connections	Clean or tighten secondary circuit wire connections
	Improper feedback system operation	Refer to Chapter 4
	Faulty ignition coil high voltage wire	Replace ignition coil high voltage wire (Distributor systems only)
	Faulty distributor cap	Replace cap (Distributor systems only)
Faulty acceleration	Incorrect ignition timing	Adjust timing
	Faulty fuel system component	Repair or replace as necessary
	Faulty spark plug(s)	Clean or replace spark plug(s)
	Improperly seated valves	Test cylinder compression, repair as necessary
	Faulty ignition coil	Test coil and replace as necessary

TCCS3C05

Troubleshooting Engine Mechanical Problems

Problem	Cause	Solution
Connecting rod bearing noise	Insufficient oil supply	Inspect for low oil level and low oil pressure
	Carbon build-up on piston	Remove carbon from piston crown
	Bearing clearance excessive or bearing missing	Measure clearance, repair as necessary
	Crankshaft connecting rod journal out-of-round	Measure journal dimensions, repair or replace as necessary
	Misaligned connecting rod or cap	Repair as necessary
	Connecting rod bolts tightened improperly	Tighten bolts with specified torque
Piston noise	Piston-to-cylinder wall clearance excessive (scuffed piston)	Measure clearance and examine piston
	Cylinder walls excessively tapered or out-of-round	Measure cylinder wall dimensions, rebore cylinder
	Piston ring broken	Replace all rings on piston
	Loose or seized piston pin	Measure piston-to-pin clearance, repair as necessary
	Connecting rods misaligned	Measure rod alignment, straighten or replace
	Piston ring side clearance excessively loose or tight	Measure ring side clearance, repair as necessary
	Carbon build-up on piston is excessive	Remove carbon from piston
Valve actuating component noise	Insufficient oil supply	Check for: (a) Low oil level (b) Low oil pressure (c) Wrong hydraulic tappets (d) Restricted oil gallery (e) Excessive tappet to bore clearance
	Rocker arms or pivots worn	Replace worn rocker arms or pivots
	Foreign objects or chips in hydraulic tappets	Clean tappets
	Excessive tappet leak-down	Replace valve tappet
	Tappet face worn	Replace tappet; inspect corresponding cam lobe for wear
	Broken or cocked valve springs	Properly seat cocked springs; replace broken springs
	Stem-to-guide clearance excessive	Measure stem-to-guide clearance, repair as required
	Valve bent	Replace valve
	Loose rocker arms	Check and repair as necessary
	Valve seat runout excessive	Regrind valve seat/valves
	Missing valve lock	Install valve lock
	Excessive engine oil	Correct oil level

TCCS3C04

Troubleshooting Engine Performance

Problem	Cause	Solution
Power not up to normal (cont.)	• Incorrect spark plug gap	• Adjust gap
	• Faulty fuel pump	• Replace fuel pump
	• Faulty fuel pump	• Replace fuel pump
	• Incorrect valve timing	• Check valve timing and repair as necessary
	• Faulty ignition coil	• Test coil and replace as necessary
	• Faulty ignition wires	• Test wires and replace as necessary
	• Improperly seated valves	• Test cylinder compression and repair as necessary
	• Blown cylinder head gasket	• Replace gasket
	• Leaking piston rings	• Test compression and repair as necessary
	• Improper feedback system operation	• Refer to Chapter 4
Intake backfire	• Improper ignition timing	• Adjust timing
	• Defective EGR component	• Repair as necessary
	• Defective TAC vacuum motor or valve	• Repair as necessary
Exhaust backfire	• Air leak into manifold vacuum	• Check manifold vacuum and repair as necessary
	• Faulty air injection diverter valve	• Test diverter valve and replace as necessary
	• Exhaust leak	• Locate and eliminate leak
Ping or spark knock	• Incorrect ignition timing	• Adjust timing
	• Distributor advance malfunction	• Inspect advance mechanism and repair as necessary (Distributor systems only)
	• Excessive combustion chamber deposits	• Remove with combustion chamber cleaner
	• Air leak into manifold vacuum	• Check manifold vacuum and repair as necessary
	• Excessively high compression	• Test compression and repair as necessary
	• Fuel octane rating excessively low	• Try alternate fuel source
	• Sharp edges in combustion chamber	• Grind smooth
	• EGR valve not functioning properly	• Test EGR system and replace as necessary
Surging (at cruising to top speeds)	• Low fuel pump pressure or volume	• Replace fuel pump
	• Improper PCV valve air flow	• Test PCV valve and replace as necessary
	• Air leak into manifold vacuum	• Check manifold vacuum and repair as necessary
	• Incorrect spark advance	• Test and replace as necessary
	• Restricted fuel filter	• Replace fuel filter
	• Restricted air cleaner	• Clean or replace air cleaner filter element
	• EGR valve not functioning properly	• Test EGR system and replace as necessary
	• Improper feedback system operation	• Refer to Chapter 4

TCCS3C07

Troubleshooting Engine Performance

Problem	Cause	Solution
Faulty acceleration (cont.)	• Improper feedback system operation	• Refer to Chapter 4
Faulty high speed operation	• Incorrect ignition timing	• Adjust timing (if possible)
	• Faulty advance mechanism	• Check advance mechanism and repair as necessary (Distributor systems only)
	• Low fuel pump volume	• Replace fuel pump
	• Wrong spark plug air gap or wrong plug	• Adjust air gap or install correct plug
	• Partially restricted exhaust manifold, exhaust pipe, catalytic converter, muffler, or tailpipe	• Eliminate restriction
	• Restricted vacuum passages	• Clean passages
	• Restricted air cleaner	• Cleaner or replace filter element as necessary
	• Faulty distributor rotor or cap	• Replace rotor or cap (Distributor systems only)
	• Faulty ignition coil	• Test coil and replace as necessary
	• Improperly seated valve(s)	• Test cylinder compression, repair as necessary
	• Faulty valve spring(s)	• Inspect and test valve spring tension, replace as necessary
	• Incorrect valve timing	• Check valve timing and repair as necessary
	• Intake manifold restricted	• Remove restriction or replace manifold
	• Worn distributor shaft	• Replace shaft (Distributor systems only)
	• Improper feedback system operation	• Refer to Chapter 4
Misfire at all speeds	• Faulty spark plug(s)	• Clean or relace spark plug(s)
	• Faulty spark plug wire(s)	• Replace as necessary
	• Faulty distributor cap or rotor	• Replace cap or rotor (Distributor systems only)
	• Faulty ignition coil	• Test coil and replace as necessary
	• Primary ignition circuit shorted or open intermittently	• Troubleshoot primary circuit and repair as necessary
	• Improperly seated valve(s)	• Test cylinder compression, repair as necessary
	• Faulty hydraulic tappet(s)	• Clean or replace tappet(s)
	• Improper feedback system operation	• Refer to Chapter 4
	• Faulty valve spring(s)	• Inspect and test valve spring tension, repair as necessary
	• Worn camshaft lobes	• Replace camshaft
	• Air leak into manifold	• Check manifold vacuum and repair as necessary
	• Fuel pump volume or pressure low	• Replace fuel pump
	• Blown cylinder head gasket	• Replace gasket
	• Intake or exhaust manifold passage(s) restricted	• Pass chain through passage(s) and repair as necessary
Power not up to normal	• Incorrect ignition timing	• Adjust timing
	• Faulty distributor rotor	• Replace rotor (Distributor systems only)

TCCS3C06

Troubleshooting the Serpentine Drive Belt

Problem	Cause	Solution
Tension sheeting fabric failure (woven fabric on outside circumference of belt has cracked or separated from body of belt)	• Grooved or backside idler pulley diameters are less than minimum recommended • Tension sheeting contacting (rubbing) stationary object • Excessive heat causing woven fabric to age • Tension sheeting splice has fractured	• Replace pulley(s) not conforming to specification • Correct rubbing condition • Replace belt • Replace belt
Noise (objectional squeal, squeak, or rumble is heard or felt while drive belt is in operation)	• Belt slippage • Bearing noise • Belt misalignment • Belt-to-pulley mismatch • Driven component inducing vibration • System resonant frequency inducing vibration	• Adjust belt • Locate and repair • Align belt/pulley(s) • Install correct belt • Locate defective driven component and repair • Vary belt tension within specifications. Replace belt.
Rib chunking (one or more ribs has separated from belt body)	• Foreign objects imbedded in pulley grooves • Installation damage • Drive loads in excess of design specifications • Insufficient internal belt adhesion	• Remove foreign objects from pulley grooves • Replace belt • Adjust belt tension • Replace belt
Rib or belt wear (belt ribs contact bottom of pulley grooves)	• Pulley(s) misaligned • Mismatch of belt and pulley groove widths • Abrasive environment • Rusted pulley(s) • Sharp or jagged pulley groove tips • Rubber deteriorated	• Align pulley(s) • Replace belt • Replace belt • Clean rust from pulley(s) • Replace pulley • Replace belt
Longitudinal belt cracking (cracks between two ribs)	• Belt has mistracked from pulley groove • Pulley groove tip has worn away rubber-to-tensile member	• Replace belt • Replace belt
Belt slips	• Belt slipping because of insufficient tension • Belt or pulley subjected to substance (belt dressing, oil, ethylene glycol) that has reduced friction • Driven component bearing failure • Belt glazed and hardened from heat and excessive slippage	• Adjust tension • Replace belt and clean pulleys • Replace faulty component bearing • Replace belt
"Groove jumping" (belt does not maintain correct position on pulley, or turns over and/or runs off pulleys)	• Insufficient belt tension • Pulley(s) not within design tolerance • Foreign object(s) in grooves	• Adjust belt tension • Replace pulley(s) • Remove foreign objects from grooves

TCCS3C09

Troubleshooting the Serpentine Drive Belt

Problem	Cause	Solution
"Groove jumping" (belt does not maintain correct position on pulley, or turns over and/or runs off pulleys)	• Excessive belt speed • Pulley misalignment • Belt-to-pulley profile mismatched • Belt cordline is distorted	• Avoid excessive engine acceleration • Align pulley(s) • Install correct belt • Replace belt
Belt broken (Note: identify and correct problem before replacement belt is installed)	• Excessive tension • Tensile members damaged during belt installation	• Replace belt and adjust tension to specification • Replace belt
	• Belt turnover • Severe pulley misalignment • Bracket, pulley, or bearing failure	• Replace belt • Align pulley(s) • Replace defective component and belt
Cord edge failure (tensile member exposed at edges of belt or separated from belt body)	• Excessive tension • Drive pulley misalignment • Belt contacting stationary object • Pulley irregularities • Improper pulley construction • Insufficient adhesion between tensile member and rubber matrix	• Adjust belt tension • Align pulley • Correct as necessary • Replace pulley • Replace pulley • Replace belt and adjust tension to specifications
Sporadic rib cracking (multiple cracks in belt ribs at random intervals)	• Ribbed pulley(s) diameter less than minimum specification • Backside bend flat pulley(s) diameter less than minimum • Excessive heat condition causing rubber to harden • Excessive belt thickness • Belt overcured • Excessive tension	• Replace pulley(s) • Replace pulley(s) • Correct heat condition as necessary • Replace belt • Replace belt • Adjust belt tension

TCCS3C10

Troubleshooting the Cooling System

Problem	Cause	Solution
High temperature gauge indication—overheating	• Coolant level low	• Replenish coolant
	• Improper fan operation	• Repair or replace as necessary
	• Radiator hose(s) collapsed	• Replace hose(s)
	• Radiator airflow blocked	• Remove restriction (bug screen, fog lamps, etc.)
	• Faulty pressure cap	• Replace pressure cap
	• Ignition timing incorrect	• Adjust ignition timing
	• Air trapped in cooling system	• Purge air
	• Heavy traffic driving	• Operate at fast idle in neutral intermittently to cool engine
	• Incorrect cooling system component(s) installed	• Install proper component(s)
	• Faulty thermostat	• Replace thermostat
	• Water pump shaft broken or impeller loose	• Replace water pump
	• Radiator tubes clogged	• Flush radiator
	• Cooling system clogged	• Flush system
	• Casting flash in cooling passages	• Repair or replace as necessary. Flash may be visible by removing cooling system components or removing core plugs.
	• Brakes dragging	• Repair brakes
	• Excessive engine friction	• Repair engine
	• Antifreeze concentration over 68%	• Lower antifreeze concentration percentage
	• Missing air seals	• Replace air seals
	• Faulty gauge or sending unit	• Repair or replace faulty component
	• Loss of coolant flow caused by leakage or foaming	• Repair or replace leaking component, replace coolant
	• Viscous fan drive failed	• Replace unit
Low temperature indication—undercooling	• Thermostat stuck open	• Replace thermostat
	• Faulty gauge or sending unit	• Repair or replace faulty component
Coolant loss—boilover	• Overfilled cooling system	• Reduce coolant level to proper specification
	• Quick shutdown after hard (hot) run	• Allow engine to run at fast idle prior to shutdown
	• Air in system resulting in occasional "burping" of coolant	• Purge system
	• Insufficient antifreeze allowing coolant boiling point to be too low	• Add antifreeze to raise boiling point
	• Antifreeze deteriorated because of age or contamination	• Replace coolant
	• Leaks due to loose hose clamps, loose nuts, bolts, drain plugs, faulty hoses, or defective radiator	• Pressure test system to locate source of leak(s) then repair as necessary

TCCS3C11

Troubleshooting the Cooling System

Problem	Cause	Solution
Coolant loss—boilover	• Faulty head gasket	• Replace head gasket
	• Cracked head, manifold, or block	• Replace as necessary
	• Faulty radiator cap	• Replace cap
Coolant entry into crankcase or cylinder(s)	• Faulty head gasket	• Replace head gasket
	• Crack in head, manifold or block	• Replace as necessary
Coolant recovery system inoperative	• Coolant level low	• Replenish coolant to FULL mark
	• Leak in system	• Pressure test to isolate leak and repair as necessary
	• Pressure cap not tight or seal missing, or leaking	• Repair as necessary
	• Pressure cap defective	• Replace cap
	• Overflow tube clogged or leaking	• Repair as necessary
	• Recovery bottle vent restricted	• Remove restriction
Noise	• Fan contacting shroud	• Reposition shroud and inspect engine mounts (on electric fans inspect assembly)
	• Loose water pump impeller	• Replace pump
	• Glazed fan belt	• Apply silicone or replace belt
	• Loose fan belt	• Adjust fan belt tension
	• Rough surface on drive pulley	• Replace pulley
	• Water pump bearing worn	• Remove belt to isolate. Replace pump.
	• Belt alignment	• Check pulley alignment. Repair as necessary.
No coolant flow through heater core	• Restricted return inlet in water pump	• Remove restriction
	• Heater hose collapsed or restricted	• Remove restriction or replace hose
	• Restricted heater core	• Remove restriction or replace core
	• Restricted outlet in thermostat housing	• Remove flash or restriction
	• Intake manifold bypass hole in cylinder head restricted	• Remove restriction
	• Faulty heater control valve	• Replace valve
	• Intake manifold coolant passage restricted	• Remove restriction or replace intake manifold

NOTE: *Immediately after shutdown, the engine enters a condition known as heat soak. This is caused by the cooling system being inoperative while engine temperature is still high. If coolant temperature rises above boiling point, expansion and pressure may push some coolant out of the radiator overflow tube. If this does not occur frequently it is considered normal.*

TCCS3C12

4

DRIVEABILITY AND EMISSION CONTROLS

AIR POLLUTION

The earth's atmosphere, at or near sea level, consists approximately of 78 percent nitrogen, 21 percent oxygen and 1 percent other gases. If it were possible to remain in this state, 100 percent clean air would result. However, many varied sources allow other gases and particulates to mix with the clean air, causing our atmosphere to become unclean or polluted.

Some of these pollutants are visible while others are invisible, with each having the capability of causing distress to the eyes, ears, throat, skin and respiratory system. Should these pollutants become concentrated in a specific area and under certain conditions, death could result due to the displacement or chemical change of the oxygen content in the air. These pollutants can also cause great damage to the environment and to the many man made objects that are exposed to the elements.

To better understand the causes of air pollution, the pollutants can be categorized into 3 separate types, natural, industrial and automotive.

Natural Pollutants

Natural pollution has been present on earth since before man appeared and continues to be a factor when discussing air pollution, although it causes only a small percentage of the overall pollution problem. It is the direct result of decaying organic matter, wind born smoke and particulates from such natural events as plain and forest fires (ignited by heat or lightning), volcanic ash, sand and dust which can spread over a large area of the countryside.

Such a phenomenon of natural pollution has been seen in the form of volcanic eruptions, with the resulting plume of smoke, steam and volcanic ash blotting out the sun's rays as it spreads and rises higher into the atmosphere. As it travels into the atmosphere the upper air currents catch and carry the smoke and ash, while condensing the steam back into water vapor. As the water vapor, smoke and ash travel on their journey, the smoke dissipates into the atmosphere while the ash and moisture settle back to earth in a trail hundreds of miles long. In some cases, lives are lost and millions of dollars of property damage result.

Industrial Pollutants

Industrial pollution is caused primarily by industrial processes, the burning of coal, oil and natural gas, which in turn produce smoke and fumes. Because the burning fuels contain large amounts of sulfur, the principal ingredients of smoke and fumes are sulfur dioxide and particulate matter. This type of pollutant occurs most severely during still, damp and cool weather, such as at night. Even in its less severe form, this pollutant is not confined to just cities. Because of air movements, the pollutants move for miles over the surrounding countryside, leaving in its path a barren and unhealthy environment for all living things.

Working with Federal, State and Local mandated regulations and by carefully monitoring emissions, big business has greatly reduced the amount of pollutant introduced from its industrial sources, striving to obtain an acceptable level. Because of the mandated industrial emission clean up, many land areas and streams in and around the cities that were formerly barren of vegetation and life, have now begun to move back in the direction of nature's intended balance.

Automotive Pollutants

The third major source of air pollution is automotive emissions. The emissions from the internal combustion engines were not an appreciable problem years ago because of the small number of registered vehicles and the nation's small highway system. However, during the early 1950's, the trend of the American people was to move from the cities to the surrounding suburbs. This caused an immediate problem in transportation because the majority of suburbs were not afforded mass transit conveniences. This lack of transportation created an attractive market for the automobile manufacturers, which resulted in a dramatic increase in the number of vehicles produced and sold, along with a marked increase in highway construction between cities and the suburbs. Multi-vehicle families emerged with a growing emphasis placed on an individual vehicle per family member. As the increase in vehicle ownership and usage occurred, so did pollutant levels in and around the cities, as suburbanites drove daily to their businesses and employment, returning at the end of the day to their homes in the suburbs.

It was noted that a smoke and fog type haze was being formed and at times, remained in suspension over the cities, taking time to dissipate. At first this "smog," derived from the words "smoke" and "fog," was thought to result from industrial pollution but it was determined that automobile emissions shared the blame. It was discovered that when normal automobile emissions were exposed to sunlight for a period of time, complex chemical reactions would take place.

It is now known that smog is a photo chemical layer which develops when certain oxides of nitrogen (NOx) and unburned hydrocarbons (HC) from automobile emissions are exposed to sunlight. Pollution was more severe when smog would become stagnant over an area in which a warm layer of air settled over the top of the cooler air mass, trapping and holding the cooler mass at ground level. The trapped cooler air would keep the emissions from being dispersed and diluted through normal air flows. This type of air stagnation was given the name "Temperature Inversion."

TEMPERATURE INVERSION

In normal weather situations, surface air is warmed by heat radiating from the earth's surface and the sun's rays. This causes it to rise upward, into the atmosphere. Upon rising it will cool through a convection type heat exchange with the cooler upper air. As warm air rises, the surface pollutants are carried upward and dissipated into the atmosphere.

When a temperature inversion occurs, we find the higher air is no longer cooler, but is warmer than the surface air, causing the cooler surface air to become trapped. This warm air blanket can extend from above ground level to a few hundred or even a few thousand feet into the air. As the surface air is trapped, so are the pollutants, causing a severe smog condition. Should this stagnant air mass extend to a few thousand feet high, enough air movement with the inversion takes place to allow the smog layer to rise above ground level but the pollutants still cannot dissipate. This inversion can remain for days over an area, with the smog level only rising or lowering from ground level to a few hundred feet high. Meanwhile, the pollutant levels increase, causing eye irritation, respiratory problems, reduced visibility, plant damage and in some cases, even disease.

This inversion phenomenon was first noted in the Los Angeles, California area. The city lies in terrain resembling a basin and with certain weather conditions, a cold air mass is held in the basin while a warmer air mass covers it like a lid.

Because this type of condition was first documented as prevalent in the Los Angeles area, this type of trapped pollution was named Los Angeles Smog, although it occurs in other areas where a large concentration of automobiles are used and the air remains stagnant for any length of time.

HEAT TRANSFER

Consider the internal combustion engine as a machine in which raw materials must be placed so a finished product comes out. As in any machine operation, a certain amount of wasted material is formed. When we relate this to the internal combustion engine, we find that through the input of air and fuel, we obtain power during the combustion process to drive the vehicle. The by-product or waste of this power is, in part, heat and exhaust gases with which we must dispose.

The heat from the combustion process can rise to over 4000°F (2204°C). The dissipation of this heat is controlled by a ram air effect, the use of cooling fans to cause air flow and a liquid coolant solution surrounding the combustion area to transfer the heat of combustion through the cylinder walls and into the coolant. The coolant is then directed to a thin-finned, multi-tubed radiator, from which the excess heat is transferred to the atmosphere by one of the three heat transfer methods, conduction, convection or radiation.

The cooling of the combustion area is an important part in the control of exhaust emissions. To understand the behavior of the combustion and transfer of its heat, consider the air/fuel charge. It is ignited and the flame front burns progressively across the combustion chamber until the burning charge reaches the cylinder walls. Some of the fuel in contact with the walls is not hot enough to burn, thereby snuffing out or quenching the combustion process. This leaves unburned fuel in the combustion chamber. This unburned fuel is then forced out of the cylinder and into the exhaust system, along with the exhaust gases.

Many attempts have been made to minimize the amount of unburned fuel in the combustion chambers due to quenching, by increasing the coolant temperature and lessening the contact area of the coolant around the combustion area. However, design limitations within the combustion chambers prevent the complete burning of the air/fuel charge, so a certain amount of the unburned fuel is still expelled into the exhaust system, regardless of modifications to the engine.

AUTOMOTIVE EMISSIONS

Before emission controls were mandated on internal combustion engines, other sources of engine pollutants were discovered along with the exhaust emissions. It was determined that engine combustion exhaust produced approximately 60 percent of the total emission pollutants, fuel evaporation from the fuel tank and carburetor vents produced 20 percent, with the final 20 percent being produced through the crankcase as a by-product of the combustion process.

Exhaust Gases

The exhaust gases emitted into the atmosphere are a combination of burned and unburned fuel. To understand the exhaust emission and its composition, we must review some basic chemistry.

When the air/fuel mixture is introduced into the engine, we are mixing air, composed of nitrogen (78 percent), oxygen (21 percent) and other gases (1 percent) with the fuel, which is 100 percent hydrocarbons (HC), in a semi-controlled ratio. As the combustion process is accomplished, power is produced to move the vehicle while the heat of combustion is transferred to the cooling system. The exhaust gases are then composed of nitrogen, a diatomic gas (N_2), the same as was introduced in the engine, carbon dioxide (CO_2), the same gas that is used in beverage carbonation, and water vapor (H_2O). The nitrogen (N_2), for the most part, passes through the engine unchanged, while the oxygen (O_2) reacts (burns) with the hydrocarbons (HC) and produces the carbon dioxide (CO_2) and the water vapors (H_2O). If this chemical process would be the only process to take place, the exhaust emissions would be harmless. However, during the combustion process, other compounds are formed which are considered dangerous. These pollutants are hydrocarbons (HC), carbon monoxide (CO), oxides of nitrogen (NOx) oxides of sulfur (SOx) and engine particulates.

HYDROCARBONS

Hydrocarbons (HC) are essentially fuel which was not burned during the combustion process or which has escaped into the atmosphere through fuel evaporation. The main sources of incomplete combustion are rich air/fuel mixtures, low engine temperatures and improper spark timing. The main sources of hydrocarbon emission through fuel evaporation on most vehicles used to be the vehicle's fuel tank and carburetor float bowl.

To reduce combustion hydrocarbon emission, engine modifications were made to minimize dead space and surface area in the combustion chamber. In addition, the air/fuel mixture was made more lean through the improved control which feedback carburetion and fuel injection offers and by the addition of external controls to aid in further combustion of the hydrocarbons outside the engine. Two such methods were the addition of air injection systems, to inject fresh air into the exhaust manifolds and the installation of catalytic converters, units that are able to burn traces of hydrocarbons without affecting the internal combustion process or fuel economy.

To control hydrocarbon emissions through fuel evaporation, modifications were made to the fuel tank to allow storage of the fuel vapors during periods of engine shut-down. Modifications were also made to the air intake system so that at specific times during engine operation, these vapors may be purged and burned by blending them with the air/fuel mixture.

CARBON MONOXIDE

Carbon monoxide is formed when not enough oxygen is present during the combustion process to convert carbon (C) to carbon dioxide (CO_2). An increase in the carbon monoxide (CO) emission is normally accompanied by an increase in the hydrocarbon (HC) emission because of the lack of oxygen to completely burn all of the fuel mixture.

Carbon monoxide (CO) also increases the rate at which the photo chemical smog is formed by speeding up the conversion of nitric oxide (NO) to nitrogen dioxide (NO_2). To accomplish this, carbon monoxide (CO) combines with oxygen (O_2) and nitric oxide (NO) to produce carbon dioxide (CO_2) and nitrogen dioxide (NO_2). ($CO + O_2 + NO = CO_2 + NO_2$).

The dangers of carbon monoxide, which is an odorless and colorless toxic gas are many. When carbon monoxide is inhaled into the lungs and passed into the blood stream, oxygen is replaced by the carbon monoxide in the red blood cells, causing a reduction in the amount of oxygen supplied to the many parts of the body. This lack of oxygen causes headaches, lack of coordination, reduced mental alertness and, should the carbon monoxide concentration be high enough, death could result.

NITROGEN

Normally, nitrogen is an inert gas. When heated to approximately 2500°F (1371°C) through the combustion process, this gas becomes active and causes an increase in the nitric oxide (NO) emission.

Oxides of nitrogen (NOx) are composed of approximately 97–98 percent nitric oxide (NO). Nitric oxide is a colorless gas but when it is passed into the atmosphere, it combines with oxygen and forms nitrogen dioxide (NO_2). The nitrogen dioxide then combines with chemically active hydrocarbons (HC) and when in the presence of sunlight, causes the formation of photo-chemical smog.

Ozone

To further complicate matters, some of the nitrogen dioxide (NO_2) is broken apart by the sunlight to form nitric oxide and oxygen. ($NO_2 + $ sunlight $= NO + O$). This single atom of oxygen then combines with diatomic (meaning 2 atoms) oxygen (O_2) to form ozone (O_3). Ozone is one of the smells associated with smog. It has a pungent and offensive odor, irritates the eyes and lung tissues, affects the growth of plant life and causes rapid deterioration of rubber products. Ozone can be formed by sunlight as well as electrical discharge into the air.

The most common discharge area on the automobile engine is the secondary ignition electrical system, especially when inferior quality spark plug cables are used. As the surge of high voltage is routed through the secondary cable, the circuit builds up an electrical field around the wire, which acts upon the oxygen in the surrounding air to form the ozone. The faint glow along the cable with the engine running that may be visible on a dark night, is called the "corona discharge." It is the result of the electrical field passing from a high along the cable, to a low in the surrounding air, which forms the ozone gas. The combination of corona and ozone has been a major cause of cable deterioration. Recently, different and better quality insulating materials have lengthened the life of the electrical cables.

Although ozone at ground level can be harmful, ozone is beneficial to the earth's inhabitants. By having a concentrated ozone layer called the "ozonosphere," between 10 and 20 miles (16–32 km) up in the atmosphere, much of the ultra violet radiation from the sun's rays are absorbed and screened. If this ozone layer were not present, much of the earth's surface would be burned, dried and unfit for human life.

OXIDES OF SULFUR

Oxides of sulfur (SOx) were initially ignored in the exhaust system emissions, since the sulfur content of gasoline as a fuel is less than 1/10 of 1 percent. Because of this small amount, it was felt that it contributed very little to the overall pollution problem. However, because of the difficulty in solving the sulfur emissions in industrial pollution and the introduction of catalytic converter to the automobile exhaust systems, a change was mandated. The automobile exhaust system, when equipped with a catalytic converter, changes the sulfur dioxide (SO_2) into sulfur trioxide (SO_3).

When this combines with water vapors (H_2O), a sulfuric acid mist (H_2SO_4) is formed and is a very difficult pollutant to handle since it is extremely corrosive. This sulfuric acid mist that is formed, is the same mist that rises from the vents of an automobile battery when an active chemical reaction takes place within the battery cells.

When a large concentration of vehicles equipped with catalytic converters are operating in an area, this acid mist may rise and be distributed over a large ground area causing land, plant, crop, paint and building damage.

PARTICULATE MATTER

A certain amount of particulate matter is present in the burning of any fuel, with carbon constituting the largest percentage of the particulates. In gasoline, the remaining particulates are the burned remains of the various other compounds used in its manufacture. When a gasoline engine is in good internal condition, the particulate emissions are low but as the engine wears internally, the particulate emissions increase. By visually inspecting the tail pipe emissions, a determination can be made as to where an engine defect may exist. An engine with light gray or blue smoke emitting from the tail pipe normally indicates an increase in the oil consumption through burning due to internal engine wear. Black smoke would indicate a defective fuel delivery system, causing the engine to operate in a rich mode. Regardless of the color of the smoke, the internal part of the engine or the fuel delivery system should be repaired to prevent excess particulate emissions.

Diesel and turbine engines emit a darkened plume of smoke from the exhaust system because of the type of fuel used. Emission control regulations are mandated for this type of emission and more stringent measures are being used to prevent excess emission of the particulate matter. Electronic components are being introduced to control the injection of the fuel at precisely the proper time of piston travel, to achieve the optimum in fuel ignition and fuel usage. Other particulate after-burning components are being tested to achieve a cleaner emission.

Good grades of engine lubricating oils should be used, which meet the manufacturers specification. Cut-rate oils can contribute to the particulate emission problem because of their low flash or ignition temperature point. Such oils burn prematurely during the combustion process causing emission of particulate matter.

The cooling system is an important factor in the reduction of particulate matter. The optimum combustion will occur, with the cooling system operating at a temperature specified by the manufacturer. The cooling system must be maintained in the same manner as the engine oiling system, as each system is required to perform properly in order for the engine to operate efficiently for a long time.

Crankcase Emissions

Crankcase emissions are made up of water, acids, unburned fuel, oil fumes and particulates. These emissions are classified as hydrocarbons (HC) and are formed by the small amount of unburned, compressed air/fuel mixture entering the crankcase from the combustion area (between the cylinder walls and piston rings) during the compression and power strokes. The head of the compression and combustion help to form the remaining crankcase emissions.

Since the first engines, crankcase emissions were allowed into the atmosphere through a road draft tube, mounted on the lower side of the engine block. Fresh air came in through an open oil filler cap or breather. The air passed through the crankcase mixing with blow-by gases. The motion of the vehicle and the air blowing past the open end of the road draft tube caused a low pressure area (vacuum) at the end of the tube. Crankcase emissions were simply drawn out of the road draft tube into the air.

To control the crankcase emission, the road draft tube was deleted. A hose and/or tubing was routed from the crankcase to the intake manifold so the blow-by emission could be burned with the air/fuel mixture. However, it was found that intake manifold vacuum, used to draw the crankcase emissions into the manifold, would vary in strength at the wrong time and not allow the proper emission flow. A regulating valve was needed to control the flow of air through the crankcase.

Testing, showed the removal of the blow-by gases from the crankcase as quickly as possible, was most important to the longevity of the engine. Should large accumulations of blow-by gases remain and condense, dilution of the engine oil would occur to form water, soots, resins, acids and lead salts, resulting in the formation of sludge and varnishes. This condensation of the blow-by gases occurs more frequently on vehicles used in numerous starting and stopping conditions, excessive idling and when the engine is not allowed to attain normal operating temperature through short runs.

Evaporative Emissions

Gasoline fuel is a major source of pollution, before and after it is burned in the automobile engine. From the time the fuel is refined, stored, pumped and transported, again stored until it is pumped into the fuel tank of the vehicle, the gasoline gives off unburned hydrocarbons (HC) into the atmosphere. Through the redesign of storage areas and venting systems, the pollution factor was diminished, but not eliminated, from the refinery standpoint. However, the automobile still remained the primary source of vaporized, unburned hydrocarbon (HC) emissions.

Fuel pumped from an underground storage tank is cool but when exposed to a warmer ambient temperature, will expand. Before controls were mandated, an owner might fill the fuel tank with fuel from an underground storage tank and park the vehicle for some time in warm area, such as a parking lot. As the fuel would warm, it would expand and should no provisions or area be provided for the expansion, the fuel would spill out of the filler neck and onto the ground, causing hydrocarbon (HC) pollution and creating a severe fire hazard. To correct this condition, the vehicle manufacturers added overflow plumbing and/or gasoline tanks with built in expansion areas or domes.

However, this did not control the fuel vapor emission from the fuel tank. It was determined that most of the fuel evaporation occurred when the vehicle was stationary and the engine not operating. Most vehicles carry 5–25 gallons (19–95 liters) of gasoline. Should a large concentration of vehicles be parked in one area, such as a large parking lot, excessive fuel vapor emissions would take place, increasing as the temperature increases.

To prevent the vapor emission from escaping into the atmosphere, the fuel systems were designed to trap the vapors while the vehicle is stationary, by sealing the system from the atmosphere. A storage system is used to collect and hold the fuel vapors from the carburetor (if equipped) and the fuel tank when the engine is not operating. When the engine is started, the storage system is then purged of the fuel vapors, which are drawn into the engine and burned with the air/fuel mixture.

EMISSION COMPONENT LOCATIONS—1993–94 MODELS

1. Power transistor
2. EGR valve
3. Mass airflow sensor
4. Throttle position sensor
5. Camshaft position sensor
6. Power steering pressure switch
7. EGR valve control solenoid
8. IACV-AAC valve
9. VTC solenoid
10. Coolant temperature sensor
11. PCV valve

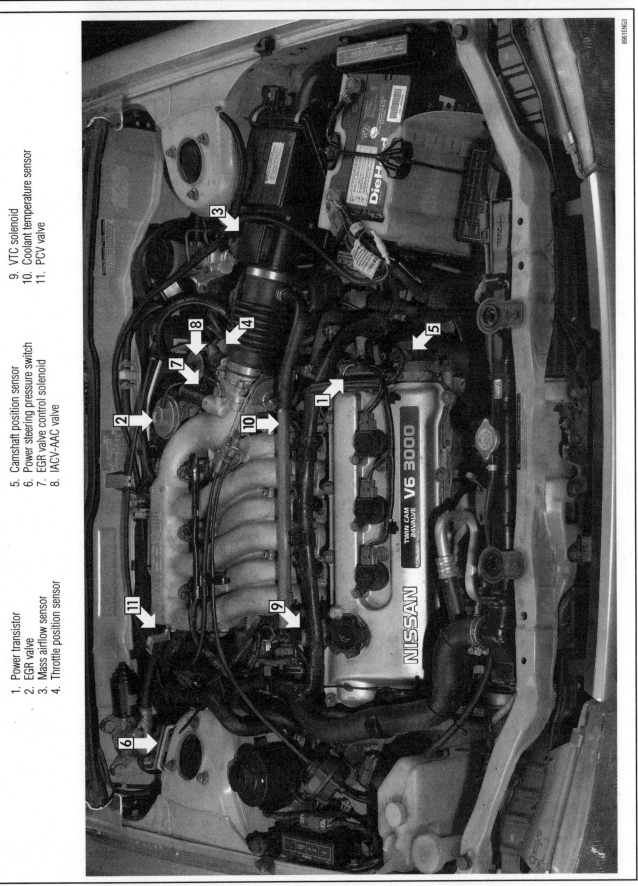

8961ENG3

EMISSION COMPONENT LOCATIONS—1995–98 ENGINES

1. Power steering pressure switch
2. Camshaft position sensor
3. PCV valve
4. Throttle position sensor
5. Mass air flow sensor
6. EVAP canister purge control valve
7. IACV-AAC valve
8. Intake air temperature sensor
9. Engine coolant temperature sensor
10. Absolute pressure sensor
11. Crankshaft position sensor (REF sensor)

Crankcase Ventilation System

OPERATION

▶ **See Figure 1**

The crankcase ventilation system returns blow-by gas to the intake manifold. A Positive Crankcase Ventilation (PCV) valve is used to meter the gas and is located in the breather separator under the intake manifold.

During partial throttle operation of the engine, manifold vacuum is high, allowing the blow-by gas to be sucked through the PCV valve into the intake manifold. Normally, the capacity of the valve is sufficient to handle any blow-by and a small amount of ventilating air. The ventilating air is drawn from the air duct into the crankcase. The ventilating air passes through the hose connecting the air inlet tube to the cylinder head cover.

Under full throttle condition, the manifold vacuum is insufficient to draw the blow-by flow through the valve. The flow reverses, coming from the crankcase, going through the ventilating hose and into the air duct.

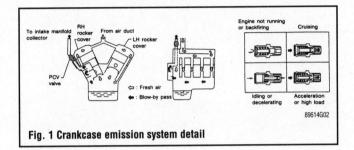

Fig. 1 Crankcase emission system detail

COMPONENT TESTING

▶ **See Figure 2**

1. Remove the PCV valve and shake it gently.
   a. If the valve rattles when shaken, connect the valve to the vacuum hose and proceed to Step 2.
   b. If the valve does not rattle, it is sticking and must be replaced.
2. Start the engine and allow it to reach normal operating temperature.
3. Check the PCV valve for vacuum by placing your finger over the end of the valve.
   a. If vacuum exists, proceed to Step 5.
   b. If vacuum does not exist, check for loose hose connections, vacuum leaks or blockage. Correct as necessary.
4. Reinstall the PCV valve.
5. With the engine running, disconnect the fresh air intake hose from the air inlet tube (which connects the air cleaner housing to the throttle body).
6. Place a stiff piece of paper over the hose end and wait 1 minute.
   a. If vacuum holds the paper in place, the system is OK; reconnect the hose.
   b. If the paper is not held in place, check for loose hose connections, vacuum leaks or blockage. Correct as necessary.

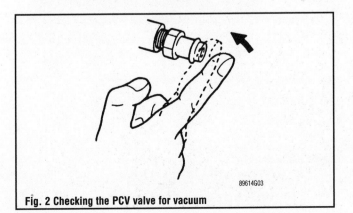

Fig. 2 Checking the PCV valve for vacuum

REMOVAL & INSTALLATION

The PCV valve is located under the intake manifold in the oil separator.
1. Disconnect the vacuum hose from the PCV valve.
2. Unscrew the PCV valve from the breather separator under the intake manifold.
To install:
3. Screw the PCV valve into the breather separator under the intake manifold.
4. Connect the vacuum hose to the PCV valve.

Evaporative Emission Controls

OPERATION

▶ **See Figure 3**

The evaporative emission control system prevents the uncontrolled release of gasoline vapors (hydrocarbons) into the atmosphere. These vapors are produced when fuel evaporates in the sealed fuel tank..

The main component of the system is the charcoal canister. The activated charcoal in the canister absorbs and stores fuel vapors generated inside the fuel tank while the engine is inoperative. When the engine is running, the vapors are drawn through the electronically controlled purge control valve and into the intake manifold. The vapors enter the air/fuel mixture and are burned in the combustion process.

➡ **Not all components are used on all vehicles.**

The purge control valve is used to time the vapor release into the intake manifold. During deceleration and idling, the purge control valve is closed and allows only a small amount of vapor to reach the intake. Under all other conditions, the valve allows vapor to be purged.

Two types of purge control valves are used: an electronic canister purge volume control valve and a purge control valve/constant purge orifice combination. The canister purge volume valve is controlled by the ECM and meters purge volume in proportion to air flow. The purge control valve/constant purge orifice combination operates mechanically. As engine speed increases and throttle vacuum rises, more vapor is purged to the intake manifold.

The canister control solenoid valve responds to signals from the ECM. When the ECM grounds the solenoid, the vacuum signal from the throttle body to the canister is cut. Generally, this is done under start-up, idling and decelerating conditions.

A fuel check valve (vacuum cut valve) is used to prevent engine vacuum from sucking fuel out of the fuel tank. The valve also functions to prevent fuel from flowing out of the fuel tank if the vehicle should roll over.

The fuel cap contains a vacuum relief valve which allows air into the fuel tank to prevent a build-up of vacuum.

The evaporative emission system canister, vacuum line and vapor hoses should be inspected every 30,000 miles (48,300 km).

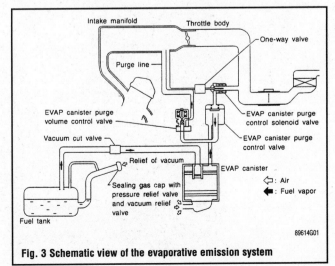

Fig. 3 Schematic view of the evaporative emission system

COMPONENT TESTING

Evaporative Canister

On all 1993–95 models, the canister is located under the battery, except the 1995 California model, which has a square canister under the left rear fénder. All 1996–98 models use the square canister under the left rear fender.

ROUND CANISTER

◆ See Figure 4

1. Refer to the illustration for port identification.
2. Blow air into port A and check for any leakage.
3. Use a vacuum pump and apply vacuum to port A.
4. Using a free hand, cover port D while blowing air into port C; air should flow out of port B.

➡The round evaporative canister is a sealed component and cannot be disassembled for inspection. Visually inspect the exterior of the canister for damage and replace as necessary.

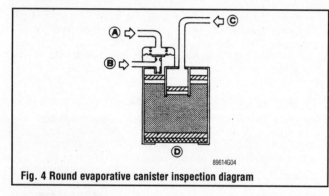

Fig. 4 Round evaporative canister inspection diagram

SQUARE CANISTER

◆ See Figures 5 and 6

1. Visually inspect the exterior of the canister for damage, and replace as necessary.
2. Label and disconnect all vacuum and vapor lines.
3. Inspect the lines for damage, and replace as necessary.
4. Inspect the canister for damage, and replace as necessary.
5. Pinch the fresh air vent hose.
6. Blow air in Port **A** and check that it flows freely out of Port **E**.
7. If air does not flow as specified, the canister may be defective.

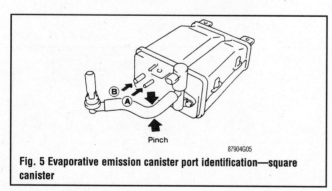

Fig. 5 Evaporative emission canister port identification—square canister

Evaporative Canister Control Solenoid Valve

◆ See Figure 7

This valve may be known as the canister purge control valve on some vehicles.

1. Label and disconnect the vacuum lines and electrical harness.
2. Inspect the lines for damage, and replace as necessary.

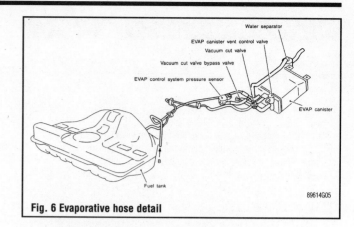

Fig. 6 Evaporative hose detail

3. Inspect the valve for damage, and replace as necessary.
4. Apply battery voltage and ground between the valve terminals.
5. Air should pass between Port **A** and Port **B**.
6. Air should not pass between Port **A** and Port **C**.
7. Remove battery voltage.
8. Air should pass between Port **A** and Port **C**.
9. Air should not pass between Port **A** and Port **B**.
10. If valve does not function as specified, it may be faulty.
11. If the valve responds as specified, check and repair power and ground circuits.

Evaporative Canister Purge Volume Control Valve

◆ See Figure 8

1. Disconnect the valve electrical harness.
2. Measure resistance between terminals, as illustrated.
3. Resistance should be 30 ohms at 77°F (25°C).
4. Remove the valve from the intake collector and disconnect the vacuum hoses.
5. With the electrical harness connected, cycle the ignition key **ON** and **OFF**.
6. Visually inspect the plunger in the valve for movement. The plunger can be seen by looking through the side vacuum port.
7. If resistance is not within specification or the valve does not move freely, the valve may be defective.
8. If the valve functions as specified, check and repair the power and ground circuits.

Fuel Cap

◆ See Figure 9

1. Wipe the valve housing clean.
2. Suck air through the cap using a vacuum pump and the proper adapters supplied with the pump.
3. A slight resistance accompanied by valve clicks indicates that the valve is in good mechanical condition.

➡By continually sucking air through the cap, the resistance should disappear.

4. Blow air through the fuel tank side of the cap and ensure that air passes through the cap.
5. If the valve in the cap is clogged or if no resistance is felt, replace the cap as an assembly.

Fuel Check Valve

◆ See Figure 10

1. Remove the valve from the vehicle.
2. Blow air through the nipple on the fuel tank side.
3. A considerable resistance should be felt and a portion of the air flow should be directed toward the canister side nipple.
4. Blow air through the nipple on the canister side.
5. Air flow should be smoothly directed toward the fuel tank side.
6. Turn the valve over and blow air through either nipple.

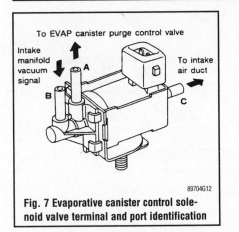

Fig. 7 Evaporative canister control solenoid valve terminal and port identification

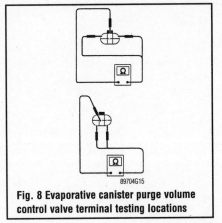

Fig. 8 Evaporative canister purge volume control valve terminal testing locations

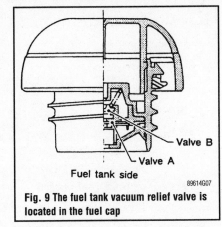

Fig. 9 The fuel tank vacuum relief valve is located in the fuel cap

7. Air should not flow in either direction.
8. If the valve does not function as specified, it may be faulty.

Purge Control Valve

ROUND CANISTER

▶ See Figure 11

1. Label and disconnect all vacuum and vapor lines.
2. Inspect the lines for damage, and replace as necessary.
3. Inspect the canister for damage, and replace as necessary.
4. Blow air in Port **A** and ensure that there is no leakage.
5. Apply a 3.94–5.91 in. Hg vacuum to port **A**.
6. Cover Port **D** with your hand.
7. Blow air into Port **C** and verify that there is a free flow of air out of Port **B**.
8. If air does not flow as specified, the canister may be defective.

SQUARE CANISTER

▶ See Figure 12

1. Label and disconnect all vacuum and vapor lines.
2. Inspect the lines for damage, and replace as necessary.
3. Inspect the valve for damage, and replace as necessary.
4. Plug Port **B**.
5. Apply an 11 psi pressure to Port **A** and hold for 15 seconds.
6. Ensure that there is no leakage.
7. Repeat the test for Port **C**.
8. If leakage occurs, the valve may be defective.

REMOVAL & INSTALLATION

On all 1993–95 models, the canister is located under the battery, except the 1995 California model, which has a square canister under the left rear fender. All 1996–98 models also use the square canister under the left rear fender.

Evaporative Canister

ROUND CANISTER

1. Label and disconnect the vacuum and vapor lines.
2. Loosen the attaching bolts.
3. Carefully remove the canister from the vehicle.
4. Inspect the canister and lines for damage. Replace components as necessary.
5. Installation is the reverse of removal. Be sure to tighten the attaching bolts securely.

SQUARE CANISTER

1. Label and disconnect the vacuum and vapor hoses.
2. Loosen the attaching bolts.
3. Carefully remove the canister from the vehicle.
4. Inspect the canister and lines for damage. Replace components as necessary.
5. Installation is the reverse of removal. Be sure to tighten the attaching bolts to 74–95 inch lbs. (8–11 Nm).

Evaporative Canister Control Solenoid Valve

The evaporative canister control solenoid valve is located on the intake manifold.
1. Label and disconnect the solenoid valve vacuum lines.
2. Loosen the solenoid valve attaching nut, then separate the valve from the intake manifold.
   To install:
3. Install the solenoid valve and tighten the mounting nut to 12–14 ft. lbs. (16–19 Nm).
4. Connect the solenoid valve vacuum lines.

Evaporative Canister Purge Volume Control Valve

1. Label and disconnect the vacuum lines and electrical harnesses.
2. Inspect the lines for damage, and replace as necessary.

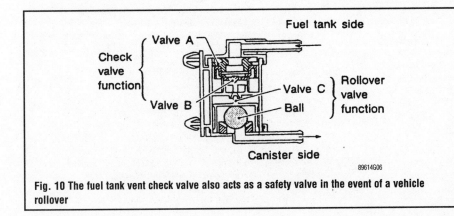

Fig. 10 The fuel tank vent check valve also acts as a safety valve in the event of a vehicle rollover

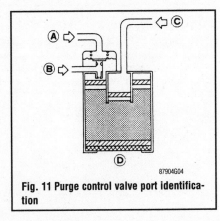

Fig. 11 Purge control valve port identification

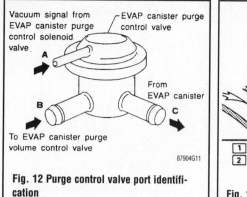

Fig. 12 Purge control valve port identification

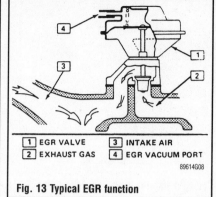

Fig. 13 Typical EGR function

1. EGR VALVE 　 3. INTAKE AIR
2. EXHAUST GAS 　 4. EGR VACUUM PORT

[Fig. 14 photo]

Fig. 14 To test the EGR valve, apply vacuum to the valve diaphragm . . .

3. Remove the valve from the intake collector.
To install:
4. Inspect valve for damage, and replace as necessary.
5. Install the valve on the collector.
6. Connect the vacuum lines and electrical harness.

Fuel Check Valve

The fuel check valve is located in the vapor vent line near the fuel tank.
1. Raise and support the vehicle safely.
2. Locate the valve in the vapor vent line.
3. Note the installed direction of the valve for installation reference.
4. Loosen the hose clamps and remove the valve.
5. Installation is the reverse of removal.

Purge Control Valve

ROUND CANISTER

On round canisters, the purge control valve is an integral part of the evaporative canister. If the valve is determined to be faulty, the canister and purge control valve must be replaced as an assembly.

SQUARE CANISTER

On square canisters, the purge control valve is a separate component mounted near the canister, at the rear of the vehicle.
1. Label and disconnect the vacuum and vapor lines.
2. Inspect the lines for damage, and replace as necessary.
3. Remove the valve from the vehicle.
To install:
4. Inspect the valve for damage, and replace as necessary.
5. Install the valve on the vehicle.
6. Connect the vacuum lines.

Exhaust Gas Recirculation (EGR) System

OPERATION

▶ **See Figure 13**

The Exhaust Gas Recirculation (EGR) system routes some of the engine exhaust gas back into the engine intake system to reduce emissions. Nissan Maximas use a system that cuts and controls vacuum applied to the EGR valve with an electric solenoid to suit engine operating conditions. This "cut and control" operation is accomplished through the Electronic Control Module (ECM), in conjunction with an EGR and canister control solenoid valve. When the ECM detects any of the following conditions, current flows through the solenoid valve:
- Low engine coolant temperature
- Engine starting
- High speed engine operation
- Engine idling
- Excessively high engine coolant temperature
- Mass air flow sensor malfunction

Such current flow through the solenoid valve causes port vacuum to be discharged into the atmosphere. The EGR valve and canister remain closed.

The EGR valve controls the amount of exhaust gas routed to the intake manifold. Vacuum is applied to the EGR valve in response to throttle valve opening. The vacuum controls the movement of a taper valve connected to the vacuum diaphragm of the EGR valve.

The EGR and canister control solenoid valve responds to signals from the ECM. When the ECM sends an ON (ground) signal, the coil in the solenoid valve is energized. A plunger will then move to cut the vacuum signal (from the throttle body to the EGR valve and canister purge valve). When the ECM sends an OFF signal, the vacuum signal passes through the solenoid valve. The signal then reaches the EGR valve and canister.

The EGR Backpressure Transducer (EGRC-BPT) valve monitors exhaust pressure to activate the diaphragm, controlling throttle body vacuum applied to the EGR valve. In this way, the recirculated exhaust gas is controlled in response to positioning of the EGR valve or to engine operation.

A negative temperature coefficient EGR temperature sensor is used to control EGR operation timing during warm-up and under conditions when the engine temperature is out of normal range.

SYSTEM TESTING

1. Start the engine and allow it to reach operating temperature.
2. Check for EGR valve movement while racing the engine from 2000–4000 rpm under no load.
3. The EGR valve diaphragm should lift up and down without restriction.
4. If the EGR valve does not respond as specified, perform component testing.

COMPONENT TESTING

EGR Valve

▶ **See Figures 14 and 15**

1. Disconnect the EGR valve vacuum hose.
2. Using a hand-held vacuum pump, slowly apply 5–10 in. Hg (17–34 kPa) of vacuum to the EGR valve nipple.
3. The EGR valve diaphragm should lift up. Release the vacuum and the EGR valve diaphragm should lower without restriction.
4. If the EGR valve does not respond as specified, remove the valve and check for obstructions. If no obstructions are found, the EGR valve may be faulty.

EGR Backpressure Transducer (EGRC-BPT) Valve

▶ **See Figure 16**

1. Label and disconnect the transducer valve's vacuum lines.
2. Plug one of the ports on top of the valve.
3. Blow into the bottom port gently while applying vacuum to the second port on top of the valve. Vacuum should hold steady and not leak.
4. Stop blowing into the bottom port and vacuum should leak out.
5. If the valve does not respond as specified, it may be faulty.

Fig. 15 . . . then quickly pull it away and listen for the valve closing

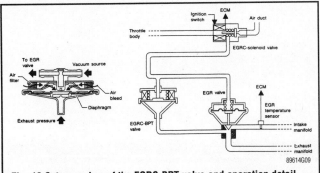

Fig. 16 Cutaway view of the EGRC-BPT valve and operation detail

EGR Control Solenoid Valve

▶ See Figures 17 and 18

1. Label and disconnect the solenoid valve electrical harness and vacuum lines.
2. Apply battery voltage as shown in the illustration (12v DC) to the solenoid terminals.
3. Air should pass through Ports **A** and **B** freely.
4. Disconnect the power supply from the solenoid.
5. Air should not pass through Ports **A** and **B** freely.
6. If the valve does not respond as specified, it may be faulty.
7. If the valve responds as specified, check and repair the power and ground circuits.

EGR Temperature Sensor

▶ See Figures 19 and 20

1. Disconnect the temperature sensor electrical harness and measure the resistance between the sensor terminals.
2. Resistance should be high when the sensor is cold and low when the sensor is hot.
3. Compare the cold and hot EGR temperature sensor resistance measurements with the accompanying chart.
4. If resistance is not within specifications or does not respond smoothly as temperature rises and falls, the sensor may be faulty.
5. If the sensor responds as specified, check and repair the power and ground circuits.

REMOVAL & INSTALLATION

EGR Valve

▶ See Figures 21, 22, and 23

The EGR valve is located on the intake manifold.
1. Disconnect the EGR vacuum lines.
2. Loosen the EGR valve attaching nuts, then separate the valve from the intake manifold.
3. Remove and discard the EGR valve gasket.

Fig. 17 Example of a EGRC control solenoid valve

Fig. 18 Checking the EGR control solenoid valve by applying voltage. Be sure to apply voltage as shown

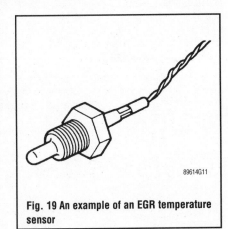

Fig. 19 An example of an EGR temperature sensor

To install:
4. Thoroughly clean the gasket mating surfaces on the valve and the intake manifold.
5. Install the EGR valve, along with a new gasket, and tighten the mounting nuts to 12–14 ft. lbs. (16–19 Nm).
6. Connect the EGR vacuum lines.

EGR Backpressure Transducer (EGRC-BPT) Valve

The EGR backpressure transducer valve is located on the intake manifold.
1. Label and disconnect the valve's vacuum lines.
2. Loosen the valve attaching bolts, then remove the valve from the mounting bracket.

EGR TEMPERATURE SENSOR

EGR temperature °C (°F)	Voltage (V)	Resistance (MΩ)
0 (32)	4.81	7.9 - 9.7
50 (122)	2.82	0.57 - 0.70
100 (212)	0.8	0.08 - 0.10

89704C01

Fig. 20 Compare the sensor resistance readings with these values

Fig. 21 Loosen the exhaust inlet pipe (arrow) before removing the mounting bolts

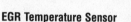

Fig. 22 Loosen the nuts securing the EGR valve . . .

Fig. 23 . . . then remove the EGR from the mounting studs on the intake manifold

To install:
3. Position the valve and tighten the mounting bolts to 12–14 ft. lbs. (16–19 Nm).
4. Connect the valve's vacuum lines.

EGR Control Solenoid Valve

The EGR and canister control solenoid valve is located on the intake manifold.
1. Label and disconnect the solenoid valve vacuum lines.
2. Loosen the solenoid valve attaching nut, then separate the valve from the intake manifold.

To install:
3. Install the solenoid valve and tighten the mounting nut to 12–14 ft. lbs. (16–19 Nm).
4. Connect the solenoid valve vacuum lines.

EGR Temperature Sensor

1. Partially drain the engine cooling system until the coolant level is below the EGR temperature sensor mounting hole.
2. Disconnect the EGR temperature sensor electrical harness.
3. Remove the sensor from the intake manifold.

To install:
4. Coat the sensor threads with Teflon® sealant.
5. Thread the sensor into the intake manifold and tighten to 11–18 ft. lbs. (15–25 Nm).
6. Connect the negative battery cable.
7. Refill the engine cooling system.
8. Start the engine and check for coolant leaks. Top off the cooling system as necessary.

ELECTRONIC ENGINE CONTROLS

Engine Control Module (ECM)

OPERATION

▶ See Figures 24 and 25

The Engine Control Module (ECM) performs many functions. The module receives data from various engine sensors and computes the required fuel flow rate necessary to maintain correct air/fuel ratio throughout the entire engine operational range.

Based on the data received and information programmed into the ECM's memory, the ECM generates output signals to control relays, actuators and solenoids. The module automatically senses and compensates for any changes in altitude when driving the vehicle.

The ECM consists of a microcomputer, inspection lamps, a diagnostic mode selector, and connectors for signal input, signal output, power supply and ground. The ECM module is located under the center console, near the accelerator pedal.

REMOVAL & INSTALLATION

▶ See Figures 26 and 27

✻✺ WARNING

Electrostatic Discharge (ESD) can ruin sensitive electronic components. Always wear a grounding strap or discharge electricity stored in your body to a good ground prior to handling any electronic components.

1. Disconnect the negative battery cable.
2. Remove the lower panel on the center console, if necessary.
3. Label and disconnect the ECM electrical harness.
4. Remove the ECM mounting screws.
5. Carefully remove the ECM from the vehicle.

To install:
6. Position the ECM in the vehicle and tighten the mounting screws securely.
7. Connect the ECM electrical harness.
8. Connect the negative battery cable.
9. Start the vehicle and verify proper operation.
10. Read and clear the ECM trouble code memory.
11. Replace the lower panel.

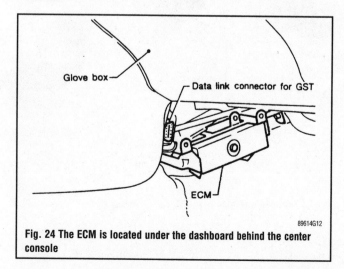

Fig. 24 The ECM is located under the dashboard behind the center console

Glove box

Data link connector for GST

ECM

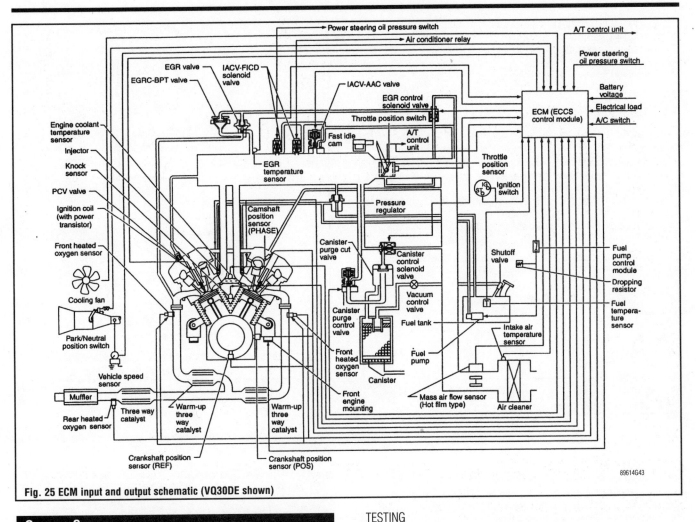

Fig. 25 ECM input and output schematic (VQ30DE shown)

Oxygen Sensor

OPERATION

▶ **See Figure 28**

The oxygen sensor supplies a signal to the ECM, which indicates a rich or lean condition during engine operation. The input data assists the computer in determining the proper air/fuel ratio. A low voltage signal from the sensor indicates too much oxygen in the exhaust (lean condition) and a high voltage signal indicates too little oxygen in the exhaust (rich condition).

Oxygen sensors are located in the exhaust system, usually in the exhaust manifold or near the catalytic converter. Heated oxygen sensors are used on some models to allow the engine to reach the closed loop state faster.

TESTING

Sensor

The ECM contains an oxygen sensor monitor function which is used to test the oxygen sensor.

1. Locate the ECM and take note of the LED and mode switch positions.
2. Turn the ignition switch **ON**.
3. Turn the mode switch screw fully clockwise.
4. Wait at least 2 seconds.
5. Turn the mode switch screw fully counterclockwise.
6. Start the engine and allow it to reach operating temperature.
7. Run the engine at approximately 2000 rpm for 2 minutes under no load.
8. Ensure that the red LED on the ECM or the Malfunction Indicator Lamp (MIL) on the dashboard flash on and off more than 5 times every 10 seconds.

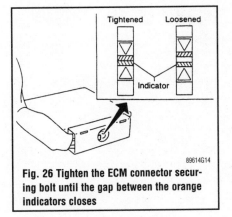

Fig. 26 Tighten the ECM connector securing bolt until the gap between the orange indicators closes

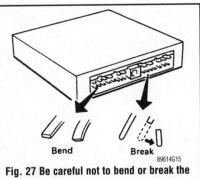

Fig. 27 Be careful not to bend or break the terminals on the ECM when installing the connector

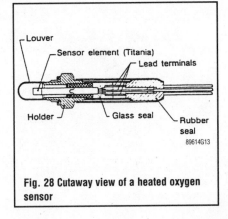

Fig. 28 Cutaway view of a heated oxygen sensor

9. If the red LED on the ECM or the MIL do not function as specified, check the oxygen sensor circuit back to the ECM for continuity.

10. If continuity exists, the oxygen sensor may be faulty.

Sensor Heater

FRONT

▶ **See Figure 29**

1. Disconnect the sensor electrical harness.
2. Measure resistance between the outer terminals of the connector.
3. Resistance should be 2.3–4.3 ohms @ 77°F (25°C).
4. Check continuity between the center terminal and each of the outer terminals. Continuity should not exist.
5. If resistance is not as specified or continuity exists, the oxygen sensor is faulty.
6. If resistance and continuity are within specification, check and repair the circuits.

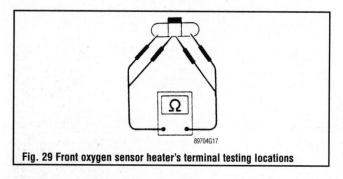

Fig. 29 Front oxygen sensor heater's terminal testing locations

REAR

▶ **See Figures 30 and 31**

1. Disconnect the sensor electrical harness.
2. On models with a three-terminal connector, measure resistance between the two outer terminals. On models with a four-terminal connector, measure resistance between the two illustrated terminals.

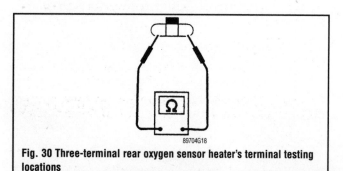

Fig. 30 Three-terminal rear oxygen sensor heater's terminal testing locations

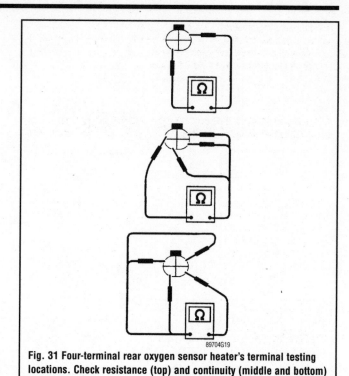

Fig. 31 Four-terminal rear oxygen sensor heater's terminal testing locations. Check resistance (top) and continuity (middle and bottom)

3. For three-terminal connectors, the resistance should be 5.2–8.2 ohms @ 77°F (25°C). For four-terminal connectors, the resistance should be 2.3–4.3 ohms @ 77°F (25°C).

4. On models with a four-terminal connector, also check continuity between the various terminal combinations, as illustrated. Continuity should not exist.

5. If resistance is not as specified or continuity exists, the oxygen sensor is faulty.

6. If resistance and continuity are within specification, check and repair the circuits.

REMOVAL & INSTALLATION

▶ **See Figures 32, 33 and 34**

Oxygen sensors are located in the exhaust manifold and may also be located in the exhaust system near the catalytic converter.

1. Raise and support the vehicle safely, as required.
2. Label and disconnect the oxygen sensor electrical harness.

➡**Lubricate the sensor threads with penetrating oil prior to removal.**

3. Remove the sensor using a box end wrench or special oxygen sensor socket.

To install:

4. Thread the sensor into the mounting boss and tighten to 30–37 ft. lbs. (40–50 Nm).

Fig. 32 Be sure to use the proper size wrench when removing the sensor from the exhaust system

Fig. 33 Some oxygen sensors have a considerable length of wire; follow the wire to the connector

Fig. 34 Be sure to coat the threads of the oxygen sensor with anti-seize compound before installation

➡Most new oxygen sensor threads are coated with anti-seize compound. If you are reinstalling a used oxygen sensor, carefully coat the threads with anti-seize compound. Take care not to allow the oxygen sensor element to be contaminated by the compound.

5. Connect the engine control electrical harness to the sensor.
6. If applicable, lower the vehicle.

Idle Air Control Valve

OPERATION

The Idle Air Control Valve-Auxiliary Air Control (IACV-AAC) functions by using a duty cycle (on/off/on), which is controlled by the ECM. The longer the "on" pulse, the greater the amount of air that will flow through the valve. The more air that flows through the valve, the higher the engine speed. Actual idle speed is the lowest speed at which the engine can operate steadily. This is computed by the ECM, taking into consideration various conditions such as warm-up, deceleration and engine load.

TESTING

▶ **See Figures 35 and 36**

1. Disconnect the electrical harness from the valve.
2. Measure the resistance between the terminals of the valve.
   a. 1993–94 VG30E engines: 0.5 ohms
   b. 1993–94 VE30DE engines: 10 ohms
   c. 1995 VQ30DE engines 0.5 ohms
   d. 1996–98 VQ30DE engines should be around 30 ohms @ 77°F (25°C).
3. If resistance is not within specification, the valve may be faulty.
4. If resistance is within specification, check the circuits back to the ECM.

REMOVAL & INSTALLATION

▶ **See Figure 37**

1. Disconnect the electrical harness from the valve.
2. Remove the valve attaching bolts.
3. Remove the valve from the assembly.

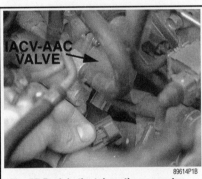

Fig. 35 Push in the tab on the connector and pull back to remove the IACV-AAC valve connector

Fig. 36 The resistance of this IACV-AAC valve confirms proper operation

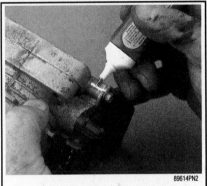

Fig. 37 Make sure the plunger slides smoothly inside the housing

➡It may be easier to remove the IACV by removing the entire IAA unit from the manifold.

To install:
4. Install the valve on the assembly.
5. Tighten the attaching bolts securely.
6. Connect the electrical harness to the valve .

Engine Coolant Temperature Sensor

OPERATION

The Engine Coolant Temperature (ECT) sensor resistance changes in response to engine coolant temperature. The sensor resistance decreases as coolant temperature increases. This provides a reference signal, which indicates engine coolant temperature, to the ECM.

TESTING

▶ **See Figures 38 and 39**

1. Disconnect the engine electrical harness from the ECT sensor.
2. Connect an ohmmeter between the ECT sensor terminals.
3. With the engine cold and the ignition switch in the **OFF** position, measure and note the ECT sensor resistance.
4. Connect the engine electrical harness to the sensor.
5. Start the engine and allow it to reach normal operating temperature.
6. Once the engine has reached normal operating temperature, turn it **OFF**.
7. Once again, disconnect the engine electrical harness from the ECT sensor.

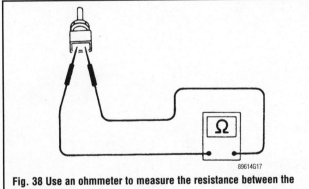

Fig. 38 Use an ohmmeter to measure the resistance between the two terminals

ENGINE COOLANT TEMPERATURE SENSOR

Temperature °C (°F)	Resistance
20 (68)	2.1 - 2.9 kΩ
50 (122)	0.68 - 1.00 kΩ
90 (194)	0.236 - 0.260 kΩ

89704C02

Fig. 39 Compare the sensor readings with these values

8. Measure and note the ECT sensor resistance with the engine hot.
9. Compare the cold and hot ECT sensor resistance measurements with the accompanying chart.
10. If readings do not approximate those in the chart, the sensor may be faulty.

REMOVAL & INSTALLATION

▶ **See Figure 40**

1. Partially drain the engine cooling system until the coolant level is below the ECT sensor mounting hole.
2. Disconnect the electrical harness from the ECT sensor.
3. Remove the coolant temperature sensor from the cylinder head.
To install:
4. Coat the sensor threads with Teflon® sealant.
5. Thread the sensor into the intake manifold and tighten securely.
6. Refill the engine cooling system.
7. Start the engine and check for coolant leaks.
8. Top off the cooling system as necessary.

Intake Air Temperature Sensor

OPERATION

▶ **See Figure 41**

The Intake Air Temperature (IAT) sensor resistance changes in response to ambient air temperature. Sensor resistance decreases as the air temperature increases, and resistance increases as the temperature decreases. This provides a signal to the ECM, indicating the temperature of the incoming air charge.

TESTING

▶ **See Figures 42 and 43**

1. Disconnect the electrical harness from the IAT sensor.
2. Measure the resistance between the sensor terminals.
3. Compare the resistance reading with the accompanying chart.
4. If the resistance is not within specification, the IAT sensor may be faulty.
5. Connect the electrical harness to the sensor.

REMOVAL & INSTALLATION

1. Disconnect the electrical harness from the IAT sensor.
2. Remove the sensor mounting screws.
3. Remove the sensor from the air cleaner housing.
To install:
4. Install the sensor in the air cleaner housing and tighten the screws securely.
5. Connect the electrical harness to the IAT sensor.

Mass Air Flow Sensor

OPERATION

The Mass Air Flow (MAF) sensor directly measures the amount of air flowing into the engine. The sensor is mounted between the air cleaner assembly and the air cleaner outlet tube.

The sensor utilizes a hot wire sensing element to measure the amount of air entering the engine. The sensor does this by sending a signal, generated by the sensor when the incoming air cools the hot wire, to the ECM. The signal is used by the ECM to calculate the injector pulse width, which controls the air/fuel ratio in the engine.

TESTING

▶ **See Figures 44, 45, 46 and 47**

1. Using a multimeter, check for voltage by backprobing the MAF sensor connector, as illustrated.
2. With the ignition switch **ON** and the engine stopped, voltage should be less than 1.0 volt.
3. With the engine idling at operating temperature, voltage should be 1.0–1.7 volts.
4. With the engine running at approximately 2,500 rpm, voltage should be 1.5–2.1volts.

➡ **It is important to watch for a linear voltage rise in response to increases in engine rpm, up to about 4000 rpm.**

5. If voltage is not within specifications, check the power and ground circuits.
6. If the power and ground circuits test okay, the MAF sensor may be faulty.

Fig. 40 Location of the thermal sending unit (A) next to the coolant temperature sensor (B)

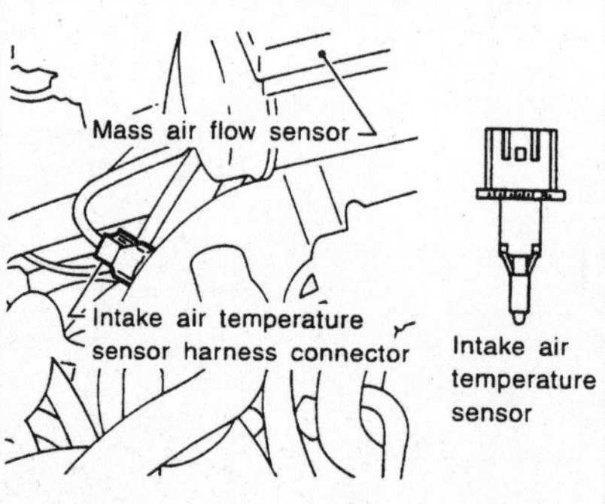

89612P50

Fig. 41 The intake air temperature sensor is located in the air intake duct

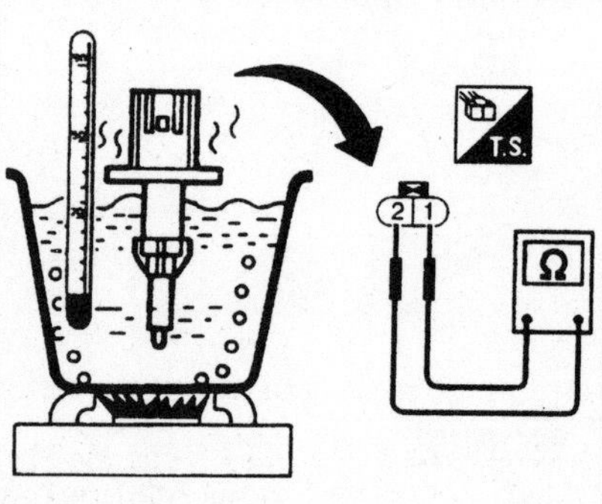

89614G18

Fig. 42 Using hot water to check intake air temperature sensor function

89614G19

INTAKE AIR TEMPERATURE SENSOR

Temperature °C (°F)	Resistance
20 (68)	2.1 - 2.9 kΩ
80 (176)	0.27 - 0.38 kΩ

89704C03

Fig. 43 Compare the sensor readings with these values

REMOVAL & INSTALLATION

▶ **See Figure 48**

1. Loosen the hose clamps securing the air tube.
2. Disconnect the air tube from the MAF sensor and throttle body.
3. Disconnect the MAF sensor electrical harness.
4. Remove the MAF sensor attaching bolts.
5. Carefully remove the MAF sensor from the air box.

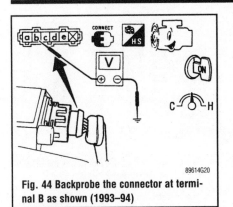

Fig. 44 Backprobe the connector at terminal B as shown (1993–94)

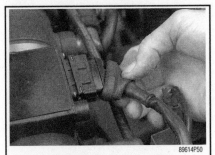

Fig. 45 On 1995–98 vehicles, backprobe terminal 1 for testing

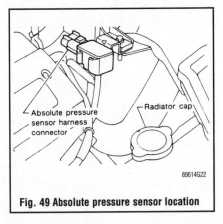

Fig. 46 To backprobe the connector, remove the rubber boot from the back of the connector

To install:

6. Position the MAF sensor in the air box.
7. Install the MAF sensor attaching bolts and tighten to 13–16 ft. lbs. (18–22 Nm).
8. Connect the MAF sensor's electrical harness.
9. Connect the air tube to the MAF sensor and throttle body.
10. Tighten the hose clamps securing the air tube.

Absolute Pressure Sensor

OPERATION

▶ See Figure 49

The absolute pressure sensor is connected to the MAP/BARO switch solenoid valve by a hose. The sensor detects ambient barometric pressure and intake manifold pressure, and sends a voltage signal to the ECM. As pressure increases, the voltage rises. The absolute pressure sensor is not used to control the engine system. It is only used for on-board diagnosis.

TESTING

▶ See Figures 50 and 51

1. Remove the absolute pressure sensor with its electrical harness connected.
2. Disconnect the vacuum hose from the sensor.
3. Turn the ignition switch **ON**.
4. Backprobe the sensor connector and check output voltage, from the white wire and ground.
5. The voltage should be 3.2–4.8 volts.
6. Connect a hand powered vacuum pump and apply a vacuum of 7.87 in. Hg (26.7 kPa).
7. Voltage should be 1.0–1.4 volts lower than the value in Step 5.
8. If voltage is not within specification or does not respond as specified, check the power and ground circuits.
9. If the power and ground circuits are okay, the sensor may be faulty.

REMOVAL & INSTALLATION

1. Label and disconnect the electrical harness from the sensor.
2. Label and disconnect the vacuum hose from the sensor.
3. Remove the sensor mounting screws.
To install:
4. Install the sensor and tighten the screws securely.
5. Connect the vacuum hose to the sensor.
6. Connect the electrical harness to the sensor.

Manifold Absolute Pressure/Barometric Pressure Switch Solenoid Valve

OPERATION

The Manifold Absolute Pressure/Barometric pressure (BARO) switch solenoid valve allows the absolute pressure sensor to monitor either ambient barometric pressure or intake manifold pressure. The solenoid switches between two passages by duty cycle (on/off) signals from the ECM.

TESTING

▶ See Figure 52

1. Label and disconnect the vacuum lines and electrical harness.
2. Inspect the lines for damage, and replace as necessary.
3. Inspect the valve for damage, and replace as necessary.
4. Apply battery voltage and ground between the valve terminals.
5. Air should pass between Port **A** and Port **B**.
6. Air should not pass between Port **A** and Port **C**.
7. Remove the battery voltage.
8. Air should pass between Port **A** and Port **C**.
9. Air should not pass between Port **A** and Port **B**.
10. If the valve does not function as specified, it may be faulty.
11. If the valve responds as specified, check and repair the power and ground circuits.

Fig. 47 The voltage should be less than 1 volt with the key in the ON position

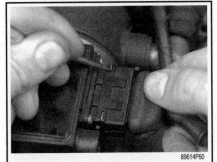

Fig. 48 Use a small pick to push the metal clip open while gently pulling back on the connector

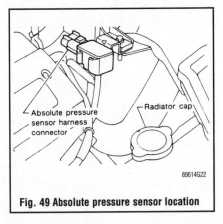

Fig. 49 Absolute pressure sensor location

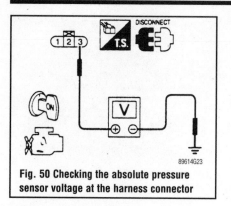

Fig. 50 Checking the absolute pressure sensor voltage at the harness connector

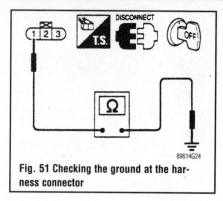

Fig. 51 Checking the ground at the harness connector

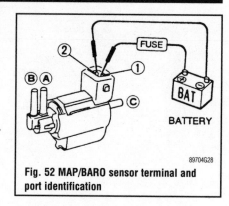

Fig. 52 MAP/BARO sensor terminal and port identification

REMOVAL & INSTALLATION

1. Label and disconnect the electrical harness from the sensor.
2. Label and disconnect the vacuum hose from the sensor.
3. Remove the sensor mounting screws.
4. Remove the sensor.

To install:

5. Install the sensor and tighten the screws securely.
6. Connect the vacuum hose to the sensor.
7. Connect the electrical harness to the sensor.

Throttle Position Sensor

OPERATION

The Throttle Position (TP) sensor is a potentiometer. It is mounted on the side of the throttle body and is connected to the throttle plate shaft. The sensor monitors throttle plate movement and position, and transmits an appropriate electrical signal to the ECM. These signals are used by the ECM to adjust the air/fuel mixture and spark timing according to engine load. The TP sensor is adjustable on some models.

Automatic transaxle TP sensors contain position switches. These switches provide a signal to the ECM when the engine is at idle and wide open throttle.

TESTING

Potentiometer

▶ **See Figures 53, 54, 55, 56 and 57**

1. Disconnect the electrical harness from the sensor.
2. Check resistance between the connector terminals.
   a. Resistance for 1993–94 model year vehicles should be as follows:
   - Throttle closed—approximately 1 kilohm
   - Throttle partially open—1–9 kilohms
   - Throttle fully open—approximately 9 kilohms

b. Resistance for 1995–98 model year vehicles should be as follows:
- Throttle closed—approximately 0.5 kilohms
- Throttle partially open—0.5–4.0 kilohms
- Throttle fully open—approximately 4.0 kilohms

3. Slowly rotate the throttle shaft and monitor the ohmmeter for a continuous, steady change in resistance. Any sudden jumps, or irregularities in resistance (such as jumping back and forth), indicates a malfunctioning sensor.

➡ **Do not perform this test on the electrical harness connector terminals, but rather on the terminals of the sensor itself.**

4. If resistance is not within specification, the sensor may be faulty.
5. If resistance is within specification, check the circuits back to the ECM.
6. Connect the electrical harness to the sensor.

Position Switches

▶ **See Figure 58**

1. Disconnect the electrical harness from the sensor.
2. Check continuity between the connector terminals.
3. When the throttle is placed in the appropriate position (idle or wide open throttle), continuity should exist.
4. When the throttle is not in the idle or wide open throttle position, continuity should not exist.

➡ **The position switches are an integral part of the TP sensor and cannot be replaced separately. If faulty, the TP sensor must be replaced as an assembly.**

5. If continuity is not as specified, the sensor is faulty.

REMOVAL & INSTALLATION

▶ **See Figure 59**

1. Label and disconnect the electrical harness from the sensor.
2. Remove the sensor mounting screws.
3. Remove the sensor from the throttle body.

To install:

4. Install the sensor on the throttle body and hand-tighten the screws.

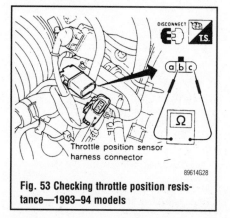

Fig. 53 Checking throttle position resistance—1993–94 models

Fig. 54 To check for throttle position sensor function, unplug the lower connector and attach the ohmmeter leads to the sensor

Fig. 55 With the throttle closed, the resistance should be around 1 kilohm (VE30DE)

Fig. 56 As you open the throttle with your hand to the fully open position, resistance should increase

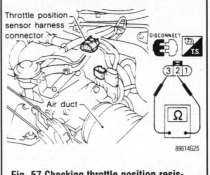

Fig. 57 Checking throttle position resistance—1995–98 models

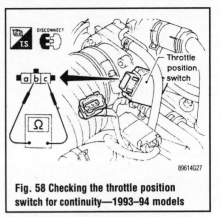

Fig. 58 Checking the throttle position switch for continuity—1993–94 models

5. Connect the electrical harness to the sensor.
6. Adjust the sensor and tighten the mounting screws securely.

ADJUSTMENT

The TP sensor is adjustable on some models. To determine if your model is adjustable, simply look for adjustment slots where the mounting bolts go through the sensor. If slots exist, the sensor is adjustable. If slots do not exist, the sensor is not adjustable.

➡ Inspect the sensor carefully, as large washers may cover the adjustment slots.

Automatic Transaxle Models

1. Start the engine and allow it to reach operating temperature.
2. Disconnect the TP sensor and closed throttle position switch electrical harness.
3. Check continuity between the closed throttle position switch connector terminals 5 and 6 (1993–94 models check terminals B and C).
4. Raise the engine speed to 2000 rpm, then gradually lower it.
5. Continuity should exist (the closed throttle position switch should close at approximately 1000 rpm with the transaxle in **N**.
6. If continuity is not as specified, loosen the TP sensor mounting bolts and slowly rotate the sensor.
7. Tighten the mounting bolts securely and recheck continuity.

Manual Transaxle Models

1. Turn the ignition switch **ON**, but do not start the engine.
2. Backprobe the connector and check voltage between the center terminal and ground.
3. With the throttle closed, voltage should be 0.3–0.7 volts.
4. If voltage is not within specification, loosen the TP sensor mounting bolts and slowly rotate the sensor.
5. Tighten the mounting bolts securely and recheck the voltage.
6. Start the engine and allow it to reach operating temperature.
7. Turn the ignition switch **OFF** and wait at least 5 seconds.

8. Disconnect the TP sensor electrical harness.
9. Start the engine and wait at least 5 seconds with the transaxle in the **N** position.
10. Reconnect the TP sensor with the engine running.

Camshaft Position Sensor

OPERATION

The Camshaft Position (CMP) sensor is a basic component of the engine control system. It monitors engine speed and piston position. These input signals to the ECM are used to control fuel injection, ignition timing and other functions.

TESTING

VG30E Engines

▶ See Figures 60 and 61

1. Remove the distributor assembly from the engine.
2. Disconnect the ignition wires and coil wire from the distributor.

➡ The camshaft position sensor electrical harness should remain connected.

3. Turn the ignition switch **ON**.
4. Measure voltage between terminals 3, 4 and ground.
5. With the engine's distributor shaft rotating slowly, voltage should fluctuate between 0 and 5 volts.

➡ If the voltage signal is checked with the engine running, the normal reading will be 2.3 volts (average voltage). An oscilloscope may also be used to view the pulse signal.

6. If voltage does not fluctuate or is not within specification, check the circuits for damage.
7. If the circuits are functional, the sensor may be faulty.
8. Install the distributor and connect the ignition and coil wires.

Fig. 59 Mark the position of the sensor before removal (throttle body removed for clarity)

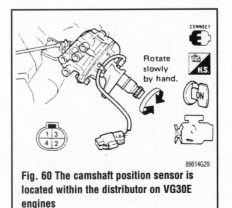

Fig. 60 The camshaft position sensor is located within the distributor on VG30E engines

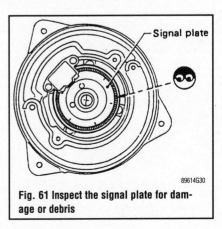

Fig. 61 Inspect the signal plate for damage or debris

VE30DE engines

▶ **See Figures 62 thru 69**

1. Mark the position of the sensor on the cylinder head so the timing is not altered when it is installed.

2. To remove the sensor from the engine, removing the two adjustment screws and pull the sensor out of the cylinder head.

3. Disconnect the power transistor.

4. Turn the ignition switch to the **ON** position.

5. Backprobe the harness connector at terminal A and ground.

6. While turning the distributor by hand, the voltage should fluctuate between 0 and 5 volts.

7. Backprobe the harness connector at terminal B and ground.

✳✳ WARNING

Do not bridge terminals A and B together while checking for sensor function. Check each terminal separately.

8. While turning the distributor by hand, the voltage should fluctuate between 0 and 5 volts.

9. If the sensor does not respond to the test as described, the sensor may be faulty.

VQ30DE Engines

▶ **See Figure 70**

1. Unplug the harness from the camshaft position sensor.

2. Remove the attachment bolt and remove the sensor.

3. Using an ohmmeter, measure the resistance between the sensor terminals.

4. The resistance for Hitachi model sensors should be 1,440–1,760 ohms @ 68°F (20°C).

5. The resistance for Mitsubishi model sensors should be 2,090–2,550 ohms @ 68°F (20°C).

6. If the resistance is not as specified, the sensor should be replaced.

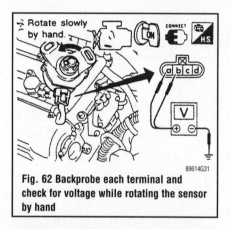

Fig. 62 Backprobe each terminal and check for voltage while rotating the sensor by hand

Fig. 63 After the position of the sensor is marked, remove the adjustment bolts . . .

Fig. 64 . . . then pull the sensor out of the cylinder head

Fig. 65 Use a small wire to backprobe terminals A and B

Fig. 66 When turning the sensor by hand, the voltage should fluctuate between 0 and 5 volts

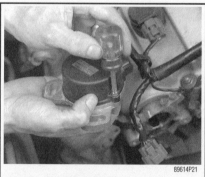

Fig. 67 To inspect the signal plate, remove the cover screws . . .

Fig. 68 . . . then lift the cover off of the sensor. Inspect the signal plate for debris or damage

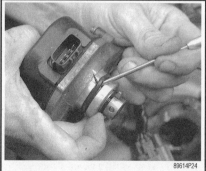

Fig. 69 Be sure to replace the O-ring when installing the sensor

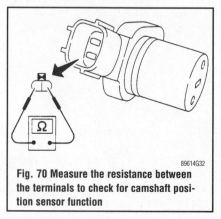

Fig. 70 Measure the resistance between the terminals to check for camshaft position sensor function

REMOVAL & INSTALLATION

VG30E Engines

The camshaft position sensor is located inside the distributor. On some distributors, the camshaft position sensor is not serviceable (replacement parts may not be available separately). If the camshaft position sensor is serviceable, use the following procedure.

1. Remove the distributor cap and wires.
2. Remove the rotor.
3. Remove the camshaft position sensor cap.
4. Remove the camshaft position sensor mounting screws.
5. Carefully remove the camshaft position sensor.

To install:

6. Position the camshaft position sensor in the distributor and tighten the mounting screws securely.
7. Install the camshaft position sensor cap.
8. Install the rotor.
9. Install the distributor cap and wires.

VE30DE and VQ30DE Engines

The camshaft position sensor on VE30DE engines is located at the rear of the left (front) cylinder bank. On VQ30DE engines, the camshaft position sensor is located on the left side of the engine, near the water pump. Unplug the electrical connector. Remove the attaching screws, then remove the sensor.

Crankshaft Position Sensor(s)

OPERATION

The Crankshaft Position Sensor (POS) is located on the transaxle housing, facing the gear teeth of the flywheel/flexplate. It detects the fluctuation of the engine revolution. The sensor consists of a permanent magnet, core and coil.

When the engine is running, the high and low parts of the teeth cause the gap with the sensor to change. This changing gap causes the magnetic field near the sensor to change. Due to the changing magnetic field, the voltage from the sensor changes.

The ECM receives this varying voltage signal and detects the fluctuation of the engine revolution.

TESTING

POS Sensor

▶ **See Figures 71 and 72**

1. Remove the sensor from the engine.
2. Inspect the sensor tip. If damage to the tip is evident, replace the sensor.
3. Plug in the sensor, but do not install it .
4. Backprobe terminals 2 and 3 with a voltmeter. Using a screwdriver, touch it against the sensor core. The voltmeter should read approximately 5 volts.
5. Slowly pull the screwdriver away; the meter should remain at 5 volts.

6. Touch the sensor core with the screwdriver; then quickly draw it away. The voltage should drop to approximately 0 volts.
7. If the sensor does not respond accordingly, the sensor may be faulty.

REF Sensor

▶ **See Figures 73 and 74**

1. Measure the resistance between the two terminals on the sensor.
2. Resistance between the terminals should be approximately 470–570 ohms @ 68°F (20°C).

REMOVAL & INSTALLATION

POS Sensor

The POS crankshaft position sensor is located on the transaxle housing facing the gear teeth of the flywheel/flexplate.

1. Disconnect the sensor electrical harness.
2. Remove the sensor mounting bolts.
3. Remove the sensor from the transaxle housing.

To install:

4. Install the sensor in the transaxle housing.
5. Tighten the sensor mounting bolts securely.
6. Connect the sensor electrical harness.

REF Sensor

The REF crankshaft position sensor is located on the oil pan, near the crankshaft damper.

1. Disconnect the sensor electrical harness.
2. Remove the sensor mounting bolts.
3. Remove the sensor from the oil pan.

To install:

4. Install the sensor in the transaxle housing.
5. Tighten the sensor mounting bolts securely.
6. Connect the sensor electrical harness.

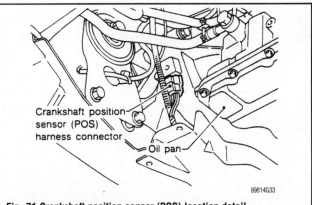

Fig. 71 Crankshaft position sensor (POS) location detail

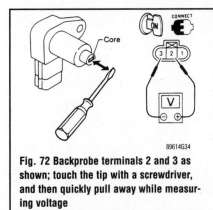

Fig. 72 Backprobe terminals 2 and 3 as shown; touch the tip with a screwdriver, and then quickly pull away while measuring voltage

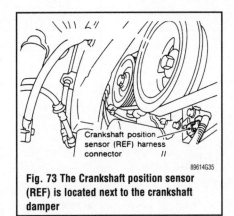

Fig. 73 The Crankshaft position sensor (REF) is located next to the crankshaft damper

Fig. 74 Measure the resistance between the two terminals to check for proper operation

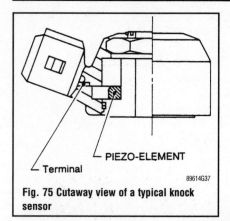

Fig. 75 Cutaway view of a typical knock sensor

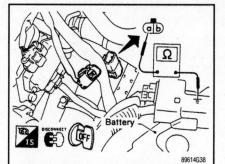

Fig. 76 Unplug the knock sensor at the sub-harness connector to check for continuity

Fig. 77 Continuity should exist between terminal A and ground when testing the knock sensor

Knock Sensor

OPERATION

▶ **See Figure 75**

The knock sensor is a piezoelectric element which is attached to the engine block, which senses engine knocking, or "pinging". The vibrational pressure is converted to a voltage signal, which is sent to the ECM. The ECM quickly processes this information and adjusts the ignition timing and fuel mixture to prevent knocking to continue.

TESTING

▶ **See Figures 76 and 77**

1. Disconnect the knock sensor at the sub-harness connector.
2. On VG30E engines, check the continuity between terminal **A** and **B**. Continuity should exist.
3. On VE30DE and VQ30DE engines, check the continuity between terminal **A** and ground. Continuity should exist.

➡ **It is necessary to use an ohmmeter which can measure more than 10 megaohms.**

REMOVAL & INSTALLATION

The knock sensor on VG30E engines is located under the rear exhaust manifold.

The knock sensor on VE30DE and VQ30DE engines is located between the cylinder banks, under the exhaust manifold. For removal, the intake manifolds must be removed.

Vehicle Speed Sensor

OPERATION

The vehicle speed sensor, located on the transaxle, sends a signal to the ECM and to the speedometer to monitor vehicle speed.

TESTING

▶ **See Figure 78**

1. Remove the sensor from the transaxle housing.
2. Connect a voltmeter to the terminals on the sensor.
3. Spin the gear on the sensor quickly by hand while noting the voltage. The sensor should produce approximately 0.5 volts of alternating current (AC).
4. If the sensor does not perform as described, it should be considered faulty.

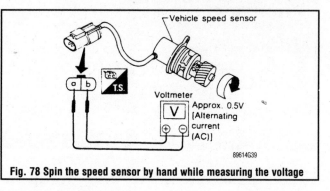

Fig. 78 Spin the speed sensor by hand while measuring the voltage

REMOVAL & INSTALLATION

1. Unplug the sensor harness connector.
2. Unscrew the retaining bolt and pull the sensor out of the transaxle housing.
   To install:
3. Inspect the O-ring on the sensor; replace it if necessary.
4. Install the sensor into the transaxle housing. Be careful the O-ring doesn't dislodge from the sensor.
5. Plug in the connector.

Valve Timing Control

OPERATION

▶ **See Figure 79**

Valve Timing Control is a system that controls the relationship between the camshaft and the crankshaft. An electronic solenoid controls the pressurized oil

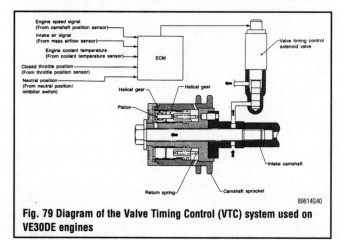

Fig. 79 Diagram of the Valve Timing Control (VTC) system used on VE30DE engines

that is routed to the mechanism mounted on the intake camshafts which alters the valve timing. This system is used on 1993–94 VE30DE Engines.

TESTING

♦ **See Figures 80 and 81**

The control solenoid for the VTC system can be tested by applying voltage to the solenoid and listening for a clicking noise.
1. Disconnect the harness from each of the VTC solenoids.
2. Apply 12 volts to the terminals as shown in the illustration.

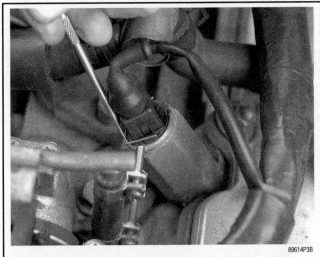

Fig. 80 Use a small pick to hold the metal clip out while pulling on the connector to remove it from the solenoid

3. Listen for a clicking noise while applying voltage; if the solenoid clicks, it can be assumed the system is functioning properly.

REMOVAL & INSTALLATION

1. Unplug the harness connector from the solenoid.
2. Using the appropriate size wrench, unbolt the solenoid from the cylinder head.
To install:
3. Screw the solenoid into the cylinder head.
4. Plug the harness connector onto the solenoid.

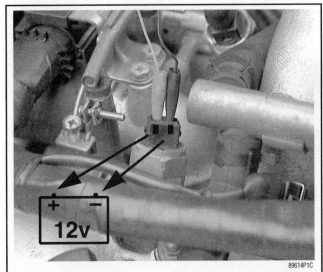

Fig. 81 Listen for a clicking noise while applying 12 volts as shown

TROUBLE CODES

General Information

♦ **See Figure 82**

Diagnostic Trouble Codes (DTC's) are indicated by the number of flashes from the red Light Emitting Diode (LED) on the ECM or the Malfunction Indicator Lamp (MIL) on the instrument panel.

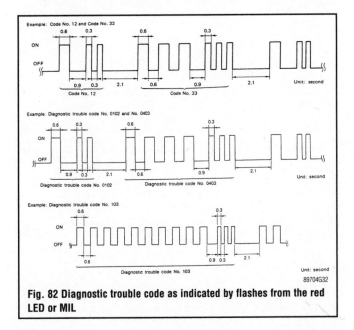

Fig. 82 Diagnostic trouble code as indicated by flashes from the red LED or MIL

On two and three-digit codes, the long (0.6 second) flashes indicate the number of tens digits and short (0.3 second) flashes indicate the number of single digits.

On four-digit codes, the long (0.6 second) flashes indicate the first two digits in the code and the short (0.3 second) flashes indicate the second two digits in the code.

Data Link Connector (DLC)

♦ **See Figure 83**

Two types of data link connectors are used on each vehicle. Each is designed to fit a specific type of tool. The data link connector for the Nissan CONSULT is located in the interior fuse panel. The data link connector for the Generic Scan Tool (GST) is usually located under the left side of the dashboard.

The data link connectors are for use with scan tools only. The terminals cannot be jumpered to read out diagnostic codes, as on some vehicles. Be sure to follow the scan tool manufacturer's instructions.

Reading Codes

♦ **See Figures 84 and 85**

Two types of diagnostic systems are used in Nissan vehicles: the two-mode diagnostic system and the five-mode diagnostic system. The five-mode system is used in 1993–94 Maximas with VG30E engines. All other vehicles use the two-mode system.

FIVE MODE DIAGNOSTIC SYSTEM

The five-mode diagnostic system is incorporated in the ECM which uses inputs from various sensors to determine the correct air/fuel ratio. If any of the

Fig. 83 When using a scan tool, make sure to follow all of the manufacturer's instructions carefully to ensure proper diagnosis

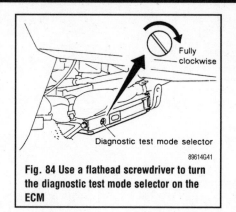

Fig. 84 Use a flathead screwdriver to turn the diagnostic test mode selector on the ECM

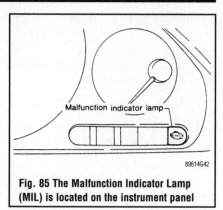

Fig. 85 The Malfunction Indicator Lamp (MIL) is located on the instrument panel

sensors malfunction the ECM will store the code in memory. The five-mode diagnostic system is capable of various tests as outlined below. When using these modes, the ECM may have to be removed from its mounting bracket to better access the mode selector switch. Vehicles are equipped with a Malfunction Indicator Light (MIL) light on the instrument panel. If any systems are malfunctioning, the (MIL) light will illuminate simultaneously with the red lamp on the ECM while the engine is running and the system is in Mode 1.

Mode I—Heated Oxygen Sensor

During closed loop operation the green lamp turns ON when a lean condition is detected and turns OFF under a rich condition. During open loop the green lamp remains ON or OFF. This mode is used to check Heated Oxygen sensor functions for correct operation. To enter Mode I, proceed as follows:
1. Turn the ignition switch ON.
2. Turn the diagnostic switch located on the side of the ECM ON by either flipping the switch to the ON position or turning the screw switch fully clockwise.
3. Turn the diagnostic switch OFF or fully counterclockwise as soon as the inspection lamp flashes once.
4. The self-diagnostic system is now in Mode I.

Mode II—Mixture Ratio Feedback Control Monitor

The green inspection lamp is operating in the same manner as in Mode I. During closed loop operation the red inspection lamp turns ON and OFF simultaneously with the green lamp when the mixture ratio is controlled within the specified value. During open loop the red lamp remains ON or OFF. Mode II is used for checking that optimum control of the fuel mixture is obtained. To enter Mode II, proceed as follows:
1. Turn the ignition switch ON.
2. Turn the diagnostic switch ON, by either flipping the switch to the ON position or use a screwdriver and turn the switch fully clockwise.
3. Turn the diagnostic switch OFF or fully counterclockwise as soon as the inspection lamps flash twice.
4. The self-diagnostic system is now in Mode II.

Mode III—Self-Diagnosis System

This mode of the self-diagnostics is for stored code retrieval.
To enter Mode III, proceed as follows:
1. Thoroughly warm the engine before proceeding. With the engine OFF, turn the ignition switch ON.
2. Turn the diagnostic switch located on the side of the ECM ON by either flipping the switch to the ON position or using a screwdriver, turn the switch fully clockwise.
3. Turn the diagnostic switch OFF or fully counterclockwise as soon as the inspection lamps flash three times.
4. The self-diagnostic system is now in Mode III.
When the battery is disconnected or self-diagnostic Mode IV is selected after using Mode III, all stored codes will be cleared. However if the ignition key is turned OFF and then the procedure is followed to enter Mode IV directly, the stored codes will not be cleared.
5. The codes will now be displayed by the red and green inspection lamps flashing. The red lamp will flash first and the green lamp will follow. The red lamp is the tens and the green lamp is the units, that is, the red lamp flashes once and the green lamp flashes twice, this would indicate a Code 12.

Mode IV—On/Off Switches

This mode checks the operation of the Vehicle Speed Sensor (VSS), Closed Throttle Position (CTP) and starter switches. Entering this mode will also clear all stored codes in the ECM. To enter Mode IV, proceed as follows:
1. Turn the ignition switch ON.
2. Turn the diagnostic switch located on the side of the ECM ON by either flipping the switch to the ON position or turning the mode switch fully clockwise.
3. Turn the diagnostic switch OFF or fully counterclockwise as soon as the inspection lamps flash 4 times.
4. The self-diagnostic system is now in Mode IV.
5. Turn the ignition switch to the START position and verify the red inspection lamp illuminates. This verifies that the starter switch is working.
6. Depress the accelerator and verify the red inspection lamp goes OFF. This verifies that the CTP switch is working.
7. Raise and properly support the vehicle and verify the lamp goes ON when the vehicle speed is above 12 mph (20 km/h). This verifies that the VSS is working.
8. Turn the ignition switch OFF.

Mode V—Real Time Diagnostics

In this mode the ECM is capable of detecting and alerting the technician the instant a malfunction in the crank angle sensor, air flow meter, ignition signal or the fuel pump occurs while operating/driving the vehicle. Items which are noted to be malfunctioning are not stored in the ECM's memory. To enter Mode V, proceed as follows:
1. Turn the ignition switch ON.
2. Turn the diagnostic switch located on the side of the ECM ON by either flipping the switch to the ON position or by turning the switch fully clockwise.
3. Turn the diagnostic switch OFF or fully counterclockwise as soon as the inspection lamps flash 5 times.
4. The self-diagnostic system is now in Mode V.
5. Ensure the inspection lamps are not flashing. If they are, count the number of flashes within a 3.2 second period:
- 1 Flash = Camshaft position sensor
- 2 Flashes = Air flow meter
- 3 Flashes = Fuel pump
- 4 Flashes = Ignition signal

TWO MODE DIAGNOSTIC SYSTEM

The 2-mode diagnostic system incorporated in the ECM which uses inputs from various sensors to determine the correct air/fuel ratio. If any of the sensors malfunction the ECM will store the code in memory. The Malfunction Indicator Light (MIL) or the red LED on the ECM is used for self-diagnostics. The 2-Mode diagnostic system is broken into two separate modes, each capable of two tests, with the ignition switch in the ON position or with the engine running.

Mode I

BULB CHECK (IGNITION ON)

In this mode the RED indicator light on the ECM and the MIL light should be ON. To enter this mode simply turn the ignition switch ON and observe the light.

MALFUNCTION WARNING (ENGINE RUNNING)

In this mode the ECM is acknowledging if there is a malfunction by illuminating the RED indicator light on the ECM and the MIL light. If the light turns OFF, the system is normal. To enter this mode, simply start the engine and observe the light. In this mode the ECM will output all malfunctions via the MIL light or the red LED on the ECM. The code may be retrieved by counting the number of flashes. The longer flashes indicate the first digit and the shorter flashes indicate the second digit.

Mode II

SELF DIAGNOSTIC RESULTS (IGNITION ON)

In this mode, Diagnostic Trouble Codes (DTC's) can be retrieved from the ECM. The DTC is indicated by the flashing sequence from the MIL or the red LED on the ECM.
1. Turn the ignition switch ON, but do not start the vehicle.
2. Turn the ECM diagnostic mode selector fully clockwise for two seconds, then turn it back fully counterclockwise.
3. Observe the red LED on the ECM or MIL light for stored codes.

➡**When the ignition is switched OFF during diagnostic modes, power to the ECM will drop after approximately five seconds. The ECM will automatically return to Mode I.**

HEATED OXYGEN SENSOR MONITOR (ENGINE RUNNING)

In this mode the red LED on the ECM or MIL light will display the condition of the fuel mixture and whether the system is in closed loop or open loop. When the light flashes ON, the exhaust gas sensor is indicating a lean mixture. When the light stays OFF, the sensor is indicating a rich mixture. If the light remains ON or OFF, it is indicating an open loop system. If the system is equipped with two exhaust gas sensors, the left side will operate first.
1. Turn the ignition switch ON.
2. Turn the diagnostic switch ON, by turning the switch fully clockwise for 2 seconds and then fully counterclockwise.
3. Start the engine and run it until it is thoroughly warm. Raise the idle to 2,000 rpm and hold for approximately two minutes. Confirm the red LED or MIL light flashes ON and OFF more than five times every ten seconds with the engine speed at 2,000 rpm.

➡**If equipped with two exhaust gas sensors, switch to the right sensor by turning the ECM mode selector fully clockwise for two seconds and then fully counterclockwise with the engine running.**

Clearing Codes

The easiest way to clear trouble codes is to turn the mode selector screw fully clockwise after all codes have been read.

➡**Turn the mode adjusting screw to the fully counterclockwise position whenever the vehicle is in use.**

The diagnostic memory will also be erased if the negative battery terminal is disconnected for 24 hours.

DIAGNOSTIC TROUBLE CODES—1993–94 (OBDII)

Diagnostic trouble code No.	Detected items	Malfunction is detected when ...	Check item (remedy)
11	Camshaft position sensor circuit	• Either 1° or 180° signal is not entered for the first few seconds during engine cranking. • Either 1° or 180° signal is not input often enough while the engine speed is higher than the specified rpm.	• Harness and connector (If harness and connector are normal, replace camshaft position sensor.)
12	Mass air flow sensor circuit	• The mass air flow sensor circuit is open or shorted. (An abnormally high or low voltage is entered.)	• Harness and connector (If harness and connector are normal, replace mass air flow sensor.)
13	Engine coolant temperature sensor circuit	• The engine coolant temperature sensor circuit is open or shorted. (An abnormally high or low output voltage is entered.)	• Harness and connector • Engine coolant temperature sensor
14	Vehicle speed sensor circuit	• The vehicle speed sensor circuit is open or shorted.	• Harness and connector • Vehicle speed sensor (pulse generator)
21	Ignition signal circuit	• The ignition signal in the primary circuit is not entered during engine cranking or running.	• Harness and connector • Power transistor unit
31	ECM	• ECM calculation function is malfunctioning.	[Replace ECM (ECCS control module).]
32	EGR function	• EGR valve does not operate. (EGR valve spring does not lift.)	• EGR valve • EGR and canister control solenoid valve
33	Oxygen sensor circuit	• The oxygen sensor circuit is open or shorted. (An abnormally high or low output voltage is entered.)	• Harness and connector • Oxygen sensor • Fuel pressure • Injectors • Intake air leaks
34	Knock sensor circuit	• The knock sensor circuit is open or shorted. (An abnormally high or low voltage is entered.)	• Harness and connector • Knock sensor
35	EGR temperature sensor circuit	• The EGR temperature sensor circuit is open or shorted. (An abnormally high or low voltage is entered.)	• Harness and connector • EGR temperature sensor
43	Throttle position sensor circuit	• The throttle position sensor circuit is open or shorted. (An abnormally high or low voltage is entered.)	• Harness and connector • Throttle position sensor
45	Injector leak	• Fuel leaks from injector.	• Injector
54	Signal circuit from A/T control unit to ECM (A/T only)	• The A/T communication line is open or shorted.	• Harness and connector
55	None	• None of the above items detected.	

89704C10

DIAGNOSTIC TROUBLE CODES—1995 (OBDII) CONT.

MIL	CONSULT GST	Detected Items	Malfunction is detected when ...	Check Items (Possible Cause)
41	P0110	Intake air temperature sensor circuit	• An excessively low or high voltage from the sensor is detected by the ECM. • Voltage sent to ECM is not practical when compared with the engine coolant temperature sensor signal.	• Harness or connectors (The sensor circuit is open or shorted.) • Intake air temperature sensor
43	P0120	Throttle position sensor circuit	• An excessively low or high voltage from the sensor is detected by the ECM. • Voltage sent to ECM is not practical when compared with the mass air flow sensor and camshaft position sensor signals.	• Harness or connectors (The sensor circuit is open or shorted.) • Throttle position sensor
55	(P0000)	No failure	• No malfunction related to OBD system is detected by either ECM or A/T control unit.	• No failure
65	P0304	No. 4 cylinder's misfire	(Three-way catalyst damage) The misfire occurs, which will damage three way catalyst by overheating.	• Improper spark plug • The ignition secondary circuit is open or shorted. • Insufficient compression • Incorrect fuel pressure • EGR valve • The injector circuit is open or shorted. • Injectors • Intake air leak • Lack of fuel • Magnetized flywheel (drive plate)
66	P0303	No. 3 cylinder's misfire		
67	P0302	No. 2 cylinder's misfire	(Exhaust quality deterioration) The misfire occurs, which will not damage three way catalyst but will affect emission deterioration.	
68	P0301	No. 1 cylinder's misfire		
71	P0300	Multiple cylinders' misfire		
72	P0420	Three way catalyst function	• Three way catalyst does not operate properly. • Three way catalyst does not have enough oxygen storage capacity.	• Three way catalyst • Exhaust tube • Intake air leak • Injectors • Injector leak
76	P0170	Fuel injection system function	• Fuel injection system does not operate properly. • The amount of mixture ratio compensation is excessive. (The mixture ratio is too lean or too rich.)	• Intake air leak • Front oxygen sensor • Injectors • Exhaust gas leak • Incorrect fuel pressure • Mass air flow sensor • Lack of fuel
77	P0136	Rear heated oxygen sensor circuit	• An excessively high voltage from the sensor is detected by the ECM. • The specified maximum and minimum voltages from the sensor are not reached. • It takes more than the specified time for the sensor to respond between rich and lean.	• Harness or connectors (The sensor circuit is open or shorted.) • Rear heated oxygen sensor • Fuel pressure • Injectors • Intake air leaks
82	P0335	Crankshaft position sensor (OBD) circuit	• The proper pulse signal from the sensor is not detected by the ECM while the engine is running at the specified rpm.	• Harness or connectors (The sensor circuit is open.) • Crankshaft position sensor (OBD)
84	P1605	A/T diagnosis communication line	• An incorrect signal from A/T control unit is detected by the ECM.	• Harness or connectors (The communication line circuit is open or shorted.) • Dead (Weak) battery • A/T control unit
95	P1336	Crankshaft position sensor (OBD)	• The chipping of the flywheel or drive plate gear tooth (cog) is detected by the ECM.	• Harness or connectors • Crankshaft position sensor (OBD) • Flywheel (Drive plate)
98	P0125	Engine coolant temperature sensor function	• Voltage sent to ECM from the sensor is not practical, even when some time has passed after starting the engine. • Engine coolant temperature is insufficient for closed loop fuel control.	• Harness or connectors (High resistance in the sensor circuit) • Engine coolant temperature sensor • Thermostat
103	P0705	Park/Neutral position switch circuit	• The signal of the park/neutral position switch is not changed in the process of engine starting and driving.	• Harness or connectors (The switch circuit is open or shorted.) • Neutral position switch • Inhibitor switch
105	P1400	EGR and canister control solenoid valve circuit	• The improper voltage signal is detected by the ECM through the solenoid valve.	• Harness or connectors (The valve circuit is open or shorted.) • EGR and canister control solenoid valve
—	P0600	Signal circuit from A/T control unit to ECM	• ECM receives incorrect voltage from A/T control unit continuously.	• Harness or connectors (The circuit between ECM and A/T control unit is open or shorted.)

89704C08

DIAGNOSTIC CODES—1995 (OBDII)

MIL	CONSULT GST	Detected Items	Malfunction is detected when ...	Check Items (Possible Cause)
11	P0340	Camshaft position sensor circuit	• Either 1° or 180° signal is not detected by the ECM for the first few seconds during engine cranking. • Either 1° or 180° signal is not detected by the ECM often enough while the engine speed is higher than the specified rpm. • The relation between 1° and 180° signals is not in the normal range during the specified rpm.	• Harness or connectors (The sensor circuit is open or shorted.) • Camshaft position sensor • Starter motor • Starting system circuit (EL section) • Dead (Weak) battery
12	P0100	Mass air flow sensor circuit	• An excessively high or low voltage is entered to ECM. • Voltage sent to ECM is not practical when compared with the camshaft position sensor signal and throttle position sensor signals.	• Harness or connectors (The sensor circuit is open or shorted.) • Mass air flow sensor
13	P0115	Engine coolant temperature sensor circuit	• An excessively high or low voltage from the sensor is detected by the ECM.	• Harness or connectors (The sensor circuit is open or shorted.) • Engine coolant temperature sensor
14	P0500	Vehicle speed sensor circuit	• The almost 0 km/h (0 MPH) signal from the sensor is detected by the ECM even when vehicle is driving.	• Harness or connectors (The sensor circuit is open or shorted.) • Vehicle speed sensor
21	P1320	Ignition signal circuit	• The ignition signal in the primary circuit is not detected by the ECM during engine cranking or running.	• Harness or connectors (The ignition primary circuit is open or shorted.) • Power transistor unit • Camshaft position sensor • Camshaft position sensor circuit
25	P0505	Idle speed control function	• The idle speed control function does not operate properly.	• Harness or connectors (The valve circuit is shorted.) • IACV-AAC valve

28	P1900	Cooling fan circuit	• Cooling fan does not operate properly.
			  (Overheat)
			• Cooling system does not operate properly.
			  (Overheat)
			• Engine coolant was not added to the system using the proper filling method.
				• Harness or connectors,
				  (The cooling fan circuit is open or shorted.)
				• Cooling fan
				• Radiator hose
				• Radiator
				• Radiator cap
				• Water pump
				• Thermostat
				• Harness or connectors
				• IACV-AAC valve

31	P0605	ECM	• ECM calculation function is malfunctioning.	• ECM (ECCS control module)
32	P0400	EGR function	• The EGR flow is excessively low or high during the specified driving condition.	• EGR valve stuck closed, open or leaking • Passage obstructed • EGR and canister control solenoid valve • Tube leaking for EGR valve vacuum • EGRC-BPT valve leaking
33	P0130	Front oxygen sensor circuit	• An excessively high voltage from the sensor is detected by the ECM. • The voltage from the sensor is constantly approx. 0.3V. • The specified maximum and minimum voltages from the sensor are not reached. • It takes more than the specified time for the sensor to respond between rich and lean.	• Harness or connectors (The sensor circuit is open or shorted.) • Front oxygen sensor • Injectors • Intake air leaks • Fuel pressure
34	P0325	Knock sensor circuit	• An excessively low or high voltage from the sensor is detected by the ECM.	• Harness or connectors (The sensor circuit is open or shorted.) • Knock sensor
35	P1401	EGR temperature sensor circuit	• An excessively low or high voltage from the sensor when engine coolant temperature is low or high.	• Harness or connectors (The sensor circuit is open or shorted.) • EGR temperature sensor
36	P0402	EGRC-BPT valve function	• EGRC-BPT valve does not operate properly.	• EGRC-BPT valve • Rubber tube (obstructed or misconnected)
37	P0130	Closed loop control	• The closed loop control function does not operate even when vehicle is driving in the specified condition.	• The front oxygen sensor circuit is open or shorted. • Front oxygen sensor

89704C07

DIAGNOSTIC CODES—1996–98 (OBDII)

Diagnostic trouble code No. (CONSULT GST)	MIL	Detected items	Malfunction is detected when …	Check Items (Possible Cause)
(P0000)	0505	No failure	• No malfunction related to OBD system is detected by either ECM or A/T control unit.	• No failure
P0100	0102	Mass air flow sensor circuit	• An excessively high or low voltage is entered to ECM.	• Harness or connectors (The sensor circuit is open or shorted.) • Mass air flow sensor
P0110	0401	Intake air temperature sensor circuit	• Voltage sent to ECM is not practical when compared with the camshaft position sensor signal and throttle position sensor signals.	• Harness or connectors (The sensor circuit is open or shorted.) • Intake air temperature sensor
P0115	0103	Engine coolant temperature sensor circuit	• An excessively low or high voltage from the sensor is detected by the ECM. • Voltage sent to ECM is not practical when compared with the engine coolant temperature sensor signal.	• Harness or connectors (The sensor circuit is open or shorted.) • Engine coolant temperature sensor
P0120	0403	Throttle position sensor circuit	• An excessively high or low voltage from the sensor is detected by the ECM.	• Harness or connectors (The sensor circuit is open or shorted.) • Throttle position sensor
P0125	0908	Engine coolant temperature sensor function	• An excessively low or high voltage from the sensor is detected by the ECM. • Voltage sent to ECM is not practical when compared with the mass air flow sensor and camshaft position sensor signals.	• Harness or connectors (High resistance in the sensor circuit.) • Engine coolant temperature sensor • Thermostat
P0130	0303	Front oxygen sensor 5 circuit	• Voltage sent to ECM from the sensor is not practical, even when some time has passed after starting the engine. • Engine coolant temperature is insufficient for closed loop fuel control.	• Harness or connectors (The sensor circuit is open or shorted.) • Front oxygen sensor • Injectors • Intake air leaks • Fuel pressure
P0130	0307	Closed loop control	• An excessively high voltage from the sensor is detected by the ECM. • The voltage from the sensor is constantly approx. 0.3V. • The specified maximum and minimum voltages from the sensor are not reached. • It takes more than the specified time for the sensor to respond between rich and lean.	• The front oxygen sensor circuit is open or shorted. • Front oxygen sensor
P0135	0901	Front heated oxygen sensor heater circuit	• The closed loop control function does not operate even when vehicle is driving in the specified condition.	• Harness or connectors (The sensor circuit is open or shorted.) • Front heated oxygen sensor heater
P0136	0707	Rear heated oxygen sensor circuit	• The current amperage in the heater circuit is out of the normal range. (An improper voltage drop signal is sent to ECM through the heater.)	• Harness or connectors • Rear heated oxygen sensor • Fuel pressure • Injectors • Intake air leaks
P0141	0902	Rear heated oxygen sensor heater circuit	• An excessively high voltage from the sensor is detected by the ECM. • The specified maximum and minimum voltages from the sensor are not reached. • It takes more than the specified time for the sensor to respond between rich and lean.	• Harness and connectors (The heater circuit is open or shorted.) • Front heated oxygen sensor heater
P0171	0115	Fuel injection system function	• The current amperage in the heater circuit is out of the normal range. (An improper voltage drop signal is sent to ECM through the heater.)	• Intake air leak • Front oxygen sensor • Injectors • Incorrect fuel pressure • Mass air flow sensor • Lack of fuel
P0172	0114	Fuel injection system function	• Fuel injection system does not operate properly. • The amount of mixture ratio compensation is too large. (The mixture ratio is too lean.)	• Front oxygen sensor • Injectors • Exhaust gas leak • Incorrect fuel pressure • Lack of fuel
P0300	0701	Multiple cylinders' misfire	(Three way catalyst damage) The misfire occurs, which will damage three way catalyst by overheating. / (Exhaust quality deterioration) The misfire occurs, which will not damage three way catalyst but will affect emission deterioration.	• Harness or connectors • Improper spark plug • The ignition secondary circuit is open or shed. • Insufficient compression • Incorrect fuel pressure • The EGR valve is open or shorted. • Injectors • Intake air leak • Lack of fuel • Magnetized flywheel (drive plate)
P0301	0608	No. 1 cylinder's misfire		
P0302	0607	No. 2 cylinder's misfire		
P0303	0606	No. 3 cylinder's misfire		
P0304	0605	No. 4 cylinder's misfire		
P0325	0304	Knock sensor circuit	• An excessively low or high voltage from the sensor is detected by the ECM.	• Harness or connectors (The sensor circuit is open or shorted.) • Knock sensor
P0335	0802	Crankshaft position sensor (OBD) circuit	• The proper pulse signal from the sensor is not detected by the ECM while the engine is running at the specified rpm.	• Harness or connectors (The sensor circuit is open.) • Crankshaft position sensor (OBD)

89704C04

DIAGNOSTIC TROUBLE CODES—1995 (OBDII) CONT.

Diagnostic trouble code No. (MIL)	CONSULT GST	Detected items	Malfunction is detected when …	Check Items (Possible Cause)
111	P0705	Inhibitor switch circuit	• A/T control unit does not receive the correct voltage signal from the switch based on the gear position.	• Harness or connectors (The switch circuit is open or shorted.) • Inhibitor switch
112	P0720	Revolution sensor	• A/T control unit does not receive the proper voltage signal from the sensor.	• Harness or connectors (The sensor circuit is open or shorted.) • Revolution sensor
113	P0731	Improper shifting to 1st gear position	• A/T can not be shifted to the 1st gear position even electrical circuit is good.	• Shift solenoid valve A • Shift solenoid valve B • Overrun clutch solenoid valve • Line pressure solenoid valve • Each clutch • Hydraulic control circuit
114	P0732	Improper shifting to 2nd gear position	• A/T can not be shifted to the 2nd gear position even electrical circuit is good.	
115	P0733	Improper shifting to 3rd gear position	• A/T can not be shifted to the 3rd gear position even electrical circuit is good.	
116	P0734	Improper shifting to 4th gear position or TCC	• A/T can not be shifted to the 4th gear position or perform lock-up even electrical circuit is good.	• T/C clutch solenoid valve
118	P0750	Shift solenoid valve A	• A/T control unit detects the improper voltage drop when it tries to operate the solenoid valve.	• Harness or connectors (The solenoid circuit is open or shorted.) • Shift solenoid valve A
121	P0755	Shift solenoid valve B	• A/T control unit detects the improper voltage drop when it tries to operate the solenoid valve.	• Harness or connectors (The solenoid circuit is open or shorted.) • Shift solenoid valve B
123	P1760	Overrun clutch solenoid valve	• A/T control unit detects the improper voltage drop when it tries to operate the solenoid valve.	• Harness or connectors (The solenoid circuit is open or shorted.) • Overrun clutch solenoid valve
124	P0740	T/C clutch solenoid valve	• A/T control unit detects the improper voltage drop when it tries to operate the solenoid valve.	• Harness or connectors (The solenoid circuit is open or shorted.) • T/C clutch solenoid valve
125	P0745	Line pressure solenoid valve	• A/T control unit detects the improper voltage drop when it tries to operate the solenoid valve.	• Harness or connectors (The solenoid circuit is open or shorted.) • Line pressure solenoid valve
126	P1705	Throttle position sensor	• A/T control unit receives an excessively low or high voltage from the sensor.	• Harness or connectors (The sensor circuit is open or shorted.) • Throttle position sensor
127	P0725	Engine speed signal	• A/T control unit does not receive the proper voltage signal from the ECM.	• Harness or connectors (The signal circuit is open or shorted.)
128	P0710	Fluid temperature sensor	• A/T control unit receives an excessively low or high voltage from the sensor.	• Harness or connectors (The sensor circuit is open or shorted.) • Fluid temperature sensor

89704C09

DIAGNOSTIC CODES—1996-98 (OBDII) CONT.

Diagnostic trouble code No. (CONSULT GST)	MIL	Detected Items	Malfunction is detected when ...	Check Items(Possible Cause)
P1320	0201	Ignition signal circuit	The ignition signal in the primary circuit is not detected by the ECM during engine cranking or running.	• Harness or connectors (The ignition primary circuit is open or shorted.) • Power transistor unit • Camshaft position sensor • Camshaft position sensor circuit
P1336	0905	Crankshaft position sensor (OBD)	The chipping of the flywheel or drive gear tooth (cog) is detected by the ECM.	• Harness or connectors • Crankshaft position sensor (OBD) • Flywheel (Drive plate)
P1400	1005	EGR valve and EVAP canister purge control solenoid valve circuit	An improper voltage signal is sent to the ECM through the solenoid valve.	• Harness or connectors (The valve circuit is open or shorted.) • EGR valve and EVAP canister purge control solenoid valve
P1401	0305	EGR temperature sensor circuit	An excessively low or high voltage from the sensor is detected by the ECM, even when engine coolant temperature is low or high.	• Harness or connectors (The sensor circuit is open or shorted.) • EGR temperature sensor
P1605	0804	A/T diagnosis communication line	An incorrect signal from A/T control unit is detected by the ECM.	• Harness or connectors (The communication line circuit is open or shorted.) • Dead (Weak) battery • A/T control unit
P1705	1206	Throttle position sensor Throttle position switch	A/T control unit receives an excessively low or high voltage from the sensor.	• Harness or connectors (The sensor circuit is open or shorted.) • Throttle position sensor • Throttle position switch
P1760	1203	Overrun clutch solenoid valve	A/T control unit detects the improper voltage drop when it tries to operate the solenoid valve.	• Harness or connectors (The solenoid circuit is open or shorted.) • Overrun clutch solenoid valve
P1900	1308 (California models) 0208 (Non-California models)	Cooling fan circuit For California models For Non-California models	Cooling fan does not operate properly. (Overheat) Cooling system does not operate properly. (Overheat) Engine coolant was not added to the system using the proper filling method.	• Harness or connectors. (The cooling fan circuit is open or shorted.) • Cooling fan • Radiator hose • Radiator • Radiator cap • Water pump • Thermostat

89704C06

DIAGNOSTIC CODES—1996-98 (OBDII) CONT.

Diagnostic trouble code No. (CONSULT GST)	MIL	Detected items	Malfunction is detected when ...	Check Items (Possible Cause)
P0340	0101	Camshaft position sensor circuit	Either 1° or 180° signal is not detected by the ECM for the first few seconds during engine cranking. Either 1° or 180° signal is not detected by the ECM often enough while the engine is running. The relation between 1° and 180° signals is not in the normal range during the specified rpm.	• Harness or connectors (The sensor circuit is open or shorted.) • Camshaft position sensor • Starter motor • Starting system circuit (EL section) • Dead (Weak) battery
P0400	0302	EGR function	The EGR flow is excessively low or high during the specified driving condition.	• Harness or connectors • EGR valve stuck closed, open or leaking • Passage blocked • EGR valve and EVAP canister purge control solenoid valve • Tube leaking for EGR valve vacuum • EGRC-BPT valve leaking • EGR temperature sensor
P0402	0306	EGRC-BPT valve function	EGRC-BPT valve does not operate properly.	• EGRC-BPT valve • Rubber tube (blocked or misconnected)
P0420	0702	Three way catalyst function	Three way catalyst does not operate properly. Three way catalyst does not have enough oxygen storage capacity.	• Three way catalyst*6 • Exhaust tube • Intake air leak • Injector leak
P0500	0104	Vehicle speed sensor circuit	The almost 0 km/h (0 MPH) signal from the sensor is detected by the ECM even when vehicle is driving.	• Harness or connectors (The sensor circuit is open.) • Vehicle speed sensor
P0505	0205	Idle speed control function	The idle speed control function does not operate properly.	• Harness or connectors (The valve circuit is open.) • IACV-AAC valve • Harness or connectors (The valve circuit is shorted.) • IACV-AAC valve
P0600		Signal circuit from A/T control unit to ECM	ECM receives incorrect voltage from A/T control unit continuously. *7 This can be detected only by "DATA MONITOR (AUTO TRIG)".	• Harness or connectors (The circuit between ECM and A/T control unit is open or shorted.)
P0605	0301	ECM	ECM calculation function is malfunctioning.	• ECM (ECCS control module)
P0705	1003	Park/Neutral position switch circuit	The signal of the park/neutral position switch is not changed in the process of engine starting and driving.	• Harness or connectors (The switch circuit is open or shorted.) • Neutral position switch • Inhibitor switch
P0705	1101	Inhibitor switch circuit	A/T control unit does not receive the correct voltage signal from the switch based on the gear position.	• Harness or connectors • Inhibitor switch
P0710	1208	Fluid temperature sensor	A/T control unit receives an excessively low or high voltage from the sensor.	• Harness or connectors (The sensor circuit is open or shorted.) • Fluid temperature sensor
P0720	1102	Revolution sensor	A/T control unit does not receive the proper voltage signal from the sensor.	• Harness or connectors (The sensor circuit is open or shorted.) • Revolution sensor
P0725	1207	Engine speed signal	A/T control unit does not receive the proper voltage signal from the ECM.	• Harness or connectors (The signal circuit is open or shorted.)
P0731	1103	Improper shifting to 1st gear position	A/T cannot be shifted to the 1st gear position even electrical circuit is good.	• Shift solenoid valve A • Shift solenoid valve B • Overrun clutch solenoid valve • Line pressure solenoid valve • Each clutch • Hydraulic control circuit
P0732	1104	Improper shifting to 2nd gear position	A/T cannot be shifted to the 2nd gear position even electrical circuit is good.	
P0733	1105	Improper shifting to 3rd gear position	A/T cannot be shifted to the 3rd gear position even electrical circuit is good.	
P0734	1106	Improper shifting to 4th gear position or TCC	A/T cannot be shifted to the 4th gear position or perform lock-up even electrical circuit is good.	
P0740	1204	T/C clutch solenoid valve	A/T control unit detects the improper voltage drop when it tries to operate the solenoid valve.	• Harness or connectors (The solenoid circuit is open or shorted.) • T/C clutch solenoid valve
P0745	1205	Line pressure solenoid valve	A/T control unit detects the improper voltage drop when it tries to operate the solenoid valve.	• Harness or connectors (The solenoid circuit is open or shorted.) • Line pressure solenoid valve
P0750	1108	Shift solenoid valve A	A/T control unit detects the improper voltage drop when it tries to operate the solenoid valve.	• Harness or connectors (The solenoid circuit is open or shorted.) • Shift solenoid valve A
P0755	1201	Shift solenoid valve B	A/T control unit detects the improper voltage drop when it tries to operate the solenoid valve.	• Harness or connectors (The solenoid circuit is open or shorted.) • Shift solenoid valve B

89704C05

VACUUM DIAGRAMS

Following are vacuum diagrams for most of the engine and emissions package combinations covered by this manual. Because vacuum circuits will vary based on various engine and vehicle options, always refer first to the vehicle emission control information label, if present. Should the label be missing, or should the vehicle be equipped with a different engine than the vehicle's original equipment, refer to the diagrams below for the same or similar configuration.

If you wish to obtain a replacement emissions label, most manufacturers make the labels available for purchase. The labels can usually be ordered from a local dealer.

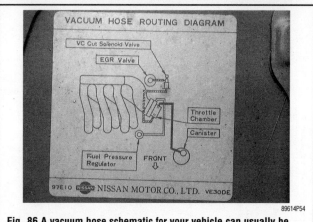

Fig. 86 A vacuum hose schematic for your vehicle can usually be found under the hood

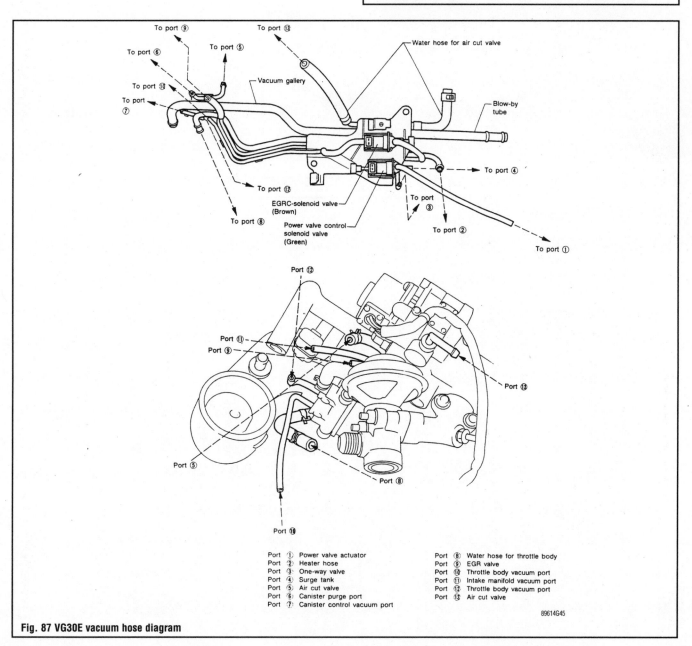

Port ①	Power valve actuator	Port ⑧	Water hose for throttle body
Port ②	Heater hose	Port ⑨	EGR valve
Port ③	One-way valve	Port ⑩	Throttle body vacuum port
Port ④	Surge tank	Port ⑪	Intake manifold vacuum port
Port ⑤	Air cut valve	Port ⑫	Throttle body vacuum port
Port ⑥	Canister purge port	Port ⑬	Air cut valve
Port ⑦	Canister control vacuum port		

Fig. 87 VG30E vacuum hose diagram

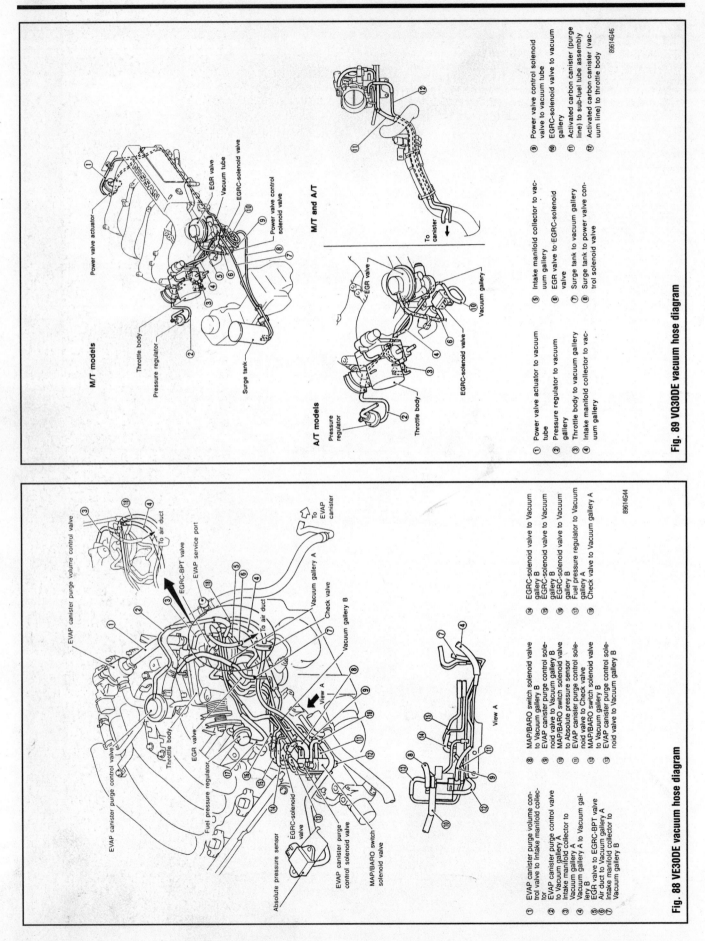

M/T models

Power valve actuator

EGR valve
Vacuum tube
EGRC-solenoid valve

Power valve control
solenoid valve

Throttle body

Pressure regulator

Surge tank

M/T and A/T

To
canister

A/T models

EGR valve

Vacuum gallery

EGRC-solenoid valve

Pressure
regulator

Throttle body

① Power valve actuator to vacuum tube
② Pressure regulator to vacuum gallery
③ Throttle body to vacuum gallery
④ Intake manifold collector to vacuum gallery
⑤ Intake manifold collector to vacuum gallery
⑥ EGR valve to EGRC-solenoid valve
⑦ Surge tank to vacuum gallery
⑧ Surge tank to power valve control solenoid valve
⑨ Power valve control solenoid valve to vacuum tube
⑩ EGRC-solenoid valve to vacuum gallery
⑪ Activated carbon canister (purge line) to sub-fuel tube assembly
⑫ Activated carbon canister (vacuum line) to throttle body

Fig. 89 VQ30DE vacuum hose diagram

EVAP canister purge volume control valve

To air duct

EGRC-BPT valve
EVAP service port

To air duct

Vacuum gallery A

Check valve

Vacuum gallery B

View A

To
EVAP
canister

EVAP canister purge volume control valve to Intake manifold collector

EVAP canister purge control valve to Vacuum gallery A

Intake manifold collector to Vacuum gallery A

Vacuum gallery A to Vacuum gallery B

EGR valve to EGRC-BPT valve

Intake manifold collector to Vacuum gallery B

Throttle body

EGR valve

Fuel pressure regulator

Absolute pressure sensor

EGRC-solenoid valve

EVAP canister purge control solenoid valve

MAP/BARO switch solenoid valve

View A

① EVAP canister purge volume control valve to Intake manifold collector
② EVAP canister purge control valve to Vacuum gallery A
③ Intake manifold collector to Vacuum gallery A
④ Vacuum gallery A to Vacuum gallery B
⑤ EGR valve to EGRC-BPT valve
⑥ Intake manifold collector to Vacuum gallery B
⑦ EVAP canister purge control solenoid valve to Vacuum gallery B
⑧ MAP/BARO switch solenoid valve to Vacuum gallery B
⑨ EVAP canister purge control solenoid valve to Vacuum gallery B
⑩ MAP/BARO switch solenoid valve to Absolute pressure sensor
⑪ EVAP canister purge control solenoid valve to Check valve
⑫ MAP/BARO switch solenoid valve to Vacuum gallery B
⑬ EVAP canister purge control solenoid valve to Vacuum gallery B
⑭ EGRC-solenoid valve to Vacuum gallery B
⑮ EGRC-solenoid valve to Vacuum gallery B
⑯ EGRC-solenoid valve to Vacuum gallery B
⑰ Fuel pressure regulator to Vacuum gallery A
⑱ Check valve to Vacuum gallery B

Fig. 88 VE30DE vacuum hose diagram

5

FUEL SYSTEM

BASIC FUEL SYSTEM DIAGNOSIS

When there is a problem starting or driving a vehicle, two of the most important checks involve the ignition and the fuel systems. The questions most mechanics attempt to answer first, "is there spark?" and "is there fuel?" will often lead to solving most basic problems. For ignition system diagnosis and testing, please refer to the information on engine electrical components and ignition systems found earlier in this manual. If the ignition system checks out (there is spark), then you must determine if the fuel system is operating properly (is there fuel?).

FUEL INJECTION SYSTEM

This section pertains to the removal, installation and adjustment of fuel system related components. For comprehensive diagnostic and testing of the emission and fuel systems, refer to Section 4.

Description Of System

The Electronic Fuel Injection (EFI) systems use various types of sensors to convert engine operating conditions into electronic signals. The generated information is fed into an Engine Control Module (ECM) where it is analyzed, then calculated electrical signals are then sent to the various equipment, to control idle speed, ignition timing and amount of fuel being injected into the engine.

Relieving Fuel System Pressure

To relieve the fuel system pressure, unplug the fuel pump fuse. Start the engine and allow it to run until it stalls out (if the vehicle does not start, just crank it for about 10 seconds). The system pressure is now relieved.

Electric Fuel Pump

REMOVAL & INSTALLATION

▶ See Figures 1 thru 8

❋ CAUTION

Observe all applicable safety precautions when working around fuel. Whenever servicing the fuel system, always work in a well ventilated area. Do not allow fuel spray or vapors to come in contact with a spark or open flame. Keep a dry chemical fire extinguisher near the work area. Always keep fuel in a container specifically designed for fuel storage; also, always properly seal fuel containers to avoid the possibility of fire or explosion.

Fig. 1 Unplug the fuel pump assembly harness connector . . .

Fig. 2 . . . then unscrew the fuel pump access cover . . .

Fig. 3 . . . then push the grommet through the cover, followed by the connector

Fig. 4 Keep in mind a small amount of fuel will escape when the lines are removed

Fig. 5 It is a good idea to plug the lines after they are removed from the pump

Fig. 6 After the lines are plugged, remove the screws that attach the fuel pump assembly to the fuel tank

Fig. 7 Be careful not to damage the fuel level sender unit when removing the assembly

Fig. 8 Be sure the O-ring doesn't fall into the fuel tank when removing the assembly

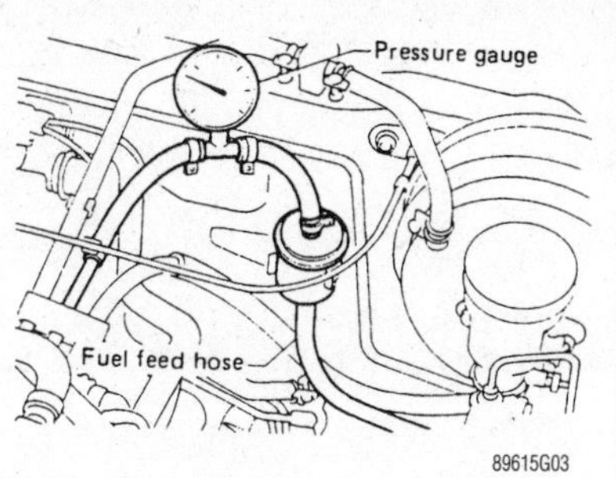

Fig. 9 Connecting a pressure gauge between the fuel filter outlet and the fuel rail inlet tube will allow an accurate reading of the fuel pressure

1. Refer to "Relieving Fuel System Pressure" procedure, in this section, and release the fuel pressure. Reducing the fuel pressure to zero is a very important step for correct removal of the electric fuel pump.
2. Disconnect the negative battery cable.
3. To access the fuel pump, the rear seat bottom must be removed.

➡ If vehicle has no fuel pump access cover the fuel tank must be lowered or removed to gain access to the in-tank fuel pump.

4. Unplug the fuel pump harness connector.
5. Remove the fuel pump access cover.
6. Disconnect the fuel outlet and the return hoses. Use rags to catch any excess fuel.
7. Remove the fuel pump assembly-to-fuel tank bolts, and carefully lift the fuel pump assembly from the fuel tank. Discard the O-ring. Place a clean rag over the fuel tank opening to prevent dirt from entering the fuel tank.

➡ When removing or installing the fuel pump assembly, be careful not to damage or deform it. It is recommended that a new O-ring is installed when replacing the fuel pump assembly.

To install:
8. Using a new O-ring, place the fuel pump assembly into the fuel tank.
9. Install the fuel pump assembly-to-fuel tank bolts and torque the bolts to 1.4-1.9 ft. lbs. (2.0-2.5 Nm).
10. Reconnect the fuel lines and the electrical connector.
11. Connect the negative battery cable, start engine and check for fuel leaks.
12. If all connections are secure, install the fuel pump access cover and the rear seat.

➡ Keep in mind that the engine may take longer to start, since the fuel pump has to prime itself and pressurize the system. Be sure the battery is in good condition.

➡ On some models, the "Check Engine Light" will stay on after installation is completed. The memory code in the control unit must be erased. To erase the code, disconnect the battery cable for 10 seconds then reconnect it after installation of fuel pump.

TESTING

♦ See Figure 9

1. To inspect the electrical condition of the fuel pump, perform the following procedure:
    a. Turn the ignition switch **OFF**.
    b. Unplug the fuel pump electrical connector.
    c. Using an ohmmeter, set on the lowest scale, connect the probes to terminals **a** and **c** (for 1995-98 models, terminals **1** and **2**). For VG30E engine models, the resistance should approximately 0 Ohms. For all other models, the resistance should be between 0.2 to 5.0 ohms; if not within specifications, the fuel pump may be faulty.
    d. If the fuel pump resistance is OK, plug in the fuel pump electrical connector.
2. Release the fuel pressure. Connect a fuel pressure gauge between the fuel filter outlet and fuel feed tube.

3. Start the engine and read the pressure; it should be:
• 1993-94 models: 36 psi (245 kPa)-At idle, fuel pressure regulator vacuum hose connected
• 1995-98 models: 34 psi (235 kPa)-At idle, fuel pressure regulator vacuum hose connected
• All models: 43 psi (294 kPa)-Disconnected fuel pressure regulator vacuum hose, and the hose plugged

➡ Make sure the fuel filter is not blocked before replacing any fuel system components.

4. Stop the engine. Disconnect the fuel pressure regulator vacuum hose from the intake manifold and plug the intake manifold opening.
5. Using a variable vacuum source, connect it to the fuel pressure regulator.
6. Start the engine and read the fuel pressure gauge as the vacuum is changed.

➡ The fuel pressure should decrease as the vacuum increases; if not, replace the fuel pressure regulator.

7. If pressure is not as specified, replace the pressure regulator and repeat the test. If the pressure is still incorrect, check for clogged or deformed fuel lines, then replace the fuel pump.

Throttle Body

REMOVAL & INSTALLATION

♦ See Figures 10 thru 16

1. Disconnect the negative battery cable.
2. Remove the intake duct from the throttle body.
3. Disconnect the vacuum hoses and the electrical harness connector(s) from the throttle body.
4. Disconnect the accelerator cable and cruise control cable from the throttle cams.
5. Label all hoses and disconnect them as necessary.
6. Remove the mounting bolts and the throttle chamber from the intake manifold.
7. If the throttle position sensor needs to be removed, refer to Section 4 for the procedure.

To install:
8. If the throttle position sensor was removed, refer to Section 4 for the installation procedure.
9. Use a new gasket, and mount the throttle body to the manifold. Torque the bolts to 6.5 ft. lbs. (8.8 Nm.) in sequence, and then to 13-16 ft. lbs. (17.7-21.6 Nm.).
10. Install and adjust the throttle cable and cruise control cable, if equipped.

➡ Check the throttle for smooth operation and make sure the bypass port is free from obstacles and is clean.

11. Connect the electrical connectors and the hoses to the throttle body.

Fig. 10 Removing the upper intake hose as an assembly will make throttle body removal easier

Fig. 11 Unclip the connector from the bracket, then it can be unplugged

Fig. 12 Rotate the cam to the full open position, then pull the cable forward and up and push the end out from the cam

Fig. 13 After the bolts are removed, pull the throttle body away from the manifold

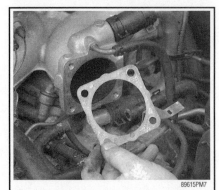

Fig. 14 Always use a new gasket when replacing the throttle body

Fig. 15 Do NOT spray the throttle position sensor with cleaner; it may be damaged. Clean only the inside of the throttle body

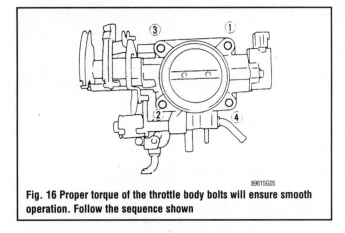

Fig. 16 Proper torque of the throttle body bolts will ensure smooth operation. Follow the sequence shown

➡ **Because of the sensitivity of the air flow meter, there cannot be any air leaks in the fuel system. Even the smallest leak could unbalance the system and affect the performance of the vehicle.**

12. Connect the air duct to the throttle body.
13. Connect the negative battery cable.
14. Start the engine, and check for air leaks and proper engine operation.
15. Adjust the idle speed as necessary.

➡ **During every check, pay attention to hose connections, dipstick and oil filler cap for evidence of air leaks. Should you encounter any, take steps to correct the problem.**

Fuel Injectors

REMOVAL & INSTALLATION

◆ **See Figures 17, 18, 19, 20 and 21**

✲✲ CAUTION

Observe all applicable safety precautions when working around fuel. Whenever servicing the fuel system, always work in a well ventilated area. Do not allow fuel spray or vapors to come in contact with a spark or open flame. Keep a dry chemical fire extinguisher near the work area. Always keep fuel in a container specifically designed for fuel storage; also, always properly seal fuel containers to avoid the possibility of fire or explosion.

1. Disconnect the negative battery cable, for safety purposes.
2. Remove the fuel rail.
3. To remove the fuel injector from the fuel rail, remove the fuel injector retainer screws and press the fuel injector out from the fuel rail. Discard the O-rings.
   To install:
4. Install new O-rings onto the fuel injector.
5. Wet the new O-rings with a thin coating of oil and press the injector into the fuel rail.
6. Install the bolts and tighten the fuel injector retainer.
7. Install the fuel rail.
8. Connect the negative battery cable.
9. Start the engine and check for leaks.

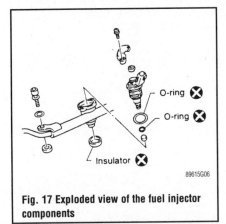

Fig. 17 Exploded view of the fuel injector components

Fig. 18 To remove the injector from the rail, remove the retainer screws and the bracket . . .

Fig. 19 . . . then pull the injector from the fuel rail

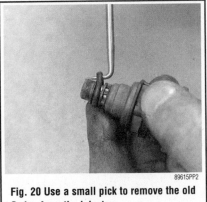

Fig. 20 Use a small pick to remove the old O-ring from the injector

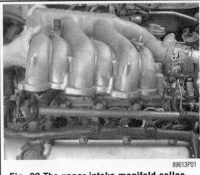

Fig. 21 The large O-ring should also be replaced

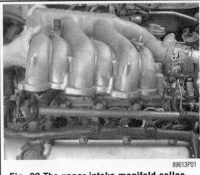

Fig. 22 The upper intake manifold collector must be removed to access the fuel injectors

➡ Keep in mind that the engine may take longer to start, since the fuel system has to pressurize. Be sure the battery is in good condition.

Fuel Rail

REMOVAL & INSTALLATION

◆ See Figures 22, 23, 24 and 25

✳✳ CAUTION

Observe all applicable safety precautions when working around fuel. Whenever servicing the fuel system, always work in a well ventilated area. Do not allow fuel spray or vapors to come in contact with a spark or open flame. Keep a dry chemical fire extinguisher near the work area. Always keep fuel in a container

specifically designed for fuel storage; also, always properly seal fuel containers to avoid the possibility of fire or explosion.

1. Disconnect the negative battery cable, for safety purposes.
2. Remove the intake manifold collector.
3. Disconnect the vacuum hose from the fuel pressure regulator.
4. Remove the fuel hoses connecting to the fuel rails, including the crossover pipe.
5. Unplug the fuel injector electrical connectors.
6. Remove the fuel rail-to-cylinder head bolts.
7. Remove the fuel rail assemblies from the engine.
To install:
8. Clean the manifold gasket area surfaces.
9. Install the fuel injector assembly by performing the following procedures:
    a. Place new injector gaskets onto the manifold.
    b. Install the fuel rail assembly to the engine.

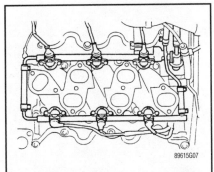

Fig. 23 After the intake manifold collector is removed, the fuel rail and the injectors can easily be accessed.

Fig. 24 Removing the fuel rail crossover pipe will make fuel rail removal easier

Fig. 25 Be sure to use new gaskets when installing the fuel rail assembly

c. Install the fuel rail-to-cylinder head bolts and torque the bolts to 6.9-8.0 ft. lbs. (9.3-10.8 Nm). Then tighten them again to 15-20 ft.lbs. (21-26 Nm).

d. Connect the fuel rail assembly to the fuel lines.

e. Connect the vacuum hose to the fuel pressure regulator.

f. Connect the electrical connectors to the fuel injectors.

10. Install the intake manifold collector.

11. Connect the negative battery cable.

12. Start the engine and check for leaks.

➥Keep in mind that the engine may take longer to start, since the fuel system has to pressurize. Be sure the battery is in good condition.

Fuel Pressure Regulator

REMOVAL & INSTALLATION

VG30E Engine

▸ See Figures 26, 27 and 28

The pressure regulator is always located on the fuel return side of the fuel injection rail and is attached to the right rear of the fuel rail assembly, at the right rear corner of the intake manifold.

✳✳ CAUTION

Observe all applicable safety precautions when working around fuel. Whenever servicing the fuel system, always work in a well ventilated area. Do not allow fuel spray or vapors to come in contact with a spark or open flame. Keep a dry chemical fire extinguisher near the work area. Always keep fuel in a container specifically designed for fuel storage; also, always properly seal fuel containers to avoid the possibility of fire or explosion.

1. Disconnect the negative battery cable and relieve the fuel pressure.

2. Disconnect the air intake duct from the dual duct housing.

3. Unplug the electrical connectors from the throttle body, the step motor AAC valve and the exhaust gas temperature sensor.

4. Disconnect and label the hoses from the rocker arm cover, the throttle body, the step motor AAC valve, the EGR control valve and the air cut valve.

5. If the spark plug wires are in the way, disconnect them and move them aside. Disconnect the accelerator cable from the throttle body.

6. Remove the upper intake manifold collector-to-intake manifold bolts, in sequence, and lift the assembly from the intake manifold. Discard the gasket.

7. Remove the lower intake manifold collector-to-intake manifold bolts, in sequence, and lift the assembly from the intake manifold. Discard the gasket.

8. Remove the fuel injector assembly by performing the following procedure:

a. Disconnect the electrical connectors from the fuel injectors.

b. Disconnect the fuel injector assembly from the fuel lines.

c. Remove the fuel rail-to-cylinder head bolts.

d. Remove the fuel rail assembly from the engine.

9. Remove the fuel pressure regulator from the fuel rail assembly.

To install:

10. Clean the gasket mounting surfaces.

11. Install the fuel injector assembly by performing the following procedure:

a. Install the fuel rail assembly to the engine.

b. Install the fuel rail-to-cylinder head bolts and torque the bolts to 1.8-2.4 ft. lbs. (2.5-3.2 Nm).

c. Connect the fuel injector assembly to the fuel lines.

d. Connect the electrical connectors to the fuel injectors.

12. Use a new gasket and install the lower intake manifold collector; torque the lower intake manifold collector-to-intake manifold bolts, in 2-3 steps, in sequence, to 13-16 ft. lbs. (18-22 Nm).

13. Use a new gasket and install the upper intake manifold collector-to-intake manifold; torque the bolts to 5.1-5.8 ft. lbs. (7-8 Nm).

14. Connect the spark plug wires, if disconnected. Connect the accelerator cable to the throttle body.

15. Connect the hoses to the rocker arm cover, the throttle body, the step motor AAC valve, the EGR control valve and the air cut valve.

16. Connect the electrical connectors to the throttle body, the step motor AAC valve and the exhaust gas temperature sensor.

17. Connect the negative battery cable.

18. Start the engine and check for leaks.

➥Keep in mind that the engine may take longer to start, since the fuel system has to pressurize. Be sure the battery is in good condition.

VE30DE and VQ30DE Engines

▸ See Figure 29

The fuel pressure regulator is attached to the fuel rail, near the throttle body, below the upper intake manifold collector.

✳✳ CAUTION

Observe all applicable safety precautions when working around fuel. Whenever servicing the fuel system, always work in a well ventilated area. Do not allow fuel spray or vapors to come in contact with a spark or open flame. Keep a dry chemical fire extinguisher near the work area. Always keep fuel in a container specifically designed for fuel storage; also, always properly seal fuel containers to avoid the possibility of fire or explosion.

1. Relieve the fuel system pressure.

2. For safety purposes, disconnect the negative battery cable.

3. Disconnect the vacuum hose attached to the regulator.

4. Disconnect the fuel hose from the regulator. Use a rag to catch any excess fuel.

5. Remove the retainer screws that hold the regulator to the fuel rail.

6. Place a rag under the regulator to contain any excess fuel, then pull it away from the fuel rail.

Fig. 26 The pressure regulator can be found attached to the fuel rail

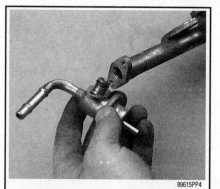

Fig. 27 After the two bolts are removed, pull the regulator from the fuel rail

Fig. 28 Always install a new O-ring when removing the fuel pressure regulator

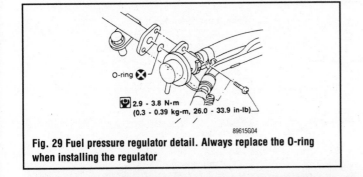

Fig. 29 Fuel pressure regulator detail. Always replace the O-ring when installing the regulator

To install:
7. Install new O-rings on the regulator.
8. Lightly lubricate the O-rings and push the regulator into the fuel rail.
9. Install the retainer screws, and attach the hoses to the regulator.
10. Connect the negative battery cable, and start the engine and check for any leaks.

➡️**Keep in mind that the engine may take longer to start, since the fuel system has to pressurize. Be sure the battery is in good condition.**

FUEL TANK

Tank Assembly

REMOVAL & INSTALLATION

◆ **See Figures 30, 31 and 32**

✳✳ CAUTION

Observe all applicable safety precautions when working around fuel. Whenever servicing the fuel system, always work in a well ventilated area. Do not allow fuel spray or vapors to come in contact with a spark or open flame. Keep a dry chemical fire extinguisher near the work area. Always keep fuel in a container specifically designed for fuel storage; also, always properly seal fuel containers to avoid the possibility of fire or explosion.

1. Relieve the fuel system pressure.
2. For safety purposes, disconnect the negative battery cable.
3. Siphon as much fuel as possible from the fuel tank, using the appropriate siphoning equipment.

➡️**Having the fuel tank as empty as possible will make removal safer and easier.**

4. Remove the lower half of the seat, and remove the fuel pump access cover.
5. Raise and safely support the vehicle.
6. Disconnect all hoses, lines and electrical connectors from the fuel tank assembly.
7. Remove the fuel tank protection panels.
8. Safely support the fuel tank, and then remove the fuel tank straps.
9. Carefully lower the fuel tank from the vehicle.

➡️**Keep in mind a small amount of fuel will be in the fuel tank; keep a drain pan and some rags handy to contain any excess fuel.**

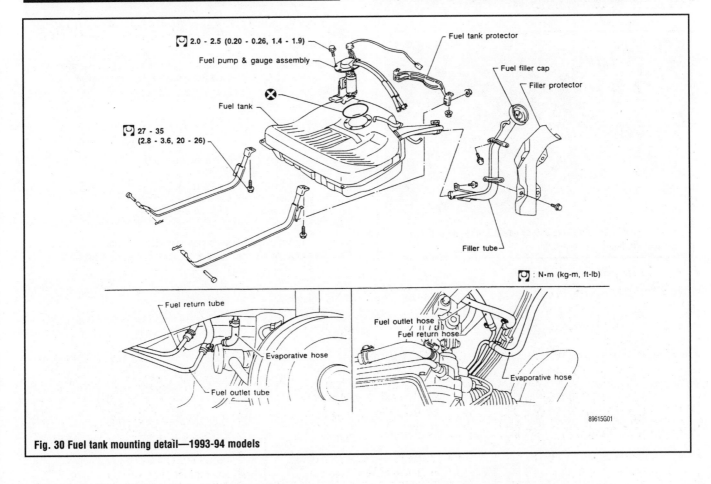

Fig. 30 Fuel tank mounting detail—1993-94 models

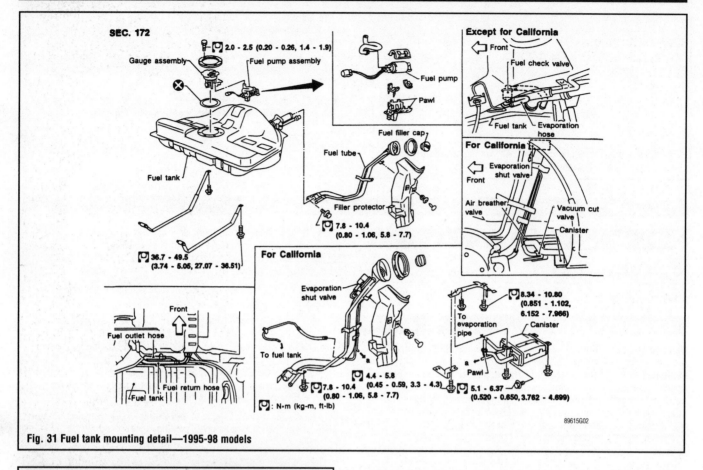

SEC. 172

2.0 - 2.5 (0.20 - 0.26, 1.4 - 1.9)

Gauge assembly

Fuel pump assembly

Fuel pump

Pawl

Fuel tank

Fuel filler cap

Fuel tube

Filler protector

7.8 - 10.4
(0.80 - 1.06, 5.8 - 7.7)

Except for California

Front

Fuel check valve

Fuel tank — Evaporation hose

For California

Front

Evaporation shut valve

Air breather valve

Vacuum cut valve

Canister

36.7 - 49.5
(3.74 - 5.05, 27.07 - 36.51)

For California

Evaporation shut valve

To fuel tank

8.34 - 10.80
(0.851 - 1.102, 6.152 - 7.966)

To evaporation pipe

Canister

Pawl

Front

Fuel outlet hose

Fuel return hose

Fuel tank

4.4 - 5.8
(0.45 - 0.59, 3.3 - 4.3)

7.8 - 10.4
(0.80 - 1.06, 5.8 - 7.7)

5.1 - 6.37
(0.520 - 0.650, 3.762 - 4.699)

: N·m (kg-m, ft-lb)

89615G02

Fig. 31 Fuel tank mounting detail—1995-98 models

89615P8H

Fig. 32 Remove the fuel pump access cover to disengage the fuel lines and the fuel pump connector

To install:

➡ **Replacing all flexible fuel lines connecting to the tank is a good idea, since they are easily accessed while the fuel tank is removed.**

10. Raise the fuel tank into position and support it.
11. Swing the fuel tank straps upward, and torque the strap bolts to 27-37 ft. lbs. (37-49 Nm.).
12. Install the fuel tank protectors to the fuel tank and/or the chassis.
13. Connect all hoses lines and electrical connectors to the fuel tank assembly. Always use new hose clamps to prevent leaks.
14. Pour one or two gallons of fuel into the tank.
15. Connect the negative battery cable.
16. Start the engine, and check for any fuel leaks.
17. If all the connections are secure, install the fuel pump access cover and the rear seat.

➡ **Keep in mind that the engine may take longer to start, since the fuel system has to pressurize. Be sure the battery is in good condition.**

6

CHASSIS ELECTRICAL

UNDERSTANDING AND TROUBLESHOOTING ELECTRICAL SYSTEMS

Basic Electrical Theory

▶ **See Figure 1**

For any 12 volt, negative ground, electrical system to operate, the electricity must travel in a complete circuit. This simply means that current (power) from the positive (+) terminal of the battery must eventually return to the negative (-) terminal of the battery. Along the way, this current will travel through wires, fuses, switches and components. If, for any reason, the flow of current through the circuit is interrupted, the component fed by that circuit will cease to function properly.

Perhaps the easiest way to visualize a circuit is to think of connecting a light bulb (with two wires attached to it) to the battery—one wire attached to the negative (-) terminal of the battery and the other wire to the positive (+) terminal. With the two wires touching the battery terminals, the circuit would be complete and the light bulb would illuminate. Electricity would follow a path from the battery to the bulb and back to the battery. It's easy to see that with longer wires on our light bulb, it could be mounted anywhere. Further, one wire could be fitted with a switch so that the light could be turned on and off.

The normal automotive circuit differs from this simple example in two ways. First, instead of having a return wire from the bulb to the battery, the current travels through the frame of the vehicle. Since the negative (-) battery cable is attached to the frame (made of electrically conductive metal), the frame of the vehicle can serve as a ground wire to complete the circuit. Secondly, most automotive circuits contain multiple components which receive power from a single circuit. This lessens the amount of wire needed to power components on the vehicle.

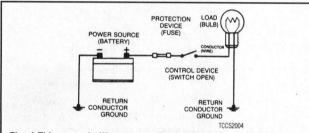

TCCS2004

Fig. 1 This example illustrates a simple circuit. When the switch is closed, power from the positive (+) battery terminal flows through the fuse and the switch, and then to the light bulb. The light illuminates and the circuit is completed through the ground wire back to the negative (-) battery terminal. In reality, the two ground points shown in the illustration are attached to the metal frame of the vehicle, which completes the circuit back to the battery

HOW DOES ELECTRICITY WORK: THE WATER ANALOGY

Electricity is the flow of electrons—the subatomic particles that constitute the outer shell of an atom. Electrons spin in an orbit around the center core of an atom. The center core is comprised of protons (positive charge) and neutrons (neutral charge). Electrons have a negative charge and balance out the positive charge of the protons. When an outside force causes the number of electrons to unbalance the charge of the protons, the electrons will split off the atom and look for another atom to balance out. If this imbalance is kept up, electrons will continue to move and an electrical flow will exist.

Many people have been taught electrical theory using an analogy with water. In a comparison with water flowing through a pipe, the electrons would be the water and the wire is the pipe.

The flow of electricity can be measured much like the flow of water through a pipe. The unit of measurement used is amperes, frequently abbreviated as amps (a). You can compare amperage to the volume of water flowing through a pipe. When connected to a circuit, an ammeter will measure the actual amount of current flowing through the circuit. When relatively few electrons flow through a circuit, the amperage is low. When many electrons flow, the amperage is high.

Water pressure is measured in units such as pounds per square inch (psi); The electrical pressure is measured in units called volts (v). When a voltmeter is connected to a circuit, it is measuring the electrical pressure.

The actual flow of electricity depends not only on voltage and amperage, but also on the resistance of the circuit. The higher the resistance, the higher the force necessary to push the current through the circuit. The standard unit for measuring resistance is an ohm Ω. Resistance in a circuit varies depending on the amount and type of components used in the circuit. The main factors which determine resistance are:

• Material—some materials have more resistance than others. Those with high resistance are said to be insulators. Rubber materials (or rubber-like plastics) are some of the most common insulators used in vehicles as they have a very high resistance to electricity. Very low resistance materials are said to be conductors. Copper wire is among the best conductors. Silver is actually a superior conductor to copper and is used in some relay contacts, but its high cost prohibits its use as common wiring. Most automotive wiring is made of copper.

• Size—the larger the wire size being used, the less resistance the wire will have. This is why components which use large amounts of electricity usually have large wires supplying current to them.

• Length—for a given thickness of wire, the longer the wire, the greater the resistance. The shorter the wire, the less the resistance. When determining the proper wire for a circuit, both size and length must be considered to design a circuit that can handle the current needs of the component.

• Temperature—with many materials, the higher the temperature, the greater the resistance (positive temperature coefficient). Some materials exhibit the opposite trait of lower resistance with higher temperatures (negative temperature coefficient). These principles are used in many of the sensors on the engine.

OHM'S LAW

There is a direct relationship between current, voltage and resistance. The relationship between current, voltage and resistance can be summed up by a statement known as Ohm's law.

Voltage (E) is equal to amperage (I) times resistance (R): $E = I \times R$
Other forms of the formula are $R = E/I$ and $I = E/R$

In each of these formulas, E is the voltage in volts, I is the current in amps and R is the resistance in ohms. The basic point to remember is that as the resistance of a circuit goes up, the amount of current that flows in the circuit will go down, if voltage remains the same.

The amount of work that the electricity can perform is expressed as power. The unit of power is the watt (w). The relationship between power, voltage and current is expressed as:

Power (w) is equal to amperage (I) times voltage (E): $W = I \times E$

This is only true for direct current (DC) circuits; The alternating current formula is a tad different, but since the electrical circuits in most vehicles are DC type, we need not get into AC circuit theory.

Electrical Components

POWER SOURCE

Power is supplied to the vehicle by two devices: The battery and the alternator. The battery supplies electrical power during starting or during periods when the current demand of the vehicle's electrical system exceeds the output capacity of the alternator. The alternator supplies electrical current when the engine is running. Just not does the alternator supply the current needs of the vehicle, but it recharges the battery.

The Battery

In most modern vehicles, the battery is a lead/acid electrochemical device consisting of six 2 volt subsections (cells) connected in series, so that the unit is capable of producing approximately 12 volts of electrical pressure. Each subsection consists of a series of positive and negative plates held a short distance apart in a solution of sulfuric acid and water.

The two types of plates are of dissimilar metals. This sets up a chemical reaction, and it is this reaction which produces current flow from the battery when its positive and negative terminals are connected to an electrical load . The power removed from the battery is replaced by the alternator, restoring the battery to its original chemical state.

The Alternator

On some vehicles there isn't an alternator, but a generator. The difference is that an alternator supplies alternating current which is then changed to direct current for use on the vehicle, while a generator produces direct current. Alternators tend to be more efficient and that is why they are used.

Alternators and generators are devices that consist of coils of wires wound together making big electromagnets. One group of coils spins within another set and the interaction of the magnetic fields causes a current to flow. This current is then drawn off the coils and fed into the vehicles electrical system.

GROUND

Two types of grounds are used in automotive electric circuits. Direct ground components are grounded to the frame through their mounting points. All other components use some sort of ground wire which is attached to the frame or chassis of the vehicle. The electrical current runs through the chassis of the vehicle and returns to the battery through the ground (-) cable; if you look, you'll see that the battery ground cable connects between the battery and the frame or chassis of the vehicle.

➡️**It should be noted that a good percentage of electrical problems can be traced to bad grounds.**

PROTECTIVE DEVICES

▶ See Figure 2

It is possible for large surges of current to pass through the electrical system of your vehicle. If this surge of current were to reach the load in the circuit, the surge could burn it out or severely damage it. It can also overload the wiring, causing the harness to get hot and melt the insulation. To prevent this, fuses, circuit breakers and/or fusible links are connected into the supply wires of the electrical system. These items are nothing more than a built-in weak spot in the system. When an abnormal amount of current flows through the system, these protective devices work as follows to protect the circuit:

• Fuse—when an excessive electrical current passes through a fuse, the fuse "blows" (the conductor melts) and opens the circuit, preventing the passage of current.

• Circuit Breaker—a circuit breaker is basically a self-repairing fuse. It will open the circuit in the same fashion as a fuse, but when the surge subsides, the circuit breaker can be reset and does not need replacement.

• Fusible Link—a fusible link (fuse link or main link) is a short length of special, high temperature insulated wire that acts as a fuse. When an excessive electrical current passes through a fusible link, the thin gauge wire inside the link melts, creating an intentional open to protect the circuit. To repair the circuit, the link must be replaced. Some newer type fusible links are housed in plug-in modules, which are simply replaced like a fuse, while older type fusible links must be cut and spliced if they melt. Since this link is very early in the

electrical path, it's the first place to look if nothing on the vehicle works, yet the battery seems to be charged and is properly connected.

✳✳ CAUTION

Always replace fuses, circuit breakers and fusible links with identically rated components. Under no circumstances should a component of higher or lower amperage rating be substituted.

SWITCHES & RELAYS

▶ See Figures 3 and 4

Switches are used in electrical circuits to control the passage of current. The most common use is to open and close circuits between the battery and the various electric devices in the system. Switches are rated according to the amount of amperage they can handle. If a sufficient amperage rated switch is not used in a circuit, the switch could overload and cause damage.

Some electrical components which require a large amount of current to operate use a special switch called a relay. Since these circuits carry a large amount of current, the thickness of the wire in the circuit is also greater. If this large wire were connected from the load to the control switch, the switch would have to carry the high amperage load and the fairing or dash would be twice as large to accommodate the increased size of the wiring harness. To prevent these problems, a relay is used.

Relays are composed of a coil and a set of contacts. When the coil has a current passed though it, a magnetic field is formed and this field causes the contacts to move together, completing the circuit. Most relays are normally open, preventing current from passing through the circuit, but they can take any electrical form depending on the job they are intended to do. Relays can be considered "remote control switches." They allow a smaller current to operate devices that require higher amperages. When a small current operates the coil, a larger current is allowed to pass by the contacts. Some common circuits which may use relays are the horn, headlights, starter, electric fuel pump and other high draw circuits.

LOAD

Every electrical circuit must include a "load" (something to use the electricity coming from the source). Without this load, the battery would attempt to deliver its entire power supply from one pole to another. This is called a "short circuit." All this electricity would take a short cut to ground and cause a great amount of damage to other components in the circuit by developing a tremendous amount of heat. This condition could develop sufficient heat to melt the insulation on all the surrounding wires and reduce a multiple wire cable to a lump of plastic and copper.

WIRING & HARNESSES

The average vehicle contains meters and meters of wiring, with hundreds of individual connections. To protect the many wires from damage and to keep them from becoming a confusing tangle, they are organized into bundles,

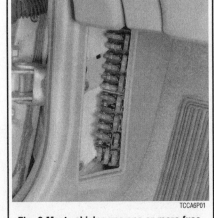

Fig. 2 Most vehicles use one or more fuse panels. This one is located on the driver's side kick panel

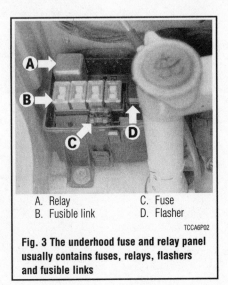

A. Relay   C. Fuse
B. Fusible link   D. Flasher

Fig. 3 The underhood fuse and relay panel usually contains fuses, relays, flashers and fusible links

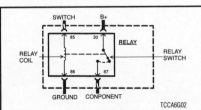

Fig. 4 Relays are composed of a coil and a switch. These two components are linked together so that when one operates, the other operates at the same time. The large wires in the circuit are connected from the battery to one side of the relay switch (B+) and from the opposite side of the relay switch to the load (component). Smaller wires are connected from the relay coil to the control switch for the circuit and from the opposite side of the relay coil to ground

enclosed in plastic or taped together and called wiring harnesses. Different harnesses serve different parts of the vehicle. Individual wires are color coded to help trace them through a harness where sections are hidden from view.

Automotive wiring or circuit conductors can be either single strand wire, multi-strand wire or printed circuitry. Single strand wire has a solid metal core and is usually used inside such components as alternators, motors, relays and other devices. Multi-strand wire has a core made of many small strands of wire twisted together into a single conductor. Most of the wiring in an automotive electrical system is made up of multi-strand wire, either as a single conductor or grouped together in a harness. All wiring is color coded on the insulator, either as a solid color or as a colored wire with an identification stripe. A printed circuit is a thin film of copper or other conductor that is printed on an insulator backing. Occasionally, a printed circuit is sandwiched between two sheets of plastic for more protection and flexibility. A complete printed circuit, consisting of conductors, insulating material and connectors for lamps or other components is called a printed circuit board. Printed circuitry is used in place of individual wires or harnesses in places where space is limited, such as behind instrument panels.

Since automotive electrical systems are very sensitive to changes in resistance, the selection of properly sized wires is critical when systems are repaired. A loose or corroded connection or a replacement wire that is too small for the circuit will add extra resistance and an additional voltage drop to the circuit.

The wire gauge number is an expression of the cross-section area of the conductor. Vehicles from countries that use the metric system will typically describe the wire size as its cross-sectional area in square millimeters. In this method, the larger the wire, the greater the number. Another common system for expressing wire size is the American Wire Gauge (AWG) system. As gauge number increases, area decreases and the wire becomes smaller. An 18 gauge wire is smaller than a 4 gauge wire. A wire with a higher gauge number will carry less current than a wire with a lower gauge number. Gauge wire size refers to the size of the strands of the conductor, not the size of the complete wire with insulator. It is possible, therefore, to have two wires of the same gauge with different diameters because one may have thicker insulation than the other.

It is essential to understand how a circuit works before trying to figure out why it doesn't. An electrical schematic shows the electrical current paths when a circuit is operating properly. Schematics break the entire electrical system down into individual circuits. In a schematic, usually no attempt is made to represent wiring and components as they physically appear on the vehicle; switches and other components are shown as simply as possible. Face views of harness connectors show the cavity or terminal locations in all multi-pin connectors to help locate test points.

CONNECTORS

▶ **See Figures 5 and 6**

Three types of connectors are commonly used in automotive applications—weatherproof, molded and hard shell.

• **Weatherproof**—these connectors are most commonly used where the connector is exposed to the elements. Terminals are protected against moisture and dirt by sealing rings which provide a weathertight seal. All repairs require the use of a special terminal and the tool required to service it. Unlike standard blade type terminals, these weatherproof terminals cannot be straightened once they are bent. Make certain that the connectors are properly seated and all of the sealing rings are in place when connecting leads.

• **Molded**—these connectors require complete replacement of the connector if

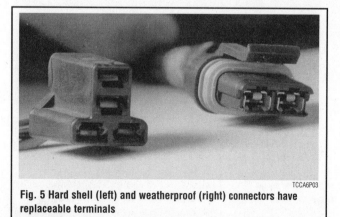

Fig. 5 Hard shell (left) and weatherproof (right) connectors have replaceable terminals

TCCA6P03

Fig. 6 Weatherproof connectors are most commonly used in the engine compartment or where the connector is exposed to the elements

TCCA6P04

found to be defective. This means splicing a new connector assembly into the harness. All splices should be soldered to insure proper contact. Use care when probing the connections or replacing terminals in them, as it is possible to create a short circuit between opposite terminals. If this happens to the wrong terminal pair, it is possible to damage certain components. Always use jumper wires between connectors for circuit checking and NEVER probe through weatherproof seals.

• **Hard Shell**—unlike molded connectors, the terminal contacts in hard-shell connectors can be replaced. Replacement usually involves the use of a special terminal removal tool that depresses the locking tangs (barbs) on the connector terminal and allows the connector to be removed from the rear of the shell. The connector shell should be replaced if it shows any evidence of burning, melting, cracks, or breaks. Replace individual terminals that are burnt, corroded, distorted or loose.

Test Equipment

Pinpointing the exact cause of trouble in an electrical circuit is most times accomplished by the use of special test equipment. The following describes different types of commonly used test equipment and briefly explains how to use them in diagnosis. In addition to the information covered below, the tool manufacturer's instructions booklet (provided with the tester) should be read and clearly understood before attempting any test procedures.

JUMPER WIRES

❋❋ CAUTION

Never use jumper wires made from a thinner gauge wire than the circuit being tested. If the jumper wire is of too small a gauge, it may overheat and possibly melt. Never use jumpers to bypass high resistance loads in a circuit. Bypassing resistances, in effect, creates a short circuit. This may, in turn, cause damage and fire. Jumper wires should only be used to bypass lengths of wire or to simulate switches.

Jumper wires are simple, yet extremely valuable, pieces of test equipment. They are basically test wires which are used to bypass sections of a circuit. Although jumper wires can be purchased, they are usually fabricated from lengths of standard automotive wire and whatever type of connector (alligator clip, spade connector or pin connector) that is required for the particular application being tested. In cramped, hard-to-reach areas, it is advisable to have insulated boots over the jumper wire terminals in order to prevent accidental grounding. It is also advisable to include a standard automotive fuse in any jumper wire. This is commonly referred to as a "fused jumper". By inserting an in-line fuse holder between a set of test leads, a fused jumper wire can be used for bypassing open circuits. Use a 5 amp fuse to provide protection against voltage spikes.

Jumper wires are used primarily to locate open electrical circuits, on either the ground (-) side of the circuit or on the power (+) side. If an electrical component fails to operate, connect the jumper wire between the component and a good ground. If the component operates only with the jumper installed, the ground circuit is open. If the ground circuit is good, but the component does not operate, the circuit between the power feed and component may be open. By moving the jumper wire successively back from the component toward the power source, you can isolate the area of the circuit where the open is located. When the component stops functioning, or the power is cut off, the open is in the segment of wire between the jumper and the point previously tested.

You can sometimes connect the jumper wire directly from the battery to the "hot" terminal of the component, but first make sure the component uses 12 volts in operation. Some electrical components, such as fuel injectors or sensors, are designed to operate on about 4 to 5 volts, and running 12 volts directly to these components will cause damage.

TEST LIGHTS

▶ See Figure 7

The test light is used to check circuits and components while electrical current is flowing through them. It is used for voltage and ground tests. To use a 12 volt test light, connect the ground clip to a good ground and probe wherever necessary with the pick. The test light will illuminate when voltage is detected. This does not necessarily mean that 12 volts (or any particular amount of voltage) is present; it only means that some voltage is present. It is advisable before using the test light to touch its ground clip and probe across the battery posts or terminals to make sure the light is operating properly.

☀ WARNING

Do not use a test light to probe electronic ignition, spark plug or coil wires. Never use a pick-type test light to probe wiring on computer controlled systems unless specifically instructed to do so. Any wire insulation that is pierced by the test light probe should be taped and sealed with silicone after testing.

Like the jumper wire, the 12 volt test light is used to isolate opens in circuits. But, whereas the jumper wire is used to bypass the open to operate the load, the 12 volt test light is used to locate the presence of voltage in a circuit. If the test light illuminates, there is power up to that point in the circuit; if the test light does not illuminate, there is an open circuit (no power). Move the test light in successive steps back toward the power source until the light in the handle illuminates. The open is between the probe and a point which was previously probed.

The self-powered test light is similar in design to the 12 volt test light, but contains a 1.5 volt penlight battery in the handle. It is most often used in place of a multimeter to check for open or short circuits when power is isolated from the circuit (continuity test).

The battery in a self-powered test light does not provide much current. A weak battery may not provide enough power to illuminate the test light even when a complete circuit is made (especially if there is high resistance in the circuit). Always make sure that the test battery is strong. To check the battery, briefly touch the ground clip to the probe; if the light glows brightly, the battery is strong enough for testing.

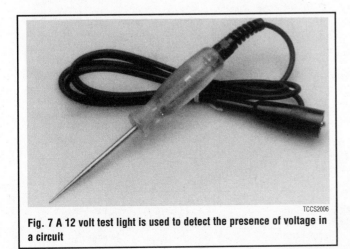

Fig. 7 A 12 volt test light is used to detect the presence of voltage in a circuit

TCCS2006

➡**A self-powered test light should not be used on any computer controlled system or component. The small amount of electricity transmitted by the test light is enough to damage many electronic automotive components.**

MULTIMETERS

Multimeters are an extremely useful tool for troubleshooting electrical problems. They can be purchased in either analog or digital form and have a price range to suit any budget. A multimeter is a voltmeter, ammeter and ohmmeter (along with other features) combined into one instrument. It is often used when testing solid state circuits because of its high input impedance (usually 10 megaohms or more). A brief description of the multimeter main test functions follows:

• Voltmeter—the voltmeter is used to measure voltage at any point in a circuit, or to measure the voltage drop across any part of a circuit. Voltmeters usually have various scales and a selector switch to allow the reading of different voltage ranges. The voltmeter has a positive and a negative lead. To avoid damage to the meter, always connect the negative lead to the negative (-) side of the circuit (to ground or nearest the ground side of the circuit) and connect the positive lead to the positive (+) side of the circuit (to the power source or the nearest power source). Note that the negative voltmeter lead will always be black and that the positive voltmeter will always be some color other than black (usually red).

• Ohmmeter—the ohmmeter is designed to read resistance (measured in ohms) in a circuit or component. Most ohmmeters will have a selector switch which permits the measurement of different ranges of resistance (usually the selector switch allows the multiplication of the meter reading by 10, 100, 1,000 and 10,000). Some ohmmeters are "auto-ranging" which means the meter itself will determine which scale to use. Since the meters are powered by an internal battery, the ohmmeter can be used like a self-powered test light. When the ohmmeter is connected, current from the ohmmeter flows through the circuit or component being tested. Since the ohmmeter's internal resistance and voltage are known values, the amount of current flow through the meter depends on the resistance of the circuit or component being tested. The ohmmeter can also be used to perform a continuity test for suspected open circuits. In using the meter for making continuity checks, do not be concerned with the actual resistance readings. Zero resistance, or any ohm reading, indicates continuity in the circuit. Infinite resistance indicates an opening in the circuit. A high resistance reading where there should be none indicates a problem in the circuit. Checks for short circuits are made in the same manner as checks for open circuits, except that the circuit must be isolated from both power and normal ground. Infinite resistance indicates no continuity, while zero resistance indicates a dead short.

☀ WARNING

Never use an ohmmeter to check the resistance of a component or wire while there is voltage applied to the circuit.

• Ammeter—an ammeter measures the amount of current flowing through a circuit in units called amperes or amps. At normal operating voltage, most circuits have a characteristic amount of amperes, called "current draw" which can be measured using an ammeter. By referring to a specified current draw rating, then measuring the amperes and comparing the two values, one can determine what is happening within the circuit to aid in diagnosis. An open circuit, for example, will not allow any current to flow, so the ammeter reading will be zero. A damaged component or circuit will have an increased current draw, so the reading will be high. The ammeter is always connected in series with the circuit being tested. All of the current that normally flows through the circuit must also flow through the ammeter; if there is any other path for the current to follow, the ammeter reading will not be accurate. The ammeter itself has very little resistance to current flow and, therefore, will not affect the circuit, but it will measure current draw only when the circuit is closed and electricity is flowing. Excessive current draw can blow fuses and drain the battery, while a reduced current draw can cause motors to run slowly, lights to dim and other components to not operate properly.

Troubleshooting Electrical Systems

When diagnosing a specific problem, organized troubleshooting is a must. The complexity of a modern automotive vehicle demands that you approach any problem in a logical, organized manner. There are certain troubleshooting techniques, however, which are standard:

• Establish when the problem occurs. Does the problem appear only under certain conditions? Were there any noises, odors or other unusual symptoms? Isolate the problem area. To do this, make some simple tests and observations, then eliminate the systems that are working properly. Check for obvious problems, such as broken wires and loose or dirty connections. Always check the obvious before assuming something complicated is the cause.

• Test for problems systematically to determine the cause once the problem area is isolated. Are all the components functioning properly? Is there power going to electrical switches and motors? Performing careful, systematic checks will often turn up most causes on the first inspection, without wasting time checking components that have little or no relationship to the problem.

• Test all repairs after the work is done to make sure that the problem is fixed. Some causes can be traced to more than one component, so a careful verification of repair work is important in order to pick up additional malfunctions that may cause a problem to reappear or a different problem to arise. A blown fuse, for example, is a simple problem that may require more than another fuse to repair. If you don't look for a problem that caused a fuse to blow, a shorted wire (for example) may go undetected.

Experience has shown that most problems tend to be the result of a fairly simple and obvious cause, such as loose or corroded connectors, bad grounds or damaged wire insulation which causes a short. This makes careful visual inspection of components during testing essential to quick and accurate troubleshooting.

Testing

OPEN CIRCUITS

▶ **See Figure 8**

This test already assumes the existence of an open in the circuit and it is used to help locate the open portion.
1. Isolate the circuit from power and ground.
2. Connect the self-powered test light or ohmmeter ground clip to the ground side of the circuit and probe sections of the circuit sequentially.
3. If the light is out or there is infinite resistance, the open is between the probe and the circuit ground.
4. If the light is on or the meter shows continuity, the open is between the probe and the end of the circuit toward the power source.

SHORT CIRCUITS

➡ **Never use a self-powered test light to perform checks for opens or shorts when power is applied to the circuit under test. The test light can be damaged by outside power.**

1. Isolate the circuit from power and ground.
2. Connect the self-powered test light or ohmmeter ground clip to a good ground and probe any easy-to-reach point in the circuit.
3. If the light comes on or there is continuity, there is a short somewhere in the circuit.
4. To isolate the short, probe a test point at either end of the isolated circuit (the light should be on or the meter should indicate continuity).

5. Leave the test light probe engaged and sequentially open connectors or switches, remove parts, etc. until the light goes out or continuity is broken.
6. When the light goes out, the short is between the last two circuit components which were opened.

VOLTAGE

This test determines voltage available from the battery and should be the first step in any electrical troubleshooting procedure after visual inspection. Many electrical problems, especially on computer controlled systems, can be caused by a low state of charge in the battery. Excessive corrosion at the battery cable terminals can cause poor contact that will prevent proper charging and full battery current flow.
1. Set the voltmeter selector switch to the 20V position.
2. Connect the multimeter negative lead to the battery's negative (-) post or terminal and the positive lead to the battery's positive (+) post or terminal.
3. Turn the ignition switch **ON** to provide a load.
4. A well charged battery should register over 12 volts. If the meter reads below 11.5 volts, the battery power may be insufficient to operate the electrical system properly.

VOLTAGE DROP

▶ **See Figure 9**

When current flows through a load, the voltage beyond the load drops. This voltage drop is due to the resistance created by the load and also by small resistances created by corrosion at the connectors and damaged insulation on the wires. The maximum allowable voltage drop under load is critical, especially if there is more than one load in the circuit, since all voltage drops are cumulative.
1. Set the voltmeter selector switch to the 20 volt position.
2. Connect the multimeter negative lead to a good ground.
3. Operate the circuit and check the voltage prior to the first component (load).
4. There should be little or no voltage drop in the circuit prior to the first component. If a voltage drop exists, the wire or connectors in the circuit are suspect.
5. While operating the first component in the circuit, probe the ground side of the component with the positive meter lead and observe the voltage readings. A small voltage drop should be noticed. This voltage drop is caused by the resistance of the component.
6. Repeat the test for each component (load) down the circuit.
7. If a large voltage drop is noticed, the preceding component, wire or connector is suspect.

RESISTANCE

▶ **See Figures 10 and 11**

✳✳ WARNING

Never use an ohmmeter with power applied to the circuit. The ohmmeter is designed to operate on its own power supply. The normal 12 volt electrical system voltage could damage the meter!

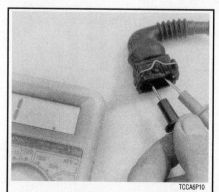

Fig. 8 The infinite reading on this multimeter indicates that the circuit is open

TCCA6P10

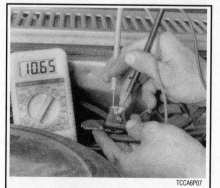

Fig. 9 This voltage drop test revealed high resistance (low voltage) in the circuit

TCCA6P07

Fig. 10 Checking the resistance of a coolant temperature sensor with an ohmmeter. Reading is 1.04 kilohms

TCCA6P08

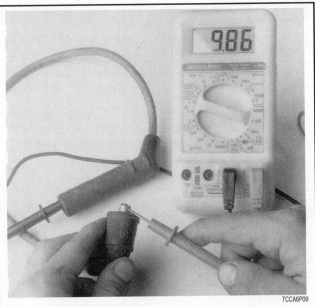

Fig. 11 Spark plug wires can be checked for excessive resistance using an ohmmeter

1. Isolate the circuit from the vehicle's power source.
2. Ensure that the ignition key is **OFF** when disconnecting any components or the battery.
3. Where necessary, also isolate at least one side of the circuit to be checked, in order to avoid reading parallel resistances. Parallel circuit resistances will always give a lower reading than the actual resistance of either of the branches.
4. Connect the meter leads to both sides of the circuit (wire or component) and read the actual measured ohms on the meter scale. Make sure the selector switch is set to the proper ohm scale for the circuit being tested, to avoid misreading the ohmmeter test value.

Wire and Connector Repair

Almost anyone can replace damaged wires, as long as the proper tools and parts are available. Wire and terminals are available to fit almost any need. Even the specialized weatherproof, molded and hard shell connectors are now available from aftermarket suppliers.

Be sure the ends of all the wires are fitted with the proper terminal hardware and connectors. Wrapping a wire around a stud is never a permanent solution and will only cause trouble later. Replace wires one at a time to avoid confusion. Always route wires exactly the same as the factory.

➡**If connector repair is necessary, only attempt it if you have the proper tools. Weatherproof and hard shell connectors require special tools to release the pins inside the connector. Attempting to repair these connectors with conventional hand tools will damage them.**

BATTERY CABLES

Disconnecting The Cables

When working on any electrical component on the vehicle, it is always a good idea to disconnect the negative (-) battery cable. This will prevent potential damage to many sensitive electrical components such as the Engine Control Module (ECM), radio, alternator, etc.

➡**Any time you disengage the battery cables, it is recommended that you disconnect the negative (-) battery cable first. This will prevent your accidentally grounding the positive (+) terminal to the body of the vehicle when disconnecting it, thereby preventing damage to the above mentioned components.**

Before you disconnect the cable(s), first turn the ignition to the **OFF** position. This will prevent a draw on the battery which could cause arcing (electricity trying to ground itself to the body of a vehicle, just like a spark plug jumping the gap) and, of course, damaging some components such as the alternator diodes.

When the battery cable(s) are reconnected (negative cable last), be sure to check that your lights, windshield wipers and other electrically operated safety components are all working correctly. If your vehicle contains an Electronically Tuned Radio (ETR), the frequencies will have to be reset, as well as the clock.

AIR BAGS (SUPPLEMENTAL RESTRAINT SYSTEM)

General Information

▶ See Figure 12

A Supplemental Restraint System (SRS), more commonly known as air bags, is installed in all 1994 and later vehicles. The system is designed to protect the driver and, on some vehicles, the front seat passenger from serious injury when the vehicle is involved in a frontal collision.

The system consists of an air bag mounted in the steering wheel, a control unit and various sensors. Those vehicles with front seat passenger protection also contain an air bag mounted above the glove box on the dash panel.

✳ WARNING

Air bag sensors are mounted behind the grille and under the console. Extreme caution should be exercised when working in these areas.

SERVICE PRECAUTIONS

- Do not use a circuit tester to check SRS function.
- Before servicing the SRS, turn the ignition **OFF**, disconnect both the negative, then the positive battery cables and wait at least 10 minutes.
- Replace the air bag module if it has been dropped or sustained any impact.
- Do not expose the air bag module to temperature exceeding 194°F (90°C).
- Do not allow oil, grease or water to come in contact with the air bag module.
- The diagnosis and sensor units must always be mounted with the arrow pointing toward the front of the vehicle.
- Check the diagnosis and sensor units for damage, deformities or rust prior to installation, and replace as required.

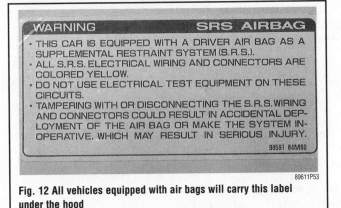

WARNING SRS AIRBAG
- THIS CAR IS EQUIPPED WITH A DRIVER AIR BAG AS A SUPPLEMENTAL RESTRAINT SYSTEM (S.R.S.).
- ALL S.R.S. ELECTRICAL WIRING AND CONNECTORS ARE COLORED YELLOW.
- DO NOT USE ELECTRICAL TEST EQUIPMENT ON THESE CIRCUITS.
- TAMPERING WITH OR DISCONNECTING THE S.R.S. WIRING AND CONNECTORS COULD RESULT IN ACCIDENTAL DEPLOYMENT OF THE AIR BAG OR MAKE THE SYSTEM INOPERATIVE, WHICH MAY RESULT IN SERIOUS INJURY.

98591 84M60

Fig. 12 All vehicles equipped with air bags will carry this label under the hood

• The spiral cable in the steering wheel must be aligned with the neutral position, since its rotations are limited. Do not attempt to turn the steering wheel or column after the steering wheel has been removed.
• Handle air bags with extreme caution. Always place them with the pad side facing upward.
• Do not use old bolts after their removal from any SRS parts. Always install SRS parts with new bolts of the proper type and strength.
• In the event of air bag inflation, the front instrument panel assembly should be replaced.

DISARMING THE SYSTEM

Before servicing the SRS, turn the ignition **OFF**. Disconnect the negative, then positive battery cables, and wait at least 10 minutes.

✷✷ CAUTION

It is still possible for the air bag to deploy for up to 10 minutes after the cables are removed. Therefore, do not work on any air bag system connectors or wires until at least 10 minutes have passed.

ARMING THE SYSTEM

Connect the positive, then the negative battery cables. Turn the ignition switch **ON** and wait for the air bag warning lamp on the instrument panel to illuminate. The warning lamp will turn off after approximately 7 seconds if no malfunctions are present. If the warning lamp does not function as stated, the SRS system should be inspected by a qualified technician.

HEATING AND AIR CONDITIONING

Blower Motor

REMOVAL & INSTALLATION

▶ **See Figures 13, 14 and 15**

The blower motor is located under the passenger's side of the dash panel, attached to the bottom of the intake unit.
1. Remove the glove box, as required.
2. Disconnect the blower motor electrical harness.
3. Disconnect the blower motor cooling tube, as required.
4. Remove the fasteners that attach the blower motor to the intake unit.
5. Remove the blower motor from the vehicle.

To install:
6. Inspect the blower wheel for damage, and replace it as necessary. Replace the blower motor mounting seal.
7. Position the blower motor on the heater unit and install the screws. Center the unit in the opening and tighten the screws securely.
8. If applicable, attach the blower motor cooling tube.
9. Connect the blower motor electrical harness.
10. Install the glove box onto the dash panel.
11. Check the blower for proper operation at all speeds.

Heater Core

REMOVAL & INSTALLATION

▶ **See Figures 16 and 17**

1. Disconnect the negative battery cable.
2. Set the TEMP lever to the HOT position.
3. Drain and recycle the engine coolant.
4. Disconnect the heater hoses from the heater unit.

5. At this point, the manufacturer suggests you remove the front seats. To do this, remove the plastic covers over the ends of the seat runners, both front and back, to expose the seat mounting bolts. Remove the bolts and remove the seats.
6. Remove the console box and the floor carpets.
7. Remove the instrument panel lower covers from both the driver's and passenger's sides of the vehicle.
8. Remove the lower cluster lids.
9. Remove the left-hand side ventilator duct.
10. Remove the radio, sound balancer and stereo cassette deck, if equipped.
11. Remove the instrument panel stay.
12. Remove the rear heater duct from the floor of the vehicle.
13. Remove the center ventilator duct.
14. Remove the left and right-hand side air guides from the lower heater outlets.
15. Label and disconnect the electrical harness.
16. Remove the screws at the bottom sides of the heater unit and the screw at the top of the unit.
17. Remove the unit, together with the heater control assembly.

➡ **On late model vehicles, the heater control cables and control assembly may have to be removed before the heater unit is removed. Always mark control cables before removing them to ensure correct adjustment and proper operation.**

To install:
18. Install the heater unit, together with the heater control assembly.
19. Install the screws at the bottom sides of the heater unit and the screw at the top of the unit.
20. Connect the electrical harness.
21. Install the left and right-hand side air guides on the lower heater outlets.
22. Install the center ventilator duct.
23. Position the rear heater duct on the floor of the vehicle.
24. Install the instrument panel stay.
25. Install the radio, sound balancer and stereo cassette deck, if equipped.

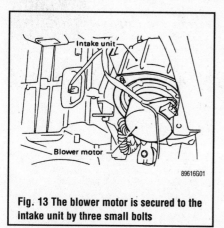

Fig. 13 The blower motor is secured to the intake unit by three small bolts

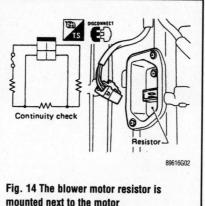

Fig. 14 The blower motor resistor is mounted next to the motor

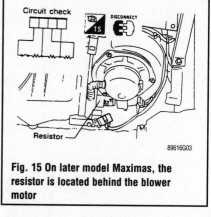

Fig. 15 On later model Maximas, the resistor is located behind the blower motor

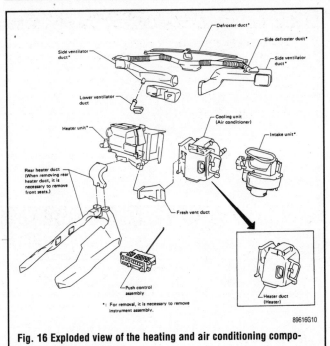

Fig. 16 Exploded view of the heating and air conditioning components—1993–94 vehicles

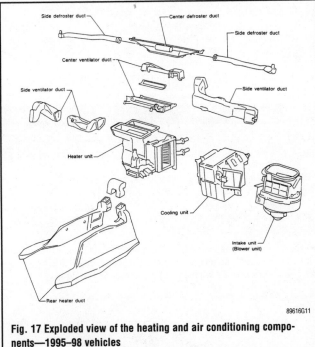

Fig. 17 Exploded view of the heating and air conditioning components—1995–98 vehicles

26. Install the left-hand side ventilator duct.
27. Install the instrument panel lower covers. Install the lower cluster lids.
28. Install the console and the floor carpets.
29. Install the front seats.
30. Connect the heater hoses to the heater unit.
31. Connect the negative battery cable.
32. Refill and bleed the engine with coolant.
33. Check for leaks. Adjust the coolant level as necessary.

Heater Water Control Valve

REMOVAL & INSTALLATION

▸ **See Figure 18**

The heater control valve is operated by a vacuum operated actuator that is controlled by a solenoid valve. The assembly is located at the rear center of the engine compartment.
1. Drain and recycle the engine coolant.
2. Unplug the harness connector from the valve.
3. Disconnect the heater hoses from the valve.

➡ **Some coolant will remain in the hoses, so place a pan under the vehicle to catch any spills.**

4. Remove the control valve from the vehicle.
To install:
5. Position the control valve in the vehicle.
6. Connect the heater hoses to the valve.
7. Connect the control cable to the valve.
8. Refill and bleed the engine with coolant.
9. Check for leaks. Adjust the coolant level as necessary.

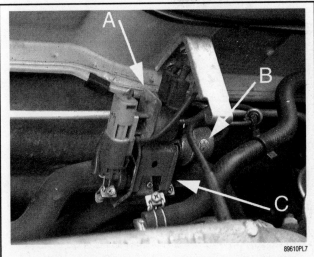

Fig. 18 Heater water control valve components—A: solenoid valve B: vacuum actuator C: heater water control valve

Air Conditioning Components

Repair or service of air conditioning components is not covered by this manual, because of the risk of personal injury or death, and because of the legal ramifications of servicing these components without the proper EPA certification and experience. Cost, personal injury or death, environmental damage, and legal considerations (such as the fact that it is a federal crime to vent refrigerant into the atmosphere), dictate that the A/C components on your vehicle should be serviced only by a Motor Vehicle Air Conditioning (MVAC) trained, and EPA certified automotive technician.

Control Cables

REMOVAL & INSTALLATION

▸ **See Figures 19 and 20**

Earlier model Maximas with manually operated climate control use cables to activate the doors which control the air flow for heating and cooling.

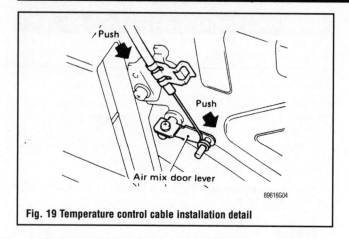

Fig. 19 Temperature control cable installation detail

1. To remove the control cables, simply remove the clip and slide the cable tip from the pin on the door lever.

To install:

2. Clamp the cable in position with the clip while pushing in the direction of the arrows in the illustrations.

3. After installing, check that the cable is adjusted properly by operating the levers on the control panel.

Control Panel

REMOVAL & INSTALLATION

1. Remove the center console trim fascia.
2. Remove the radio to allow access to reach behind the control panel.
3. Remove the control panel attaching screws.
4. Remove the center console bracket, if necessary, to allow for easier removal.

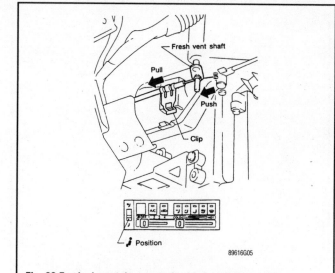

Fig. 20 Fresh air vent door control cable installation detail

5. Separate the control panel from the trim panel.
6. Unplug the harness connectors and vacuum lines from the control panel.

To install:

7. Plug in the harness connectors and vacuum lines from the control panel.
8. Install the control panel into the trim panel.
9. Install the center console bracket, if removed.
10. Install the control panel attaching screws. Do not overtighten them, as they are screwed into plastic.
11. Install the radio.
12. Install the center console trim fascia.
13. Operate the climate controls and check for proper operation.

CRUISE CONTROL

▶ **See Figures 21 and 22**

Nissan refers to their cruise control as the Automatic Speed Control Device (ASCD) system. The ASCD system maintains a desired speed of the vehicle under normal driving conditions. However, steep grades up or down may cause variations in the selected speeds. The electronic cruise control system has the capability to cruise, coast, resume speed, accelerate, "tap-up" and "tap-down".

The cruise control system components include the control switches, control unit, actuator, speed sensor, vacuum pump, vacuum pump relay, vacuum switch, electrical release switches and electrical harness.

The cruise control system uses the ASCD control unit to obtain the desired operation. The controller monitors the vehicle speed and operates the vacuum pump, which controls the actuator. The actuator controls vehicle speed with a cable attached to the throttle body.

The release switches are mounted on the brake/clutch/accelerator pedal bracket. When the brake or clutch pedal is depressed, the cruise control system is electrically disengaged and the throttle is returned to the idle position. The cruise control module assembly contains a circuit which will prevent system engagement below 25 mph (40 km/h).

➡**The use of the speed control is not recommended when driving conditions do not permit maintaining a constant speed, such as in heavy traffic or on roads that are winding, icy, snow covered or slippery.**

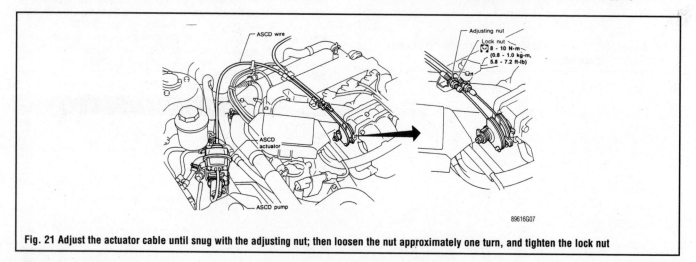

Fig. 21 Adjust the actuator cable until snug with the adjusting nut; then loosen the nut approximately one turn, and tighten the lock nut

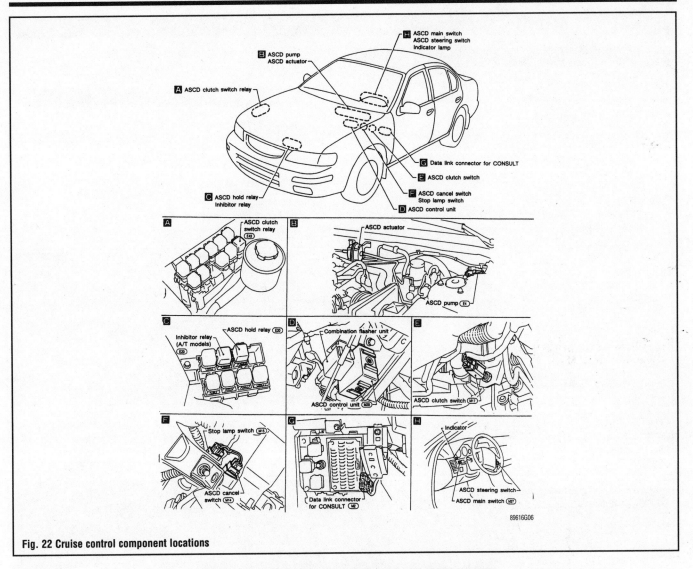

Fig. 22 Cruise control component locations

89616G06

CRUISE CONTROL TROUBLESHOOTING

Problem	Possible Cause
Will not hold proper speed	Incorrect cable adjustment
	Binding throttle linkage
	Leaking vacuum servo diaphragm
	Leaking vacuum tank
	Faulty vacuum or vent valve
	Faulty stepper motor
	Faulty transducer
	Faulty speed sensor
	Faulty cruise control module
Cruise intermittently cuts out	Clutch or brake switch adjustment too tight
	Short or open in the cruise control circuit
	Faulty transducer
	Faulty cruise control module
Vehicle surges	Kinked speedometer cable or casing
	Binding throttle linkage
	Faulty speed sensor
	Faulty cruise control module
Cruise control inoperative	Blown fuse
	Short or open in the cruise control circuit
	Faulty brake or clutch switch
	Leaking vacuum circuit
	Faulty cruise control switch
	Faulty stepper motor
	Faulty transducer
	Faulty speed sensor
	Faulty cruise control module

Note: Use this chart as a guide. Not all systems will use the components listed.

TCCA6C01

ENTERTAINMENT SYSTEMS

Radio

REMOVAL & INSTALLATION

▶ **See Figures 23 thru 30**

1. Remove the dash panel trim panel that surrounds the radio.
2. Remove the screws securing the radio.
3. Carefully pull the radio from the dash panel.
4. Label and disconnect the electrical harnesses and antenna wire.
5. Remove the radio from the vehicle.

To install:

6. Connect the electrical harnesses and antenna wire.
7. Carefully position the radio in the dash panel.

8. Install the four radio attaching screws and tighten securely.
9. Install the trim panel that surrounds the radio.

Speakers

REMOVAL & INSTALLATION

Front

▶ **See Figures 31 and 32**

1. Remove the front door panel.
2. Remove the speaker attaching bolts.

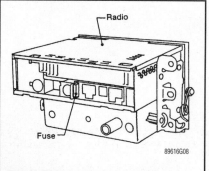

Fig. 23 There is a fuse on the back of the radio that can only be accessed by removing the radio

Fig. 24 Unclip the trim panel surrounding the shifter to allow for removal of the fascia surrounding the radio

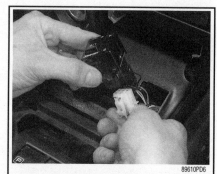

Fig. 25 Pull the shift mode switch (automatic models) out of the lower fascia and disconnect it

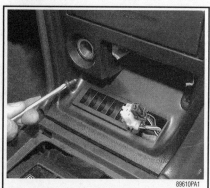

Fig. 26 Remove the two screws on the bottom of the fascia . . .

Fig. 27 . . . then carefully unclip it by pulling outward

Fig. 28 Unclip the connectors from the cigarette lighter and set the panel aside

Fig. 29 Remove the radio retaining screws and slide the radio out of the center console

Fig. 30 Pull out on the connectors to remove them from the radio

Fig. 31 After the door panel is removed, the speakers bolts can easily be accessed

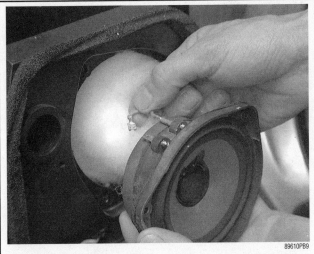

Fig. 32 Pull the connectors from the speaker and remove it from the door

➡Take care not to damage the speaker cone.

3. Pull the speaker from the plastic housing.
4. Depress the clip and disconnect the electrical harness.

WINDSHIELD WIPERS AND WASHERS

Windshield Wiper Blade and Arm

REMOVAL & INSTALLATION

▶ **See Figures 33 and 34**

➡On most models, the wiper arms are of different lengths. Label the wiper arms when removing to ensure that they are installed in their correct positions on the vehicle.

1. Remove the wiper arm pivot nut.
2. Matchmark the wiper arm and the pivot stud for installation reference.
3. Use a battery post puller or equivalent tool if necessary to extract the wiper arm from the pivot shaft.

➡The wiper arm pivot shaft is splined and tapered. Considerable force may be needed to remove the wiper arm from the stud. Work carefully and use the proper tools to avoid damage to the vehicle.

4. Remove the wiper blade and arm assembly from the vehicle.
To install:
5. Align the matchmarks on the pivot shaft and wiper arm.
6. If matchmarks were not made, proceed as follows:

To install:
5. Connect the speaker electrical harness.
6. Position the speaker in the plastic housing.
7. Install and tighten the speaker attaching bolts.

➡**Hand-tighten the screws only. Overtightening can damage the plastic housing.**

8. Install the front door panel.

Rear

➡**The speaker grilles on this vehicle are attached to the package shelf from the underside by four screws. The package shelf must be removed to remove the speaker grilles.**

1. Remove the rear seat.
2. Remove the package shelf.
3. Remove the four speaker attaching screws.

➡**Take care not to damage the speaker cone.**

4. Pull the speaker from the plastic housing.
5. Depress the clip and disconnect the electrical harness.
To install:
6. Connect the speaker electrical harness.
7. Position the speaker, then install and tighten the four speaker attaching screws.
8. Install the package shelf.
9. Install the rear seat.

a. Position the wiper arms so they are approximately horizontal.
b. Measure the distance between the bottom edge of the windshield and the center of the wiper blade.
c. Adjust the wiper arms until the measured distance is 0.71–1.30 in. (18–33mm) for the driver's side arm and 0.67–1.26 in. (17–32mm) for the passenger's side arm.
d. Install the wiper arm on the pivot stud and ensure that the splines engage fully.
7. Install the wiper arm and pivot shaft nut. Tighten the nut to 34–45 inch lbs. (4–5 Nm).

Windshield Wiper Motor

REMOVAL & INSTALLATION

▶ **See Figures 35 thru 45**

1. Remove the wiper arm assemblies.
2. Remove the cowl cover. The cowl cover is attached by plastic rivets, a screw in the center position and weatherstripping clips along the edge.
3. Unplug the wiper motor harness connector.

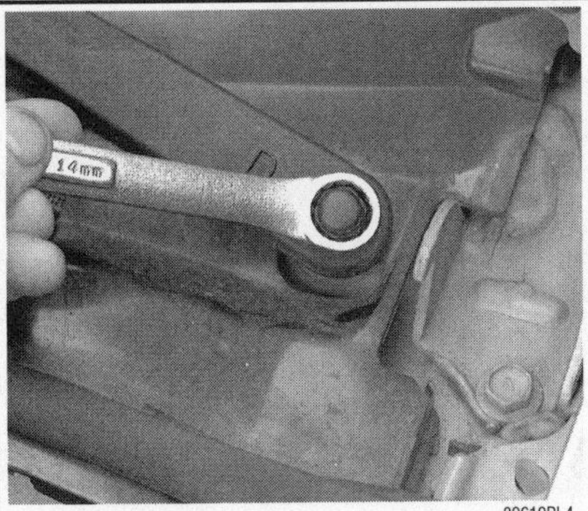

Fig. 33 Remove the cap nut that secures the wiper arm to the shaft . . .

Fig. 34 . . . then rock the arm up and down until it comes loose from the tapered shaft

Fig. 35 Gently pry upward to remove the covers to access the plastic rivets

Fig. 36 The rivets must be pried away from the body; usually they are not reusable

Fig. 37 There is one screw near the center of the cowl cover

Fig. 38 The weatherstrip has plastic retainer clips; be careful not to tear the weatherstrip when prying on the clips

Fig. 39 Carefully lift the cowl cover from the vehicle; the plastic can crack if bent too far

Fig. 40 Unplug the harness connector from the wiper motor . . .

Fig. 41 . . . then remove the bolts that secure the wiper motor

Fig. 42 Carefully position the motor so the crank arm nut can be removed

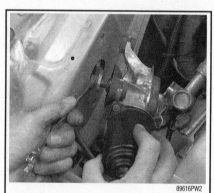

Fig. 43 Use a wrench to remove the crank arm nut

Fig. 44 Mark the motor shaft and crank arm before removal

Fig. 45 The motor can now be removed from the vehicle

4. Remove the wiper motor retaining bolts.

5. Pull out the wiper motor from the cowl and remove the nut retaining the crank arm to the motor.

6. Using a paint pen or a scribe, mark the crank arm/wiper motor shaft relationship. This will help preventing the wiper arm motor from being out of phase with the wiper arm assemblies.

7. Remove the wiper motor from the vehicle.

To install:

8. Position the wiper motor onto the crank arm, and install the nut.

9. Attach the wiper motor to the cowl with the retaining bolts.

10. Connect the wiper motor electrical harness.

11. Install the cowl cover.

12. With the ignition switch in the **ON** position, cycle the wipers a few times.

13. Turn the ignition switch **OFF**, and install the wiper arms onto the shafts.

14. Flip the wiper arms up, away from the windshield. Cycle the wipers again a few times as described above. Verify that the wipers stop in the proper position.

Windshield Washer Motor

REMOVAL & INSTALLATION

The windshield washer motor is either mounted to or contained in the washer reservoir.

1. Label and disconnect the washer motor electrical harness.

NSTRUMENTS AND SWITCHES

Instrument Cluster

REMOVAL & INSTALLATION

▶ **See Figures 46 thru 52**

1. Disarm the Supplemental Restraint System (SRS) and remove the air bag from the steering wheel.
2. Remove the steering wheel.

➡**On some models, the steering wheel may not have to be removed to remove the instrument panel.**

3. Remove the center console fascia.
4. Remove the instrument panel lower panel on the driver's side.
5. Remove the dash panel lower reinforcement panel.

2. Label and disconnect the washer motor hoses.

➡**Position a drain pan under the washer reservoir to catch any washer fluid which leaks out.**

3. Remove the washer reservoir from the vehicle.
4. Remove the washer pump from the reservoir.
To install:
5. Install the washer pump on the reservoir.
6. Install the washer reservoir in the vehicle.
7. Connect the washer motor hoses.
8. Connect the washer motor electrical harness.

6. Remove the steering column covers, spiral cable and combination switch.
7. Unfasten the cluster fascia.
8. Unscrew the instrument cluster from the dash panel. Unplug the harness connectors from the rear of the cluster and remove it from the vehicle.
To install:
9. Plug in the harness connectors into the instrument cluster and place the cluster inside the dash panel.
10. Install the instrument cluster fascia.
11. Install the spiral cable, combination switch and steering column covers.
12. Install the dash panel lower reinforcement panel.
13. Install the instrument panel lower panel on the driver's side.
14. Install the kick plate and dash panel side finisher on the driver's side.
15. Install the center console fascia.
16. Install the steering wheel.
17. Install the air bag assembly, then arm the SRS.

Fig. 46 Remove the upper screws retaining the instrument cluster fascia

Fig. 47 There are also screws on the lower half of the fascia that can only be accessed by removing the lower panels

Fig. 48 Carefully remove the instrument cluster fascia from the dash panel

Fig. 49 There are four screws that hold the instrument cluster inside the dash panel (arrows)

Fig. 50 Pull the instrument cluster outward . . .

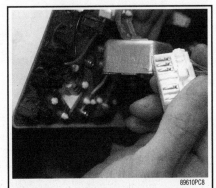
Fig. 51 . . . and unplug the harness connectors from the rear

Fig. 52 After the instrument cluster is removed, the bulbs can easily be changed. Twist the bulb holder, and pull the bulb out

Gauges

REMOVAL & INSTALLATION

The gauges are an integral part of the instrument cluster. If the gauges are determined to be faulty, the entire instrument cluster usually must be replaced as an assembly.

Check with your local authorities about laws concerning the replacement of speedometer/odometers.

LIGHTING

▶ See Figure 53

Headlights

REMOVAL & INSTALLATION

▶ See Figures 54, 55 and 56

1. Open the vehicle's hood and secure it in an upright position.
2. Unplug the harness connector that attaches to the rear of the headlight.

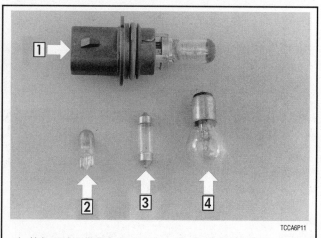

1. Halogen headlight bulb
2. Side marker light bulb
3. Dome light bulb
4. Turn signal/brake light bulb

Fig. 53 Examples of various types of automotive light bulbs

3. Unfasten the locking ring which secures the bulb and socket assembly, then withdraw the assembly rearward.
4. If necessary, gently pry the socket's retaining clip over the projection on the bulb (use care not to break the clip.) Pull the bulb from the socket.
   To install:
5. Before installing a light bulb into the socket, ensure that all electrical contact surfaces are free of corrosion or dirt.
6. Line up the replacement headlight bulb with the socket. Firmly push the bulb onto the socket until the spring clip latches over the bulb's projection.

✴✴ WARNING

Do not touch the glass bulb with your fingers ! Oil from your fingers can severely shorten the life of the bulb. If necessary, wipe off any dirt or oil from the bulb with rubbing alcohol before completing installation.

7. To ensure that the replacement bulb functions properly, activate the applicable switch to illuminate the bulb which was just replaced. (If this is a combination low and high beam bulb, be sure to check both intensities.) If the replacement light bulb does not illuminate, either it too is faulty or there is a problem in the bulb circuit or switch. Correct if necessary.
8. Position the headlight bulb and secure it with the locking ring.
9. Close the vehicle's hood.

HEADLIGHT AIMING

▶ See Figures 57, 58 and 59

The headlights must be properly aimed to provide the best, safest road illumination. The lights should be checked for proper aim and adjusted as necessary. Certain state and local authorities have requirements for headlight aiming; these should be checked before adjustment is made.

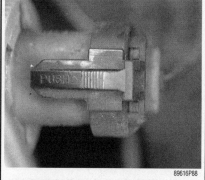

Fig. 54 Push down on the tab while pulling the connector from the headlight

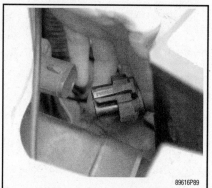

Fig. 55 Notice the tab on the headlight; this helps the connector to stay seated

Fig. 56 After the connector is removed, twist the retainer ring counterclockwise and pull the bulb from the lens

Fig. 57 The star wheels behind the head-lights are used for aiming

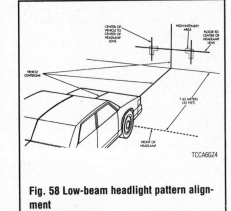

Fig. 58 Low-beam headlight pattern alignment

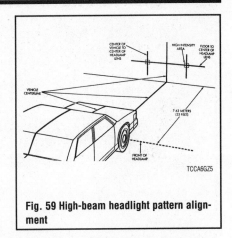

Fig. 59 High-beam headlight pattern alignment

❊❊ CAUTION

About once a year, when the headlights are replaced or any time front end work is performed on your vehicle, the headlight should be accurately aimed by a reputable repair shop using the proper equipment. Headlights not properly aimed can make it virtually impossible to see and may blind other drivers on the road, possibly causing an accident. Note that the following procedure is a temporary fix, until you can take your vehicle to a repair shop for a proper adjustment.

Headlight adjustment may be temporarily made using a wall, as described below, or on the rear of another vehicle. When adjusted, the lights should not glare in oncoming vehicle9 windshields, nor should they illuminate the passenger compartment of vehicles driving in front of you. These adjustments are rough and should always be fine-tuned by a repair shop which is equipped with headlight aiming tools. Improper adjustments may be both dangerous and illegal.

For most of the vehicles covered by this manual, horizontal and vertical aiming of each sealed beam unit is provided by two adjusting screws which move the retaining ring and adjusting plate against the tension of a coil spring. There is no adjustment for focus; this is done during headlight manufacturing.

➡ Because the composite headlight assembly is bolted into position, no adjustment should be necessary or possible. Some applications, however, may be bolted to an adjuster plate or may be retained by adjusting screws. If so, follow this procedure when adjusting the lights, BUT always have the adjustment checked by a reputable shop.

Before removing the headlight bulb or disturbing the headlamp in any way, note the current settings in order to ease headlight adjustment upon reassembly. If the high or low beam setting of the old lamp still works, this can be done using the wall of a garage or a building:

1. Park the vehicle on a level surface, with the fuel tank about ½ full and with the vehicle empty of all extra cargo (unless normally carried). The vehicle should be facing a wall which is no less than 6 feet (1.8m) high and 12 feet (3.7m) wide. The front of the vehicle should be about 25 feet from the wall.

2. If aiming is to be performed outdoors, it is advisable to wait until dusk in order to properly see the headlight beams on the wall. If done in a garage, darken the area around the wall as much as possible by closing shades or hanging cloth over the windows.

3. Turn the headlights **ON** and mark the wall at the center of each light's low beam, then switch on the brights and mark the center of each light's high beam. A short length of masking tape which is visible from the front of the vehicle may be used. Although marking all four positions is advisable, marking one position from each light should be sufficient.

4. If neither beam on one side is working, and if another like-sized vehicle is available, park the second one in the exact spot where the vehicle was and mark the beams using the same-side light. Then switch the vehicles so the one to be aimed is back in the original spot. It must be parked no closer to or farther away from the wall than the second vehicle.

5. Perform any necessary repairs, but make sure the vehicle is not moved, or is returned to the exact spot from which the lights were marked. Turn the headlights **ON** and adjust the beams to match the marks on the wall.

6. Have the headlight adjustment checked as soon as possible by a reputable repair shop.

Signal and Marker Lights

REMOVAL & INSTALLATION

Front Turn Signal and Parking Lights

◆ See Figures 60 thru 68

1. If necessary, unfasten and remove the lens housing.
2. Disengage the bulb and socket assembly from the lens housing.
3. Gently grasp the light bulb and remove it from the socket. Depending on the type of bulb, you must either depress and twist the bulb ⅛ or pull it straight out of its socket. Refer to the illustrations.

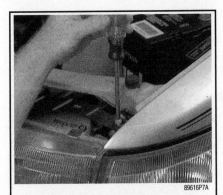

Fig. 60 Front upper signal lights are attached to the vehicle by a single screw

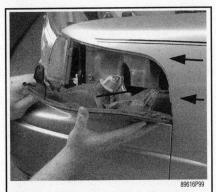

Fig. 61 After the screw is removed, carefully pull forward and out

Fig. 62 Remove the socket by twisting counterclockwise, then depress and twist the bulb ⅛ turn

Fig. 63 To remove the bumper mounted parking/turn indicators, remove the two screws on the sides of the lens

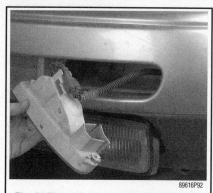

Fig. 64 The entire lens and reflector assembly can be pulled from the bumper

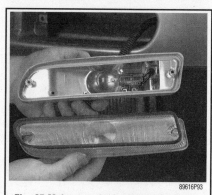

Fig. 65 Make sure the gasket on the lens is properly positioned during installation

Fig. 66 Note the small tab on the upper portion of the lens; this is installed first

Fig. 67 The bulb is removed by pushing in and twisting, and then pulling it out of the socket

To install:

4. Before installing the light bulb into the socket, ensure that all electrical contact surfaces are free of corrosion or dirt.

5. Line up the base of the light bulb with the socket, then insert the light bulb into the socket until it is fully seated. If the (turn signal) bulb has pins on its base, be sure that they are properly oriented.

6. To ensure that the replacement bulb functions properly, activate the applicable switch to illuminate the bulb which was just replaced. If the replacement light bulb does not illuminate, either it too is faulty or there is a problem in the bulb circuit or switch. Correct as necessary.

7. Install the socket and bulb assembly into the lens housing.

8. If applicable, position and reattach the lens housing.

Side Marker Lights

▶ **See Figures 68 and 69**

1. Disengage the bulb and socket assembly from the lens housing, accessed from the trunk.

2. Gently grasp the light bulb and pull it straight out of the socket.

To install:

3. Before installing the light bulb into the socket, ensure that all electrical contact surfaces are free of corrosion or dirt.

4. Line up the base of the light bulb with the socket, then insert the light bulb into the socket until it is fully seated.

5. To ensure that the replacement bulb functions properly, activate the applicable switch to illuminate the bulb which was just replaced. If the replacement light bulb does not illuminate, either it too is faulty or there is a problem in the bulb circuit or switch. Correct as necessary.

6. Install the socket and bulb assembly into the lens housing.

Tail and Brake Lights

▶ **See Figures 70 and 71**

1. Depending on the vehicle and bulb application, either unscrew and remove the lens or disengage the bulb and socket assembly from the rear of the lens housing.

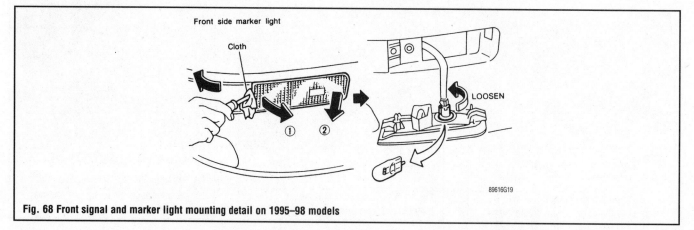

Front side marker light

Cloth

LOOSEN

① ②

Fig. 68 Front signal and marker light mounting detail on 1995–98 models

Fig. 69 The rear side marker lights are accessed from the trunk, behind the small flap of carpet

2. To remove a light bulb with retaining pins from its socket, grasp the bulb, then gently depress and twist it 1/8 turn counterclockwise, and pull it from the socket.

To install:

3. Before installing a light bulb into the socket, ensure that all electrical contact surfaces are free of corrosion or dirt.

➡**Before installing the light bulb, note the positions of the two retaining pins on the bulb. They will likely be at different heights on the bulb, to ensure that the bulb is installed correctly. If, when installing the bulb, it does not turn easily, do not force it. Remove the bulb and rotate it 180 degrees from its former position, then reinsert it into the bulb socket.**

4. Insert the light bulb into the socket and, while depressing the bulb, twist it 1/8 turn clockwise until the two pins on the light bulb are properly engaged in the socket.

5. To ensure that the replacement bulb functions properly, activate the applicable switch to illuminate the bulb which was just replaced. If the replacement light bulb does not illuminate, either it too is faulty or there is a problem in the bulb circuit or switch. Correct if necessary.

6. If applicable, install the socket and bulb assembly into the rear of the lens housing; otherwise, install the lens over the bulb.

Dome Light

1. Using a small prytool, carefully remove the cover lens from the lamp assembly.

2. Remove the bulb from its retaining clip contacts. If the bulb has tapered ends, gently depress the spring clip/metal contact and disengage the light bulb, then pull it free of the two metal contacts.

To install:

3. Before installing the light bulb into the metal contacts, ensure that all electrical conducting surfaces are free of corrosion or dirt.

4. Position the bulb between the two metal contacts. If the contacts have small holes, be sure that the tapered ends of the bulb are situated in them.

5. To ensure that the replacement bulb functions properly, activate the applicable switch to illuminate the bulb which was just replaced. If the replacement light bulb does not illuminate, either it is faulty or there is a problem in the bulb circuit or switch. Correct as necessary.

6. Install the cover lens until its retaining tabs are properly engaged.

Trunk, License Plate and High-Mount Brake Lights

▶ See Figures 72, 73, 74 and 75

These lights are very easy to replace. It usually involes simply removing a lens, then pulling or twisting the bulb from its socket. Refer to the illustrations.

Fig. 70 To replace the brake and taillights, lift up on the tabs and hinge the flap upward to access the taillight bulbs

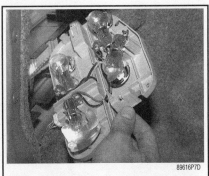

Fig. 71 Depress the clip and pull the back of the lens housing away to reveal the lamps

Fig. 72 The trunk lamp is covered by a plastic lens and is located under the package shelf

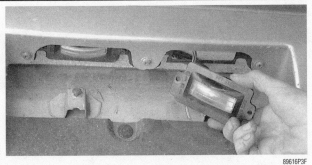

Fig. 73 To access the license plate lights, unscrew the lens assembly; the bulb is removed by twisting the bulb holder and pulling outward

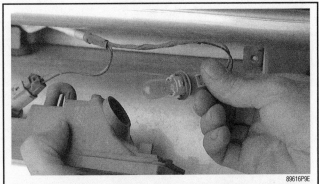

Fig. 74 Unscrew the high-mount brake light assembly, and twist the bulb holder from the lens; the bulb pulls straight out

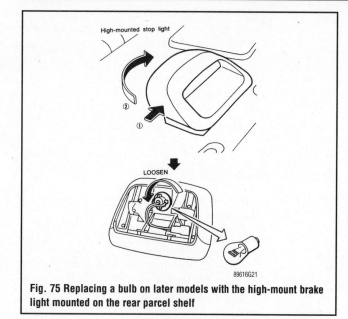

Fig. 75 Replacing a bulb on later models with the high-mount brake light mounted on the rear parcel shelf

Fog/Driving Lights

REMOVAL & INSTALLATION

▶ See Figures 76 thru 83

1. Remove the fasteners attaching the fog lamp to the bumper.
2. Unplug the electrical harness connector from the fog light.
3. Remove the fog light assembly from the bumper.

4. Unscrew the lens and separate the light assembly.
5. Disengage the spring clip and remove the bulb from the lens.

✸✸ WARNING

Do not touch the glass bulb with your fingers! Oil from your fingers can severely shorten the life of the bulb. If necessary, wipe off any dirt or oil from the bulb with rubbing alcohol before completing installation.

To install:
6. Place the bulb in the recess of the rear of the lens and engage the spring clip.
7. Assemble the two halves of the light assembly.
8. Plug in the electrical harness connector to the fog light.
9. Install the fog light assembly into the bumper. Be careful not to over-tighten the fasteners.
10. Check the fog lights for proper operation.

INSTALLING AFTERMARKET AUXILIARY LIGHTS

➡Before installing any aftermarket light, make sure it is legal for road use. Most acceptable lights will have a DOT approval number. Also check your local and regional inspection regulations. In certain areas, aftermarket lights must be installed in a particular manner or they may not be legal for inspection.

1. Disconnect the negative battery cable.
2. Unpack the contents of the light kit purchased. Place the contents in an open space where you can easily retrieve a piece if needed.
3. Choose a location for the lights. If you are installing fog lights, below the bumper and apart from each other is desirable. Most fog lights are mounted below or very close to the headlights. If you are installing driving lights, above the bumper and close together is desirable. Most driving lights are mounted between the headlights.

Fig. 76 After the two bracket bolts are removed, pull the light forward to slide the front lens bracket from the bumper

Fig. 77 Press down on the connector tab, then pull it from the light

Fig. 78 The lens screws can now be accessed; remove them to separate the light

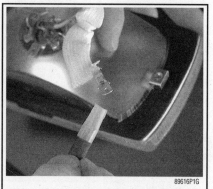

Fig. 79 Pull back the insulation and disconnect the positive lead . . .

Fig. 80 . . . followed by the ground lead

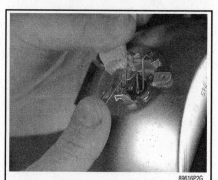

Fig. 81 Push down on the clip and remove it from the hook, then hinge the clip back . . .

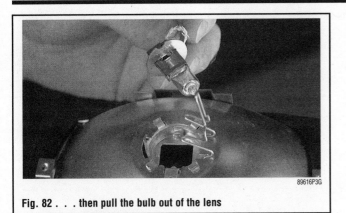

Fig. 82 . . . then pull the bulb out of the lens

4. Drill the needed hole(s) to mount the light. Install the light, and secure using the supplied retainer nut and washer. Tighten the light mounting hardware, but not the light adjustment nut or bolt.

5. Install the relay that came with the light kit in the engine compartment, in a rigid area, such as a fender. Always install the relay with the terminals facing down. This will prevent water from entering the relay assembly.

6. Using the wire supplied, locate the ground terminal on the relay, and connect a length of wire from this terminal to a good ground source. You can drill a hole and screw this wire to an inside piece of metal; just scrape the paint away from the hole to ensure a good connection.

7. Locate the light terminal on the relay; and attach a length of wire between this terminal and the fog/driving lamps.

8. Locate the ignition terminal on the relay, and connect a length of wire between this terminal and the light switch.

9. Find a suitable mounting location for the light switch and install. Some examples of mounting areas are a location close to the main light switch, auxiliary light position in the dash panel, if equipped, or in the center of the dash panel.

10. Depending on local and regional regulations, the other end of the switch can be connected to a constant power source such as the battery, an ignition opening in the fuse panel, or a parking or headlight wire.

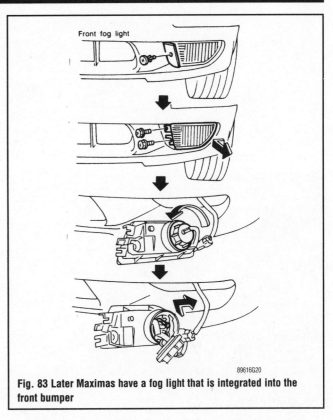

Fig. 83 Later Maximas have a fog light that is integrated into the front bumper

11. Locate the power terminal on the relay, and connect a wire with an in-line fuse of at least 10 amperes between the terminal and the battery.

12. With all the wires connected and tied up neatly, connect the negative battery cable.

13. Turn the lights ON and adjust the light pattern, if necessary.

TRAILER WIRING

Wiring the vehicle for towing is fairly easy. There are a number of good wiring kits available and these should be used, rather than trying to design your own.

All trailers will need brake lights and turn signals as well as tail lights and side marker lights. Most areas require extra marker lights for overwide trailers. Also, most areas have recently required back-up lights for trailers, and most trailer manufacturers have been building trailers with back-up lights for several years.

Additionally, some Class I, most Class II and just about all Class III and IV trailers will have electric brakes. Add to this number an accessories wire, to operate trailer internal equipment or to charge the trailer's battery, and you can have as many as seven wires in the harness.

Determine the equipment on your trailer and buy the wiring kit necessary. The kit will contain all the wires needed, plus a plug adapter set which includes the female plug, mounted on the bumper or hitch, and the male plug, wired into, or plugged into the trailer harness.

When installing the kit, follow the manufacturer's instructions. The color cod-

ing of the wires is usually standard throughout the industry. One point to note: some domestic vehicles, and most imported vehicles, have separate turn signals. On most domestic vehicles, the brake lights and rear turn signals operate with the same bulb. For those vehicles with separate turn signals, you can purchase an isolation unit so that the brake lights won't blink whenever the turn signals are operated, or, you can go to your local electronics supply house and buy four diodes to wire in series with the brake and turn signal bulbs. Diodes will isolate the brake and turn signals. The choice is yours. The isolation units are simple and quick to install, but far more expensive than the diodes. The diodes, however, require more work to install properly, since they require the cutting of each bulb's wire and soldering in place of the diode.

One, final point, the best kits are those with a spring loaded cover on the vehicle mounted socket. This cover prevents dirt and moisture from corroding the terminals. Never let the vehicle socket hang loosely; always mount it securely to the bumper or hitch.

CIRCUIT PROTECTION

Fuses

REPLACEMENT

▶ **See Figures 84, 85 and 86**

Fuses are located either in the engine compartment or passenger compartment fuse and relay panels. If a fuse blows, a single component or single circuit will not function properly.

1. Remove the fuse and relay panel cover.

2. Inspect the fuses to determine which is faulty.

3. Unplug and discard the fuse.

4. Inspect the panel terminals and clean if corroded. If any terminals are damaged, replace the terminals.

5. Plug in a new fuse of the same amperage rating.

✳✳ WARNING

Never exceed the amperage rating of a blown fuse. If the replacement fuse also blows, check for a problem in the circuit.

6. Check for proper operation of the affected component or circuit.

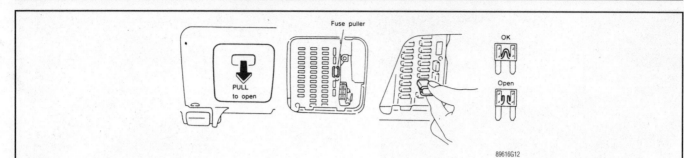

Fig. 84 The fuse panel is located on the left lower kick panel

Fig. 85 There are also fuses in the engine compartment

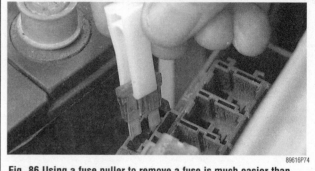

Fig. 86 Using a fuse puller to remove a fuse is much easier than using your fingernails

Maxi-Fuses (Fusible Links)

Maxi-fuses are located in the engine compartment relay boxes near the battery. If a maxi-fuse blows, an entire circuit or several circuits will not function properly.

REPLACEMENT

▶ **See Figures 87 and 88**

1. Remove the fuse and relay box cover.
2. Inspect the fusible links to determine which is faulty.
3. Unplug and discard the fusible link.
4. Inspect the box terminals and clean if corroded. If any terminals are damaged, replace the terminals.
5. Plug in a new fusible link of the same amperage rating.

✳✳ WARNING

Never exceed the amperage rating of a blown maxi-fuse. If the replacement fuse also blows, check for a problem in the circuit(s).

6. Check for proper operation of the affected circuit(s).

Flasher Unit and Relays

The combination flasher relay is located under the dash panel, next to the center console near the Automatic Speed Control Device (ACSD) control box. If the turn signals operate in only one direction, a bulb is probably burned out. If they do not operate in either direction, a bulb on each side may be burned out, or the flasher may be defective.

REPLACEMENT

▶ **See Figures 89 thru 98**

1. Remove the passenger compartment fuse and relay box cover, noting which position the flasher unit occupies.
2. Unplug and discard the flasher.
3. Inspect the box terminals and clean if corroded. If any terminals are damaged, replace the terminals.
4. Plug in a new flasher of the same type.
5. Operate the turn signals and hazard lights. Check for proper operation.

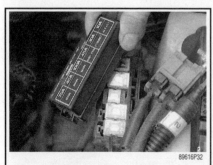

Fig. 87 Maxi-fuses are usually located in the engine compartment. The covers are removed by unhooking the tabs on the sides

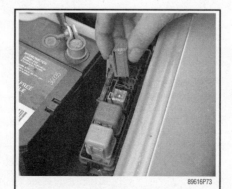

Fig. 88 Pinch the tab on the side of the maxi-fuse and pull it upward

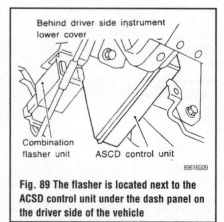

Fig. 89 The flasher is located next to the ACSD control unit under the dash panel on the driver side of the vehicle

Fig. 90 Relays are found in various locations, usually within the engine compartment. The relay cover identifies each relay function

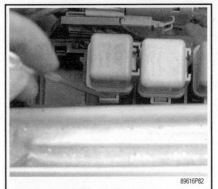

Fig. 91 To remove a relay, use a small metal pick to depress the tab . . .

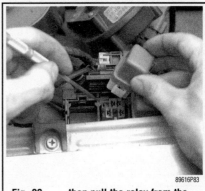

Fig. 92 . . . then pull the relay from the base

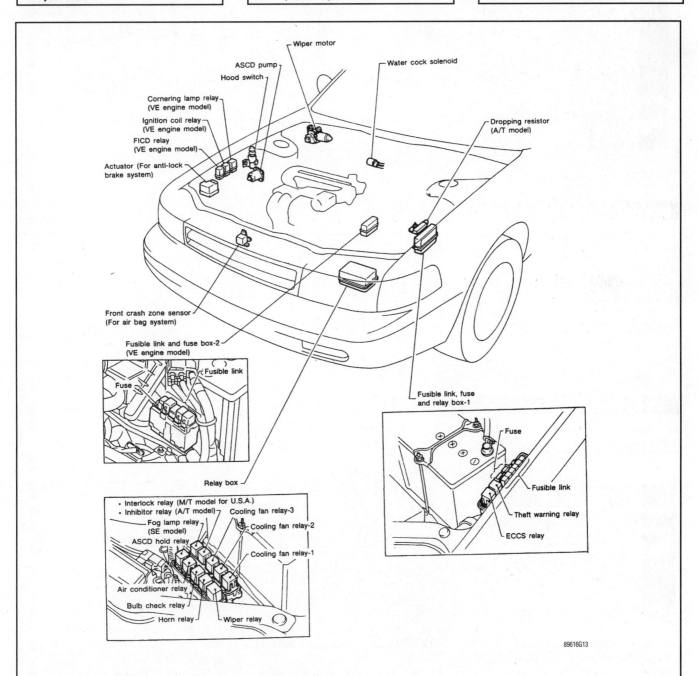

Fig. 93 Engine compartment electrical unit locations on 1993–94 models

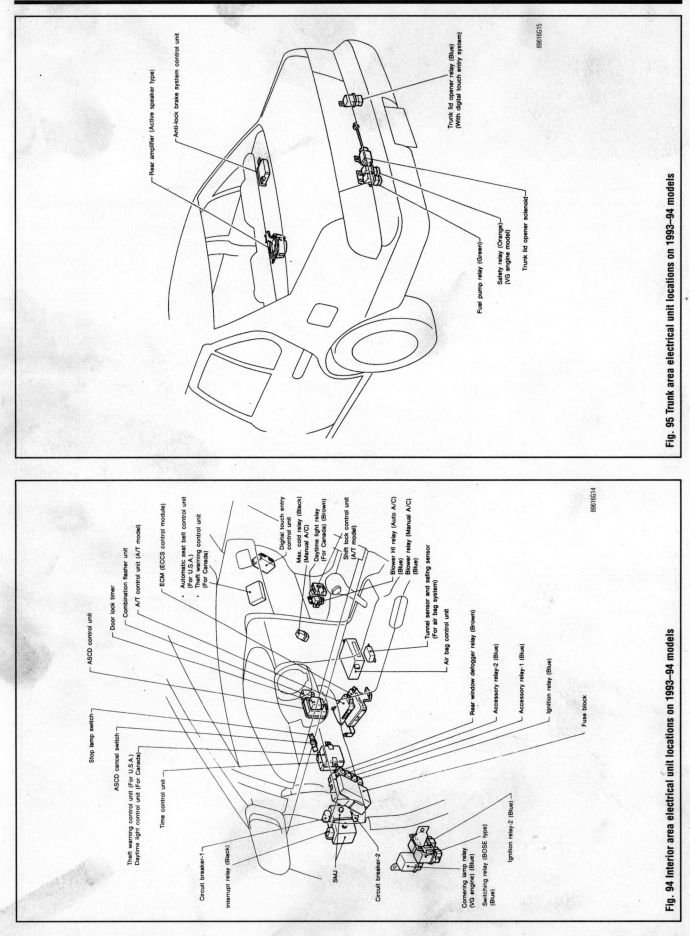

Fig. 95 Trunk area electrical unit locations on 1993–94 models

Rear amplifier (Active speaker type)
Anti-lock brake system control unit
Trunk lid opener relay (Blue)
(With digital touch entry system)
Fuel pump relay (Green)
Safety relay (Orange)
(VG engine model)
Trunk lid opener solenoid

Fig. 94 Interior area electrical unit locations on 1993–94 models

ASCD control unit
Door lock timer
Combination flasher unit
A/T control unit (A/T model)
ECM (ECCS control module)
Automatic seat belt control unit
(For U.S.A.)
Theft warning control unit
(For Canada)
Digital touch entry control unit
Max. cold relay (Black)
(Manual A/C)
Daytime light relay
(For Canada) (Brown)
Shift lock control unit
(A/T model)
Blower HI relay (Auto A/C)
(Blue)
Blower relay (Manual A/C)
(Blue)
Tunnel sensor and safing sensor
(For air bag system)
Air bag control unit
Rear window defogger relay (Brown)
Accessory relay-2 (Blue)
Accessory relay-1 (Blue)
Ignition relay (Blue)
Fuse block

Stop lamp switch
ASCD cancel switch
Theft warning control unit (For U.S.A.)
Daytime light control unit (For Canada)
Time control unit
Circuit breaker-1
Interrupt relay (Black)
SMJ
Circuit breaker-2
Cornering lamp relay
(VG engine) (Blue)
Switching relay (BOSE type)
(Blue)
Ignition relay-2 (Blue)

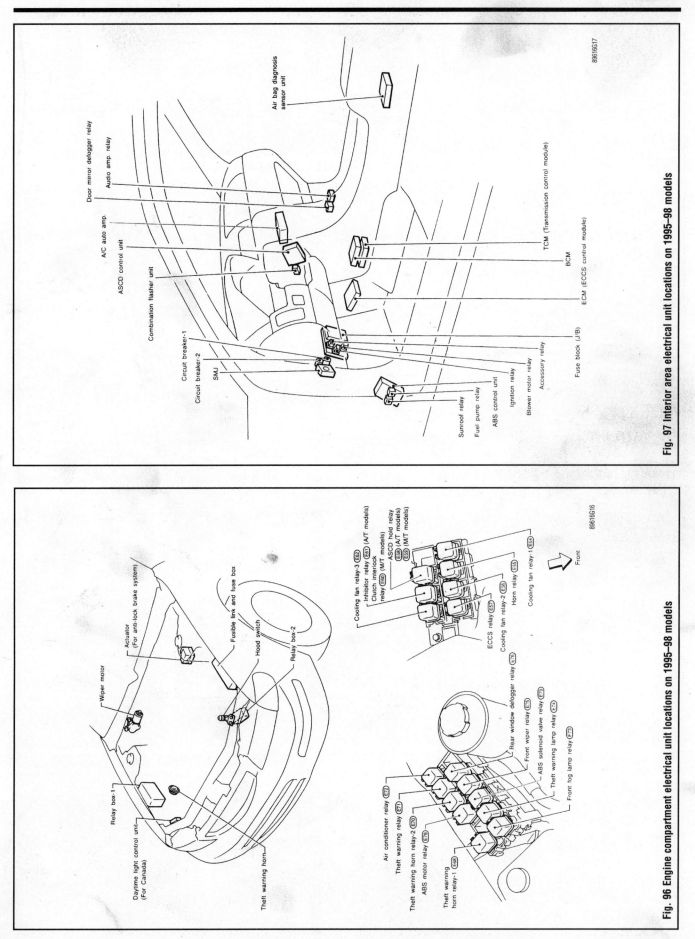

Fig. 97 Interior area electrical unit locations on 1995–98 models

Fig. 96 Engine compartment electrical unit locations on 1995–98 models

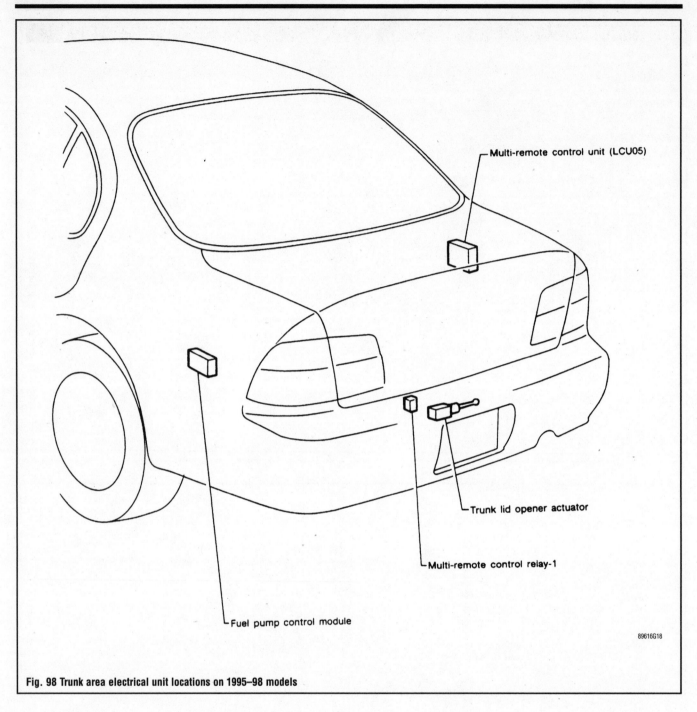

Multi-remote control unit (LCU05)

Trunk lid opener actuator

Multi-remote control relay-1

Fuel pump control module

89616G18

Fig. 98 Trunk area electrical unit locations on 1995–98 models

WIRING DIAGRAMS

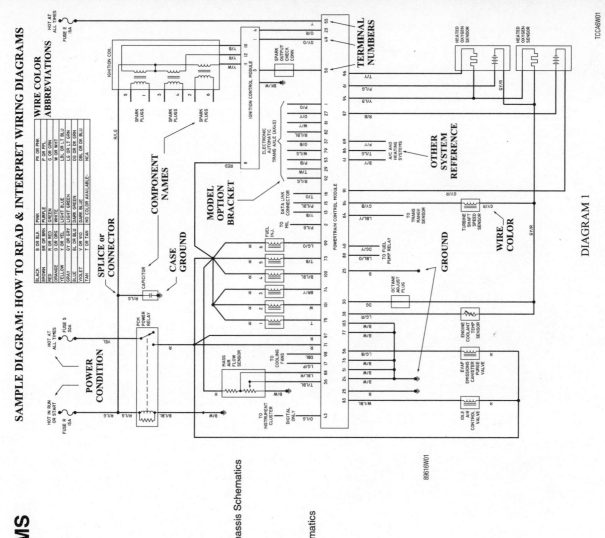

SAMPLE DIAGRAM: HOW TO READ & INTERPRET WIRING DIAGRAMS

DIAGRAM 1

INDEX OF WIRING DIAGRAMS

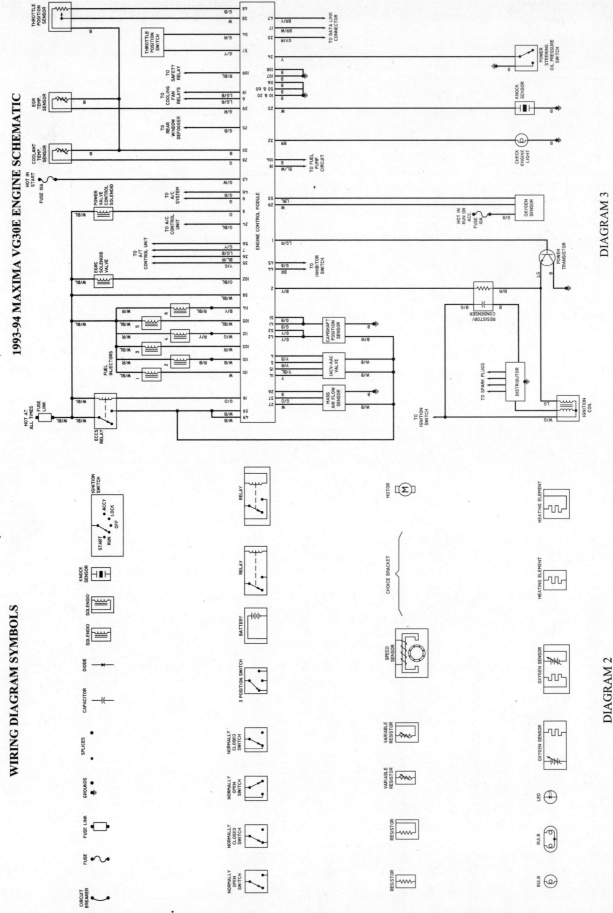

1993-94 MAXIMA VG30E ENGINE SCHEMATIC

DIAGRAM 3

WIRING DIAGRAM SYMBOLS

DIAGRAM 2

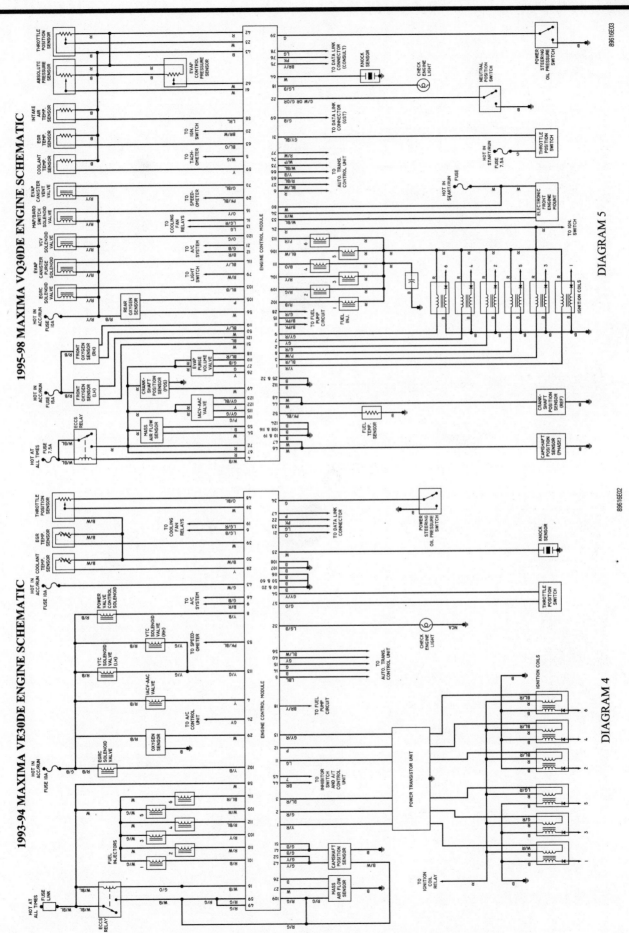

1995-98 MAXIMA VQ30DE ENGINE SCHEMATIC

1993-94 MAXIMA VE30DE ENGINE SCHEMATIC

DIAGRAM 5

DIAGRAM 4

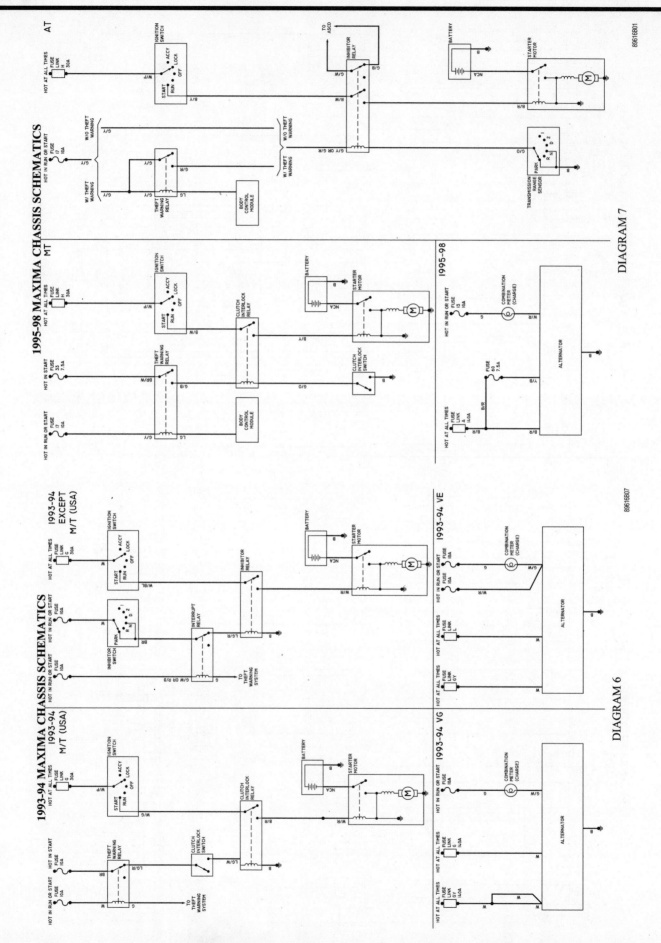

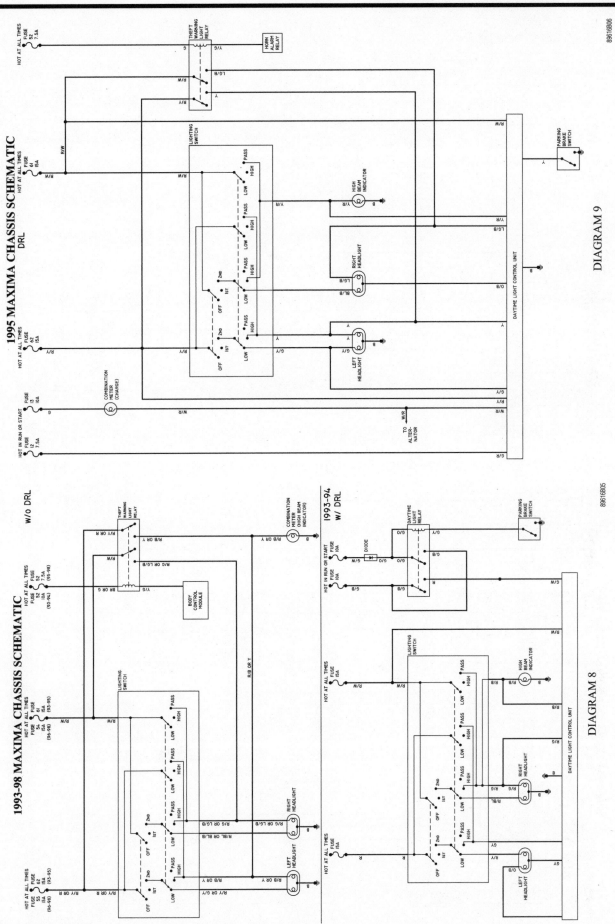

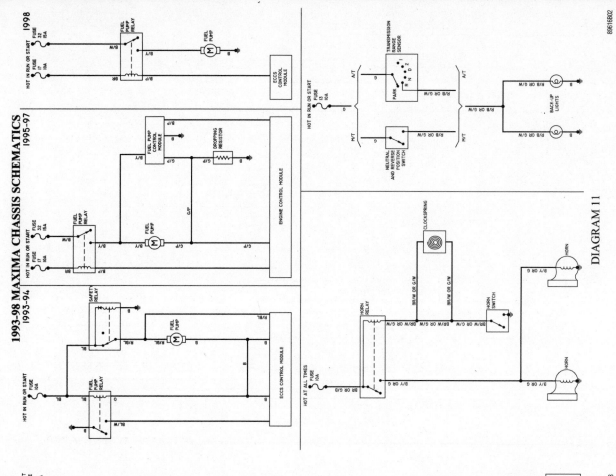

DIAGRAM 11

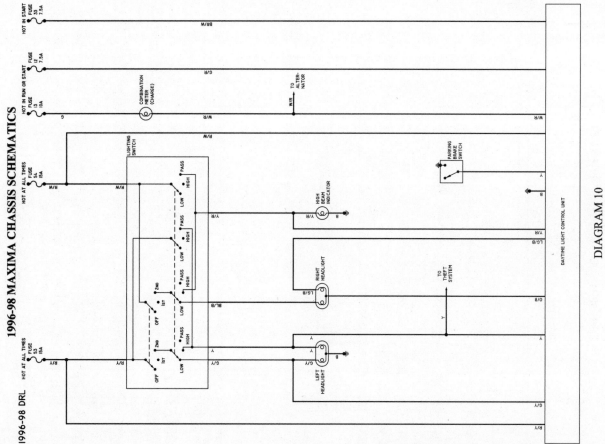

DIAGRAM 10

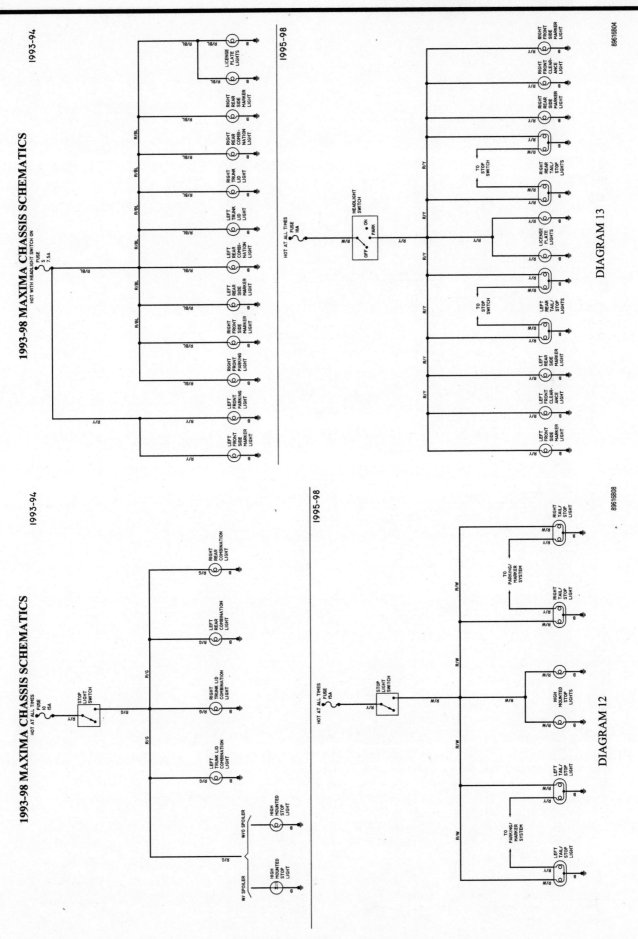

1993-98 MAXIMA CHASSIS SCHEMATICS

DIAGRAM 13

DIAGRAM 12

89616B04

89616B08

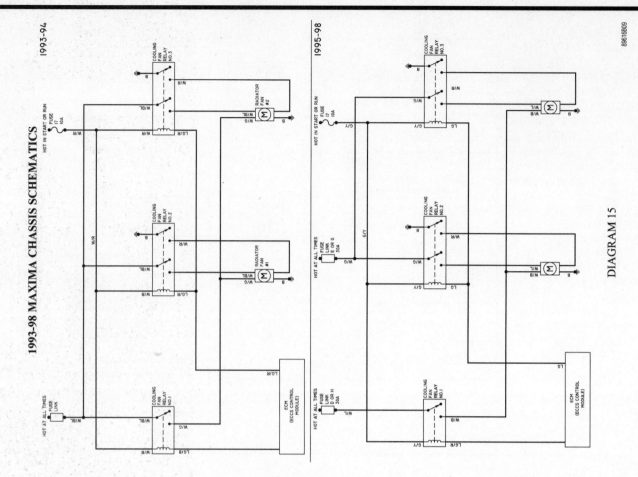

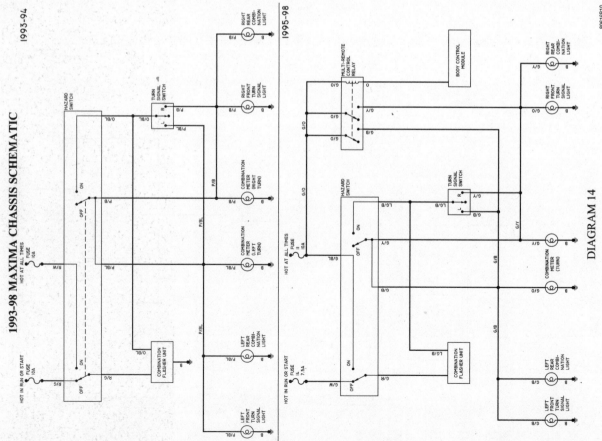

7

DRIVE TRAIN

MANUAL TRANSAXLE

Understanding the Manual Transaxle

Because of the way an internal combustion engine breathes, it can produce torque, or twisting force, only within a narrow speed range. Most modern, overhead valve pushrod engines must turn at about 2500 rpm to produce their peak torque. By 4500 rpm they are producing so little torque that continued increases in engine speed produce no power increases. The torque peak on overhead camshaft engines is generally much higher, but much narrower.

The manual transaxle and clutch are employed to vary the relationship between engine speed and the speed of the wheels so that adequate engine power can be produced under all circumstances. The clutch allows engine torque to be applied to the transaxle input shaft gradually, due to mechanical slippage. Consequently, the vehicle may be started smoothly from a full stop. The transaxle changes the ratio between the rotating speeds of the engine and the wheels by the use of gears. The gear ratios allow full engine power to be applied to the wheels during acceleration at low speeds and at highway/passing speeds.

In a front wheel drive transaxle, power is usually transmitted from the input shaft to a mainshaft or output shaft located slightly beneath and to the side of the input shaft. The gears of the mainshaft mesh with gears on the input shaft, allowing power to be carried from one to the other. All forward gears are in constant mesh and are free from rotating with the shaft unless the synchronizer and clutch is engaged. Shifting from one gear to the next causes one of the gears to be freed from rotating with the shaft and locks another to it. Gears are locked and unlocked by internal dog clutches which slide between the center of the gear and the shaft. The forward gears employ synchronizers; friction members which smoothly bring gear and shaft to the same speed before the toothed dog clutches are engaged.

Back-up Light Switch

REMOVAL & INSTALLATION

▶ **See Figure 1**

The back-up lamp/neutral position switch is located at the bottom of the transaxle. The switch connector is located at the top of the transaxle, with the wire running down the side of the case.
1. Raise and safely support the vehicle.
2. Disconnect the switch electrical harness.

➡**Before removing the switch, place a drain pan beneath the transaxle to catch dripping fluid.**

3. Unfasten the screw and remove the switch from the transaxle.
To install:
4. Position the switch in the transaxle and tighten its attaching bolt to 24–36 inch lbs. (3–4 Nm).
5. Connect the switch electrical harness.
6. Lower the vehicle.

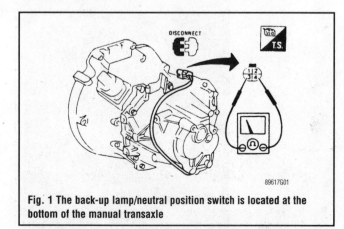

Fig. 1 The back-up lamp/neutral position switch is located at the bottom of the manual transaxle

Manual Transaxle Assembly

REMOVAL & INSTALLATION

▶ **See Figures 2 thru 7**

1. Disonnect the negative, then the positive battery cables.
2. Remove the battery and battery bracket.
3. Remove the air cleaner box and mass air flow sensor.
4. Remove the air duct.
5. Remove the clutch operating cylinder from the transaxle.
6. Remove the starter.
7. Disconnect the back-up lamp switch harness connector.
8. Remove the crankshaft position sensor.

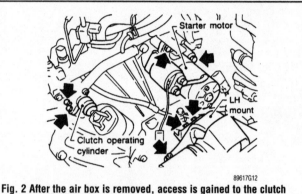

Fig. 2 After the air box is removed, access is gained to the clutch operating cylinder and starter

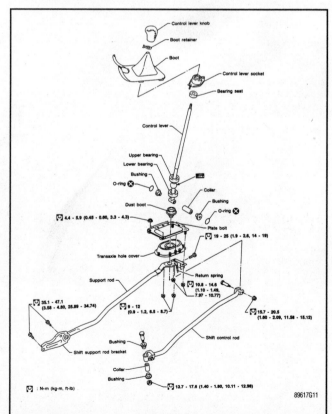

Fig. 3 Exploded view of the 1995–96 manual shifter assembly. Other models similar

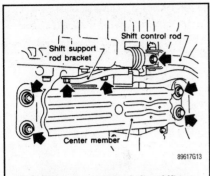
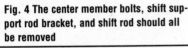

Fig. 4 The center member bolts, shift support rod bracket, and shift rod should all be removed

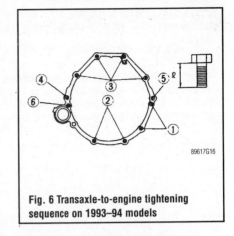

Fig. 5 The engine must be safely supported when the transaxle is removed from the vehicle

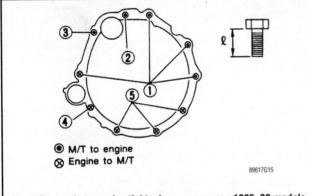

Fig. 6 Transaxle-to-engine tightening sequence on 1993–94 models

Fig. 7 Transaxle-to-engine tightening sequence on 1995–98 models

➡**Take care not to damage the sensor tip.**

9. Unplug the speed sensor, position switch and ground harness connectors.
10. Remove the shift control rod and support bracket from the transaxle. Refer to the illustrations.
11. Drain and recycle the gear oil from the transaxle.

➡**Take note of the condition of the oil as it is draining. Milky oil (which shows up as streaks of white) indicates the presence of moisture. Silvery streaks in the oil indicate the presence of metal. If either condition exists, serious problems may exist inside the transaxle.**

12. Remove the halfshafts, as described later in this section.
13. Support the engine by placing a jack beneath the oil pan. Use a piece of wood between the jack and oil pan as a cushion.
14. Using a transmission jack, support the transaxle.
15. Remove the center member, and the left engine mount.

✳✳ CAUTION

Be certain the engine is secure before removing the engine/transaxle mounts.

16. Raise the jacks slightly to access the lower housing bolts.
17. Remove the lower housing bolts and lower the jacks.
18. Remove the upper housing bolts.
19. Pull the transaxle away from the engine and carefully lower it from the vehicle.
To install:
20. Position the transaxle on the engine and install the transaxle-to-engine attaching bolts. Refer to the charts for torque specifications.

➡**Bolts are of varying lengths. Install the bolts in their proper positions.**

21. For 1993–1994 vehicles, tighten the bolts as follows:
• 1—0.98 in. (25 mm.) bolts tighten to 12–15 ft. lbs. (16–21 Nm.).

• 2—1.10 in. (28 mm.) bolts tighten to 22–30 ft. lbs. (30–40 Nm.).
• 3—2.24 in. (57 mm.) bolts tighten to 29–36 ft. lbs. (39–49 Nm.).
• 4—2.24 in. (57 mm.) bolts tighten to 29–36 ft. lbs. (39–49 Nm.).
• 5—2.52 in. (64 mm.) bolts tighten to 29–36 ft. lbs. (39–49 Nm.).
• 6—1.18 in. (30 mm.) bolts tighten to 15–20 ft. lbs. (21–27 Nm.).
• Gusset-to-engine bolts tighten to 22–30 ft. lbs. (30–40 Nm.).
22. For 1995–98 vehicles, tighten the bolts as follows:
• 1—1.77 in. (52 mm.) bolts tighten to 51–59 ft. lbs. (70–79 Nm.).
• 2—1.18 in. (65 mm.) bolts tighten to 51–59 ft. lbs. (70–79 Nm.).
• 3—1.57 in. (124 mm.) bolts tighten to 51–59 ft. lbs. (70–79 Nm.).
• 4—1.77 in. (40 mm.) bolts tighten to 26–35 ft. lbs. (35–47 Nm.).
• 5—3.15 in. (40 mm.) bolts tighten to 26–35 ft. lbs. (35–47 Nm.).
23. The remainder of the installation procedure is the reverse of removal.

Halfshafts

REMOVAL & INSTALLATION

▸ **See Figures 8 thru 24**

✳✳ WARNING

If the vehicle is going to be removed while the halfshafts are out of the vehicle, use 2 outer CV joints and install them in the hubs to obtain the proper torque to the front wheel bearings. Rolling the vehicle without outer CV joints installed will destroy the front wheel bearings.

➡**To remove the left halfshaft on vehicles equipped with an automatic transaxle, the right halfshaft must be removed first.**

1. Raise and safely support the vehicle.
2. Remove the wheel.
3. Remove the locknut that attaches the outer CV joint.

Fig. 8 This cracked CV joint boot has allowed most of the grease to escape; if not replaced promptly, the CV joint will quickly fail

➡The brake caliper does not need to be removed to perform this service. Do not twist or stretch the brake hose when moving components.

4. Disconnect the lower suspension arm from the wheel hub by unbolting the ball joint.

➡Later models use a unified lower ball joint/suspension arm assembly. The ball joint can be separated from the wheel hub by tapping a hammer on the area where the ball joint is mounted to the hub (after the bolt is removed) while applying downward force to the suspension arm.

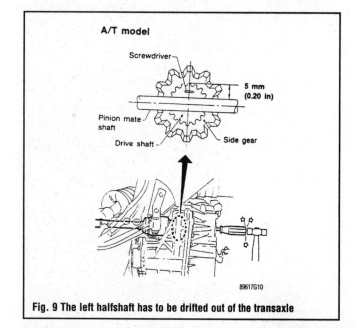

Fig. 9 The left halfshaft has to be drifted out of the transaxle

If the ball joint will not pop out, the use of a ball joint separator is recommended.

5. Separate the halfshaft from the knuckle by tapping it lightly. If it is hard to remove, a halfshaft removal tool can be mounted on the wheel studs to press the halfshaft from the hub.

6. If removing the right halfshaft, remove the bolts securing the support bearing.

7. Carefully pry the support bearing out of its housing. The support bearing will not fully slide out of its housing until the halfshaft is removed from the transaxle.

8. Remove the halfshafts from the transaxle by gently prying them from the housing.

9. On automatic transaxles, the left halfshaft should be removed by using a suitable tool as shown in the illustration. Use caution when performing this procedure, as the gear and pinion mate shaft are easily damaged.

To install:

10. Using an oil seal cover tool to protect the inner diameter of the oil seal, install the halfshafts.

11. Properly align the serrations and then withdraw the oil seal cover tool.

12. Push on the halfshaft to press the circlip on the halfshaft into the groove on the side gear.

13. After inserting the halfshaft, attempt to gently pull the halfshaft out of the transaxle. If it pulls out, the circlip is not properly meshed with the side gear.

14. If installing the right halfshaft, tighten the bolts holding the support bearing.

15. Connect the tie rod ball joint.

16. Connect the lower ball joint to the suspension arm with the three bolts. Tighten the bolts to 56–80 ft. lbs. (118–147 Nm.)

17. The ball joint nut on later models should be tightened to 46–56 ft. lbs. (62–76 Nm.).

18. Install the wheel bearing locknut. Tighten the locknut to 174–231 ft. lbs. (235–314 Nm).

19. Install the wheel.

20. Lower the vehicle.

Fig. 10 Straighten the cotter pin and pull it out . . .

Fig. 11 . . . and remove the adjusting cap and insulator

Fig. 12 Use a large prybar to hold the hub in place while loosening the nut

Fig. 13 When installing the halfshaft, be sure to lubricate the washer with oil to obtain a proper torque reading

Fig. 14 The ball joint is attached to the suspension arm by three bolts which are unified with a plate

Fig. 15 After the ball joint is removed from the suspension arm, the wheel hub and caliper assembly can be pulled away

Fig. 16 Use a punch to tap the outer CV joint from the hub. Do not hit it directly with a hammer; the threads will be distorted

Fig. 17 The halfshaft can now be removed from the vehicle

Fig. 18 Carefully remove the support bearing from the bracket

Fig. 19 Apply anti-seize compound to the support bearing to prevent rust build-up

Fig. 20 Using a wire brush, clean any surface rust build-up from the bearing . . .

Fig. 21 . . . and the support bracket

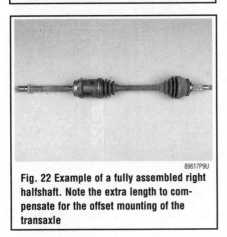

Fig. 22 Example of a fully assembled right halfshaft. Note the extra length to compensate for the offset mounting of the transaxle

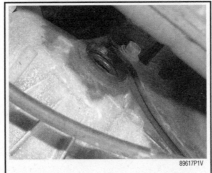

Fig. 23 This seal on the transaxle is leaking; while the halfshaft is removed, replacement is recommended

Fig. 24 The front wheel bearing seal is pressed into the wheel hub and can be changed separately of the bearing

CV-JOINT OVERHAUL

♦ See Figure 25

Transaxle Side

♦ See Figures 26, 27 and 28

1. Remove the boot bands.
2. Matchmark the slide joint housing and inner race, prior to separating the joint assembly.
3. Pry off the snap ring and remove the ball cage, inner race and balls as a unit.
4. Remove the snap ring and withdraw the boot.
5. The right halfshaft uses a support bearing with a longer inner CV joint to compensate for the offset of the transaxle. Removing the support bearing from the halfshaft requires a press. Do not attempt to hammer the bearing from the halfshaft.

To assemble:

➡Cover the halfshaft serrations with tape, so as not to damage the boot.

6. Throughly clean all parts in solvent and dry with compressed air. Check parts for evidence of damage, and replace as necessary.
7. Install the boot and new boot band on the halfshaft.
8. Install a new inner snap ring.
9. Install the ball cage, inner race and balls as a unit. Confirm that the matchmarks are aligned.
10. Install a new outer snap ring.
11. Pack the CV joint with 5.0–6.0 ounces of grease.
12. Ensure that the boot is properly installed on the halfshaft groove.
13. Set the boot so that it does not swell or deform when its length is 3.82–3.90 in. (97–99mm).
14. Lock the new boot bands securely.

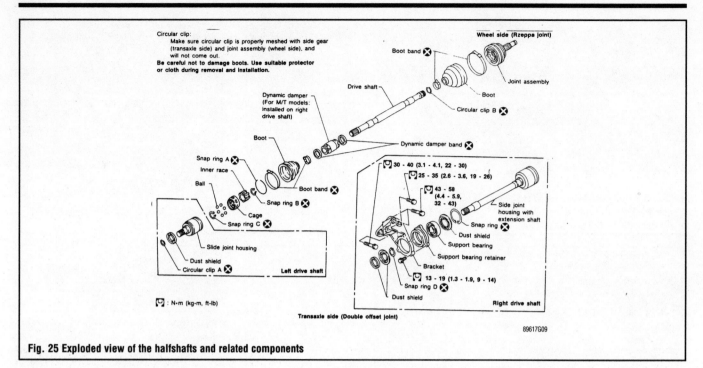

Fig. 25 Exploded view of the halfshafts and related components

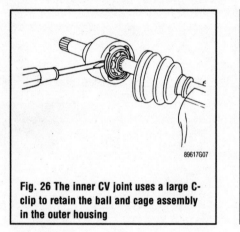

Fig. 26 The inner CV joint uses a large C-clip to retain the ball and cage assembly in the outer housing

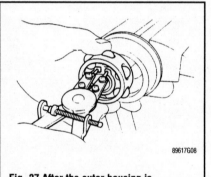

Fig. 27 After the outer housing is removed, the ball and cage assembly can slide from the shaft by removing the C-clip

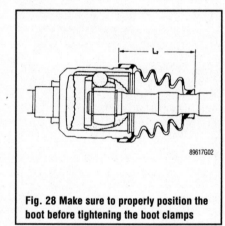

Fig. 28 Make sure to properly position the boot before tightening the boot clamps

Wheel Side

▶ **See Figures 29 and 30**

The joint on the wheel side cannot be disassembled.

1. Prior to separating the joint assembly, matchmark the halfshaft and joint assembly.

2. Separate the joint using a slide hammer.

3. Remove the boot bands.

To assemble:

4. Throughly clean all parts in solvent and dry with compressed air. Check parts for evidence of damage and replace as necessary.

➡**Cover the halfshaft serrations with tape, so as not to damage the boot.**

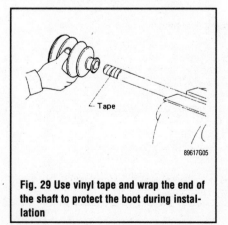

Fig. 29 Use vinyl tape and wrap the end of the shaft to protect the boot during installation

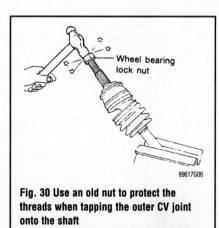

Fig. 30 Use an old nut to protect the threads when tapping the outer CV joint onto the shaft

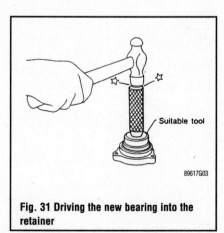

Fig. 31 Driving the new bearing into the retainer

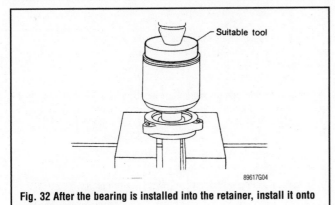

Fig. 32 After the bearing is installed into the retainer, install it onto the shaft with a press

5. Install the boot and small boot band on the halfshaft.
6. Set the joint assembly onto the halfshaft and align the matchmarks.
7. Attach the joint assembly to the halfshaft by lightly tapping the serrated end with a plastic hammer.

➡**Using a metal hammer may damage the threads on the end of the joint.**

CLUTCH

Understanding the Clutch

♦ See Figure 33

✳✳ CAUTION

The clutch driven disc may contain asbestos, which has been determined to be a cancer causing agent. Never clean clutch surfaces with compressed air! Avoid inhaling any dust from any clutch surface! When cleaning clutch surfaces, use a commercially available brake cleaning fluid.

The purpose of the clutch is to disconnect and connect engine power at the transaxle. A vehicle at rest requires a lot of engine torque to get all that weight moving. An internal combustion engine does not develop a high starting torque (unlike steam engines) so it must be allowed to operate without any load until it builds up enough torque to move the vehicle. Torque increases with engine rpm. The clutch allows the engine to build up torque by physically disconnecting the engine from the transaxle, relieving the engine of any load or resistance.

The transfer of engine power to the transaxle (the load) must be smooth and gradual; if it weren't, drive line components would wear out or break quickly. This gradual power transfer is made possible by gradually releasing the clutch pedal. The clutch disc and pressure plate are the connecting link between the engine and transaxle. When the clutch pedal is released, the disc and plate contact each other (the clutch is engaged) physically joining the engine and transaxle. When the pedal is pushed inward, the disc and plate separate (the clutch is disengaged) disconnecting the engine from the transaxle.

Most clutches utilize a single plate, dry friction disc with a diaphragm-style spring pressure plate. The clutch disc has a splined hub which attaches the disc to the input shaft. The disc has friction material where it contacts the flywheel and pressure plate. Torsion springs on the disc help absorb engine torque pulses. The pressure plate applies pressure to the clutch disc, holding it tight against the surface of the flywheel. The clutch operating mechanism consists of a release bearing, fork and cylinder assembly.

The release fork and actuating linkage transfer pedal motion to the release bearing. In the engaged position (pedal released) the diaphragm spring holds the pressure plate against the clutch disc, so engine torque is transmitted to the input shaft. When the clutch pedal is depressed, the release bearing pushes the diaphragm spring center toward the flywheel. The diaphragm spring pivots the fulcrum, relieving the load on the pressure plate. Steel spring

8. Pack the CV joint with 3.5–4.0 ounces of grease.
9. Ensure that the boot is properly installed on the halfshaft groove.
10. Set the boot so that it does not swell or deform when its length is 3.327–3.406 in. (84.5–86.5mm).
11. Lock the new boot bands securely.

Support Bearing

♦ See Figures 31 and 32

1. Remove the dust shield.
2. Remove the snap ring.
3. Press the support bearing assembly from the halfshaft using a hydraulic press and the appropriate adapters.
4. Separate the support bearing from the retainer using a bearing driver.

To assemble:
5. Throughly clean all parts in solvent and dry with compressed air. Check the parts for evidence of damage.
6. Ensure that the wheel bearing rolls freely and is free from noise, cracks, pitting and wear.
7. Check the support bearing bracket for cracks, and replace as necessary.
8. Install the bearing into the retainer using a bearing driver.
9. Press the support bearing onto the shaft using a hydraulic press.
10. Install the new snap ring.
11. Install the new dust shield.

straps riveted to the clutch cover lift the pressure plate from the clutch disc, disengaging the engine drive from the transaxle and enabling the gears to be changed.

The clutch is operating properly if:
1. It will stall the engine when released with the vehicle held stationary.
2. The shift lever can be moved freely between 1st and reverse gears when the vehicle is stationary and the clutch disengaged.

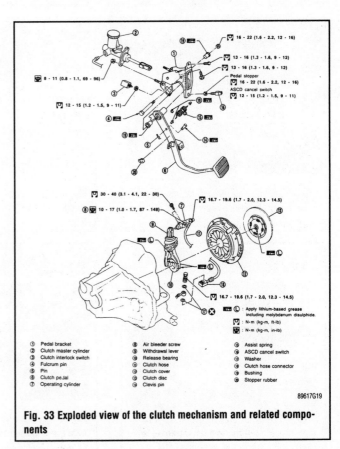

Fig. 33 Exploded view of the clutch mechanism and related components

✳✳ CAUTION

The clutch driven disc may contain asbestos, which has been determined to be a cancer causing agent. Never clean clutch surfaces with compressed air! Avoid inhaling any dust from any clutch surface! When cleaning clutch surfaces, use a commercially available brake cleaning fluid.

Driven Disc And Pressure Plate

REMOVAL & INSTALLATION

♦ See Figures 34 thru 47

1. Remove the transmission/transaxle from the engine.
2. Insert a clutch alignment tool all the way into the clutch disc hub. This must be done to support the weight of the clutch disc during removal.

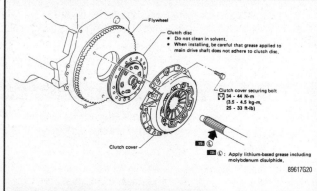

Fig. 34 Exploded view of the clutch assembly

3. Matchmark the pressure plate/flywheel relationship for installation reference.
4. Loosen the pressure plate bolts in sequence, a turn at a time.
5. Remove the pressure plate and clutch disc.

To install:

6. Inspect all components and replace as necessary.

➡The clutch cover and pressure plate are balanced as an assembly. If replacement of either part becomes necessary, replace all components as an assembly (clutch disc, pressure plate and release bearing).

7. Lightly lubricate the transaxle/transmission splines with grease.
8. Install the disc on the splines and slide it back and forth a few times. Remove the disc and remove any excess grease.

➡Be sure no grease contacts the disc or pressure plate.

9. Remove the release mechanism from the transmission/transaxle housing.
10. Lubricate the bearing sleeve inside groove, the contact point of the withdrawal lever and bearing sleeve, the contact surface of the lever ball pin and the lever with a lithium based molybdenum disulfide grease.
11. Install the clutch disc on the alignment tool.
12. Install the pressure plate and evenly tighten the bolts to 25–33 ft. lbs. (34–44 Nm).
13. Remove the clutch alignment tool.
14. Install the transmission/transaxle.
15. Bleed the clutch hydraulic system.
16. If necessary, adjust the clutch pedal.

ADJUSTMENTS

Pedal Height

♦ See Figure 48

1. Adjust the pedal height by using the ASCD (cruise control) cancel switch.
2. Pedal height should be 6.50–6.89 in (165–175 mm.).

Fig. 35 Loosen and remove the clutch and pressure plate bolts evenly, a little at a time . . .

Fig. 36 . . . then carefully remove the clutch and pressure plate assembly from the flywheel

Fig. 37 Check across the flywheel surface; it should be flat

Fig. 38 If necessary, lock the flywheel in place and remove the retaining bolts . . . .

Fig. 39 . . . then remove the flywheel from the crankshaft in order to replace it or have it machined

Fig. 40 Upon installation, it is usually a good idea to apply a threadlocking compound to the flywheel bolts

Fig. 41 Be sure that the flywheel surface is clean, before installing the clutch

Fig. 42 Install a clutch alignment arbor, to align the clutch assembly during installation

Fig. 43 Clutch plate and pressure plate installed with the alignment arbor in place

Fig. 44 The pressure plate-to-flywheel bolt holes should align

Fig. 45 You may want to use a threadlocking compound on the clutch assembly bolts

Fig. 46 Be sure to use a torque wrench to tighten all bolts

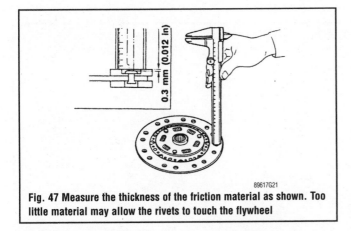

Fig. 47 Measure the thickness of the friction material as shown. Too little material may allow the rivets to touch the flywheel

➥After the pedal height and free play are properly adjusted, Make sure the clutch interlock switch is in the fully depressed position when the pedal is at the top of its stroke.

Free-Play

♦ See Figure 48

1. Loosen the locknut and adjust the pedal free-play by means of the master cylinder pushrod.
2. Pedal free-play should be 0 .039–0.118 in. (1.0–3.0 mm.) for 1993–96 models and 0.35–.063 in. (9–16 mm.) for 1997–98 models.
3. Tighten the locknut securely.

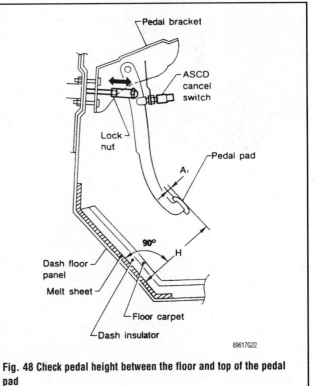

Fig. 48 Check pedal height between the floor and top of the pedal pad

Clutch Interlock Switch

♦ See Figure 49

1. Loosen the locknut and adjust the clearance between the stopper rubber and the clutch interlock switch threads.

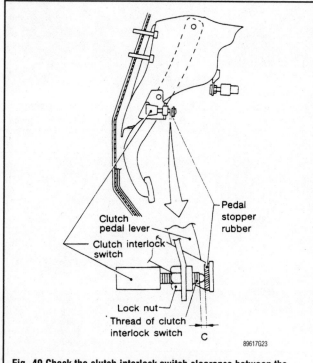

Fig. 49 Check the clutch interlock switch clearance between the stopper rubber and the clutch interlock switch threads

2. Clearance should be 0.004–.039 in. (0.1–1.0 mm.)
3. Tighten the locknut securely.

Master Cylinder

♦ See Figure 50

REMOVAL & INSTALLATION

1. Disconnect the clutch pedal arm from the pushrod clevis in the passenger compartment.
2. Disconnect and cap the hydraulic line at the clutch master cylinder.

✳✳ WARNING

Any brake fluid that is removed from the system should be discarded. Also, do not allow any brake fluid to come in contact with a painted surface; it will damage the paint. Place a rag under the cylinder to absorb any spilled fluid.

3. Remove the nuts attaching the master cylinder to the firewall.
4. Remove the master cylinder from the engine compartment.
To install:
5. Install the master cylinder and tighten the attaching nuts to 5–8 ft. lbs. (8–11 Nm).
6. Connect the clutch hydraulic line to the master cylinder. Tighten the fitting securely.
7. Connect the clutch pedal arm to the pushrod clevis.
8. Bleed the clutch hydraulic system.

Slave Cylinder

REMOVAL & INSTALLATION

♦ See Figure 51

1. Raise and safely support the vehicle.

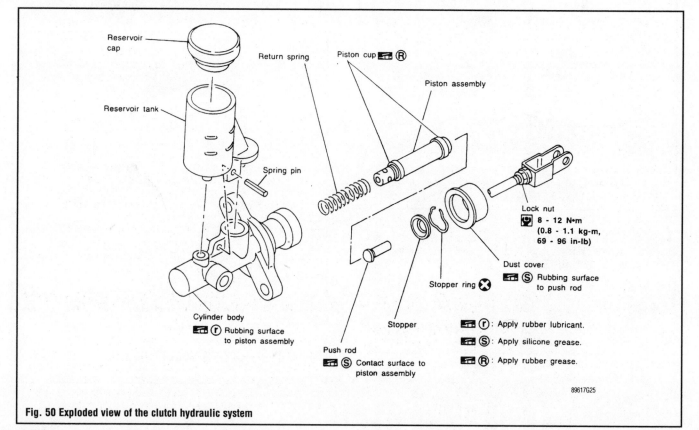

Fig. 50 Exploded view of the clutch hydraulic system

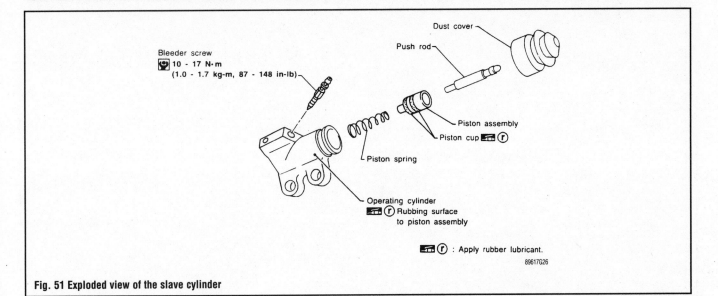

Fig. 51 Exploded view of the slave cylinder

2. Disconnect and cap the hydraulic line at the slave cylinder.
3. Remove the nuts attaching the slave cylinder to the transmission/transaxle.
4. Remove the slave cylinder.

To install:
5. Install the slave cylinder and tighten the attaching nuts to 22–30 ft. lbs. (30–40 Nm).
6. Connect the clutch hydraulic line to the slave cylinder. Tighten the fitting securely.
7. Bleed the clutch hydraulic system.

HYDRAULIC SYSTEM BLEEDING

▶ See Figure 52

❋ CAUTION

Brake fluid contains polyglycol ethers and polyglycols. Avoid contact with the eyes and wash your hands thoroughly after handling brake fluid. If you do get brake fluid in your eyes, flush your eyes with clean, running water for 15 minutes. If eye irritation persists, or if you have taken brake fluid internally, IMMEDIATELY seek medical assistance.

❋❋ WARNING

Clean, high quality brake fluid is essential to the safe and proper operation of the clutch hydraulic system. You should always buy the highest quality brake fluid that is available. If the clutch hydraulic system becomes contaminated, drain and flush the system, then refill the master cylinder with new fluid. Never reuse any brake fluid. Any brake fluid that is removed from the system should be discarded. Also, do not allow any brake fluid to come in contact with a painted surface; it will damage the paint.

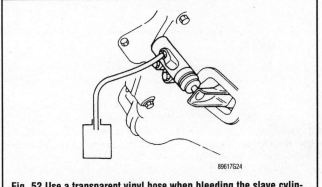

Fig. 52 Use a transparent vinyl hose when bleeding the slave cylinder so the air bubbles can be seen

1. Check the level of fluid in the clutch master cylinder reservoir and fill to the specified level. During the bleeding process, continue to check and replenish the reservoir to prevent the fluid level from getting lower than ½ the specified level.
2. Remove the dust cap from the bleeder screw on the clutch slave cylinder and connect a clear tube to the bleeder screw. Insert the other end of the tube into a clean, clear plastic or glass container half filled with brake fluid.
3. Pump the clutch pedal SLOWLY several times.
4. Hold the clutch pedal down and loosen the bleeder screw.
5. Tighten the bleeder screw and release the clutch pedal gradually.
6. Repeat until all evidence of air bubbles completely disappears from the brake fluid being pumped out through the tube.
7. When the air is completely removed, securely tighten the bleeder screw and replace the dust cap.
8. Check the level of fluid in the clutch master cylinder reservoir and fill as necessary.
9. Depress the clutch pedal several times to check the operation of the clutch hydraulic system. Check for leaks.

AUTOMATIC TRANSAXLE

Understanding the Automatic Transaxle

▶ See Figure 53

The automatic transaxle allows engine torque and power to be transmitted to the front wheels within a narrow range of engine operating speeds. It will allow the engine to turn fast enough to produce plenty of power and torque at very low speeds, while keeping it at a sensible rpm at high vehicle speeds

(and it does this job without driver assistance). The transaxle uses a light fluid as the medium for the transmission of power. This fluid also works in the operation of various hydraulic control circuits and as a lubricant. Because the transaxle fluid performs all of these functions, trouble within the unit can easily travel from one part to another. For this reason, and because of the complexity and unusual operating principles of the transaxle, a very sound understanding of the basic principles of operation will simplify troubleshooting.

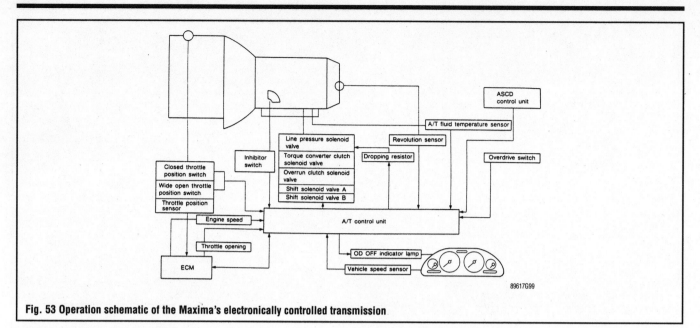

Fig. 53 Operation schematic of the Maxima's electronically controlled transmission

TORQUE CONVERTER

▶ **See Figure 54**

The torque converter replaces the conventional clutch. It has three functions:

1. It allows the engine to idle with the vehicle at a standstill, even with the transaxle in gear.

2. It allows the transaxle to shift from range-to-range smoothly, without requiring that the driver close the throttle during the shift.

3. It multiplies engine torque to an increasing extent as vehicle speed drops and throttle opening is increased. This has the effect of making the transaxle more responsive and reduces the amount of shifting required.

The torque converter is a metal case which is shaped like a sphere that has been flattened on opposite sides. It is bolted to the rear end of the engine's crankshaft. Generally, the entire metal case rotates at engine speed and serves as the engine's flywheel.

The case contains three sets of blades. One set is attached directly to the case. This set forms the torus or pump. Another set is directly connected to the output shaft, and forms the turbine. The third set is mounted on a hub which, in turn, is mounted on a stationary shaft through a one-way clutch. This third set is known as the stator.

A pump, which is driven by the converter hub at engine speed, keeps the torque converter full of transmission fluid at all times. Fluid flows continuously through the unit to provide cooling.

Under low speed acceleration, the torque converter functions as follows:

The torus is turning faster than the turbine. It picks up fluid at the center of the converter and, through centrifugal force, slings it outward. Since the outer edge of the converter moves faster than the portions at the center, the fluid picks up speed.

The fluid then enters the outer edge of the turbine blades. It then travels back toward the center of the converter case along the turbine blades. In impinging upon the turbine blades, the fluid loses the energy picked up in the torus.

If the fluid was now returned directly into the torus, both halves of the converter would have to turn at approximately the same speed at all times, and torque input and output would both be the same.

In flowing through the torus and turbine, the fluid picks up two types of flow, or flow in two separate directions. It flows through the turbine blades, and it spins with the engine. The stator, whose blades are stationary when the vehicle is being accelerated at low speeds, converts one type of flow into another. Instead of allowing the fluid to flow straight back into the torus, the stator's curved blades turn the fluid almost 90° toward the direction of rotation of the engine. Thus the fluid does not flow as fast toward the torus, but is already spinning when the torus picks it up. This has the effect of allowing the torus to turn much faster than the turbine. This difference in speed may be compared to the difference in speed between the smaller and larger gears in any gear train. The result is that engine power output is higher, and engine torque is multiplied.

As the speed of the turbine increases, the fluid spins faster and faster in the direction of engine rotation. As a result, the ability of the stator to redirect the fluid flow is reduced. Under cruising conditions, the stator is eventually forced to rotate on its one-way clutch in the direction of engine rotation. Under these conditions, the torque converter begins to behave almost like a solid shaft, with the torus and turbine speeds being almost equal.

PLANETARY GEARBOX

▶ **See Figures 55, 56 and 57**

The ability of the torque converter to multiply engine torque is limited. Also, the unit tends to be more efficient when the turbine is rotating at relatively high speeds. Therefore, a planetary gearbox is used to carry the power output of the turbine to the driveshaft.

Planetary gears function very similarly to conventional transaxle gears. However, their construction is different in that three elements make up one gear system, and, in that all three elements are different from one another. The three elements are: an outer gear that is shaped like a hoop, with teeth cut into the inner surface; a sun gear, mounted on a shaft and located at the very center of the outer gear; and a set of three planet gears, held by pins in a ring-like planet carrier, meshing with both the sun gear and the outer gear. Either the outer gear or the sun gear may be held stationary, providing more than one possible torque multiplication factor for each set of gears. Also, if all three gears are forced to rotate at the same speed, the gearset forms, in effect, a solid shaft.

Most automatics use the planetary gears to provide various reductions ratios. Bands and clutches are used to hold various portions of the gearsets to the transaxle case or to the shaft on which they are mounted. Shifting is accomplished, then, by changing the portion of each planetary gearset which is held to the transaxle case or to the shaft.

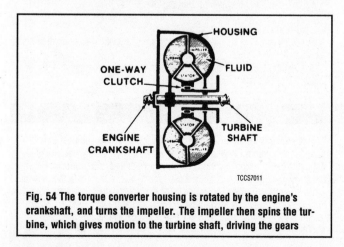

Fig. 54 The torque converter housing is rotated by the engine's crankshaft, and turns the impeller. The impeller then spins the turbine, which gives motion to the turbine shaft, driving the gears

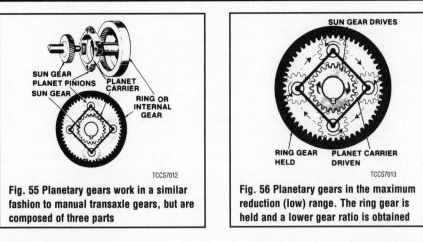

Fig. 55 Planetary gears work in a similar fashion to manual transaxle gears, but are composed of three parts

Fig. 56 Planetary gears in the maximum reduction (low) range. The ring gear is held and a lower gear ratio is obtained

Fig. 57 Planetary gears in the minimum reduction (drive) range. The ring gear is allowed to revolve, providing a higher gear ratio

SERVOS & ACCUMULATORS

▶ **See Figure 58**

The servos are hydraulic pistons and cylinders. They resemble the hydraulic actuators used on many other machines, such as bulldozers. Hydraulic fluid enters the cylinder, under pressure, and forces the piston to move to engage the band or clutches.

The accumulators are used to cushion the engagement of the servos. The transmission fluid must pass through the accumulator on the way to the servo. The accumulator housing contains a thin piston which is sprung away from the discharge passage of the accumulator. When fluid passes through the accumulator on the way to the servo, it must move the piston against spring pressure, and this action smoothes out the action of the servo.

HYDRAULIC CONTROL SYSTEM

The hydraulic pressure used to operate the servos comes from the main transaxle oil pump. This fluid is channeled to the various servos through the shift valves. There is generally a manual shift valve which is operated by the transaxle selector lever and an automatic shift valve for each automatic upshift the transaxle provides.

➡**Many new transaxles are electronically controlled. On these models, electrical solenoids are used to better control the hydraulic fluid. Usually, the solenoids are regulated by an electronic control module.**

There are two pressures which affect the operation of these valves. One is the governor pressure which is effected by vehicle speed. The other is the modulator pressure which is effected by intake manifold vacuum or throttle position. Governor pressure rises with an increase in vehicle speed, and modulator pressure rises as the throttle is opened wider. By responding to these two pressures, the shift valves cause the upshift points to be delayed with increased throttle opening to make the best use of the engine's power output.

Most transaxles also make use of an auxiliary circuit for downshifting. This circuit may be actuated by the throttle linkage the vacuum line which actuates

the modulator, by a cable or by a solenoid. It applies pressure to a special downshift surface on the shift valve or valves.

The transaxle modulator also governs the line pressure, used to actuate the servos. In this way, the clutches and bands will be actuated with a force matching the torque output of the engine.

Neutral Safety Switch

REMOVAL & INSTALLATION

▶ **See Figure 59**

The inhibitor switch is bolted to the transaxle case, behind the shift lever. The switch prevents the engine from being started in any transaxle position except **P** or **N**. It also controls the back-up lights.

1. Raise and safely support the vehicle.
2. Disconnect the manual control linkage from the manual shaft.
3. Remove the switch attaching bolts.
4. Remove the switch from the transaxle.

To install:

5. Mount the switch on the transaxle and hand-tighten the attaching bolts.
6. Adjust the switch and tighten the bolts securely.
7. Connect the manual control linkage to the manual shaft.
8. Adjust the manual control linkage as necessary.
9. Lower the vehicle.

ADJUSTMENT

▶ **See Figure 60**

1. Place the transaxle selector lever in **N**.
2. Loosen the attaching bolts.
3. Insert a 0.16 in. (4mm) diameter aligning pin into the switch, then move the switch until the pin falls into the hole in the rotor.

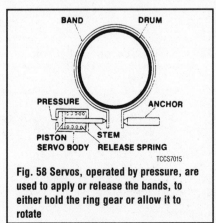

Fig. 58 Servos, operated by pressure, are used to apply or release the bands, to either hold the ring gear or allow it to rotate

Fig. 59 The back-up light switch is integrated into the inhibitor switch

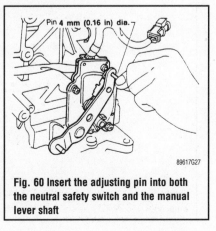

Fig. 60 Insert the adjusting pin into both the neutral safety switch and the manual lever shaft

4. Tighten the attaching bolts securely.
5. Ensure that the engine will start only in **P** or **N**.
6. Ensure that the back-up lights go on only in **R**.

Automatic Transaxle Assembly

REMOVAL & INSTALLATION

▶ **See Figures 61 thru 66**

1. Disconnect the negative, then the positive battery cables.
2. Remove the battery and battery bracket.
3. Remove the air cleaner box and mass air flow sensor.
4. Label and disconnect the transaxle electrical harnesses.
5. Remove the crankshaft position (POS) sensor.
6. Remove the passenger's side mounting bracket from the vehicle.
7. Disconnect the control cable at the transaxle.
8. Drain and recycle the transmission fluid.

➡ **Take note of the condition of the fluid as it is draining. Milky fluid (which shows up as streaks of white) indicates the presence of moisture. Silvery streaks in the fluid indicate the presence of metal. If either condition exists, serious problems may exist inside the transaxle.**

9. Remove the halfshafts.
10. Disconnect and cap the oil cooler pipes.
11. Remove the starter motor.
12. Support the engine by placing a jack beneath the oil pan. Use a piece of wood between the jack and oil pan as a cushion.
13. Remove the center member.
14. Remove the rear plate cover and disconnect the torque converter from the driveplate.
15. Remove the transaxle-to-engine bolts.
16. Pull the transaxle away from the engine and lower it from the vehicle carefully.

To install:

➡ **Bolts are of varying lengths. Install the bolts in their proper positions.**

17. Make certain the torque converter is fully seated in the transaxle.
18. Position the transaxle to the engine and install the transaxle-to-engine attaching bolts.
19. For 1993–94 vehicles with RE4F02A transaxles, tighten the bolts as follows:

- 1—2.36 in. (60 mm.) bolts tighten to 22–30 ft. lbs. (30–40 Nm.).
- 2—1.77 in. (45 mm.) bolts tighten to 29–36 ft. lbs. (39–49 Nm.).
- 3—0.98 in. (25 mm.) bolts tighten to 22–30 ft. lbs. (30–40 Nm.).
- 4—0.79 in. (20 mm.) bolts tighten to 4.3–5.8 ft. lbs. (6–8 Nm.).
- 5—1.10 in. (28 mm.) nuts tighten to 22–30 ft. lbs. (30–40 Nm.).

20. For 1993–94 vehicles with RE4F04V transaxles, tighten the bolts as follows:

- 1—2.36 in. (60 mm.) bolts tighten to 29–36 ft. lbs. (39–49 Nm.).
- 2—2.36 in. (60 mm.) bolts tighten to 29–36 ft. lbs. (39–49 Nm.).
- 3—0.98 in. (25 mm.) bolts tighten to 22–30 ft. lbs. (30–40 Nm.).
- 4—0.98 in. (25 mm.) bolts tighten to 22–30 ft. lbs. (30–40 Nm.).
- 5—tighten nuts to 22–30 ft. lbs. (30–40 Nm.).
- 6—4.53 in. (115 mm.) bolts tighten to 32–43 ft. lbs. (43–58 Nm.).
- Front gusset-to-engine bolts tighten to 22–30 ft. lbs. (30–40 Nm.).

21. For 1995–97 vehicles, tighten all bolts to 51–59 ft. lbs. (70–79 Nm.). Be sure the bolts are in their proper locations.
22. For 1998 vehicles, tighten the bolts as follows:

- 1—1.77 in. (45 mm.) bolts tighten to 29–36 ft. lbs. (39–49 Nm.).
- 2—1.18 in. (30 mm.) bolts tighten to 22–27 ft. lbs. (30–36 Nm.).
- 3—1.57 in. (40 mm.) bolts tighten to 22–27 ft. lbs. (30–36 Nm.).
- 4—1.77 in. (45 mm.) bolts tighten to 54–61 ft. lbs. (74–83 Nm.).
- 5—3.15 in. (80 mm.) bolts tighten to 22–27 ft. lbs. (30–36 Nm.).
- 6—2.56 in. (65 mm.) bolts tighten to 22–27 ft. lbs. (30–36 Nm.).

23. After the transaxle is properly secured to the engine, connect the drive plate to the torque converter. Use thread locking compound on the torque converter bolts, and tighten them securely.
24. The remainder of the installation procedure is the reverse of removal.

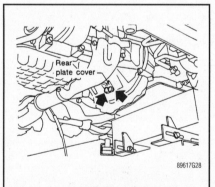

Fig. 61 Remove the rear plate cover to access the torque converter bolts

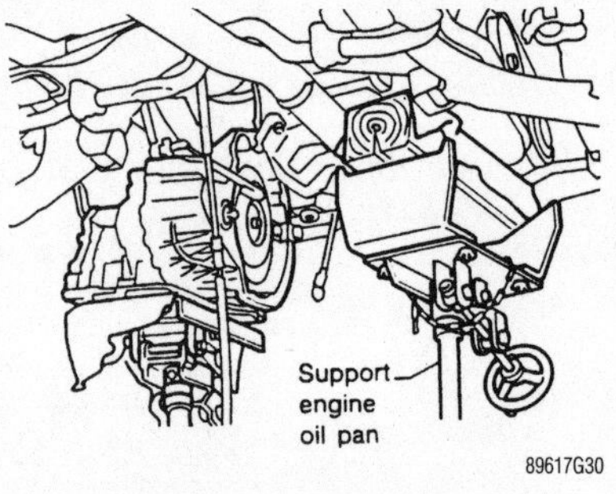

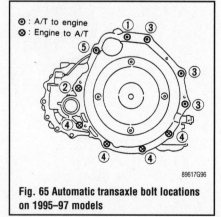

Fig. 62 The engine must be supported on a separate jack when removing the transaxle

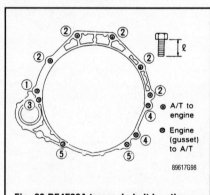

Fig. 63 RE4F02A transaxle bolt locations on 1993–94 models

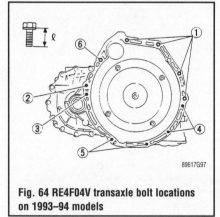

Fig. 64 RE4F04V transaxle bolt locations on 1993–94 models

Fig. 65 Automatic transaxle bolt locations on 1995–97 models

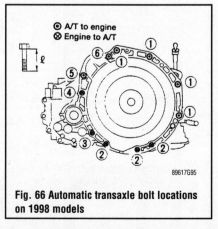

Fig. 66 Automatic transaxle bolt locations on 1998 models

Halfshafts

Halfshaft removal, installation and overhaul is the same for manual and automatic transaxles. Refer to the appropriate section under Manual Transaxle.

TORQUE SPECIFICATIONS

Component	English Specification	Metric Specification
Manual transaxle		
Transaxle to engine bolts		
VG30E and VE30DE engines ①		
.98 in (25mm) bolts	12–15 ft lbs	16–21 Nm
1.10 in. (28mm) bolts	22–30 ft lbs	30–40 Nm
2.24 in. (57mm) bolts	29–36 ft lbs	39–49 Nm
2.52 in. (64mm) bolts	29–36 ft lbs	39–49 Nm
1.18 in. (30mm) bolts	15–20 ft lbs	21–27 Nm
VQ30DE engines ①		
2.05 in (52mm) bolts	51–59 ft lbs	70–79 Nm
2.56 in. (65mm) bolts	51–59 ft lbs	70–79 Nm
4.88 in. (124mm) bolts	51–59 ft lbs	70–79 Nm
1.57 in. (40mm) bolts	26–35 ft lbs	35–47 Nm
Automatic transaxle		
Transaxle to engine bolts		
1993-94 RE4F04A transaxle ①		
2.36 in (60mm) bolts	22–30 ft lbs	30–40 Nm
1.77 in. (45mm) bolts	29–36 ft lbs	39–49 Nm
0.98 in. (25mm) bolts	22–30 ft lbs	30–40 Nm
0.79 in. (20mm) bolts	4.3–5.8 ft lbs	6–8 Nm
1.10 in. (28mm) bolts	22–30 ft lbs	30–40 Nm
1993-94 RE4F04AV transaxle ①		
2.36 in (60mm) bolts	29–36 ft lbs	39–49 Nm
0.98 in. (25mm) bolts	22–30 ft lbs	30–40 Nm
4.53 in. (115mm) bolts	32–43 ft lbs	43–58 Nm
nuts	22–30 ft lbs	30–40 Nm
Gusset to engine bolt	22–30 ft lbs	30–40 Nm
1995-97 transaxles ①	51–59 ft lbs	70–79 Nm
1998 transaxles ①		
1.77 in (45mm) bolts	29–36 ft lbs	39–49 Nm
1.18 in. (30mm) bolts	22–27 ft lbs	30–36 Nm
1.57 in. (40mm) bolts	22–27 ft lbs	30–36 Nm
1.77 in. (45mm) bolts	54–61 ft lbs	74–83 Nm
3.15 in. (80mm) bolts	22–27 ft lbs	30–36 Nm
2.56 in. (65mm) bolts	22–27 ft lbs	30–36 Nm
Transaxle Mounts		
Center member-to-body	57–72 ft lbs	77–98 Nm
Engine mount-to-bracket	57–72 ft lbs	77–98 Nm
Engine mount-to-center member	57–72 ft lbs	77–98 Nm
Transaxle mount	47-54 ft. lbs.	64-74 Nm
Body-to-transaxle bolt ②	32-41 ft. lbs.	43-55 Nm
Clutch		
Pressure plate-to-flywheel	25–33 ft lbs	34–44 Nm
Slave cylinder-to-transaxle	22–30 ft lbs	30–40 Nm
Master cylinder-to-body	5–8 ft lbs	8–11 Nm

TORQUE SPECIFICATIONS

Component	English Specification	Metric Specification
Flywheel/drive plate		
Flywheel-to-crankshaft	61–69 ft lbs	83–93 Nm
Drive plate-to-crankshaft	61–69 ft lbs	83–93 Nm
Torque converter-to-driveplate	33–43 ft lbs	44–59 Nm
Back-up switch		
Manual models	2.2–3.0 ft lbs	3–4 Nm
Automatic models (inhibitor switch)	1.8–2.9 ft lbs	2.5–3.9 Nm
Halfshafts		
Axle nuts	174–231 ft lbs	235–314 Nm
Supprt bearing-to-bracket	9–14 ft lbs	13–19 Nm
Support bearing bracket-to-engine	19–26 ft lbs	25–35 Nm
Suspension/steering		
Suspension arm-to-ball joint	46–56 ft lbs	62–76 Nm
Ball joint nut	56–80 ft lbs	118–147 Nm
Tie rod ball joint nut	22–29 ft lbs	29–39 Nm

① Refer to illustrations for additional information.

② Refer to the illustrations for additional torque specifications.

89617C02

8

SUSPENSION AND STEERING

WHEELS

Wheel Assembly

REMOVAL & INSTALLATION

▶ See Figure 1

1. Park the vehicle on a level surface.
2. Remove the jack, tire iron and, if necessary, the spare tire from their storage compartments.
3. Check the owner's manual or refer to Section 1 of this manual for the jacking points on your vehicle. Then, place the jack in the proper position.
4. If equipped with lug nut trim caps, remove them by either unscrewing or pulling them off the lug nuts, as appropriate. Consult the owner's manual, if necessary.
5. If equipped with a wheel cover or hub cap, insert the tapered end of the tire iron in the groove and pry off the cover.
6. Apply the parking brake and block the diagonally opposite wheel with a wheel chock or two.

➡ Wheel chocks may be purchased at your local auto parts store, or a block of wood cut into wedges may be used. If possible, keep one or two of the chocks in your tire storage compartment, in case any of the tires has to be removed on the side of the road.

7. If equipped with an automatic transaxle, place the selector lever in **P** or Park; with a manual transaxle, place the shifter in Reverse.
8. With the tires still on the ground, use the tire iron/wrench to break the lug nuts loose.

➡ If a nut is stuck, never use heat to loosen it or damage to the wheel and bearings may occur. If the nuts are seized, one or two heavy hammer blows directly on the end of the bolt usually loosens the rust. Be careful, as continued pounding will likely damage the brake drum or rotor.

9. Using the jack, raise the vehicle until the tire is clear of the ground. Support the vehicle safely using jackstands.
10. Remove the lug nuts, then remove the tire and wheel assembly.
To install:
11. Make sure the wheel and hub mating surfaces, as well as the wheel lug studs, are clean and free of all foreign material. Always remove rust from the wheel mounting surface and the brake rotor or drum. Failure to do so may cause the lug nuts to loosen in service.
12. Install the tire and wheel assembly and hand-tighten the lug nuts.
13. Using the tire wrench, tighten all the lug nuts, in a crisscross pattern, until they are snug.
14. Raise the vehicle and withdraw the jackstand, then lower the vehicle.

15. Using a torque wrench, tighten the lug nuts in a crisscross pattern to 72–87 ft. lbs. (98–118 Nm).

✳✳ WARNING

Do not overtighten the lug nuts, as this may cause the wheel studs to stretch or the brake disc (rotor) to warp.

16. If so equipped, install the wheel cover or hub cap. Make sure the valve stem protrudes through the proper opening before tapping the wheel cover into position.
17. If equipped, install the lug nut trim caps by pushing them or screwing them on, as applicable.
18. Remove the jack from under the vehicle, and place the jack and tire iron/wrench in their storage compartments. Remove the wheel chock(s).
19. If you have removed a flat or damaged tire, place it in the storage compartment of the vehicle and take it to your local repair station to have it fixed or replaced as soon as possible.

INSPECTION

Inspect the tires for lacerations, puncture marks, nails and other sharp objects. Repair or replace as necessary. Also check the tires for treadwear and air pressure as outlined in Section 1 of this manual.
Check the wheel assemblies for dents, cracks, rust and metal fatigue. Repair or replace as necessary.

Wheel Lug Studs

REMOVAL & INSTALLATION

With Disc Brakes

▶ See Figures 2, 3 and 4

1. Raise and support the appropriate end of the vehicle safely using jackstands, then remove the wheel.
2. Remove the brake pads and caliper. Support the caliper aside using wire or a coat hanger. For details, please refer to Section 9 of this manual.
3. Remove the outer wheel bearing and lift off the rotor. For details on wheel bearing removal, installation and adjustment, please refer to Section 1 of this manual.
4. Properly support the rotor using press bars, then drive the stud out using an arbor press.

➡ If a press is not available, CAREFULLY drive the old stud out using a blunt drift. MAKE SURE the rotor is properly and evenly supported or it may be damaged.

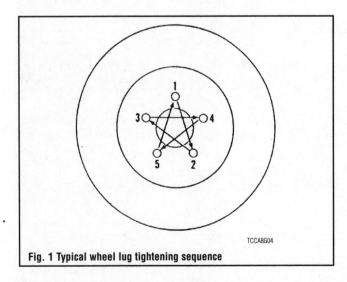

Fig. 1 Typical wheel lug tightening sequence

TCCA8G04

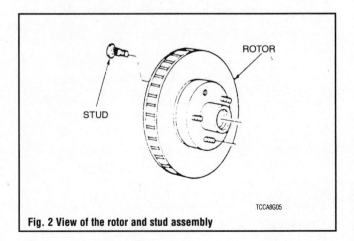

Fig. 2 View of the rotor and stud assembly

TCCA8G05

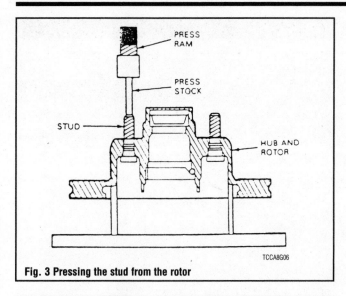

Fig. 3 Pressing the stud from the rotor

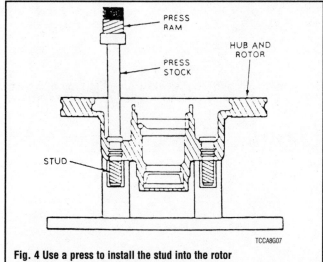

Fig. 4 Use a press to install the stud into the rotor

To install:

5. Clean the stud hole with a wire brush and start the new stud with a hammer and drift pin. Do not use any lubricant or thread sealer.

6. Finish installing the stud with the press.

➡ **If a press is not available, start the lug stud through the bore in the hub, then position about 4 flat washers over the stud and thread the lug nut. Hold the hub/rotor while tightening the lug nut, and the stud should be drawn into position. MAKE SURE THE STUD IS FULLY SEATED, then remove the lug nut and washers.**

7. Install the rotor and adjust the wheel bearings.
8. Install the brake caliper and pads.
9. Install the wheel, then remove the jackstands and carefully lower the vehicle.
10. Tighten the lug nuts to the proper torque.

With Drum Brakes

▶ See Figures 5, 6 and 7

1. Raise the vehicle and safely support it with jackstands, then remove the wheel.
2. Remove the brake drum.
3. If necessary to provide clearance, remove the brake shoes, as outlined in Section 9 of this manual.

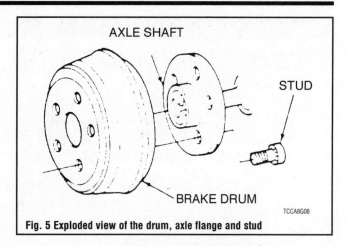

Fig. 5 Exploded view of the drum, axle flange and stud

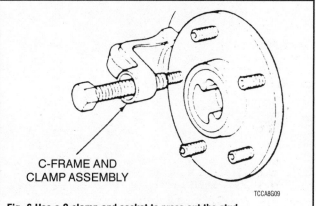

Fig. 6 Use a C-clamp and socket to press out the stud

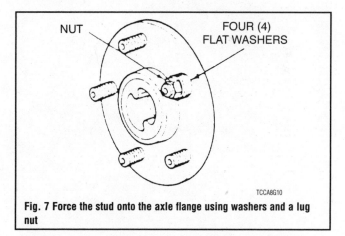

Fig. 7 Force the stud onto the axle flange using washers and a lug nut

4. Using a large C-clamp and socket, press the stud from the axle flange.
5. Coat the serrated part of the stud with liquid soap and place it into the hole.

To install:

6. Position about 4 flat washers over the stud and thread the lug nut. Hold the flange while tightening the lug nut, and the stud should be drawn into position. MAKE SURE THE STUD IS FULLY SEATED, then remove the lug nut and washers.

7. If applicable, install the brake shoes.
8. Install the brake drum.
9. Install the wheel, then remove the jackstands and carefully lower the vehicle.
10. Tighten the lug nuts to the proper torque.

FRONT SUSPENSION

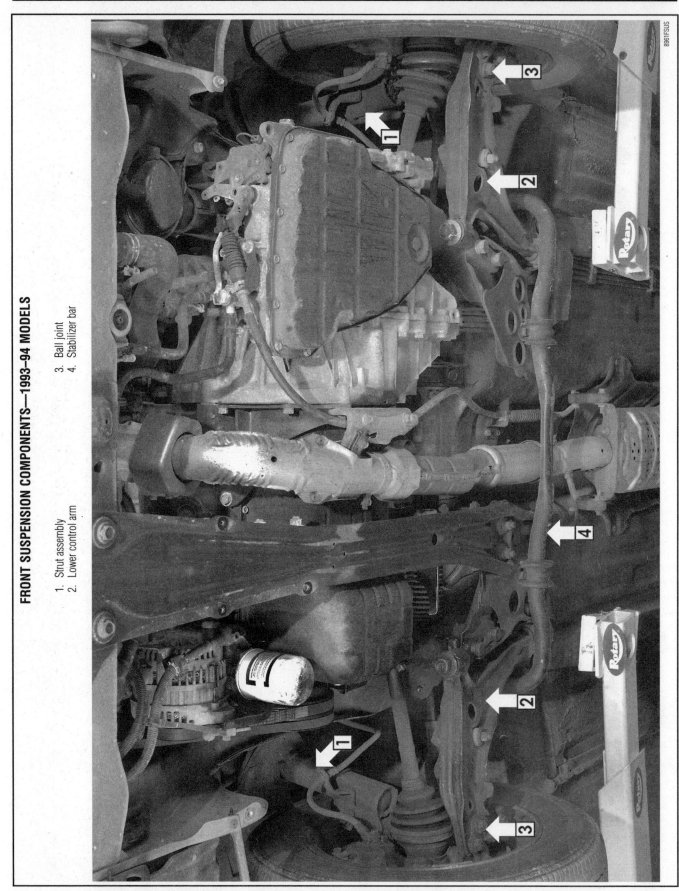

FRONT SUSPENSION COMPONENTS—1993–94 MODELS

1. Strut assembly
2. Lower control arm
3. Ball joint
4. Stabilizer bar

FRONT SUSPENSION COMPONENT LOCATIONS—1995–98 MODELS

1. Strut assembly
2. Stabilizer bar
3. Outer tie rod
4. Lower control arm
5. Ball joint

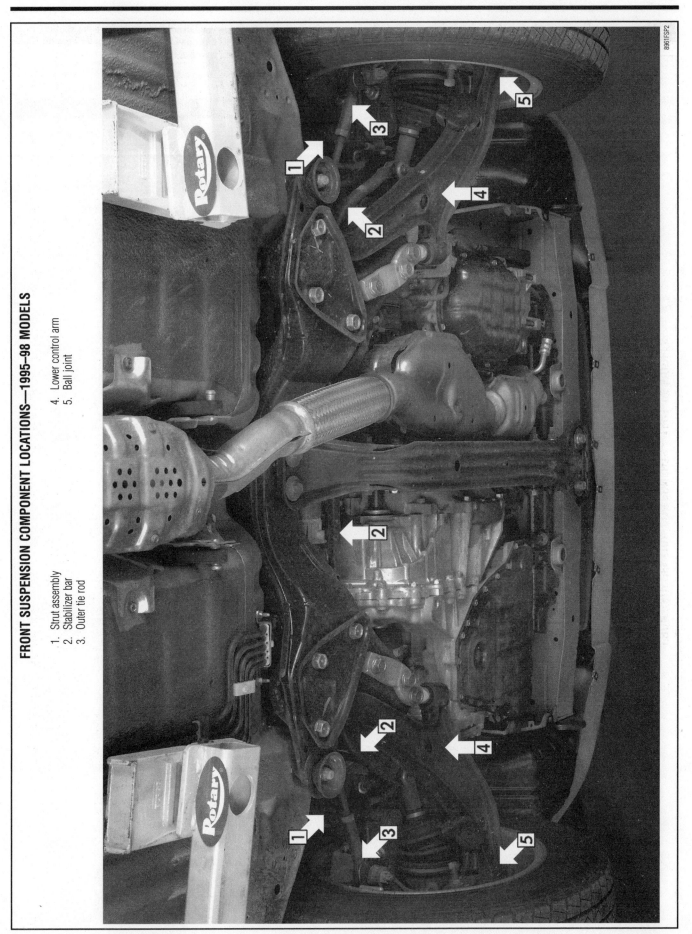

8961FSP2

MacPherson Strut

REMOVAL & INSTALLATION

1993–94 Models

♦ **See Figures 8 thru 23**

1. Disconnect the negative battery cable. If equipped with adjustable struts, disconnect the sub-harness connector at the strut tower.
2. Raise and safely support the vehicle.
3. Remove the wheel. Mark the position of the strut-to-steering knuckle location.
4. Detach the brake tube from the strut.
5. Support the control arm.
6. Remove the strut-to-steering knuckle bolts.

➡ On models equipped with adjustable struts, remove the shock absorber actuator-to-plate bolts and separate the actuator from the plate; the plate is located on top of the strut.

7. Support the strut and remove the 3 upper strut-to-chassis nuts. Remove the strut from the vehicle.

❋❋ WARNING

Never loosen the strut center nut until the spring is compressed or serious injury or vehicle damage may occur.

8. Secure the assembly in a vise.
9. Attach the spring compressor to the spring, leaving the top few coils free.
10. Remove the dust cap from the top of the strut to expose the center nut, if a dust cap is provided. Loosen the nut.

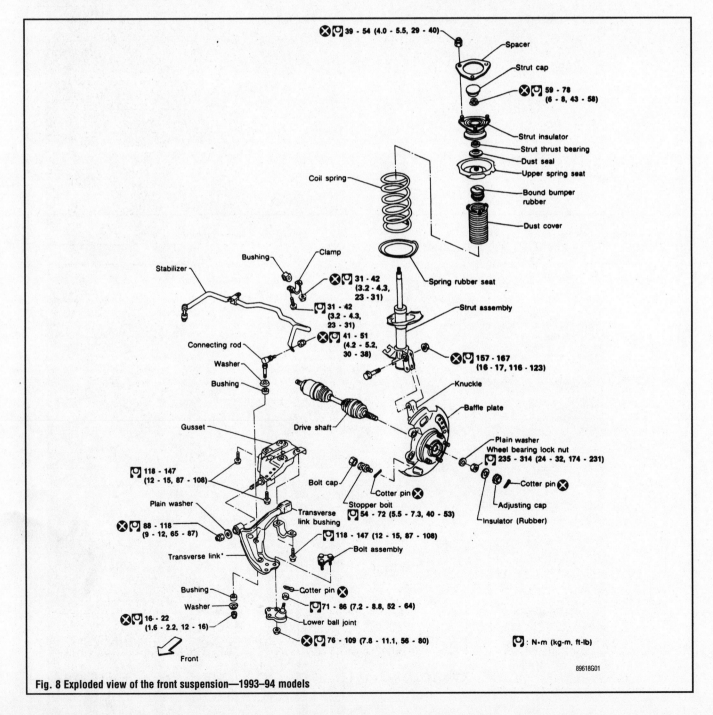

Fig. 8 Exploded view of the front suspension—1993–94 models

89618G01

Fig. 9 After marking the position of the knuckle, loosen the securing bolts

Fig. 10 Keep the nut on the bolt and use a hammer to loosen it from the knuckle

Fig. 11 Pull the bottom of the strut from the knuckle

Fig. 12 Remove the three upper strut mounting nuts

Fig. 13 The strut can now be removed from the vehicle

Fig. 14 Remove the dust cap . . .

Fig. 15 . . . then loosen the center nut

Fig. 16 Compress the spring . . .

Fig. 17 . . . then remove the center nut

Fig. 18 Remove the strut insulator . . .

Fig. 19 . . . then the bearing and seal

Fig. 20 Remove the spring seat . . .

Fig. 21 . . . and the spring with the compressor attached

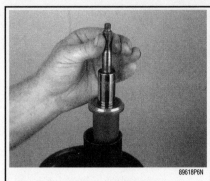

Fig. 22 If necessary, remove the strut insert cap then remove the insert

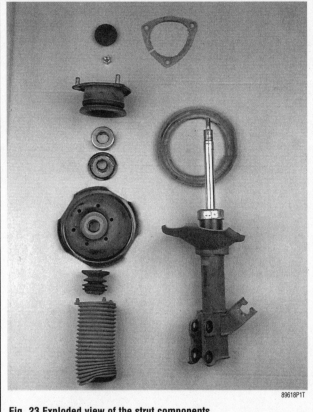

Fig. 23 Exploded view of the strut components

11. Compress the spring just far enough to permit the strut insulator to be turned by hand. Remove the self locking center nut.

12. Take out the strut insulator, strut bearing, oil seal, upper spring seat and bound bumper rubber from the top of the strut. Note their sequence of removal and be sure to assemble them in the same order.

13. Remove the spring with the spring compressor still attached.

To install:

14. Reassemble the strut assembly and observe the following:

a. Make sure you assemble the unit with the shock absorber piston rod fully extended.

b. When assembling, take care that the rubber spring seats, both top and bottom, and the spring are positioned in their grooves before releasing the spring.

15. Tighten the strut locknut.

16. Install the strut assembly onto the vehicle and tighten the strut-to-body nuts. Tighten the strut-to-knuckle bolts.

17. If equipped with a shock absorber actuator, install the actuator and tighten the actuator-to-plate bolts.

18. If the brake hose was disconnected from the brake caliper, bleed brakes and install the wheel. Reattach the brake hose to the strut.

19. Connect the negative battery cable and engage the adjustable strut electrical connectors, if equipped.

20. Check and/or adjust the wheel alignment.

1995–98 Models

▶ See Figures 24, 25 and 26

1. Disconnect the negative battery cable.
2. Raise and safely support the vehicle.
3. Remove the wheel. Matchmark the position of the strut-to-steering knuckle location.
4. Disconnect the brake hose from the strut.
5. Remove the ABS wheel sensor and move it out of the way.
6. Matchmark and remove the bolts attaching the steering knuckle to the strut.
7. Open the hood and remove the strut attaching nuts while holding the strut.

✳✳ CAUTION

Do not remove the center locknut from the strut assembly until the strut is safely compressed.

8. Remove the strut from the vehicle.
9. Place the strut assembly in a vise with the special holding tool ST35652000 or in a spring compressor.
10. Loosen the piston rod locknut.

✳✳ CAUTION

Do not remove the piston rod locknut, the spring is under tension and can cause serious personal injury.

11. Compress the spring with the spring compressor then remove the piston rod locknut.

➡ Before removing the strut from the coil spring, note the positioning of the strut in relationship to the coil spring for reassembly.

12. Remove the strut mounting insulator bracket, strut mounting bearing, upper spring seat, and the upper spring rubber seat.
13. Remove the strut, leaving the coil spring compressed.
14. Remove the piston boot and rebound bumper from the strut.

To install:

15. Install the rebound bumper and the boot to the strut piston.
16. Install the strut into the coil spring, make sure the strut and spring are properly positioned.
17. Install the upper spring rubber seat, upper spring seat, strut mounting bearing, and the strut mounting insulator bracket. Make sure that the cutout on the upper spring seat is facing the outside of the vehicle.
18. Install the piston rod locknut then remove the spring compressor.
19. Tighten the piston rod locknut.
20. Install the strut into the strut tower and install new attaching nuts.
21. Install the bolts attaching the steering knuckle to the strut and align the matchmarks.
22. Install the ABS wheel sensor and tighten the attaching bolt.
23. Install the brake hose to the strut.

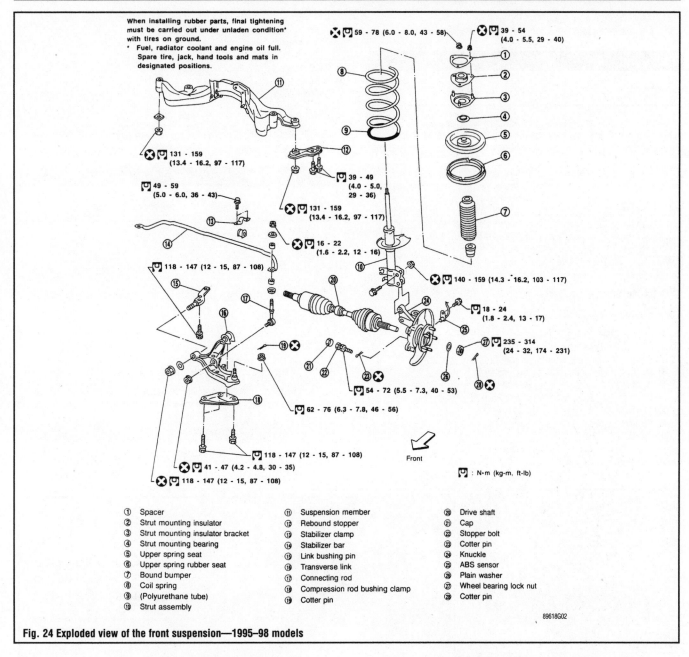

When installing rubber parts, final tightening must be carried out under unladen condition*
with tires on ground.
* Fuel, radiator coolant and engine oil full. Spare tire, jack, hand tools and mats in designated positions.

⊗ ☐ 59 - 78 (6.0 - 8.0, 43 - 58)

⊗ ☐ 39 - 54 (4.0 - 5.5, 29 - 40)

⊗ ☐ 131 - 159 (13.4 - 16.2, 97 - 117)

☐ 49 - 59 (5.0 - 6.0, 36 - 43)

⊗ ☐ 39 - 49 (4.0 - 5.0, 29 - 36)

⊗ ☐ 131 - 159 (13.4 - 16.2, 97 - 117)

⊗ ☐ 16 - 22 (1.6 - 2.2, 12 - 16)

⊗ ☐ 140 - 159 (14.3 - 16.2, 103 - 117)

☐ 118 - 147 (12 - 15, 87 - 108)

☐ 18 - 24 (1.8 - 2.4, 13 - 17)

⊗ ☐ 235 - 314 (24 - 32, 174 - 231)

☐ 54 - 72 (5.5 - 7.3, 40 - 53)

☐ 62 - 76 (6.3 - 7.8, 46 - 56)

Front

☐ 118 - 147 (12 - 15, 87 - 108)

⊗ ☐ 41 - 47 (4.2 - 4.8, 30 - 35)

⊗ ☐ 118 - 147 (12 - 15, 87 - 108)

☐ : N·m (kg-m, ft-lb)

① Spacer
② Strut mounting insulator
③ Strut mounting insulator bracket
④ Strut mounting bearing
⑤ Upper spring seat
⑥ Upper spring rubber seat
⑦ Bound bumper
⑧ Coil spring
⑨ (Polyurethane tube)
⑩ Strut assembly

⑪ Suspension member
⑫ Rebound stopper
⑬ Stabilizer clamp
⑭ Stabilizer bar
⑮ Link bushing pin
⑯ Transverse link
⑰ Connecting rod
⑱ Compression rod bushing clamp
⑲ Cotter pin

⑳ Drive shaft
㉑ Cap
㉒ Stopper bolt
㉓ Cotter pin
㉔ Knuckle
㉕ ABS sensor
㉖ Plain washer
㉗ Wheel bearing lock nut
㉘ Cotter pin

89618G02

Fig. 24 Exploded view of the front suspension—1995–98 models

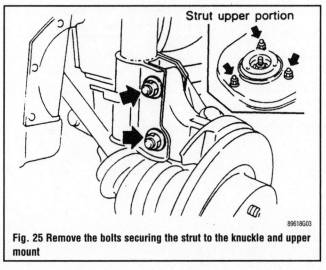

Strut upper portion

89618G03

Fig. 25 Remove the bolts securing the strut to the knuckle and upper mount

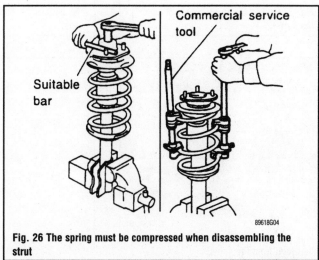

Commercial service tool

Suitable bar

89618G04

Fig. 26 The spring must be compressed when disassembling the strut

24. Install the front wheels and lower the vehicle.
25. Check and/or adjust the wheel alignment as necessary.

Ball Joint

INSPECTION

The lower ball joint should be replaced when play becomes excessive. An effective way to determine ball joint play is to raise the vehicle until the wheel is just a couple of inches off the ground and the ball joint is unloaded (meaning you can't raise directly under the ball joint). Place a long bar under the tire and move the wheel and tire assembly up and down. Keep one hand on top of the tire while you are doing this. If there is over ¼ in. of play at the top of the tire, the ball joint is probably bad. This is assuming that the wheel bearings are in good shape and properly adjusted. As a double check on this, have someone watch the ball joint while you move the tire up and down with the bar. If you can see considerable play, besides feeling play at the top of the wheel, the ball joint needs replacing.

REMOVAL & INSTALLATION

1993–94 Models

▶ See Figures 8, 27, 28, 29 and 30

1. Raise and safely support the vehicle.
2. Remove the wheel assembly.
3. Loosen the lower ball joint-to-traverse link securing bolts/nuts.
4. Remove the ball joint cotter pin and castle nut.
5. Remove the lower ball joint-to-traverse link securing bolts/nuts.
6. Using the Ball Joint Remover tool HT72520000 or equivalent, separate the ball joint from the steering knuckle.
7. Remove the ball joint.
To install:
8. Install the ball joint in the spindle and tighten the ball joint-to-steering knuckle nut. Install a new cotter pin.

9. Install the ball joint-to-traverse link securing bolts. Tighten the ball joint-to-traverse link bolts/nuts.
10. Install the wheel assembly.
11. Lower the vehicle.
12. Check the vehicle for proper alignment.

1995–98 Models

▶ See Figure 24

The lower ball joint is not replaceable, if the ball joint is defective the lower control arm or transverse link must be replaced.

Stabilizer Bar

REMOVAL & INSTALLATION

▶ See Figures 8, 24, 31, 32 and 33

1. Raise and safely support the vehicle.
2. Remove the ball joint socket nuts connecting the stabilizer bar to the lower control arm.
3. Remove the 4 stabilizer bar bracket bolts and then pull the bar from the vehicle.
To install:
4. Make sure the stabilizer ball joint socket is positioned properly.
5. Install the stabilizer bar and mounting brackets. Never fully tighten the mounting bolts unless the vehicle is resting on the ground with normal weight upon the wheels. Be sure the stabilizer bar ball joint socket is properly positioned.

➡ **When installing the stabilizer bar, make sure the paint mark and the bushings are aligned. Make sure the clamp is facing in the right direction.**

6. Lower the vehicle.
7. Bounce the vehicle to stabilize the suspension. Tighten the stabilizer bar bracket bolts.
8. Tighten the nuts connecting the stabilizer bar to the control arm.

Fig. 27 Loosen the lower ball joint securing nuts

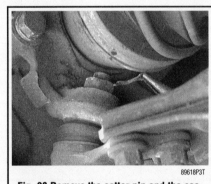

Fig. 28 Remove the cotter pin and the castle nut

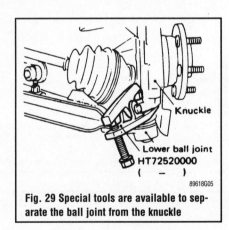

Fig. 29 Special tools are available to separate the ball joint from the knuckle

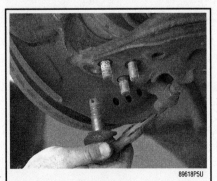

Fig. 30 After it is separated, remove the ball joint from the vehicle

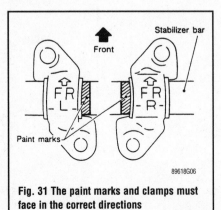

Fig. 31 The paint marks and clamps must face in the correct directions

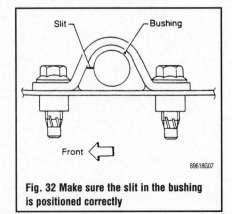

Fig. 32 Make sure the slit in the bushing is positioned correctly

Lower Control Arm (Transverse Link)

REMOVAL & INSTALLATION

▶ **See Figures 8, 24, 34, 35, 36, and 37**

1. Raise and safely support the vehicle.
2. Remove the front wheels.
3. Remove the ABS wheel sensor and move it out of the way.
4. Remove the wheel bearing locknut.
5. Disconnect the tie rod from the steering knuckle.
6. Matchmark then remove the bolts attaching the strut to the steering knuckle.
7. Separate the halfshaft from the steering knuckle by lightly tapping the end of the shaft.
8. Separate the steering knuckle and the lower ball joint.
9. Disconnect the stabilizer bar from the lower control arm.
10. Remove the bolts attaching the link bushing pin to the chassis. If necessary, remove the nut attaching the link to the control arm and remove the link.
11. Remove the bolts attaching the compression rod bushing clamp and remove the lower control arm/traverse link.

To install:

12. Install the lower control arm and the compression rod bushing clamp into the vehicle.
13. Install the link bushing pin, if removed from the control arm.
14. Tighten all bolts and nuts until they are snug enough to support the weight of the vehicle but not fully tight, the bolts should be torqued to specification with the vehicle on the floor. Refer to the illustrations for tightening torques and sequences.
15. Install the steering knuckle to the lower control arm and connect the ball joint.

➡ **Always use a new nut when installing the ball joint to the control arm.**

16. Connect the steering knuckle to the strut and to the halfshaft.
17. Install the strut mounting bolts and align the matchmarks.
18. Install the tie rod ball joint and tighten the nut.
19. Install the wheel bearing locknut
20. Install the ABS wheel sensor and tighten the attaching bolt.
21. Install the front wheels, lower the vehicle and tighten hub locknut.
22. Tigthen the bolts attaching the compression rod bushing clamp and the link bushing pin, in the proper sequence.
23. If the link bushing pin was removed from the control arm, tighten the attaching nut.
24. Tighten the sway bar attaching nut.
25. Have the vehicle alignment checked.

Steering Knuckle and Hub Assembly

REMOVAL & INSTALLATION

▶ **See Figures 38 and 39**

1. Raise and support the front of the vehicle safely and remove the wheels.
2. Remove wheel bearing locknut.
3. Remove brake caliper assembly. Make sure not to twist the brake hose.
4. Remove tie rod ball joint.

➡ **Cover axle boots with waste cloth or equivalent so as not to damage them when removing driveshaft. Make a matching mark on strut housing and adjusting pin before removing them.**

5. Separate the halfshaft from the knuckle by slightly tapping it.
6. Mark and remove the steering knuckle-to-strut mounting bolts.
7. Remove the lower ball joint from knuckle.
8. Remove the steering knuckle from lower control arm.

To install:

9. Install the steering knuckle to the lower control arm and connect the ball joint.

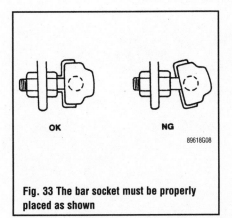

Fig. 33 The bar socket must be properly placed as shown

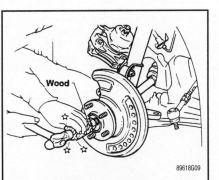

Fig. 34 Tap the shaft out of the hub. Use a block of wood to protect the shaft

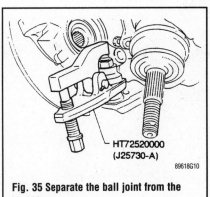

Fig. 35 Separate the ball joint from the knuckle

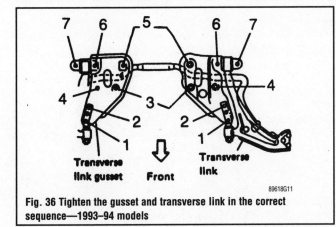

Fig. 36 Tighten the gusset and transverse link in the correct sequence—1993–94 models

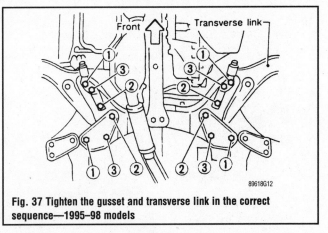

Fig. 37 Tighten the gusset and transverse link in the correct sequence—1995–98 models

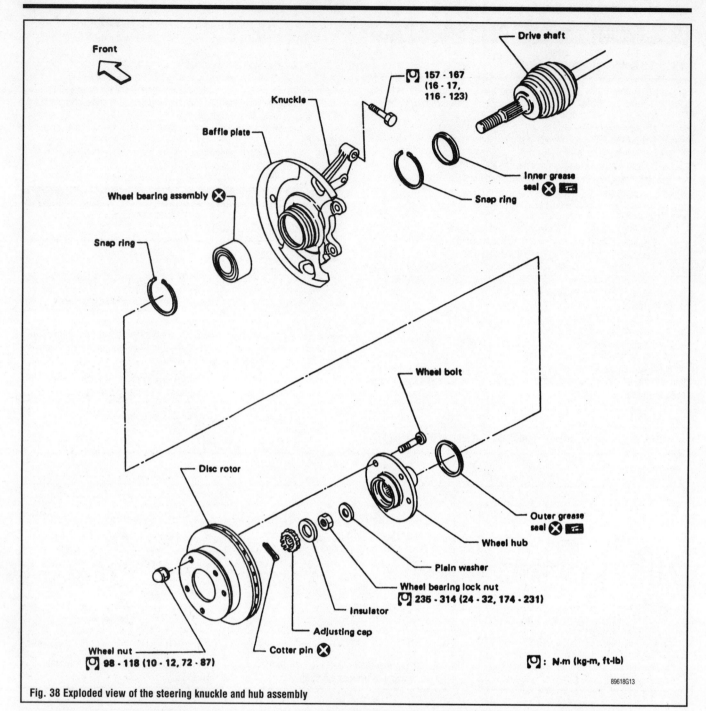

Front

Drive shaft

Knuckle

Baffle plate

157 - 167 (16 - 17, 116 - 123)

Inner grease seal ⊗ 🔒

Snap ring

Wheel bearing assembly ⊗

Snap ring

Wheel bolt

Disc rotor

Outer grease seal ⊗ 🔒

Wheel hub

Plain washer

Wheel bearing lock nut
235 - 314 (24 - 32, 174 - 231)

Insulator

Adjusting cap

Cotter pin ⊗

Wheel nut
98 - 118 (10 - 12, 72 - 87)

🔧 : N·m (kg-m, ft-lb)

89618G13

Fig. 38 Exploded view of the steering knuckle and hub assembly

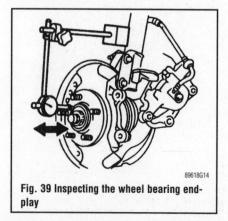

89618G14

Fig. 39 Inspecting the wheel bearing end-play

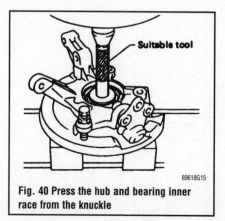

Suitable tool

89618G15

Fig. 40 Press the hub and bearing inner race from the knuckle

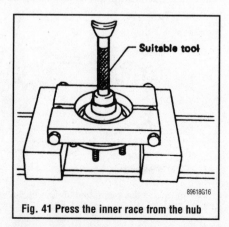

Suitable tool

89618G16

Fig. 41 Press the inner race from the hub

10. Connect the steering knuckle to the strut and to the halfshaft.
11. Install the tie rod ball joint.
12. Install the brake caliper assembly.
13. Install the wheel bearing locknut
14. Install the front wheels, lower the vehicle and tighten hub locknut.
15. Using a dial micrometer, measure the wheel bearing endplay; it should be less than 0.0020 in. (0.05mm).

Front Wheel Bearings

REMOVAL & INSTALLATION

▶ **See Figures 40 thru 50**

1. Using a shop press and a suitable tool, press the hub with the inner race from the steering knuckle.
2. Using a shop press and a suitable tool, press the bearing inner race from the hub and remove the grease seal.

3. Using a prybar, pry the inner grease seal from the steering knuckle.
4. Using snapring pliers to remove the inner and outer snaprings from the steering knuckle.
5. Using a shop press and a suitable tool, press the bearing outer race from the steering knuckle.
6. Inspect the hub, steering knuckle and snaprings for cracks and/or wear; if necessary, replace the damaged part(s).
   To install:
7. Install the inner snapring in the steering knuckle groove.
8. Using a shop press and a suitable tool, press the new wheel bearing assembly into the steering knuckle, until it seats, using a maximum pressure of 3 tons.
9. Pack the new grease seal lip with multi-purpose grease.
10. Using a shop press and a suitable tool, press the new outer grease seal into the steering knuckle.
11. Using a shop press and a suitable tool, press the new inner grease seal into the steering knuckle.
12. Using a shop press and a suitable tool, press the hub into the steering

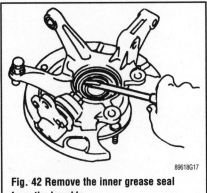

Fig. 42 Remove the inner grease seal from the knuckle

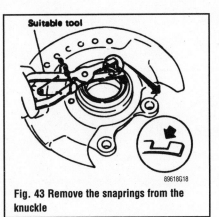

Fig. 43 Remove the snaprings from the knuckle

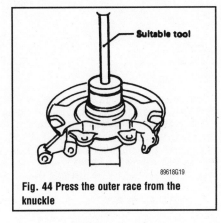

Fig. 44 Press the outer race from the knuckle

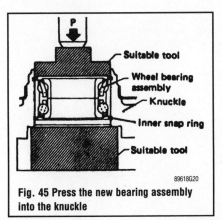

Fig. 45 Press the new bearing assembly into the knuckle

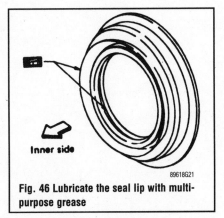

Fig. 46 Lubricate the seal lip with multi-purpose grease

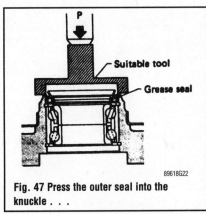

Fig. 47 Press the outer seal into the knuckle . . .

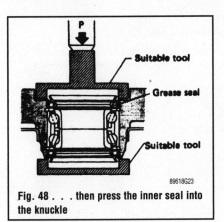

Fig. 48 . . . then press the inner seal into the knuckle

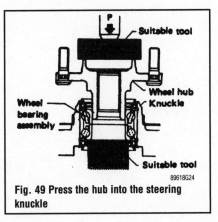

Fig. 49 Press the hub into the steering knuckle

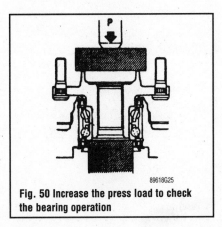

Fig. 50 Increase the press load to check the bearing operation

knuckle, until it seats, using a maximum pressure of 3 tons; be careful not to damage the grease seal.

13. To check the bearing operation, perform the following procedure:
    a. Increase the press pressure to 3.5–5.0 tons.
    b. Spin the steering knuckle, several turns, in both directions.
    c. Make sure the wheel bearings operate smoothly.

Front End Alignment

If the tires are worn unevenly, if the vehicle is not stable on the highway or if the handling seems uneven in spirited driving, the wheel alignment should be checked. If an alignment problem is suspected, first check for improper tire inflation and other possible causes. These can be worn suspension or steering components, accident damage or even unmatched tires. If any worn or damaged components are found, they must be replaced before the wheels can be properly aligned. Wheel alignment requires very expensive equipment and involves minute adjustments which must be accurate; it should only be performed by a trained technician. Take your vehicle to a properly equipped shop.

Following is a description of the alignment angles which are adjustable on most vehicles and how they affect vehicle handling. Although these angles can apply to both the front and rear wheels, usually only the front suspension is adjustable.

CASTER

▶ **See Figure 51**

Looking at a vehicle from the side, caster angle describes the steering axis rather than a wheel angle. The steering knuckle is attached to a control arm or strut at the top and a control arm at the bottom. The wheel pivots around the line between these points to steer the vehicle. When the upper point is tilted back, this is described as positive caster. Having a positive caster tends to make the wheels self-centering, increasing directional stability. Excessive positive caster makes the wheels hard to steer, while an uneven caster will cause a pull to one side. Overloading the vehicle or sagging rear springs will affect caster, as will raising the rear of the vehicle. If the rear of the vehicle is lower than normal, the caster becomes more positive.

CAMBER

▶ **See Figure 52**

Looking from the front of the vehicle, camber is the inward or outward tilt of the top of wheels. When the tops of the wheels are tilted in, this is negative camber; if they are tilted out, it is positive. In a turn, a slight amount of negative camber helps maximize contact of the tire with the road. However, too much negative camber compromises straight-line stability, increases bump steer and torque steer.

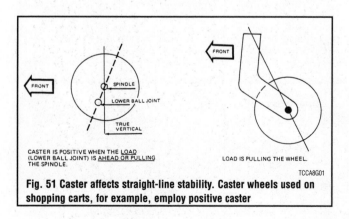

CASTER IS POSITIVE WHEN THE LOAD (LOWER BALL JOINT) IS AHEAD OR PULLING THE SPINDLE.

LOAD IS PULLING THE WHEEL.

TCCA8G01

Fig. 51 Caster affects straight-line stability. Caster wheels used on shopping carts, for example, employ positive caster

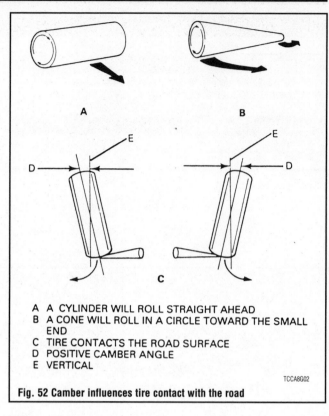

A A CYLINDER WILL ROLL STRAIGHT AHEAD
B A CONE WILL ROLL IN A CIRCLE TOWARD THE SMALL END
C TIRE CONTACTS THE ROAD SURFACE
D POSITIVE CAMBER ANGLE
E VERTICAL

TCCA8G02

Fig. 52 Camber influences tire contact with the road

TOE

▶ **See Figure 53**

Looking down at the wheels from above the vehicle, toe angle is the distance between the front of the wheels, relative to the distance between the back of the wheels. If the wheels are closer at the front, they are said to be toed-in or to have negative toe. A small amount of negative toe enhances directional stability and provides a smoother ride on the highway.

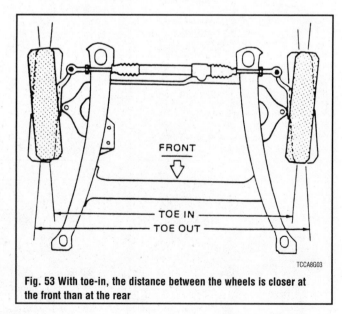

FRONT

TOE IN
TOE OUT

TCCA8G03

Fig. 53 With toe-in, the distance between the wheels is closer at the front than at the rear

REAR SUSPENSION

REAR SUSPENSION COMPONENTS—1993–94 MODELS

1. Strut assembly
2. Stabilizer bar
3. Parallel links
4. Radius rod

896TRSUS

REAR SUSPENSION COMPONENTS—1995–98 MODELS

1. Strut assembly
2. Lateral link
3. Control rod (inside lateral link)
4. Torsion beam

MacPherson Strut

REMOVAL & INSTALLATION

1993–94 Models

♦ **See Figures 54 thru 65**

1. Disconnect the negative battery cable.
2. Remove the rear seat and the parcel shelf.
3. If equipped with an adjustable shock absorber, unplug the electrical connector from the sensor unit.
4. If equipped, remove the shock absorber actuator bracket bolts and the shock absorber actuator.
5. If necessary, remove the actuator bracket-to-strut nut and the bracket.
6. Raise and safely support the vehicle; do not raise the vehicle at the parallel links or radius links. Remove the wheel(s).

7. Uncouple the rear brake hydraulic line from the strut. Then, unbolt and remove the brake assembly, wheel bearings and backing plate.

➡ **If equipped with disc brakes, suspend the brake caliper so the hydraulic line will not be stressed. If equipped with drum brakes, remove the entire brake assembly**

8. Remove the radius rod-to-strut bolt, stabilizer bar-to-radius rod bracket bolt, radius rod bracket-to-strut bolts and both parallel links-to-strut nut/bolt.
9. Remove the strut mounting cap from the strut.
10. Support the strut from underneath and remove the 3 strut-to-chassis nuts and lower the strut from the vehicle.

❋❋ WARNING

Never loosen the strut center nut until the spring is compressed or serious injury or vehicle damage may occur.

11. Loosen the piston rod locknut.

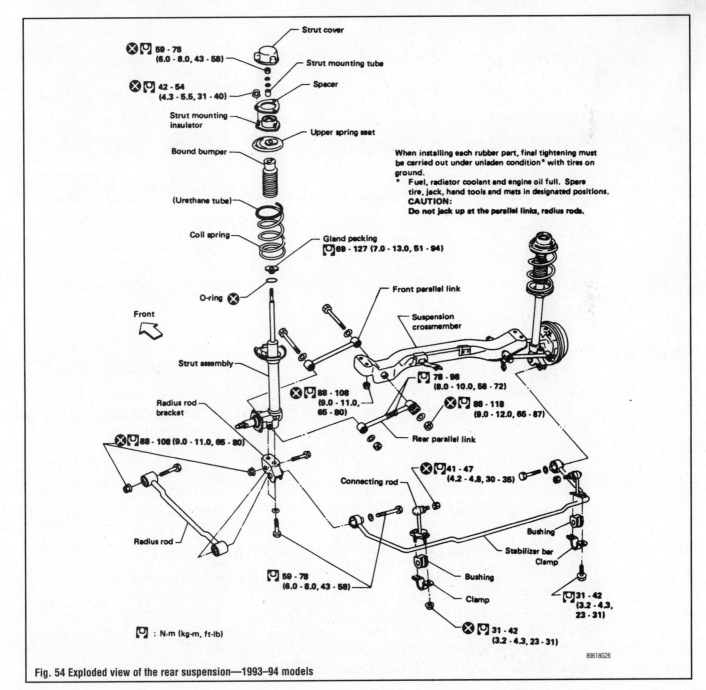

Fig. 54 Exploded view of the rear suspension—1993–94 models

Fig. 55 Remove the bolts securing the stabilizer bar . . .

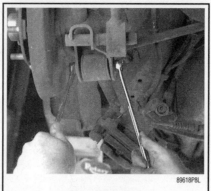

Fig. 56 . . . the radius rod . . .

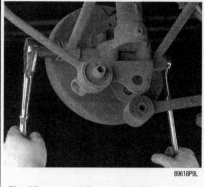

Fig. 57 . . . and the parallel links

Fig. 58 Remove the strut cap, then remove the bolts securing the strut. Make sure the strut is supported

Fig. 59 The strut can now be removed from the vehicle

Fig. 60 Install the spring compressor and remove the piston locknut

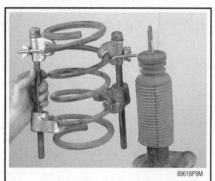

Fig. 61 Remove the upper spring seat components and the spring

Fig. 62 Attach the strut to the rear wheel to make loosening of the strut cap easier

Fig. 63 The strut cartridge can now be removed from the casing

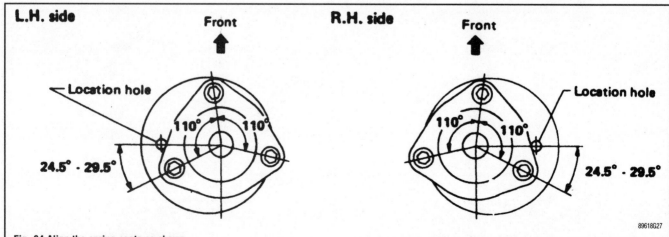

Fig. 64 Align the spring seats as shown

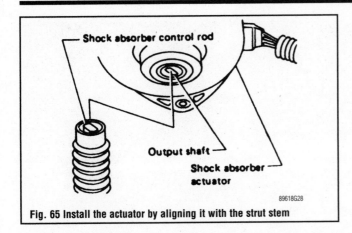

Fig. 65 Install the actuator by aligning it with the strut stem

Do not remove the piston rod locknut, the spring is under tension and can cause serious personal injury.

12. Compress the spring with the spring compressor then remove the piston rod locknut.

➡ **Before removing the strut from the coil spring, note the positioning of the strut in relationship to the coil spring for reassembly.**

13. Remove the strut mounting insulator bracket, strut mounting bearing, upper spring seat, and the upper spring rubber seat.
14. Remove the piston boot and rebound bumper from the strut.
15. Remove the strut cap and remove the insert.
To install:
16. If removed, install the strut cartridge and cap.

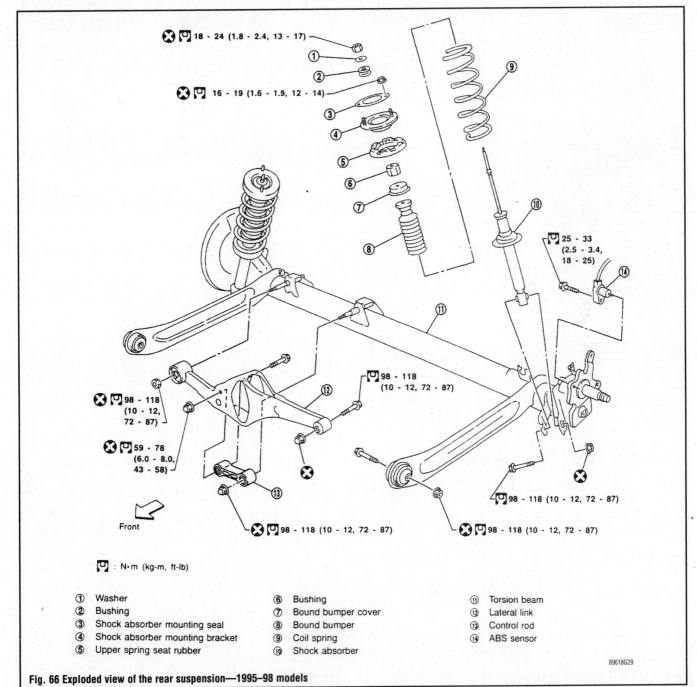

☒ ⬚ 18 - 24 (1.8 - 2.4, 13 - 17)

☒ ⬚ 16 - 19 (1.6 - 1.9, 12 - 14)

⬚ 25 - 33 (2.5 - 3.4, 18 - 25)

☒ ⬚ 98 - 118 (10 - 12, 72 - 87)

☒ ⬚ 98 - 118 (10 - 12, 72 - 87)

☒ ⬚ 59 - 78 (6.0 - 8.0, 43 - 58)

⬚ 98 - 118 (10 - 12, 72 - 87)

☒ ⬚ 98 - 118 (10 - 12, 72 - 87)

Front

☒ ⬚ 98 - 118 (10 - 12, 72 - 87)

☒ ⬚ 98 - 118 (10 - 12, 72 - 87)

⬚ : N•m (kg-m, ft-lb)

① Washer	⑥ Bushing	⑪ Torsion beam
② Bushing	⑦ Bound bumper cover	⑫ Lateral link
③ Shock absorber mounting seal	⑧ Bound bumper	⑬ Control rod
④ Shock absorber mounting bracket	⑨ Coil spring	⑭ ABS sensor
⑤ Upper spring seat rubber	⑩ Shock absorber	

Fig. 66 Exploded view of the rear suspension—1995–98 models

17. Install the rebound bumper and the boot to the strut piston.
18. Install the strut into the coil spring, make sure the strut and spring are properly positioned.
19. Install the upper spring rubber seat, upper spring seat, strut mounting bearing, and the strut mounting insulator bracket. Refer to the illustrations for proper alignment.
20. Install the piston rod locknut then remove the spring compressor.
21. Tighten the piston rod locknut.
22. Install in the strut onto the vehicle and support it with the 3 mounting nuts.
23. Install both parallel links-to-strut nut and bolt, radius rod bracket-to-strut bolts, stabilizer bar-to-radius rod bracket bolt and the radius rod-to-strut bolt.
24. If removed, install the brake assembly.
25. Tighten all bolts sufficiently to safely support the vehicle; then, lower the vehicle to the ground. The final tightening of all the suspension components must be carried out with the vehicle in an unloaded condition.
26. Connect the brake line to the strut housing.
27. If equipped, connect the electrical harness connector and the shock absorber actuator.
28. Install the strut mounting cap.
29. If the brake line was disconnected, bleed the brake system.
30. Install the rear seat and the parcel shelf.
31. Install the wheels and connect the negative battery cable.
32. Check and/or adjust the wheel alignment.

1995–98 Models

▶ **See Figures 66, 67, 68 and 69**

1. Raise and safely support the vehicle.
2. Remove the rear wheels.
3. Support the rear torsion beam assembly with a jack.
4. Open the trunk and remove the two nuts attaching the strut to the vehicle.

✳✳ CAUTION

Do not remove the center locknut from the strut assembly until the strut is safely compressed.

5. Remove the bolt attaching the strut to the rear torsion beam assembly and remove the strut.
6. Place the strut assembly in a vise with the special holding tool HT71780000 or in a spring compressor.
7. Loosen the piston rod locknut.

✳✳ CAUTION

Do not remove the piston rod locknut, the spring is under tension and can cause serious personal injury.

8. Compress the spring with the spring compressor then remove the piston rod locknut.

➡ **Before removing the strut from the coil spring, note the positioning of the strut in relationship to the coil spring for reassembly.**

9. Remove the bushing, strut mounting bracket, and the upper spring seat rubber.
10. Remove the strut, leaving the coil spring compressed.
11. Remove the bushing, bound bumper cover, and the bound bumper.
To install:
12. Install the bound bumper, bound bumper cover, and the bushing.
13. Install the strut into the coil spring, make sure the strut and spring are properly positioned.
14. Install the upper spring seat rubber, strut mounting bracket, and the bushing. Make sure that the mounting bracket is properly positioned.
15. Install the piston rod locknut then remove the spring compressor.
16. Tighten the piston rod locknut.
17. Install the strut into the vehicle and install new attaching nuts.
18. Position the strut on the rear torsion beam and install the bolt.
19. Remove the support from the rear torsion beam.
20. Install the rear wheels and lower the vehicle.
21. Check the vehicle's alignment and adjust as necessary.

Radius Rod

REMOVAL & INSTALLATION

▶ **See Figure 54**

➡ **This procedure applies to 1993–94 models only.**

1. Raise and safely support the vehicle; do not raise the vehicle at the parallel links or radius links. If necessary, remove the wheel.
2. Remove the radius rod-to-strut nut/bolt.
3. Remove the radius rod-to-chassis nut/bolt and the radius rod.
To install:
4. Install in the radius rod onto the vehicle.
5. Tighten all bolts sufficiently to safely support the vehicle. If the wheel was removed, install it. Lower the vehicle to the ground.
6. Final tighten the nuts and bolts.

Parallel Link

REMOVAL & INSTALLATION

▶ **See Figure 54**

➡ **This procedure applies to 1993–94 models only.**

1. Raise and safely support the vehicle; do not raise the vehicle at the parallel links or radius links. If necessary, remove the wheel.
2. Remove the parallel links-to-strut nut/bolt.
3. Remove the parallel links-to-suspension member nut/bolt and the parallel links.
To install:
4. Install in the parallel links onto the vehicle.
5. Tighten all bolts sufficiently to safely support the vehicle. If the wheel was removed, install it. Lower the vehicle to the ground.
6. Final tighten the nuts and bolts.

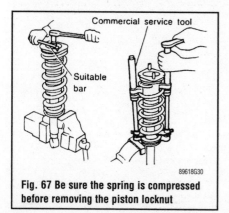

Fig. 67 Be sure the spring is compressed before removing the piston locknut

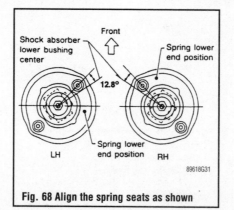

Fig. 68 Align the spring seats as shown

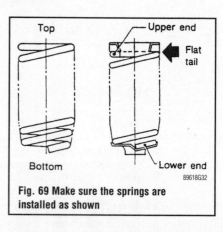

Fig. 69 Make sure the springs are installed as shown

Stabilizer Bar

REMOVAL & INSTALLATION

▶ **See Figure 54**

➡**This procedure applies to 1993–94 models only.**

1. Raise and safely support the vehicle.
2. Remove the mounting nuts connecting the stabilizer bar to the radius rod brackets.
3. Remove the 4 bolts holding the stabilizer bar bracket to the chassis and then pull the bar from the vehicle.
   To install:
4. Install the stabilizer bar and mounting brackets. Never fully tighten the mounting bolts unless the vehicle is resting on the ground with normal weight upon the wheels.

➡ **When installing the stabilizer bar, make sure the paint mark is aligned with the bushing and the clamp is facing in the correct direction.**

5. Tighten the bolts connecting the stabilizer bar bracket to the chassis.
6. Tighten the nuts connecting the stabilizer bar to the radius rod brackets.
7. Make sure the stabilizer bar connecting rods are installed on their correct sides.
8. Lower the vehicle.

Torsion Beam, Lateral Link and Control Rod

REMOVAL & INSTALLATION

▶ **See Figures 66, 70, 71, 72 and 73**

➡**This procedure applies to 1995–98 models only.**

1. Loosen the lug nuts.
2. Raise and safely support the vehicle securely on jackstands. Remove the wheels.

✳✳ WARNING

Be sure to disconnect the ABS wheel sensor from the assembly. Failure to do so may result in damage to the sensor wire and the sensor becoming inoperative.

3. Remove the brake calipers and suspend them with a piece of wire. Do not let them hang by the hose.
4. Using a transmission jack, raise the torsion beam a little, then remove the suspension mounting bolts.
5. Lower the jack and remove the suspension assembly.
6. The lateral link and control rod can now be removed.
7. Inspect the torsion beam and control rod for cracks, wear and deformation. The length of the lateral link and control rod is as follows:

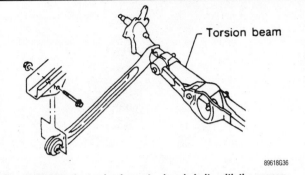

Fig. 73 Tighten the torsion beam-to-chassis bolts with the suspension unloaded

- A—8.15–8.19 in. (207–208mm)
- B—15.51–15.55 in. (394–395mm)
- C—23.66–23.74 in. (601–603mm)
- D—4.17–4.25 in. (106–108mm)

To install:

8. When installing the control rod, connect the bushing with the smaller inner diameter to the lateral link. Install the lateral link and the control rod on the torsion beam. Place the lateral link with the arrow topside.
9. Place the lateral link and control rod horizontally against the beam, and tighten the bolts. Refer to the illustration.
10. Secure the torsion beam to the vehicle. Make sure the lateral link is horizontal, then tighten the link to the chassis.
11. Attach the struts to the torsion beam and tighten the fasteners.
12. Tighten the torsion beam-to-chassis bolts.
13. Install the calipers, ABS sensor and wheels. Lower the vehicle to the ground. Final tighten the lug nuts.

Rear Wheel Bearings

REMOVAL & INSTALLATION

▶ **See Figures 74 thru 82**

➡**If the vehicle is equipped with ABS, the sensor must be removed to protect the sensor and its wiring.**

1. Raise and safely support the vehicle. Remove the rear wheel(s).
2. If equipped with disc brakes, perform the following procedures:
   a. Remove the brake caliper and hang it by a piece of wire.
   b. Remove the brake caliper support.
   c. Remove the disc brake pads.
   d. Remove the brake disc.
3. If equipped with drum brakes, perform the following procedures:
   a. Remove the brake drum.
   b. If necessary, remove the brake shoe assembly.
4. Remove the grease cap.

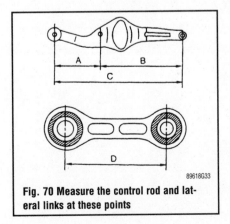

Fig. 70 Measure the control rod and lateral links at these points

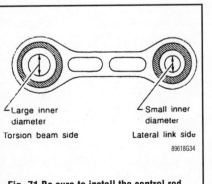

Fig. 71 Be sure to install the control rod correctly

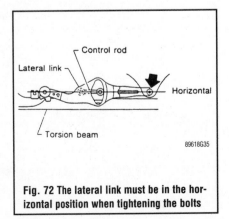

Fig. 72 The lateral link must be in the horizontal position when tightening the bolts

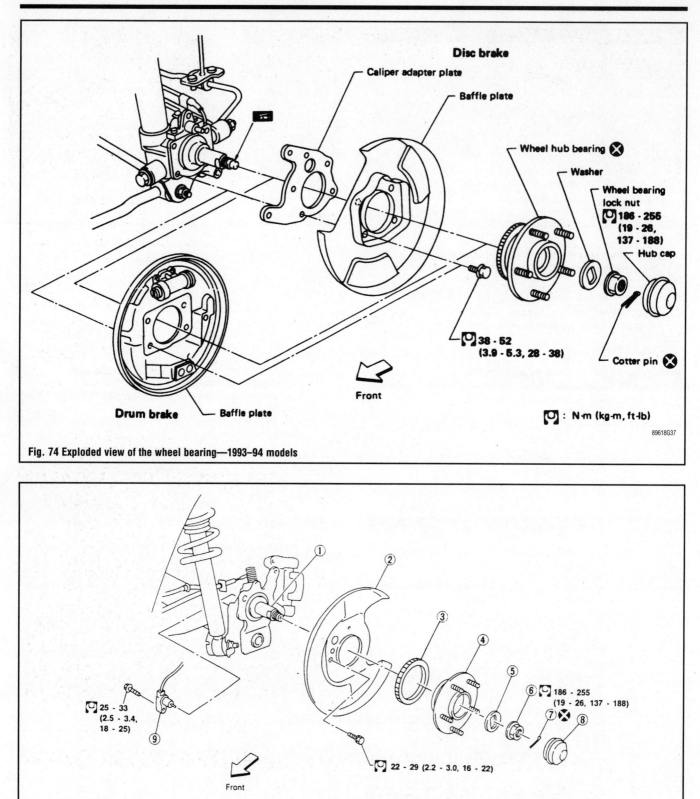

Fig. 74 Exploded view of the wheel bearing—1993–94 models

Fig. 75 Exploded view of the wheel bearing— 1995–98 models

①	Spindle	④	Wheel hub bearing	⑦	Cotter pin
②	Baffle plate	⑤	Washer	⑧	Hub cap
③	ABS sensor rotor	⑥	Wheel bearing lock nut	⑨	ABS sensor

89618P8N

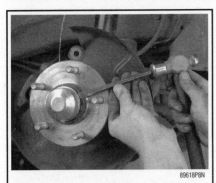

Fig. 76 Remove the grease cap from the hub . . .

89618P10

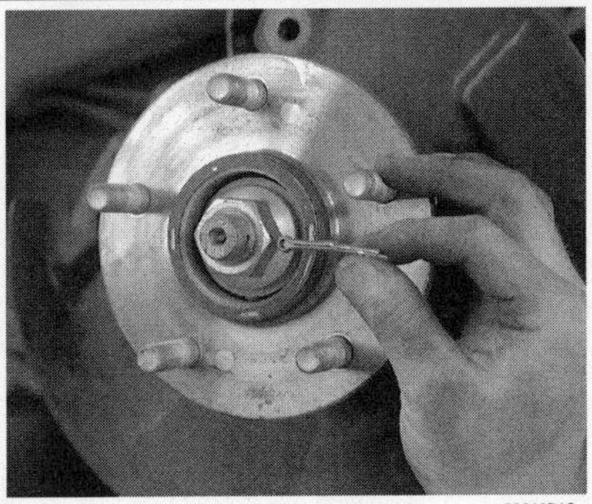

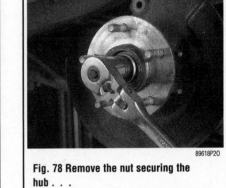

Fig. 77 . . . and the cotter pin

89618P20

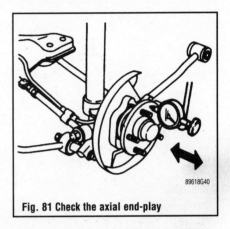

Fig. 78 Remove the nut securing the hub . . .

89618P40

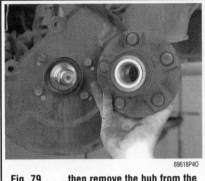

Fig. 79 . . . then remove the hub from the spindle

89618G39

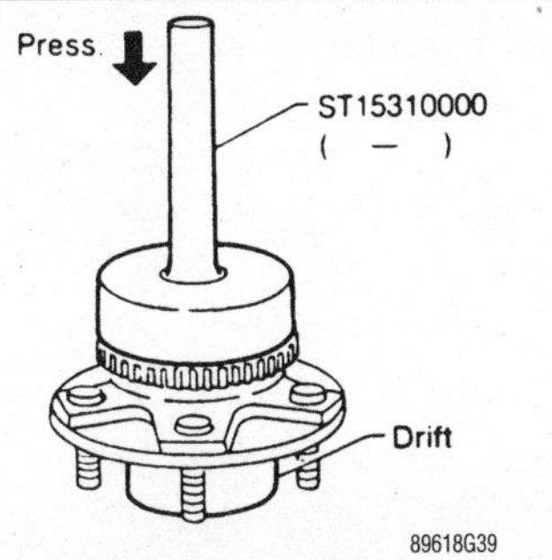

Fig. 80 If equipped with ABS a sensor ring must be installed. Measure the old hub assembly for the press depth

89618G40

Fig. 81 Check the axial end-play

5. Remove the cotter pin, wheel bearing locknut, washer, and the wheel hub bearing assembly. A slide hammer may be needed to remove the hub bearing assembly.

➡ **The wheel hub bearing assembly is not repairable; it must be replaced when defective.**

To install:

6. If the vehicle is equipped with ABS, the sensor ring must be removed and installed on the new hub.
7. Install the wheel hub bearing assembly, the washer and the wheel bearing locknut. Tighten the wheel bearing locknut to 138–188 ft. lbs. (187–255 Nm).
8. Verify that the wheel bearings operate smoothly.
9. Install a new cotter pin into the spindle to hold the wheel bearing locknut.
10. Install a dial micrometer to the rear wheel hub bearing assembly and check the axial end-play; it should be less than 0.0020 in. (0.05 mm).
11. Install the grease cap.
12. If removed, install the ABS sensor and its wiring.
13. Install the brake assembly and the wheels.

89618P60

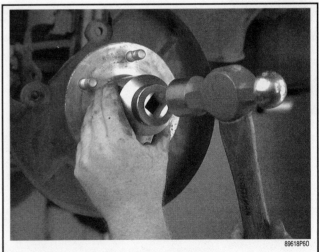

Fig. 82 Use a socket to drive the grease cap on

STEERING

Steering Wheel

REMOVAL & INSTALLATION

Without Air Bag

➧ See Figure 83

1. Position the wheels in the straight-ahead direction. The steering wheel should be right side up and level.
2. Disconnect the negative battery cable.
3. Pull out the horn pad. If the vehicle has a horn wire running from the pad to the steering wheel, disconnect it.
4. Remove the rest of the horn switching mechanism, noting the relative location of the parts. Remove the mechanism only if it hinders subsequent wheel removal procedures.
5. Matchmark the top of the steering column shaft and the steering wheel flange.
6. Remove the steering wheel-to-steering column nut. Using the steering wheel puller tool ST27180001, or equivalent, pull the steering wheel from the steering column.

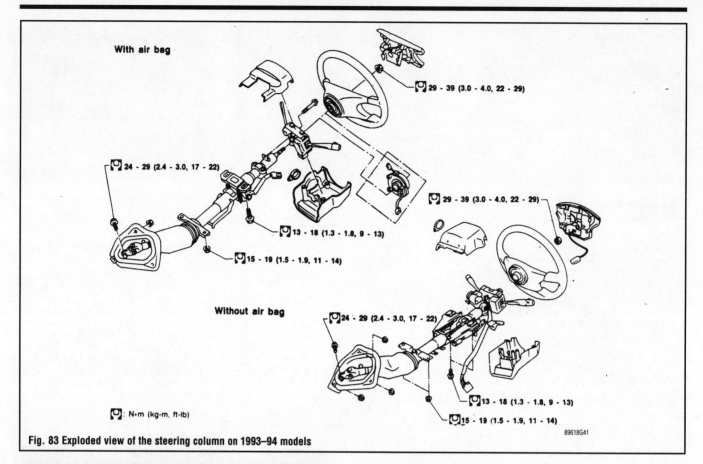

With air bag

$\boxed{\downarrow}$ 29 - 39 (3.0 - 4.0, 22 - 29)

$\boxed{\downarrow}$ 24 - 29 (2.4 - 3.0, 17 - 22)

$\boxed{\downarrow}$ 29 - 39 (3.0 - 4.0, 22 - 29)

$\boxed{\downarrow}$ 13 - 18 (1.3 - 1.8, 9 - 13)

$\boxed{\downarrow}$ 15 - 19 (1.5 - 1.9, 11 - 14)

Without air bag

$\boxed{\downarrow}$ 24 - 29 (2.4 - 3.0, 17 - 22)

$\boxed{\downarrow}$ 13 - 18 (1.3 - 1.8, 9 - 13)

$\boxed{\downarrow}$ 15 - 19 (1.5 - 1.9, 11 - 14)

$\boxed{\downarrow}$: N•m (kg-m, ft-lb)

Fig. 83 Exploded view of the steering column on 1993–94 models

89618G41

❈❈ WARNING

Do not strike the shaft with a hammer, which may cause the column to collapse.

To install:

7. Apply multi-purpose grease to the entire surface of the turn signal cancel pin (both portions) and the horn contact slip ring.

8. Install the steering wheel by aligning the matchmarks. Do not drive or hammer the steering wheel into place or the steering column will be damaged.

9. Tighten the steering wheel-to-steering column nut.

10. Install the horn pad and connect the negative battery cable.

With Air Bag

♦ See Figures 83, 84 and 85

1. Position the wheels in the straight-ahead direction. The steering wheel should be right side up and level.

2. Disconnect the negative battery cable.

❈❈ CAUTION

Wait 10 minutes after the battery cable has been disconnected, before attempting to work on the air bag unit. The air bag unit is still armed and can inflate, during the 10 minute period, and possibly causing bodily injury.

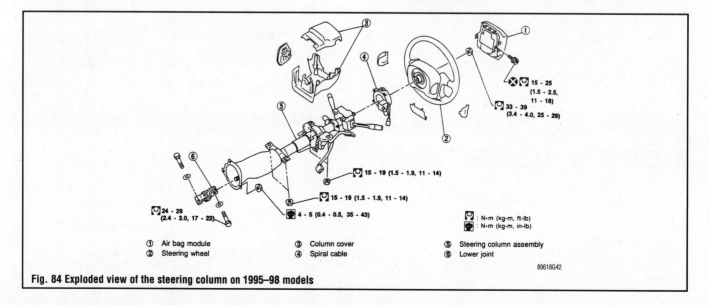

$\boxed{\otimes}$ 15 - 25 (1.5 - 2.5, 11 - 18)

$\boxed{\downarrow}$ 33 - 39 (3.4 - 4.0, 25 - 29)

$\boxed{\downarrow}$ 15 - 19 (1.5 - 1.9, 11 - 14)

$\boxed{\downarrow}$ 15 - 19 (1.5 - 1.9, 11 - 14)

$\boxed{\otimes}$ 4 - 5 (0.4 - 0.5, 35 - 43)

$\boxed{\downarrow}$ 24 - 29 (2.4 - 3.0, 17 - 22)

$\boxed{\downarrow}$: N•m (kg-m, ft-lb)
$\boxed{\otimes}$: N•m (kg-m, in-lb)

① Air bag module
② Steering wheel
③ Column cover
④ Spiral cable
⑤ Steering column assembly
⑥ Lower joint

Fig. 84 Exploded view of the steering column on 1995–98 models

89618G42

3. Remove the lower lid from the steering wheel and unplug the air bag unit electrical connector.

4. Remove both side lids from the steering wheel.

5. Using a T50H Torx® bit, remove the air bag-to-steering wheel bolts from both sides of the steering wheel; discard the bolts.

6. Lift the air bag unit upward and place it in a safe, clean, dry place with the pad side facing upward; be sure the temperature in the area will not exceed 212°F (100°C).

7. Unplug the horn connector and remove the nuts.

8. Matchmark the top of the steering column shaft and the steering wheel flange.

9. Remove the steering wheel-to-steering column nut. Using the steering wheel puller tool ST27180001, or equivalent, pull the steering wheel from the steering column.

✳✳ WARNING

Do not strike the shaft with a hammer, which may cause the column to collapse.

To install:

10. Apply multi-purpose grease to the entire surface of the turn signal cancel pin (both portions) and the horn contact slip ring.

11. Install the steering wheel by aligning the matchmarks. Do not drive or hammer the steering wheel into place or you may cause the (collapsible) steering column to collapse, in which case you'll have to buy a whole new steering column unit.

12. Tighten the steering wheel-to-steering column nut.

13. Engage the horn electrical connector and install the nuts.

14. If it was removed, make sure the spiral cable is aligned.

15. Using new air bag-to-steering wheel Torx® bolts, install them into both sides of the steering wheel.

16. Install both side lids to the steering wheel.

17. Engage the air bag unit electrical connector and install the lower lid to the steering wheel.

18. Connect the negative battery cable and make sure the air bag indicator light turns on. The AIR BAG light should extinguish after about seven seconds. If the light does not extinguish, have the air bag self diagnostic system checked.

Spiral Cable

REMOVAL & INSTALLATION

▶ **See Figures 86 and 87**

1. Position the wheels in the straight-ahead direction. The steering wheel should be right side up and level.

2. Disconnect the negative battery cable.

✳✳ CAUTION

Wait 10 minutes after the battery cable has been disconnected, before attempting to work on the air bag unit. The air bag unit is still armed and can inflate, during the 10 minute period, and possibly causing bodily injury.

3. Remove the steering wheel.

4. Remove the steering wheel covers.

5. On 1993–94 models, attach the spiral cable to the stopper.

6. Unplug the connector and remove the screws securing the spiral cable.

To install:

7. Make sure the spiral cable is properly aligned:

➡ **On 1993–94 models, this step is not necessary if the stopper was engaged.**

a. On 1993–94 models, turn the cable clockwise until it catches the stopper. Back the cable of approximately two turns until the yellow alignment mark appears on the left gear. Align the arrow with this yellow mark.

b. On 1995–98 models, turn the cable left about 2.5 turns from the right end position and align the two arrows.

8. Attach the spiral cable and engage the connector. Disengage the stopper if applicable.

9. Installation of the remaining components is the reverse of removal.

Combination Switch

REMOVAL & INSTALLATION

▶ **See Figure 88**

✳✳ CAUTION

The air bag system (SRS or SIR) must be disarmed before removing the combination switch. Failure to do so may cause accidental deployment, property damage, or personal injury.

1. Disarm the air bag, if equipped and disconnect the battery ground cable.

2. Remove the steering wheel. Remove the spiral cable from the steering column, if equipped.

3. Remove the steering column covers.

➡ **At this point, the individual switch assemblies can be removed without removing the combination switch base assembly. To service an indi-**

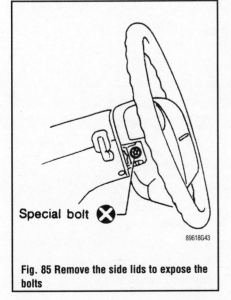

Fig. 85 Remove the side lids to expose the bolts

Special bolt ⊗

89618G43

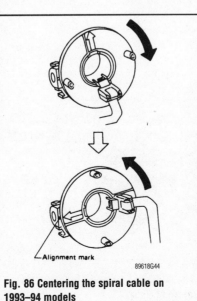

Alignment mark

89618G44

Fig. 86 Centering the spiral cable on 1993–94 models

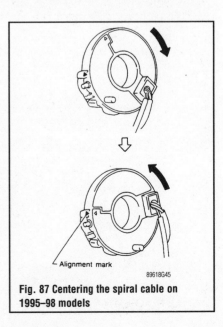

Alignment mark

89618G45

Fig. 87 Centering the spiral cable on 1995–98 models

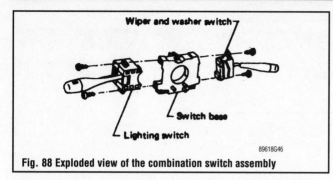

Fig. 88 Exploded view of the combination switch assembly

vidual switch/stalk assembly, disconnect the electrical lead and remove the two stalk-to-base mounting screws. If the switch base must be removed, proceed with the remainder of the removal procedure.

4. Disconnect the electrical plugs from the switch.
5. Remove the retaining screws, push down on the base of the switch with moderate pressure and twist the switch and pull it from the steering wheel shaft.
To install:
6. Install the remaining components in the reverse order of removal.
7. Check the switch functions for proper operation. Many vehicles have turn signal switches that have a tab which must fit into a hole in the steering shaft. This fit is necessary in order for the system to return the switch to the neutral position after the turn has been made. Be sure to align the tab and the hole when installing the combination switch. Be sure to align the spiral cable.

Steering Lock Cylinder

REMOVAL & INSTALLATION

▶ **See Figures 89 and 90**

✳✳ CAUTION

The air bag system (SRS or SIR) must be disarmed before removing the combination switch. Failure to do so may cause accidental deployment, property damage, or personal injury.

1. Disconnect the battery ground cable.
2. Remove the steering wheel. Observe the caution on the collapsible steering column.
3. Remove the steering column covers.
4. Using a drill, drill the heads from the steering lock-to-steering shaft clamp screws.
5. Unplug the electrical harness connector and remove the steering lock from the vehicle.
To install:
6. Install the steering lock cylinder in the proper position.
7. Using new shear screws, install and tighten them until the heads break off.
8. Connect the steering lock electrical connector.

9. On airbag models, make sure the spiral cable is aligned. Install the steering column covers and steering wheel.
10. Reconnect the battery cable. Turn key to the **ON** position and check system for proper operation.

Ignition Switch

REMOVAL & INSTALLATION

▶ **See Figure 91**

➡**The ignition switch or warning switch can be replaced without removing the steering lock assembly. The ignition switch is on the back of the assembly and the warning switch on the side.**

1. Disconnect the negative battery cable and insulate the terminal end.

✳✳ CAUTION

The air bag system must be disarmed before removing the steering wheel. Failure to do so may cause accidental deployment, property damage or personal injury.

2. Remove the steering wheel and the steering column upper and lower covers.
3. Remove the spiral cable assembly.
4. Remove the combination switch from the steering column.
5. Remove steering column support nuts and lower the steering column.
6. Disconnect the ignition switch wiring and interlock cable (if equipped).
7. Remove the bolts that secure the steering lock and remove steering lock assembly.
To install:
8. Install the steering lock assembly and secure with new shear type bolts.
9. Connect the ignition switch wiring harness and the interlock cable.
10. Raise the steering column and secure with mounting nuts.
11. Install the spiral cable assembly.
12. Install the combination switch, steering column covers, and the steering wheel.
13. Connect the negative battery cable and enable the air bag system.

Tie Rod Ends

REMOVAL & INSTALLATION

▶ **See Figures 92 thru 97**

1. Raise the front of the vehicle and support it on jackstands. Remove the wheel.
2. Remove the cotter pin and the tie rod ball joint stud nut. Note the position of the steering linkage.
3. Loosen the tie rod-to-steering gear locknut.
4. Using a suitable ball joint separator tool remove the tie rod ball joint from the steering knuckle.

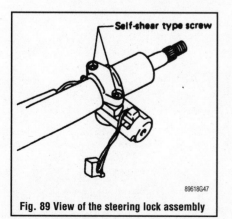

Fig. 89 View of the steering lock assembly

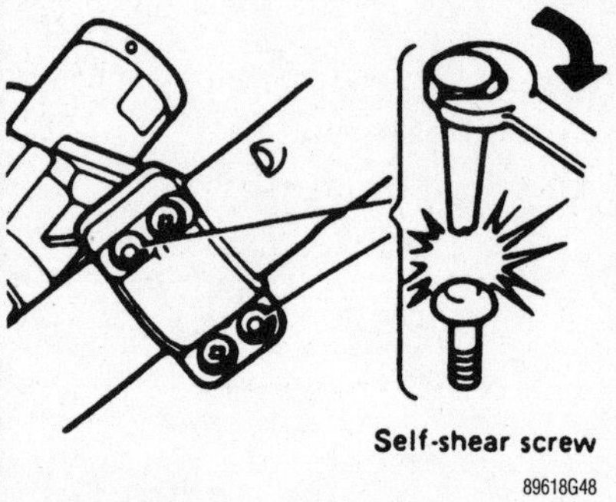

Fig. 90 Tighten the shear bolts until the heads break off

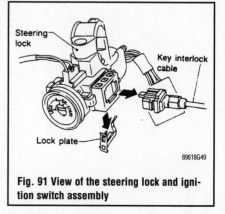

Fig. 91 View of the steering lock and ignition switch assembly

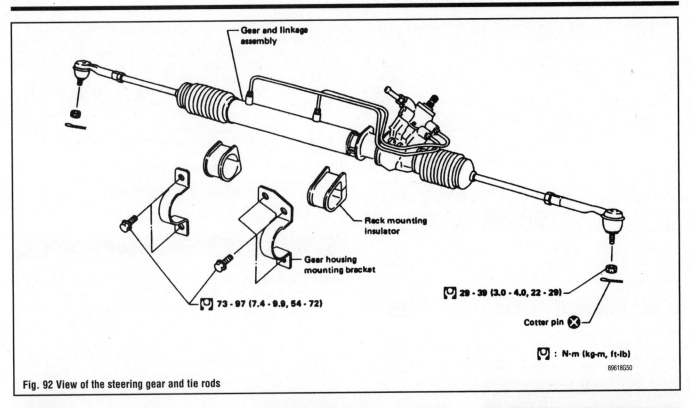

Fig. 92 View of the steering gear and tie rods

Fig. 93 Loosen the locknuts from the steering gear

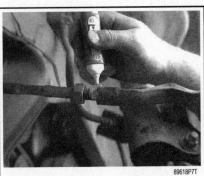

Fig. 94 Matchmark the position of the tie rod

Fig. 95 Remove the cotter pin and loosen the nut . . .

Fig. 96 . . . then break the tie rod taper from the knuckle. Leave the nut on to protect the threads

Fig. 97 Count the number of turns to remove the tie rod

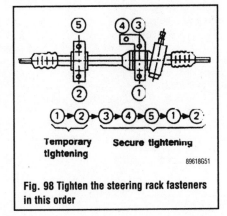

Fig. 98 Tighten the steering rack fasteners in this order

5. Loosen the locknut and remove the tie rod end from the tie rod, counting the number of complete turns it takes to completely free it.

To install:

6. Install the new tie rod end, turning it in exactly as far as you screwed out the old one. Make sure it is correctly positioned in relationship to the steering linkage.

7. Fit the ball joint and nut, tighten them and install a new cotter pin. Torque the ball joint stud nut to specifications. Check front end alignment.

8. The outer tie rod end-to-steering knuckle torque specification is 22–29 ft. lbs. (29–39 Nm.).

➡ **Always replace the cotter pins and if necessary replace the retaining nut.**

9. Check and adjust the front end alignment as necessary.

Power Steering Gear

REMOVAL & INSTALLATION

▸ **See Figures 92 and 98**

❊❊ CAUTION

The air bag system must be disarmed before removing the steering wheel. Failure to do so may cause accidental deployment, property damage or personal injury.

1. Point the front tires straight ahead and lock the steering in this position.

❊❊ WARNING

Do not turn the steering wheel or column with the lower joint removed from the steering column or the spiral cable may be damaged.

2. Remove the steering wheel.

➡ **The steering wheel must be removed before disconnecting the steering column lower joint to avoid damaging the SRS spiral cable.**

3. Raise and support the vehicle safely and remove the front wheels.
4. Disconnect the tie rod ends from the steering knuckles.
5. Remove the carbon canister from the vehicle.
6. Support the engine then remove the bolts attaching the engine mounts to the engine mounting center member. Remove the engine mounting center member.
7. Remove the front stabilizer bar from the vehicle.
8. Remove the nuts attaching the hole cover to the bulkhead.
9. Move the hole cover aside and disconnect the lower joint from the rack and pinion. Matchmark the pinion shaft and the pinion housing to record the steering neutral position.
10. Disconnect the power steering fluid pipes from the rack and pinion. •
11. Remove the bolts attaching the mounting brackets and remove the rack and pinion from the vehicle.

To install:

12. Position the rack and pinion in the vehicle and install the mounting brackets. Tighten the mounting nuts and bolts in the proper sequence.

13. Install new O-rings to the power steering fluid pipes and connect them to the rack and pinion. Tighten the low pressure line 20–29 ft. lbs. (27–39 Nm). Tighten the high pressure line to 11–18 ft. lbs. (15–25 Nm).

14. Align the lower steering joint to the pinion shaft and install the joint onto the pinion shaft. Install the bolt and tighten to 17–22 ft. lbs. (24–29 Nm).

15. Properly position the hole cover and install the attaching nuts, tighten the nuts to 2.9–3.6 ft. lbs. (4–5 Nm).

16. Install the front stabilizer.

17. Install the engine mounting center member and tighten the attaching bolts. Attach the engine mounts to the center member and tighten the bolts. Remove the support from the engine.

18. Install the remaining components in the reverse order of removal.

19. Tighten the tie rod end nuts, then install a new cotter pin.

20. Fill the power steering reservoir with fluid and bleed the air from the power steering system.

21. Check the vehicle front end alignment and adjust as necessary.

Power Steering Pump

REMOVAL & INSTALLATION

1. Disconnect the negative battery cable.
2. If necessary, remove the air cleaner duct and the air cleaner.
3. Remove the drive belt from the air conditioning compressor, if equipped.
4. Loosen power steering pump belt adjustment as follows:
   a. Loosen the pivot and mounting bolts.
   b. Loosen the idler pulley locknut and turn the adjusting nut counterclockwise to remove the power steering belt.
5. Loosen the power steering hoses at the pump and remove the bolts holding the power steering pump to the bracket.
6. Disconnect and plug the power steering hoses and remove the pump from the vehicle.

To install:

7. Using new O-rings, connect the power steering hoses to the steering pump.

8. Install the power steering pump and secure it with its mounting bolts. Tighten the front and rear mounting bolts to specifications.

9. Install the remaining components in the reverse order from which they were removed.

10. Connect the negative battery cable.

11. Fill the power steering system, start the engine and turn the steering wheel from side-to-side to bleed air from system.

BLEEDING

1. Fill the pump reservoir and allow to remain undisturbed for a few minutes.

2. Raise the vehicle until the front wheels are clear of the ground.

3. With the engine off, quickly turn the wheels right and left several times, lightly contacting the stops.

4. Add fluid if necessary.

5. Start the engine and let it idle.

6. Repeat Steps 3 and 4 with the engine idling.

7. Stop the engine, lower the vehicle until the wheels just touch the ground. Start the engine, allow it to idle, and turn the wheels back and forth several times. Check the fluid level and refill, if necessary.

9

BRAKES

BRAKE OPERATING SYSTEM

Basic Operating Principles

Hydraulic systems are used to actuate the brakes of all modern automobiles. The system transports the power required to force the frictional surfaces of the braking system together from the pedal to the individual brake units at each wheel. A hydraulic system is used for two reasons.

First, fluid under pressure can be carried to all parts of an automobile by small pipes and flexible hoses without taking up a significant amount of room or posing routing problems.

Second, a great mechanical advantage can be given to the brake pedal end of the system, and the foot pressure required to actuate the brakes can be reduced by making the surface area of the master cylinder pistons smaller than that of any of the pistons in the wheel cylinders or calipers.

The master cylinder consists of a fluid reservoir along with a double cylinder and piston assembly. Double type master cylinders are designed to separate the front and rear braking systems hydraulically in case of a leak. The master cylinder coverts mechanical motion from the pedal into hydraulic pressure within the lines. This pressure is translated back into mechanical motion at the wheels by either the wheel cylinder (drum brakes) or the caliper (disc brakes).

Steel lines carry the brake fluid to a point on the vehicle's frame near each of the vehicle's wheels. The fluid is then carried to the calipers and wheel cylinders by flexible tubes in order to allow for suspension and steering movements.

In drum brake systems, each wheel cylinder contains two pistons, one at either end, which push outward in opposite directions and force the brake shoe into contact with the drum.

In disc brake systems, the cylinders are part of the calipers. At least one cylinder in each caliper is used to force the brake pads against the disc.

All pistons employ some type of seal, usually made of rubber, to minimize fluid leakage. A rubber dust boot seals the outer end of the cylinder against dust and dirt. The boot fits around the outer end of the piston on disc brake calipers, and around the brake actuating rod on wheel cylinders.

The hydraulic system operates as follows: When at rest, the entire system, from the piston(s) in the master cylinder to those in the wheel cylinders or calipers, is full of brake fluid. Upon application of the brake pedal, fluid trapped in front of the master cylinder piston(s) is forced through the lines to the wheel cylinders. Here, it forces the pistons outward, in the case of drum brakes, and inward toward the disc, in the case of disc brakes. The motion of the pistons is opposed by return springs mounted outside the cylinders in drum brakes, and by spring seals, in disc brakes.

Upon release of the brake pedal, a spring located inside the master cylinder immediately returns the master cylinder pistons to the normal position. The pistons contain check valves and the master cylinder has compensating ports drilled in it. These are uncovered as the pistons reach their normal position. The piston check valves allow fluid to flow toward the wheel cylinders or calipers as the pistons withdraw. Then, as the return springs force the brake pads or shoes into the released position, the excess fluid reservoir through the compensating ports. It is during the time the pedal is in the released position that any fluid that has leaked out of the system will be replaced through the compensating ports.

Dual circuit master cylinders employ two pistons, located one behind the other, in the same cylinder. The primary piston is actuated directly by mechanical linkage from the brake pedal through the power booster. The secondary piston is actuated by fluid trapped between the two pistons. If a leak develops in front of the secondary piston, it moves forward until it bottoms against the front of the master cylinder, and the fluid trapped between the pistons will operate the rear brakes. If the rear brakes develop a leak, the primary piston will move forward until direct contact with the secondary piston takes place, and it will force the secondary piston to actuate the front brakes. In either case, the brake pedal moves farther when the brakes are applied, and less braking power is available.

All dual circuit systems use a switch to warn the driver when only half of the brake system is operational. This switch is usually located in a valve body which is mounted on the firewall or the frame below the master cylinder. A hydraulic piston receives pressure from both circuits, each circuit's pressure being applied to one end of the piston. When the pressures are in balance, the piston remains stationary. When one circuit has a leak, however, the greater pressure in that circuit during application of the brakes will push the piston to one side, closing the switch and activating the brake warning light.

In disc brake systems, this valve body also contains a metering valve and, in some cases, a proportioning valve. The metering valve keeps pressure from traveling to the disc brakes on the front wheels until the brake shoes on the rear wheels have contacted the drums, ensuring that the front brakes will never be used alone. The proportioning valve controls the pressure to the rear brakes to lessen the chance of rear wheel lock-up during very hard braking.

Warning lights may be tested by depressing the brake pedal and holding it while opening one of the wheel cylinder bleeder screws. If this does not cause the light to go on, substitute a new lamp, make continuity checks, and, finally, replace the switch as necessary.

The hydraulic system may be checked for leaks by applying pressure to the pedal gradually and steadily. If the pedal sinks very slowly to the floor, the system has a leak. This is not to be confused with a springy or spongy feel due to the compression of air within the lines. If the system leaks, there will be a gradual change in the position of the pedal with a constant pressure.

Check for leaks along all lines and at wheel cylinders. If no external leaks are apparent, the problem is inside the master cylinder.

DISC BRAKES

Instead of the traditional expanding brakes that press outward against a circular drum, disc brake systems utilize a disc (rotor) with brake pads positioned on either side of it. An easily-seen analogy is the hand brake arrangement on a bicycle. The pads squeeze onto the rim of the bike wheel, slowing its motion. Automobile disc brakes use the identical principle but apply the braking effort to a separate disc instead of the wheel.

The disc (rotor) is a casting, usually equipped with cooling fins between the two braking surfaces. This enables air to circulate between the braking surfaces making them less sensitive to heat buildup and more resistant to fade. Dirt and water do not drastically affect braking action since contaminants are thrown off by the centrifugal action of the rotor or scraped off the by the pads. Also, the equal clamping action of the two brake pads tends to ensure uniform, straight line stops. Disc brakes are inherently self-adjusting. There are three general types of disc brake:

1. A fixed caliper.
2. A floating caliper.
3. A sliding caliper.

The fixed caliper design uses two pistons mounted on either side of the rotor (in each side of the caliper). The caliper is mounted rigidly and does not move.

The sliding and floating designs are quite similar. In fact, these two types are often lumped together. In both designs, the pad on the inside of the rotor is moved into contact with the rotor by hydraulic force. The caliper, which is not held in a fixed position, moves slightly, bringing the outside pad into contact with the rotor. There are various methods of attaching floating calipers. Some pivot at the bottom or top, and some slide on mounting bolts. In any event, the end result is the same.

DRUM BRAKES

Drum brakes employ two brake shoes mounted on a stationary backing plate. These shoes are positioned inside a circular drum which rotates with the wheel assembly. The shoes are held in place by springs. This allows them to slide toward the drums (when they are applied) while keeping the linings and drums in alignment. The shoes are actuated by a wheel cylinder which is mounted at the top of the backing plate. When the brakes are applied, hydraulic pressure forces the wheel cylinder's actuating links outward. Since these links bear directly against the top of the brake shoes, the tops of the shoes are then forced against the inner side of the drum. This action forces the bottoms of the two shoes to contact the brake drum by rotating the entire assembly slightly (known as servo action). When pressure within the wheel cylinder is relaxed, return springs pull the shoes back away from the drum.

Most modern drum brakes are designed to self-adjust themselves during application when the vehicle is moving in reverse. This motion causes both shoes to rotate very slightly with the drum, rocking an adjusting lever, thereby causing rotation of the adjusting screw. Some drum brake systems are designed to self-adjust during application whenever the brakes are applied. This on-board adjustment system reduces the need for maintenance adjustments and keeps both the brake function and pedal feel satisfactory.

POWER BOOSTERS

Virtually all modern vehicles use a vacuum assisted power brake system to multiply the braking force and reduce pedal effort. Since vacuum is always available when the engine is operating, the system is simple and efficient. A vacuum diaphragm is located on the front of the master cylinder and assists the driver in applying the brakes, reducing both the effort and travel he must put into moving the brake pedal.

The vacuum diaphragm housing is normally connected to the intake manifold by a vacuum hose. A check valve is placed at the point where the hose enters the diaphragm housing, so that during periods of low manifold vacuum brakes assist will not be lost.

Depressing the brake pedal closes off the vacuum source and allows atmospheric pressure to enter on one side of the diaphragm. This causes the master cylinder pistons to move and apply the brakes. When the brake pedal is released, vacuum is applied to both sides of the diaphragm and springs return the diaphragm and master cylinder pistons to the released position.

If the vacuum supply fails, the brake pedal rod will contact the end of the master cylinder actuator rod and the system will apply the brakes without any power assistance. The driver will notice that much higher pedal effort is needed to stop the car and that the pedal feels harder than usual.

Vacuum Leak Test

1. Operate the engine at idle without touching the brake pedal for at least one minute.
2. Turn off the engine and wait one minute.
3. Test for the presence of assist vacuum by depressing the brake pedal and releasing it several times. If vacuum is present in the system, light application will produce less and less pedal travel. If there is no vacuum, air is leaking into the system.

System Operation Test

1. With the engine **OFF**, pump the brake pedal until the supply vacuum is entirely gone.
2. Put light, steady pressure on the brake pedal.
3. Start the engine and let it idle. If the system is operating correctly, the brake pedal should fall toward the floor if the constant pressure is maintained.

Power brake systems may be tested for hydraulic leaks just as ordinary systems are tested.

❊❊ WARNING

Clean, high quality brake fluid is essential to the safe and proper operation of the brake system. You should always buy the highest quality brake fluid that is available. If the brake fluid becomes contaminated, drain and flush the system, then refill the master cylinder with new fluid. Never reuse any brake fluid. Any brake fluid that is removed from the system should be discarded.

Adjustments

DRUM TYPE BRAKES

1. Raise and support the rear of the vehicle on jackstands.
2. Remove the rubber cover from the backing plate.
3. Insert a brake adjusting tool through the hole in the brake backing plate. Turn the toothed adjusting nut to spread the brake shoes, making contact with the brake drum.

➡**When adjusting the brake shoes, turn the wheel until considerable drag is felt.**

4. When considerable drag is felt, back off the adjusting nut a few notches, so the correct clearance is maintained between the brake drum and the brake shoes. Make sure the wheel rotates freely.

BRAKE PEDAL

◆ See Figures 1 and 2

1. Before adjusting the pedal, make sure the wheel brakes are correctly adjusted.
2. To adjust the pedal free height, perform the following procedure:
   a. Loosen the input rod locknut.
   b. Adjust the pedal free height to 6.26–6.50 in. (159–165mm) for manual transaxles or 6.65–6.85 in. (169–174mm) with an automatic transaxle.
   c. Torque the locknut to 12–16 ft. lbs. (16–22 Nm); make sure the input rod tip stays inside the clevis.
3. To adjust the brake light and/or ASCD cancel switch(s)-to-pedal clearance, perform the following procedures:
   a. Disconnect the electrical connector from the brake light and/or ASCD cancel switch(s).
   b. Loosen the brake light switch and the ASCD cancel switch locknuts.
   c. Turn the switch(s) to adjust the clearance between the pedal stopper and the threaded end; the clearance should be 0.012–0.039 in. (0.3–1.0mm).
   d. Torque the brake light and/or ASCD cancel switch locknuts to 9–11 ft. lbs. (12–15 Nm).
   e. Connect the electrical connector to the brake light switch and/or the ASCD cancel switch.
4. Check the pedal free-play; it should be 0.040.12 in. (13mm). Make sure the brake light is off when the pedal is released.
5. Check the brake pedal depressed height with the engine running. It should be 3.54 in. (90mm) for 1993–94 models. For 1995–98 models it should be 2.76 in. (70mm) for manual transaxles or 2.95 (75mm) for automatics. If the height is under these specifications, check the system for leaks, accumulation of air or damage to the components, such as: master cylinder, wheel cylinder or etc.; make the necessary repairs.

Brake Light Switch

REMOVAL & INSTALLATION

1. Unplug the electrical connector from the brake light switch.
2. Loosen the brake light switch locknuts.
3. Remove the brake light switch.
   To install:
4. Install the switch. Turn the switch to adjust the clearance between the pedal stopper and the threaded end; the clearance should be 0.012–0.039 in. (0.3–1.0mm).
5. Tighten the brake light switch locknuts to 9–11 ft. lbs. (12–15 Nm).

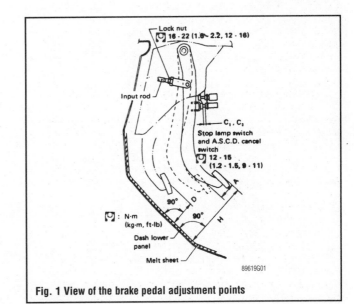

Fig. 1 View of the brake pedal adjustment points

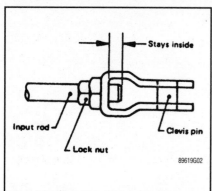

Fig. 2 Make sure the input rod stays inside the clevis when tightening the locknut

Fig. 3 Unplug the electrical connector

Fig. 4 Drain all the fluid from the reservoir

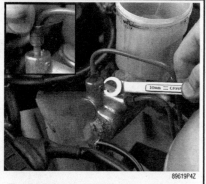

Fig. 5 Loosen the fluid lines from the master cylinder

Fig. 6 Remove the nuts securing the master cylinder to the booster . . .

Fig. 7 . . . then remove the master cylinder from the vehicle

6. Engage the electrical connector to the brake light switch. Make sure the brake light is off when the pedal is released.

Master Cylinder

REMOVAL & INSTALLATION

▶ **See Figures 3 thru 9**

1. Unplug the electrical connector from the reservoir.
2. Clean the outside of the master cylinder thoroughly, particularly around the cap and fluid lines.
3. Disconnect the brake fluid tubes, then plug the openings to prevent dirt from entering the system.
4. Remove the master cylinder mounting nuts and remove the master cylinder from the vehicle.

To install:

➡ **At this point it will be necessary to adjust the output rod length.**

5. Apply 19.69 in. Hg of vacuum to the brake booster using a vacuum pump.
6. Measure the output rod length from the end of the rod to the front face of the booster.
7. The adjustment of the rod should be 0.4045–0.4144 in. (10.275–10.525mm).
8. Bench bleed the master cylinder assembly prior to installation.
9. Install the master cylinder and tighten the mounting nuts to 9–11 ft. lbs. (12–15 Nm).
10. Connect the brake lines.

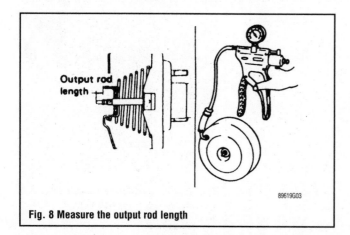

Fig. 8 Measure the output rod length

Fig. 9 Install the fluid lines to the proper ports

11. Refill the reservoir with brake fluid and bleed the system.
12. Engage the electrical connector to the bottom of the reservoir.
13. Check for fluid leaks and verify proper brake system operation.

Power Brake Booster

REMOVAL & INSTALLATION

⬧ **See Figure 8**

1. Remove the master cylinder mounting nuts and pull the master cylinder assembly (brake lines connected) away from the power booster.
2. Detach the vacuum line from the booster.
3. Detach the booster pushrod at the pedal clevis.
4. Unbolt the booster from under the dash and lift it out of the engine compartment.

To install:

5. Install the brake booster assembly to the vehicle; tighten the booster-to-chassis nuts to 9–12 ft. lbs. (13–16 Nm).
6. Install the master cylinder assembly. Be sure to perform the output rod length.
7. Connect the booster pushrod to the pedal clevis. Connect the vacuum lines to brake booster.
8. Connect the battery. Start the engine and check brake operation.

Brake Proportioning Valve

REMOVAL & INSTALLATION

The master cylinders are equipped with integral dual proportioning valves that are not to be disassembled. If necessary, replace the master cylinder.

Brake Hoses and Pipes

Metal lines and rubber brake hoses should be checked frequently for leaks and external damage. Metal lines are particularly prone to crushing and kinking under the vehicle. Any such deformation can restrict the proper flow of fluid and therefore impair braking at the wheels. Rubber hoses should be checked for cracking or scraping; such damage can create a weak spot in the hose and it could fail under pressure.

Any time the lines are removed or disconnected, extreme cleanliness must be observed. Clean all joints and connections before disassembly (use a stiff bristle brush and clean brake fluid); be sure to plug the lines and ports as soon as they are opened. New lines and hoses should be flushed clean with brake fluid before installation to remove any contamination.

REMOVAL & INSTALLATION

⬧ **See Figures 10, 11, 12 and 13**

1. Disconnect the negative battery cable.
2. Raise and safely support the vehicle on jackstands.

3. Remove any wheel and tire assemblies necessary for access to the particular line you are removing.
4. Thoroughly clean the surrounding area at the joints to be disconnected.
5. Place a suitable catch pan under the joint to be disconnected.
6. Using two wrenches (one to hold the joint and one to turn the fitting), disconnect the hose or line to be replaced.
7. Disconnect the other end of the line or hose, moving the drain pan if necessary. Always use a back-up wrench to avoid damaging the fitting.
8. Disconnect any retaining clips or brackets holding the line and remove the line from the vehicle.

➡ If the brake system is to remain open for more time than it takes to swap lines, tape or plug each remaining clip and port to keep contaminants out and fluid in.

To install:

9. Install the new line or hose, starting with the end farthest from the master cylinder. Connect the other end, then confirm that both fittings are correctly threaded and turn smoothly using finger pressure. Make sure the new line will not rub against any other part. Brake lines must be at least 1/2 in. (13mm) from the steering column and other moving parts. Any protective shielding or insulators must be reinstalled in the original location.

❊ WARNING

Make sure the hose is NOT kinked or touching any part of the frame or suspension after installation. These conditions may cause the hose to fail prematurely.

10. Using two wrenches as before, tighten each fitting.
11. Install any retaining clips or brackets on the lines.
12. If removed, install the wheel and tire assemblies, then carefully lower the vehicle to the ground.
13. Refill the brake master cylinder reservoir with clean, fresh brake fluid, meeting DOT 3 specifications. Properly bleed the brake system.
14. Connect the negative battery cable.

Brake System Bleeding

BLEEDING PROCEDURE

⬧ **See Figures 14 and 15**

The purpose of bleeding the brakes is to expel air trapped in the hydraulic system. The system must be bled whenever the pedal feels spongy, indicating that compressible air has entered the system. It must also be bled whenever the system has been opened or repaired. You will need a helper for this job.

❊ WARNING

Be careful! Brake fluid is extremely harmful to painted surfaces. Brake fluid picks up moisture from the air. Don't leave the master cylinder or the fluid container uncovered any longer than necessary. Never reuse brake fluid which has been bled from the brake system.

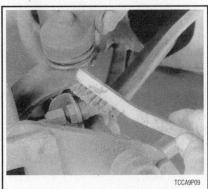

TCCA9P09

Fig. 10 Use a brush to clean the fittings of any debris

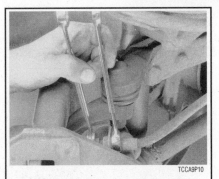

TCCA9P10

Fig. 11 Use two wrenches to loosen the fitting. If available, use flare nut type wrenches

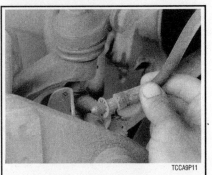

TCCA9P11

Fig. 12 Any gaskets/crush washers should be replaced with new ones during installation

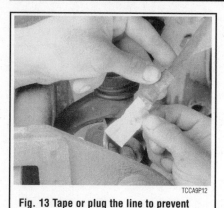

Fig. 13 Tape or plug the line to prevent contamination

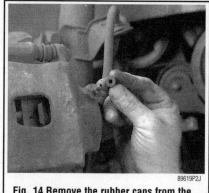

Fig. 14 Remove the rubber caps from the bleeder screws

Fig. 15 Attach the hose and jar to the bleeder screw

1. The sequence for bleeding is as follows:
- Models not equipped with ABS: left rear wheel cylinder, right rear wheel cylinder, left front caliper, right front caliper.
- Model equipped with ABS: left rear caliper or wheel cylinder, right rear caliper or wheel cylinder, left front caliper, right front caliper, ABS actuator.

➡ **On models with ABS, be sure to turn the ignition OFF and unplug the actuator connector.**

2. Clean all the bleeder screws. You may want to give each one a shot of a penetrating lubricant to loosen it up; seizure is a common problem with bleeder screws, which then break off, usually requiring replacement of the part to which they are attached.
3. Fill the master cylinder with DOT 3 brake fluid.

➡ **Check the level of the fluid often when bleeding, and refill the reservoirs as necessary. Don't let them run dry, or you will have to repeat the process.**

4. Attach a length of clear vinyl tubing to the bleeder screw on the wheel cylinder (or master cylinder). Insert the other end of the tube into a clear, clean jar half filled with brake fluid.
5. Have you helper slowly depress the brake pedal. As this is done, open the bleeder screw ⅓–½ of a turn, and allow the fluid to run through the tube. Then close the bleeder screw before the pedal reaches the end of its travel. Have you assistant slowly release the pedal. Repeat this process until no air bubbles appear in the expelled fluid.

➡ **If the brake pedal is depressed too fast, small air bubbles will form in the brake fluid.**

6. Repeat the procedure on the other remaining bleeder screws, checking the level of fluid in the cylinder reservoirs often.
7. When all the air has been bleed from the system, perform the following steps:
   a. If disconnected, reconnect the actuator.
   b. Pressurize the system and check for leaks.
   c. Check and fill the fluid reservoir.

DISC BRAKES

✱✱ CAUTION

Brake pads may contain asbestos, which has been determined to be a cancer causing agent. Never clean the brake surfaces with compressed air! Avoid inhaling any dust from any brake surface! When cleaning brake surfaces, use a commercially available brake cleaning fluid.

Brake Pads

REMOVAL & INSTALLATION

FRONT

♦ **See Figures 16 thru 21**

1. Raise and support the front of the vehicle, then remove the wheels.
2. Remove the bottom guide pin from the caliper and swing the caliper cylinder body upward.
3. Remove the brake pad retainers and the pads.
To install:
4. Compress the piston of the disc brake caliper.
5. Install the brake pads and caliper assembly.
6. Lubricate the guide pin. Tighten the guide pin to 16–23 ft. lbs. (22–31 Nm).
7. Install the wheels.
8. Apply the brakes a few times to seat the pads. Check the master cylinder and add fluid if necessary. Bleed the brakes, if necessary.

REAR

♦ **See Figures 22 thru 30**

✱✱ WARNING

Do not press the piston into the bore as performed on the front disc brakes. Due to the parking brake mechanism, the caliper piston must be turned into the bore.

1. Raise and support the vehicle safely.
2. Remove the rear wheels.
3. Release the parking brake and remove the cable bracket bolt.
4. Remove the bottom pin bolt and lift off the caliper body.
5. Pull out the pad springs and then remove the pads and shims.
To install:
6. Clean the piston end of the caliper body and the area around the pin holes. Be careful not to get oil on the rotor.
7. Carefully turn the piston clockwise back into the caliper body (this can be done with a pair of needle nose pliers). Take care not to damage the piston boot.
8. Coat the pad contact area on the mounting support with a silicone based grease.
9. Install the pads, shims, and the pad springs. Always use new shims.
10. Position the caliper body in the mounting support and tighten the pin bolt. Be sure to lubricate it first.
11. Install the wheels and lower the vehicle.
12. Apply the brakes a few times to seat the pads. Check the master cylinder and add fluid if necessary. Bleed the brakes, if necessary.

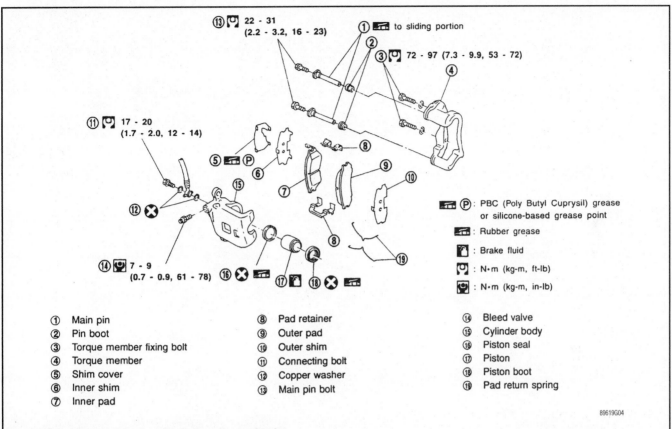

⑬ 🔧 22 - 31 (2.2 - 3.2, 16 - 23)

① ⬛ to sliding portion

② 🔧 72 - 97 (7.3 - 9.9, 53 - 72)

④

⑪ 🔧 17 - 20 (1.7 - 2.0, 12 - 14)

⑤ ⬛ Ⓟ
⑥
⑧
⑨
⑩

⑮
⑫ ✖
⑦
⑧

⬛ Ⓟ : PBC (Poly Butyl Cuprysil) grease or silicone-based grease point

⬛ : Rubber grease

🔧 : Brake fluid

🔧 : N·m (kg-m, ft-lb)

🔧 : N·m (kg-m, in-lb)

⑭ 🔧 7 - 9 (0.7 - 0.9, 61 - 78)

⑯ ✖ ⬛ ⑰ 🔧 ⑱ ✖ ⬛

⑲

① Main pin	⑧ Pad retainer	⑭ Bleed valve
② Pin boot	⑨ Outer pad	⑮ Cylinder body
③ Torque member fixing bolt	⑩ Outer shim	⑯ Piston seal
④ Torque member	⑪ Connecting bolt	⑰ Piston
⑤ Shim cover	⑫ Copper washer	⑱ Piston boot
⑥ Inner shim	⑬ Main pin bolt	⑲ Pad return spring
⑦ Inner pad		

89619G04

Fig. 16 Exploded view of the front disc brake caliper and pads

89619P4J
Fig. 17 Loosen and remove the bottom guide pin . . .

89619P6J
Fig. 18 . . . then rotate the caliper upwards

89619P9J
Fig. 19 Remove the pads from the caliper mount

89619P7Q
Fig. 20 Compress the piston into the caliper

89619P8J
Fig. 21 Lubricate the guide pin before installing it

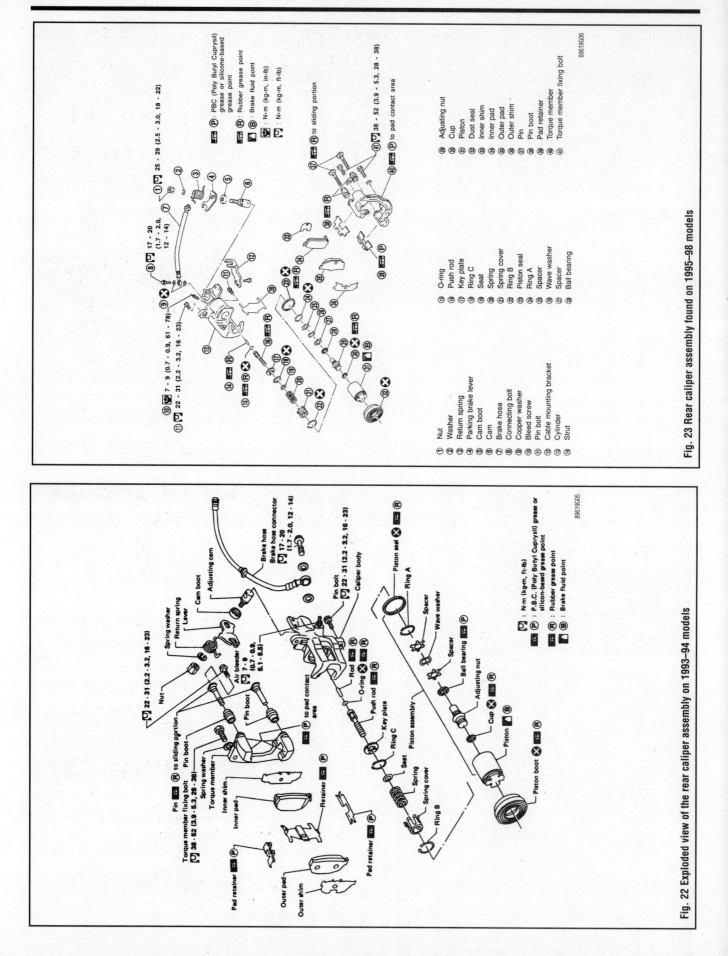

89619G06

① Nut
② Washer
③ Return spring
④ Parking brake lever
⑤ Cam
⑥ Cam boot
⑦ Brake hose
⑧ Connecting bolt
⑨ Copper washer
⑩ Bleed screw
⑪ Pin bolt
⑫ Cable mounting bracket
⑬ Cylinder
⑭ Strut

⑮ O-ring
⑯ Push rod
⑰ Key plate
⑱ Ring C
⑲ Seat
⑳ Spring
㉑ Spring cover
㉒ Ring B
㉓ Piston seal
㉔ Ring A
㉕ Spacer
㉖ Wave washer
㉗ Spacer
㉘ Ball bearing

㉙ Adjusting nut
㉚ Cup
㉛ Piston
㉜ Dust seal
㉝ Inner shim
㉞ Inner pad
㉟ Outer pad
㊱ Outer shim
㊲ Pin
㊳ Pin boot
㊴ Pad retainer
㊵ Torque member
㊶ Torque member fixing bolt

Fig. 23 Rear caliper assembly found on 1995–98 models

Fig. 22 Exploded view of the rear caliper assembly on 1993–94 models

89619G05

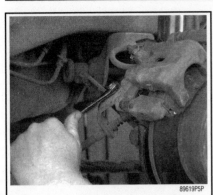

Fig. 24 Remove the cable bracket bolt then pull the bracket from the caliper

Fig. 25 Remove the bottom caliper pin bolt . . .

Fig. 26 . . . then rotate the caliper upwards

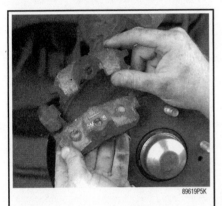

Fig. 27 Remove the pads from the mount

Fig. 28 A special tool is available to rotate the caliper piston

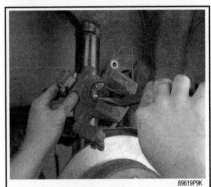

Fig. 29 As an alternative, a pair of needle nose pliers can be used

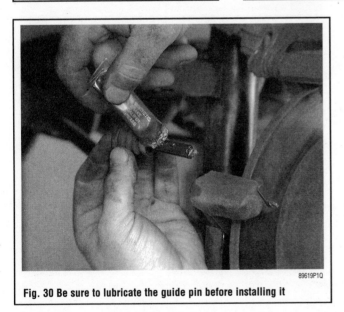

Fig. 30 Be sure to lubricate the guide pin before installing it

INSPECTION

Brake pad lining thickness can be checked without removing the pads. When replacing pads, always check the surface of the rotors for scoring or wear. The rotors should be removed for resurfacing or replacement if badly scored. Replace the pads if they have reached the wear limit, are worn unevenly or if the friction material is cracked. If the pads are worn unevenly, the caliper may be frozen or binding.

Brake Caliper

REMOVAL & INSTALLATION

FRONT

▶ See Figure 16

1. Raise and safely support vehicle.
2. Remove the front wheels.
3. Remove both guide pin bolts and brake fluid hose connector; be sure to plug the openings to prevent dirt from entering the system.
4. Remove the caliper assembly and pads from the vehicle.
   To install:
5. Install the pads, shims and retainer(s).
6. Install the brake caliper and tighten the caliper-to-torque member pin bolts to 16–23 ft. lbs. (22–31 Nm).
7. Using new copper washers, install the brake line to the brake caliper and tighten the connecting bolt to 12–14 ft. lbs. (17–20 Nm).
8. Install the wheels and tighten the lug nuts to the proper specification.
9. Bleed the brake system and top off the master cylinder as necessary.

☀ WARNING

Make sure you pump the brakes and get a hard pedal before moving the vehicle!

REAR

▶ See Figures 22 and 23

1. Raise and safely support the vehicle. Remove the rear wheels.
2. Remove the parking brake cable stay fixing bolt and the lockspring.

3. Remove the brake fluid hose from the caliper.

4. Remove the lower caliper-to-torque member pin bolt and raise the caliper.

5. Remove the pad retainers, the pads and the shims.

6. Remove the upper caliper-to-torque member pin bolt and remove the caliper.

To install:

7. Clean the piston end of the caliper body and the area around the pin holes. Be careful not to get oil on the rotor.

8. Using a pair of needle nose pliers, carefully turn the piston clockwise back into the caliper body; remove some brake fluid from the master cylinder, if necessary. Take care not to damage the piston boot.

9. Coat the pad contact area on the mounting support with a silicone based grease.

10. Install pads, shims and the pad springs.

11. Install the caliper body into position and tighten the caliper-to-torque member pin bolts to 16–23 ft. lbs. (22–31 Nm).

12. Reconnect the brake fluid hose and tighten the flare nut to 12–14 ft. lbs. (17–20 Nm).

13. Install the lockspring and the parking brake stay fixing bolt.

14. Bleed the brake system and top off the master cylinder as necessary.

15. Install the wheels, lower the vehicle.

✳✳ WARNING

Make sure you pump the brakes and get a hard pedal before moving the vehicle!

OVERHAUL

▶ **See Figures 31 thru 38**

➡ Some vehicles may be equipped dual piston calipers. The procedure to overhaul the caliper is essentially the same with the exception of multiple pistons, O-rings and dust boots.

1. Remove the caliper from the vehicle and place on a clean workbench.

✳✳ CAUTION

NEVER place your fingers in front of the pistons in an attempt to catch or protect the pistons when applying compressed air. This could result in personal injury!

➡ Depending upon the vehicle, there are two different ways to remove the piston from the caliper. Refer to the brake pad replacement procedure to make sure you have the correct procedure for your vehicle.

2. The first method is as follows:

a. Stuff a shop towel or a block of wood into the caliper to catch the piston.

b. Remove the caliper piston using compressed air applied into the caliper inlet hole. Inspect the piston for scoring, nicks, corrosion and/or worn or damaged chrome plating. The piston must be replaced if any of these conditions are found.

3. For the second method, you must rotate the piston to retract it from the caliper.

4. If equipped, remove the anti-rattle clip.

5. Use a prytool to remove the caliper boot, being careful not to scratch the housing bore.

6. Remove the piston seals from the groove in the caliper bore.

7. Carefully loosen the brake bleeder valve cap and valve from the caliper housing.

8. Inspect the caliper bores, pistons and mounting threads for scoring or excessive wear.

9. Use crocus cloth to polish out light corrosion from the piston and bore.

10. Clean all parts with denatured alcohol and dry with compressed air.

To assemble:

11. Lubricate and install the bleeder valve and cap.

12. Install the new seals into the caliper bore grooves, making sure they are not twisted.

Fig. 31 For some types of calipers, use compressed air to drive the piston out of the caliper, but make sure to keep your fingers clear

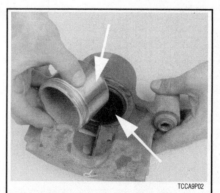

Fig. 32 Withdraw the piston from the caliper bore

Fig. 33 On some vehicles, you must remove the anti-rattle clip

Fig. 34 Use a prytool to carefully pry around the edge of the boot . . .

Fig. 35 . . . then remove the boot from the caliper housing, taking care not to score or damage the bore

Fig. 36 Use extreme caution when removing the piston seal; DO NOT scratch the caliper bore

Fig. 37 Use the proper size driving tool and a mallet to properly seal the boots in the caliper housing

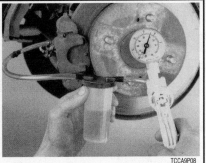

Fig. 38 There are tools, such as this Mighty-Vac, available to assist in proper brake system bleeding

Fig. 39 Remove the caliper and suspend it with wire. The disc can now be removed

13. Lubricate the piston bore.
14. Install the pistons and boots into the bores of the calipers and push to the bottom of the bores.
15. Use a suitable driving tool to seat the boots in the housing.
16. Install the caliper in the vehicle.
17. Install the wheel and tire assembly, then carefully lower the vehicle.
18. Properly bleed the brake system.

Brake Disc (Rotor)

REMOVAL & INSTALLATION

▶ See Figure 39

1. Raise and support the vehicle safely.
2. Remove the wheel assembly.
3. Remove the disc brake caliper assembly. Using a wire, support the caliper assembly; do not disconnect the brake line from the caliper.
4. Remove the caliper mounting bolts and remove the mount.
5. Remove the brake disc (rotor) from the wheel hub.

➡ On some rotors there are two threaded holes in the rotor. Two 8mmx1.25 bolts can be placed in these holes. When the bolts are turned evenly, the rotor is pressed away from the hub.

6. Inspect the disc for wear, cracks, runout and thickness; if necessary, replace the disc.

To install:
7. Install disc onto the wheel hub.
8. Install the disc caliper mount and tighten the mounting bolts.
9. Install the caliper assembly to the caliper mounting bracket.
10. Check the level of fluid in the master cylinder. Top off fluid as necessary.
11. Install the wheels and tighten the wheel lug nuts to the proper specification.
12. If the brake system was opened, bleed the brake system.

❄❄ WARNING

Make sure to pump the brakes and get a hard pedal before driving the vehicle!

INSPECTION

▶ See Figures 40 and 41

1. Check the brake rotor for roughness, cracks or chips; if necessary, replace the disc.
2. To inspect the disc runout, perform the following procedure:
   a. Secure the disc to the wheel hub with 2 nuts.

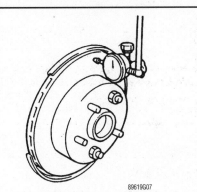

Fig. 40 Use a dial indicator to inspect the runout

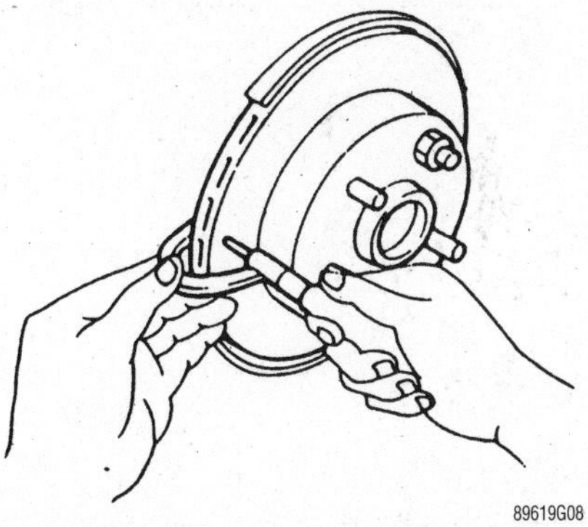

Fig. 41 Use a micrometer to check the disc thickness

   b. Make sure the wheel bearing end play is within specifications.
   c. Using a dial indicator, rotate the wheel disc and check the disc runout.
   d. If the runout exceeds specifications, move the disc to another position on the wheel hub and re-perform the dial indicator test.
   e. If the runout still exceeds specifications, machine the disc to specifications or replace it.

➡ The rotor can be machined on a brake lathe; most auto parts stores have complete machine shop service. The rotors should be machined or replaced during every front disc brake pad replacement.

3. Using a micrometer, check the disc thickness at about 8 positions; if the thickness variation is greater than 0.0004 in. (0.01mm), replace or resurface the disc.

DRUM BRAKES

> **⁑ CAUTION**
>
> Brake shoes may contain asbestos, which has been determined to be a cancer causing agent. Never clean the brake surfaces with compressed air! Avoid inhaling any dust from any brake surface! When cleaning brake surfaces, use a commercially available brake cleaning fluid.

Brake Drums

REMOVAL & INSTALLATION

▶ **See Figure 42**

1. Raise the rear of the vehicle and support it on jackstands.
2. Remove the wheels.
3. Release the parking brake.
4. Remove the brake drum from the brake shoes. If necessary, back off the brakes to remove the drum.

➡ On some models there are 2 threaded service holes in each brake drum. If the drum will not come off, fit two M8x1.25mm bolts in the service holes and screw them in: this will force the drum away from the axle.

To install:
5. Install the drum assembly to the vehicle.
6. Install the wheels.
7. Adjust the rear brakes.

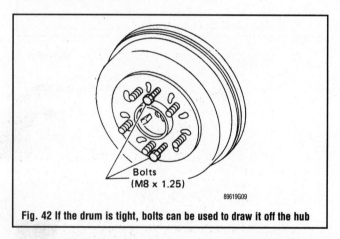

Bolts
(M8 x 1.25)

89619G09

Fig. 42 If the drum is tight, bolts can be used to draw it off the hub

INSPECTION

1. After removing the brake drum, wipe out the accumulated dust with a damp cloth.

> **⁑ CAUTION**
>
> Do not blow the brake dust out of the drums with compressed air or lung power. Brake linings may contain asbestos, a known cancer causing substance. Dispose of the cloth after use.

2. Inspect the drum for cracks, deep grooves, roughness, scoring or out-of-roundness. Replace any brake drum which is cracked. The drums should also be checked for maximum inside diameter.
3. Smooth any slight scores by polishing the friction surface with the fine emery cloth or have the drum machined (trued) at a machine shop. Heavy or extensive scoring will cause excessive brake lining wear and should be removed from the brake drum through resurfacing.

Brake Shoes

INSPECTION

1. Remove the brake drum.
2. Using a ruler, measure the shoe lining thickness. Be sure the shoes are not worn unevenly.
3. When replacing brake shoes, always check the surface of the brake drums for scoring or wear. The brake drums should resurfaced or machined if badly scored.

REMOVAL & INSTALLATION

▶ **See Figure 43**

➡ If you are not thoroughly familiar with the procedures involved in brake replacement, disassemble and assemble one side at a time, leaving the other wheel intact, as a reference. This will reduce the risk of assembling brakes incorrectly. Special brake tools are available to make this repair easier.

1. Raise the vehicle and remove the rear wheels.
2. Release the parking brake and remove the brake drum.
3. Place a heavy rubber band or clamp around the wheel cylinder to prevent the piston from coming out.
4. Remove the return springs, adjuster assembly, hold-down springs, and brake shoes.
5. Disconnect the parking brake cable from the toggle lever.

To install:
6. Clean the backing plate and check the wheel cylinder for leaks.
7. The brake drums must be machined if scored or out of round.
8. Reconnect the parking brake cable.
9. Hook the return springs into the new shoes. The return spring ends should be between the shoes and the backing plate. The longer return spring must be adjacent to the wheel cylinder. A very thin film of lithium grease may be applied to the pivot points at the ends of the brake shoes. Grease the shoe locating buttons on the backing plate, also. Be careful not to get grease on the linings or drums.
10. Install the adjuster assembly (rotate nut until adjuster rod is at its shortest point) between brake shoes. Place one shoe in the adjuster and piston slots and pry the other shoe into position. Install hold-down springs and reconnect the return springs.
11. Install the drums and wheels. Adjust the brakes and bleed the hydraulic system, if necessary.
12. Make sure the shoes do not drag when the parking brake is applied and then is released.

ADJUSTMENT

1. Raise and support the rear of the vehicle on jackstands.
2. Remove the rubber cover from the backing plate.
3. Insert a brake adjusting tool through the hole in the brake backing plate. Turn the toothed adjusting nut to spread the brake shoes, making contact with the brake drum.

➡ When adjusting the brake shoes, turn the wheel until considerable drag is felt.

4. When considerable drag is felt, back off the adjusting nut a few notches, so the correct clearance is maintained between the brake drum and the brake shoes. Make sure the wheel rotates freely.

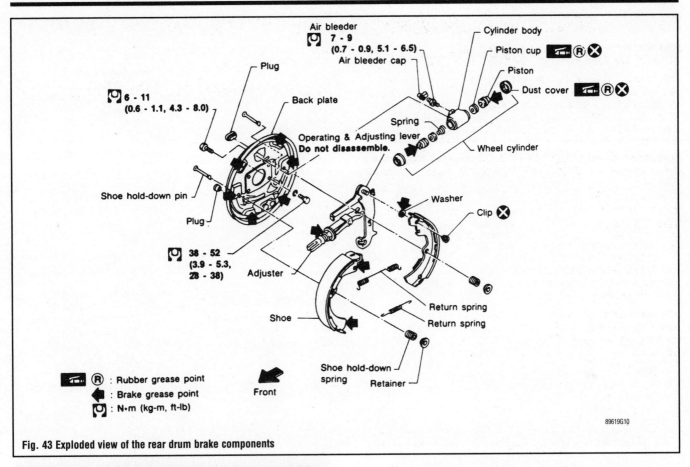

Fig. 43 Exploded view of the rear drum brake components

Wheel Cylinder

REMOVAL & INSTALLATION

▶ See Figure 43

1. Raise and safely support vehicle.
2. Remove the rear wheels and the brake drums.
3. Disconnect the flare nut and the brake tube from the wheel cylinder, then plug the line to prevent dirt from entering the system.
4. Remove the brake shoes from the backing plate.

5. Remove the wheel cylinder-to-backing plate bolts and the wheel cylinders.

➡ If the wheel cylinder is difficult to remove, bump it with a soft hammer to release it from the backing plate.

To install:

6. Install the wheel cylinder assembly to the backing plate. Tighten the wheel cylinder-to-backing plate bolts.
7. Connect the brake line(s) and install the rear brake shoes.
8. Install the brake drum.
9. Bleed the brake system.
10. Adjust the rear brakes as necessary.

PARKING BRAKE

Cables

REMOVAL & INSTALLATION

▶ See Figures 44 and 45

Front Cable

1. Remove the center console assembly.
2. Loosen and remove the parking brake cable adjusting nut at the base of the parking brake lever.
3. From under the vehicle, disconnect the parking brake cables at the equalizer.
4. Unbolt the parking brake lever from the center console.
5. Unbolt and remove the front parking brake cable from the vehicle.

To install:

6. Install the front parking brake cable into the parking brake lever and start the adjusting nut on the front cable.
7. Install the lever and cable assembly into the vehicle. Tighten the mounting bolts to 9–12 ft. lbs. (13–16 Nm).

8. From under the vehicle, connect the parking brake cables at the equalizer.
9. Install the center console assembly.

Rear Cable

1. Remove the rear wheel and the brake drum or disc assembly.
2. At the cable adjuster, loosen the adjusting nut, then separate the rear cable from the equalizer.
3. On rear drum brakes, remove the brake shoes from the backing plate, then separate the rear cable from the toggle lever.
4. On rear disc brakes, remove the cable retainer and the cable end from the toggle lever.
5. Remove the bolts that secure the cable to the vehicle under body.
6. Pull the cable through the backing plate and remove it from the vehicle.

To install:

7. Connect the cable to the toggle lever and tighten the cable retainer nut on the backing plate to 9–12 ft. lbs. (13–16 Nm).
8. Install the bolts that secure the cable to the vehicle under body and tighten the bolt to 45–57 inch lbs. (5.1–6.5 Nm).

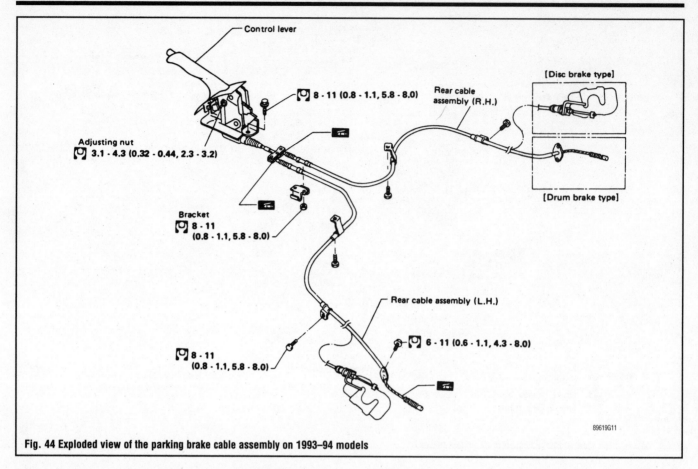

Fig. 44 Exploded view of the parking brake cable assembly on 1993–94 models

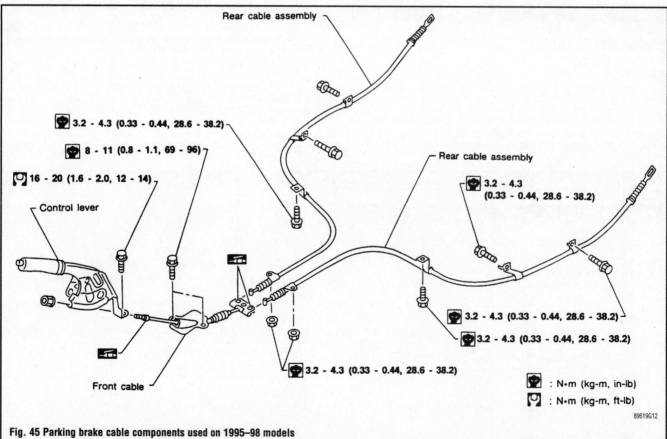

Fig. 45 Parking brake cable components used on 1995–98 models

9. At the cable equalizer, connect the parking brake cable and tighten the bolt or mounting nut to 9–12 ft. lbs. (13–16 Nm).

10. Install the disc brake rotor and wheel assembly.

11. Adjust the parking brake cable.

ADJUSTMENT

➡ **Make sure the rear brakes are properly adjusted prior to adjusting the parking brake.**

1. Pull the parking brake lever with 44 lbs. of force and note the number of notches.

2. The parking brake lever should raise 8–11 notches.

3. Locate the parking brake adjuster at the base of the hand lever and rotate the adjuster nut on the threaded rod to obtain the proper parking brake lever adjustment.

4. Bend the parking brake warning lamp switch plate so that brake warning light comes on when parking brake lever is pulled up 1 notch. The brake light should turn off when the lever is fully released.

ANTI-LOCK BRAKE SYSTEM

General Information

▸ **See Figures 46 and 47**

The Anti-Lock Brake System (ABS) is designed to prevent locked wheel skidding during hard braking or during braking on slippery surfaces. The front wheels of a vehicle cannot apply steering force if they are locked and sliding; the vehicle will continue in its previous direction of travel. The anti-lock brake systems found on these vehicles hold the wheels just below the point of locking, thereby allowing some steering response and preventing the rear of the vehicle from sliding sideways while braking.

There are conditions for which ABS provides no benefit. Hydroplaning is possible when the tires ride on a film of water, losing contact with the paved surface. This renders the vehicle totally uncontrollable until road contact is regained. Extreme steering maneuvers at high speed, or cornering beyond the limits of tire adhesion, can result in skidding which is independent of vehicle braking.

Under normal braking conditions, ABS functions in the same manner as a standard brake system. The system is merely a combination of electrical and hydraulic components, working together, to control the flow of brake fluid to the wheels when necessary.

The ABS control unit is the electronic brain of the system, receiving and

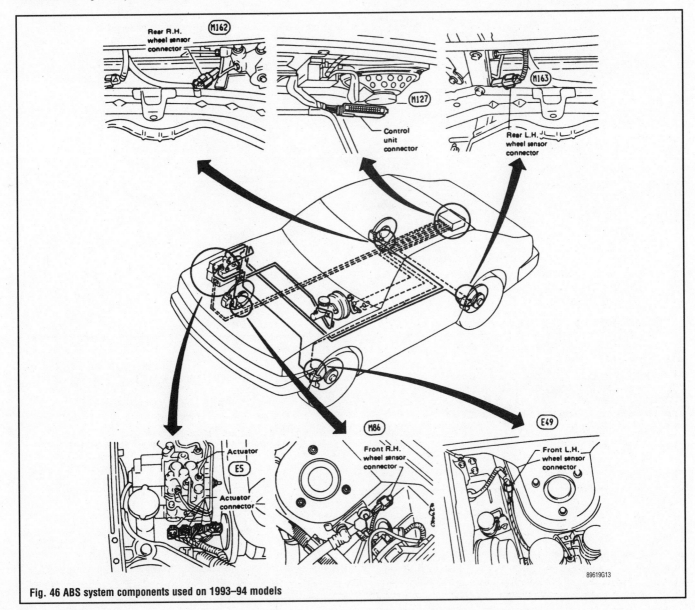

Fig. 46 ABS system components used on 1993–94 models

89619G13

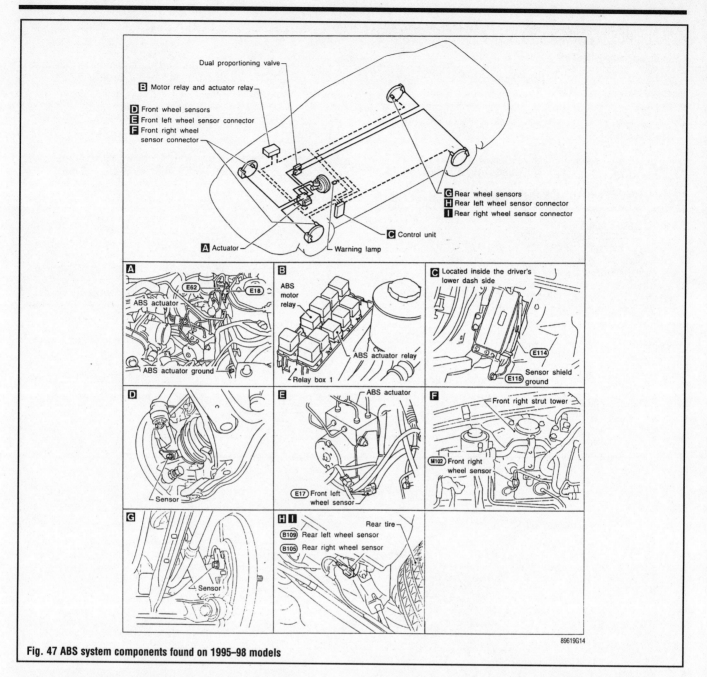

Fig. 47 ABS system components found on 1995–98 models

interpreting speed signals from the speed sensors. The control unit will enter anti-lock mode when it senses impending wheel lock at any wheel, and immediately control the brake line pressure to the affected wheel.

The actuator assembly is separate from the master cylinder and booster. It contains the wheel circuit valves used to control brake fluid pressure to each wheel circuit.

The wheel speed sensors monitor decelerating wheel speed and provide data to the control module.

PRECAUTIONS

• Certain components within the Anti-lock Brake System (ABS) are not intended to be serviced or repaired individually. Only those components with removal and installation procedures should be serviced.

• Do not use rubber hoses or other parts not specifically identified for an ABS system. When using repair kits, replace all parts included in the kit. Partial or incorrect repair may lead to functional problems and require the replacement of components.

• Lubricate rubber parts with clean, fresh brake fluid to ease assembly. Do not use lubricated shop air to clean parts; damage to rubber components may result.

• Use only specified brake fluid from an unopened container.

• If any hydraulic component or line is removed or replaced, it may be necessary to bleed the entire system.

• A clean repair area is essential. Always clean the reservoir and cap thoroughly before removing the cap. The slightest amount of dirt in the fluid may plug an orifice and impair the system function. Perform repairs after components have been thoroughly cleaned; use only denatured alcohol to clean components. Do not allow ABS components to come into contact with any substance containing mineral oil; this includes used shop rags.

• The ABS control unit is a microprocessor similar to other computer units in the vehicle. Ensure that the ignition switch is **OFF** before removing or installing controller harnesses. Avoid static electricity discharge at or near the controller.

• If any arc welding is to be done on the vehicle, the control unit should be unplugged before welding operations begin.

Reading Codes

▶ **See Figures 48, 49 and 50**

On 1993–94 models, drive the vehicle over 20 mph (32 km/h) for at least one minute. With the engine running, inspect the LED on the control unit. The codes will appear as flashes of the LED.

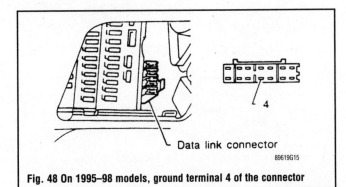

Data link connector

89619G15

Fig. 48 On 1995–98 models, ground terminal 4 of the connector

No. of L.E.D. flashes	Malfunctioning part or unit
1	Left front actuator solenoid circuit
2	Right front actuator solenoid circuit
3	Right rear actuator solenoid circuit
4	Left rear actuator solenoid circuit
5	Left front wheel sensor circuit
6	Right front wheel sensor circuit
7	Right rear wheel sensor circuit
8	Left rear wheel sensor circuit
9	Motor and motor relay
10	Solenoid valve relay
16 or continuous	Control unit
Warning activates and L.E.D. "OFF"	Power supply or ground circuit for control unit

89619G16

Fig. 49 ABS system trouble codes used on 1993–94 models

Code No. (No. of LED flashes)	Malfunctioning part
12	Self-diagnosis could not detect any malfunctions.
45	Actuator front left outlet solenoid valve
46	Actuator front left inlet solenoid valve
41	Actuator front right outlet solenoid valve
42	Actuator front right inlet solenoid valve
51	Actuator rear right outlet solenoid valve
52	Actuator rear right inlet solenoid valve
55	Actuator rear left inlet solenoid valve
56	Actuator rear left inlet solenoid valve
25	Front left sensor (open-circuit)
26	Front left sensor (short-circuit)
21	Front right sensor (open-circuit)
22	Front right sensor (short-circuit)
35	Rear left sensor (open-circuit)
36	Rear left sensor (short-circuit)
31	Rear right sensor (open-circuit)
32	Rear right sensor (short-circuit)
18	Sensor rotor
61	Actuator motor or motor relay
63	Solenoid valve relay
57	Power supply (Low voltage)
71	Control unit
Warning lamp stays on continuously.	Control unit power supply circuit Warning lamp bulb circuit Control unit or control unit connector Solenoid valve relay stuck Power supply for solenoid valve relay coil
Warning lamp stays on, during self-diagnosis.	Control unit
Warning lamp does not work before engine starts.	Fuse, warning lamp bulb or warning lamp circuit Control unit
Warning lamp does not come on during self-diagnosis.	Control unit

89619G17

Fig. 50 ABS system trouble codes used on 1995–98 models

On 1995–98 models, drive the vehicle over 20 mph (32 km/h) for at least one minute. Turn the ignition **OFF**. Ground the **4** terminal of the data link connector under the dashboard, then turn the ignition **ON**. The codes will appear as flashes of the ABS lamp on the dashboard.

➡**Do not press the brake pedal while reading codes.**

Clearing Codes

On 1993–94 models, clear the codes by disconnecting the negative battery cable for at least one minute.

On 1995–98 models, clear the codes by grounding and ungrounding the **L** terminal of the data link connector under the dashboard three times within 12.5 seconds. Each ground should last more than one second. The ABS warning lamp on the dashboard will go out after the erasing operation has been completed.

ABS Control Unit

REMOVAL & INSTALLATION

▶ **See Figures 46 and 47**

On 1993–94 models, the ABS control unit is located in the trunk, next to the rear speaker. On 1995–98 models, it is under the driver's side of the dashboard.
1. Disconnect the negative battery cable.
2. Unplug the electrical connector from the control unit.
3. Remove the control unit-to-chassis bolts and the control unit.
4. To install, reverse the removal procedures.
5. Connect the electrical harness to the ABS control unit. Connect the negative battery cable.

ABS Actuator

REMOVAL & INSTALLATION

▶ **See Figures 46 and 47**

The ABS actuator is located in the engine compartment.
1. Relieve the pressure from the ABS system.
2. Disconnect the negative battery cable.
3. Unplug the electrical harness from the actuator.
4. Disconnect the fluid lines from the actuator. Plug the ends of the lines to prevent leakage.
5. Remove the actuator-to-bracket mounting nuts.
6. Remove the actuator from the mounting bracket.
To install:
7. Position the actuator onto the mounting bracket.
8. Install the actuator mounting fasteners.
9. Connect the fluid lines and the electrical harness.
10. Connect the negative battery cable.
11. Bleed the brake system.

Front Wheel Sensor

REMOVAL & INSTALLATION

▶ **See Figures 46 and 47**

1. Raise and safely support the vehicle.
2. Remove the front wheels.
3. Unplug the sensor harness connector.
4. Detach the sensor-to-steering knuckle bolts.
5. Unbolt the sensor from the rear of the steering knuckle.
6. Withdraw the sensor from the sensor rotor. Remove the sensor mounting brackets from the sensor wiring.

➡**During removal and installation, take care not to damage the sensor or the teeth of the rotor.**

To install:
7. Transfer the mounting brackets to the new sensor. Insert the sensor through the opening in the rear of the knuckle and engage the sensor with the rotor teeth.
8. Install the sensor mounting bolts. Check and adjust the sensor-to-rotor clearance. Once the clearance is set, tighten the sensor-to-steering knuckle bolts to 13–17 ft. lbs. (18–24 Nm).
9. Position and install the sensor mounting brackets. Make the sure the sensor wiring is routed properly.
10. Engage the sensor harness connector.
11. Mount the front wheels and lower the vehicle.

TESTING

1. Check the clearance between the edge of the sensor and rotor teeth using a feeler gauge; the clearance should be 0.008–0.039 in. (0.2–1.0mm) on 1993–94 models. On 1995–98 models, it should be 0.0071–0.0343 in. (0.18–0.87mm). To adjust the clearance, loosen the sensor mounting bolt(s) and move the sensor back and forth until the clearance is as specified.
2. Using an ohmmeter, measure the resistance between the harness terminals. It should be 0.8–1.2k ohms.

Rear Wheel Sensor

REMOVAL & INSTALLATION

▶ **See Figures 46 and 47**

1. Raise and safely support the vehicle.
2. Remove the rear wheels.
3. Unplug the sensor harness connector.
4. Detach the sensor-to-mounting bracket bolt.
5. Remove the sensor mounting bolts.
6. Withdraw the sensor from the rear gusset.
7. Remove the sensor mounting brackets from the sensor wiring.
To install:
8. Transfer the mounting brackets to the new sensor.
9. Install the sensor. Check and adjust the sensor-to-rotor clearance. Once the clearance is set, tighten the sensor mounting bolt to 13–17 ft. lbs. (18–24 Nm).
10. Install the sensor mounting brackets. Make the sure the sensor wiring is routed properly.
11. Engage the sensor harness connector.
12. Mount the rear wheels and lower the vehicle.

TESTING

1. Check the clearance between the edge of the sensor and rotor teeth using a feeler gauge; the clearance should be 0.008–0.039 in. (0.2–1.0mm) on 1993–94 models. On 1995–98 models, it should be 0.0091–0.0283 in. (0.23–0.72mm). To adjust the clearance, loosen the sensor mounting bolt(s) and move the sensor back and forth until the clearance is as specified.
2. Using an ohmmeter, measure the resistance between the harness terminals. It should be 0.8–1.2k ohms.

Bleeding the ABS System

PRECAUTIONS

• Carefully monitor the brake fluid level in the master cylinder at all times during the bleeding procedure. Keep the reservoir full at all times.
• Only use brake fluid that meets or exceeds DOT 3 specifications.
• Place a suitable container under the master cylinder to avoid spillage of brake fluid.
• Do not allow brake fluid to come in contact with any painted surface. Brake fluid makes excellent paint remover.
• Make sure to use the proper bleeding sequence.

BLEEDING PROCEDURE

1. Turn the ignition switch **OFF** and unplug the electrical connectors from the ABS actuator.

2. Clean all dirt from around the master cylinder reservoir caps. Remove the caps and fill the master cylinder to the proper level with clean, fresh brake fluid meeting DOT 3 specifications.

→Brake fluid picks up moisture from the air, which reduces its effectiveness and causes brake line corrosion. Don't leave the master cylinder or the fluid container open any longer than necessary. Be careful not to spill brake fluid on painted surfaces. Wipe up any spilled fluid immediately and rinse the area with clear water.

3. Clean all the bleeder screws. You may want to give each one a shot of penetrating solvent to loosen it. Seizure is a common problem with bleeder screws, which then break off, sometimes requiring replacement of the part to which they are attached.

4. Attach a length of clear vinyl tubing to the bleeder screw on the left rear wheel cylinder or caliper (right rear on 1995–98 models). Insert the other end of the tube into a clear, clean jar ½ filled with brake fluid.

5. Have your helper SLOWLY depress the brake pedal. As this is done, open the bleeder (follow the correct bleeding order) screw ⅓–½ of a turn, and allow the fluid to run through the tube. Close the bleeder screw before the pedal reaches the end of its travel. Have your assistant slowly release the pedal. Repeat this process until no air bubbles appear in the expelled fluid.

6. Repeat the procedure on the other wheels in the following order:
1993–94 models:
  a. Right front caliper
  b. Right rear wheel cylinder or caliper
  c. Left front caliper
1995–98 models:
  a. Left front caliper
  b. Left rear wheel cylinder or caliper
  c. Right front caliper

7. Be sure to check the fluid level in the master cylinder reservoirs often. Do not allow the reservoirs to run dry or the bleeding process will have to be repeated.

BRAKE SPECIFICATIONS
All measurements in inches unless noted

Year	Model	Master Cylinder Bore	Brake Disc Original Thickness	Brake Disc Minimum Thickness	Brake Disc Maximum Runout	Brake Drum Diameter Original Inside Diameter	Brake Drum Diameter Max. Wear Limit	Brake Drum Diameter Max. Machine Diameter	Minimum Lining Thickness Front	Minimum Lining Thickness Rear
1993	Disc/Drum	①	0.870	0.787	0.0028	9.000	0.060	9.060	0.079	0.059
	Rear Disc	—	0.350	0.315	0.0028	—	—	—	—	0.079
1994	Disc/Drum	①	0.870	0.787	0.0028	9.000	0.060	9.060	0.079	0.059
	Rear Disc	—	0.350	0.315	0.0028	—	—	—	—	0.079
1995	Front Disc	0.937	0.870	0.787	0.0031	—	—	—	0.079	—
	Rear Disc	—	0.350	0.310	0.0059	—	—	—	—	0.059
1996	Front Disc	0.937	0.870	0.787	0.0031	—	—	—	0.079	—
	Rear Disc	—	0.350	0.310	0.0059	—	—	—	—	0.059
1997	Front Disc	0.937	0.870	0.787	0.0031	—	—	—	0.079	—
	Rear Disc	—	0.350	0.310	0.0059	—	—	—	—	0.059
1998	Front Disc	0.937	0.870	0.787	0.0031	—	—	—	0.079	—
	Rear Disc	—	0.350	0.310	0.0059	—	—	—	—	0.059

① Without ABS = 0.937 in.
  With ABS = 1.000 in.

89619C01

Troubleshooting the Brake System

Problem	Cause	Solution
Low brake pedal (excessive pedal travel required for braking action.)	Excessive clearance between rear linings and drums caused by inoperative automatic adjusters	Make 10 to 15 alternate forward and reverse brake stops to adjust brakes. If brake pedal does not come up, repair or replace adjuster parts as necessary.
	Worn rear brakelining	Inspect and replace lining if worn beyond minimum thickness specification.
	Bent, distorted brakeshoes, front or rear	Replace brakeshoes in axle sets
	Air in hydraulic system	Remove air from system. Refer to Brake Bleeding.
Low brake pedal (pedal may go to floor with steady pressure applied.)	Fluid leak in hydraulic system	Fill master cylinder to fill line; have helper apply brakes and check calipers, wheel cylinders, differential valve, tubes, hoses and fittings for leaks. Repair or replace as necessary.
	Air in hydraulic system	Remove air from system. Refer to Brake Bleeding.
	Incorrect or non-recommended brake fluid (fluid evaporates at below normal temp).	Flush hydraulic system with clean brake fluid. Refill with correct-type fluid.
	Master cylinder piston seals worn, or master cylinder bore is scored, worn or corroded	Repair or replace master cylinder
Low brake pedal (pedal goes to floor on first application—o.k. on subsequent applications.)	Disc brake pads sticking on abutment surfaces of anchor plate. Caused by a build-up of dirt, rust, or corrosion on abutment surfaces	Clean abutment surfaces
Fading brake pedal (pedal height decreases with steady pressure applied.)	Fluid leak in hydraulic system	Fill master cylinder reservoirs to fill mark, have helper apply brakes, check calipers, wheel cylinders, differential valve, tubes, hoses, and fittings for fluid leaks. Repair or replace parts as necessary.
	Master cylinder piston seals worn, or master cylinder bore is scored, worn or corroded	Repair or replace master cylinder
Decreasing brake pedal travel (pedal travel required for braking action decreases and may be accompanied by a hard pedal.)	Caliper or wheel cylinder pistons sticking or seized	Repair or replace the calipers, or wheel cylinders
	Master cylinder compensator ports blocked (preventing fluid return to reservoirs) or pistons sticking or seized in master cylinder bore	Repair or replace the master cylinder
	Power brake unit binding internally	Test according to the following procedure: (a) Shift transmission into neutral and start engine (b) Increase engine speed to 1500 rpm, close throttle and fully depress brake pedal (c) Slow release brake pedal and stop engine (d) Have helper remove vacuum check valve and hose from power unit. Observe for backward movement of brake pedal. (e) If the pedal moves backward, the power unit has an internal bind—replace power unit

TCCA9001

Troubleshooting the Brake System (cont.)

Problem	Cause	Solution
Spongy brake pedal (pedal has abnormally soft, springy, spongy feel when depressed.)	Air in hydraulic system	Remove air from system. Refer to Brake Bleeding.
	Brakeshoes bent or distorted	Replace brakeshoes
	Brakelining not yet seated with drums and rotors	Burnish brakes
	Rear drum brakes not properly adjusted	Adjust brakes
Hard brake pedal (excessive pedal pressure required to stop vehicle. May be accompanied by brake fade.)	Loose or leaking power brake unit vacuum hose	Tighten connections or replace leaking hose
	Incorrect or poor quality brake lining	Replace with lining in axle sets
	Bent, broken, distorted brakeshoes	Replace brakeshoes
	Calipers binding or dragging on mounting pins. Rear brakeshoes dragging on support plate.	Replace brake mounting pins and bushings. Clean rust or burrs from rear brake support plate ledges and lubricate ledges with molydisulfide grease. NOTE: If ledges are deeply grooved or scored, do not attempt to sand or grind them smooth—replace support plate.
	Caliper, wheel cylinder, or master cylinder pistons sticking or seized	Repair or replace parts as necessary
	Power brake unit vacuum check valve malfunction	Test valve according to the following procedure: (a) Start engine, increase engine speed to 1500 rpm, close throttle and immediately stop engine (b) Wait at least 90 seconds then depress brake pedal (c) If brakes are not vacuum assisted for 2 or more applications, check valve is faulty
	Power brake unit has internal bind	Test unit according to the following procedure: (a) With engine stopped, apply brakes several times to exhaust all vacuum in system (b) Shift transmission into neutral, depress brake pedal and start engine (c) If pedal height decreases with foot pressure and less pressure is required to hold pedal in applied position, power unit vacuum system is operating normally. Test power unit. If power unit exhibits a bind condition, replace the power unit.
	Master cylinder compensator ports (at bottom of reservoirs) blocked by dirt, scale, rust, or have small burrs (blocked ports prevent fluid return to reservoirs).	Repair or replace master cylinder CAUTION: Do not attempt to clean blocked ports with wire, pencils, or similar implements. Use compressed air only.
	Brake hoses, tubes, fittings clogged or restricted	Use compressed air to check or unclog parts. Replace any damaged parts.
	Brake fluid contaminated with improper fluids (motor oil, transmission fluid, causing rubber components to swell and stick in bores	Replace all rubber components, combination valve and hoses. Flush entire brake system with DOT 3 brake fluid or equivalent.
	Low engine vacuum	Adjust or repair engine

TCCA9002

10

BODY AND TRIM

EXTERIOR

Doors

REMOVAL & INSTALLATION

✳✳ WARNING

To prevent damage to the vehicle, two people should perform this procedure.

1. Open the door and support it under its center using a floor jack.
2. Matchmark the door hinge for installation reference.
3. Label and disconnect the electrical harnesses.
4. Remove the door hinge-to-body attaching bolts and washers.
5. Carefully remove the door from the vehicle.

To install:

6. Position the door on the vehicle, carefully aligning the matchmarks made during removal.
7. Tighten the attaching bolts to 22–27 ft. lbs. (29–37 Nm).
8. Carefully close the door to check for proper alignment.
9. Readjust the door hinges as necessary.
10. Once the door is properly aligned, adjust the door lock (striker).

ADJUSTMENT

▶ **See Figures 1 and 2**

1. Determine which hinge bolts must be loosened to move the door in the desired direction.
2. Matchmark the hinge to the door as a starting reference.
3. Loosen the hinge bolts just enough to permit movement of the door with a padded prybar, but not loose enough to permit the door to move on its own.
4. Move the door the distance estimated to obtain the desired fit.
5. Tighten the door hinge-to-body bolts to 22–27 ft. lbs. (29–37 Nm).
6. Check the door to ensure that it closes properly and that there is no binding or interference with the adjacent panel.
7. Repeat the operation until the desired fit is obtained.
8. Check the door lock (striker) alignment for proper door closing, and adjust as necessary.

Hood

REMOVAL & INSTALLATION

▶ **See Figures 3, 4 and 5**

✳✳ WARNING

To prevent damage to the vehicle, two people should perform this procedure.

1. Open and support the hood.
2. Matchmark the hood hinges to the hood for installation reference.
3. Note the spacing between the front fender and hood for alignment reference.
4. Protect the body with a cover to prevent damage to the paint.
5. Remove the hood hinge-to-hood attaching bolts.

➡ Take care not to let the hood slip when the bolts are removed.

6. Remove the hood from the vehicle.

To install:

7. Position the hood on the vehicle and hand-tighten the retaining bolts.
8. Align the matchmarks and tighten the hood hinge bolts securely.
9. Carefully lower the hood to check for proper alignment.
10. Adjust the hood alignment as necessary.

ALIGNMENT

1. The hood can be adjusted fore-and-aft and side-to-side by loosening the hood hinge retaining bolts.
2. Reposition the hood as required and tighten the hood hinge bolts to 12–15 ft. lbs. (16–21 Nm).
3. To raise or lower the hood in relation to the fenders, add spacers between the hood and hinges.
4. Check the hood lock (striker) alignment for proper hood closing, and adjust as necessary.

Trunk Lid

REMOVAL & INSTALLATION

▶ **See Figures 6 and 7**

✳✳ WARNING

To prevent damage to the vehicle, two people should perform this procedure.

1. Open and support the trunk lid.
2. Matchmark the trunk lid hinges to the trunk lid for installation reference.
3. Note the spacing between the rear fender and trunk lid for alignment reference.
4. Protect the body with a cover to prevent damage to the paint.
5. Using a pry tool, carefully disengage the torsion bars.

✳✳ CAUTION

The trunk torsion bars are under spring tension. Wear eye protection, and be careful.

6. Carefully pry back the spring clip and push out the pivot pins.

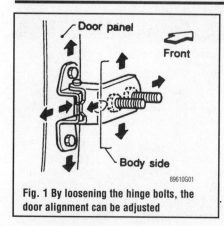

Fig. 1 By loosening the hinge bolts, the door alignment can be adjusted

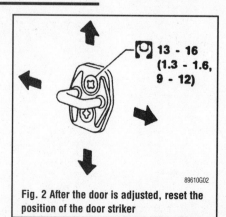

Fig. 2 After the door is adjusted, reset the position of the door striker

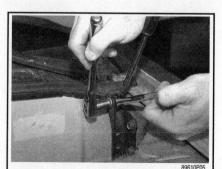

Fig. 3 Use a back up wrench to hold the strut mount in place while the nut is removed

Fig. 4 Be sure to matchmark the hood hinges before removing the hood

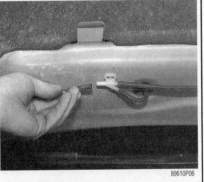

Fig. 5 Don't forget to unplug the windshield washer line

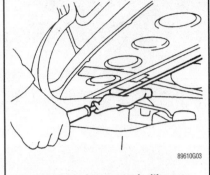

Fig. 6 Use a pry bar wrapped with a rag and carefully disengage the torsion bars

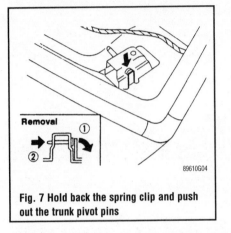

Fig. 7 Hold back the spring clip and push out the trunk pivot pins

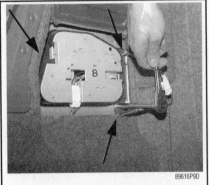

Fig. 8 Remove the nuts from the studs which secure the lens to the body

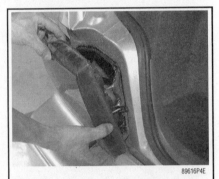

Fig. 9 It may take some force to remove the lens; do not pry on the light, as it may crack

➡Take care not to let the trunk lid slip when the bolts are removed.

    7. Remove the trunk lid from the vehicle.

To install:

    8. Position the trunk lid on the vehicle and hand-tighten the retaining bolts.

    9. Align the matchmarks and tighten the trunk lid bolts securely.

    10. Carefully lower the trunk lid to check for proper alignment.

    11. Adjust the trunk lid alignment as necessary.

ALIGNMENT

    1. The trunk lid can be adjusted fore-and-aft and side-to-side by loosening the trunk lid bolts.

    2. Reposition the trunk lid as required and tighten the trunk lid bolts securely.

    3. To raise or lower the trunk lid in relation to the fenders, add spacers between the trunk lid and hinges.

    4. Check the trunk lid lock (striker) alignment for proper trunk lid closing, and adjust as necessary.

Tail Light Lens

REMOVAL & INSTALLATION

▶ **See Figures 8 and 9**

    1. Remove the nuts which secure the tail light lens to the body.

    2. Remove the bulb holder which attaches to the tail light.

    3. Carefully pull the tail light from the vehicle. If necessary, use a heat gun to soften the butyl sealant.

To install:

    4. Apply new butyl sealant to the new lens.

    5. Install the tail light. Tighten the nuts securely, but don't overtighten them.

    6. Install the bulb holder to the tail light.

Grille

REMOVAL & INSTALLATION

    1. Open and support the hood.

    2. Locate the grille attaching clips.

    3. Using a long, straight bladed screwdriver, reach in through the grille and rotate the attaching clips ¼ turn. This will align the square head of the clip with the square hole in the grille.

    4. Carefully remove the grille from the vehicle.

To install:

    5. Remove any clips still left in the holes on the body and properly position them in the grille.

    6. Position the grille on the body and align all the attaching clips with their respective holes.

    7. Carefully push the grille into position, making sure all attaching clips engage properly.

Outside Mirrors

REMOVAL & INSTALLATION

▶ **See Figures 10, 11, 12, 13 and 14**

    1. Remove the interior door panel.

    2. Carefully pry up the plastic cover.

    3. Remove the sail trim panel.

    4. On power mirrors, disconnect the mirror electrical harness.

    5. Remove the mirror attaching screws, then carefully pull the mirror from the door.

To install:

    6. Position the mirror on the vehicle, making sure the rubber molding around the mirror is installed correctly.

Fig. 10 Pop off the plastic cover that covers the mirror mounting screws

Fig. 11 Then remove the plastic trim cover

Fig. 12 Remove the three bolts that attach the mirror to the door

Fig. 13 After the bolts are removed, the mirror is easily removed. Don't forget to unplug the harness connector

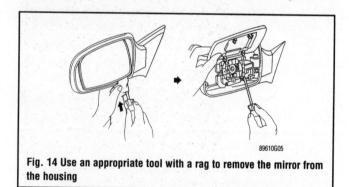

Fig. 14 Use an appropriate tool with a rag to remove the mirror from the housing

7. Install the mirror attaching screws and tighten securely.
8. On power mirrors, connect the mirror electrical harness.
9. Install the sail trim panel.
10. Position the plastic cover and push into place to engage the tangs.
11. Install the interior door panel.

Antenna

➡️On some vehicles, the antenna is impregnated in the rear window glass. On these vehicles, the antenna can be repaired using an antenna repair kit.

REPLACEMENT

Fixed Mast

1. Remove the antenna mast by unscrewing it from the base.
2. Remove the antenna nut and base.
3. Disconnect the antenna cable at the antenna.
4. Remove the mounting bolt at the bottom of the antenna.

5. Remove the antenna through the trunk.
6. Installation is the reverse of removal.
7. Tighten the mounting bolt securely.

Power Antenna

▶ See Figure 15

MOTOR

1. Remove the antenna nut and base.
2. Disconnect the antenna cable at the antenna.
3. Remove the mounting bolts at the bottom of the power unit.
4. Remove the power unit through the trunk.
5. Installation is the reverse of removal.
6. Tighten the mounting bolts securely.

ROD

1. Remove the antenna nut and base.
2. Remove the antenna rod while raising it by operating the antenna motor.

To install:

3. Lower the antenna rod by operating the antenna motor.
4. Insert the gear section of the antenna rope into place with it facing toward the antenna motor.
5. As soon as rope is wound onto the antenna motor, stop the motor.
6. Insert the antenna rod lower end into the antenna motor pipe.
7. Retract the antenna rod completely by operating the antenna motor.
8. Install the antenna nut and base.

Fenders

REMOVAL & INSTALLATION

1. Remove the front bumper.
2. Remove the headlamp lens assembly.

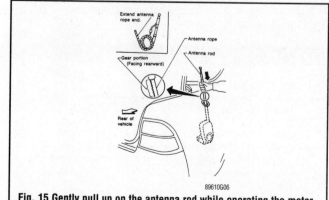

Fig. 15 Gently pull up on the antenna rod while operating the motor to the UP position

3. Remove the front wheel inner splash shield.
4. Remove the rocker panel trim, as necessary.
5. Remove the hood, as necessary.
6. Locate and remove the fender mounting bolts and clips.

➡**Some of the fender mounting bolts may be under a considerable amount of undercoating. Scrape off the undercoating from the bolt heads as necessary to avoid stripping them.**

7. Carefully remove the fender from the vehicle. It may be necessary to cut the body sealant with a sharp blade to allow the fender to be removed.
8. Installation is the reverse of removal.
9. Carefully align the fender to allow proper clearance to open the front door.

Power Sunroof

REMOVAL & INSTALLATION

Motor

▶ **See Figure 16**

1. Remove the sunroof switch panel by pushing it to the side and disengaging the pawl, then pulling it downward.
2. Remove the sunroof switch bracket.
3. Unplug the sunroof motor wiring harness connectors.
4. Remove the sunroof motor mounting screws.

➡**Disassembly of the sunroof motor is not recommended.**

To install:

5. Lightly lubricate the drive gear with grease and install the sunroof motor to the sunroof assembly.
6. Plug in the electrical harness connectors to the sunroof motor.
7. Operate the sunroof to verify proper operation.
8. Install the sunroof switch bracket and the sunroof switch panel.

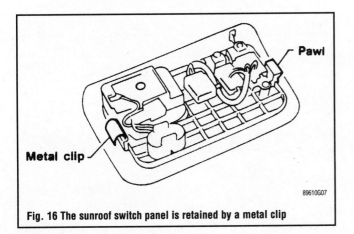

Fig. 16 The sunroof switch panel is retained by a metal clip

Sunroof

▶ **See Figures 17 and 18**

1. Tilt up the sunroof lid.
2. Remove the lid side trim.
3. Remove the lid bolts and the lid assembly.
4. Remove the rear drain mount screws and the drain.
5. Remove the shade assembly holders from the sunroof frame.
6. Remove the shade assembly.
7. Remove the sunroof switch, interior accessories and headliner.
8. Remove the switch bracket.
9. Remove the motor assembly, spacer and clip.
10. Remove the wind deflector mount holders from the sunroof frame.
11. Remove the wind deflector.
12. Disconnect the drain hose.
13. Remove the sunroof brackets.

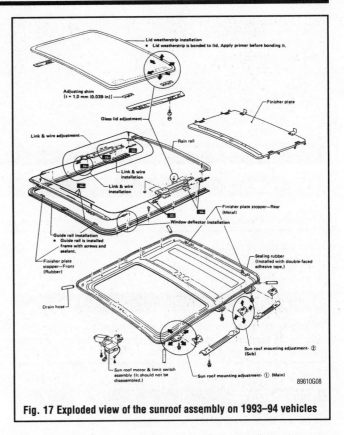

Fig. 17 Exploded view of the sunroof assembly on 1993–94 vehicles

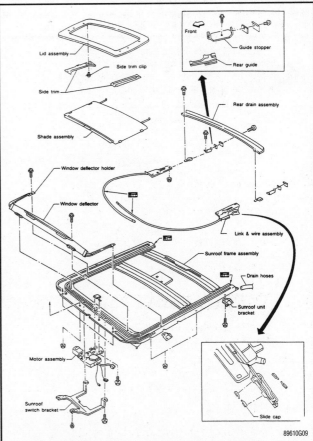

Fig. 18 Exploded view of the sunroof assembly on 1995–97 vehicles—1998 models similar

14. Remove the sunroof frame assembly.
15. Remove the link and wire assemblies.
To install:
16. Tilt up the sunroof lid.
17. Install the link and wire assemblies.
18. Install the sunroof frame assembly.
19. Install the sunroof brackets.
20. Connect the drain hose.
21. Install the wind deflector.

22. Install the wind deflector mount holders on the sunroof frame.
23. Install the motor assembly, spacer and clip.
24. Install the switch bracket.
25. Install the sunroof switch, interior accessories and headliner.
26. Install the shade assembly.
27. Install the shade assembly holders on the sunroof frame.
28. Install the rear drain mount screws and the drain.
29. Install the lid bolts and the lid assembly.
30. Install the lid side trim.

INTERIOR

Dash Panel

REMOVAL & INSTALLATION

♦ **See Figures 19 and 20**

1. Disconnect the negative battery cable.
2. Disable the air bag and remove it from the steering wheel.

❊❊ CAUTION

Be sure to place the air bag module on a flat surface with the pad side facing upward. In the event of accidental deployment, this will minimize the chance of injury.

3. Remove the steering wheel.

❊❊ CAUTION

Some models covered by this manual may be equipped with a Supplemental Restraint System (SRS), which uses an air bag. Whenever working near any of the SRS components, such as the impact sensors, the air bag module, steering column and instrument panel, or the front seats, disable the SRS, as described in Section 6.

4. Remove the glove box assembly from the dash panel.
5. Disconnect the passenger side air bag.
6. Remove the kick panel on the driver side of the vehicle.
7. Remove the driver side knee pad assembly.

8. Remove the steering column covers.
9. Unplug the connectors and remove the combination switch.
10. Remove the instrument cluster fascia.
11. Remove the instrument cluster from the dash panel.
12. Remove the center grille from the dash panel.
13. Remove the shifter fascia.
14. Remove the center console fascia, and the radio.
15. Remove the climate control unit.
16. Remove the center console.
17. Remove the trim panels on the front windshield pillars.
18. Carefully pry the defroster grille(s) from the dash panel. This will allow access to the upper dash panel bolts.
19. Remove the bolts securing the dash panel to the vehicle.
20. With the help of an assistant, remove the dash panel from the vehicle.
To install:
21. With the help of an assistant, place the dash panel into the vehicle.
22. Install the defroster grille(s) onto the dash panel.
23. Install the trim panels on the front windshield pillars.
24. Install the center console.
25. Install the climate control unit.
26. Install the radio, and the center console fascia.
27. Snap the shifter fascia into place.
28. Install the center grille to the dash panel.
29. Install the instrument cluster from the dash panel.

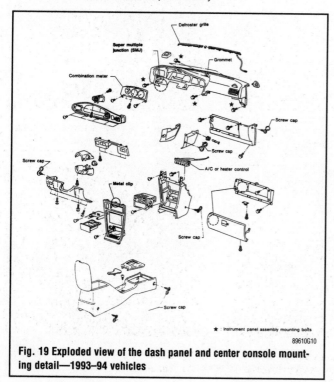

Fig. 19 Exploded view of the dash panel and center console mounting detail—1993–94 vehicles

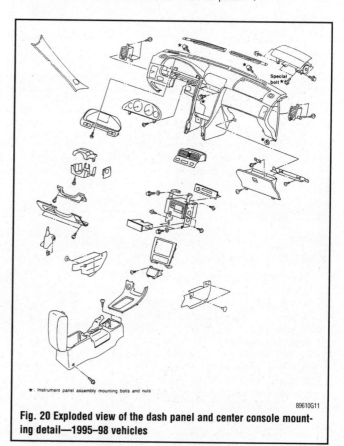

Fig. 20 Exploded view of the dash panel and center console mounting detail—1995–98 vehicles

30. Install the instrument cluster fascia.
31. Install the combination switch.
32. Install the steering column covers.
33. Install the driver side knee pad assembly.
34. Install the kick panel on the driver side of the vehicle.
35. Connect the passenger side air bag.
36. Install the glove box assembly to the dash panel.
37. Install the steering wheel.
38. Install the air bag into the steering wheel.
39. Connect the negative battery cable.

Console

REMOVAL & INSTALLATION

1. Unsnap and remove the A/T fascia or M/T boot.
2. Remove the cluster lid, as required to gain clearance.
3. Remove the center console attaching screws.
4. Lift the console slightly and disconnect the electrical harnesses.
5. Carefully lift the center console from the vehicle.

To install:
6. Position the center console in the vehicle.
7. Install and securely tighten all attaching screws.
8. Install the cluster lid.
9. Install the A/T fascia or M/T boot.

Door Panels

REMOVAL & INSTALLATION

▶ See Figures 21 thru 32

1. Open the door fully.
2. Remove the inside latch escutcheon.
3. Remove the pull handle.
4. If so equipped, remove the power window switch trim and switch assembly.
5. If applicable, disconnect the switch assembly wiring harness.

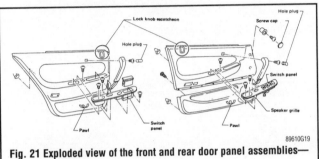

Fig. 21 Exploded view of the front and rear door panel assemblies—1993–94 vehicles

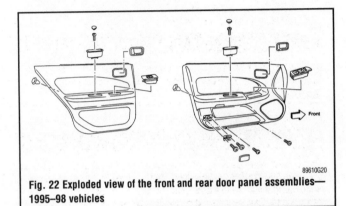

Fig. 22 Exploded view of the front and rear door panel assemblies—1995–98 vehicles

Fig. 23 Use a small metal pick to lift the escutcheon from the door latch recess

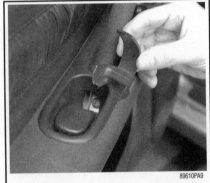

Fig. 24 With the escutcheon removed, the door pull handle screws can be accessed

Fig. 25 Remove the plastic cap to access the upper door handle screw

Fig. 26 After the screws are removed, the door handle can be removed

Fig. 27 There is usually a screw that attaches the inner door panel to the door

Fig. 28 Carefully lift the switch panel from the door panel . . .

Fig. 29 . . . then unplug the switch harness connectors

Fig. 30 Pop off the screw covers . . .

Fig. 31 . . . then carefully remove the door panel

Fig. 32 After the door panel is free, reach behind and disconnect the courtesy light and trunk switch

➡The door panel is held in place by several clips. Use a door panel clip removal tool to avoid damaging the clips, door panel or the door.

6. Carefully pry the door panel from the door.
7. Lift the door panel straight up to release it from the lip at the top of the door.

To install:

8. Replace any damaged clips.
9. Position the door panel on the door frame and ensure that the panel fits over the lip at the top of the door.
10. Align the clips with the holes in the door and, using your fist, tap the door panel into place.
11. Connect the switch assembly wiring harness, if so equipped.
12. If applicable, install the power window switch trim and switch assembly.
13. Install the pull handle.
14. Install the inside handle escutcheon.

Door Locks

REMOVAL & INSTALLATION

◆ **See Figures 34, 35, 36 and 37**

➡When a lock cylinder is replaced, all the door lock cylinders should be replaced in a set, or have a qualified locksmith rekey the replacement door lock cylinder. This will eliminate carrying an extra key which will only fit one lock.

Lock Cylinders

1. Remove the door panel and moisture barrier.
2. Disconnect the lock cylinder from the rod by turning the resin clip.
3. Loosen the nuts attaching the outside door handle and remove the outside door handle.
4. Remove the lock cylinder by removing the retaining clip.

To install:

5. Install the lock cylinder and clip on the door handle.
6. Install the outside door handle.
7. Connect the rod to the lock cylinder and securely fasten the resin clip.
8. Install the moisture barrier and door panel.

Power Door Lock Actuators

1. Disconnect the negative battery cable.
2. Remove the door panel and moisture barrier.
3. Unfasten the actuator's electrical connector.
4. Disconnect the required linkage rods.
5. Remove the actuator assembly retaining screws.
6. Remove the actuator from the door.

To install:

7. Install the actuator in the door and tighten the retaining screws securely.
8. Connect the required linkage rods.
9. Fasten the actuator's electrical connector.
10. Install the moisture barrier and door panel.
11. Connect the negative battery cable.

Trunk Lock

REMOVAL & INSTALLATION

◆ **See Figure 33**

➡When a lock cylinder is replaced, all the door lock cylinders should be replaced in a set, or have a qualified locksmith rekey the replacement door lock cylinder. This will eliminate carrying an extra key which will only fit one lock.

1. Remove the interior trim, as required.
2. Loosen the nuts/bolts attaching the striker to the trunk lid.
3. Remove the striker.
4. Withdraw the lock cylinder after removing the retaining clip.

To install:

5. Position the lock cylinder and install the retaining clip.
6. Install the striker and tighten the attaching nuts/bolts securely.
7. Install the interior trim, as required.

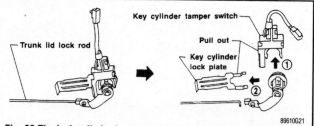

Fig. 33 The lock cylinder is secured to the trunk with a spring metal plate

Electric Window Motor and Regulator

REMOVAL & INSTALLATION

▶ See Figures 34, 35, 36 and 37

1. Ensure that the window is fully closed.
2. Disconnect the negative battery cable.
3. Open the door fully.
4. Remove the inner door panel and moisture barrier.
5. Disconnect the electric window motor harness.
6. Remove the electric window motor and regulator, using the illustrations as a guide.

To install:

7. Install the electric window motor and regulator. Tighten the attaching bolts to the illustrated specifications.
8. Connect the electric window motor harness.
9. Connect the negative battery cable.
10. Operate the window to ensure proper functioning.
11. Adjust the window regulator mechanism, as required.
12. Install the moisture barrier and inner door panel.

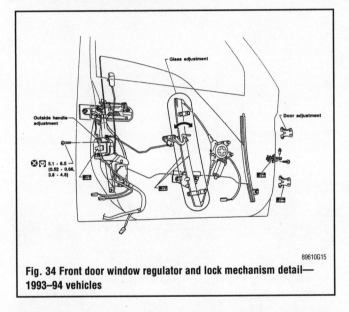

Fig. 34 Front door window regulator and lock mechanism detail— 1993–94 vehicles

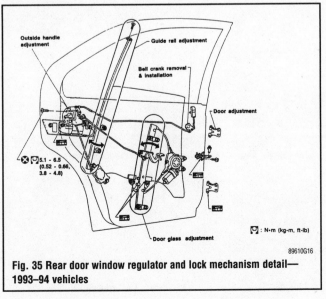

Fig. 35 Rear door window regulator and lock mechanism detail— 1993–94 vehicles

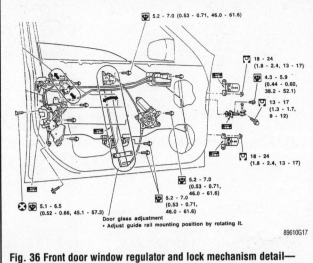

Fig. 36 Front door window regulator and lock mechanism detail— 1995–98 vehicles

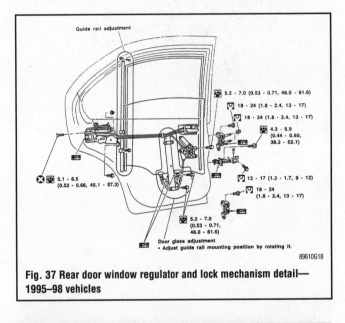

Fig. 37 Rear door window regulator and lock mechanism detail— 1995–98 vehicles

Windshield and Fixed Glass

REMOVAL & INSTALLATION

If your windshield, or other fixed window, is cracked or chipped, you may decide to replace it with a new one yourself. However, there are two main reasons why replacement windshields and other window glass should be installed only by a professional automotive glass technician: safety and cost.

The most important reason a professional should install automotive glass is for safety. The glass in the vehicle, especially the windshield, is designed with safety in mind in case of a collision. The windshield is specially manufactured from two panes of specially-tempered glass with a thin layer of transparent plastic between them. This construction allows the glass to "give" in the event that a part of your body hits the windshield during the collision, and prevents the glass from shattering, which could cause lacerations, blinding and other harm to passengers of the vehicle. The other fixed windows are designed to be tempered so that if they break during a collision, they shatter in such a way that there are no large pointed glass pieces. The professional automotive glass technician knows how to install the glass in a vehicle so that it will function optimally during a collision. Without the proper experience, knowledge and tools, installing a piece of automotive glass yourself could lead to additional harm if an accident should ever occur.

Cost is also a factor when deciding to install automotive glass yourself. Performing this could cost you much more than a professional may charge for the same job. Since the windshield is designed to break under stress, an often life saving characteristic, windshields tend to break VERY easily when an inexperienced person attempts to install one. Do-it-yourselfers buying two, three or even four windshields from a salvage yard because they have broken them during installation are common stories. Also, since the automotive glass is designed to prevent the outside elements from entering your vehicle, improper installation can lead to water and air leaks. Annoying whining noises at highway speeds from air leaks or inside body panel rusting from water leaks can add to your stress level and subtract from your wallet. After buying two or three windshields, installing them and ending up with a leak that produces a noise while driving and water damage during rainstorms, the cost of having a professional do it correctly the first time may be much more alluring. We here at Chilton,

therefore, advise that you have a professional automotive glass technician service any broken glass on your vehicle.

WINDSHIELD CHIP REPAIR

♦ See Figures 38 thru 52

➥Check with your state and local authorities on the laws for state safety inspection. Some states or municipalities may not allow chip repair as a viable option for correcting stone damage to your windshield.

Although severely cracked or damaged windshields must be replaced, there is something that you can do to prolong or even prevent the need for replacement of a chipped windshield. There are many companies which offer windshield chip repair products, such as Loctite's® Bullseye™ windshield repair kit. These kits usually consist of a syringe, pedestal and a sealing adhesive. The syringe is mounted on the pedestal and is used to create a vacuum which pulls

Fig. 38 Small chips on your windshield can be fixed with an aftermarket repair kit, such as the one from Loctite®

Fig. 39 To repair a chip, clean the windshield with glass cleaner and dry it completely

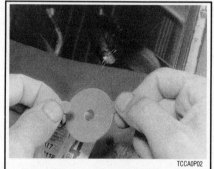

Fig. 40 Remove the center from the adhesive disc and peel off the backing from one side of the disc . . .

Fig. 41 . . . then press it on the windshield so that the chip is centered in the hole

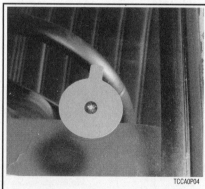

Fig. 42 Be sure that the tab points upward on the windshield

Fig. 43 Peel the backing off the exposed side of the adhesive disc . . .

Fig. 44 . . . then position the plastic pedestal on the adhesive disc, ensuring that the tabs are aligned

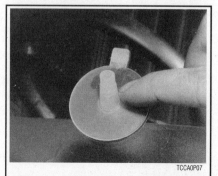

Fig. 45 Press the pedestal firmly on the adhesive disc to create an adequate seal . . .

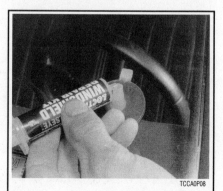

Fig. 46 . . . then install the applicator syringe nipple in the pedestal's hole

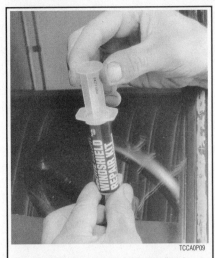

Fig. 47 Hold the syringe with one hand while pulling the plunger back with the other hand

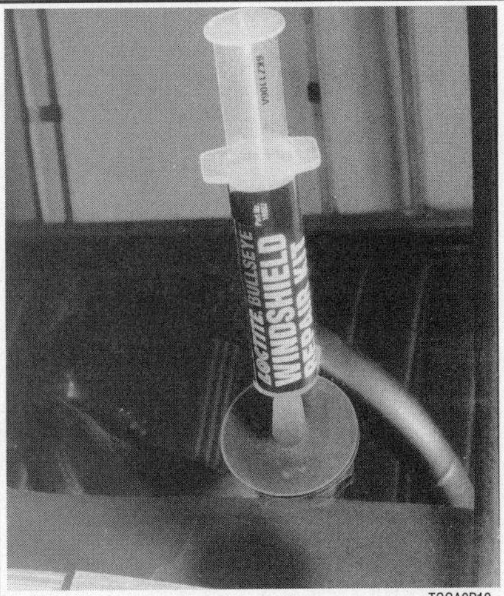

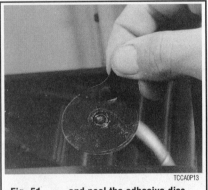

Fig. 48 After applying the solution, allow the entire assembly to sit until it has set completely

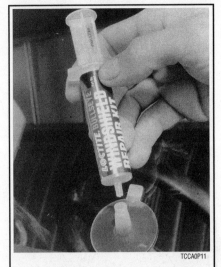

Fig. 49 After the solution has set, remove the syringe from the pedestal . . .

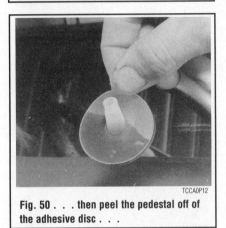

Fig. 50 . . . then peel the pedestal off of the adhesive disc . . .

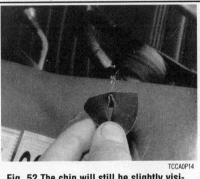

Fig. 51 . . . and peel the adhesive disc off of the windshield

Fig. 52 The chip will still be slightly visible, but it should be filled with the hardened solution

the plastic layer against the glass. This helps make the chip transparent. The adhesive is then injected which seals the chip and helps to prevent further stress cracks from developing. Refer to the sequence of photos to get a general idea of what windshield chip repair involves.

➡**Always follow the specific manufacturer's instructions.**

Inside Rear View Mirror

REPLACEMENT

1. The rear view mirror is attached to the inner roof panel with three screws. To remove the mirror, simply remove the plastic screw cover, and unscrew the mirror base from the roof of the vehicle.

Seats

REMOVAL & INSTALLATION

Front

▶ See Figures 53 and 54

✳✳ CAUTION

Some models covered by this manual may be equipped with a Supplemental Restraint System (SRS), which uses an air bag. When-

ever working near any of the SRS components, such as the impact sensors, the air bag module, steering column and instrument panel, and front seats, disable the SRS, as described in Section 6.

1. Locate and remove the four seat mounting bolts.
2. Disconnect any electrical harnesses attached to the seat.
3. Carefully lift the seat from the vehicle.
4. Installation is the reverse of removal.
5. Tighten the seat mounting bolts to 32–41 ft. lbs. (43–55 Nm).

Rear

▶ See Figures 55, 56, 57 and 58

1. Remove the lower seat cushion by pulling straight up on the front portion and disengaging the clips. Then hinge the seat upward to release the rear clips.
2. Remove upper rear seat back-to-chassis bolts.
3. Remove rear seat back by tilting forward and pulling straight up.
To install:
4. Install the lower seat cushion and torque the lower rear seat-to-chassis bolts to 15–20 ft. lbs. (21–26 Nm).
5. Install the upper rear seat back cushion and torque the upper rear seat back-to-chassis bolts to 15–20 ft. lbs. (21–26 Nm)

Power Seat Motor

REMOVAL & INSTALLATION

1. Remove the seat.

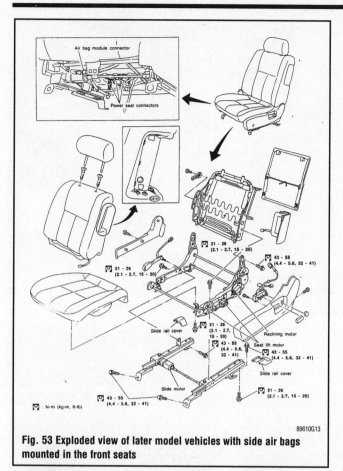

Fig. 53 Exploded view of later model vehicles with side air bags mounted in the front seats

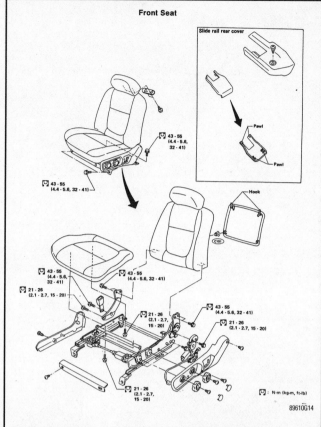

Fig. 54 Exploded view of a powered front seat assembly

Fig. 55 Pull up on the front of the lower seat cushion and disengage the clips

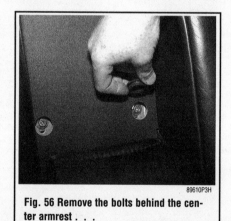

Fig. 56 Remove the bolts behind the center armrest . . .

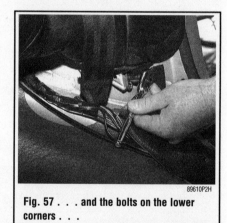

Fig. 57 . . . and the bolts on the lower corners . . .

Fig. 58 . . . Then pull up on the seat to disengage the three clips on the top of the seat

⁂ CAUTION

Some models covered by this manual may be equipped with a Supplemental Restraint System (SRS), which uses an air bag. Whenever working near any of the SRS components, such as the impact sensors, the air bag module, steering column and instrument panel, and front seats, disable the SRS, as described in Section 6.

2. Turn the seat upside down to access all seat adjusting motors.
3. Remove the seat trim panels.
4. Remove the seat motor mounting bolts.
5. Remove the seat motors.
6. Installation is the reverse of removal.
7. Tighten the seat mounting bolts to 15–20 ft. lbs. (21–26 Nm).

Rear

▶ **See Figure 59**

1. Locate and remove the two mounting bolts under the bench portion of the rear seat.
2. Locate and remove the two mounting bolts at the bottom of the seat back.

3. If equipped with a pass-through opening/center armrest, remove the two screws from the frame.
4. Lift the seat back straight up to release it from the clips which attach it to the package shelf.
5. Carefully remove the seat from the vehicle.
6. Installation is the reverse of removal.
7. Tighten the seat mounting bolts to 32–41 ft. lbs. (43–55 Nm).

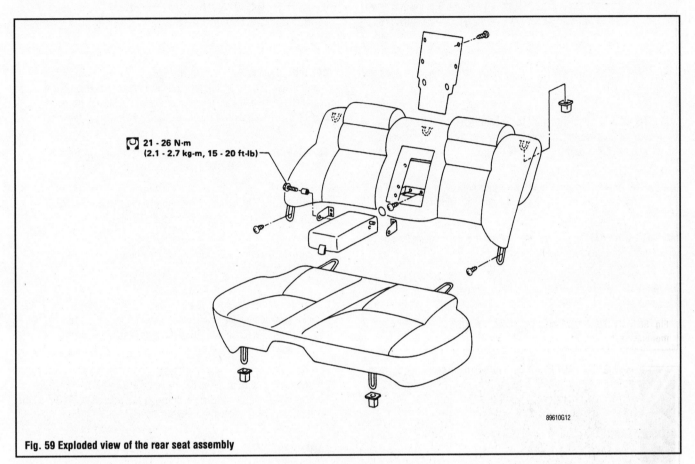

21 - 26 N·m
(2.1 - 2.7 kg-m, 15 - 20 ft-lb)

89610G12

Fig. 59 Exploded view of the rear seat assembly

TORQUE SPECIFICATIONS

Component	English Specification	Metric Specification
Exterior		
Door	13–17 ft lbs	18–24 Nm
Hood	12–15 ft lbs	16–21 Nm
Hood latch	15–20 ft lbs	21–26 Nm
Trunk lid	12–15 ft lbs	21–21 Nm
Interior		
Seats	32–41 ft lbs	43–55 Nm
Power seat motor	15–20 ft lbs	21–26 Nm
Power window motor	3.8–5.1 ft lbs	5.2–7.0 Nm

89610C01

GLOSSARY

AIR/FUEL RATIO: The ratio of air-to-gasoline by weight in the fuel mixture drawn into the engine.

AIR INJECTION: One method of reducing harmful exhaust emissions by injecting air into each of the exhaust ports of an engine. The fresh air entering the hot exhaust manifold causes any remaining fuel to be burned before it can exit the tailpipe.

ALTERNATOR: A device used for converting mechanical energy into electrical energy.

AMMETER: An instrument, calibrated in amperes, used to measure the flow of an electrical current in a circuit. Ammeters are always connected in series with the circuit being tested.

AMPERE: The rate of flow of electrical current present when one volt of electrical pressure is applied against one ohm of electrical resistance.

ANALOG COMPUTER: Any microprocessor that uses similar (analogous) electrical signals to make its calculations.

ARMATURE: A laminated, soft iron core wrapped by a wire that converts electrical energy to mechanical energy as in a motor or relay. When rotated in a magnetic field, it changes mechanical energy into electrical energy as in a generator.

ATMOSPHERIC PRESSURE: The pressure on the Earth's surface caused by the weight of the air in the atmosphere. At sea level, this pressure is 14.7 psi at 32°F (101 kPa at 0°C).

ATOMIZATION: The breaking down of a liquid into a fine mist that can be suspended in air.

AXIAL PLAY: Movement parallel to a shaft or bearing bore.

BACKFIRE: The sudden combustion of gases in the intake or exhaust system that results in a loud explosion.

BACKLASH: The clearance or play between two parts, such as meshed gears.

BACKPRESSURE: Restrictions in the exhaust system that slow the exit of exhaust gases from the combustion chamber.

BAKELITE: A heat resistant, plastic insulator material commonly used in printed circuit boards and transistorized components.

BALL BEARING: A bearing made up of hardened inner and outer races between which hardened steel balls roll.

BALLAST RESISTOR: A resistor in the primary ignition circuit that lowers voltage after the engine is started to reduce wear on ignition components.

BEARING: A friction reducing, supportive device usually located between a stationary part and a moving part.

BIMETAL TEMPERATURE SENSOR: Any sensor or switch made of two dissimilar types of metal that bend when heated or cooled due to the different expansion rates of the alloys. These types of sensors usually function as an on/off switch.

BLOWBY: Combustion gases, composed of water vapor and unburned fuel, that leak past the piston rings into the crankcase during normal engine operation. These gases are removed by the PCV system to prevent the buildup of harmful acids in the crankcase.

BRAKE PAD: A brake shoe and lining assembly used with disc brakes.

BRAKE SHOE: The backing for the brake lining. The term is, however, usually applied to the assembly of the brake backing and lining.

BUSHING: A liner, usually removable, for a bearing; an anti-friction liner used in place of a bearing.

CALIPER: A hydraulically activated device in a disc brake system, which is mounted straddling the brake rotor (disc). The caliper contains at least one piston and two brake pads. Hydraulic pressure on the piston(s) forces the pads against the rotor.

CAMSHAFT: A shaft in the engine on which are the lobes (cams) which operate the valves. The camshaft is driven by the crankshaft, via a belt, chain or gears, at one half the crankshaft speed.

CAPACITOR: A device which stores an electrical charge.

CARBON MONOXIDE (CO): A colorless, odorless gas given off as a normal byproduct of combustion. It is poisonous and extremely dangerous in confined areas, building up slowly to toxic levels without warning if adequate ventilation is not available.

CARBURETOR: A device, usually mounted on the intake manifold of an engine, which mixes the air and fuel in the proper proportion to allow even combustion.

CATALYTIC CONVERTER: A device installed in the exhaust system, like a muffler, that converts harmful byproducts of combustion into carbon dioxide and water vapor by means of a heat-producing chemical reaction.

CENTRIFUGAL ADVANCE: A mechanical method of advancing the spark timing by using flyweights in the distributor that react to centrifugal force generated by the distributor shaft rotation.

CHECK VALVE: Any one-way valve installed to permit the flow of air, fuel or vacuum in one direction only.

CHOKE: A device, usually a moveable valve, placed in the intake path of a carburetor to restrict the flow of air.

CIRCUIT: Any unbroken path through which an electrical current can flow. Also used to describe fuel flow in some instances.

CIRCUIT BREAKER: A switch which protects an electrical circuit from overload by opening the circuit when the current flow exceeds a predetermined level. Some circuit breakers must be reset manually, while most reset automatically.

COIL (IGNITION): A transformer in the ignition circuit which steps up the voltage provided to the spark plugs.

COMBINATION MANIFOLD: An assembly which includes both the intake and exhaust manifolds in one casting.

COMBINATION VALVE: A device used in some fuel systems that routes fuel vapors to a charcoal storage canister instead of venting them into the atmosphere. The valve relieves fuel tank pressure and allows fresh air into the tank as the fuel level drops to prevent a vapor lock situation.

COMPRESSION RATIO: The comparison of the total volume of the cylinder and combustion chamber with the piston at BDC and the piston at TDC.

CONDENSER: 1. An electrical device which acts to store an electrical charge, preventing voltage surges. 2. A radiator-like device in the air conditioning system in which refrigerant gas condenses into a liquid, giving off heat.

CONDUCTOR: Any material through which an electrical current can be transmitted easily.

CONTINUITY: Continuous or complete circuit. Can be checked with an ohmmeter.

COUNTERSHAFT: An intermediate shaft which is rotated by a mainshaft and transmits, in turn, that rotation to a working part.

CRANKCASE: The lower part of an engine in which the crankshaft and related parts operate.

CRANKSHAFT: The main driving shaft of an engine which receives reciprocating motion from the pistons and converts it to rotary motion.

CYLINDER: In an engine, the round hole in the engine block in which the piston(s) ride.

CYLINDER BLOCK: The main structural member of an engine in which is found the cylinders, crankshaft and other principal parts.

CYLINDER HEAD: The detachable portion of the engine, usually fastened to the top of the cylinder block and containing all or most of the combustion chambers. On overhead valve engines, it contains the valves and their operating parts. On overhead cam engines, it contains the camshaft as well.

DEAD CENTER: The extreme top or bottom of the piston stroke.

DETONATION: An unwanted explosion of the air/fuel mixture in the combustion chamber caused by excess heat and compression, advanced timing, or an overly lean mixture. Also referred to as "ping".

DIAPHRAGM: A thin, flexible wall separating two cavities, such as in a vacuum advance unit.

DIESELING: A condition in which hot spots in the combustion chamber cause the engine to run on after the key is turned off.

DIFFERENTIAL: A geared assembly which allows the transmission of motion between drive axles, giving one axle the ability to turn faster than the other.

DIODE: An electrical device that will allow current to flow in one direction only.

DISC BRAKE: A hydraulic braking assembly consisting of a brake disc, or rotor, mounted on an axle, and a caliper assembly containing, usually two brake pads which are activated by hydraulic pressure. The pads are forced against the sides of the disc, creating friction which slows the vehicle.

DISTRIBUTOR: A mechanically driven device on an engine which is responsible for electrically firing the spark plug at a predetermined point of the piston stroke.

DOWEL PIN: A pin, inserted in mating holes in two different parts allowing those parts to maintain a fixed relationship.

DRUM BRAKE: A braking system which consists of two brake shoes and one or two wheel cylinders, mounted on a fixed backing plate, and a brake drum, mounted on an axle, which revolves around the assembly.

DWELL: The rate, measured in degrees of shaft rotation, at which an electrical circuit cycles on and off.

ELECTRONIC CONTROL UNIT (ECU): Ignition module, module, amplifier or igniter. See Module for definition.

ELECTRONIC IGNITION: A system in which the timing and firing of the spark plugs is controlled by an electronic control unit, usually called a module. These systems have no points or condenser.

END-PLAY: The measured amount of axial movement in a shaft.

ENGINE: A device that converts heat into mechanical energy.

EXHAUST MANIFOLD: A set of cast passages or pipes which conduct exhaust gases from the engine.

FEELER GAUGE: A blade, usually metal, or precisely predetermined thickness, used to measure the clearance between two parts.

FIRING ORDER: The order in which combustion occurs in the cylinders of an engine. Also the order in which spark is distributed to the plugs by the distributor.

FLOODING: The presence of too much fuel in the intake manifold and combustion chamber which prevents the air/fuel mixture from firing, thereby causing a no-start situation.

FLYWHEEL: A disc shaped part bolted to the rear end of the crankshaft. Around the outer perimeter is affixed the ring gear. The starter drive engages the ring gear, turning the flywheel, which rotates the crankshaft, imparting the initial starting motion to the engine.

FOOT POUND (ft. lbs. or sometimes, ft.lb.): The amount of energy or work needed to raise an item weighing one pound, a distance of one foot.

FUSE: A protective device in a circuit which prevents circuit overload by breaking the circuit when a specific amperage is present. The device is constructed around a strip or wire of a lower amperage rating than the circuit it is designed to protect. When an amperage higher than that stamped on the fuse is present in the circuit, the strip or wire melts, opening the circuit.

GEAR RATIO: The ratio between the number of teeth on meshing gears.

GENERATOR: A device which converts mechanical energy into electrical energy.

HEAT RANGE: The measure of a spark plug's ability to dissipate heat from its firing end. The higher the heat range, the hotter the plug fires.

HUB: The center part of a wheel or gear.

HYDROCARBON (HC): Any chemical compound made up of hydrogen and carbon. A major pollutant formed by the engine as a byproduct of combustion.

HYDROMETER: An instrument used to measure the specific gravity of a solution.

INCH POUND (inch lbs.; sometimes in.lb. or in. lbs.): One twelfth of a foot pound.

INDUCTION: A means of transferring electrical energy in the form of a magnetic field. Principle used in the ignition coil to increase voltage.

INJECTOR: A device which receives metered fuel under relatively low pressure and is activated to inject the fuel into the engine under relatively high pressure at a predetermined time.

INPUT SHAFT: The shaft to which torque is applied, usually carrying the driving gear or gears.

INTAKE MANIFOLD: A casting of passages or pipes used to conduct air or a fuel/air mixture to the cylinders.

JOURNAL: The bearing surface within which a shaft operates.

KEY: A small block usually fitted in a notch between a shaft and a hub to prevent slippage of the two parts.

MANIFOLD: A casting of passages or set of pipes which connect the cylinders to an inlet or outlet source.

MANIFOLD VACUUM: Low pressure in an engine intake manifold formed just below the throttle plates. Manifold vacuum is highest at idle and drops under acceleration.

MASTER CYLINDER: The primary fluid pressurizing device in a hydraulic system. In automotive use, it is found in brake and hydraulic clutch systems and is pedal activated, either directly or, in a power brake system, through the power booster.

MODULE: Electronic control unit, amplifier or igniter of solid state or integrated design which controls the current flow in the ignition primary circuit based on input from the pick-up coil. When the module opens the primary circuit, high secondary voltage is induced in the coil.

NEEDLE BEARING: A bearing which consists of a number (usually a large number) of long, thin rollers.

OHM: (Ω) The unit used to measure the resistance of conductor-to-electrical flow. One ohm is the amount of resistance that limits current flow to one ampere in a circuit with one volt of pressure.

OHMMETER: An instrument used for measuring the resistance, in ohms, in an electrical circuit.

OUTPUT SHAFT: The shaft which transmits torque from a device, such as a transmission.

OVERDRIVE: A gear assembly which produces more shaft revolutions than that transmitted to it.

OVERHEAD CAMSHAFT (OHC): An engine configuration in which the camshaft is mounted on top of the cylinder head and operates the valve either directly or by means of rocker arms.

OVERHEAD VALVE (OHV): An engine configuration in which all of the valves are located in the cylinder head and the camshaft is located in the cylinder block. The camshaft operates the valves via lifters and pushrods.

OXIDES OF NITROGEN (NOx): Chemical compounds of nitrogen produced as a byproduct of combustion. They combine with hydrocarbons to produce smog.

OXYGEN SENSOR: Use with the feedback system to sense the presence of oxygen in the exhaust gas and signal the computer which can reference the voltage signal to an air/fuel ratio.

PINION: The smaller of two meshing gears.

PISTON RING: An open-ended ring with fits into a groove on the outer diameter of the piston. Its chief function is to form a seal between the piston and cylinder wall. Most automotive pistons have three rings: two for compression sealing; one for oil sealing.

PRELOAD: A predetermined load placed on a bearing during assembly or by adjustment.

PRIMARY CIRCUIT: the low voltage side of the ignition system which consists of the ignition switch, ballast resistor or resistance wire, bypass, coil, electronic control unit and pick-up coil as well as the connecting wires and harnesses.

PRESS FIT: The mating of two parts under pressure, due to the inner diameter of one being smaller than the outer diameter of the other, or vice versa; an interference fit.

RACE: The surface on the inner or outer ring of a bearing on which the balls, needles or rollers move.

REGULATOR: A device which maintains the amperage and/or voltage levels of a circuit at predetermined values.

RELAY: A switch which automatically opens and/or closes a circuit.

RESISTANCE: The opposition to the flow of current through a circuit or electrical device, and is measured in ohms. Resistance is equal to the voltage divided by the amperage.

RESISTOR: A device, usually made of wire, which offers a preset amount of resistance in an electrical circuit.

RING GEAR: The name given to a ring-shaped gear attached to a differential case, or affixed to a flywheel or as part of a planetary gear set.

ROLLER BEARING: A bearing made up of hardened inner and outer races between which hardened steel rollers move.

ROTOR: 1. The disc-shaped part of a disc brake assembly, upon which the brake pads bear; also called, brake disc. 2. The device mounted atop the distributor shaft, which passes current to the distributor cap tower contacts.

SECONDARY CIRCUIT: The high voltage side of the ignition system, usually above 20,000 volts. The secondary includes the ignition coil, coil wire, distributor cap and rotor, spark plug wires and spark plugs.

SENDING UNIT: A mechanical, electrical, hydraulic or electro-magnetic device which transmits information to a gauge.

SENSOR: Any device designed to measure engine operating conditions or ambient pressures and temperatures. Usually electronic in nature and designed to send a voltage signal to an on-board computer, some sensors may operate as a simple on/off switch or they may provide a variable voltage signal (like a potentiometer) as conditions or measured parameters change.

SHIM: Spacers of precise, predetermined thickness used between parts to establish a proper working relationship.

SLAVE CYLINDER: In automotive use, a device in the hydraulic clutch system which is activated by hydraulic force, disengaging the clutch.

SOLENOID: A coil used to produce a magnetic field, the effect of which is to produce work.

SPARK PLUG: A device screwed into the combustion chamber of a spark ignition engine. The basic construction is a conductive core inside of a ceramic insulator, mounted in an outer conductive base. An electrical charge from the spark plug wire travels along the conductive core and jumps a preset air gap to a grounding point or points at the end of the conductive base. The resultant spark ignites the fuel/air mixture in the combustion chamber.

SPLINES: Ridges machined or cast onto the outer diameter of a shaft or inner diameter of a bore to enable parts to mate without rotation.

TACHOMETER: A device used to measure the rotary speed of an engine, shaft, gear, etc., usually in rotations per minute.

THERMOSTAT: A valve, located in the cooling system of an engine, which is closed when cold and opens gradually in response to engine heating, controlling the temperature of the coolant and rate of coolant flow.

TOP DEAD CENTER (TDC): The point at which the piston reaches the top of its travel on the compression stroke.

TORQUE: The twisting force applied to an object.

TORQUE CONVERTER: A turbine used to transmit power from a driving member to a driven member via hydraulic action, providing changes in drive ratio and torque. In automotive use, it links the driveplate at the rear of the engine to the automatic transmission.

TRANSDUCER: A device used to change a force into an electrical signal.

TRANSISTOR: A semi-conductor component which can be actuated by a small voltage to perform an electrical switching function.

TUNE-UP: A regular maintenance function, usually associated with the replacement and adjustment of parts and components in the electrical and fuel systems of a vehicle for the purpose of attaining optimum performance.

TURBOCHARGER: An exhaust driven pump which compresses intake air and forces it into the combustion chambers at higher than atmospheric pressures. The increased air pressure allows more fuel to be burned and results in increased horsepower being produced.

VACUUM ADVANCE: A device which advances the ignition timing in response to increased engine vacuum.

VACUUM GAUGE: An instrument used to measure the presence of vacuum in a chamber.

VALVE: A device which control the pressure, direction of flow or rate of flow of a liquid or gas.

VALVE CLEARANCE: The measured gap between the end of the valve stem and the rocker arm, cam lobe or follower that activates the valve.

VISCOSITY: The rating of a liquid's internal resistance to flow.

VOLTMETER: An instrument used for measuring electrical force in units called volts. Voltmeters are always connected parallel with the circuit being tested.

WHEEL CYLINDER: Found in the automotive drum brake assembly, it is a device, actuated by hydraulic pressure, which, through internal pistons, pushes the brake shoes outward against the drums.

MASTER
INDEX